CompTIA®

Tech+®

Study Guide

Third Edit

CompTIA®

Tech+®

Study Guide

Exam FC0-U71

Third Edition

Quentin Docter

Published by John Wiley & Sons, Inc., Hoboken, New Jersey.
Published simultaneously in Canada and the United Kingdom.

ISBNs: 9781394288793 (paperback), 9781394288816 (ePDF), 9781394288809 (ePub)

For general information on our other products and services, please contact our Customer Care Department within the United States at (800) 762-2974, outside the United States at (317) 572- 3993. For product technical support, you can find answers to frequently asked questions or reach us via live chat at https://sybexsupport.wiley.com.

Wiley also publishes its books in a variety of electronic formats. Some content that appears in print may not be available in electronic formats. For more information about Wiley products, visit our web site at www.wiley.com.

Library of Congress Cataloging in Publication data available on request.

Cover image: © Jeremy Woodhouse/Getty Images, Inc.
Cover design: Wiley

SKY10082703_082324

In memory of Grandpa Joe, who fostered my love of technology and so much more

Acknowledgments

First and foremost, I need to thank my family. Without their support and patience, I would never be able to work on projects like this.

They say it takes a village to produce a book, and it always amazes me at the number of people who are involved. I have been fortunate to work with a great Sybex crew yet again. Liz Britten was the project manager. Thanks, Liz, for keeping us on track and answering all of my random questions. Kenyon Brown was the senior acquisitions editor for this book—thank you, Kenyon, for asking me to take on this book.

Chris Crayton, my technical editor, is the best in the business. Thank you, Chris, for always challenging me with ideas to improve the book, as well as catching my silly mistakes. In addition, Satish Gowrishankar, Saravanan Dakshinamurthy, and Hariharan Jayamoorthy all played excellent roles in ensuring the quality of this work. Thank you, gentlemen. To Liz Welch, my copy editor, thank you for correcting my grammar mistakes over and over again. I saw you fixing the same ones chapter after chapter—my grammar might not be the best, but at least I am consistent! Finally, Nancy Carrasco, thank you for being the final set of eyes to make sure we didn't miss anything. I very much so appreciate you all!

About the Author

Quentin Docter started in the IT industry as a tech support agent for Packard Bell in 1994. Since then he has worked in tech support, network administration, consulting, training, web development, and project management. During his career, he has achieved certifications from CompTIA (including Tech+, A+, and Cloud Essentials+), Microsoft, Cisco, Novell, and Sun Microsystems. He is the author of several books, including the *CompTIA A+ Complete Study Guide* from Sybex, 2022, an imprint of Wiley.

About the Technical Editor

Chris Crayton, MCSE, CISSP, CASP+, PenTest+, CySA+, Cloud+, S+, N+, A+, ITF+, is a technical consultant, trainer, author, and industry-leading technical editor. He has worked as a computer technology and networking instructor, information security director, network administrator, network engineer, and PC specialist. Chris has served as technical editor and content contributor on numerous technical titles for several of the leading publishing companies. He has also been recognized with many professional and teaching awards.

Contents at a Glance

Contents

Table of Exercises

Introduction

If you're picking up this book, it means it's likely that either you're thinking about getting into the IT industry, or you are relatively new to it. Either way, you are probably getting advice from nearly everyone you meet. One of the common refrains you probably hear is "Get certified!" With so many certifications out there, you might wonder where to start—CompTIA Tech+ is that place.

Certification is one of the best things you can do for your career if you are working in, or want to break into, the IT profession, because it proves that you know what you're talking about regarding the subjects in which you're certified. It also powerfully endorses you as a professional in a way that's similar to a physician being board certified in a certain area of expertise. It can add to your résumé and make you more attractive to potential employers and more valuable as an employee. Anything you can do to stay ahead of the competition—even standing out among your present colleagues—could make a big difference in whether or not you gain a promotion!

In this book, you'll find out what the Tech+ exam is all about because each chapter covers a part of the exam. I've included some great review questions at the end of each chapter to help crystallize the information you learned and solidly prepare you to ace the exam. This book covers more than just the exam, though. I believe in providing my students with a foundation of IT knowledge that will prepare them for real jobs, not just to pass a test. After all, life is not a multiple-choice test with the answers clearly laid out in front of you!

A really cool thing about working in IT is that it's constantly evolving, so there are always new things to learn and fresh challenges to master. Once you obtain your Tech+ certification and discover that you're interested in taking it further by getting into more complex topics (and making more money), the CompTIA A+ certification is definitely your next step.

What Is the CompTIA Tech+ Certification?

Tech+ is a certification developed by the Computing Technology Industry Association (CompTIA) that exists to provide resources and education for the computer and technology community. This is the same body that developed the A+ exam for PC technicians, Network+ for networking experts, and Security+ for security practitioners.

Way back in 1995, members of the organization got together to develop a new certification that tests skills for IT. To ensure industrywide support, it was sponsored by many past and present IT industry leaders like these:

- Compaq Computers
- Digital Equipment Corporation (a part of Compaq)
- IBM

- Lotus
- Microsoft
- Novell
- TSS
- U.S. Robotics
- US West
- Wave Technologies

The Tech+ exam was designed to test the skills of those with little to no experience in the field but who want to show that they have a broad general understanding of core IT topics. It tests areas such as computer hardware, operating systems and applications, basic networking, security, and setting up and maintaining a computer.

Why Become Tech+ Certified?

Because CompTIA is a well-respected developer of vendor-neutral industry certifications, becoming Tech+ certified proves that you have a base level of knowledge in the specific areas tested by the Tech+ objectives.

Four major benefits are associated with becoming Tech+ certified:

Proof of Professional Achievement Computer professionals are pretty competitive when it comes to collecting more certifications than their peers. And because the Tech+ certification broadly covers the entire field of computers, it's a great stepping-stone to prove that you have what it takes to succeed in this industry. Because it's rare to gain something that's worth a lot with little effort, I'll be honest—preparing for the Tech+ exam isn't exactly a lazy day at the beach. But passing the test is worth it because it will get the attention of potential employers.

Opportunity for Advancement We all like to get ahead in our careers—advancement results in more responsibility and prestige, and it usually means a fatter paycheck, greater opportunities, and added options. In the IT sector, a great way to make sure all that good stuff happens is by earning a lot of technology certifications, including Tech+.

Fulfillment of Training Requirements Tech+, because of its wide-reaching industry support, is recognized as a baseline of computer knowledge. This can potentially fulfill IT-related training requirements set forth by your company.

Customer Confidence As companies discover the CompTIA advantage, they will undoubtedly require qualified staff to achieve these certifications. Many companies outsource their work to consulting firms with experience working with security. Firms that have certified staff have a definite advantage over firms that don't.

How to Become Tech+ Certified

As this book goes to press, Pearson VUE is the sole Tech+ exam provider. The following is the necessary contact information and exam-specific details for registering. Exam pricing might vary by country or by CompTIA membership.

Vendor	Website	Phone Number
Pearson VUE	https://home.pearsonvue.com/comptia	U.S. and Canada: 877-551-PLUS (7587)

When you schedule the exam, you'll receive instructions regarding appointment and cancellation procedures, ID requirements, and information about the testing center location. In addition, you'll receive a registration and payment confirmation letter. Exams can be scheduled up to six weeks out or as late as the next day (or, in some cases, even the same day).

Exam prices and codes may vary based on the country in which the exam is administered. For detailed pricing and exam registration procedures, refer to CompTIA's website at www.comptia.org.

After you've successfully passed your Tech+ exam, CompTIA will award you a certification. Within four to six weeks of passing the exam, you'll receive your official CompTIA Tech+ certificate and ID card. (If you don't receive these within eight weeks of taking the test, contact CompTIA directly using the information found in your registration packet.)

Tips for Taking the Tech+ Exam

Here are some general tips for taking your exam successfully:

- Bring two forms of ID with you. One must be a photo ID, such as a driver's license. The other can be a major credit card or a passport. Both forms must include a signature.
- Arrive early at the exam center so you can relax and review your study materials, particularly tables and lists of exam-related information. Once you are ready to enter the testing room, you will need to leave everything outside; you won't be able to bring any materials into the testing area.
- Read the questions carefully. Don't be tempted to jump to an early conclusion. Make sure you know exactly what each question is asking.
- Don't leave any unanswered questions. Unanswered questions are scored against you. There will be questions with multiple correct responses. When there is more than one correct answer, a message at the bottom of the screen will prompt you either to "choose two" or "choose all that apply." Be sure to read the messages displayed to know how many correct answers you must choose.
- When answering multiple-choice questions about which you're unsure, use a process of elimination to get rid of the obviously incorrect answers first. Doing so will improve your odds if you need to make an educated guess.
- On form-based tests (nonadaptive), because the hard questions will take the most time, save them for last. You can move forward and backward through the exam.
- For the latest pricing on the exams and updates to the registration procedures, visit CompTIA's website at www.comptia.org.

Who Should Read This Book?

You—if want to pass the Tech+ exam and pass it confidently! This book is chock-full of the exact information you need and directly maps to Tech+ exam objectives (listed later in this introduction), so if you use it to study for the exam, your odds of passing shoot way up.

In addition to including every bit of knowledge you need to learn to pass the exam, I've included some really great tips and solid wisdom to equip you even further to work successfully in the real IT world.

What Does This Book Cover?

This book covers everything you need to know to pass the CompTIA Terch+ exam. But in addition to studying the book, it's a good idea to practice on actual computers if you can.

Here's a list of the 12 chapters in this book:

Chapter 1, "Core Hardware Components" This chapter introduces you to the core insides of a computer, specifically motherboards, processors, memory, storage, expansion slots, power, and cooling systems.

Chapter 2, "Peripherals and Connectors" While core hardware is important, users can truly customize their computer experience by adding peripheral hardware. To connect all of those toys to your system, you need to know which connectors to use, and this chapter teaches you all of that.

Chapter 3, "Computing Devices and the Internet of Things" Now that you've learned about all of the individual hardware components, how do they all work together? This chapter discusses features of servers, workstations, laptops, tablets, smartphones, and gaming consoles. It also introduces the Internet of Things (IoT), which can turn practically anything into a device.

Chapter 4, "Operating Systems" Without an operating system, computer hardware makes a pretty good doorstop. The operating system is the most critical piece of software on a computer, because it coordinates the efforts of the hardware and provides an interface for the user to interact with the machine.

Chapter 5, "Software Applications" This chapter covers a variety of common application types that reside on computers, such as productivity software, collaboration software, utility software, and web browsers. It also teaches you about software management and the proper ways to install, uninstall, and manage applications.

Chapter 6, "Software Development" Have you ever wondered how applications get created? This chapter will teach you the characteristics of several classes of programming languages. You will also see examples of code, programming logic, and organizational methods.

Chapter 7, "Database Fundamentals" Databases are a key part of computing systems today. Data is the new currency, and therefore databases are like a bank vault. This chapter walks you through database concepts and structures, and it shows you some methods to interact with databases.

Chapter 8, "Networking Concepts and Technologies" Who doesn't want to get on the Internet? Wireless networks are popular today as a method to get Internet connectivity. You'll learn about key networking technologies and how to configure a wireless router in this chapter.

Chapter 9, "Cloud Computing and Artificial Intelligence" These are two of the biggest trends in IT today, the cloud and AI. First you will learn what the cloud is, and isn't (for example, it's neither fluffy nor in the sky). Then you will learn how AI works and explore different AI applications.

Chapter 10, "Security Concepts and Threats" The downside to computers is that it seems like hackers are everywhere. This chapter will introduce you to common threats posed by would-be attackers so you know how to avoid them. It also introduces a security framework and access control concepts.

Chapter 11, "Security Best Practices" This chapter builds on Chapter 10 by showing you how to set up your system to protect it against attacks. You will learn about hardening devices, managing users, and using data encryption.

Chapter 12, "Data Continuity and Computer Support" Inevitably, computers will run into problems—it's the nature of electronic components. This chapter will show you how to troubleshoot any issues that pop up. *Warning*: After reading this chapter, all of your family members will call on you for technical support (if they don't already)! This chapter also shows you how to plan for eventual computer problems so that you don't totally lose your data.

What's Included in the Book

I've included the following study tools throughout the book:

Assessment Test At the end of this introduction is an Assessment Test that you can use to check your readiness for the exam. Take this test before you start reading the book; it will help you determine the areas where you might need to brush up. The answers to the Assessment Test questions appear on a separate page after the last question of the test. Each answer includes an explanation and a note telling you the chapter in which the material appears.

Objective Map and Opening List of Objectives Just before the Assessment Test, you'll find a detailed exam objective map, showing you where each of the CompTIA exam objectives is covered in this book. In addition, each chapter opens with a list of the exam objectives it covers. Use these to see exactly where each of the exam topics is covered.

Exam Essentials Each chapter, just after the summary, includes a number of exam essentials. These are the key topics that you should take from the chapter in terms of areas to focus on when preparing for the exam.

Lab Exercises Each chapter includes a hands-on lab to give you more experience. These exercises map to the exam objectives. Some ask specific questions, and you can find the answers to those questions in Appendix A.

Chapter Review Questions To test your knowledge as you progress through the book, there are 20 review questions at the end of each chapter. As you finish each chapter, answer the review questions and then check your answers—the correct answers and explanations are in Appendix B. You can go back to reread the section that deals with each question you got wrong in order to ensure that you answer correctly the next time you're tested on the material.

Go to `http://www.wiley.com/go/sybextestprep` to register and gain access to this interactive online learning environment and test bank with study tools.

Interactive Online Learning Environment and Test Bank

The interactive online learning environment that accompanies *CompTIA Tech+ Study Guide: Exam FC0-U71, Third Edition*, provides a test bank with study tools to help you prepare for the certification exam and increase your chances of passing it the first time! The test bank includes the following:

Sample Tests All of the questions in this book are provided, including the Assessment Test, which you'll find at the end of this introduction, and the review questions at the end of each chapter. In addition, there are two Practice Exams with more than 60 questions each. Use these questions to test your knowledge of the study guide material. The online test bank runs on multiple devices.

Flashcards Questions are provided in digital flashcard format (a question followed by a single correct answer). You can use the flashcards to reinforce your learning and provide last-minute test prep before the exam.

Other Study Tools A glossary of key terms from this book and their definitions is available as a fully searchable PDF.

Like all exams, the Tech+ certification from CompTIA is updated periodically and may eventually be retired or replaced. At some point after CompTIA is no longer offering this exam, the old editions of our books and online tools will be retired. If you have purchased this book after the exam was retired, or are attempting to register in the Sybex online learning environment after the exam was retired, please know that we make no guarantees that this exam's online Sybex tools will be available once the exam is no longer available.

How to Use This Book

If you want a solid foundation for the serious effort of preparing for the Tech+ exam, then look no further because I've spent countless hours putting together this book with the sole intention of helping you to pass it!

This book is loaded with valuable information, and you will get the most out of your study time if you understand how I put the book together. Here's a list that describes how to approach studying:

1. Take the Assessment Test immediately following this introduction. (The answers are at the end of the test, but no peeking!) It's okay if you don't know any of the answers—that's what this book is for. Carefully read over the explanations for any question you get wrong, and make note of the chapters where that material is covered.
2. Study each chapter carefully, making sure you fully understand the information and the exam objectives listed at the beginning of each one. Again, pay extra-close attention to any chapter that includes material covered in questions you missed on the Assessment Test.
3. Complete the lab exercise at the end of each chapter. Do *not* skip these exercises. One reason is that they directly map to the CompTIA objectives and reinforce the material. Another reason is that it gives you hands-on experience, which is crucial.
4. Answer all the review questions related to each chapter. Specifically, note any questions that confuse you, and study the corresponding sections of the book again. And don't just skim these questions—make sure you understand each answer completely.
5. Try your hand at the Practice Exams. The more questions you practice, the better you will be when you sit for the real exam.
6. Test yourself using all of the electronic flashcards. This is a new and updated flashcard program to help you prepare for the latest CompTIA Tech+ exam, and it is a really great study tool.

Learning every bit of the material in this book is going to require you to apply yourself with a good measure of discipline. So, try to set aside the same time period every day to study, and select a comfortable and quiet place to do so. If you work hard, you will be surprised at how quickly you learn this material.

If you follow the steps listed here and study with the Review Questions, Practice Exams, electronic flashcards, and all of the written labs, I'm confident you have a great chance of passing the CompTIA Tech+ exam. However, studying for the Tech+ exam is a little like training for a marathon—if you don't go for a good run every day, you're not likely to finish very well.

Exam Objectives

Speaking of objectives, you're probably pretty curious about them, right? CompTIA asked groups of IT professionals to fill out a survey rating the skills they felt were important in their jobs, and the results were grouped into objectives for the exam and divided into six domains.

This table gives you the extent by percentage in which each domain is represented on the actual examination.

Domain	% of Examination
1.0 IT Concepts and Terminology	13%
2.0 Infrastructure	24%
3.0 Applications and Software	18%
4.0 Software Development Concepts	13%
5.0 Data and Database Fundamentals	13%
6.0 Security	19%
Total	100%

Exam objectives are subject to change at any time without prior notice and at CompTIA's sole discretion. Please visit CompTIA's website (www.comptia.org) for the most current listing of exam objectives.

CompTIA Tech+ Study Guide

FC0-U71 Exam Objectives

Objective	Chapter(s)
1.0 IT Concepts and Terminology	
1.1 Explain the basics of computing.	1
1.2 Identify notational systems.	6
1.3 Compare and contrast common units of measure.	1, 2, 8
1.4 Explain the troubleshooting methodology.	12
2.0 Infrastructure	
2.1 Explain common computing devices and their purposes.	3
2.2 Explain the purpose of common internal computing components.	1
2.3 Compare and contrast storage types.	1, 2, 8
2.4 Given a scenario install and configure common peripheral devices.	2
2.5 Compare and contrast common types of input/output device interfaces.	2
2.6 Compare and contrast virtualization and cloud technologies.	9
2.7 Compare and contrast Internet service types.	8
2.8 Identify basic networking concepts.	8
2.9 Explain the basic capabilities of a small wireless network.	8

Objective	Chapter(s)
3.0 Applications and Software	
3.1 Identify components of an OS.	4
3.2 Explain the purpose of operating systems.	4
3.3 Explain the purpose and proper use of software.	5
3.4 Given a scenario, configure and use web browser features.	5
3.5 Identify common uses of artificial intelligence (AI).	9
4.0 Software Development Concepts	
4.1 Compare and contrast programming language categories.	6
4.2 Identify fundamental data types and their characteristics.	6
4.3 Explain the purpose and use of programming concepts.	6
4.4 Identify programming organizational techniques and logic concepts.	6
5.0 Data and Database Fundamentals	
5.1 Explain the value of data and information.	10
5.2 Explain database concepts and the purpose of a database.	7
5.3 Compare and contrast various database structures.	7
5.4 Explain basic data backup concepts.	12
6.0 Security	
6.1 Explain fundamental security concepts and frameworks.	10
6.2 Explain methods to secure devices and security best practices.	5, 11
6.3 Explain password best practices.	11
6.4 Identify common use cases for encryption.	11
6.5 Given a scenario, configure security settings for a small wireless network.	8

How to Contact the Publisher

If you believe you have found a mistake in this book, please bring it to our attention. At John Wiley & Sons, we understand how important it is to provide our customers with accurate content, but even with our best efforts an error may occur.

In order to submit your possible errata, please email it to our Customer Service Team at `wileysupport@wiley.com` with the subject line “Possible Book Errata Submission.”

Assessment Test

1. Which of the following optical discs will store the most data?
   A. CD-ROM
   B. DVD-ROM DL
   C. DVD-ROM DS
   D. RS-ROM
2. Which of the following devices are used to permanently store user data in a computer? (Choose two.)
   A. HDD
   B. RAM
   C. ROM
   D. SSD
3. Which of the following on your computer is considered firmware?
   A. RAM
   B. SSD
   C. CMOS
   D. BIOS
4. What was the first widely adopted video connector standard?
   A. HDMI
   B. VGA
   C. USB
   D. DVI
5. What type of removable storage is often used in digital cameras?
   A. Flash drive
   B. NAS
   C. Memory card
   D. Mobile media card
6. Which of the following network speeds provides the greatest throughput?
   A. 100 Gbps
   B. 100 Mbps
   C. 1 Kbps
   D. 1000 bps

7. Angela has an iPhone with a biometric scanner enabled. She powered the device off, and just turned it back on. What methods can she use to unlock her phone?
   - **A.** Facial recognition only
   - **B.** Passcode only
   - **C.** Facial recognition or passcode
   - **D.** Facial recognition, fingerprint ID, or passcode

8. You are setting up a new Wi-Fi connection on your iPad. What is the first step in the process?
   - **A.** Enter wireless password.
   - **B.** Verify Internet connection.
   - **C.** Verify wireless capabilities.
   - **D.** Locate SSID.
   - **E.** Turn on Wi-Fi.

9. What type of security is involved when pairing two Bluetooth devices together?
   - **A.** SSL certificates are exchanged.
   - **B.** A PIN is provided by the Bluetooth device.
   - **C.** The Bluetooth security layer negotiates the security mechanism.
   - **D.** There is no security involved.

10. You install a new video card into a computer but it only gives you basic resolution. A friend suggests you check the driver version. Where would you do that in Windows?
    - **A.** Device Manager
    - **B.** Video Card Manager
    - **C.** Task manager
    - **D.** Services Manager

11. Which Windows feature helps prevent against catastrophic system changes such as accidentally installing malware?
    - **A.** Application Manager
    - **B.** UAC
    - **C.** Encryption
    - **D.** Task Manager

12. If you buy a new Apple tablet computer, what operating system can you expect to find on it?
    - **A.** Android
    - **B.** iOS
    - **C.** iPadOS
    - **D.** macOS

13. Which of the following is not considered productivity software?
    A. Spreadsheet software
    B. Web browser
    C. Online workspace
    D. Visual diagramming software

14. Which of the following is the most legitimate place to download a software application from?
    A. Perpetual website
    B. Piracy website
    C. OEM website
    D. Third-party website

15. The cache in a web browser stores what?
    A. The list of favorite websites
    B. User configuration information
    C. Private browsing settings
    D. Temporary files

16. Which data type exists only in true and false states?
    A. Binary
    B. Boolean
    C. Char
    D. Float

17. Code that is not part of the functionality of the program but that is intended to be easy for people to read is called what?
    A. Compiled
    B. Interpreted
    C. Commented
    D. Pseudocode

18. Which of the following container types has a fixed length?
    A. Constant
    B. Array
    C. Vector
    D. String

19. When creating a relational database, what is the name of the rules and structure?
    A. Forms
    B. Tables

C. Schema

D. Constraints

20. Which of the following statements is true regarding a foreign key in a relational database?

A. They are required.

B. There can be only one per table.

C. They are automatically indexed.

D. Null values are allowed.

21. David, a database administrator, needs to remove a column from an existing database. Which command should he use?

A. `ALTER`

B. `DELETE`

C. `DROP`

D. `REMOVE`

22. You open your web browser and type in `www.google.com`, but your computer can't find the website. Your neighbor's computer finds it just fine. What is most likely the cause?

A. Incorrect DNS configuration.

B. Incorrect DHCP configuration.

C. Incorrect WPA2 configuration.

D. The website is down.

23. Your friend Marcos asks you which of the following are the most secure. What do you tell him?

A. 802.11n

B. Infrared

C. Fiber-optic

D. UTP

24. Your need to set up a wireless router for a friend. He wants to be sure that his network is secure. Which wireless security method should you implement?

A. WPA2

B. WPA

C. WPA3

D. WEP

25. Which hypervisor is typically used in server-side virtualization?

A. Type 1

B. Type 2

C. Type 3

D. Type 4

26. If an operating system resides within a hypervisor, what is that operating system called?
    - A. Host OS
    - B. Guest OS
    - C. Parasite OS
    - D. Hybrid OS

27. Which of the following types of AI is most likely to be used to show you similar products to the one you searched for on an online retailer site?
    - A. AI chatbot
    - B. AI assistant
    - C. Generative AI
    - D. Predictive AI

28. When setting up authorization on a network, what should the administrator consider using?
    - A. Least privilege model
    - B. Multifactor
    - C. Single sign-on
    - D. Location tracking

29. A user has been accused of hacking into a server. Which of the following would keep them from denying that they did it?
    - A. Authentication
    - B. Authorization
    - C. Accounting
    - D. Nonrepudiation

30. Your manager read about a replay attack and is worried a hacker will try to use it on your network. What type of concern is this?
    - A. Confidentiality
    - B. Integrity
    - C. Availability
    - D. Authentication

31. Which of the following are considered device hardening techniques? (Choose two.)
    - A. Disabling AutoPlay
    - B. Requiring security certificates
    - C. Enabling single sign-on
    - D. Installing antimalware software

32. What is the name of an organization that is responsible for ensuring websites are legitimate and can send and receive secure traffic?

    A. CA

    B. SSL

    C. TLS

    D. HTTPS

33. You are browsing the Internet to purchase a gift for a friend. What should you look for to ensure it's safe to enter your credit card information?

    A. Security seal of approval

    B. RSA Secure Access symbol

    C. OEM validation

    D. `HTTPS://`

34. You just installed a new HP printer on your Dell computer, and it's not printing. What is the first source to check for information on the problem?

    A. Dell's website

    B. HP's website

    C. Google Search

    D. Internet technical community groups

35. When configuring a backup solution for your computer, you decide that speed is the most important factor. Which storage option should you choose?

    A. Locally attached storage

    B. Network attached storage

    C. Cloud storage

    D. Offline storage

36. You have just completed a backup of your PC onto a USB flash drive. What is the next step you need to take?

    A. Store the backup in a secure location.

    B. Burn the disc to ensure the data is saved.

    C. Test the backup to verify it works.

    D. Copy the backup data to the cloud.

Answers to the Assessment Test

1. C. A double-sided DVD-ROM can store more data than a dual-layer DVD-ROM, and both can store much more than a CD-ROM. There is no RS-ROM. See Chapter 1 for more information.

2. A, D. Hard disk drives (HDDs) are used to permanently store user data. Solid-state drives (SSDs) are one type of hard drive. See Chapter 1 for more information.

3. D. The basic input output system (BIOS) is firmware. It's stored on a hardware chip called the CMOS. See Chapter 1 for more information.

4. B. VGA was the first widely used video connector standard, and it was released in 1987. HDMI, DVI, and USB can all be used for video but are newer. See Chapter 2 for more information.

5. C. Digital cameras use memory cards. The most popular form of memory card in the market today is the SD card. See Chapter 2 for more information.

6. A. 100 gigabits per second (Gbps) is the fastest of these options. Megabits per second, kilobits per second, and bits per second are all slower. See Chapter 2 for more information.

7. B. With biometrics such as facial scanning enabled, you can use either the passcode or your face. However, if it was just powered off, the only option is to enter the passcode. See Chapter 3 for more information.

8. C. The proper steps in order are to verify wireless capabilities, turn on Wi-Fi, locate SSID, enter wireless password, and verify Internet connection. See Chapter 3 for more information.

9. B. When pairing two Bluetooth devices, you need to enter the PIN into your mobile device that allows it to connect to the Bluetooth device. See Chapter 3 for more information.

10. A. Drivers can be checked and updated in Windows Device Manager. See Chapter 4 for more information.

11. B. User Account Control (UAC) manages security settings such as the ability to install new software. See Chapter 4 for more information.

12. C. New Apple iPads will have the iPadOS, which is an offshoot from iOS. See Chapter 4 for more information.

13. C. Online workspace is an example of collaboration software. See Chapter 5 for more information.

14. C. The original equipment manufacturer (OEM) website is the best place to download software from. See Chapter 5 for more information.

15. D. The cache stores temporary Internet files. See Chapter 5 for more information.

16. B. The Boolean data type only uses true and false. Oftentimes they are represented with a 1 for True and a 0 for False, but this does not have to be the case. See Chapter 6 for more information.

17. D. Pseudocode is used for annotation, and it does not affect the functionality of the program. See Chapter 6 for more information.

18. B. Arrays and vectors are the two container types. Arrays have a fixed length, and vectors can have a dynamically allocated length. See Chapter 6 for more information.

19. C. The schema is the rules and structure of a relational database. See Chapter 7 for more information.

20. D. A foreign key is one or more columns in a table that refers to the primary key in another table. Unlike primary keys, null values are allowed. Foreign keys are not required, there can be more than one per table, and they are not automatically indexed. See Chapter 7 for more information.

21. A. The `ALTER` command is used to add, remove, or modify columns in a database. `DROP` is used to remove a table or database. `DELETE` is used to delete a record, and there is no `REMOVE` command. See Chapter 7 for more information.

22. A. DNS servers resolve hostnames to IP addresses. It's possible that your computer has the wrong address for the DNS sever. DHCP automatically configures TCP/IP clients, and WPA2 is a wireless security protocol. If the website was down, your neighbor would not be able to access it either. See Chapter 8 for more information.

23. C. Wired connections are more secure than wireless ones. Fiber-optic cable is also immune to wiretaps, which makes it more secure than UTP. See Chapter 8 for more information.

24. C. WPA3 is the most secure wireless security protocol in use today. See Chapter 8 for more information.

25. A. A Type 1 hypervisor, also known as a bare metal hypervisor, is used in server-side virtualization. Type 2 hypervisors are used in client-side virtualization. There are no Type 3 or Type 4 hypervisors. See Chapter 9 for more information.

26. B. An OS residing within a hypervisor is called a guest OS. If the hypervisor is running on an OS, the OS running the hypervisor is called the host OS. See Chapter 9 for more information.

27. D. The AI most likely behind this product suggestion is AI predictions and suggestions. See Chapter 9 for more information.

28. A. The least privilege model is a framework that administrators should use for authorizing users to access resources. Multifactor and single sign-on are examples of authentication, not authorization. Location tracking is a form of accounting. See Chapter 10 for more information.

29. D. The framework for access control is AAA—authentication, authorization, and accounting. Nonrepudiation is added, which makes it so people can't deny that an event took place. See Chapter 10 for more information.

30. B. A replay attack is an example of an integrity concern. Other examples are on-path attacks, impersonation, and unauthorized information alteration. See Chapter 10 for more information.

31. A, D. Device hardening makes it harder for attackers to gain access to your system by reducing the potential areas of attack. Two examples of device hardening are disabling unused or unneeded services such as AutoPlay and installing antimalware. See Chapter 11 for more information.

32. A. A certificate authority (CA) issues SSL certificates to websites so they can use the HTTPS protocol. See Chapter 11 for more information.

33. D. Secure websites will start with `HTTPS://` instead of `HTTP://`. See Chapter 11 for more information.

34. B. Always check the manufacturer's website first. Since it's an HP printer, check their site and not Dell's. See Chapter 12 for more information.

35. A. When choosing a backup solution, know that locally attached storage devices will always be faster than network storage or cloud-based solutions. See Chapter 12 for more information.

36. C. After completing a backup, you should verify that the backup is working properly. See Chapter 12 for more information.

Core Hardware Components

THE FOLLOWING COMPTIA TECH+ FC0-U71 EXAM OBJECTIVES ARE COVERED IN THIS CHAPTER:

✓ **1.0 IT Concepts and Terminology**

✓ **1.1 Explain the basics of computing.**

- Input
- Processing
- Output
- Storage

✓ **1.3 Compare and contrast common units of measure.**

- Storage unit
  - Bit
  - Byte
  - Kilobyte (KB)
  - Megabyte (MB)
  - Gigabyte (GB)
  - Terabyte (TB)
  - Petabyte (PB)
- Processing speed
  - Megahertz (MHz)
  - Gigahertz (GHz)

✓ **2.0 Infrastructure**

✓ **2.2 Explain the purpose of common internal computing components.**

- Motherboard/system board
- Firmware/basic input/output system (BIOS)

- Random-access memory (RAM)
- Central processing unit (CPU)
- Graphics processing unit (GPU)
- Storage
- Network interface card (NIC)
    - Wired vs. wireless
    - Onboard vs. expansion card

✓ **2.3 Compare and contrast storage types.**

- Volatile vs. non-volatile
- Local storage
    - RAM
    - Read-only memory (ROM)
    - Storage drive
        - Magnetic disks/hard disk drive (HDD)
        - Solid-state drive (SSD)
        - Non-volatile memory express (NVMe)
    - Optical
    - External flash drives

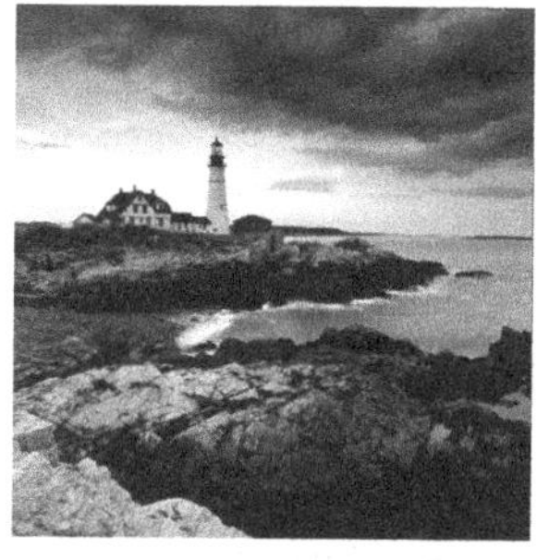

What better way to kick off a book on computing technology fundamentals than to talk about the most fundamental components of all—core hardware. When you break it down to the basics, computers are simply collections of specialized hardware devices that work together (with software) to provide you with the functionality you want. For most users, the desired functionality is to take input, such as from a keyboard, a mouse, or a touchscreen; somehow process it; produce output (video or printed); and store data. Sometimes the hardware is in your hands, and at other times it's halfway around the world—but it's always necessary. Even soft and fluffy-sounding terms such as "the cloud" (which I will introduce in Chapter 9, "Cloud Computing and Artificial Intelligence") rely on much of the same hardware that sits snugly within your tablet or smartphone case.

To begin your journey of understanding fundamental computing technology concepts, I will discuss components that are commonly included inside the computer case. Some are critical, whereas others just provide features that are nice to have, such as sound or a network connection. In this way, I'll start from the inside out so that you understand what makes computers work the way they do.

Introducing Internal Components

In this section, I will talk about the components that are generally inside the computer case. Some of them are exclusively found inside the case, such as the motherboard and the processor, whereas others can be internal or external. For example, internal hard drives (for storage) are standard in desktop and laptop computers, but you can also buy external hard drives for expanded storage. Network cards are another great example. Today, the circuitry is generally built into the computer, but you can easily find external ones as well. Regardless of the location of your hard drive or network card, it still provides the same functionality.

Most home computer components are modular. That is, they can be removed and replaced by another piece of hardware that does the same thing, provided that it's compatible and that it fits. For example, if the hard drive in your laptop fails, it can be removed and replaced by another hard drive. This isn't always the case, of course, and the general rule is that the smaller the device, the less modular it is. This is because to achieve the smaller size, manufacturers need to integrate more functionality into the same component. It's usually quicker and just as cost-effective to replace a device such as a smartphone rather than repair it if a part fails. If a component is modular and can be replaced, you will sometimes hear it referred to as a *field-replaceable unit (FRU)*.

Since I'm talking about components that are inside the case, it would be unfortunate to ignore the case itself. Cases are usually a combination of metal and plastic and serve these three primary functions:

- Keeping all the components securely in place
- Protecting the components from harm
- Providing adequate airflow to keep components from overheating

Protecting the components is the key. Water and other liquids are obviously bad for electronic devices, and direct exposure to sunlight and dust can cause parts to overheat and fail. The case guards against all these things. Moreover, in some cases (pun intended), it can make your device easily mobile.

Throughout this section, I will specifically talk about *personal computer (PC)* (laptop and desktop) hardware. Many of the principles here apply to smaller devices such as smartphones as well.

Exploring Motherboards, Processors, and Memory

These three components—motherboards, processors, and memory—are the holy trinity of computers. Pretty much every personal computing device made today requires all three of these parts. So, without further ado, let's dive in.

Motherboards

The *motherboard* is the most important component in the computer because it connects all the other components. Functionally, it acts much like the nervous system of the computer. You will also hear it called the system board or the *mainboard*. With this introduction, you might think that this piece of hardware is complex—and you'd be right! Manufacturers and hardware resellers don't make it easy to understand what you're dealing with either. Here's the description of a motherboard for sale on an Internet hardware site:

> Asus ROG Strix Z790-E Gaming WiFi II LGA 1700 DDR5 ATX Motherboard, DDR5 8000+, 1x PCIe 5.0x16, 2x PCIe 4.0x16, 5x M.2 slots, 1x HDMI, 1x DisplayPort, 1x USB 20 Gbps port, 11x USB 10 Gbps ports, Wi-Fi 7

What does that all mean? Is it even human language? Don't worry. By the end of this section on motherboards, you will understand what it all means.

Tech+ exam objective 2.2, "Explain the purpose of common internal computing components," lists motherboard/system board as a subobjective. I'll explain the motherboard in depth here, probably in more detail than you will need to know for the exam. It's better to be over-prepared, though, and the knowledge you gain here will help you in the real world as well.

The first thing to know about motherboards is that they are a *printed circuit board (PCB)*—that is, a conductive series of pathways laminated to a nonconductive substrate that lines the bottom of the computer. Most of the time they are green, but you will also see them in a rainbow of colors, including black, brown, blue, red, and white ones. If you look at the bottom of a motherboard, you will see all the conductive pathways. Some of the most popular brands right now are ASUS, GIGABYTE, and Micro-Star (MSI). Figure 1.1 shows a typical motherboard.

FIGURE 1.1 A motherboard

All other components are attached to this circuit board. Some are physically attached directly to the board and aren't intended to be removed, such as the underlying circuitry, the central processing unit (CPU) slot, random access memory (RAM) slots, expansion slots, and a variety of other chips. Components such as the CPU and the RAM get physically attached to the motherboard. Other devices, such as hard drives and power supplies, are attached via their own cables and connectors.

Manufacturers can also integrate components such as the CPU, video card, network card, and others directly onto the motherboard as opposed to having slots into which they are inserted. As a rule of thumb, the smaller the motherboard, the more likely it is to have integrated components.

Let's start breaking down the features and components typically associated with motherboards. The following list might look long, but breaking each one down separately will help you to understand the importance of each one. Here are the topics coming up shortly:

- Form factors
- Chipsets
- Processor sockets
- Memory slots
- Expansion slots
- Disk controllers
- Power connectors
- BIOS/firmware
- CMOS and CMOS battery
- Back-panel connectors
- Front-panel connectors

In the following sections, you will learn about some of the most common components of a motherboard and what they do. I'll show you what each component looks like so that you can identify it on almost any motherboard you run across.

Form Factors

Motherboards are classified by their design, which is called a *form factor*. There are dozens of form factors in existence. Because motherboards mount to the system case, it's important to know what types of motherboards your case supports before replacing one. Desktop computer cases often support multiple sizes of motherboards, but laptops are another story. With laptops, you almost always need to replace an old motherboard with the same version.

The most common form factors used today are Advanced Technology Extended (ATX), microATX, and Information Technology Extended (ITX).

ITX is not one specific form factor but a collection of small form factor (SFF) boards.

The form factors differ in size and configuration of the components on the motherboard. In addition, they may have different power requirements. MicroATX and ITX are specifically designed to be paired with low-wattage power supplies, which consume and produce less power and therefore generate less heat, to reduce the amount of heat produced by the computer. Because these two are smaller, they also offer fewer options for adding expansion cards versus the ATX design.

Here's a quick history lesson. The XT form factor was developed by IBM in 1983, and it is generally considered the first industry-standard PC form factor. In 1985, IBM released the Baby-AT, which because of its smaller size quickly became the most popular form factor in the market. The Baby-AT was king until 1996 when Intel released the ATX standard. As of this writing, the ATX and microATX (which is similar in configuration to ATX, only smaller) are still the most popular desktop computer form factors.

Table 1.1 provides the dimensions of common motherboard form factors.

TABLE 1.1 Motherboard form factors

Form factor	Release year	Size
Baby-AT	1985	8.5 × 10 – 13 in (216 × 254 – 330 mm)
ATX	1996	12 × 9.6 in (305 × 244 mm)
microATX	1996	9.6 × 9.66 in (244 × 244 mm)
Mini-ITX	2001	6.7 × 6.7 in (170 × 170 mm)
Nano-ITX	2003	4.7 × 4.7 in (120 × 120 mm)
Pico-ITX	2007	3.9 × 2.8 in (100 × 72 mm)
Mobile-ITX	2007	2.95 × 1.77 in (75 × 45 mm)
Neo-ITX	2012	6.7 × 3.35 in (170 × 85 mm)

In view of how quickly computer technology evolves, it is amazing that the form factors remain popular for as long as they do. The advent of smaller devices such as tablets and smartphones has driven the most recent form factor design changes.

Chipsets

The motherboard's *chipset* is a collection of chips or circuits that perform interface and peripheral functions for the processor. Said differently, this collection of chips provides interfaces for memory, expansion cards, and onboard peripherals, and it generally dictates how a motherboard will communicate with the installed peripherals.

Chipsets are usually given a name and model number by the original manufacturer—for example, Intel's Z790. What features make the Z790 so great? I will be honest; I have no idea. There are so many chipsets out there that it's impossible to memorize the features of each one. But, if you need to know, having the manufacturer and model can help you look up the features of that particular chipset, such as the type of RAM supported, the type and brand of onboard video, and so on.

In the motherboard example at the beginning of this section, you saw an ASUS Z790-E motherboard. The best place to look for motherboard specifications is on the manufacturer's website. For example, `https://rog.asus.com/us/motherboards/rog-strix/rog-strix-z790-e-gaming-wifi-model/spec` tells you everything that you need to know about the ASUS ROG Strix Z790-E motherboard.

The functions of chipsets can be divided into two major groups: Northbridge and Southbridge. It's highly unlikely that you'll be tested on these on the Tech+ exam, but I want to introduce them just in case you hear the terms. Plus, I think it helps better explain exactly what the chipset does.

Northbridge The Northbridge subset of a motherboard's chipset performs one important function: management of high-speed peripheral communications. The Northbridge is responsible primarily for communications with integrated video and processor-to-memory communications.

The communications between the CPU and memory occur over what is known as the *front-side bus (FSB)*, which is just a set of signal pathways connecting the CPU and main memory. The *back-side bus (BSB)*, if present, is a set of signal pathways between the CPU and any external cache memory.

Southbridge The Southbridge subset of the chipset is responsible for providing support to the onboard slower peripherals (PS/2, parallel ports, serial ports, Serial and Parallel ATA, and so on) and managing their communications with the rest of the computer and the resources given to them. If you're thinking about any component other than the CPU, memory and cache, or integrated video, the Southbridge is in charge.

As of 2023, most PCs don't separate out the Northbridge and Southbridge into two physically distinct chips. Instead, a single chip typically handles both functions of the chipset. In addition, some manufacturers will refer to their chipsets as a *platform controller hub (PCH)* or integrate the functionality directly into the central processing unit (CPU).

Figure 1.2 shows the chipset of a motherboard, with the heat sink of the Northbridge, at the top left, connected to the heat-spreading cover of the Southbridge, at the bottom right.

FIGURE 1.2 Northbridge and Southbridge

Real World Scenario

Who's Driving the Bus?

When talking about the Northbridge, I mentioned a bus (specifically a front-side bus), so now is a good time to talk about what a bus does and to give you some historical context. You'll probably hear the term come up often when talking about computer hardware, such as in discussions about the system bus, expansion bus, parallel bus, and serial bus.

A *bus* is a common collection of signal pathways over which related devices communicate within the computer system. It refers specifically to a data path or the way that the computer communicates over that path.

Take serial and parallel buses, for example. A serial bus communicates one *bit* (short for binary digit, which is the smallest unit of data in computing), either a 0 (in an off state) or a 1 (in an on state) of data at a time, whereas a parallel bus communicates in several parallel channels (eight, for example) at once. Based on this explanation, you might think that parallel is faster than serial. After all, eight lanes should move more data than one lane, right? Sometimes, but not always. It depends on how fast you can get each lane to move.

Serial was developed before parallel, because at its core it's an easier technology to implement. In the late 1980s, parallel became much more popular for printers because it was a lot faster. The only downside to parallel was that the different streams of data needed to be carefully synchronized. This slowed down transmissions so that they weren't exactly eight times faster than the comparable serial connections.

By 1996, manufacturers had advanced the speed of serial technology enough so that it was faster than parallel, and the world saw the introduction of Universal Serial Bus (USB). It was faster than parallel, and it had a lot of additional features, such as the ability to hot-plug devices (that is, plug and unplug them without needing to shut down the system). Today, all of the fastest peripheral-connection technologies in use, such as USB, Peripheral Component Interconnect Express (PCIe), and Serial ATA (SATA), are all serial.

Thus, although parallel was king for a day, it's now outdated and rarely used. You can get faster transmissions via serial technology.

Processor Sockets

The *central processing unit (CPU)* is the "brain" of any computer. There are many different types of processors for computers, and the processor you have must fit into the socket on the motherboard. Typically, in today's computers, the processor is the easiest component to identify on the motherboard. It is usually the component that has either a large fan and/or a *heat sink* (usually both) attached to it. You will learn more about types of CPUs in the "Processors" section, later in this chapter.

CPU sockets are almost as varied as the processors they hold. Sockets are basically flat and have several columns and rows of holes or pins arranged in a square, as shown in Figure 1.3. You'll hear terms like *pin grid array (PGA)* or *land grid array (LGA)* to describe the socket type. In Figure 1.3, the left socket is PGA (socket AM4), and the right one is an LGA 1200. PGA sockets have holes, and the processors have pins that fit into the holes. LGA sockets have contacts (often pins) built into them, which connect with contacts on the CPU. Both sockets have locking mechanisms to hold the processor in place. PGA uses a simple lever, whereas LGA has a more complex locking harness (which is closed in Figure 1.3). You might also see *ball grid array (BGA)* sockets, which use small balls as their contact points.

FIGURE 1.3 CPU sockets

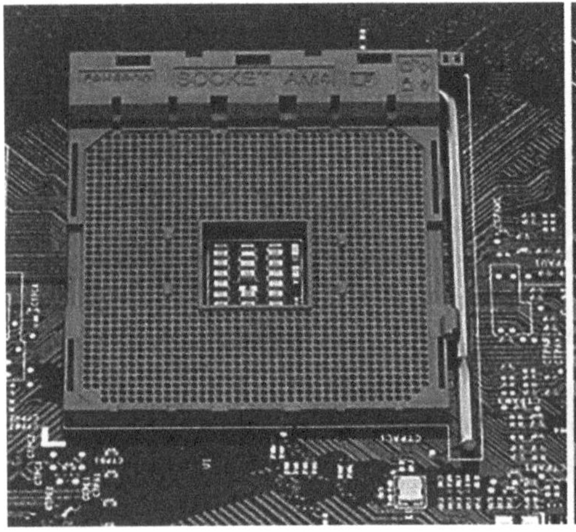

At the beginning of this section, I gave you a description of a motherboard for sale. LGA 1700 is the socket shown in the example.

Memory Slots

Random access memory (RAM) slots are for the modules that hold memory chips. RAM is the primary memory used to store currently used data and instructions for the CPU. Think of it as volatile, short-term memory; it's volatile in the sense that its contents will be lost if it's not continuously powered. (This is in contrast to *persistent* storage, which hard drives offer. I'll talk more about those later in this chapter, in the "Storage Devices" section.) Many and varied types of memory are available for PCs today. Examples include *Double Data Rate 4 (DDR4)* and DDR5. Memory for desktops comes on circuit boards called *dual inline memory modules (DIMMs)* and for laptops on *small outline DIMMs (SODIMMs)*. (I will talk about what these acronyms mean in the "Memory" section later in this chapter.)

Memory slots are easy to identify on a motherboard. First, they are long and slender and generally close to the CPU socket. Classic DIMM slots were usually black and, like all memory slots, were placed very close together. (Today manufacturers make memory slots of various colors.) Metal pins in the bottom make contact with the metallic pins on each memory module. Small metal or plastic tabs on each side of the slot keep the memory module securely in its slot. Figure 1.4 shows some memory slots on a desktop motherboard.

FIGURE 1.4 DIMM slots

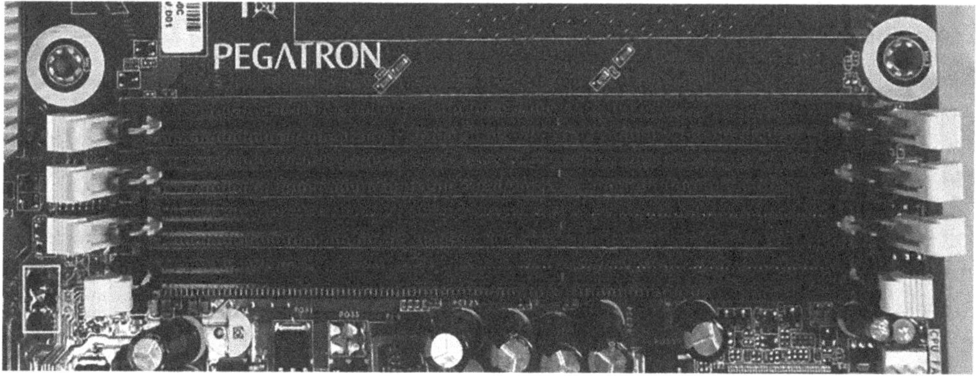

Laptops are space constrained, so they use the smaller form factor SODIMM chips. SODIMM slots are configured so that the chips lie nearly parallel to the motherboard, as shown in Figure 1.5.

FIGURE 1.5 SODIMM slots

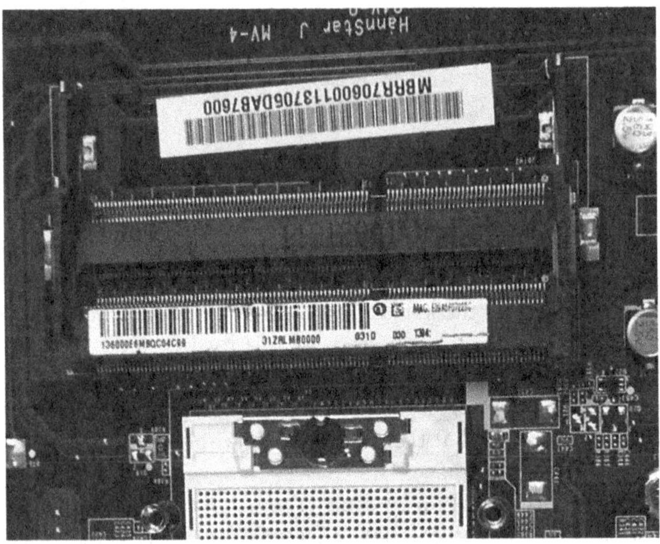

Motherboard designers can also speed up the system by adding *cache memory* between the CPU and RAM. Cache is a fast form of memory, and it improves system performance by predicting what the CPU will ask for next and prefetching this information before being asked. I will talk about cache more in the "Processors" section later in this chapter.

If there is cache on your motherboard, it is not likely to be a removable component. Therefore, it does not have a slot or connector like RAM does.

Expansion Slots

The most visible parts of any motherboard are the *expansion slots*. These are small plastic slots, usually from 1 to 6 inches long and approximately ½″ wide. As their name suggests, these slots are used to install various devices in the computer to expand its capabilities. Some expansion devices that might be installed in these slots include video, network, sound, and disk interface cards.

If you look at the motherboard in your computer, you will more than likely see one of these main types of expansion slots used in computers today:

- PCI
- AGP
- PCIe

Each type differs in appearance and function. In the following sections, I will cover how to identify visually the different expansion slots on the motherboard.

PCI Expansion Slots

For years, the most common expansion slots were the 32-bit *Peripheral Component Interconnect (PCI)* slots. They are easily recognizable because they are only around 3 inches long and classically white, although modern boards take liberties with the color. Although popularity has shifted from PCI to PCIe, the PCI slot's service to the industry cannot be ignored; it has been an incredibly prolific architecture for many years.

At the time PCI came out, the bus speed (how fast the data gets from point A to point B) was considered fast. You could get data throughput rates of 133 megabytes per second (MBps) and 266 MBps, with 133 MBps being the most common. Eventually, advances in the technology would double PCI speeds up to 533 Mbps. (Yes, 266 × 2 = 532, not 533. Hardware developers take a little creative license with rounding here and there.) By today's standards, the best PCI throughput is extremely slow, as you will see when we discuss newer technologies such as AGP and PCIe in the next two sections.

PCI slots and adapters are manufactured in 3.3V and 5V versions. The notch (also called a key) in the card edge of the common 5V slots and adapters is oriented toward the front of the motherboard, and the notch in the 3.3V adapters is oriented toward the rear. Figure 1.6 shows three PCI expansion slots; notice how the keys are in different positions on the connectors. The 5V slot is in the foreground and the two 3.3V slots are behind it. Also notice that a universal card, which has notches in both positions, is inserted into and operates fine in the 3.3V slot in the background.

FIGURE 1.6 PCI expansion slots

AGP Expansion Slots

Accelerated Graphics Port (AGP) slots are known mostly for legacy video card use and have been supplanted in new installations by PCI Express slots and their adapters. While AGP is almost extinct today, you can still buy motherboards that have it. AGP slots were designed to be a direct connection between the video circuitry and the PC's memory. They are also easily recognizable because they are usually brown and located right next to the PCI slots on the motherboard. AGP slots are slightly shorter than PCI slots and are pushed back from the rear of the motherboard in comparison with the position of the PCI slots. Figure 1.7 shows an example of an older AGP slot, along with a white PCI slot for comparison. Notice the difference in length between the two.

In the tech world, the word "legacy" means old and outdated, and the technology is likely no longer used. It's not meant as a compliment!

FIGURE 1.7 An AGP slot compared to a PCI slot

AGP performance is based on the original specification, known as AGP 1x, which has a data rate of 266 MBps. AGP 2x, 4x, and 8x specifications increase throughput linearly. For instance, AGP 8x produces an effective throughput of 2133 MBps. (266 × 8 = 2128, not 2133. This is another example of hardware developers creatively rounding numbers.) Note that this maximum throughput is only a fraction of the throughput of PCIe x16, which is covered in the following section.

PCIe Expansion Slots

Today's most common expansion slot architecture on motherboards is *PCI Express (PCIe)*. It was designed to be a replacement for AGP and PCI. PCIe has the advantage of being faster than AGP while maintaining the flexibility of PCI. PCIe has no plug compatibility with either AGP or PCI. As a result, some modern PCIe motherboards still have a regular PCI slot for backward compatibility, but AGP slots are rarely included.

There are seven different speeds supported by PCIe, designated × 1 (pronounced "by 1"), × 2, × 4, × 8, × 12, × 16, and × 32, with × 1, × 4, and × 16 being the most common. A slot that supports a particular speed will be of a specific physical size because faster cards require more wires and therefore are longer. As a result, a × 8 slot is longer than a × 1 slot but shorter than a × 16 slot. Every PCIe slot has a 22-pin portion in common toward the rear of the motherboard, as shown in Figure 1.8, in which the rear of the motherboard is to the left. These 22 pins comprise mostly voltage and ground leads. Figure 1.8 shows, from top to bottom, a × 16 slot, two × 1 slots, and a legacy PCI slot.

FIGURE 1.8 PCIe expansion slots

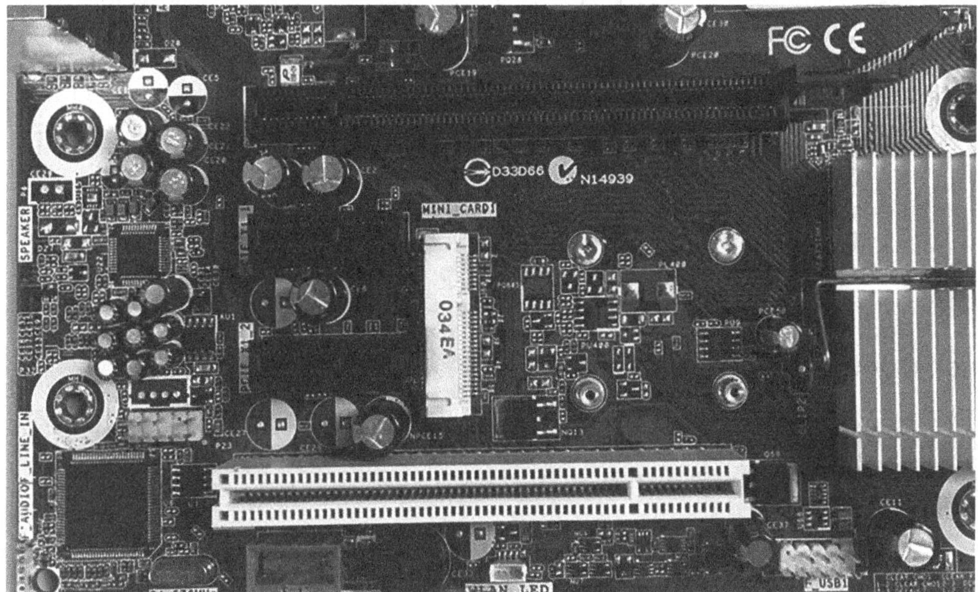

Compared to its predecessors, PCIe is fast. Even at the older PCIe 2.0 standard, a PCIe × 1 card will run at 500 MBps, which is comparable to the best that PCI can offer (533 MBps). The current in-market PCIe standard is PCIe 5.0, and with it a × 16 card can operate at a screaming 63 GBps, or about 118 times as fast as PCI. All PCIe slots are backward compatible with older PCIe cards. So, you can put a PCIe 2.0 card in a PCIe 5.0 slot—you just won't get the speed of PCIe 5.0, of course.

Real World Scenario

The Speed of Innovation

Newer standards always offer faster data transfer rates and greater throughput. Usually when the standard is released, people shake their heads at how mind-bogglingly fast they are, and then the cycle repeats itself a few years later. Hardware devices that support the standard are often one or two years behind the release of the standard.

For example, PCIe 4.0 came out in October 2017, seven years after PCIe 3.0. It doubled the data rates of the previous standard and provided good performance for virtual and augmented reality applications.

PCIe 5.0 was released in May 2019 and of course doubled up on PCIe 4.0. This helped support machine learning and artificial intelligence, as well as high-speed data transfers needed in data centers.

Continuing the journey is PCIe 6.0, released in January 2022. Devices supporting this standard are expected to hit the market in 2024. And right around the corner is PCIe 7.0, with a 2025 release date and devices expected in 2027. Some technology experts say that it's hard to imagine any device needing the crazy 256 GBps of bandwidth that PCIe 7.0 will provide, but I'm sure someone will figure out an application for it.

Its high data rate makes PCIe the current choice of gaming aficionados. The only downside with PCIe (and with later AGP slots) is that any movement of these high-performance devices can result in temporary failure or poor performance. Consequently, both PCIe and AGP slots have a latch and tab that secure the adapters in place.

Disk Controllers

One of the endearing features of computers is that they store data and allow it to be retrieved later. (It's true that they sometimes mysteriously lose our data too, but that's another story.) The long-term storage device is called a *hard drive*, and it plugs into the motherboard.

Stored data is sometimes called data at rest, as opposed to moving across a network (data in transit) or being used by a program (data in use). The state of the data makes a difference in how the data must be secured. Securing data in transit is covered more in Chapter 8, "Networking Concepts and Technologies," and securing data at rest is in Chapter 11, "Security Best Practices."

There are a few different hard drive standard connectors. The older one that you will run into is called *Integrated Drive Electronics (IDE)* or *Parallel Advanced Technology Attachment (PATA)*. The newer and much faster one is called *Serial Advanced Technology Attachment (SATA)*. Figure 1.9 shows the two IDE connectors (the black and white ones are the same). Figure 1.10 shows four SATA connectors. Notice how they are conveniently labeled for you on the motherboard!

FIGURE 1.9 IDE hard drive connectors

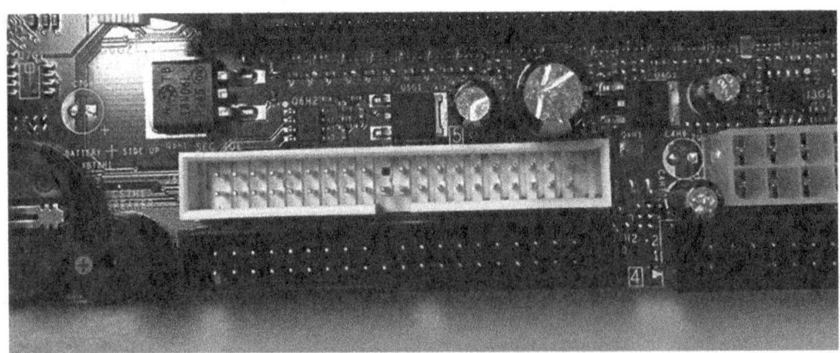

FIGURE 1.10 SATA hard drive connectors

Power Connectors

Computers are obviously electronic devices, and electronics, of course, require power. In addition to the other sockets and slots on the motherboard, a special connector (the 24-pin block connector shown in Figure 1.11) allows the motherboard to be connected to the power supply to receive power. This connector is where the ATX power adapter plugs in. Older AT-style motherboards used a 20-pin connector, and other devices such as hard drives and optical drives use smaller connectors that we will talk about later.

FIGURE 1.11 A 24-pin ATX power connector

BIOS/Firmware

Firmware is the name given to any software that is encoded in hardware, usually a *read-only memory (ROM)* chip, and can be run without extra instructions from the operating system. Firmware is great for situations where a specific computing routine that never (or rarely) changes needs to be run. Most computing devices and printers use firmware in some sense. The best example of firmware is a computer's *basic input/output system (BIOS)* routine, which is burned into a flash memory chip located on the motherboard. Also, some expansion cards, such as video cards, use their own firmware utilities for setting up peripherals.

Tech+ exam objective 2.2 lists firmware/basic input/output system (BIOS) as a subobjective. Be sure to know what it does.

Aside from the processor, the most important chip on the motherboard is the BIOS chip. This special memory chip contains the BIOS system software that boots the system and initiates the memory and hard drive to allow the operating system to start.

The BIOS chip is easily identified. If you have a brand-name computer, this chip might have the name of the manufacturer on it and usually the word *BIOS*. For clones, the chip usually has a sticker or printing on it from one of the major BIOS manufacturers (AMI, Phoenix/Award, Winbond, and so on). Figure 1.12 gives you an idea of what a BIOS chip might look like. This one is made by Fintek.

FIGURE 1.12 A BIOS chip on a motherboard

When you power on your computer, the BIOS initializes and runs a system-checking routine called the *power-on self-test (POST)*. The POST routine does the following things:

- Verifies the integrity of the BIOS itself
- Verifies and confirms the size of primary memory
- Analyzes and catalogs other forms of hardware, such as buses and boot devices
- Offers the user a key sequence to enter the configuration screen
- Hands over control to the boot device (usually a hard drive) highest in the configured boot order to load the operating system

If all its tests complete successfully, the POST process finishes. If there is an error, it can produce a beep code or displayed code that indicates there is an issue. Each BIOS publisher has its own series of codes that can be generated.

The BIOS on most modern computers has been replaced by a Unified Extensible Firmware Interface (UEFI), first introduced in 2002. It supports all the functions BIOS did, and it has updated features such as a graphical interface, support for larger hard drives, embedded security, and a faster boot time. In practice, the terms BIOS and UEFI are essentially interchangeable. In this book, I will use BIOS as that's the term specified in the exam objectives and acronym list.

As mentioned, the POST routine offers the user a chance to enter the BIOS and change the configuration settings. This is usually done by pressing a key during the boot process, such as F2, F12, or the Delete key. The computer may prompt you, but usually the prompt goes by quickly. If you don't see anything, an Internet search for the motherboard manufacturer will give you instructions on how to get into the BIOS. Once you get a screen showing that the operating system has started, you're too late. Figure 1.13 shows a BIOS (technically UEFI) configuration page.

FIGURE 1.13 BIOS settings

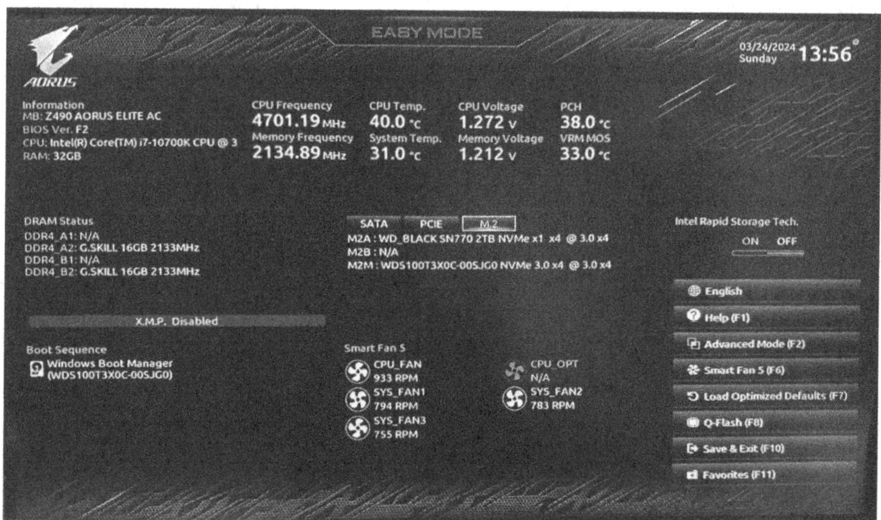

Inside the BIOS, you can make system configuration selections such as changing the system time, selecting a preferred boot device, or enabling/disabling features such as virtualization support or BIOS security and save the results. In the BIOS shown in Figure 1.13, you would press F2 or click Advanced Mode to make these changes. Also, many BIOSs offer diagnostic routines that you can use to have the BIOS analyze the state and quality of the same components it inspects during bootup but at a much deeper level.

Flashing the BIOS

When you upgrade your system's hardware, the system BIOS typically recognizes it upon bootup. If you upgraded your hard drive, processor, or memory and it's not recognized, though, you might need to update your system BIOS. This is done through a process called *flashing the BIOS*.

To flash the BIOS, you will need to download the most current version from the manufacturer of your computer (or motherboard, if you built your own system) and follow the instructions. As a warning, you should always be very careful when flashing a BIOS and follow the manufacturer's instructions to the letter. Messing it up could cause the motherboard to become inoperable.

CMOS and CMOS Battery

Your PC has to keep certain settings when it's turned off and its power cord is unplugged, such as the date and time, hard drive configuration, memory and CPU settings, boot sequence, and power management features.

These settings are kept in a special memory chip called the *complementary metal oxide semiconductor (CMOS)*. CMOS (pronounced *see-moss*) is actually a manufacturing technology for integrated circuits, but since the first commonly used chip made from CMOS technology was a BIOS memory chip, the terms have become somewhat interchangeable. To be technically correct, though, the name of the chip is the CMOS, and the BIOS settings are stored on the chip.

The CMOS chip must have power constantly or it will lose its information (just like RAM does when your computer is powered off). To prevent CMOS from losing its rather important information, motherboard manufacturers include a small battery called the *CMOS battery* to power the CMOS memory. Most CMOS batteries look like watch batteries or small cylindrical batteries. If you look back at Figure 1.12, you will see the CMOS battery next to the BIOS.

If your system does not retain its configuration information after it's been powered off, it's possible that the CMOS battery has failed. Replacing it is similar to replacing a watch battery.

Back-Panel Connectors

If you've ever looked at the back of a computer, you know that there's a lot going on back there. There could be a dozen or so different types of connectors, including ones for power, video, audio, a keyboard and mouse, networking (such as Gigabit Ethernet), and other devices. Generally speaking, all of these connectors are connected to one of two things: the motherboard or an expansion card that's attached to the motherboard. I will talk about all of these in Chapter 2, "Peripherals and Connectors." For now, I offer you Figure 1.14, showing several connectors on the back panel.

FIGURE 1.14 Motherboard back panel

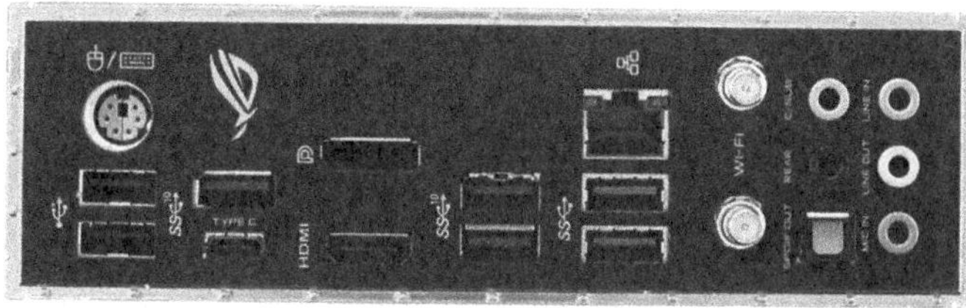

Front-Panel Connectors

Even though the front panel of the computer isn't as chaotic as the back panel, there's still a lot happening. The front of your computer might have one or more memory card readers or optical drives such as a DVD-ROM. It's kind of old-school to have these devices accessible from the front of your system. Years ago, you might have had 3½″ or even 5¼″ floppy drives on the front of your system too. (Google them!)

With the obsolescence of floppy drives, a lot more real estate opened up on the front of your computer. Computer manufacturers realized that accessibility was a big deal and started moving connectors that used to be found only on the backs of systems to the front. Now, your system will likely have most if not all of the following types of connectors on the front panel or top of the case. All of them get connected to the motherboard in some fashion.

Power Button Having a *power button* in an easily accessible place seems kind of obvious, doesn't it? Well, they used to be on the back or side of computers, too. Many times, your power button will also double as a power light, letting you know that the system is on.

Reset Button Reset buttons are hit-or-miss on computers today. The idea is that this button would reboot your computer from a cold startup without removing power from the components. The reset button is incredibly handy to have when a software application locks up your entire system. Because power is not completely lost, the reset button may not help if you had a memory issue.

Drive Activity Lights These little lights often look like circular platters (like a hard drive) or have a hard drive icon next to them. They let you know that your hard drive is working.

Audio Ports The front of most computers now has a port for headphones as well as a microphone. Long gone are the days where you had to put your computer in a certain spot on or under your desk, just so your short headphones cord could reach all the way to the back of the box.

Other Connectors Trying to get to the back of your computer to plug in a flash drive is about as convenient as ripping out the back seat of your car to get stuff out of the trunk. It might actually be faster just to remove your hard drive and give it your friend so they can copy the files they need. (Okay, not really.) Fortunately, most new computers have one or more USB ports on the front or top of the case. Other systems will have memory card readers built into the front of the case as well. I will cover these different connectors in Chapter 2.

Real World Scenario

Motherboard, Revisited

At the beginning of this section, I gave you a description of a motherboard for sale.

> Asus ROG Strix Z790-E Gaming WiFi II LGA 1700 DDR5 ATX Motherboard, DDR5 8000+, 1x PCIe 5.0x16, 2x PCIe 4.0x16, 5x M.2 slots, 1x HDMI, 1x DisplayPort, 1x USB 20 Gbps port, 11x USB 10 Gbps ports, Wi-Fi 7

Now that you've learned about motherboards, let's translate the acronym string. "Asus ROG Strix Z790-E Gaming WiFi II" is the manufacturer and model of the motherboard. It has the LGA 1700 CPU socket, and uses DDR5 RAM (which you will learn about in the "Memory" section later in this chapter). It's an ATX-style motherboard (again, supporting DDR5) with one PCIe 5.0× 16 slot, two PCIe 4.0× 16 slots, five M.2 slots (covered in the "Hard Drives" section later in this chapter), one HDMI and one DisplayPort (to connect monitors), one USB 20 Gbps port and 11 USB 10 Gbps ports for external peripherals, and it supports Wi-Fi 7 (which I will talk about in Chapter 8; sometimes you will see it written as WiFi, but the correct standard per the accrediting agency is Wi-Fi, with a hyphen).

Armed with this information, you can now compare motherboards to each other to determine which one has some of the features you are seeking!

Processors

The processor is the most important component on the motherboard. The role of the *central processing unit (CPU)* is to control and direct all the activities of the computer. Because of this role, the CPU often is called the brain of the computer. The analogy isn't perfect because the processor isn't capable of thinking independently. It just does what it's instructed to do, which is processing math. Still, the analogy of the processor as the computer's brain is close enough.

Tech+ exam objective 2.2 lists central processing unit (CPU) as a subobjective. Be sure to know what it is and what it does!

Processors are small silicon chips consisting of an array of *millions* of transistors. Intel and Advanced Micro Devices (AMD) are the two largest PC-compatible CPU manufacturers.

The terms *processor* and *CPU* are interchangeable.

CPUs are generally square, with contacts arranged in rows of pins. Older CPU sockets were in a configuration called a *pin grid array (PGA)*. The newer version uses a configuration called the *land grid array (LGA)*. LGA is sturdier than PGA because it has the pins in the socket versus on the processor, which results in less damage to processors from trying to insert them incorrectly into their sockets. Figure 1.15 shows an Intel Core i7 processor sitting in an open LGA socket.

FIGURE 1.15 Intel Core i7 processor

As powerful as processors are, they don't look that impressive from the outside. Moreover, rarely will you see a processor without an accompanying heat-removal system. Your processor will have either a metal heat sink (it looks like rows of aluminum fins sticking up from it), a fan, or a combination of the two. Without a heat sink and/or fan, a modern processor would generate enough heat to destroy itself within a few seconds.

CPU Characteristics

The most important characteristic your processor can have is compatibility. Does it fit into your motherboard? Beyond this, there are literally dozens of different characteristics that CPUs have, such as hyperthreading and virtualization support. Most of those topics are beyond the scope of this book. Here, I'll focus on three key characteristics: architecture, speed, and cache.

Architecture

Three architecture-related terms with which you should be familiar are 32-bit, and 64-bit, and ARM. Processors that you find today will be labeled as 32-bit or 64-bit. What this refers to is the set of data lines between the CPU and the primary memory of the system; they can be 32- or 64-bits wide, among other widths. The wider the bus, the more data that can be processed per unit of time, and hence, the more work that can be performed. For true 64-bit CPUs, which have 64-bit internal registers and can run x64 versions of Microsoft operating systems, the external system data bus will always be 64 bits wide or some larger multiple thereof. You will find 32-bit and 64-bit processors designed for all types of computers, such as laptops, desktops, workstations, and servers. In today's world, though, using a 32-bit processor on a server would be a little like entering a bicycle into a sports car race.

Advanced RISC Machines (ARM) refers to a type of processor that uses an architecture known as *reduced instruction set computing (RISC)*. That's in contrast to Intel's (and clones) x86 architecture, which employs *complex instruction set computing (CISC)*. Confused yet? Remember that processors do math. The differences between RISC and CISC is how the processors do the math and the instructions that the software needs to give them to do the math. Long story short, RISC processors may take more steps to do the same math problem than would a CISC processor. While that might sound inefficient and therefore slower, RISC processors have some advantages that compensate, eliminating most performance gaps. On the positive side, RISC processors can be made much smaller than their CISC cousins and produce less heat. The differences between RISC and CISC are way beyond the scope of the Tech+ exam, but the context helps me explain these two key things that you *do* need to know about ARM:

- ARM processors are made in both 32-bit and 64-bit versions, so you will find them in workstations and servers, albeit not very often.
- Because they can be made smaller and produce less heat, ARM processors are generally used in devices that are tablet-sized and smaller, like mobile phones. Roughly 90 percent of all small devices use ARM chips.

Another term that you will hear in terms of architecture is the number of cores a processor has. You might see something labeled dual-core, quad-core, or even 128-core. To keep making better and faster processors every year, manufacturers constantly have to find ways to increase the number of instructions a processor can handle per second. Since about 2004, they've done it mostly by adding cores to desktop processors. Multicore means that the CPU is actually made up of several processors working in unison within the same package.

Speed

Hertz (Hz) are electrical cycles per second. Each time the internal clock of the processor completes a full cycle, a single Hz has passed. Back in 1981, IBM's first PC ran at 4.77 *megahertz (MHz)*, which is 4.77 million cycles per second. Modern processors operate at billions of cycles per second, or *gigahertz (GHz)*. For example, you might see a processor that runs at 3.5 GHz. Generally speaking, faster is better, although it generates more heat.

To save power during times when it's not busy, many CPUs can throttle down their speed to reduce the amount of energy used. CPU throttling is common in processors for mobile devices, where heat generation and system-battery drain are key issues of full power usage.

For the Tech+ exam objective 1.3, "Compare and contrast common units of measure," you need to be familiar with megahertz (*MHz)* and gigahertz *(GHz)* in reference to processing speed.

Cache

I already mentioned cache when discussing motherboards, but most processors also include their own built-in cache. Cache is a quick form of memory that greatly speeds up the performance of your computer.

You'll see three different cache designations. Level 1 cache (*L1 cache*) is the smallest and fastest, and it's on the processor die itself. In other words, it's an integrated part of the manufacturing pattern that's used to stamp the processor pathways into the silicon chip. You can't get any closer to the processor than that.

While the definition of L1 cache has not changed much over the years, the same is not true for other cache levels. L2 and L3 cache used to be on the motherboard but now have moved on the die in most processors as well. The biggest differences are the speed and whether they are shared. L2 cache is larger but a little slower than L1 cache. For processors with multiple cores, each core will generally have its own dedicated L1 and L2 caches. A few processors share a common L2 cache among the cores. L3 cache is larger and slower than L1 or L2, and it is usually shared among all processor cores.

The typical increasing order of capacity and distance from the processor die is L1 cache, L2 cache, L3 cache, and RAM. This is also the typical decreasing order of speed. The following list includes representative capacities of these memory types. The cache capacities are for each core of the original Intel Core i7 processor. The RAM capacity is simply a modern example.

- *L1 cache:* 64 KB (32 KB each for data and instructions)
- *L2 cache:* 256 KB
- *L3 cache:* 4 MB–12 MB
- *RAM:* 4 GB–64 GB

CPU Functionality

Processors are made up of millions of transistors, which are electrical gates that let power through or not depending on their current state. They're the basis of *binary* processing, that is, processing (doing math) based on things being in one of two states: on or off, 1 or 0.

At their most basic level, all that computers understand is 1s and 0s; it's the processor's job to do math on strings of 1s and 0s. The math that it performs is based on what's known as an *instruction set*—rules on how to do the math. It accepts numbers as input, performs calculations on them, and delivers other numbers as output. How many numbers the processor can accept at a time varies. Earlier, I mentioned 32-bit versus 64-bit architecture. Processors with 64-bit architecture can accept more data at once, and as you can imagine, that can make them much faster than their 32-bit cousins.

Tech+ exam objective 1.1, "Explain the basics of computing," lists input, processing, output, and storage as subobjectives. Have a high-level understanding of how each works.

Binary notation is a bit unfamiliar to most people, because we're more accustomed to using the decimal numbering system (0–9). Exercise 1.1 will get you more familiar with binary notation.

I'll talk a lot more about binary, decimal, and hexadecimal in Chapter 6, "Software Development."

EXERCISE 1.1

Converting Between Decimal and Other Numbering Systems

1. In Windows, open the Calculator application by typing **calc** in the search box and pressing Enter.
2. Click the Calculator button (the three parallel lines near the upper-left corner), and choose Programmer to switch to Programmer view, as shown in Figure 1.16. Notice on the left that there is a mark next to the Dec option because that is what's selected. Dec is short for Decimal.

FIGURE 1.16 Calculator in Programmer view

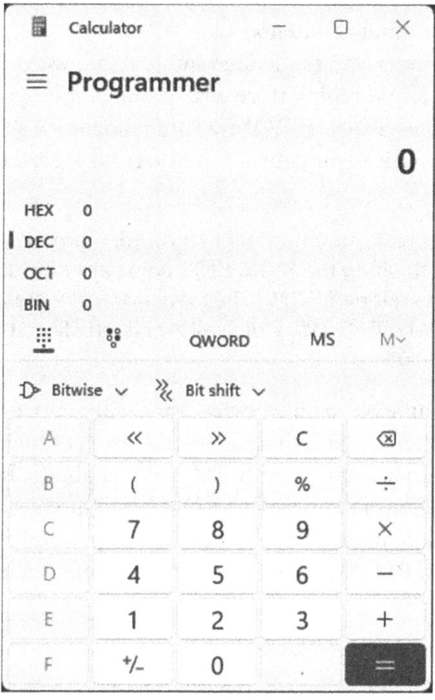

3. Enter the number **267**.
4. Notice that the calculator shows you the hexadecimal (HEX), decimal (DEC), octal (OCT), and binary (BIN) conversions of the number. If you have an older version of Calculator, you will need to click the radio buttons next to these options to perform the conversion. The number in binary is 100001011.
5. Click BIN. Notice that all your number keys are now grayed out except 0 and 1.
6. Click HEX. Now you can also use all your number keys, as well as the letter keys A–F.
7. Click DEC again to return to decimal.
8. Experiment with other numbers. What would your birth date look like in binary or hex? Close the calculator when you are finished.

Memory

Memory, generically speaking, is data storage that uses on/off states on a chip to record patterns of binary data. (Remember, computers deal only with 1s and 0s!) Inside a memory chip is a grid of on/off switches. An on value represents 1, and an off value represents 0.

Memory can be either static or dynamic. *Static memory* (aka *nonvolatile memory*) doesn't require power to maintain its contents. *Dynamic memory* (aka *volatile memory*) has to be constantly powered on to retain its contents.

Broadly speaking, all memory can be divided into one of two types: ROM and RAM. *Read-only memory (ROM)* chips store data permanently; you can't make changes to their content at all. (It takes a special ROM-writing machine to write one.) This type of memory is always static. The BIOS on your motherboard is stored on a ROM chip.

BIOS chips today are updatable through a process mentioned earlier called flashing the BIOS. BIOS chips are now stored on a newer, modified version of ROM called *electronically erasable programmable ROM (EEPROM)*, which allows the ROM to be updated by using electronic pulses.

The programming on simple electronic devices that will never need to be user-updated, like the computer on an exercise treadmill that stores various fitness programs, will also be stored on ROM. The main advantage of ROM is its reliability. It can never be accidentally changed or deleted. The disadvantages of ROM are that it's slow compared to RAM and that you can't ever update it; you have to pull the chip out of the system and replace it. Because of these drawbacks, ROM isn't used as a PC's primary memory source; a PC has only a small amount of ROM.

Tech+ exam objective 2.2 lists random access memory (RAM) as a subobjective. In addition, objective 2.3, "Compare and contrast storage types," lists volatile vs. non-volatile, RAM, and ROM as subobjectives.

Random access memory (RAM) can be written and rewritten on the device in which it's installed. It's called *random access* because the data is stored in whatever locations are available in it, and when reading data back from RAM, only the required data is read, not the entire contents.

You can never have too much RAM.

RAM can be either static or dynamic. Static RAM (SRAM), also called flash RAM, is the type you use when you store files on a USB flash drive. Static RAM is nonvolatile; you can disconnect a flash RAM device and carry it with you, and the next time you connect it to a computer, the data will still be there. Most of the memory on a PC's motherboard is dynamic RAM (DRAM), so when someone refers to a computer's memory or RAM, you can generally assume that they mean the DRAM on the motherboard. Dynamic RAM is volatile; when you turn off your computer, its content is gone.

The motherboard's RAM functions as a work area when the computer is on. The OS is loaded into it, as are any applications that you have open and any data associated with those applications. The more free RAM in the computer, the larger the available workspace, so the more applications and data files you'll be able to have open at once. If your system runs low on RAM, it can use slower virtual memory to compensate. Exercise 1.2 shows you how to configure your virtual memory. Note that for exercises and examples in this book I am using Windows 11 Home. Older Windows operating systems will have similarly or identically named utilities to perform these tasks. If you are unsure, an Internet search for the utility name should help you out.

Real World Scenario

Virtual Memory

Many OSs, including Microsoft Windows, use a tremendous amount of RAM as they operate. They sometimes do this to the point that even a well-equipped PC might not have enough RAM to do everything that a user wants. To prevent the user from being denied an activity because of a lack of available memory, these OSs employ virtual memory to take up the slack.

With virtual memory, a portion of the hard disk is set aside as a holding area for the contents of RAM. When there isn't enough space in RAM to hold the data that needs to be placed there, the OS's virtual memory management utility temporarily moves some of the least recently used data in RAM onto the hard disk, making room for the new incoming data. Then, if an application calls for the data that was moved out, the virtual memory manager moves something else out and swaps the needed data back in again.

Because of all this data swapping, the reserved area on the hard disk for virtual memory is sometimes called a *swap file, page file,* or *paging file.*

The main drawback of virtual memory is its speed, which is limited to the speed at which the hard drive can store and retrieve data. Compared to the speed of the processor and memory, the hard disk is very slow. Therefore, the less physical RAM available in a system and the more that system has to rely on virtual memory, the more slowly applications will run on that system. That's why adding more RAM to a system is often a worthwhile upgrade.

EXERCISE 1.2

Assessing Your Computer's RAM and Virtual Memory in Windows 11

1. In the Windows search box (located next to the Start button), type **about**, which will show the About Your PC desktop app. Click the app name to open it. (Alternatively, open Control Panel ➢ System.) You will get a screen similar to the one shown in Figure 1.17.

EXERCISE 1.2 ***(continued)***

FIGURE 1.17 About your PC

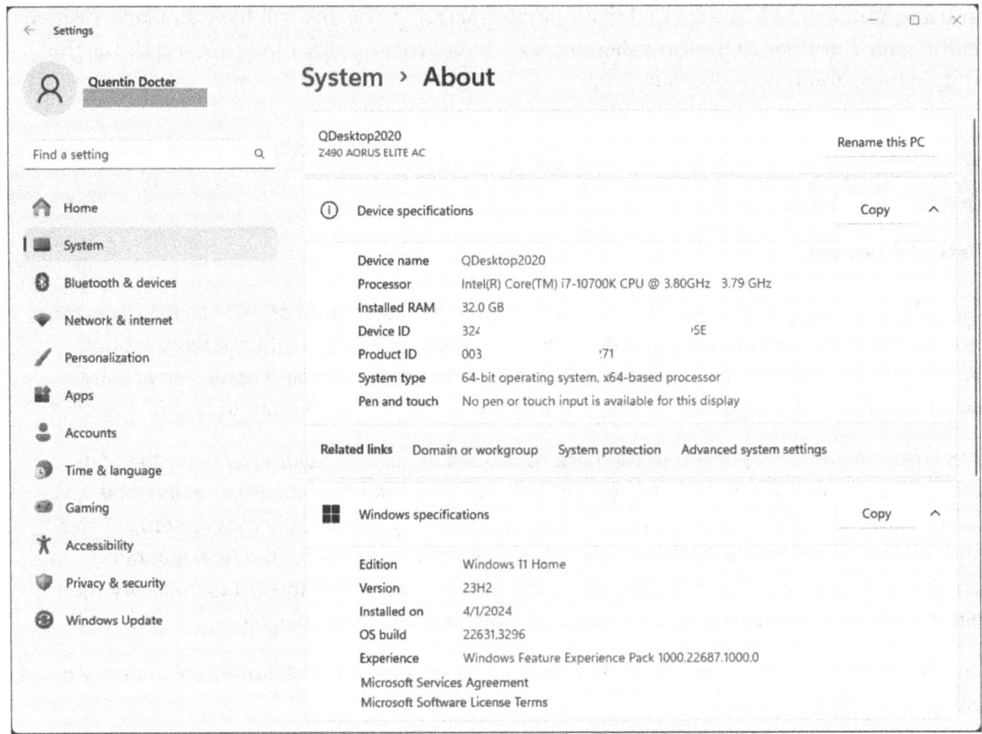

2. In the Device Specifications section of the page that appears, note the amount of installed memory (RAM). This is the total physical amount of RAM.
3. Under the Device Specifications box, click Advanced System Settings. The System Properties dialog box opens.
4. On the Advanced tab, in the Performance section, click Settings. The Performance Options dialog box opens.
5. Click the Advanced tab, and in the Virtual Memory section, note the total paging file size for all drives, as shown in Figure 1.18. This is the amount of virtual memory set aside for the system's use.

FIGURE 1.18 Virtual memory

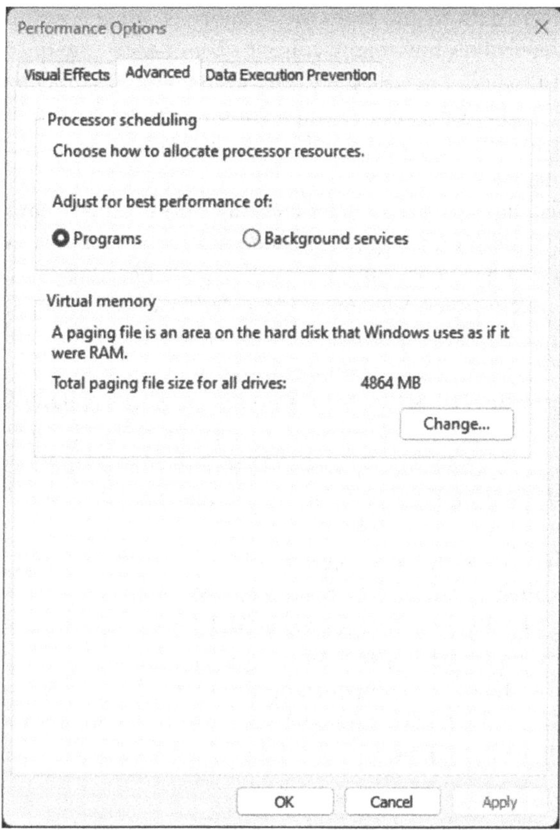

6. Click the Change button. The Virtual Memory dialog box opens.
7. Click Cancel to close the dialog box without making any changes. (It's usually best to continue to let this setting be automatically managed by the system.)
8. Click Cancel to close the Performance Options dialog box.
9. Click Cancel to close the System Properties dialog box.
10. Close the Control Panel window.

Memory Bus Speeds

The pathway that delivers data to and from the memory is called a *memory bus*. Memory has a bus width that determines how many columns are in each row of storage. All the bits in a single row are read together as a single value, so the wider the memory bus width, the more data that can be read at once. For example, in memory with an 8-bit width, you might have a number like 01001100. In memory with a 32-bit width, you could have a number with up to 32 binary digits.

The memory bus also has a speed, which determines how quickly data will travel on its pathway. Memory on modern PCs is synchronized with the system bus, which in turn is controlled by the system timer on the motherboard. (Remember the Northbridge? It controls all of that.) The system timer determines the speed at which data enters the processor. Memory that operates at the same speed as the front-side bus is called *single data rate (SDR) synchronous dynamic random-access memory (SDRAM)*.

The original successor to SDR SDRAM was *double data rate (DDR) SDRAM*, also sometimes called DDR1. It makes higher transfer rates achievable by strictly controlling the timing of the electrical data and clock signals so that data can be double-pumped into the RAM. The term *double data rate* is a reference to DDR's capability of achieving nearly twice the bandwidth of SDR.

After DDR1 came DDR2 SDRAM, which enables greater throughput and requires lower power by running the internal clock at half the speed of the data bus in addition to double-pumping the bus. This effectively multiplies the DDR1-level performance by two so that there is a total of four data transfers per internal clock cycle.

DDR3, DDR4, and DDR5 go even further, doubling the data rate from each previous version and using less power. The DDR6 standard, expected to be finalized in late 2024 or early 2025, will double the speed of DDr4.

Video cards with DDR6 RAM are already on the market; you will see it labeled as GDDR6 (the leading G indicates it's memory optimized for graphics cards). The DDR6 dates are for system RAM.

Motherboards typically accept only one type of RAM: SDR, DDR, DDR2, DDR3, DDR4, or DDR5. Even if the motherboard is physically compatible with other types, it's programmed to work with RAM at a certain speed.

Physical Characteristics of RAM

There have been various sizes and shapes of RAM modules in PCs over the years. For the most part, PCs today use memory chips arranged on a small circuit board; an example is the *dual inline memory module (DIMM)*. The *dual* in DIMM refers to the fact that the module uses pins on both sides of the circuit board. DIMMs differ in the number of conductors, or pins, that each particular physical form factor uses. Some common examples include 168-, 184-, 240-, and 288-pin configurations. In addition, laptop memory comes in smaller form factors known as a *small outline DIMM (SODIMM)*. (Some laptops also use a smaller version known as a MicroDIMM.) Figure 1.19 shows the form factors for some popular memory modules. From the top down are DDR4, DDR3, DDR2, and a laptop DDR3

SODIMM. Notice how the desktop DDR RAM is all basically the same size but the keying notches on the bottom of the modules are in different places.

FIGURE 1.19 Memory module form factors

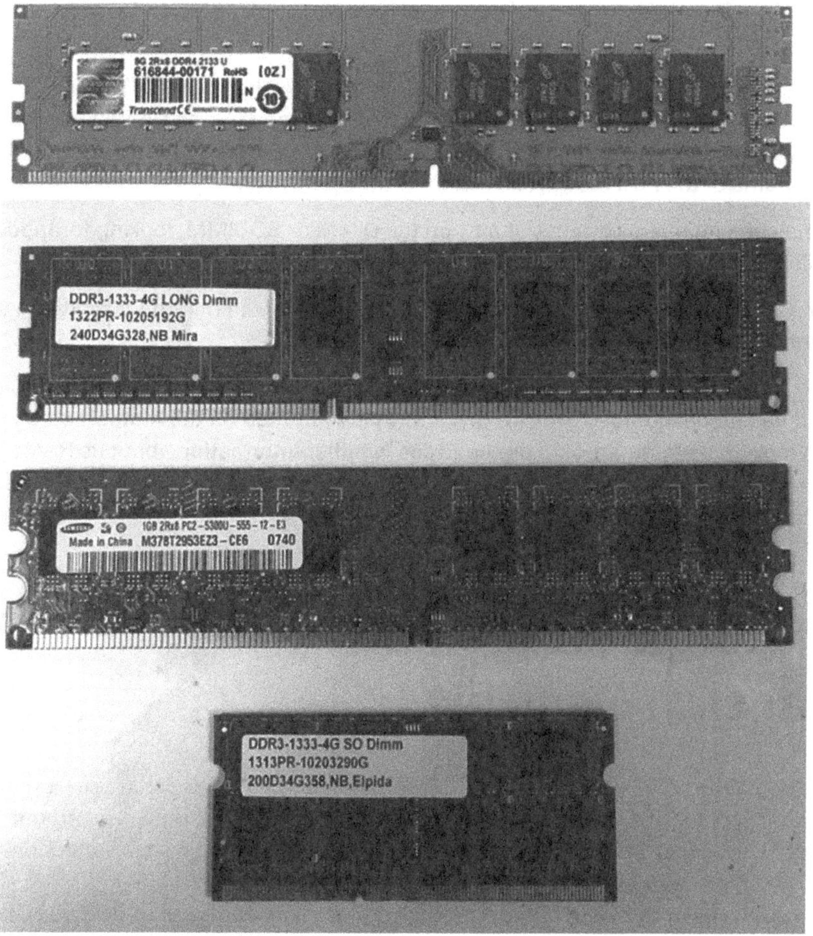

Different types of DIMMs and SODIMMs may be similar or even identical in overall size and shape and may even have the same number of pins. For example, DDR2 and DDR3 DIMMs both have 240 pins. DDR4 and DDR5 have 288 pins, but are the same length as DDR2 and DDR3. The good news is that each type of RAM has a uniquely placed notch in the edge that contains the pins. That notch makes the RAM fit only into a slot that has a correspondingly placed spacer, and it prevents people from installing the wrong type of memory. You could try, but the memory stick would likely break before you got it in there.

Exercise 1.3 helps you determine what type of RAM you have in your computer.

EXERCISE 1.3

Determining the Type of Installed RAM

1. Look in the documentation that came with your computer to see whether there is anything about the RAM specifications. In the documentation, locate the information about installing a RAM upgrade. This will tell you where to find the RAM on your system.
2. Open the computer's case and locate the RAM. Identify whether it's DIMM or SODIMM. (Most laptops use SODIMM, and most desktop PCs use DIMM.) To avoid damaging it with static electricity, avoid touching it. If you need to touch it, touch the metal frame of the PC's case first.
3. Examine the numbers or codes, if any, on the DIMM or SODIMM, looking for model numbers, speeds, or any other pertinent information.
4. Look at the data you gathered online to see whether you can determine anything about the memory based on those numbers.
5. If you can't determine the RAM type by any of these methods, find the motherboard's brand and model number (look for this information printed on the motherboard itself). Then look up the motherboard online to see whether information about its RAM requirements is available.

Exploring Storage and Expansion Devices

Beyond the "big three" of the motherboard, processor, and RAM, there are several other important devices located inside your computer. Broadly speaking, they fall into one of two camps. They either provide long-term storage or expand your system's functionality by giving you features such as video, audio, or network access.

In the following sections, I will introduce you to six different types of devices. The first two, hard drives and optical drives, give you the ability to store data on a long-term basis. The last four, video cards, sound cards, network cards, and modems, provide features that take your computer from being a really good paperweight to being a helpful and fun device to use.

Storage Devices

So far in this chapter we've covered details related to system RAM, which is a short-term, volatile storage component. In this section, we will switch to discussing long-term, nonvolatile, or *persistent* storage options (meaning they don't lose their data when powered off) including hard disk drives, solid-state drives, optical discs, and flash drives.

Storage is mentioned in Tech+ objective 1.1 and again in objective 2.2. Objective 2.3 goes even further and lists several local storage options you need to be familiar with, including magnetic disks/hard disk drive (HDD), solid-state drive (SSD), nonvolatile memory express (NVMe), optical, and external flash drives. It's clearly an important topic!

Hard Drives

Computers would be a lot less useful to us if they weren't able to store our data long-term. This is where hard drives come in. *Hard disk drive (HDD)* systems (called hard disks or *hard drives* for short) are used for permanent storage and quick access. They hold our data as well as files the system needs to operate smoothly. Drives differ in their capacity, their speed (access time), and the type of materials they are made from (metal or glass platters coated with a magnetic coating).

Hard disks typically reside inside the computer, where they are semipermanently mounted with no external access (although there are external and removable hard drives), and can hold more information than other forms of storage. Hard drives use a magnetic storage medium and are known as conventional drives to differentiate them from newer solid-state storage media.

Inside a conventional, spinning disk hard drive, you will find a sealed stack of metal platters, each with a read-write head on a retractable arm that reads data from and writes data to the platters by magnetizing bits of iron oxide particles on the platters in patterns of positive and negative polarity. As a hard disk operates, the platters rotate at a high speed, and the read/write heads hover just over the disk surfaces on a cushion of air generated by the spinning. Normally, you won't see the inside of a hard drive, so you can see one in Figure 1.20. Once you open the metal box in which it's encased, you ruin the drive. The drives are typically 3½″ in diameter for full-size hard disk drives (for desktop PCs) and 2½″ for smaller hard disk drives used in laptops.

FIGURE 1.20 Inside a hard drive

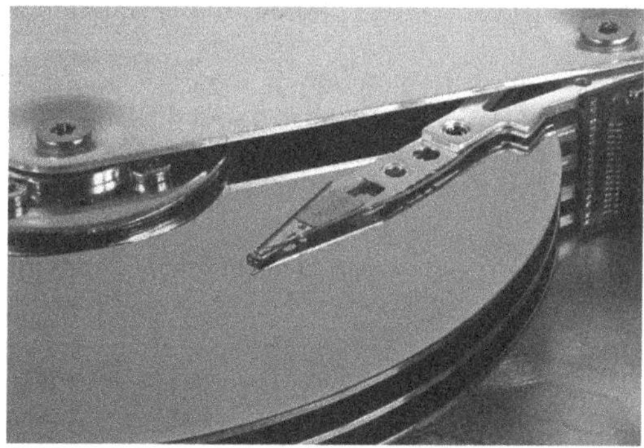

Source: Seagate Technology LLC / Wikimedia Commons / CC BY SA 3.0.

You might hear old-timers talk about floppy disks and floppy disk drives (FDDs). Floppy disks were square and held a thin, pliable disk of magnetic material. They were written to and read from magnetically, just like hard drives. You would insert them into an FDD, which performed the reading and writing functions on the disk.

The two most common sizes were 3½″ and 5¼″, and they held 1.44 MB and 1.2 MB, respectively. You won't need to know those numbers for the exam, but they give you good perspective on how little data they could hold. The one advantage they had was that they were portable. Now we have USB flash drives, with capacities in the gigabytes (and no special read/write device required), which make floppy disks obsolete.

Hard Drive Characteristics

When evaluating hard drives, there are really two factors that determine their performance: size and speed.

Size is fairly self-evident. Hard drives with larger capacity store more data. There isn't anything too tricky about it. You can easily find hard drives with capacities from several hundred gigabytes up to 20 terabytes or more. Table 1.2 has some conversions that will likely come in handy.

TABLE 1.2 Bit and byte conversions

How many	Equals	Example
1 bit	1 bit	A single 0 or 1.
8 bits	1 byte	One text character.
1,000 bytes	1 kilobyte (KB)	A 1,000-character plain-text file or a small icon.
1,000 kilobytes	1 megabyte (MB)	A small photograph or one minute of music.
1,000 megabytes	1 gigabyte (GB)	A full-length audio CD is about 800 MB; a two-hour DVD movie is about 4 GB.
1,000 gigabytes	1 terabyte (TB)	A large business database.
1,000 terabytes	1 petabyte (PB)	Data from a large government institution, such as the U.S. Internal Revenue Service.

How many	Equals	Example
1,000 petabytes	1 exabyte (EB)	It's rumored that YouTube stores just over 1 EB of data, but it's hard to confirm that claim.
1,000 exabytes	1 zettabyte (ZB)	In 2013, NPR and Forbes reported that the U.S. National Security Agency's new Utah data center could store up to 5 ZB of data. But it's the NSA, so of course there is no official confirmation of this.

The historical convention was always that the next level up equaled 1,024 of the previous level, such that 1 MB = 1,024 KB. Now, it's more or less accepted that we just round everything off to 1,000 to make it easier to do the math.

Most people assume that they don't need to think in terms of exabytes or zettabytes (not to mention yottabytes, which are 1,000 zettabytes), but with 18–20 TB hard drives being relatively common today, these larger measures are probably right around the corner.

Tech+ exam objective 1.3 specifically calls out all storage units of measure from bit up to petabyte, so it may be helpful to review Table 1.2 a few times so you understand the order from smallest to largest.

Speed is the other thing you will want to look at when considering a hard drive. Hard drive access is much slower than RAM access, so hard drives can often be the bottleneck in system performance. Over the years, though, technology has evolved to improve hard drive access time. To speed up data access, manufacturers increase the speed at which the platters spin from one generation of drives to the next, with multiple speeds coexisting in the marketplace for an unpredictable period until demand dies down for one or more speeds.

The following spin rates, in revolutions per minute (rpm), have been used in the industry for the platters in conventional magnetic hard disk drives:

- 5400 rpm
- 7200 rpm
- 10,000 rpm
- 12,000 rpm
- 15,000 rpm

A higher rpm rating results in the ability to move data more quickly. The lower speeds can be better for laptops, where heat production and battery usage can be issues with the higher-speed drives. For desktop HDDs, 7200 rpm is the most common speed in use today.

Connecting a Hard Drive

There are two common hard drive standards in the marketplace today: Parallel ATA (PATA), also known as Integrated Drive Electronics (IDE), and Serial ATA (SATA). PATA/IDE has been around a lot longer (IDE came out in the late 1980s), and SATA is the newer and faster technology, launched in 2003.

Regardless of the standard, hard drives need two connections to function properly: power and the data cable. The power comes from the power supply, and the data cables connect to the motherboard. Figure 1.21 shows the back of two standard 3½″ desktop hard drives. The top one is PATA/IDE, and the bottom one is SATA.

FIGURE 1.21 PATA/IDE and SATA hard drives

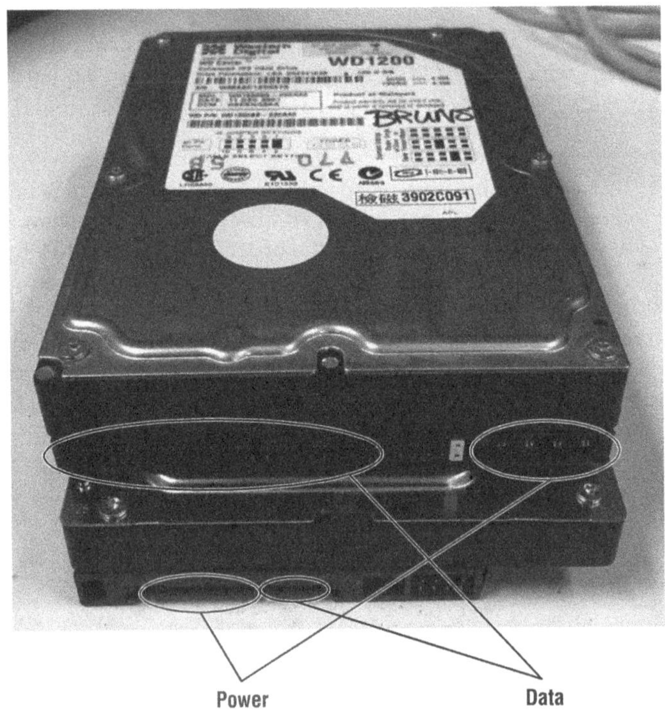

Figure 1.22 shows the ends of the data cables. Again, the top one is PATA, and the bottom one is SATA. The connectors where the data cables plug into the motherboard were shown in Figure 1.9 and Figure 1.10.

FIGURE 1.22 PATA and SATA data cables

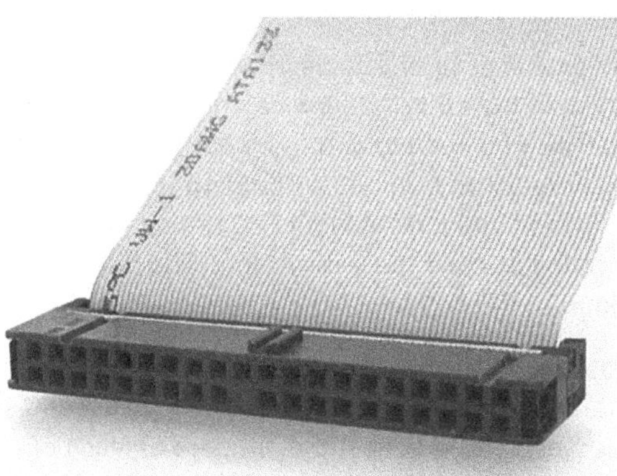

There's a third connector type, called Small Computer System Interface (SCSI, pronounced *scuzzy*), that you might hear about. It uses a ribbon cable similar to IDE but wider. It was once popular for high-end systems, but the speed and lower cost of SATA has made SCSI fade in popularity. Few motherboards had SCSI controllers built onto them. If you wanted a SCSI hard drive, you needed to add an internal expansion board with a SCSI controller on It.

 **Real World Scenario**

Connecting Multiple PATA Devices

Hard drives are important, and for many years the most common hard drive standard was PATA (at the time called IDE). Most motherboards came with two connectors; today, motherboards will have one, if they support PATA at all. When CD-ROM drives came out, they too used the same 40-pin connector as hard drives. If you had only two devices, this wasn't a problem. But what if you wanted two hard drives *and* a CD-ROM?

The 40-pin PATA ribbon cable has three connectors on it. One goes to the motherboard, and the other two—one in the middle of the cable and one at the other end—go to drives. If you have only one PATA drive, you use the connector at the far end of the cable, and the extra connector in the middle of the cable goes unused.

If you need to connect two devices to one cable, then you also need to tell the computer which device has priority over the other. Otherwise, they fight like spoiled children and neither one will work. To do that, you need to configure each drive as either the primary or the secondary on that cable. Primary and secondary configuration is performed via jumpers on the back of the hard drive. If you look at Figure 1.21, the jumper block is the 10-pin block between the PATA data connector and the power block. The right two pins have a jumper placed over them, configuring the drive.

Some PATA cables will assign a role to a drive based on the connector into which it's plugged. (That's called Cable Select [CS], with the primary at the end and the secondary in the middle.) To make this work, you must set the jumpers on each of the drives to the CS setting. Fortunately, they are usually set to CS by default. The top of the hard drive might have a sticker showing you the jumper settings (the one in Figure 1.21 does), or you can check the manufacturer's documentation.

When a newly installed PATA drive doesn't work, it could be because the jumpers aren't set correctly.

Solid-State Drives

Unlike conventional hard drives, a *solid-state drive (SSD)* has no moving parts but uses the same solid-state memory technology found in the other forms of flash memory. You can think of them as bigger versions of the flash drives that are so common.

SSDs are expected to behave like traditional HDDs. That is, they retain their contents even when the system is powered off. As you might expect, SSDs have several advantages over their mechanical counterparts. These include the following:

- Faster start-up and read times
- Less power consumption and heat produced
- Silent operation
- Generally more reliable because of a lack of moving parts
- Less susceptible to damage from physical shock and heat production
- Higher data density per square centimeter

Disadvantages of SSDs are as follows:

- The technology to build an SSD is more expensive per byte.
- All solid-state memory is limited to a finite number of write (including erase) operations. Lack of longevity could be an issue.

To summarize, SSDs are faster and produce less heat but are generally more expensive than conventional mechanical hard drives. There is also a lot more variety when it comes to shapes and sizes of SSDs as well as how they are connected to the motherboard.

Internal SSD Technologies

SSDs are one area that can cause a lot of confusion for new and experienced technicians alike. There are several standards that sound similar to each other and multiple connection methods as well. Old conventional HDDs might be slow and bulky, but at least they are simple to understand and install!

Terms that you will hear referring specifically to SSDs include *nonvolatile memory express (NVMe)* and M.2 (pronounced *m dot two*). While these terms are often used interchangeably, they are different things. One of the newest SSD technologies, NVMe is a standard regulating data transfers. It's incredibly fast—Generation 4 NVMe drives can transfer more than 7000 MB/s (megabytes per second) compared to SATA SSDs, which top out at about 600 MB/s. But there is no such thing as an NVMe slot, and NVMe drives can be made in form factors such as PCIe. Figure 1.23 shows a PCIe NVMe SSD.

FIGURE 1.23 PCIe NVMe SSD

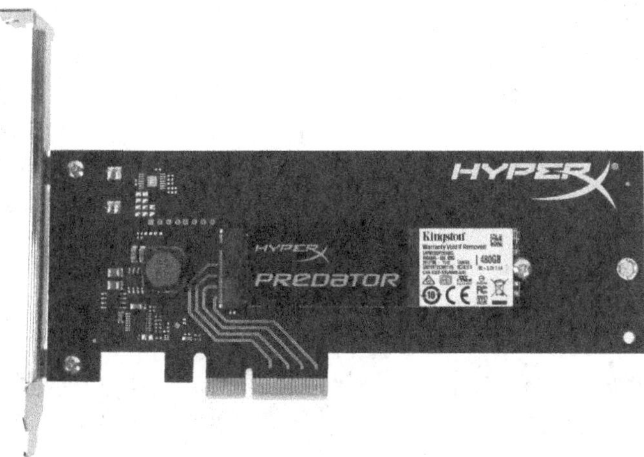

M.2, on the other hand, is a *form factor*—that is, the size and physical configuration of the drive. It also shares its name with M.2 slots on the motherboard. It's not a coincidence—as you would expect, M.2 drives fit into M.2 slots. Figure 1.24 shows an M.2 NVMe SSD.

FIGURE 1.24 M.2 NVMe SSD

To further complicate things, M.2 drives come in NVMe and SATA varieties. An NVMe M.2 drive will greatly outperform a SATA M.2 drive. Still, any SATA SSD will be several times faster than a conventional HDD.

When it comes to selecting an SSD, make sure that the motherboard supports the drive you want to install, and confirm you have an open slot of the right type—M.2, SATA, or PCIe. We've already looked at PCIe (Figure 1.8) and SATA (Figure 1.10) slots in this chapter; Figure 1.25 shows an M.2 connector. It's in the center pointing downward. To get to it, you will need to loosen a screw that holds a protective cover in place over the slot and remove the cover. The protective cover is shown in Figure 1.26, with the screw on the left.

FIGURE 1.25 M.2 connector on motherboard

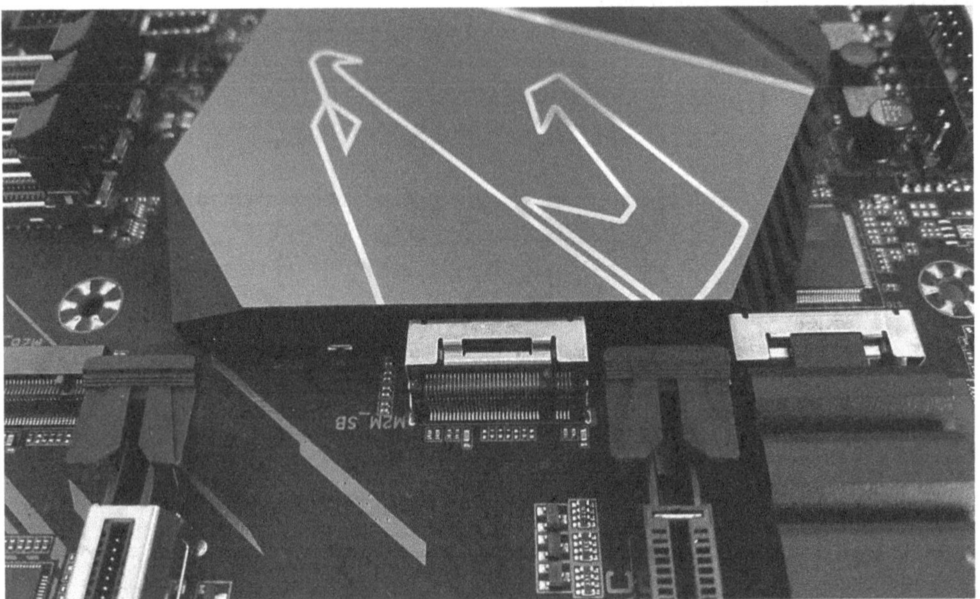

External Flash Drives

An *external flash drive* is a small, portable SSD that connects through a USB port. You will hear them called thumb drives as well, because they are often about the size of a human thumb. The capacity will be less than an internal or external SSD, typically the maximum size is 256 GB, but the primary benefit is portability. Figure 1.27 shows two flash drives.

Exercise 1.4 shows how to view information about your storage drives in Windows.

FIGURE 1.26 M.2 slot protective cover

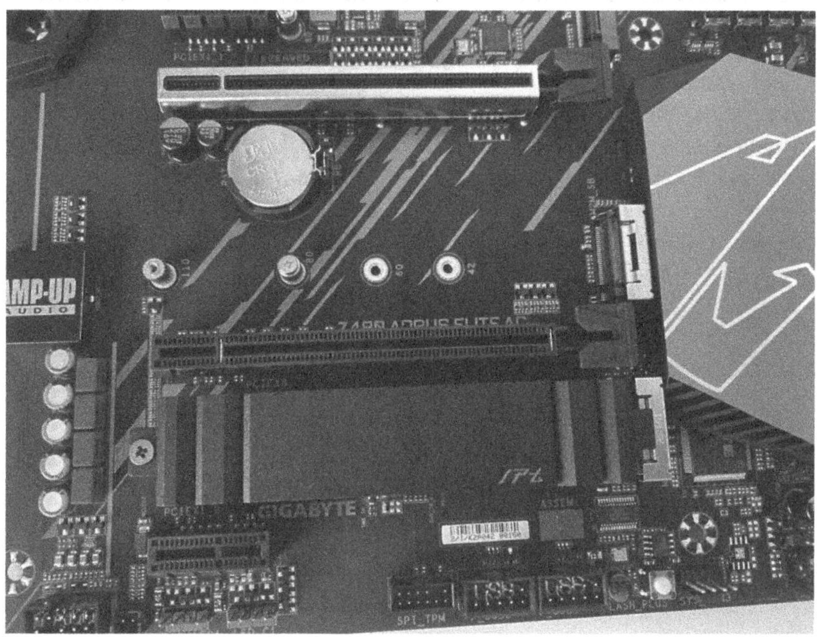

FIGURE 1.27 Two USB flash drives

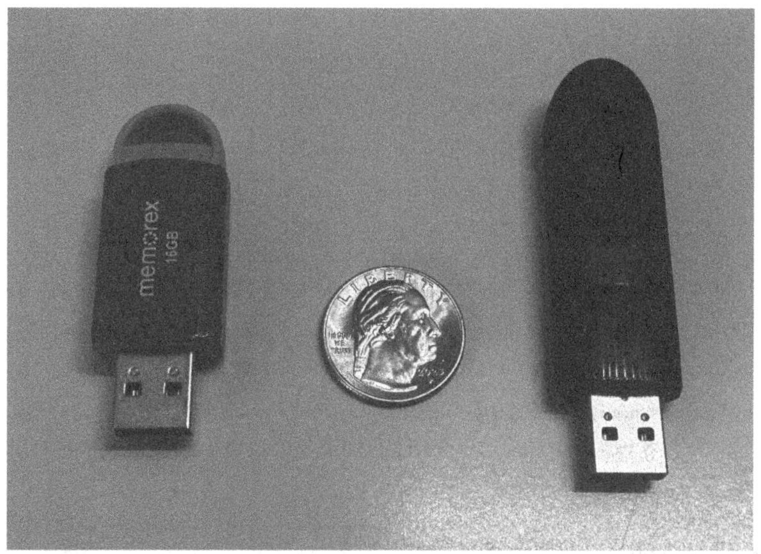

EXERCISE 1.4

Examining Storage Drives in Windows 11

1. Open File Explorer in Windows 11 by pressing the Windows key on your keyboard plus the E key. (In the future, I will shorten this by saying "press Windows + E.") In the left navigation pane, click This PC. This will show the This PC desktop app. A list of the drives on your PC appears, like the one shown in Figure 1.28.

FIGURE 1.28 Installed disk drives

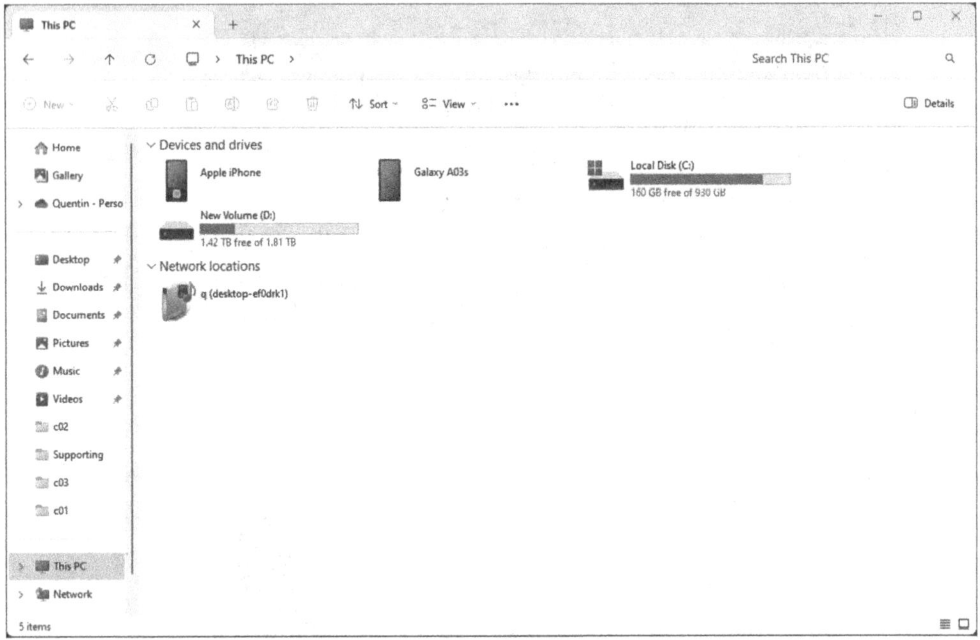

2. Examine the primary hard disk (C:). You can see a bar that shows you how much storage space it has as well as how much space is free. Figure 1.28 shows an example.
3. Right-click the primary hard disk (C:), and click Properties. A Properties dialog box opens for that drive, as shown in Figure 1.29.
4. Examine the information about the file system, used space, free space, and capacity. If free space is low (under about 10 percent), your computer could run slower than it should.
5. Click the Hardware tab. Information appears about all of the disk drives, including any connected USB storage devices and your optical drive if you have one. Here you can see the brand name and model number of each drive, like in Figure 1.30.
6. Click Cancel to close the dialog box, and close the This PC window.

FIGURE 1.29 Hard disk properties

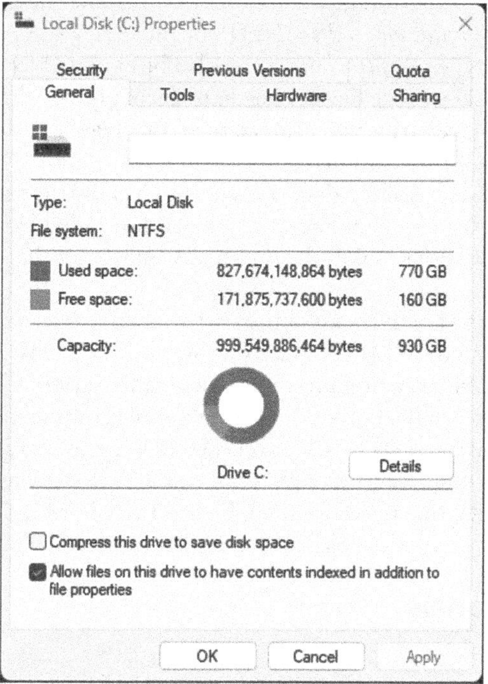

FIGURE 1.30 Disk drives

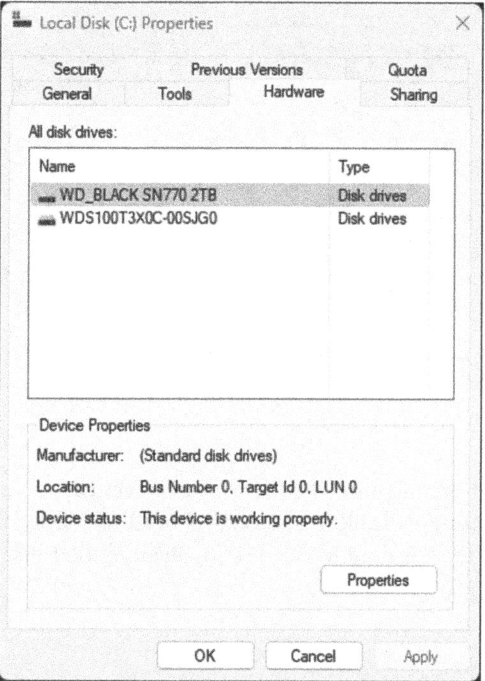

Optical Drives

Computers can have an optical storage drive capable of reading the latest *Blu-ray Disc (BD)*, a digital versatile disc or *digital video disc (DVD)*, or the legacy *compact disc (CD)* that you have lying around. Each type of *optical drive* can also be expected to support the technology that came before it. Optical storage devices began replacing floppy drives in the late 1990s. Even though these discs have greater data capacity and increased performance over floppies, they are not intended to replace hard drives.

The BDs, DVDs, and CDs used for data storage are virtually the same as those used for permanent recorded audio and video. The way data, audio, and video information is written to consumer-recordable versions makes them virtually indistinguishable from professionally manufactured discs.

Each of these media types requires an optical drive capable of reading them. Those devices are designated with a *-ROM* ending, for example, *BD-ROM*, *DVD-ROM*, or *CD-ROM*. If the drive is capable of writing to these discs (called a *burner*), it will have a different ending, such as *-R* (recordable) or *-RW* (rewritable). To confuse matters further, there are two standards of DVD burners: DVD-RW and DVD+RW. Today's DVD readers can generally handle both formats, but older devices might not be able to do so. Burnable BD drives are designated BD-R or BD-RE (for re-recordable). Figure 1.31 shows a DVD-ROM. It's really hard to tell optical drives apart from each other, unless you see the logo that's on it.

FIGURE 1.31 A DVD-ROM

Each of the formats I have mentioned so far has different capacities. Table 1.3 lists the most common. Before getting to Table 1.3, though, I need to define a few more acronyms. Discs can be single-sided (SS) or double-sided (DS), meaning that information is written to one or both faces of the disc. In addition, DVDs and BDs can have multiple layers on the same side, otherwise known as *dual-layer* (DL). The ability to create dual layers nearly doubles the capacity of one side of the disc. Boldfaced capacities in the table are the commonly accepted values for their respective formats.

TABLE 1.3 Optical discs and their capacities

Disc format	Capacity
CD SS (includes recordable versions)	650 MB, **700 MB**, 800 MB, 900 MB
DVD-R/RW SS, SL	4.71 GB (**4.7 GB**)
DVD+R/RW SS, SL	4.70 GB (**4.7 GB**)
DVD-R, DVD+R DS, SL	**9.4 GB**
DVD-R SS, DL	8.54 GB (**8.5 GB**)
DVD+R SS, DL	8.55 GB (**8.5 GB**)
DVD+R DS, DL	17.1 GB
BD-R/RE SS, SL	25 GB
BD-R/RE SS, DL	50 GB
BD-R/RE DS, DL	100 GB

SS: single-sided; DS: double-sided; SL: single-layer; DL: dual-layer

A double-sided, single-layer DVD will give you more storage space than a single-sided, dual-layer DVD. This is because there is a bit of inefficiency when writing a second layer on one side, so the second layer doesn't quite give you double the storage space versus just one layer.

Now you know why Blu-ray movies are so much better than those on DVD. Even the simplest BD can store nearly 50 percent more data than the most advanced DVD!

Other Internal Expansion Devices

Beyond storage, there are other internal devices that add functionality to a computer as well. A computer with no video output won't be of use to most people, so there's a device that enables images to appear on a screen. Audio output isn't always critical, but anyone who has been on a business or school conference call where the audio doesn't work might beg to differ. Finally, computing today necessarily means communicating with other computers, and network cards help out with that. Let's take a look at them.

Video Cards

A video adapter (more commonly called a *graphics adapter* or even more commonly a *video card*) is the expansion card you put into a computer to allow the computer to display output on some kind of monitor. A video card is responsible for converting the data sent to it by the CPU into the pixels, addresses, and other items required for display.

Tech+ exam objective 2.2, "Explain the purpose of common internal computing components," lists graphics processing unit (GPU) as a subobjective.

Modern video cards include dedicated chips to perform some of these functions, thus accelerating the speed of display. This type of chip is called a *graphics processing unit (GPU)*. Some of the common GPUs are AMD Radeon and NVIDIA GeForce. Most video cards also have their own onboard RAM. This is a good thing, and just like the RAM on your motherboard, the more the better. Figure 1.32 shows a video card.

FIGURE 1.32 An EVGA GeForce video card

Most video cards sold today use the PCIe interface, but you might still see some older AGP cards out there. They both work the same way, except that AGP is very slow compared to PCIe.

Video cards can have one or more external plug-ins for monitors or other display devices. These will be covered in more detail in Chapter 2. Also notice that this card has two rather large fans attached to it—in fact, that's about all you can see. This is because the card has its own processor and memory and generates a lot of heat. Secondary cooling is necessary to keep this card from melting down.

To save space and money, some systems (primarily laptops) will have the GPU built into the CPU or otherwise located on the motherboard. These systems will also split the system RAM between video and other system functions. (Usually, in these cases, the amount of RAM dedicated to video can be configured in the BIOS or in Windows.) There's nothing wrong with this type of configuration, other than it's slower than having separate components. If you are a gamer or otherwise have high video processing needs, you will want a separate video card with as much RAM on it as you can get.

Sound Cards

Just as there are devices to convert computer signals into printouts and video information, there are devices to convert those signals into sound. These devices are known as *sound cards* (or audio cards). Although sound cards started out as pluggable adapters, this functionality is one of the most common integrated technologies found on motherboards today. A sound card typically has small, round, 1/8″ (3.5 mm) jacks on the back of it for connecting microphones, headphones, and speakers, as well as other sound equipment. Many sound cards used to have a DA15 game port, which could be used either for joysticks or for musical instrument digital interface (MIDI) controllers, used with external keyboards and so forth. Figure 1.33 shows an example of a legacy sound card with a DA15 game port.

FIGURE 1.33 A legacy sound card

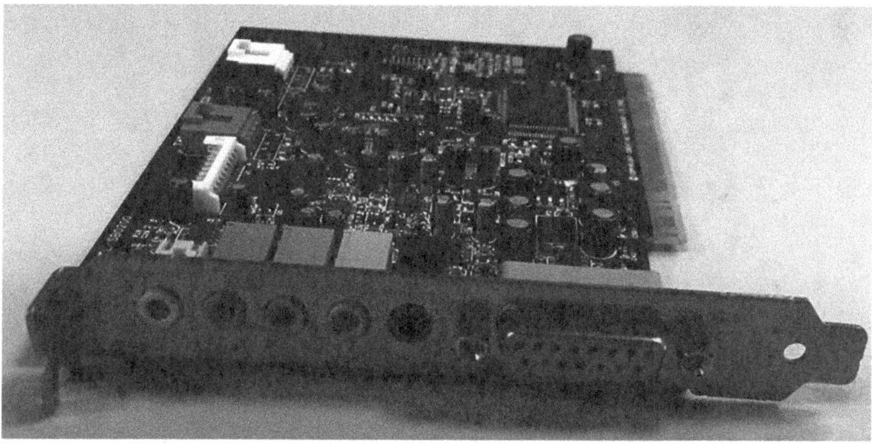

The most popular sound card standard in the market is the Sound Blaster, which is made by Creative Labs.

Network Cards

It seems like every computer participates on a network these days, whether it's at the office or at home. A *network interface card (NIC)* is an expansion card that connects a computer to a network so that it can communicate with other computers on that network. It translates the data from the parallel data stream used inside the computer into the serial data stream that makes up the frames used on the network. It has a connector for the type of expansion bus on the motherboard (PCIe, PCI, and so on) as well as a connector for the type of network (wired connectors such as fiber or RJ45, or an antenna for wireless). Figure 1.34 shows a wireless network card designed for a desktop PC.

Tech+ exam objective 2.2 lists network interface card (NIC) as a subobjective. You should be familiar with wired and wireless cards as well as onboard (integrated into the motherboard) versus expansion cards. NICs will also be covered again in Chapter 8.

FIGURE 1.34 A wireless desktop NIC

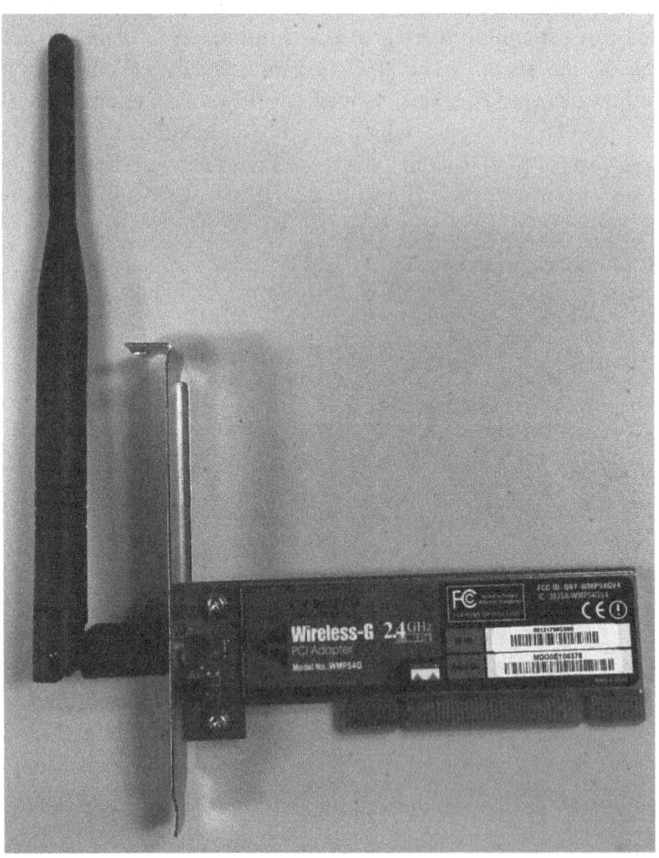

Most computers today have the NIC circuitry integrated into their motherboards. A computer with an integrated NIC wouldn't need to have a NIC add-on card installed unless it was faster or if you were using the second NIC for load balancing, security, or fault tolerance.

Modems

Any computer that connects to the Internet using an analog dial-up connection needs a modem, or *mo*dulator/*dem*odulator. A *modem* is a device that converts digital signals from a computer into analog signals that can be transmitted over phone lines and back again. These expansion card devices are easy to identify because they have phone connectors on the plate. Usually, as you can see in Figure 1.35, there are two RJ-11 ports: one for connection to the telephone line and the other for connection to a telephone. This is primarily so that a phone can gain access to the same wall jack to which the computer connects without swapping their cords. Keep in mind, though, that you won't be able to use the phone while the computer is connected to the Internet.

FIGURE 1.35 A modem

Before high-speed Internet became popular, a modem was the device people used to get on the Internet. Of course, this meant that the phone line was in use and no one could call your home phone. This was back in the days when people still had land phone lines and when mobile phones were a rare luxury. (I feel like my grandpa talking about the "olden days" when I say these things!) Modems are rarely used today.

Although modems qualify as legacy technology, they are mentioned in Tech+ exam objective 2.8, "Identify basic networking concepts." Like network cards, they will be covered again in Chapter 8.

Exploring Power and Cooling

Without electricity, there wouldn't be any computers. With too much electricity, you'll fry everything inside the box. The goal is to find a happy medium and provide consistent power to your computer.

Electronics components produce heat. The amount of heat depends on a variety of things, such as the number of transistors it has, the size of the piece, and the ventilation provided. Having components overheat is the most surefire way of having them fail, except perhaps for dousing them with water.

In the next two sections, you'll learn about providing your computer components with the right amount of power and then cooling them off so that they last as long as possible.

Power Supplies

The device in the computer that provides power is appropriately named the power supply (see Figure 1.36), sometimes called a power supply unit (PSU). That nondescript black box converts 110V or 220VAC current into the DC voltages that a computer needs to operate. These are +3.3VDC, +5VDC, and –5VDC (on older systems) and +12VDC and –12VDC on newer ones.

FIGURE 1.36 A desktop power supply

The abbreviation *VDC* stands for *volts DC. DC* is short for *direct current.* Unlike alternating current (AC), DC does not alter the direction in which the electrons flow. AC for standard power distribution does so 50 or 60 times per second (50 Hz or 60 Hz, respectively).

Power supplies contain transformers and capacitors that can discharge *lethal* amounts of current even when disconnected from the wall outlet for long periods. They are not meant to be serviced, especially by untrained personnel. *Do not* attempt to open them or do any work on them. Simply replace and recycle them when they go bad.

Power supplies are rated in watts. A *watt* is a unit of power. The higher the number, the more power your computer can draw from the power supply. Think of this rating as the capacity of the device to supply power. Most computers require power supplies in the 250-watt to 500-watt range. Higher-wattage power supplies might be required for more advanced systems that employ power-hungry graphics technologies or multiple disk drives, for instance. It is important to consider the draw that the various components and subcomponents of your computer place on the power supply before choosing one or its replacement.

Power supplies have an input plug for the power cord (shown on the left in Figure 1.37), a connector to power the motherboard, and then other connectors to power peripherals such as hard drives and optical drives. Each has a different appearance and way of connecting to the device. Newer PSUs have a variety of similar, replacement, and additional connectors, such as dedicated power connectors for SATA and PCIe, additional power connectors for the motherboard, and even modular connections for these leads back to the power supply instead of a permanent wiring harness. Figure 1.38 shows the ATX power connector that goes to the motherboard. Notice that it's keyed so that it can't be put in the wrong way. Figure 1.39 shows three different types of peripheral power connectors: a 4-pin Molex connector for PATA hard drives and optical drives, a 6-pin PCIe (called a PEG connector), and a SATA connector.

FIGURE 1.37 Power supply in the case

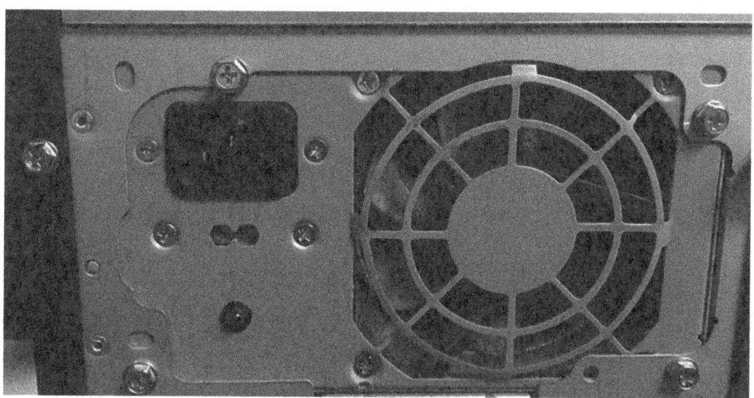

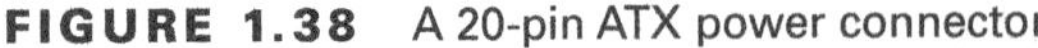

FIGURE 1.38 A 20-pin ATX power connector

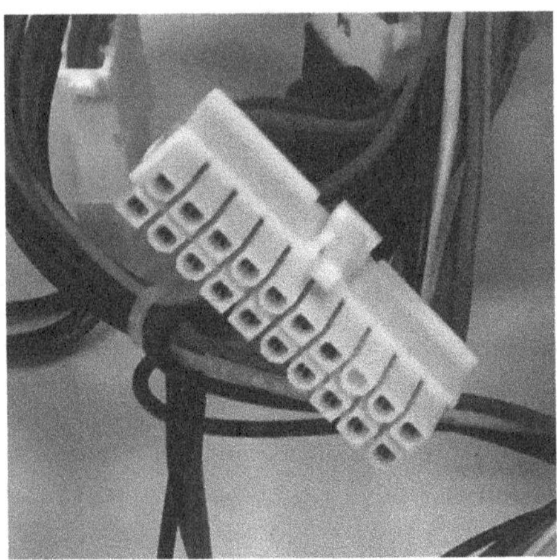

FIGURE 1.39 Peripheral power connectors

Most power supplies have a recessed, two-position slider switch, often a red one, on the rear that is exposed through the case. You can see it in Figure 1.37. Selections read 110 and 220, 115 and 230, or 120 and 240. This dual-voltage selector switch is used to adjust for the voltage level used in the country where the computer is in service. For example, in the United States, the power grid supplies anywhere from 110VAC to 120VAC. However, in Europe, for instance, the voltage supplied is double, ranging from 220VAC to 240VAC.

Although the voltage is the same as what is used in the United States to power high-voltage appliances, such as electric ranges and clothes driers, the amperage is much lower. The point is the switch is not there to match the type of outlet used in the same country. If the wrong voltage is chosen in the United States, the power supply expects more voltage than it receives and might not power up at all. If the wrong voltage is selected in Europe, however, the power supply receives more voltage than its setting. The result could be disastrous for the entire computer. Sparks could also ignite a fire that could destroy nearby property and endanger lives. Always check the switch before powering up a new or recently relocated computer. In the United States and other countries that use the same voltage, check the setting of this switch if the computer fails to power up.

Laptop computers don't have big, bulky power supplies like the one shown in Figure 1.36, but instead they use smaller AC adapters. They function the same way, converting AC current into DC power for the laptop's components. AC adapters are also rated in watts and selected for use with a specific voltage the same as power supplies. One difference is that AC adapters are also rated in terms of DC volts out to the laptop or other device, such as certain brands and models of printers. Figure 1.40 shows a laptop AC adapter. You can see the circular connector on the laptop for the adapter. Many newer laptops use a power supply with a USB-C connector at the end instead of the older circular one.

FIGURE 1.40 Laptop power supply

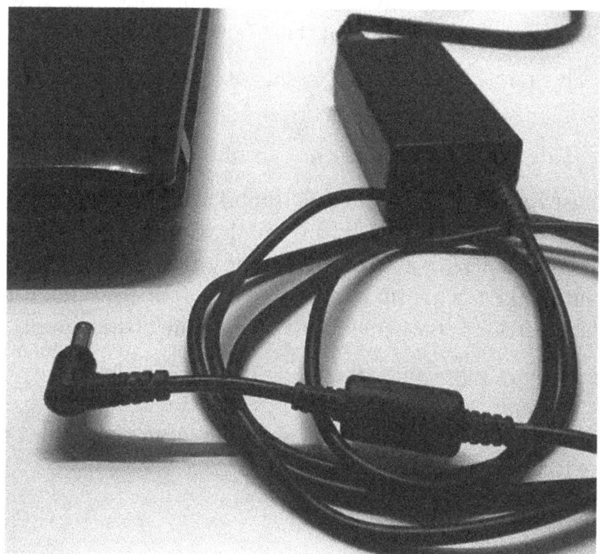

Because both power supplies and AC adapters go bad on occasion, you should replace them both and not attempt to repair them yourself. When replacing an AC adapter, be sure to match the size, shape, and polarity of the tip with the adapter you are replacing. However, because the output DC voltage is specified for the AC adapter, be sure to replace it with one of equal output voltage, an issue not seen when replacing desktop power supplies that have standard outputs. Additionally, and as with power supplies, you can replace an AC adapter with a model that supplies more watts to the component because the component uses only what it needs.

Cooling Systems

The downside of providing power to electronic components is that they produce heat. The excess heat must be dissipated, or it will shorten the life of the components. In some cases (as with the CPU), the component will produce so much heat that it can destroy itself in a matter of seconds if there is not some way to remove this extra heat. All computer systems today come with some cooling systems to reduce and remove heat. Here I'll discuss two broad categories of cooling systems: case cooling and CPU cooling.

Case Cooling

The most common method used to cool computers is air cooling. With air cooling, the movement of air removes the heat from the component. Sometimes, large blocks of metal called *heat sinks* are attached to a heat-producing component to dissipate the heat more rapidly.

When you turn on a computer, you will often hear lots of whirring. Most of this noise is coming from the various fans inside the computer. Fans provide airflow within the computer.

Most desktop PCs have a combination of these fans:

Front Intake Fan This fan is used to bring fresh, cool air into the computer for cooling purposes.

Rear Exhaust Fan This fan is used to take hot air out of the case.

Power Supply Exhaust Fan This fan is usually found at the back of the power supply and is used to cool the power supply. In addition, this fan draws air from inside the case into vents in the power supply. This pulls hot air through the power supply so that it can be blown out of the case. The front intake fan assists with this airflow. The rear exhaust fan supplements the power supply fan to achieve the same result outside the power supply.

In addition, you can buy supplemental cooling devices for almost any component inside your computer. For example, you can get cooling systems specifically for hard drives, RAM, chipsets, and video cards. Ideally, the airflow inside a computer should resemble what is shown in Figure 1.41.

FIGURE 1.41 System unit airflow

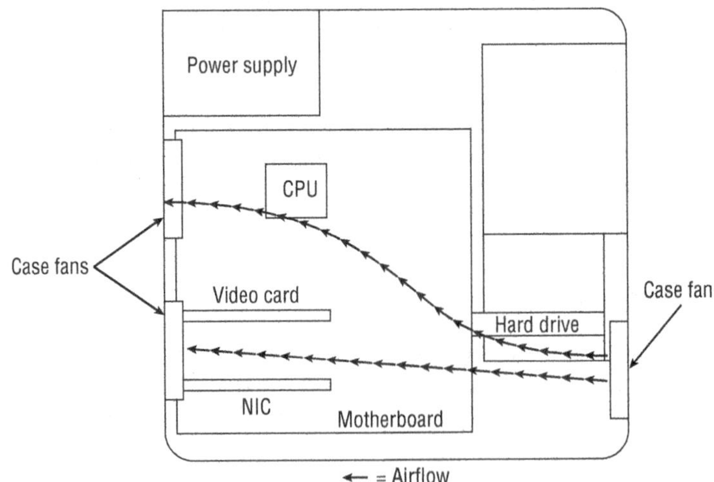

Note that you must pay attention to the orientation of the power supply's airflow. If the power supply fan is an exhaust fan, as assumed in this discussion, the front and rear fans will match their earlier descriptions: front, intake; rear, exhaust. If you run across a power supply that has an intake fan, the orientation of the supplemental chassis fans should be reversed as well. The rear chassis fan (or fans) should always be installed in the same orientation as the power supply fan runs to avoid creating a small airflow circuit that circumvents the cross flow of air through the case. The front chassis fan and the rear fans should always be installed in the reverse orientation to prevent them from fighting against each other and reducing the internal airflow.

CPU Cooling

Without a doubt, the greatest challenge in computer cooling is keeping the CPU's temperature in check. It is the component that generates the most heat in a computer; if left unchecked, it will fry itself in a matter of seconds. That's why most motherboards have an internal CPU heat sensor and a CPU fan sensor. If no cooling fan is active, these devices will shut down the computer before damage occurs.

There are a few different types of CPU cooling methods, but the two most common can be grouped into two categories: air cooling and liquid cooling.

Air Cooling

The parts inside most computers are cooled by air moving through the case. The CPU is no exception. However, because of the large amount of heat produced, the CPU must have (proportionately) the largest surface area exposed to the moving air in the case. Therefore, the heat sinks on the CPU are the largest of any inside the computer. Figure 1.42 shows a CPU heat sink. This one is a beast, at about 6″ across.

FIGURE 1.42 CPU heat sink

The metal fins on the heat sink in Figure 1.42 attach to the processor, and the fan in between helps dissipate the heat. You will find a variety of different types of processor heat sinks on the market, but most of them involve both the metal heat spreaders and a fan.

Don't touch a CPU heat sink until your computer has been turned off for at least several minutes!

The CPU fan often blows air down through the body of the heat sink to force the heat into the ambient internal air, where it can join the airflow circuit for removal from the case. However, in some cases, you might find that the heat sink extends up farther, using radiator-type fins, and the fan is placed at a right angle and to the side of the heat sink. This design moves the heat away from the heat sink immediately instead of pushing the air down through the heat sink. CPU fans can be purchased that have an adjustable rheostat to allow you to dial in as little airflow as you need, aiding in noise reduction but potentially leading to accidental overheating.

Liquid Cooling

Liquid cooling is the second most popular way to cool processors. Liquid cooling uses a special water block to conduct heat away from the processor (as well as from the chipset). Water is circulated through this block to a radiator, where it is cooled. The most common type of liquid cooler for a home PC is called an all-in-one (AIO) cooler. An AIO cooler will be much smaller than an air cooler and has one to three fans installed. AIO systems are comparably priced to air coolers. There are other, fancier, and more expensive water cooling systems that require the user to buy separate components and put them all together.

The theory is that you could achieve better cooling performance through the use of liquid cooling. For the most part, this is true. However, with traditional cooling methods (which use air and water), the lowest temperature you can achieve is room temperature. Plus, with liquid cooling, the pump is submerged in the coolant (generally speaking), so as it works, it produces heat, which adds to the overall liquid temperature.

The primary market for liquid cooling is high-performance systems and servers.

Summary

In this chapter, you began your survey of fundamental IT concepts with a tour inside the case of a computer. Considering that computers are collections of hardware, with software that lets you interact with that hardware, it makes sense to know what all the components inside that metal and plastic box do.

First, you looked at motherboards, CPUs, and memory. The motherboard is the most important component in the system because it connects everything and provides pathways for communication. If the motherboard fails, your computer will not work. Processors are analogous to the brain of the computer, but what they really do is math and logic operations. They do it very quickly, and they generate a ton of heat. Much like the motherboard, if the processor fails, you don't have a computer. Memory is critical, too. It's a temporary storage area for data; that data is lost when your system is turned off. Generally speaking, the more memory your system has, the better.

Second, you looked at storage and expansion devices. Hard drives give you the permanent storage you need to make computers useful. They can be either conventional hard drives or newer solid-state drives. You can also store data on optical discs such as BD-ROMs, DVD-ROMs, or CD-ROMs. Expansion devices add functionality to your computers. Video cards let you see pictures on your screens, sound cards give you music, network cards are pretty much necessary to communicate with other computers, and modems, well, modems used to be important for getting on the Internet but are now nearly extinct.

Finally, I talked about power supplies and system cooling. Computers are electronics, so of course they need power. Power supplies take AC power from wall outlets and convert it into DC power that the computer components need. The use of all this electricity generates heat, and too much heat can cause your components to fail. Most systems have built-in heat-mitigation systems such as fans and heat sinks. CPUs generate the most heat and therefore have the most pressing need to be adequately cooled.

Exam Essentials

Explain the basics of computing and processing. At a fundamental level, most users want computers to do four things: take input, provide processing on the input, produce output, and provide long-term storage.

Understand how to compare common data units of measure. A bit is either a 0 or a 1. Eight bits are 1 byte. Further, 1,000 bytes equal 1 kilobyte; 1,000 kilobytes equal 1 megabyte; 1,000 megabytes equal 1 gigabyte; 1,000 gigabytes equal 1 terabyte; and 1,000 terabytes equal 1 petabyte.

Compare and contrast megahertz and gigahertz. Hertz measures the number of electronic cycles in one second. Megahertz (MHz) means one million cycles, and gigahertz (GHz) means one billion cycles per second.

Understand the purpose of motherboards, CPUs, and RAM. Motherboards connect all the components together and provide electrical pathways for data. CPUs perform mathematical and logic operations on data, and RAM is used as a temporary storage area for data that the processor and applications need.

Explain what the BIOS does. The BIOS loads the POST routine, which starts the computer's boot process. It also stores configuration information such as the date and time, amount of RAM, and which device to load the operating system from.

Know the difference between conventional hard drives and solid-state drives. First, they both do the same thing, which is to provide long-term, nonvolatile data storage (as opposed to RAM which is volatile storage). Conventional hard disk drives have spinning platters and read/write heads, whereas SSDs use flash memory. SSDs are faster but generally more expensive than their conventional HDD counterparts. A newer SSD technology is NVMe, which speeds up the rate at which SSDs can transfer data.

Know what a GPU is. A graphics processing unit (GPU) is the main processor for a video card, specially designed for that purpose.

Know the features of optical discs. Optical discs store data but are not designed to replace hard drives. BD-ROMs store more data than DVD-ROMs, which store more than CD-ROMs.

Understand what different expansion devices do. Video cards produce images for display devices such as monitors. Audio (sound) cards produce sound. Network cards and modems are for communication. Network cards communicate via network cable or wirelessly, whereas modems use conventional telephone lines.

Understand the importance of power and system cooling. Computers need power to operate, and that is provided by the power supply unit (PSU) which is plugged into the wall. Computer components generate heat, in particular, the processor. They need to be cooled off to survive. Case fans are generally good enough for computers. CPUs require more active cooling methods, such as a combination of a heat sink and a fan or advanced systems such as liquid cooling.

Chapter 1 Lab

You can find the answers in Appendix A.

In this lab, you are being given the task of buying a new computer for a relative. You've been given a strict budget. Based on that budget, you found three systems at the same price. Your relative will use the computer for browsing the Internet, paying bills, and occasionally playing some games. They also take a lot of family photos and videos and like to edit them on their computer. See Table 1.4 for the specifications of each of the three systems you found.

TABLE 1.4 Shopping comparison

Specification	System J	System L	System S
Processor	2.0 GHz AMD Ryzen 7	1.3 GHz Intel Core i5	2.5 GHz Intel Core i5
System memory (RAM)	16 GB DDR4	16 GB DDR5	8 GB DDR4
RAM expandable to	Non-expandable	32 GB	32 GB
Hard drive type	SATA SSD	SATA SSD	SATA SSD
Hard drive size	1 TB	512 GB	256 GB
Screen size	16 inches	14 inches	15.6 inches

Specification	System J	System L	System S
Touch screen	No	Yes	Yes
Graphics	AMD Radeon	Intel Iris XE integrated	Intel UHD integrated
Video memory	2 GB dedicated	Shared	Shared
Sound card	7.1-channel integrated	5.1-channel integrated	7.1 channel integrated
Network card	Wireless AC	Wireless AX	Wireless AC
USB ports	4 USB-A	1 USB-A 3.2	2 USB-A 3.2, 1 USB-A 2.0
Display ports	HDMI	HDMI, 2 Thunderbolt	HDMI
Operating system	Windows 11 Home	Windows 11 Home	Windows 11 Home
Battery life	12.8 hours	16.5 hours	15.1 hours
Weight	4.1 lbs	3.4 lbs	3.7 lbs

1. Based on the system specifications, which one would you recommend and why?
2. What specifications made you not choose the others?
3. If you were looking for a computer for someone who played a lot of online action games, would you change your recommendation? Why?
4. If this laptop were for a relative who traveled a lot, would you change your recommendation and why?

Review Questions

You can find the answers in Appendix B.

1. Which components in your computer store data? (Choose three.)
   - A. RAM
   - B. SSD
   - C. PCI
   - D. PSU
   - E. BD-ROM
2. What type of expansion card allows your computer to talk to other computers without wires?
   - A. Modem
   - B. NIC
   - C. PSU
   - D. PCIe
3. Which type of expansion slot provides the fastest data transfer speeds?
   - A. PCI
   - B. PCIe x1
   - C. PCIe x16
   - D. PCIe x64
4. Which of the following optical discs will store the most data?
   - A. CD-ROM
   - B. DVD-ROM DL
   - C. DVD-ROM DS
   - D. BD-ROM
5. Data needs to be stored on a computer and access speed is the most important thing. The data does not need to be persistent. What is the best option for storing this data?
   - A. Database
   - B. RAM
   - C. SSD
   - D. HDD
6. Your friend Joe wants to add another hard drive to his computer. What should he check to make sure that his system will support it?
   - A. PSU
   - B. Expansion slots
   - C. CPU
   - D. RAM

7. If a user wants to play live-action video games, which component will they want to upgrade first in their computer?
   A. CPU
   B. GPU
   C. PSU
   D. NVMe
8. You want to upgrade your computer to give it a faster boot time and more space for your files. What should you purchase?
   A. RAM
   B. HDD
   C. SSD
   D. CPU
9. If your computer runs low on RAM, what will it use instead?
   A. Cache
   B. SSD
   C. Optical drive
   D. Virtual memory
10. Order the storage unit sizes from largest to smallest.
   A. MB, KB, GB, TB
   B. KB, MB, GB, PB
   C. TB, GB, MB, KB
   D. PB, GB, TB, MB
11. When you turn on your computer, it tells you that it does not have the time and date set and asks you to enter setup. What likely needs to be replaced?
   A. CMOS battery
   B. BIOS chip
   C. CPU
   D. Time controller
12. A user named Monika wants to upgrade the memory in her laptop. What type of memory will she need?
   A. DIMM
   B. SODIMM
   C. DDR5
   D. DDR4

13. Which device is connected to the motherboard with a 24-pin block connector?
    - A. HDD
    - B. SSD
    - C. RAM
    - D. PSU

14. Which of the following are connectors for internal storage devices? (Choose two.)
    - A. SATA
    - B. HHD
    - C. SSD
    - D. M.2
    - E. NVMe

15. Which of the following processor types is most likely to be found in a smartphone?
    - A. 32-bit
    - B. GPU
    - C. Intel
    - D. ARM

16. You just installed more memory in your computer, but it's not recognized. Your friend suggests that you upgrade your BIOS. What's the best way to do this?
    - A. Order a new BIOS chip from the motherboard manufacturer.
    - B. Order a new BIOS chip from the memory manufacturer.
    - C. Flash the BIOS.
    - D. You can't upgrade a BIOS.

17. Which component inside a computer produces the most heat?
    - A. PSU
    - B. CPU
    - C. GPU
    - D. RAM

18. Which of the following are nonvolatile data storage options for user data? (Choose two.)
    - A. SSD
    - B. HDD
    - C. RAM
    - D. ROM

19. Your boss wants you to justify your suggestion to purchase solid-state hard drives. What are advantages of solid-state drives? (Choose three.)
    - A. Faster than HDDs
    - B. Generate less heat than HDDs
    - C. Quieter than HDDs
    - D. Cheaper than HDDs
20. Which of the following are communications devices for computers? (Choose two.)
    - A. NIC
    - B. Modem
    - C. PCIe
    - D. Sound card

Peripherals and Connectors

THE FOLLOWING COMPTIA TECH+ FC0-U71 EXAM OBJECTIVES ARE COVERED IN THIS CHAPTER:

✓ **1.0 IT Concepts and Terminology**

✓ **1.3: Compare and contrast common units of measure.**

- Throughput unit
  - Bits per second (bps)
  - Kilobits per second (Kbps)
  - Megabits per second (Mbps)
  - Gigabits per second (Gbps)
  - Terabytes per second (Tbps)

✓ **2.0 Infrastructure**

✓ **2.3: Compare and contrast storage types.**

- Local network storage
  - Network-attached storage (NAS)

✓ **2.4: Given a scenario, install and configure common peripheral devices.**

- Devices
  - Printer
  - Scanner
  - Keyboard
  - Mouse
  - Web camera
  - External drive

        - Speakers/headset
        - Display
            - SmartTV
            - Projector
            - Monitor
        - Uninterruptible power supply (UPS)
    - Installation types
        - Plug-n-play vs. driver installation
        - Other required steps
        - IP-based peripherals
        - Web-based configuration steps

✓ **2.5: Compare and contrast common types of input/output device interfaces.**

- Networking
    - Wired
        - Ethernet connector (RJ45)
        - Fiber connector small form-factor pluggable (SFP)
    - Wireless
        - Bluetooth
        - Near-field communication (NFC)
        - 802.11X
    - Networking devices and tools
        - Crimpers
        - Cable testers
- Peripheral devices
    - USB (A/B/C)
    - Thunderbolt
    - Bluetooth
    - Radio frequency (RF)
    - Lightning

- Display ports
  - Video Graphics Array (VGA)
  - Digital Visual Interface (DVI)
  - High Definition Media Interface (HDMI)
  - DisplayPort
  - USB-C
- Display Technology
  - Mirroring
  - Casting

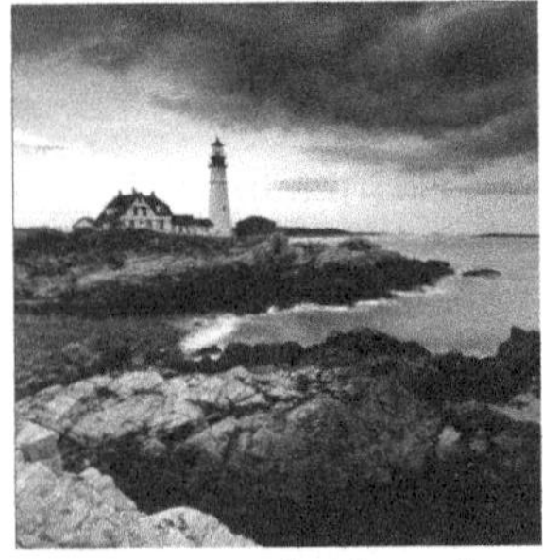

The hardware inside your computer's case is critical to its operation, no doubt about it. By contrast, the peripheral hardware outside the case is optional. Your computer doesn't need a monitor or a keyboard to work properly. Granted, these devices add functionality that you really want. No one is going to bother using a computer without a display for very long.

Dozens of different types of peripherals can be attached to a computer. It would be impractical to cover all possible peripherals here, so let's focus on some of the most common ones that you will encounter. Each one, of course, provides specific functionality to make a computer do the things you want it to do. Some devices have one specific function—take the keyboard, for example. It's designed solely to provide input. Other peripherals can do multiple things, such as many printers. Not only do they print, but most can also scan and maybe even send and receive faxes. In this way, a multifunctional printer is both an input and an output device.

In this chapter, you'll learn about three different categories of computer peripherals: those that provide audio and video, those that allow for external storage and communication, and those that perform input and output functions and manage power. I will group the peripheral devices the best I can, but know that there will be some overlap because of their functionality or the technologies used. For example, audio and video are clearly output, but they're so specialized that they deserve their own sections. In addition, some of the connectors used for external storage can also be used for video or other devices. Some technologies are multipurpose, so they naturally fall into multiple camps.

Along with the devices themselves, there are lots of different connector types to address. Even though I have many to discuss, the good news is that it's hard to plug something into the wrong spot. I'm not saying that you can't do it (I know some of you like a good challenge), but it's pretty tough to do.

Finally, at the end of the chapter, I'll explain installation steps for various devices. Topics will include driver installation as well as special considerations for IP- and web-based peripherals. Then, there will be one final review of all the connectors covered in this chapter.

Installing and Configuring Audio and Video Devices

While it might be hard to believe such a scenario, the first computers didn't have video output. In those now-ancient times, output could have been delivered via punch cards, a series of lights, or printed paper. Back then, computers were basically used as giant calculators so the output didn't require fancy graphics. Fortunately, monitors started making common appearances in the mid-1970s, and the technology has steadily improved. The inclusion of audio output, other than basic beeping, wasn't common for another decade.

In this first section, you'll look at audio and video peripherals, which are generally classified as output devices. Now this designation doesn't completely hold true, as you will see. For example, sound cards have connections for microphones, which allow users to input as well as output sound, and touchscreens allow for user input as well. Regardless, most of what I cover here will be specifically related to computer output, and I'll talk about the exceptions as I move through the chapter objectives.

Audio Connectors

Audio and audio connectors are a pretty easy topic in the grand scheme of computers, so let's tackle it first and get it out of the way. As you learned in Chapter 1, "Core Hardware Components," computers can have internal sound cards (or audio cards) that will let the computer produce music, sound for games, or even the voices of your friends and loved ones.

To hear the sound, though, you need speakers. Speakers come in a variety of shapes and sizes, from simple and cheap headphones to complex speaker systems that rival those found in high-end home theaters. Depending on for what purpose you intend to use your computer, you can choose the right kind for your needs. Laptops almost always have speakers built into their case.

Figure 2.1 shows you the back-panel connectors of a desktop system. You can tell that these connectors are all built into the motherboard because of their location. If this system had a separate sound card, the audio connectors would be in an expansion slot instead. On the right side you see three round audio connectors designed for 1/8″ (3.5 mm) plugs. This system also gives you a handy icon next to each plug, letting you know which one is for audio input, which one is for speakers (it's usually green), and which one is for the microphone (usually pink).

FIGURE 2.1 Audio connectors

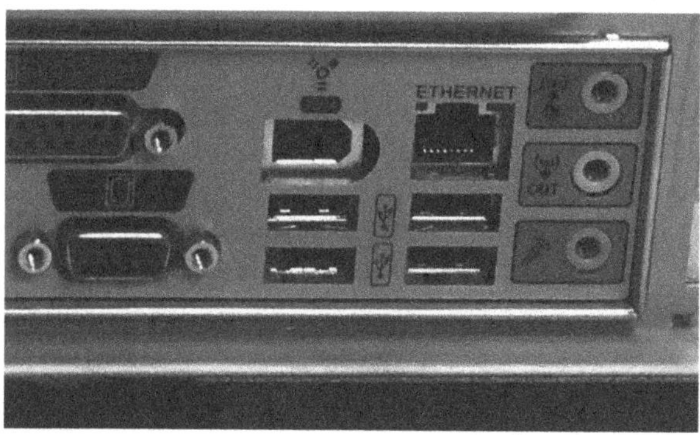

The example in Figure 2.1 is pretty basic. Some sound cards give you a few more plugs, such as the one in Figure 2.2. In this one, the black plug is for a subwoofer (if you have one), green is for speakers, and pink is still for the microphone. It's really hard to see, but on sound cards such as this, there are small icons etched into the metal plate to let you know what should be plugged into each port. To me, decoding them is a little like trying to read hieroglyphics. This sound card also has a DA15 connector on the right, called a *game port*, which can be used to plug in older-style joysticks.

FIGURE 2.2 Sound card with game port

Game ports have been made obsolete by USB ports, which I will talk about shortly. Any joysticks that you find today will most likely be USB.

So, this is the first example of a component (the sound card) handling both input and output duties. Speakers most definitely provide output, and microphones and joysticks are input devices. But they both plug into the same device—either the sound card or the audio ports built into the motherboard.

Tech+ exam objective 2.4, "Given a scenario, install and configure common peripheral devices," includes speakers/headset as a subobjective.

If your neighbors don't want to hear your music, or if you want to have a private conversation, a *headset* is a better choice than external speakers. Headsets combine speakers and a microphone into one device, conveniently worn on your head. (Of course, earbuds and other in-ear devices count, too.) Nearly all wired headsets, like the one shown in Figure 2.3, will connect via USB. Wireless headsets will either have a USB dongle or use Bluetooth, which we will get into later in this chapter.

FIGURE 2.3 A USB headset

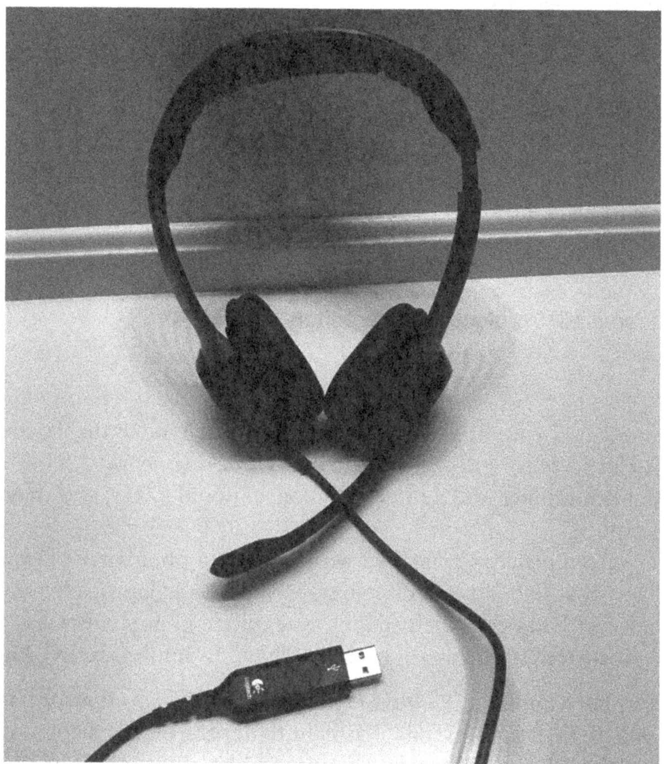

Display Devices and Connectors

Can you imagine not having monitors on computers? Well, the earliest computers didn't have video output, and academics and scientists still used them. Granted, the machines also took up the entire room and had a fraction of the computing power of your wristwatch, but they were still computers. It's a good thing that technology has come a long way since then. It's doubtful that computers would enjoy the popularity they have today if they weren't visual.

In Chapter 1, you learned about video cards. Here, I'll talk about the other end of that system, which is the display device. After that, I'll spend some time talking about the types of connectors that you will use to join the display and computer together. Finally, you will look at how to configure some common video settings on your computer.

Display Devices

When it comes to display devices, you have quite a few choices in the marketplace. In many ways, choosing a display device for a computer is much like shopping for a television.

They use similar technologies and give you similar features. Here, I'll group display devices into these four broad categories:

- Monitors
- Smart TVs
- Touchscreens
- Projectors

In upcoming sections, I'll discuss each one in order.

Tech+ exam objective 2.4 lists Display as a subobjective that includes smart TV, projector, and monitor.

Monitors

Flat-screen *monitors* are by far and away the most popular type of display device you will encounter today. Flat screens replaced old and bulky *cathode ray tube (CRT)* monitors because they are much thinner and lighter than conventional CRTs, and they also consume significantly less power.

The rise of flat-screen displays coincided with the rise in popularity of laptops. Said a better way, it's likely that flat-screen technology—which made laptops far smaller and more portable than they ever had been—helped laptops explode in popularity.

Monitors are mostly based on one of two underlying technologies, LCD and LED:

Liquid Crystal Display Monitor A *liquid crystal display (LCD) monitor* has two polarized filters, between which are liquid crystals. For light to appear on the display screen, it must pass through both filters and the crystals. The second filter, however, is at an angle to the first, so by default nothing passes through. By applying current to the crystal, you can cause it to twist, which also twists the light passing through it. If the light twists so that it matches the angle of the second filter, it can pass through the filter and light up an area of the display. On a color LCD, an additional filter splits the light into separate cells for red, green, and blue. An LCD monitor needs a light source, which is called a *backlight* and is either behind or near the edge of the display.

Light-Emitting Diode Monitor If you can't tell the difference between an LCD display and a *light-emitting diode (LED) monitor*, you're not alone. LED displays are just LCD panels with light-emitting diodes (LEDs) as light sources instead of the cold cathode fluorescent (CCFL) backlighting used by conventional LCD monitors. This results in brighter colors and darker blacks.

There are of course offshoots to these technologies. If you go monitor shopping today you will be introduced to:

- In-plane switching (IPS), which delivers wide viewing angles but has slower response times, so it isn't as good for fast-motion video such as games or live sports.
- Organic light-emitting diode (OLED), where the pixels themselves emit their own light without the need of a backlight. OLEDs have good response times, but more limited

viewing angles, may not be as bright (but have darker black versus backlight monitors that might look a little gray when images are dark), and can be susceptible to image burn-in.

- Quantum dot LED (QLED) screens need a backlight. They use an LCD screen overlaid with very small quantum dots to sharpen the picture. Their primary advantage is that they are brighter than OLEDs.

It's unlikely that the Tech+ exam will quiz you in much detail about how IPS, OLED, or QLED work, but knowing the basics is still useful. For the real world, understand that different technologies exist, and each has pros and cons that may better suit a user's needs.

Smart TVs

A *smart TV* is very much so like a monitor. The biggest differences are that smart TVs are usually larger and they have built-in Internet connectivity as well as preinstalled apps. Because of their larger size, they often won't produce as crisp of an image as a monitor will. I will talk about this more in the "Adjusting and Configuring Displays" section later in this chapter. Connecting a smart TV is just like connecting a monitor.

Just like when you are shopping for a computer or monitor, the specs of similarly sized or priced smart TVs might be very different. It's best to shop around to see what features each has to determine what's best for your needs and budget. Table 2.1 shows some sample specifications for three similarly priced 75″ smart TVs. Don't worry if you're not familiar with all of the specification types; we will cover the ones you need to know throughout this chapter.

TABLE 2.1 Smart TV specifications

Brand	LG	Hisense	Samsung	Sony
Resolution	4K (2160p)	4K (2160p)	4K (2160p)	4K (2160p)
Backlight	Edge lit	Full array local dimming	Full array local dimming	Direct lit
Voice assistant	Amazon Alexa	Google Assistant	Amazon Alexa	Google Assistant
LED panel type	QNED	QLED	QLED	Standard LED
Picture quality enhancement	Active HDR	4K Active HDR	Quantum HDR 4X	4K HDR Processor X1
Motion enhancement	None	Motion Rate 480	Motion Xcelerator Turbo+	Motionflow XR960
Refresh rate	120 Hz	144 Hz	120 Hz	120 Hz
Smart platform (OS)	webOS	Google TV	Tizen	Google TV

TABLE 2.1 SmartTV specifications *(continued)*

Brand	LG	Hisense	Samsung	Sony
Major streaming services	11	8	11	7
HDMI inputs	4	4	4	4
Weight (lbs)	72.8	79.4	72.1	74.5

Touchscreens

Touchscreens have exploded in popularity in recent years. They are pretty much standard fare for smartphones and tablets, and most laptop computers (except for lower-end models) offer them as well. The idea is pretty simple; it looks like any other display device, but you can touch the screen and the system senses it. It can be as simple as registering a click, like a mouse, or it can be more advanced such as capturing handwriting and saving it as a digital note. It's both an output device and an input device.

Although the technical details of how touchscreens work are beyond the scope of this book, there are a few things to know. One is that some touchscreens will work with any object touching them, whereas others require a conductive input, such as your finger. Smartphones are a great example of this, as anyone who lives in cold climates and wears gloves can attest. The second thing is that some touchscreens are coated with a film that is sensitive to touch. Cleaning these screens with regular glass cleaner can ruin the touchscreen nature of the device. It's best to clean those devices only with a damp cloth as needed.

What About Webcams?

Since I'm discussing video devices in this section, this is probably the best place to talk about web cameras, or webcams. A *webcam* is a small camera attached or built into your computer that allows you to capture video. It does not record the video itself, but it transmits the video signals to the computer for display or processing. Those signals can be recorded or streamed live in a webcast or video chat. Almost all laptops now have webcams built into their cases, whereas desktop webcams generally connect to the computer via USB.

Web cameras are a subobjective of Tech+ exam objective 2.4, so ensure you are familiar with them.

Projectors

Another major category of display device is the video projection system, or projector. Portable *projectors* are incredibly useful if you travel a lot or if you can't afford projectors for every conference room in your office. Interactive whiteboards allow presenters to project an image onto the board as they use virtual markers to draw electronically on the displayed image. Remote participants can see the slide on their computer, as well as the markups made by the presenter. The presenter can see the same markups because the board transmits them to the computer to which the projector is attached, causing them to be displayed by the projector in real time.

Projection systems are required to produce a lighted image and display it many feet away from the system. The inherent challenge to this is that ambient light tends to interfere with the image's projection. The best way to fight this problem is to ensure that your projector has a high brightness rating, which is measured in lumens. Projection systems are usually rated and chosen for purchase based on lumens of brightness, once a maximum supported resolution has been chosen. In a relatively darkened room, a projector producing as little as 1,300 lumens is adequate. However, in a very well-lit area, you may need 5,000 to 6,000 lumens for the image to be readily visible to viewers. By way of comparison, standard indoor light bulbs typically produce between 800 lumens and 1,200 lumens.

Bulb replacements tend to be relatively expensive, so treat your projector with care when moving it!

Video Connectors

Now that I have talked about the characteristics of different display devices, let's discuss how to plug them into a computer. I will start with the oldest technologies and work toward the present, and I'll show you what each connector and port looks like.

The Tech+ exam objective 2.5, "Compare and contrast common types of input/output device interfaces," lists several display ports (video connectors) you need to know for the exam:

- Video Graphics Array (VGA)
- Digital Visual Interface (DVI)
- High Definition Media Interface (HDMI)
- DisplayPort
- USB-C

VGA

The *video graphics array (VGA)* connector was the de facto video standard for computers for years and is still in use today. First introduced in 1987 by IBM, it was quickly adopted by other PC manufacturers. The term *VGA* is often used interchangeably to refer to generic analog video, the 15-pin video connector I'm talking about here, or a 640 × 480 screen resolution (even though the VGA standard can support much higher resolutions). Figure 2.4 shows a VGA connector, as well as the male connector that plugs into the monitor. Nearly all VGA connectors are blue in color.

FIGURE 2.4 VGA connectors

VGA technology is the only one on the objectives list that is analog. It has been superseded by newer digital standards such as DVI (discussed next), and it was supposed to be phased out starting in 2013. A technology this widely used will be around for quite a while, though, and you'll still see a lot of these in the wild.

All of the video connector types introduced from here on are digital standards.

DVI

Digital visual interface (DVI) was introduced in 1999. It's the first widely used digital video standard for computers, but it also supports analog signals. On video cards, it's a white blocky connector about an inch long. Figure 2.5 shows what the connector looks like coming from the monitor.

FIGURE 2.5 DVI connector

The designers of DVI were smart to make it compatible with analog signals, as well as VGA technology. If you have a monitor with a DVI cable but a computer with only a VGA port (or vice versa), you can buy an adapter to connect the two.

USB

Universal serial bus (USB) is a ubiquitous connector, so it should come as no surprise that there are USB display devices. The first widely used standard was USB 1.1, which was released in 1998, but it was pretty slow (only 12 Mbps), so it was really only used for keyboards, mice, and printers. When USB 2.0 came out in 2000 with a high-speed transfer rate of 480 Mbps, video devices were possible. I am guessing that everyone has seen USB, and the familiar connector is technically USB-A. USB-C is the newest connector, and it's an elongated oval shape, as shown in Figure 2.6. It was designed to replace older USB connectors, and it's reversible, meaning that you can plug it in with either edge up—there is no such thing as "upside down" with USB-C.

The current fastest USB standard is USB 4, which supports data transfer speeds of up to 40 Gbps. Keep in mind that to achieve these speeds, all of the relevant components, including the motherboard, cable, and USB device, need to support that standard. If not, the chain will work only as fast as the slowest link.

FIGURE 2.6 USB-C (top) and USB-A (bottom) connectors

Just How Fast Is It?

It's important to understand the different throughput units of measure. For example, I will refer to speeds in terms of *bits per second (bps)* throughout this chapter. In the case of the old USB 1.1, it's *megabits per second (Mbps)*, whereas USB 4 is *gigabits per second (Gbps)*. In the field, you will also see *kilobits per second (Kbps)* and *terabits per second (Tbps)*. The good news is that the naming conventions are similar to the storage units you learned about in Chapter 1. The math is the same. If the speed is 1,000 bits per second, that equals 1 kilobit per second, and a speed of 1,000 Kbps is the same as 1 Mbps.

Just to confuse things a little, some devices will have throughput rated in *bytes* per second. Remember that a byte is 8 bits, so it's a big difference! In terms of abbreviations, bits per second (bps) uses a lowercase *b*, and bytes per second (Bps) uses an uppercase *B*.

Tech+ exam objective 1.3, "Compare and contrast common units of measure," asks you to be familiar with these throughput units. In the exam objectives, Tbps is incorrectly labeled terabytes per second. Remember that bytes will always have an uppercase *B*, and bits will always use a lowercase *b*.

Perhaps the nicest feature of USB display devices is that they can draw their power from the USB cable, so you do not need to plug in a separate power cord for the display.

HDMI

One of the newest standards, and a very popular one in the home theater market today, is *high-definition multimedia interface (HDMI)*. (The exam objectives also call it high-definition media interface, but the difference is unimportant.) It was introduced in 2002, which makes it seem old in technology years, but it's a great, fast, reliable connector that will probably be around for several years to come. Figure 2.7 shows an HDMI cable and port on a motherboard.

FIGURE 2.7 HDMI cable and connector

The HDMI standard is very fast; the most current version, HDMI 2.1 (released in November 2017), has a data rate of 48 Gbps. HDMI 2.1 supports 4K and 8K video at a 120 Hz refresh rate. Like USB, HDMI also has an advantage over DVI and other older standards in that it can carry audio signals and network connectivity as well as video.

Even though HDMI can transmit more than video, it's nearly always considered a "video standard."

DisplayPort and Thunderbolt

DisplayPort was introduced in 2008 by the Video Electronics Standards Association (VESA). It was designed to be an industry standard and replace VGA and DVI. It's also backward compatible with VGA and DVI through the use of adapters. Figure 2.8 shows a DisplayPort port on a laptop and a connector. A DisplayPort port is intended to be for video devices only, but like HDMI and USB, it can transmit audio and video simultaneously.

FIGURE 2.8 DisplayPort port and connector

Thunderbolt was developed as an offshoot of the DisplayPort technology. The short history is that Apple announced a mini DisplayPort (MDP) standard in late 2008 and stated that the standard would have no licensing fee. In early 2009, VESA responded by saying that MDP would be included in the upcoming DisplayPort 1.2 specification. Apple was not pleased about this, and it teamed up with Intel to rework the specification. It added in support for PCIe, renamed it Thunderbolt, and launched it in 2011. Thunderbolt supports not only video devices but also several other types of peripherals. In terms of versatility, it's really only second to USB. I'll talk more about Thunderbolt in the "External Storage Connectors" section later in this chapter. All Apple laptops made today contain a Thunderbolt port; other laptops can too if the manufacturer licenses the technology from Apple. It looks a lot like a DisplayPort, only smaller, and has the characteristic lightning bolt icon, as shown in Figure 2.9.

FIGURE 2.9 Two Thunderbolt ports

Looking at Figure 2.9, you might think that Thunderbolt ports look a lot like USB-C ones, and you're right. They use the same connectors, and a device supporting one technology can be plugged into a port supporting the other. Without getting into too much detail, most USB-C devices will work in a Thunderbolt port, but Thunderbolt devices likely will not work if plugged into a computer that only supports USB.

Adjusting and Configuring Displays

Now that we've talked about the different types of display devices and how you can hook them up to your computer, let's shift gears a bit and talk about how to keep monitors behaving properly once they're connected. First, we'll start with the adjustments on the monitor itself.

When you change the monitor resolution (via the display driver properties in Control Panel in Windows, for example), the on-screen image may shift in one direction or become slightly larger or smaller than it was before. Most monitors have on-screen controls that can be used to adjust the image size, image position, contrast, brightness, and other factors. Inexpensive or old monitors may have just a couple of buttons for monitor adjustment; nearly all newer monitors will have a complete digital menu system of controls that pop up when you press a certain button. You then move through the menu system by clicking buttons to change the setting you want. If you're unsure of what the buttons do, check the monitor's manual to figure out how the controls work; they're different for each model.

Four key concepts to know for adjusting and configuring displays are resolution, refresh rate, mirroring, and casting.

Resolution *Resolution* is defined by how many software picture elements (pixels) are used to draw the screen. Resolution is described in terms of the visible image's dimensions, which indicate how many rows and columns of pixels are used to draw the screen. For example, a resolution of 1024 × 768 means 1,024 pixels across (columns) and 768 pixels down (rows) were used to draw the pixel matrix. Resolution is a software setting that is common among all display devices.

An advantage of higher resolutions is that more information can be displayed in the same screen area. A disadvantage is that the same objects and text displayed at a higher resolution appear smaller and might be harder to see. Some displays will only support specific resolutions. If set to an incorrect option, the image will become warped or distorted.

Refresh Rate The *refresh rate* is the frequency (times per second) at which the image on the screen is completely redrawn. It's measured in screen draws per second, or hertz (Hz). Imagine taking a long ruler and placing it horizontally at the bottom of the display, and then leaving it parallel to the bottom of the display as you move the ruler to the top of the display. That's analogous to a screen draw. Images are refreshed on a display multiple times per second. The lowest common refresh rate is 60 Hz and is fine for most users and applications. Higher refresh rates translate to more fluid video motion. Gamers and others who watch fast action will use displays with at least 144Hz, and some displays support 240 Hz.

Refresh rates are typically preset in the display and often can't be changed. However, some displays will let you adjust the refresh rate up or down.

Mirroring In some instances, a user will want to have multiple displays, such as when working on a project that requires referencing a spreadsheet and a presentation at the same time, or when projecting a visual to an audience. If two or more displays are used at the same time to project the same image, that is called *mirroring*. Mirroring can be done with a wired (HDMI, DisplayPort) or wireless (Bluetooth, Miracast, Apple's AirPlay, or other apps) connection. We will look at how to configure mirroring on a laptop in Exercise 2.1. When mirroring, all actions performed on one display (such as moving the mouse or changing slides) will be shown on the mirrored display.

Casting Screen *casting* is when someone streams media from one device to another over an Internet connection. For example, you can cast music or a movie from a tablet to a smart TV. The music or movie then appears on the smart TV and not on the tablet, allowing the tablet to be used for other things such as Internet surfing. Google's Chromecast is a popular example of casting technology.

Mirroring and casting are in Tech+ exam objective 2.5, so be able to compare and contrast the two.

Exercise 2.1 gives you practice in adjusting display settings.

EXERCISE 2.1

Adjusting a Desktop Monitor

1. Locate the buttons on your monitor that control its image. They are usually on the side or back of the monitor's case.
2. Experiment with the buttons to see whether you can determine what they do. Or, look up the buttons in the monitor's documentation or on the manufacturer's website.

EXERCISE 2.1 *(continued)*

On a laptop's built-in monitor, adjustment controls are usually not on the monitor itself but built into the keyboard. Several of the keys on your keyboard, most often the *Function (Fn) keys* near the top of the keyboard, will have extra symbols, sometimes in a contrasting color. In Figure 2.10, you can see several of these on a laptop's F3–F8 keys.

FIGURE 2.10 Video adjustment keys including F4 (LCD toggle), F7 (dim), and F8 (brighten)

Pressing these keys in combination with the Function (Fn) key, as shown in Figure 2.11, activates that special function. For example, there may be a key with a picture of the sun with an up arrow that increases the display brightness, like the F8 key in Figure 2.10.

FIGURE 2.11 Function (Fn) key

It's fairly common for laptop users to plug in an external display device such as a larger monitor or a projector. When you do this, you might need to toggle your video output to the correct device. In the example shown in Figure 2.10, you would press Fn and F4 at the same time. Options usually include displaying on the internal or external monitor only, displaying the same image on both, or extending the desktop to stretch across both devices. Figure 2.12 shows you what these options might look like on your laptop.

FIGURE 2.12 Laptop video toggle

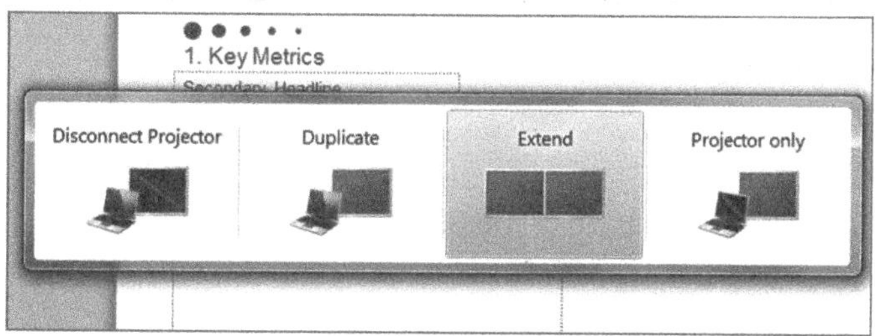

Some older laptops just cycle through the choices without giving you this visual, but most newer laptops show you what's happening. Once you have a second monitor attached, you can configure various aspects of it, such as if it's the primary or secondary display and if it appears to the left or the right of your laptop monitor (so if you move your mouse to the edge of one screen, it automatically flows to the other screen). Exercise 2.2 walks you through some multiple-monitor configuration options.

EXERCISE 2.2

Changing the Settings for Multiple Monitors

1. Right-click a blank portion of the desktop.
2. Click Display Settings, as shown in Figure 2.13. If you have multiple displays, you will see a screen similar to the one in Figure 2.14.

Note that if you have a single display, you won't see the same screen as the one in Figure 2.14. The display settings will start off with the Brightness & Color section instead. You can still make display settings changes, just not configure multiple displays.

FIGURE 2.13 Display Settings

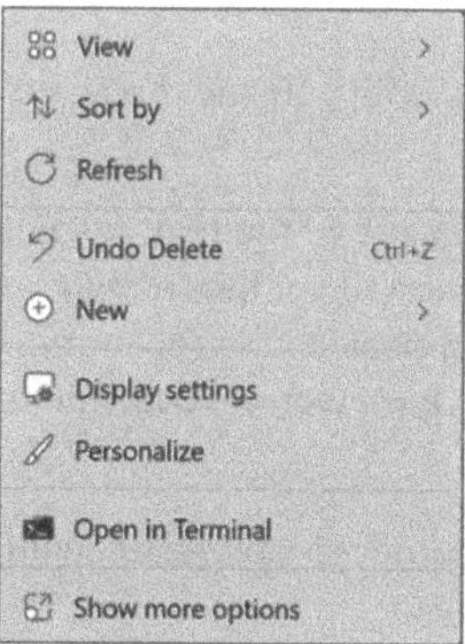

EXERCISE 2.2 *(continued)*

FIGURE 2.14 Multiple displays

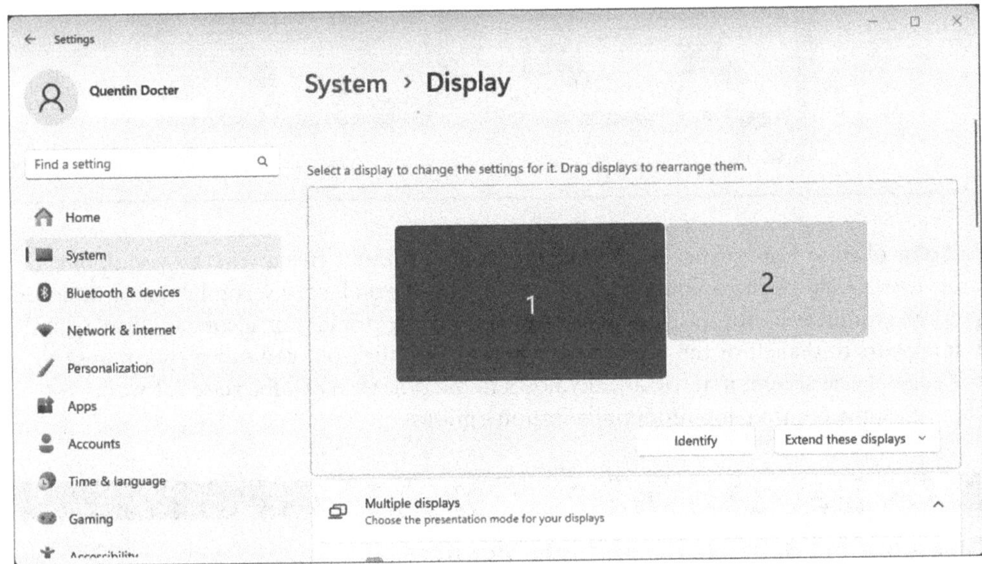

3. Click and drag the second monitor to the desired virtual position around the primary monitor. This affects the direction in which you drag objects from one display to the other. You can see in Figure 2.14 that I placed the secondary display to the right of the primary one built into the laptop. This affects how your mouse will move between the two screens.
4. Click the down arrow next to Extend These Displays. You will get a screen similar to the one in Figure 2.15.

Here you can choose to duplicate the displays (mirroring), extend the displays for a larger desktop, or show on only one or the other screens.

5. Scroll down in Display settings until you see the Scale & Layout section, like what's shown in Figure 2.16.

Notice that here you can change the size of the text, resolution, and orientation. On some displays, you may also have an option to set the refresh rate. As an optional step, change the display resolution to something besides the recommended setting and see what happens to the images on the screen. Don't worry—you will be able to change it back if you don't like it!

6. Click the X in the upper-right corner to save your changes and exit.

FIGURE 2.15 Multiple display options

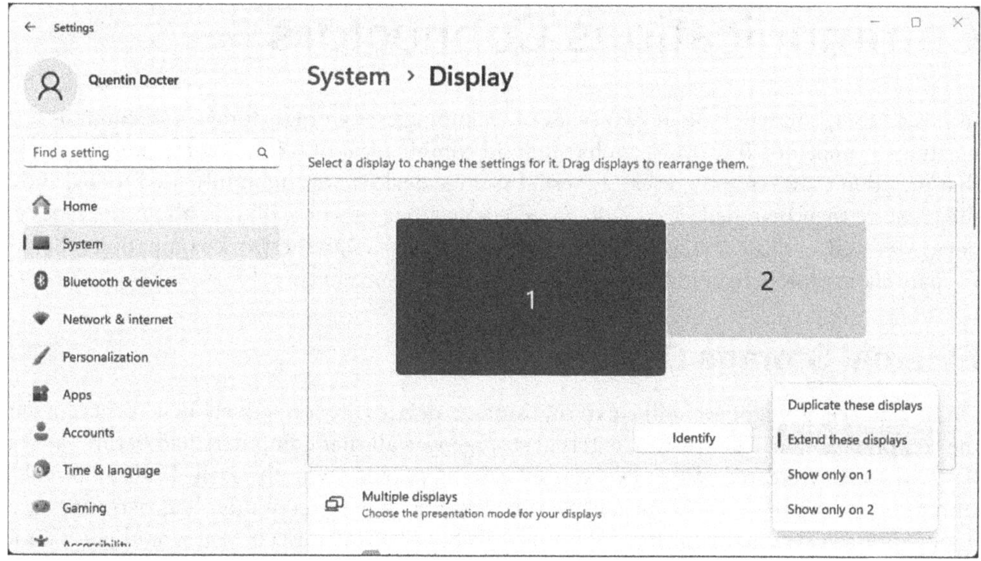

FIGURE 2.16 Scale & Layout

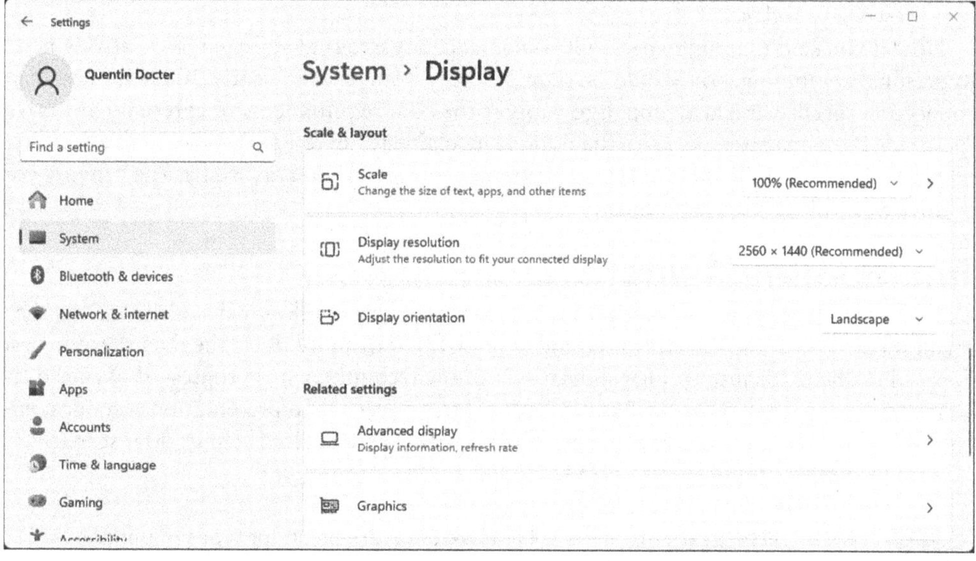

Understanding External Storage and Communications Connectors

In this section, you will look at two types of technologies: external storage and communications connectors. It might seem like an odd combination of technologies, and it's true that they don't always go together. External storage devices are commonly used today, and they require their own dedicated high-speed connections to work. I'll talk about the types of devices as well as those connections. Many external devices are network-compatible, though, so that relates closely to communications (network) connections.

External Storage Devices

On first glance, it might seem like external storage devices are a relatively new technology in the computer world. The truth is, external storage was all that computers had before internal hard drives were created. When PCs started gaining popularity in the early 1980s, internal storage was more the exception than the rule. Practically every computer had two external floppy disk drives, usually of the 5¼″ variety. To boot your computer, you would put a boot disk in the primary floppy drive and then turn on the computer. It would read the floppy drive and load the operating system into memory from there. Once the operating system was loaded, you would then take that disk out and put another one in with the program or data you needed. External storage was the norm, but it didn't resemble the external storage options we have today.

Now if you said that high-speed, ultra-high-capacity external storage was relatively new to personal computing, you would be right. It's only been since the early 2000s that external connection speeds were fast enough to support the data requirements of external hard drives. As speeds have increased, so have the options available for external storage. In this section, I will talk about several common types of external storage options, as well as the primary connectors you will see used with them.

Types of External Storage

As I have said before, we've come a long way since the days of floppy disk drives. Even the smallest external storage devices used today hold 1,000 or more times the data that the best floppy disks held. It's just another indication of how technology has progressed. We need the larger storage space because we have lots of pictures, videos, and presentations on our computers, and we need to store and transfer them easily. These devices help us do just that.

Tech+ exam objective 2.4 lists external drives under types of peripheral devices you should know how to install and configure. It doesn't specify which type of external drives, so all of the ones listed here may be fair game.

Flash Drives

We talked about *flash drives* in Chapter 1, but since we're specifically covering external storage options here let's do a quick review. Flash drives have, for all practical purposes, replaced external floppy disk drives in computers. They're compact and cheap, store a lot, and are easy to use. As you can see in Figure 2.17, they have USB connectors. All you have to do is to plug in the drive, wait for the system to detect it, and away you go. Most flash drives have a small light on them that illuminates when they're ready for use and that blinks when data is being written to or read from it.

FIGURE 2.17 A flash drive

Internally, flash drives use the same technology as solid-state drives (SSDs). There are no moving parts. Flash drives are small and can be misplaced, and have about a 10-year shelf life, which could be considered downsides. In 10 years, the flash drive you have will be so hopelessly outdated, you will want a new one anyway.

Memory Cards

From an internal composition standpoint, *memory cards* use the same technology as flash drives. They look a little different, though (see Figure 2.18), and they require a special card

FIGURE 2.18 SD memory cards

reader. Desktops, laptops, and printers may have memory card readers built into them, like the laptop shown in Figure 2.19, where it is located next to the USB port. It's becoming less and less common to see these readers built into systems today, though, because users have gravitated towards easy-to-use flash drives. If your system doesn't have a memory card reader, you can buy an external one that plugs into a USB port.

FIGURE 2.19 SD memory card slot and USB port

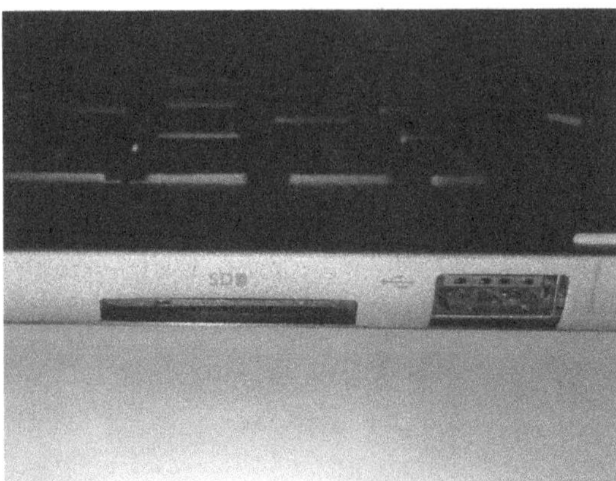

There are several different standards of memory cards, and they're all slightly different sizes. Three prominent standards are as follows:

- Smart media
- Compact flash
- Secure digital (SD)

Of the three, SD is the most popular and the one most likely to be built into your laptop or other device today. The standard *secure digital (SD) cards* are tiny—barely over an inch long (32 mm) and 0.08″ (2.1 mm) thick. You can easily find SD cards up to 512 GB in size, although the theoretical maximum for the current standard (called SD Extended Capacity, or SDXC) is 2 TB. Memory cards are more expensive than flash drives of the same capacity.

SD cards also come in two smaller sizes, the mini SD and the micro SD. Smaller cards will fit into devices built for larger cards, if you use an adapter.

Memory cards are capable of storing any type of data, but their small size makes them popular for inserting into devices such as digital cameras and video cameras, as well as small portable gaming devices.

External Hard Drives

An *external hard drive* is basically the same thing as an internal hard drive, except that it's enclosed in a protective case and connects via an external connector. External drives can be conventional HDDs or SSDs. You can see that the one in Figure 2.20 has a USB connector on the back. This example is a little older; it's about 6 inches tall and can be set upright as pictured or laid flat. It has a light on the front to let you know that it's working, and the light flashes when the drive is reading or writing.

FIGURE 2.20 External hard drive

External hard drives will connect via USB or Thunderbolt connectors. I'll discuss the differences in the "External Storage Connectors" section later in this chapter.

With current technology, regardless of the type of external hard drive connection you have, an external drive will be slower than using an internal SATA hard drive. USB 4 and Thunderbolt are faster than internal PATA hard drives, however. (USB 4 and Thunderbolt specifications are outlined in the upcoming "USB" and "Thunderbolt" sections.)

External Optical Drives

In the "External Hard Drives" section, I said that external drives are basically just like internal drives but with different connectors. The same holds true for external optical drives, whether they are CD, DVD, or Blu-ray devices. Like their external hard drive cousins, they will connect via USB or Thunderbolt.

Network-Attached Storage

A *network-attached storage (NAS)* device takes hard drive storage to the next level. Based on its name, you can probably guess that it's attached to the network, which it is, but that's just the beginning. First, take a look at a simple NAS device in Figure 2.21.

FIGURE 2.21 Netgear NAS device

Source: PJ / Wikimedia Commons / CC BY-SA 3.0

Looking at Figure 2.21, you can see that this is a self-enclosed unit that can hold up to four hard drives. Some hold more; some hold less. Nicer NAS systems will allow you to hot-swap hard drives, meaning that if one fails, you can remove it and replace it without shutting the NAS down. Additionally, most NAS systems will have built-in fault tolerance as well, meaning that if one drive fails, your data will still be protected.

In Tech+ exam objective 2.3, "Compare and contrast storage types," network-attached storage (NAS) is listed under Local Network Storage.

In addition to the hardware, the NAS device contains its own operating system, meaning that it acts like its own file server. In most cases, you can plug it in, do some very minor configuration, and have instant storage space on your network.

As far as connectivity goes, NAS systems will connect to a PC through a USB or Thunderbolt port, but that is primarily so you can use that PC to run the configuration software for the NAS. The NAS also connects to the network, and that is how all of the network users access the storage space.

If you are running a small office and need additional centralized storage, a NAS system is a good way to go.

Accessing a NAS server over the network will generally be slower than having an external hard drive on your computer. The advantage is that if you have multiple users on a network, everyone can easily get to it.

External Storage Connectors

In this section, I want to focus on the three types of connectors that you're most likely to see with external hard drives and other peripherals. I've mentioned their names throughout this chapter, and I've already covered USB in a bit of depth. It's important, though, to cover all of them in the same place so that you're able to compare and contrast the benefits of each, as well as to differentiate what they look like.

USB (A/B/C), Thunderbolt, and Lightning are all subobjectives of Tech+ exam objective 2.5. You should be able to compare and contrast these different peripheral connection types.

USB

USB is the connector I have talked about the most, but it's such a critical one that it's good to review again. And here, I'll get into a bit more depth than I did before.

Like all other standards, USB has gone through several stages of evolution. The first published standard was USB 1.0, released in 1986. Because of some technical limitations, it didn't really catch on. Those limitations were fixed by 1998 when USB 1.1 was released. It caught fire in a hurry. It was slow (only 12 Mbps), so it was primarily used for keyboards, mice, and printers. Since 1998, there have been four major upgrades to the USB standard; Table 2.2 shows the dates and important facts.

TABLE 2.2 USB specifications

Version	Year	Speed	Port/color	Trade name
USB 1.1	1998	12 Mbps	USB-A White	Full Speed
USB 2.0	2000	480 Mbps	USB-A Black	High Speed
USB 3.0	2008	5 Gbps	USB-A Blue, USB-C	SuperSpeed
USB 3.1	2013	10 Gbps	USB-A Teal, USB-C	SuperSpeed+
USB 3.2	2017	20 Gbps	USB-C	SuperSpeed 20 Gbps
USB 4	2019	40 Gbps	USB-C	USB4 40 Gbps

USB 3.1 had people really excited because that version put USB in the same ballpark as the fastest standards at the time, which were FireWire, eSATA, and Thunderbolt. USB 3.2, which was finalized in September 2017, doubled the speed of USB 3.1, delivering 20 Gbps over standard USB-C cables up to 3 meters in length. USB 4 again doubled the speed, but with a maximum cable length of 0.8 meters.

The majority of USB ports that you see in the market today are still USB 2.0. If you have a newer USB device, it will work while plugged into a USB 2.0 port, but it will just run at the slower speed. SuperSpeed USB-A ports and connectors are all supposed to be colored blue or teal to differentiate them easily from older versions. USB-C connectors won't be color-coded.

There is some confusion in the marketplace over USB versions and adapters. For example, what is the difference, if anything, between USB Type-C (or USB-C) cables and USB 3.1? They are very different things. If you see USB-A, USB-B, or USB-C, this refers to the connection type on the USB cable. The current gold standard is USB-C. The versions, which define speed, are given numbers, such as USB 3.1, USB 3.2, and USB 4.

Regardless of the standard, low-power devices can get their power from the USB port itself. Devices with higher power requirements (such as the external hard drive shown in Figure 2.20) can still use their own power sources. Up to 127 devices can be connected to one USB bus at once. As far as the types of devices that can be connected to USB, it's almost limitless. If you can think of a computer peripheral, odds are it comes in a USB version.

The Standards Graveyard

If you think there are a lot of computer technology standards to know, you're right. The list of outdated standards, though, dwarfs what we currently have in-market. Two of them that related to external peripherals were eSATA and FireWire.

External Serial ATA (eSATA) used the same technology as internal SATA, with a smaller connector. It entered the market in 2003 and was intended mostly for hard drive use. It topped out at about 6 Gbps, and most versions did not provide power to the device. Now, the speed and lack of power are antiquated, and the standard has fallen by the wayside in favor of USB-C and Thunderbolt.

FireWire was developed by Apple and released in 2000. Its maximum throughput was 3.2 Gbps, which was fast at the time, but again, antiquated today. In 2011, Apple started installing Thunderbolt connectors on its laptops instead, and FireWire disappeared as well.

Thunderbolt

I already talked about Thunderbolt a bit in the context of video connectors because the technology was developed as an offshoot of DisplayPort technology. As a quick review, remember that Apple partnered with Intel and launched Thunderbolt in 2011. Consequently, you will find Thunderbolt ports as standard features on Apple laptops, but they are hit-or-miss on other brands. Figure 2.9 has a picture of the port, which has a lightning bolt next to it. In terms of versatility, Thunderbolt is second only to USB in the types of devices made for it. You will find video devices, hard drives, printers, laptop docking stations, audio devices, and PCIe expansion enclosures that use Thunderbolt. Table 2.3 compares Thunderbolt standards.

TABLE 2.3 Thunderbolt standards

Version	Year	Speed	Connector
1.0	2011	10 Gbps	Mini DisplayPort
2.0	2013	20 Gbps	Mini DisplayPort
3.0	2015	40 Gbps	USB-C
4.0	2020	40 Gbps	USB-C

You've seen the trend with other technologies where the newer version doubles the speed of the previous one, and Thunderbolt for the most part is no different. Version 4.0 didn't double the throughput of 3.0, but it does add support for dual 4k video displays. The first two versions used the now-outdated mini DisplayPort (shown in Figure 2.22), but current versions use USB-C.

FIGURE 2.22 mini DisplayPort on a MacBook Pro

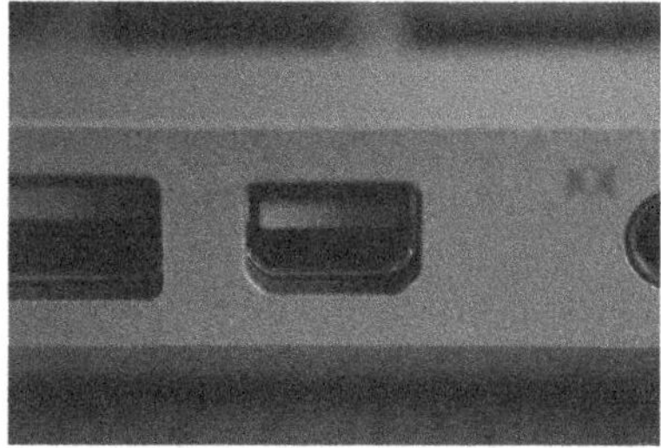

Source: Jena Selle / Wikimedia Commons / CC BY-SA 2.0

Lightning

Where there is a thunderbolt there must be lightning, right? Bad joke attempts aside, *Lightning* is an Apple proprietary connector introduced in 2012 with the iPhone 5 and is used with iPhones and iPads. It's an 8-pin connector, shown in Figure 2.23, that is not keyed, meaning that you can put it in with either edge up.

FIGURE 2.23 Lightning cable

Lightning cables support USB 2.0. You will find cables that are USB-A to Lightning, USB-C to Lightning, as well as various Lightning adapters, such as those to HDMI, DisplayPort, audio, power, and Lightning to female USB Type-A (so you can plug a USB device into an iPad or iPhone).

For years (since about 2017), there have been rumors that Apple may do away with the Lightning connector in a future iPhone release and instead move to USB-C. After all, Apple had added USB-C ports to laptops and iPads, and USB-C is the port of the future. This rumor finally came true with the iPhone 15 released in 2023, when Lightning was replaced with USB-C. It would make sense that future iPhones will have USB-C as well.

Communications Connectors

The last three connectors I will talk about in this section are for communications. Two will get you onto a wired network, and the other is designed to use telephone lines.

Network Connectors

To be fair, there are more than a dozen different types of network connectors in existence. The connector used depends on the type of network cable you're using. For example, old-school coaxial cable (similar to cable TV cabling) uses different connectors than does twisted pair, and there are probably a dozen different fiber-optic cables alone. The good news for the CompTIA Tech+ test is that there's only two you have to know about. One is used with copper cables, and the other with fiber-optic ones.

You will learn more about different cable types in Chapter 8, "Networking Concepts and Technologies."

RJ45

The most common connector on the end of a copper network cable in use today is the *registered jack 45 (RJ45)* connector, also known as an *Ethernet connector*. You'll find RJ45 connectors on the ends of twisted-pair network cables, which you will hear people call Ethernet cables or sometimes Cat 5 or Cat 6 cables (*Cat* is short for *category*). It looks like a telephone plug, except that it's wider. A twisted-pair cable has four pairs of wires, so there are eight leads on the connector. You plug it in just as you would a telephone cord. The maximum speed depends on a lot of factors, such as the communication standard you are using and distance, but the maximum you'll get from twisted pair is 40 Gbps. Figure 2.24 shows two RJ connectors: *registered jack 11 (*RJ11) on the left and RJ45 on the right.

FIGURE 2.24 RJ11 and RJ45 connectors

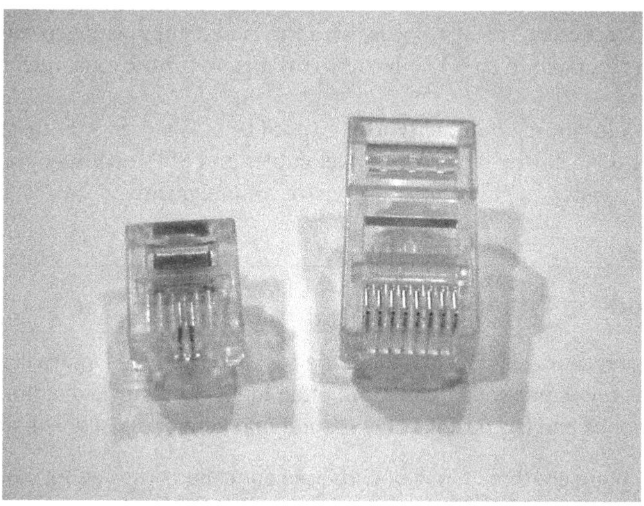

RJ45 and SFP are subobjectives of Tech+ exam objective 2.5. Be able to compare and contrast them.

SFP

Of the myriad fiber-optic cable connectors, the one you need to know is the *small form-factor pluggable (SFP)* connector. Fiber-optic network cables provide significantly higher throughput rates over longer distances than copper cables do. They are also immune to eavesdropping (someone physically hacking in and listening to network traffic between two computers), which can improve network security. The SFP connector (Figure 2.25) is an easy-to-use, hot-pluggable (you can plug in or unplug a device while the power is on) connector. The connector slides into place much like an RJ45 and clicks when it's locked in. To unplug it, you press on the latch and pull straight out.

FIGURE 2.25 SFP connector

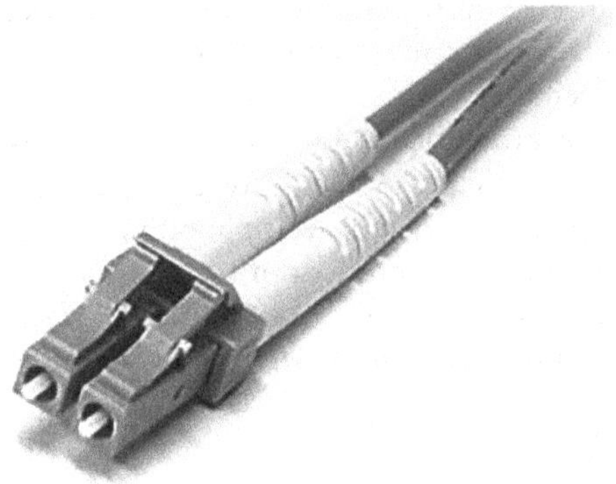

There are many different SFP standards, with the fastest supporting speeds at 400 Gbps over 40 kilometers, compared to 40 Gbps up to 50 meters for the most advanced copper cabling.

You will learn a lot more about networking specifics in Chapter 8. For now, though, remember there is RJ45 for twisted-pair copper cables and SFP for fiber-optic cables. Fiber connections will be faster, but also more expensive to implement.

Wireless Networking Options

The networking connectors I just talked about are for wired networking; it's likely, though, that you've used wireless networking far more often than wired. In view of the ubiquitous nature of smartphones and laptops, it's only natural that wireless is everywhere.

For our purposes, there are three types of wireless connection types about which you should be aware:

- Wi-Fi (802.11x)
- Bluetooth
- Radio frequency (RF)

Wi-Fi is the global de facto wireless networking standard. To connect to a Wi-Fi network, you need a wireless network card and some sort of central connectivity device, such as a wireless router or access point. Devices that are Bluetooth-enabled can communicate directly from peer to peer. No special network card or central hub is needed.

Devices that use *radio frequency (RF)* transmit a very limited range, typically only a few inches or so. This technology is fairly common in mobile payment applications. Because of the short distances involved, a related term you'll see is *near-field communication (NFC)*. Again, no extra hardware is needed, just NFC-enabled sending and receiving devices.

> This section covers connectors and interfaces, but there really isn't a picture I can show you of built-in Bluetooth or RF. If your smartphone (or other device) has them, you just enable them with software settings. Networking is an important topic, and wireless networking is given ample coverage in Chapter 8.

Networking Devices and Tools

Most users are perfectly happy to buy premade network cables from a store. There are times, though, when off-the-shelf solutions don't work. Perhaps you need a longer cable than you can find, or perhaps your boss realizes that making cables in-house is cheaper than purchasing them premade.

Bulk cable and connectors are sold separately and can be connected together with a tool called a crimper. A *crimper* is basically a fancy pair of pliers with a wire cutter/stripper, specifically designed to fasten a connector to a cable. An RJ45 crimper and a few connectors are shown in Figure 2.26.

FIGURE 2.26 RJ45 crimper

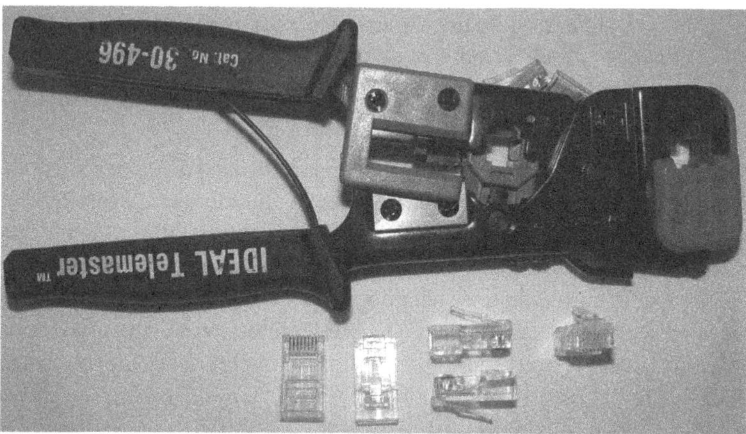

While it's relatively easy to make an RJ45 cable once you get the hang of it, making fiber-optic cables is far more difficult and requires greater precision. It's doable but most likely relegated to a specialist.

Once the cable is made, how do you know if it works? Or, if you have an existing cable that appears to have failed, how do you check it? In situations like these, you need a cable tester. This is an indispensable tool for any network technician. Usually, you would use a cable tester before you install a cable to make sure it works. Of course, you can test them after they've been run as well. A decent cable tester will tell you the type of cable, and more elaborate models will have connectors for multiple types of cables. Figure 2.27 shows a TRENDnet cable tester.

FIGURE 2.27 ATRENDnet cable tester

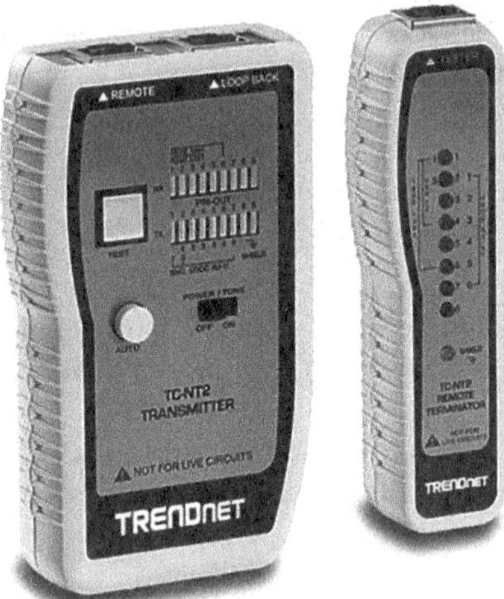

Source: With permission ofTRENDnet, Inc.

Crimpers and cable testers are called out as networking devices and tools to understand in Tech+ exam objective 2.5.

Telephone Connectors

Back before high-speed Internet was the norm, computers used a device called a *modem* to get online. Modems used the analog telephone lines to communicate back and forth. Users would call in to an *Internet service provider (ISP)*, log in to the ISP's network, and then have Internet access. While nearly obsolete today, modems are still listed in the networking objectives of the Tech+ exam, so I will cover telephone line connectors here too. The telephone connector that you will see in use is called *RJ11*. Telephone cables often have two pairs of wires, but only one is used. Figure 2.24 shows an RJ11. In Figure 2.28, you can see an RJ11 port next to an RJ45 port on a laptop.

FIGURE 2.28 RJ11 and RJ45 ports

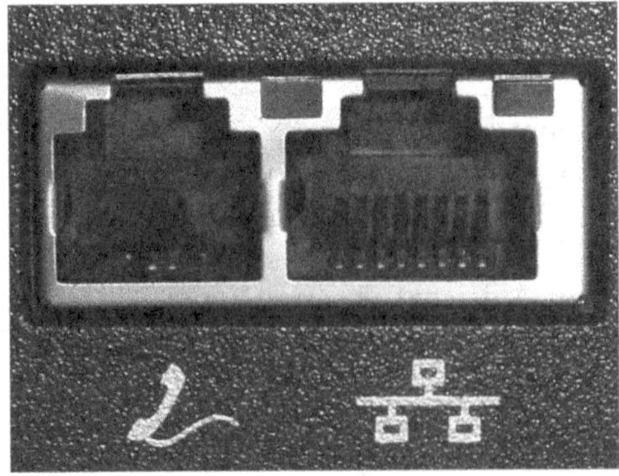

The biggest reason modems are no longer used is lack of speed. The fastest modems ever produced had a transfer rate of 56 Kbps, but in practice the most you ever really got out of the connection was around 40 Kbps. That's barely fast enough to download text files without pulling out your hair, never mind music or videos! The only reason they would be used today is if there is no other possible option (wired, satellite, cellular, anything) to connect to the Internet.

Both RJ45 and RJ11 connectors have been in existence for nearly 70 years, but they were mandated as standards in 1976.

Understanding Input, Output, and Power Devices

Even though artificial intelligence has made rapid strides in recent years, computers are still unable truly to "think" for themselves. This is probably a good thing, but my goal isn't to kick off a debate on cyber-ethics here. The point is that computers don't do anything until they are given input telling them what to do. The input can be as simple as a single keystroke or click or as complicated as millions of lines of computer code. Either way, input is critical.

The earliest computers used punch cards as input; for example, ENIAC (which is recognized as the first electronic general-purpose computer) used punch cards for input and output in 1946. Keyboards were already widely available in the form of typewriters and were introduced as computer input devices by 1948. Pointing devices actually preceded them, with the trackball being invented in 1946. (Mice didn't really become popular until much later, in 1984.) Today, a keyboard and a mouse is still the most common duo of input devices, so I'll discuss both of them in the upcoming sections.

After that, we will look at an input device of sorts of an entirely different variety. You know that computers need power to work, but what if the power is lost? An uninterruptible power supply can help resolve loss-of-power issues as well as help protect from damaging power surges.

Providing output is also a critical function of computers. Having a "black box" where input goes in but nothing comes out isn't very useful—although we probably all know some devices or even people like this! There are several kinds of output, with the most common being video and printing. Since we've already talked about video devices, the output section here will focus on printers. But first, let's talk about input devices.

Keyboards

The *keyboard* owes its history to that of the typewriter. The typewriter was first patented in 1868, and as of 1877 they were in mass production. In the 1930s, the keyboard was combined with the telegraph and also with punch card systems to create keypunches. For entering data, the typewriter keyboard was the technology of choice. So, it shouldn't come as a surprise that computer makers adopted the technology as well.

The most common keyboard configuration for Latin script languages is called QWERTY, named for the first six letters on the top row, from left to right. Keys were laid out as they were to minimize jamming of the metal arms within mechanical typewriters; the most commonly used letters were spaced farther apart to avoid issues. The Remington company, which was the leader in typewriter production in the 1870s, popularized the design, and the rest, as they say, is history.

Today, of course, we still use keyboards that have this configuration even though we don't need to worry about mechanical arms running into each other in the inner workings of our typewriters. Even when keyboards are built into devices such as the BlackBerry or reproduced on our smartphone screens, the default layout has not changed. After video displays, keyboards are pretty much the most essential thing that we plug into our computer.

Connecting Keyboards

The most common way to connect keyboards today is through your USB port. But wait, what about wireless keyboards, you ask? They're also usually connected via USB, just with a wireless USB receiver, as shown in Figure 2.29.

FIGURE 2.29 Wireless USB receiver

Prior to USB, the standard for several years was the *PS/2 port* (also known as a mini-DIN 6 connector), which was a keyboard and mouse interface port first found on the IBM PS/2 (hence the name). It is smaller than previous interfaces (the DIN 5 keyboard port and serial mouse connector), and thus its popularity increased quickly. It's shown in Figure 2.30. You'll notice that in addition to having an icon next to each port, the keyboard port is usually purple, and the mouse port is usually green. You will rarely see these connectors in the wild today. If you run into a keyboard that has a PS/2 connector (and it's not in a museum), you can buy a PS/2 to USB adapter. Or you could buy a new keyboard.

FIGURE 2.30 Keyboard and mouse PS/2 ports

Keyboard Configuration Options

There are two directions I am going to take this. First, let's talk about the physical configuration of your keyboard. Keyboards haven't changed a great deal over the last 140 or so years, but newer advances in ergonomics have led to some more comfortable (and interesting-looking) typing options. If your wrists or arms get sore or numb from typing too much, you might have bad form, and typing on a standard keyboard (or especially a small laptop keyboard) can be part of the problem. One design that's been out for several years is called the *natural keyboard*. It's shown in Figure 2.31, and it is designed to promote more natural hand and arm positions. And as a bonus, the keyboard in Figure 2.31 is vintage and has a PS/2 connector and a USB adapter!

FIGURE 2.31 A natural keyboard

Other types of ergonomic keyboards are on the market, too, ranging from the interesting looking to downright bizarre. If a natural keyboard does not help ease the pain in your wrists, a different kind might do the trick.

Second, you have some configuration options within your operating system. One of the more interesting ones is that you can change your keyboard layout. If you have programs in which you type using a different alphabet than Latin-based, you can change it to a different character type. In addition, there's another Latin-based layout called Dvorak, which is an alternative to QWERTY. It's designed to place more commonly used letters in better spots, increasing your typing speed. After all, we don't need to worry about mechanical keys sticking together on our typewriters any longer! Personally, I think it would take a lot of frustrating time to get used to it, but a former boss of mine used it and swore by its efficiency. It could also be fun to change it on an unsuspecting co-worker, not that I would recommend that. Exercise 2.3 shows you how to change your keyboard layout in Windows 10.

EXERCISE 2.3

Changing Your Keyboard Layout in Windows 11

1. Open the Language & Region settings app by typing **language** into the Windows search box. Click Language Settings. You will get a screen similar to the one shown in Figure 2.32.

FIGURE 2.32 Language & Region Settings

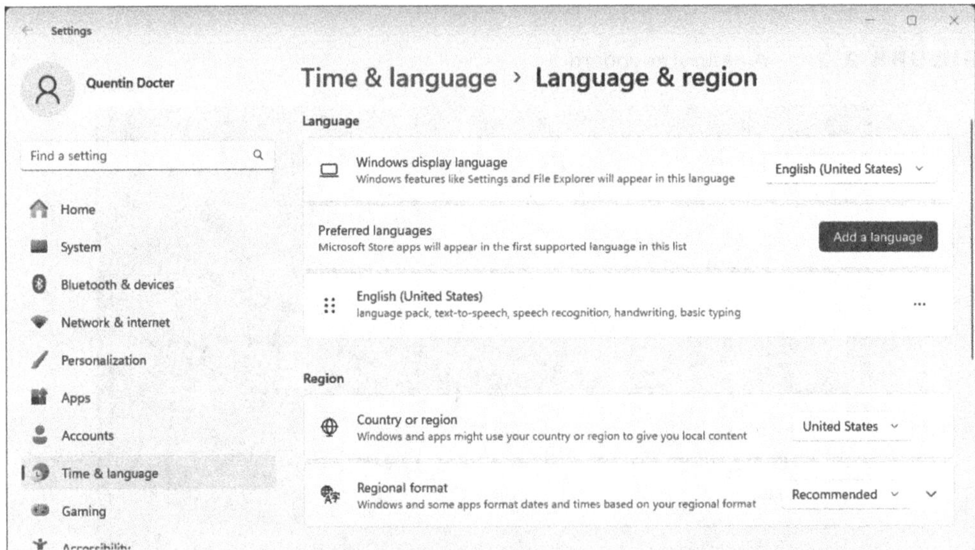

2. This computer has English installed. Click the more options button (it's the three dots in a horizontal line) to the right of English (United States) and then click Language Options. If you scroll down, you will see the Keyboards section, like the one in Figure 2.33.

FIGURE 2.33 Language & Region options

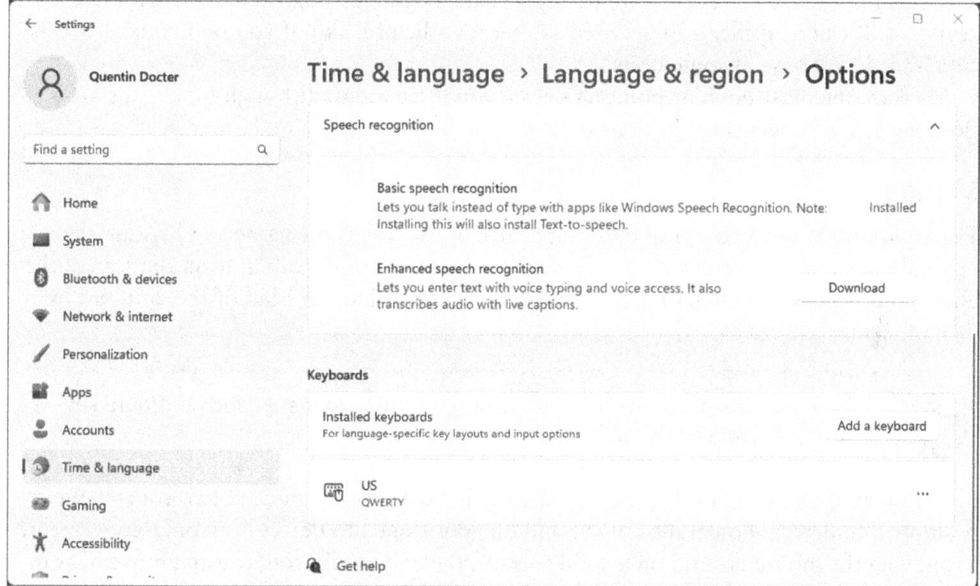

3. Click Add A Keyboard, and from the list choose United States-Dvorak. That will add Dvorak to your list of keyboards at the bottom of Figure 2.33. Close the window to save your changes.
4. In the system tray (just to the left of the clock in your taskbar, by default in the lower-right corner of your screen) you should now see an option that says ENG US. Click it.
5. In the window that appears, choose the option that says United States-Dvorak. Now your keyboard is set to use the Dvorak layout. Good luck!
6. To change it back, click ENG DV in the system tray and then choose ENG US. You can also change input options by pressing the Windows key and the spacebar.

Pointing Devices

Pointing devices are so named because they allow you to move your cursor around the screen and point at what you want; they're a convenient handheld tool that lets you easily navigate on-screen. Pointing devices have been in use since the beginning of humankind, if you include the index finger. They've pretty much been available for computers as long as computers have existed. For example, the trackball was developed in 1946 to replace the joystick as an input device for an early electronic radar-plotting system. The mouse came along in the 1960s, but it didn't gain much popularity until Apple came out with the Macintosh 128K in 1984.

You might think that a mouse or another pointing device is basically required for today's PCs, but it's not. When I teach classes for computer technicians, one of the activities I like to have them do is disconnect their mouse and then navigate through Windows with just their keyboard. It can be difficult to get used to, but it's a helpful skill if you find yourself stuck with a broken mouse at some point.

Mice are the most popular pointing device you'll see today, although touchpads are a close second. I'll cover them both next.

Mouse

The *mouse* is the most common pointing device in use today. It's named so because the original mice that were created had the connector cord (a tail) leading from the rear of their body, pointing toward the user. Later designs put the cord at the head of the unit, but by then the name had stuck.

Per exam objective 2.4, you should be able to install and configure keyboards and mice.

For most of its existence, the mouse had a ball inside it that touched two rollers: one positioned to detect vertical movement and one positioned to detect horizontal movement. By moving the mouse around on a solid surface, the ball would roll, causing movement in the rollers, which would get translated into electrical signals and move the cursor on your screen. Slippery surfaces would cause the ball to skid, making the mouse less useful, so people started using mouse pads to compensate.

The progression of technology allowed mice to lose their tails and their balls (replaced by a light that senses movement), and so most mice today are wireless or optical or both. Figure 2.34 shows a typical wireless optical mouse.

FIGURE 2.34 Wireless optical mouse

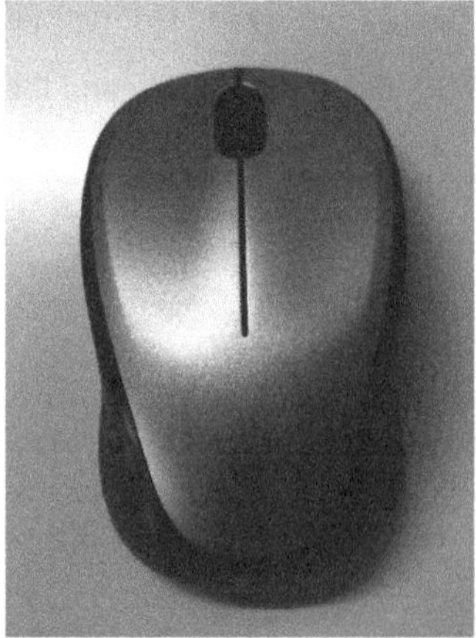

Mice come in a variety of shapes, sizes, and styles. Some are very small, designed to be more portable and used with laptops and tablets. As with keyboards, ergonomic designs exist as well. Most mice will have two or more buttons for left- and right-clicking, as well as a wheel to scroll up and down. You'll find some variance, such as mice for Macs, which have historically had only one button.

Touchpad

Instead of using an external device such as a mouse, you can do as our ancient ancestors did and point at something using your finger. Granted, they didn't have a *touchpad* to use because touchpads didn't rise to prominence until the laptop computer became commonplace. Functionally, a touchpad works just like a mouse in that you can move your finger around to control the cursor, and you'll often have two buttons, one for left-clicking and one for right-clicking. Many touchpads also let you tap the pad itself to indicate a click. Figure 2.35 shows a typical touchpad.

FIGURE 2.35 Touchpad

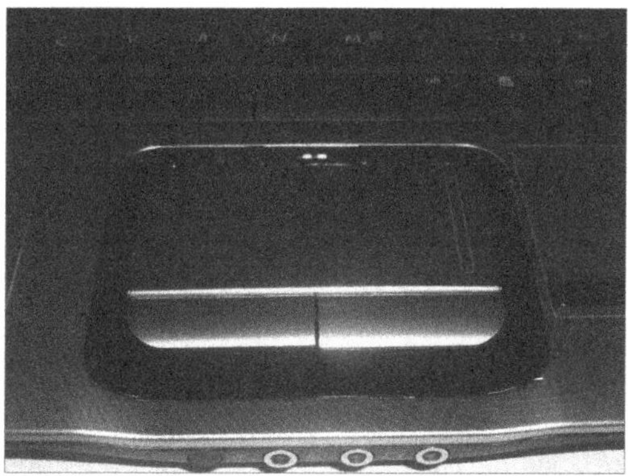

You'll notice that the touchpad is conveniently placed right below the laptop keyboard, which happens to be where your palms rest when you type. Sometimes this will cause problems because you can inadvertently cause your mouse cursor to do random things such as jump across the screen. Most touchpads today have settings to allow you to control the sensitivity, and they will also differentiate between a palm touching them and a finger. In addition, if you have a sensitive touchpad that is giving you trouble, you can disable it altogether. Let's do that in Exercise 2.4.

EXERCISE 2.4

Disabling a Touchpad in Windows 11

1. Open the Touchpad Settings app by typing **touchpad** into the Windows search box and pressing Enter. You will get a screen like the one shown in Figure 2.36.

EXERCISE 2.4 *(continued)*

FIGURE 2.36 Touchpad settings

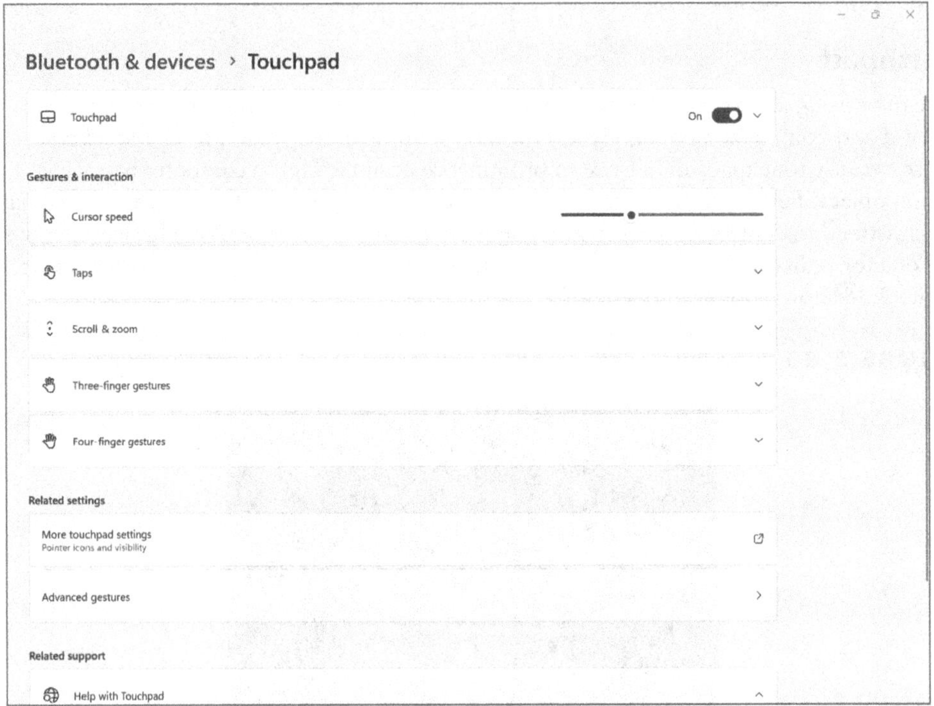

2. To disable the touchpad, simply slide the Touchpad toggle from on to off. With the down arrow to the right of the toggle, you can automatically disable the touchpad when a mouse is connected, and below there is a slider to change the cursor speed.
3. (Optional) Scroll down through the Touchpad settings to see what else you can configure. Options include tapping, scroll and zoom, and gesture settings. For example, you can make it so a down motion scrolls up, or a down motion scrolls down, whichever you prefer.
4. Close the Touchpad Settings window.

Although touchpads are primarily used with laptop computers, you can also buy external touchpads that connect to a computer just as a mouse would.

Connecting Pointing Devices

This section can almost be summed up with one acronym: USB. By far and away, USB is the most common connector you will see used with pointing devices.

Before USB was invented, mice would be connected via PS/2 ports, just like keyboards. For a refresher on what that looks like, refer to Figure 2.30. The mouse port is the green one at the top. Prior to PS/2, mice and other pointing devices were connected via RS-232 serial ports.

Pointing Device Configuration Options

For as simple as pointing devices such as mice are, there are a few configuration options you can set on them. For example, you can change the button configuration so that the mouse becomes more natural for left-handed people. You can also change how fast the cursor moves across the screen, what it looks like, and how quickly you need to click for the system to register it as a double click. In Windows, all of these settings are configured through Mouse Properties in the Mouse app within Control Panel. Exercise 2.5 walks you through a few of the convenience-related options. Note that some of these are purely aesthetic, but others are useful to some people with disabilities or who would otherwise have difficulty using the pointing device.

EXERCISE 2.5

Configuring a Mouse in Windows 11

1. Open the Mouse Settings app by typing **mouse** into the Windows search box and pressing Enter. A window similar to the one shown in Figure 2.37 will appear.

FIGURE 2.37 Mouse settings

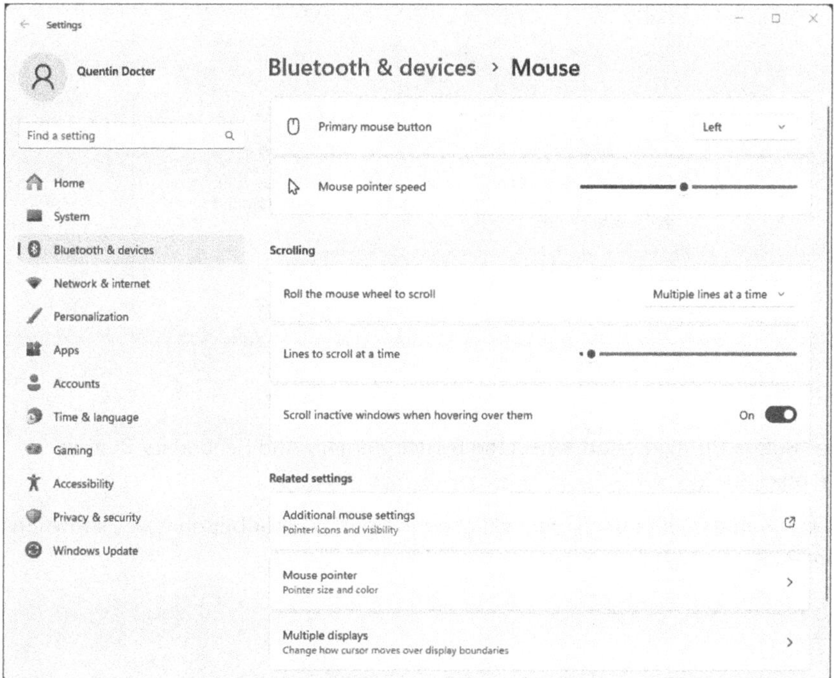

EXERCISE 2.5 ***(continued)***

2. Notice that in the Mouse settings there are basic options such as switching the primary button, setting the cursor speed, and choosing how much to scroll when the mouse wheel is used.

3. Under Related Settings, click Additional Mouse Settings to open Mouse Properties, as shown in Figure 2.38. This is where more options such as accessibility can be configured.

FIGURE 2.38 Mouse Properties window

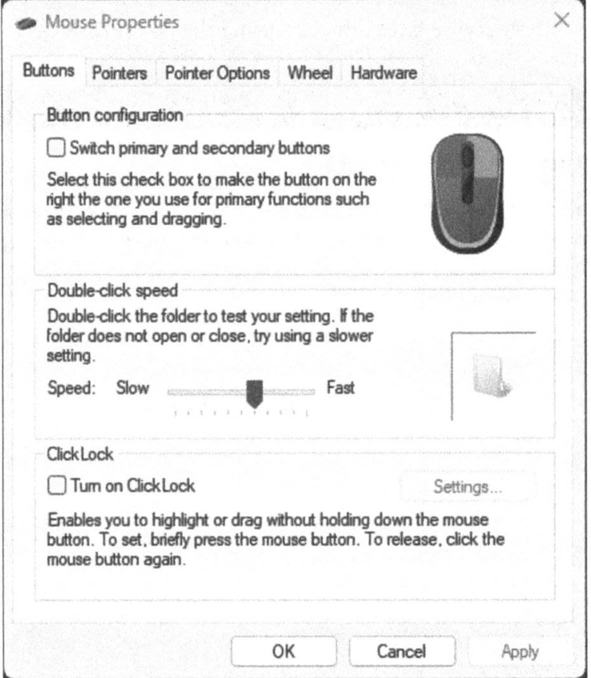

4. Under Button Configuration, select the Switch Primary And Secondary Buttons check box.

5. Click the Pointer Options tab (you will need to use the other button now), shown in Figure 2.39.

FIGURE 2.39 Pointer Options tab

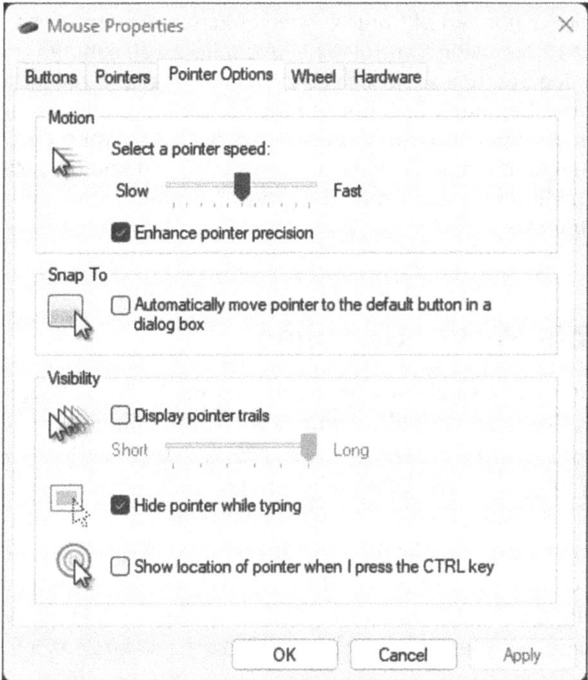

6. In the Motion section, drag the pointer speed all the way to the Slow end. Notice how slowly the mouse moves. Slide the bar all the way to Fast to see the difference.
7. Click OK to save the changes if you like or click Cancel.

Windows 11 will often provide multiple ways to get to similar settings, and occasionally it can be confusing. You might have noticed this with Exercise 2.5. In the paragraph preceding it, I mentioned Mouse Properties in Control Panel. You can get to this in two ways:

- Opening Control Panel, selecting View By: Category in the upper right corner, then clicking Hardware and Sound, and then clicking Mouse under Devices and Printers.
- Opening Control Panel, selecting View By: Large icons (or Small icons) in the upper right corner, then clicking Mouse.

In the exercise, I instead had you type **mouse** into the Windows search box and press Enter. This opened the Mouse settings app shown in Figure 2.37, which is not part of Control Panel. (Microsoft seems to be slowly moving away from using Control Panel to configure all settings and is instead promoting Settings apps such as this.) Then in step 3 you clicked Additional Mouse Settings which opened the Mouse Properties window—the same one you can open through Control Panel. It's not so important how you get there when multiple paths exist, as long as you can find the setting you need. Sometimes it's just a matter of playing around with it until you find the path you prefer.

Uninterruptible Power Supplies

Nearly every computer has a single power supply. Normally this is fine, but if the computer is vital enough that a power failure will cause catastrophic harm, a redundant option should be considered. An *uninterruptible power supply (UPS)* is a battery backup system that a computer can plug into. The UPS plugs into the wall, which keeps its batteries charged. In the event of a power outage or a *brownout* (sometimes called an *undervoltage event*) where power isn't completely lost but there is a drop in voltage, the UPS can supply the attached computer with power for a limited amount of time and provide for a graceful shutdown. Figure 2.40 shows a small UPS and Figure 2.41 shows the back of the device, where the computer plugs into. Other UPSs can be as large as a generator or several feet tall.

FIGURE 2.40 An uninterruptible power supply

Source: With permission of Schneider Electric

FIGURE 2.41 The back of an uninterruptible power supply

Inside the UPS are one or more batteries and fuses. Much like a surge suppressor, a UPS is designed to protect everything that's plugged into it from power surges. UPSs are also designed to protect against power sags and even power outages. Energy is stored in the batteries, and if the power fails, the batteries can power the computer for a period of time so that someone can then safely power it down.

Per Tech+ exam objective 2.4, you should understand the basics of installing and configuring a UPS.

Many UPSs and operating systems will also work together to (and safely) power down automatically a system that gets switched to UPS power. Notice on Figure 2.41 that the back of this UPS has an RJ45 data port. A network cable attached to that port, along with the right software such as APC's PowerChute, allow for configuration. Configuration options will include how long to leave the computer running before it shuts down and if it will send any connected users a warning message (if it's a server, for example). These types of devices may be overkill for Uncle Bob's machine at home, but they're critically important fixtures in server rooms.

The UPS should be checked periodically to make sure that its battery is operational. Most UPSs have a test button that you can press to simulate a power outage. You will find that batteries wear out over time, and you should replace the battery in the UPS every couple of years to keep the UPS dependable.

UPSs all have a limit as to how many devices they can handle at once. These power limitations should be strictly observed. Overloading the UPS can cause a short, which could potentially result in fire.

Printers

Printers are electromechanical output devices that are used to put information from the computer onto paper. They have been around since the introduction of the computer and are still popular today. Even though our society keeps inching closer toward electronic documents, there are times when a paper copy makes more sense or is required.

In this section, I will discuss the details of the two most common printer technologies: inkjet printers and laser printers. I will also talk about additional functionality that many printers now have built in, such as scanning and faxing. Once I cover printer technologies, I'll talk about how to connect a printer to a computer.

Printer Technologies

At the end of the day, all the printer needs to do is make an image appear on paper. Most of the time this is done with ink, but there are other ways, too. You can use several different technologies to get an image on paper; the list of printer types includes impact, solid ink, dye-sublimation, inkjet, thermal, laser, and plotters. The two you will see the most often today are inkjet and laser printers.

Inkjet Printers

For home use, *inkjet printers* are the most popular choice, although you will see them used in businesses as well. You might also hear these types of printers referred to as *bubble-jet printers*, but the term *Bubble Jet* is copyrighted by Canon. These printers spray ink on the page to form the image. Older inkjet printers used a reservoir of ink, a pump, and a nozzle to accomplish this. They were messy, noisy, and inefficient. Bubble Jet printers and newer inkjet printers work much more efficiently and are much cheaper. For all practical purposes, consider them one and the same because their components and printing processes are nearly identical.

Inkjet printers are simple devices. They contain very few parts and thus are inexpensive to manufacture. It's common today to have a $40 to $50 inkjet printer with print quality that rivals that of basic laser printers. These types of printers can use normal copy paper, and most of them can print fairly high-quality photos on glossy photo paper as well.

The primary consumable for inkjet printers is the *ink cartridge*. This is a small plastic container that holds the liquid ink the printer uses to create images. Printers that print only in black and white need only a black cartridge, whereas color printers need black in addition to cyan, magenta, and yellow. Color printers can have one of three cartridge configurations:

- All ink in one cartridge. These are often referred to as CMYK (cyan, magenta, yellow, black) cartridges.
- One black cartridge and a separate CMY color cartridge.
- Four cartridges total, one for each color.

From a print-quality standpoint, it doesn't matter that much which configuration you get. From a money standpoint, though, it can matter quite a bit. Most people use a lot more black ink than color ink. If you have a CMYK cartridge and run out of black, you'll need to replace the entire cartridge even if there are other colors remaining. In Figure 2.42, you can see a printer that has two cartridges: one color and one black.

FIGURE 2.42 Inkjet printer cartridges

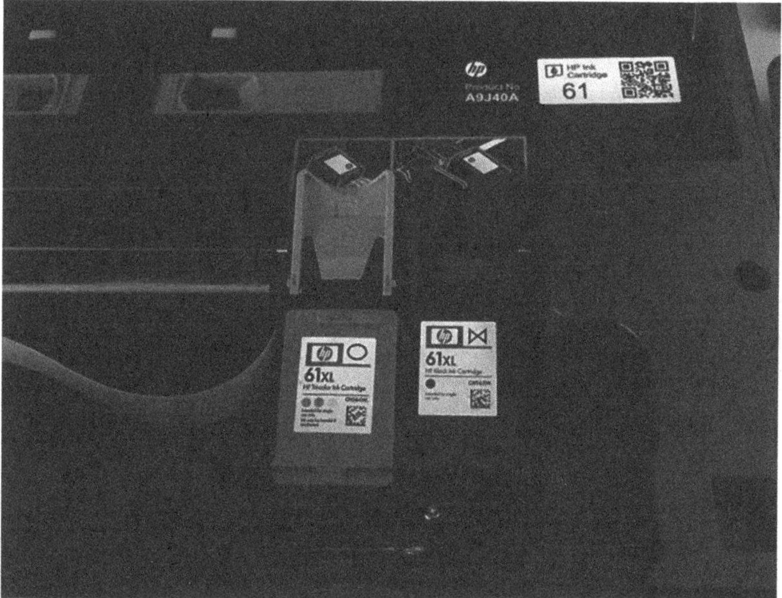

Ink cartridges are held in place by plastic clips. They are folded back above the cartridges in Figure 2.42. To replace a cartridge, you release the clip, slide out the old cartridge, slide in the new one, and lock it into place. Make sure that the ink cartridges are the right size for your printer—in Figure 2.42, you can see that these are HP 61 (the XL on these cartridges indicate that they have more ink than a standard HP 61 cartridge).

Laser Printers

A *laser printer* works much like a photocopier. The main difference is that a photocopier scans a document to produce an image, whereas the laser printer receives digitized data from a computer. Laser printers are generally bigger, faster, and more expensive than inkjet printers. Thus, you're more likely to find them in office settings than in homes. Laser printers also do not use ink. They use a dry powdery plastic resin called *toner*, which is stored in a replaceable toner cartridge. Toner cartridges are more expensive than ink cartridges, but they produce many more pages and are generally more cost-effective on a per-page basis. Figure 2.43 shows a small laser printer's toner carriage with four cartridges—black, cyan, magenta, and yellow from front to back.

FIGURE 2.43 Laser printer toner cartridges in a printer

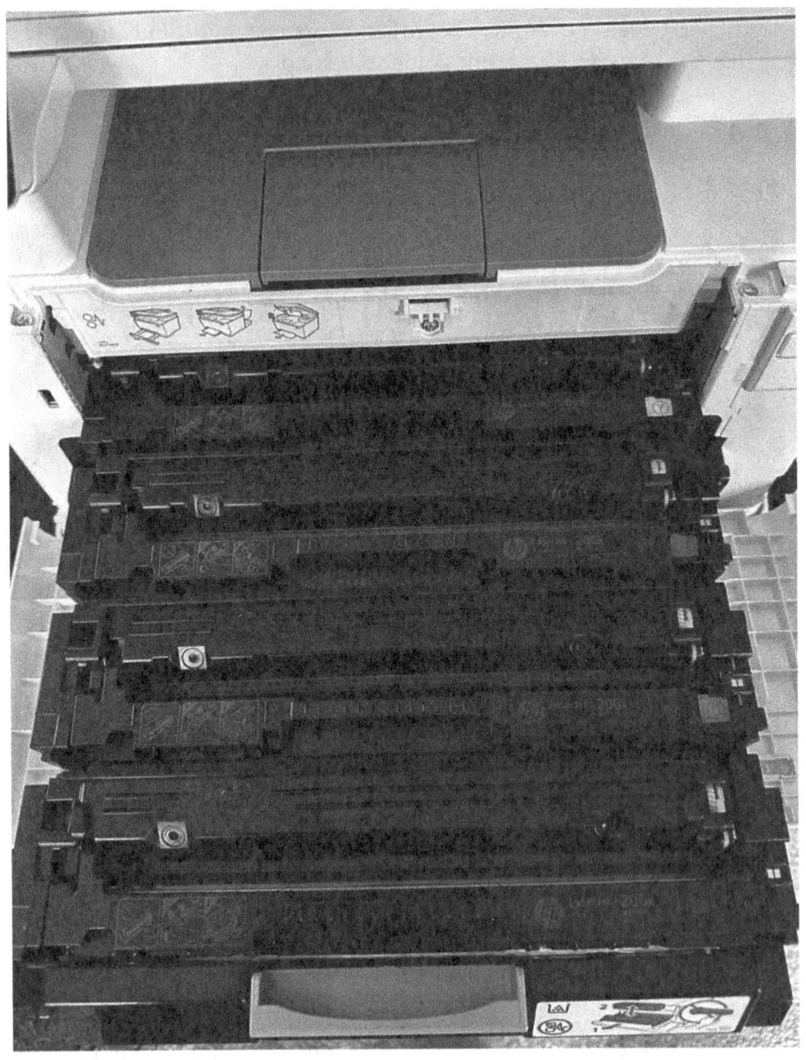

A laser printer contains a large cylinder known as a *drum*, which carries a high negative electrical charge. During the print process, the printer directs a laser beam to partially neutralize the charge in certain areas of the drum. When the drum rotates past a toner reservoir, the toner clings to the areas of lesser charge, and the page image is formed on the drum. The drum then rotates past positively charged paper, and the toner jumps off onto the paper. The paper then passes through a fuser that melts the plastic particles of the toner so that they stick to the paper.

Laser printers are available in color or monochrome models. To print in color, a laser printer must make four passes across the same page, laying down a different color each time. Such a printer has four separate toner cartridges: cyan, magenta, yellow, and black.

Although you're unlikely to do so, if you spill any toner, let it settle before you clean it up. Toner is a fine powder and is carcinogenic. A *carcinogen* is a product that, with long-term continued exposure, may cause cancer. Also, don't use a normal vacuum cleaner to try to pick up toner. The powder is so fine that it will pass through the vacuum's filters and out the vent. Use a special computer vacuum that is designed with finer filters to catch the toner.

Other Technologies Often Bundled with Printers

A lot of the printers you see on the market today combine printing with additional features, such as scanning, copying, and faxing. Such printers are called *multifunctional printers* or *all-in-one printers*. Adding features changes the printer from being solely an output device to being an input device as well. Printers with a built-in scanner usually incorporate them as a flat-bed scanner on top of the printer; they generally don't cost much more than a single-function printer and can be handy to have around. In Figure 2.44, you can see a laser printer with its top slightly opened. To scan or copy a document, you would either place it into the paper feed mechanism on top (which is handy for multipage documents) or lay it on the glass and close the lid. Scanning or copying is initiated from the touchscreen or from software on a connected computer, such as the HP Scan utility shown in Figure 2.45. The difference between scanning and copying is simple—scanning sends it to a computer either directly or via email, whereas copying produces a physical replica on the printer.

Nowadays, you will rarely see stand-alone scanners, which are input devices, or fax machines, which can be input and output devices.

Per Tech+ exam objective 2.4, given a scenario, you should know how to install and configure printers and scanners.

FIGURE 2.44 Laser printer with lid ajar to reveal scanning glass

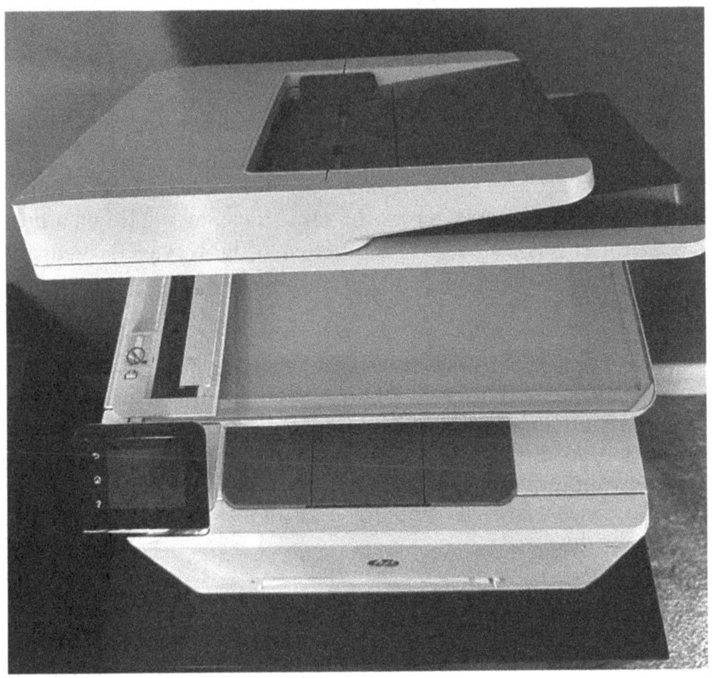

FIGURE 2.45 HP Scan utility

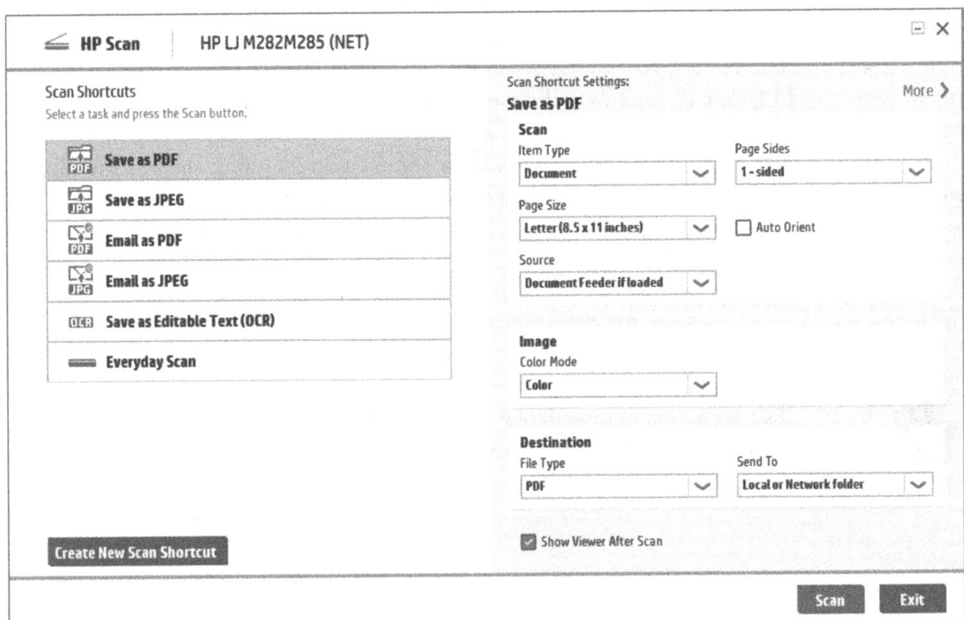

Connecting Printers

For your printer to work properly, you must have a connection to it. The printer can be connected directly to your computer, or you can connect to one via a network. In this section, we'll look at various types of connectors that have been popular for printers over the years.

Serial Connections

When computers send data serially, they send it 1 bit at a time, one after another. The bits stand in line like people waiting to get into a movie theater. In Chapter 1, I talked about how old-time serial connections were painfully slow but that new serial technology makes it a more viable option than parallel. In this particular instance, the serial I'm talking about is the old-school variety.

Specifically, older-style serial connectors were based on a standard called RS-232 and were called *serial ports*. They came in 9-pin (DE9) and 25-pin (DB25) varieties; Figure 2.46 shows the male DE9. It's aqua colored and conveniently labeled "Serial."

FIGURE 2.46 Back-panel connectors, including serial and parallel ports

Serial connections like this really aren't used for printers anymore. Modems used serial connectors, too, but they have also gone the way of the dinosaur. About the only time that you will see serial connections used today are for server, router, and switch consoles that can be used for management and diagnostics.

Parallel Connections

When a printer uses parallel communication, it is receiving data 8 bits at a time over eight separate wires (one for each bit). Parallel communication was the most popular way of communicating from computer to printer for many years, mainly because it was faster than serial. In fact, the *parallel port* became so synonymous with printing that a lot of companies simply started referring to parallel ports as *printer ports*. In Figure 2.46, the pink 25-pin parallel port has a printer icon above it.

A parallel cable consists of a male DB25 connector that connects to the computer and a male 36-pin Centronics connector that connects to the printer. Parallel cables work best when they are less than 10′ long, and they should be IEEE 1284 compliant. Figure 2.47 shows a typical printer cable, with the parallel connector on the left and the Centronics connector on the right.

FIGURE 2.47 Parallel cable

USB

Earlier in the chapter, you learned that USB stands for Universal Serial Bus, but the *U* could as easily stand for "ubiquitous." USB is everywhere and seemingly connects everything. Printers are no exception. USB is the most common physical connector type that you will see used with printers today.

Networked Printers

Rather than connect the printer to your computer, you can connect it to the network. This setup is popular in businesses and is becoming more popular in home networks as well. When connecting a printer to the network, you have two choices. The first is to connect it via a network cable, which typically uses an RJ45 connector. The second is to connect it via wireless networking. You'll examine wireless networking in detail in Chapter 8.

In addition to connecting the printer, you need to install a special piece of software called a *printer driver* so the operating system knows how to talk to the printer. I will talk about drivers and how to install them in Chapter 5, "Software Applications."

Configuring Printers

Once the printer is installed you may want to configure various settings, such as if users can print in color or if the printer is shared on the network for others to use. Many printers today come with their own configuration software, downloaded with the driver, and it would be impractical to cover them all here. Instead, let's take a look at some common configuration options available through Windows.

Printers are managed through the Printers & Scanners settings app. To open it, type **printers** in the Windows search box and press Enter. It will look similar to Figure 2.48. Click the printer you want to configure, and it will take you to the printer management window like the one in Figure 2.49.

FIGURE 2.48 Printers & Scanners

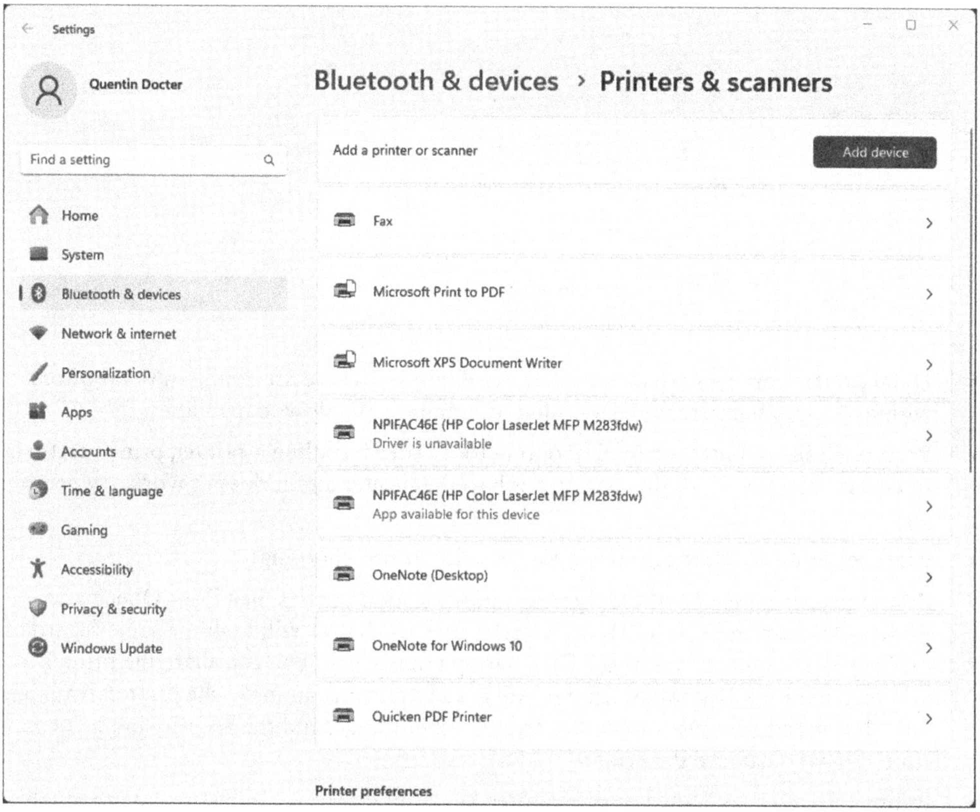

Let's take a look at the options in Figure 2.49 from the top down:

- The print queue is where print jobs are sent and held until they are printed. **Open print queue** lets you look at the jobs waiting in line. If a job has stalled, it might hold up other jobs. In here you can cancel or delete waiting print jobs.

FIGURE 2.49 Managing a printer

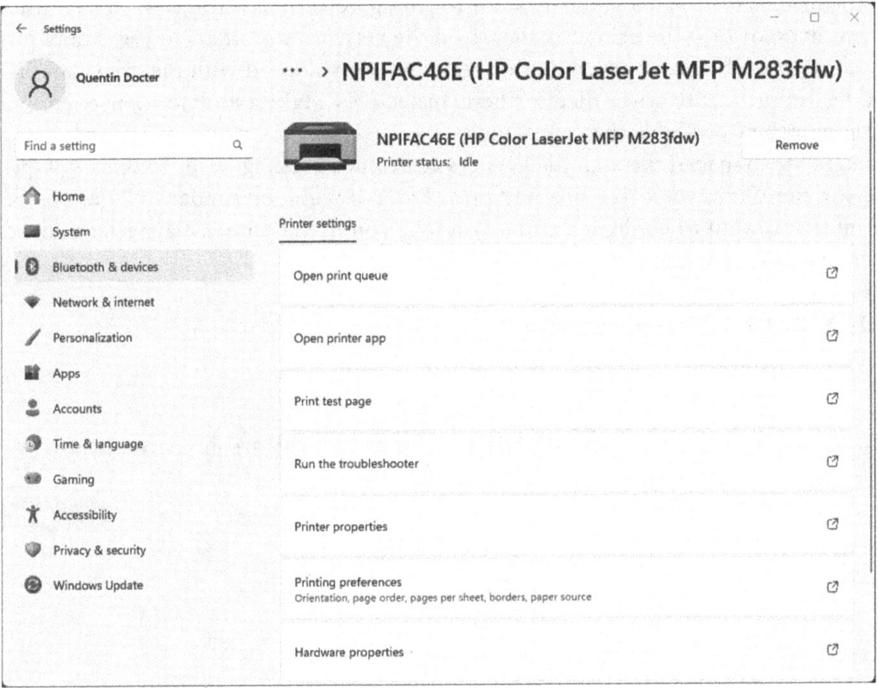

- **Open printer app** does what you might think it does. There are configuration options within the app, but here we're focusing on standard Windows capabilities.
- **Print test page** is a useful troubleshooting tool. After installing a printer, print a test page to ensure it works. Also, if you send a job to the printer and it doesn't work, try printing a test page.
- **Run the troubleshooter** runs basic connectivity troubleshooting.
- **Printer properties** is one of the three key utilities, along with Open Print Queue and Printing Preferences. It's shown in Figure 2.50, and all tabs will look the same regardless of the printer you have installed. The Sharing tab is where you can share the printer for others to use on the network. On the Advanced tab, you can make the printer available only during certain times of the day, among other things, and the Security tab lets you configure who can use the printer.
- **Printing preferences** is the last of the three key utilities, shown in Figure 2.51. Available options will be somewhat customized based on the printer's capabilities. Here you can manage the printer quality, effects, finishing, and color options.
- **Hardware properties** lets you look at basic stuff like the printer name and when it was installed.

FIGURE 2.50 Printer properties

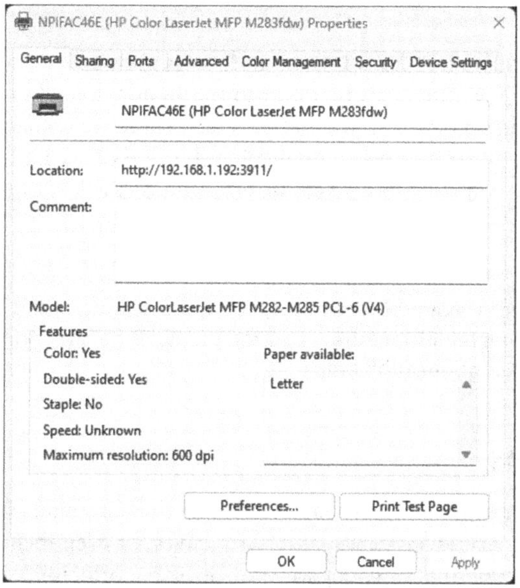

NPIFAC46E (HP Color LaserJet MFP M283fdw) Properties
General
Sharing
Ports
Advanced
Color Management
Security
Device Settings
NPIFAC46E (HP Color LaserJet MFP M283fdw)
Location:
http://192.168.1.192:3911/
Comment:
Model:
HP ColorLaserJet MFP M282-M285 PCL-6 (V4)
Features
Color: Yes
Double-sided: Yes
Staple: No
Speed: Unknown
Maximum resolution: 600 dpi
Paper available:
Letter
Preferences...
Print Test Page
OK
Cancel
Apply

FIGURE 2.51 Printing preferences

NPIFAC46E (HP Color LaserJet MFP M283fdw)
Printing Shortcuts
Paper/Quality
Effects
Finishing
Color
Advanced
A printing shortcut is a collection of saved print settings that you can select with a single click.
Printing shortcuts:
Factory defaults
General Everyday Printing
Envelopes
Cardstock/Heavy
Labels
Transparencies
Save As...
Delete
Reset
Paper sizes:
8.5 x 11.0 inches
Letter
Paper source:
Printer auto select
Paper type:
Unspecified
Print on both sides:
Yes, flip over
Pages per sheet:
1 page per sheet
Print in Grayscale
Off
About...
Help
OK
Cancel

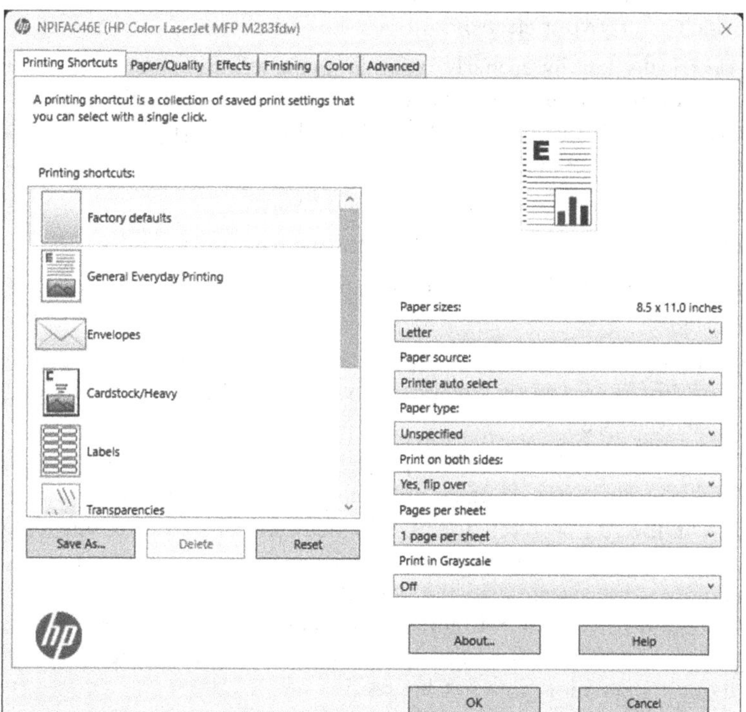

Understanding Installation Basics

So far in this chapter, you've learned a lot about different types of devices and connectors. Perhaps you still have a few questions on your mind, though, like "How do I get these devices to work? Do I just plug them in and that's it?" There isn't a simple answer because a lot depends on the type of device you're connecting. Instead of trying to cover each possible type of device, I'll show you some principles to help you regardless of the situation or device you're trying to connect.

Per Tech+ exam objective 2.4, you should understand plug-n-play versus driver installation, other required steps, IP-based peripherals, and web-based configuration steps.

Internal Devices

By an internal device, I mean anything that goes inside the computer case. This can include sound cards, network cards, video cards, and hard drives, or even memory or a processor. (I know, the last two aren't peripherals, but some of the same principles apply.) Here are some good steps to follow:

1. *Always* make sure that the computer is powered off. Most technicians will leave it plugged in to help electrically ground the components and prevent disastrous static discharge (which can fry your electronics).
2. Practice electrical safety by properly grounding yourself. Either use an antistatic wrist strap (it secures to your wrist and connects to the case using an alligator clip) or maintain contact with a metal part of the plugged-in (but turned off) computer while handling sensitive components.
3. Remove the component you are replacing, if necessary.
4. Identify the slot or connection you will use for the new device.
5. Insert the new device. Make sure to connect power if it requires a direct connection to the power supply.
6. Turn the computer back on. (Replacing the case is optional at this point. Some techs like to leave it off just in case something doesn't work right. But once it's working properly, always replace the case.)

One of two things should happen when you reboot the computer: Either the operating system will automatically detect the device or you will need to install a driver. Let's take a scenario using Windows 11. You replace an old video card with a newer one and reboot Windows. Windows might automatically detect the new video card and install the proper driver. When an operating system does this, it's referred to as *plug-and-play*. Literally, you plug the device in and you can play. If not, you will need to install the driver manually. You might have gotten it on a CD or flash drive, or you may need to download it from the Internet. I'll talk about drivers a lot more in Chapter 5.

Sometimes the OS will recognize the device but install the incorrect or an older driver. In these cases, you will want to install the driver manually.

Processors, memory, and internal hard drives don't require you to install drivers. They will need to be properly detected by the system BIOS, however. If the BIOS doesn't see them, there's no way the operating system can use them.

During or after driver installation, you might be asked to perform other required steps, such as configuring the device. It all really depends on what you're installing.

External Devices

Installing an external device (one that resides outside the case) is often much easier than installing an internal device. Namely, you don't have to turn the power off and open the case! Most external devices will connect via USB, Thunderbolt, or one of the video connections you learned about earlier.

So, plug it in, and if it has its own external power source, make sure that's plugged in, too. Then let plug-and-play do its thing. In fact, installing an external device is really the type of scenario for which plug-and-play was designed. Using Windows as an example again, when the device is plugged in, Windows should recognize it as an attempt to install a driver. If Windows is successful, you will get a message from your system tray saying that the device was installed successfully and is ready to use. Otherwise, you will get a message saying it was detected but a driver could not be installed. Then it's your turn to install it manually.

IP- and Web-Based Devices

As of this writing, printers are pretty much the only peripherals that you will install that may require IP- or web-based configuration steps. Let's take a quick look at each.

IP-Based Printers

In some cases, you might want to print to a printer that's not attached directly to your computer, but it is on the same network as you. In scenarios like this, you will need to install an IP printer. It's usually pretty straightforward. Exercise 2.6 shows you how to do this in Windows 11.

EXERCISE 2.6

Installing an IP Printer

1. Open the Printers & Scanners app by typing **printers** into the Windows search box and pressing Enter.
2. In the Printers & Scanners app, click the Add Device button at the top of the screen.

EXERCISE 2.6 *(continued)*

3. Regardless of whether your computer finds a printer, click the Add Manually link next to The Printer That I Want Isn't Listed, as shown in Figure 2.52.

FIGURE 2.52 Adding a new printer

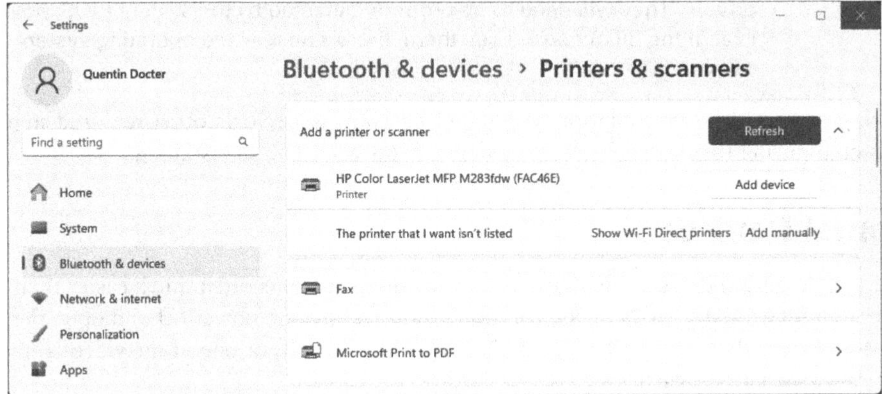

4. In the Add Printer window that pops up, click the Add A Printer Using An IP Address Or Hostname radio button and click Next.
5. In the next window, like the one shown in Figure 2.53, choose TCP/IP Device as the device type and enter the IP address of the printer you want to install. Click Next.

FIGURE 2.53 Entering the IP address of the printer

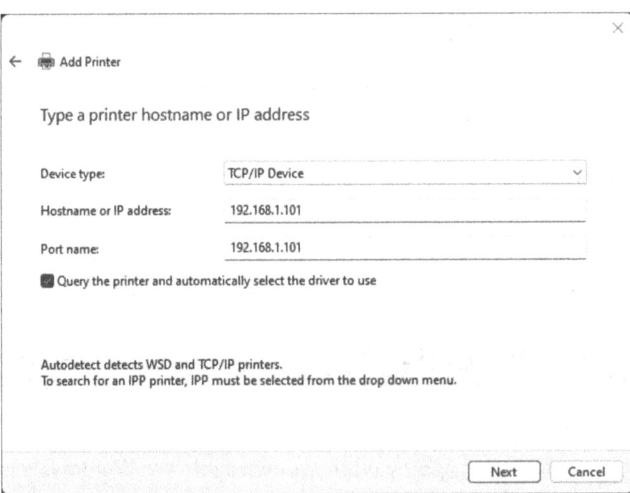

6. Windows will attempt to contact the printer and, once connected, install the appropriate driver.

Web-Based Printers

Several printer manufacturers allow you to configure a printer to be available via the Internet or by sending it an email. For example, many HP printers are compatible with HP ePrint, giving you access to your printer from anywhere in the world. Imagine being on vacation and being able to print your favorite photo on your home printer—before you even get home! Granted, you won't be there to see it, but it's still pretty cool. If you have an HP printer, here are the basic steps to get started:

1. Go to `www.hpsmart.com` and create a user account.
2. Enable web services on your printer, and link it to the HP Smart account.
3. Set up an email address for the printer, and configure proper security, such as who can print to the printer.

In the example shown in Figure 2.54, you can see an HP Envy 5530 series printer, already configured for HP ePrint. Options that you can configure include the email address of the printer (`whatever@hpeprint.com`) and who is allowed to send jobs to the printer. The security list is configured by email address, so it's not foolproof from a security standpoint.

FIGURE 2.54 HP ePrint configuration

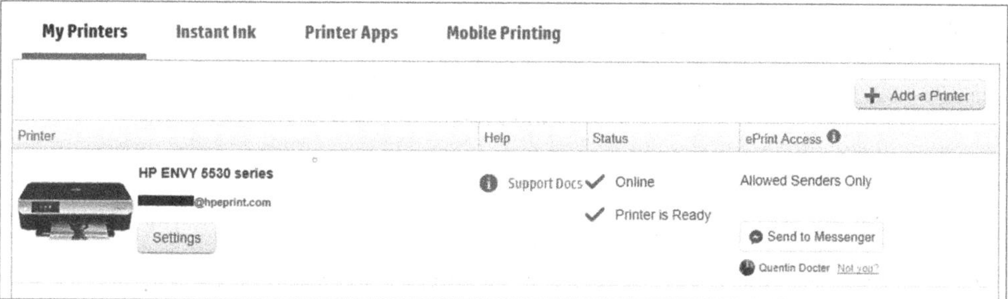

To use the service, open your email, create a new email to the printer's email address, and then attach the document or file you want to print. Provided that the printer is powered on and available, the job will print.

Reviewing Connector Types

We've covered a lot of different types of connectors in this chapter. Instead of having you bounce around between pages to compare and contrast them to each other, Table 2.4 lists them all. In it, I've included the approximate release date, the maximum speed of the newest standard in that family, and the types of devices that you will commonly see associated with the connector. For some of the maximum speeds, I listed n/a because no one ever really talks about the speed of those connections. In cases like that, just assume that they're slow!

TABLE 2.4 Summary of connectors

Type	Released	Max speed	Primary uses
VGA	1987	n/a	Video (analog)
DVI	1999	3.96 Gbps	Video (digital and analog)
HDMI	2002	48 Gbps	Video (digital)
DisplayPort	2008	25.9 Gbps	Video (digital)
Thunderbolt	2011	40 Gbps	Video, hard drives, audio, docks, PCIe expansion
Lightning	2012	480 Mbps	iPhones and iPads; earbuds/headsets, power, and other accessories
USB-A	1998	10 Gbps	Keyboards, mice, printers, and many others
USB-C	2014	40 Gbps	Keyboards, mice, printers, and many others
PS/2	1987	n/a	Keyboards and mice
Parallel	1970	20 Mbps	Printers
Serial (RS-232)	1962	115 Kbps	Modem, printers, mice, control console for server and router management
RJ45	1976	40 Gbps	Network cards
RJ11	1976	56 Kbps	Modems

Summary

In this chapter, you learned about external peripheral devices and the connector types used to hook them to your computer. There are dozens of different types of external peripherals in the marketplace, but we covered some of the most common ones, such as audio and video, external storage, networking, and input and output.

First, I covered audio and video devices. To hear sound, you need a sound card in your system as well as a set of speakers or headphones. Video devices are critical to modern computers; I talked about different types of monitors and projectors as well as the different video connectors that have been used in the past or are in use today.

Second, you learned about external storage and communications devices. There are many different types of external storage devices that you'll use, from tiny memory cards and small thumb drives to large-capacity network-attached storage to mobile devices such as media players and smartphones. Communications devices such as network cards and modems help computers connect with each other.

Third, I covered input and output devices. Input devices include keyboards and pointing devices like the mouse and touchpad. For output devices, I specifically covered printers, which put ink on paper. Printers are one example of a device that can fall into multiple camps as far as input and output goes. A basic printer is just for output, but a multifunctional printer that also has scanning or faxing capabilities can be considered an input device as well.

Finally, we covered some principles for installing peripherals. Concepts included drivers (which I'll cover in more detail in Chapter 5), plug-and-play, and the steps required for IP-based peripherals and web-based configuration.

Exam Essentials

Be able to compare and contrast common throughput units. From slowest to fastest, know bits per second (bps), kilobits per second (Kbps), megabits per second (Mbps), gigabits per second (Gbps), and terabits per second (Tbps). Anything with a capital *B* would be bytes.

Understand the features of common video connectors. The video connectors you need to know are VGA, DVI, HDMI, DisplayPort, Thunderbolt, and USB.

Understand the way in which laser printers and inkjet printers create images. Laser printers use a powdery toner, and inkjet printers use liquid ink in small cartridges.

Know which connection types are used for external storage. Connections that are used for external storage devices are USB and Thunderbolt.

Understand what a UPS does. A uninterruptible power supply (UPS) is a battery backup for a computer that can provide power in the event of a power failure, and most often protect against power surges as well.

Know how best to connect keyboards and mice to computers. Keyboards and mice today all use USB. In the past, the PS/2 connector was used. Before PS/2, mice could use serial ports.

Know the two key wired networking connectors and telephone line connector. Twisted-pair copper cables use an RJ45 connector, also called an Ethernet connector. Fiber-optic cables can use a small form-factor pluggable (SFP) connector. If you have a modem, it will use telephone lines and an RJ11 connector.

Know which tools are used to create and test network cables. Network cables are created using a crimper and tested using a cable tester.

Know which connector types are used for peripheral devices. The most common connector types are USB-A, USB-C, Thunderbolt, and Lightning.

Understand the difference between mirroring and casting. In mirroring, the exact same image is shown on both displays. In casting, one device sends the image to a second display, where it is displayed, and the casting device can perform other tasks.

Know the common wireless networking technologies. Wi-Fi is the most common wireless networking technology. Mobile devices can also use Bluetooth and radio frequency (RF) for near-field communication (NFC).

Given a scenario, understand how to install and configure common peripherals. Steps will vary based on the peripheral. However, in general, you need to plug the device in, install the driver (or let plug-and-play install it), and configure the device.

Chapter 2 Lab

You can find the answers in Appendix A.

Your friend Elise comes to you looking for help. You know that she is talented at producing videos and has recently started her own company to make videos for local restaurants and entertainment venues to put on their websites.

Elise tells you that her business is growing quickly, and she's very excited. She's had so much business that she needed to bring in another friend, James, to do some work for her, and both of them have been very busy. Elise had purchased an external hard drive for additional storage, but now she is running out of room and needs a better solution, preferably one that both she and James can use. Elise uses a MacBook Pro. James has some sort of Mac as well, but it's a few years old.

In order, Elise's goals are to increase storage space, make it easily available for her and James, and have some protection against losing all of the data she has compiled to date. She also doesn't want to spend a fortune, because she needs to keep costs down for her business to keep growing.

1. What types of hardware does Elise need to accomplish her goals?
2. Are there any peripherals that would let her accomplish all of her goals with one device?
3. How much will that option cost if she wants to get 10 TB of storage space?
4. Are there other options Elise has that might save her money?

Feel free to use the Internet to research and come up with at least two options for Elise.

Review Questions

You can find the answers in Appendix B.

1. Which of the following ports was developed by Apple and is found on MacBooks?
   A. eSATA
   B. USB
   C. Thunderbolt
   D. Mac Video
2. If you want to plug in a keyboard, which types of connectors might you use? (Choose two.)
   A. Parallel
   B. Serial
   C. USB
   D. PS/2
3. What is the name of the connector that you are likely to find at the end of a twisted-pair network cable?
   A. RJ11
   B. RJ45
   C. HDMI
   D. TPI
4. You want to use the video connector with the best resolution. Which one should you pick?
   A. HDMI
   B. HEMI
   C. DVI
   D. VGA
5. Which of the following connectors provides support for dual 4k displays?
   A. DVI
   B. USB
   C. RJ45
   D. Thunderbolt
6. Which type of printer uses a powdery substance to create images on paper?
   A. Powder
   B. Thermal
   C. Inkjet
   D. Laser

7. Rebecca points at a flat square below her keyboard on her laptop and asks what that is. What is it?
   - A. Trackpad
   - B. Touchpad
   - C. Touchstick
   - D. Webcam
8. Which of the following are wireless networking technologies? (Choose two.)
   - A. NFC
   - B. DVI
   - C. RJ45
   - D. Bluetooth
9. If you are installing a peripheral device and plug-and-play works as expected, which of the following is true?
   - A. You will need to install the device driver to make the peripheral work.
   - B. The peripheral should function normally.
   - C. You will need to complete web-based configuration steps for the peripheral to work.
   - D. You will need to configure IP-based options for the peripheral to work.
10. You want to install a device in your office that allows for extra storage and has built-in fault tolerance. Which device do you need?
    - A. NAS
    - B. RAS
    - C. SAS
    - D. External hard drive
11. One of your friends asks you if you have any SuperSpeed devices. What type of device is she talking about?
    - A. SSD
    - B. OLED
    - C. USB
    - D. eSATA
12. You have a color inkjet printer. What type of ink cartridge does it most likely use?
    - A. CMYB
    - B. CMYK
    - C. RGB
    - D. ROYGBIV

13. In your office, you need to set up your computer for a video teleconference with another office. What peripheral do you need to make this work?
    - **A.** Scanner
    - **B.** CRT
    - **C.** Projector
    - **D.** Webcam
14. Which of the following devices can provide power to a computer in the event of a power outage?
    - **A.** UPS
    - **B.** PSU
    - **C.** USB
    - **D.** RF
15. Which of the following connectors does not provide digital video output?
    - **A.** HDMI
    - **B.** DVI
    - **C.** VGA
    - **D.** Thunderbolt
16. List the units of throughput from fastest to slowest.
    - **A.** Tbps, Gbps, Mbps, Kbps
    - **B.** Tbps, Mbps, Gbps, Kbps
    - **C.** Kbps, Mbps, Gbps, Tbps
    - **D.** Kbps, Gbps, Mbps, Tbps
17. You are asked to create a working twisted-pair cable from a bulk roll and some extra connectors. Which device would you use?
    - **A.** Cable tester
    - **B.** Crimper
    - **C.** Splicer
    - **D.** Multimeter
18. Which of the following statements is true about DVI connectors?
    - **A.** They are digital only.
    - **B.** They are analog only.
    - **C.** They are digital and analog.
    - **D.** They support hybrid video technology.

19. You just installed a printer and want to share it on the network. Where do you perform this task in Windows?
    A. Printing preferences
    B. Printer properties
    C. Print queue
    D. IP printing configuration

20. Robert complains that the cursor on his laptop screen often jumps around unexpectedly when he's typing. What can he do to solve the problem?
    A. Reinstall the mouse driver.
    B. Reinstall the video driver.
    C. Reboot the computer.
    D. Disable the touchpad.
    E. Stop typing.

Computing Devices and the Internet of Things

THE FOLLOWING COMPTIA TECH+ FC0-U71 EXAM OBJECTIVES ARE COVERED IN THIS CHAPTER:

✓ **2.0 Infrastructure**

✓ **2.1 Explain common computing devices and their purposes.**

- Smartphones
- Tablets
- E-readers
- Laptops
- Workstations
- Servers
- Gaming consoles
- Virtual reality systems
- Augmented reality systems
- Internet of Things (IoT)
  - Home appliances
  - Home automation devices
    - Thermostats
    - Security systems
    - Home assistants
    - Deadbolts/door locks
    - Video doorbells

- Vehicles
- Internet Protocol (IP)/security cameras
- Streaming media devices
- Medical devices
- Exercise equipment Wearable devices

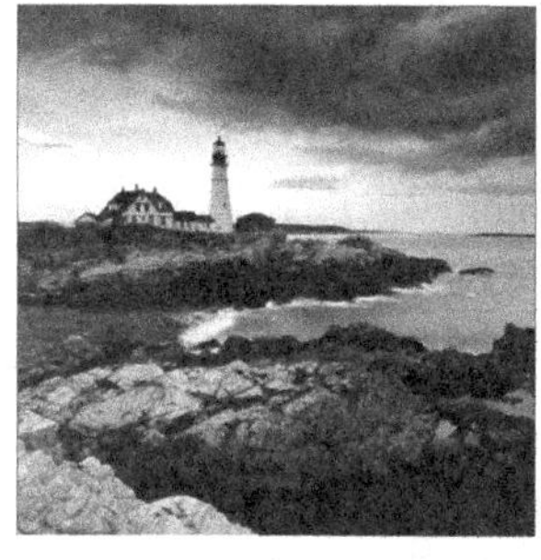

Understanding how individual computer components work is important for anyone working in information technology (IT). But what we and our users work with every day are collections of components that we colloquially call *computers*. Of course, since there are different types of tasks that we need computers to perform, there are different types of computers. After all, traveling for work and lugging around a desktop computer and a 21″ monitor isn't very practical.

In addition, the natural progression of technology evolution usually means that devices get smaller, faster, and cheaper. As those three things happen, manufacturers start bundling technologies together that previously resided on separate devices, such as a telephone and a GPS. For evidence of all of those factors coming together, you need to look no further than smartphones or tablets.

You can be certain that the inventors of early computers would be absolutely astonished by the capability of the smartphones in the market today, ones that are easily several thousands of times more powerful than the room-sized behemoths of their day. And in another 40 or 50 years, who knows what types of devices will exist? The youth of that generation may look back on our smartphones as quaint curiosities, much like the youth of today look at black-and-white televisions or cassette tapes.

Communications methods have also evolved dramatically in concurrence with hardware. Twenty years ago, wireless networking was slow and uncommonly used. Mobile phones were starting to become more popular, but they were used for voice calls and maybe a text or two. Cellular networks couldn't handle much more than that. Today, it seems that every home has a wireless network, and relatively high-speed cellular networks penetrate every corner of the civilized world.

The combination of smaller hardware and ubiquitous communications has enabled connectivity like the world has never seen before. One of the outcroppings of this is the Internet of Things (IoT). Literally, it's the promise of all electronics devices connected to each other and accessible from anywhere. This has profound implications on how we can live our lives, as well as our security—both good and bad.

This chapter starts by covering various types of computing devices with which you'll be working, moving from larger to smaller, with particular emphasis on using mobile devices. The end of the chapter focuses on explaining one of the hottest topics in technology today, the Internet of Things.

Exploring Larger Computing Devices

It's likely that you work with computing devices every day. You might even be reading this book on one. Most people have smartphones, which are certainly computers, and it's hard to imagine life before they existed. How did we possibly survive without having the answer to every imaginable question right at our fingertips?

The demarcation line between types of devices seems to be between larger devices, such as desktops and laptops, that can run traditional software applications, and smaller handheld devices. In this section, I will discuss three different types of larger computing devices and the roles they play. In the next section, we will work our way to the smaller ones that seemingly everyone carries around with them. By no means will this chapter cover an exhaustive list of all types of computers, but it will give you a good understanding of the similarities and differences between different types of devices in the marketplace.

Servers and Workstations

Computer networks are everywhere. A *network* is a collection of computers and other devices connected together somehow to share resources. Chapter 8, "Networking Concepts and Technologies," will give you a great foundation for understanding networks. For now, though, let's focus on two different types of computing devices that you will commonly find on a network: servers and workstations.

Tech+ exam objective 2.1, "Explain common computing devices and their purposes," includes servers, workstations, and laptops. Understand the different roles each one plays in a computing environment.

Servers

Servers come in many shapes and sizes. They are a core component of the network, providing resources necessary for users to perform tasks. Said differently, they serve resources up to network users—hence their name.

Servers offer networks the ability to centralize the control of resources and security, thereby reducing administrative difficulties. They can be used to distribute processes for balancing the load on computers and can thus increase speed and performance. They can also compartmentalize files for improved reliability. That way, if one server goes down, not all of the files are lost.

Servers can perform several different critical roles on a network. For example, servers that provide files to the users on the network are called *file servers*. Likewise, servers that host printing services for users are called *print servers*. (Servers can be used for other tasks as well, such as authentication, remote access services, administration, email, and so on.) Networks can include single-purpose and multipurpose servers. If the server is a single-purpose server, it is a file server only or a print server only. A multipurpose server can be, for example, both a file server and a print server at the same time. Another distinction that we use in categorizing servers is whether they are dedicated or nondedicated.

Dedicated Servers A *dedicated server* is assigned to provide specific applications or services for the network and nothing else. End users don't sit at these machines to do their daily work. Because a dedicated server specializes in only a few tasks, it requires fewer resources than a nondedicated server might require from the computer that is hosting it. This savings may translate to efficiency and can thus be considered as having a beneficial impact on network performance. A *web server* is an example of a dedicated server. It is dedicated to the task of serving up web pages and nothing else.

More and more, companies are choosing *cloud-based* servers for their dedicated servers. These servers are administered by a third party and accessed through an Internet connection. This saves the company the overhead of buying and managing server hardware. You will learn a lot more about the cloud in Chapter 9, "Cloud Computing and Artificial Intelligence."

Nondedicated Servers Nondedicated servers are assigned to provide one or more network services *and* local access for a user. A *nondedicated server* is expected to be slightly more flexible in its day-to-day use than a dedicated server. Nondedicated servers can be used to direct network traffic and perform administrative actions, but they also are often used to serve as a front end for the administrator to work with other applications or services or perform services for more than one network. For example, a dedicated web server might serve out one or more websites, whereas a nondedicated web server serves out websites but might also function as a print server on the local network, or as the administrator's workstation.

Many networks use both dedicated and nondedicated servers to incorporate the best of both worlds, offering improved network performance with the dedicated servers and flexibility with the nondedicated servers.

Workstations

Workstations are the computers on which network users do their work, performing activities such as word processing, data analysis, database design, graphic design, email, and other office or personal tasks. Workstations are basically everyday computers, except for the fact that they are connected to a network that offers additional resources. Workstations can range from diskless computer systems (computers that don't have their own hard drives, and instead save all files on a server) to desktops or laptops. In network terms, workstations are also known as *client computers*. As clients, they are allowed to communicate with the servers in the network to use the network's resources.

It takes several items to make a workstation into a network client. You must install a *network interface card (NIC)*, an expansion card that allows the PC to talk on a network. You must connect it to a cabling system that connects to other computers (unless your NIC supports wireless networking). You must also install special software, called *client software*, which allows the computer to talk to the servers and request resources from them. Once all this has been accomplished, the computer is "on the network."

Network client software comes with all operating systems today. When you configure your computer to participate on a network, the operating system utilizes this software.

Clients might or might not know that resources they are using are on a server. Or, they might not realize that the accounting files they access are on one server, but the print job they just sent went to a completely different one. In the end, the goal is to provide seamless access to resources that the client needs, and the client shouldn't have to worry about where the resources are physically located.

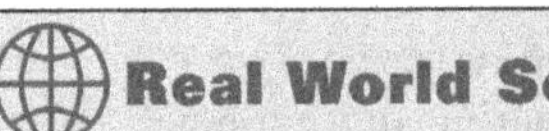

Real World Scenario

Is That a Server or a Workstation?

This is one of the things I like to do when teaching novice technicians. In the room, there will be a standard-looking mini-tower desktop computer. I point to it and ask, "Is that a server or a workstation?" A lot of techs will look at it and say it's a workstation because it is a desktop computer. The real answer is, "It depends."

Although people may have a perception that servers are ultra-fancy, rack-mounted behemoths, that isn't necessarily true. It's true that servers typically need more powerful hardware than do workstations because of their role on the network, but that doesn't have to be the case. (Granted, having servers that are less powerful than your workstations doesn't make logical sense.) What really differentiates a workstation from a server is what operating system it has installed and what role it plays on the network.

For example, if that system has Microsoft Windows Server 2022 installed on it, you can be pretty sure that it's a server. If it has Windows 10 or Windows 11, it's more than likely going to be a client, but not always. Computers with operating systems such as Windows 11 can be both clients on the network and nondedicated servers, as would be the case if you share your local printer with others on the network.

The moral of the story? Don't assume a computer's role simply by looking at it. You need to understand what is on it and what role it plays on the network to make that determination.

Laptops

The original portable computers were hardly portable. They were the size of a small suitcase and could weigh 50 pounds. Not only were they greatly inferior to desktops in technology, they were also outrageously expensive. It's no wonder few people purchased them. As technology improved and components were made smaller and lighter, laptops evolved from their suitcase-sized cousins to what you see today.

The purpose of a laptop, for the most part, is to do everything a desktop computer can, but to be portable. They contain a built-in keyboard, pointing device, and flatscreen display in a clamshell design. They are also often called *notebook* computers because they resemble large notebooks. Most portable computers in use today are laptop computers.

This section focuses on laptops, and there are many similar devices in the marketplace that fall under this umbrella. For example, Google Chromebooks are a type of laptop, and I've already mentioned notebooks. Throughout this section, assume those terms are interchangeable unless otherwise indicated. Later in the chapter I'll get into tablets, which are smaller still and deserve their own special discussion.

Laptop Architecture

Laptops are similar to desktop computers in architecture in that they contain many parts that perform similar functions. However, the parts that make up a laptop are completely different from those that are inside desktop computers. The obvious major difference is size; laptops are space challenged. Another primary concern is heat. Restricted space means less airflow, meaning parts can heat up and overheat faster.

To overcome space limitations, laptop parts are physically much smaller and lighter, and they must fit into the compact space of a laptop's case. It might not sound like much, but there really is a major difference between a 4.5-pound laptop and a 5.5-pound laptop if you're hauling it around in its carrying case all day. Also, laptop parts are designed to consume less power and to shut themselves off when not being used, although many desktops also have components that go into a low-power state when not active, such as video circuitry.

Working With Laptop Hardware

Most integrated laptop hardware is proprietary, meaning that to replace a part, you need to use a component built specifically for that laptop. Table 3.1 lists some common laptop components and replacement considerations.

TABLE 3.1 Laptop hardware replacement considerations

Component	Notes
Motherboard	Almost always proprietary; need to order from the manufacturer.
CPU	Almost always built into the motherboard.
RAM	Usually industry-standard small outline dual inline memory modules (SODIMMs).
Hard drive	Industry-standard sized, almost always solid-state drives (SSDs) today.

TABLE 3.1 Laptop hardware replacement considerations *(continued)*

Component	Notes
Video, sound, and network cards	Almost always integrated into the motherboard. Can add an external network card if the integrated one fails.
Case	Proprietary.
Display	Proprietary.
Battery	Proprietary.

For a review of motherboard, CPU, RAM, and hard drive functions, see Chapter 1, "Core Hardware Components." Video, sound, and network cards were introduced in Chapter 2, "Peripherals and Connectors." In addition to standard computer hardware, laptop users frequently make use of external power adapters, docking stations, and cable locks.

External Power Adapters

Even though they have internal batteries, laptops of course need to be plugged into a power source to recharge that battery. Some users like to have an extra power adapter. For example, they might have one at home and at work, so they don't need to carry one around in their laptop bag. Different power adapters can plug into alternating current (AC) sources, such as a wall outlet, or direct current (DC) sources, such as in automobiles or airplanes. Figure 3.1 shows a basic AC power adapter. Almost all of them today will have a USB-C connector.

FIGURE 3.1 Laptop AC power adapter

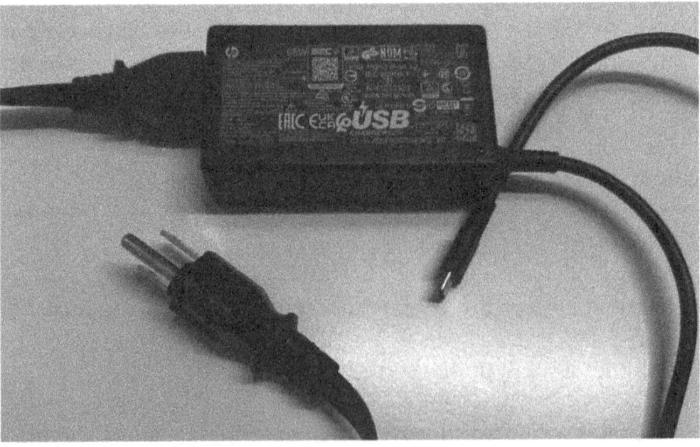

Power adapters are easily replaceable, but be sure to get one that is compatible with the laptop. You should choose one rated for the same or higher wattage than the original. If it's an older laptop, you may need to pay special attention to the *polarity* of the plug—that is, whether the center or tip of the power connector is positive or negative—that interfaces with the laptop. If the laptop requires the positive lead to be the center conductor, for instance, then you must take care not to reverse the polarity. Doing so could cause damage to the electronic components. Look for symbols like the ones shown in Figure 3.2 on the power supply, and make sure that the new power supply is the same as the old one. If the symbol doesn't exist, and it won't on USB-C power adapters, then don't worry about it.

FIGURE 3.2 Polarity symbols

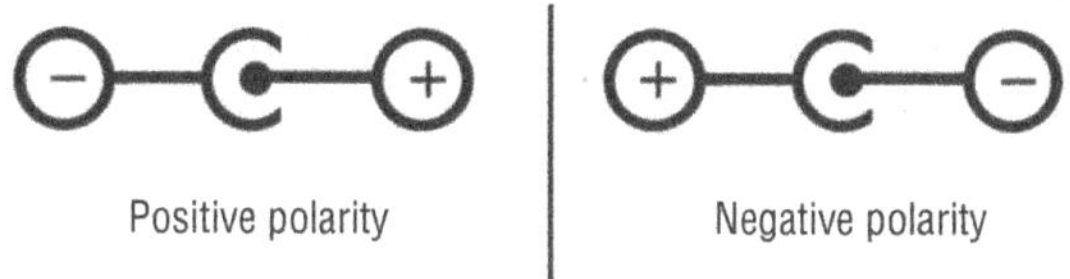

Docking Stations

While users love laptops for their portability, sometimes a user simply needs to work with a full-sized keyboard or monitor. In addition, some users might have other external peripherals they need to plug in, such as external storage or a printer. It can be a pain to plug and unplug these devices constantly.

A docking station (shown in Figure 3.3) is a laptop-only peripheral that is basically an extension of the motherboard of a laptop. Because a docking station is designed to stay behind when the laptop is removed, it can contain things like a full-sized drive bay and expansion slots. The docking station in Figure 3.3 has the following ports: four USB (two are on the side), two DisplayPort, one HDMI, one RJ45, and a cable lock. It connects to the PC through a USB-C connection. It's about 5″ square and 2″ high.

FIGURE 3.3 A docking station

Also, the docking station can function as a port replicator. A port replicator reproduces the functions of the ports on the back of a laptop so that peripherals such as monitors, keyboards, printers, and so on that don't travel with the laptop can remain connected to the dock and don't all have to be unplugged physically each time the laptop is taken away.

Older laptops will have a connector on the bottom to connect to a specific type of docking port, making docking ports proprietary. These ports work only with docking stations designed by the laptop's manufacturer, and vice versa. Newer docking stations connect via USB-C, typically in the same port that would have been otherwise used for the power cord.

Cable Locks

To a thief, laptops can be a pretty easy target. One way that you can help to secure your laptop physically is through the use of a cable lock, sometimes called a *Kensington lock* (named after a company that makes them) or a *K-lock*. Essentially, a cable lock anchors your device to a physical structure, making it nearly impossible for someone to walk off with it. Figure 3.4 shows a cable lock with a number combination lock. With others, small keys are used to unlock the lock. If you grew up using a bicycle lock, these will look really familiar.

FIGURE 3.4 Cable lock

Here's how it works. First, find a secure structure, such as the permanent metal supports of your desk at work. Then, wrap the lock cord around the structure, putting the lock through the loop at the other end. Finally, secure the lock into your cable lock hole on the back or side of your laptop (Figure 3.5), and you're secure. If you forget your combination or lose your key, you're most likely going to have to cut through the cord, which will require a large cable cutter or a hacksaw.

If someone wants your laptop badly enough, they can break the case and dislodge your lock. Having the lock in place will deter most people looking to make off with it, though.

FIGURE 3.5 Cable lock insertion point

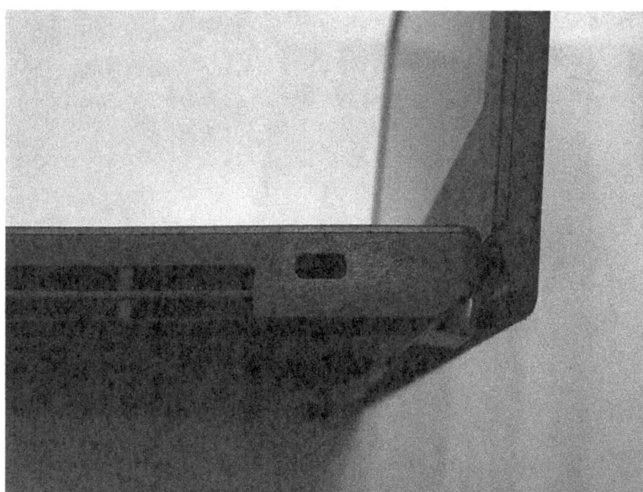

Working With Laptop Interfaces

Laptops are smaller versions of desktop computers; users are expected to do much of the same kinds of work on each. As such, the inputs for a laptop aren't drastically different than they are on a desktop, only smaller. The keyboard must fit into the design of the case, and the pointing device should as well. (You can plug in an external mouse or trackball, but you don't need to.)

Keyboards

The smaller keyboard on a laptop needs to provide all of the functionality that its larger cousins do, and in fact even more. But because of the smaller amount of space, multiple features might be combined onto one key. For example, there might not be enough space for a 0–9 number pad, so the number pad might be combined with letter keys and then activated with another key.

Another feature of laptop keyboards is the special *function (Fn) key*, which you were introduced to in Chapter 2. Recall that it's typically near the Windows key on the keyboard. To use a multifunction key, you press and hold the Fn key (as you would the Shift, Ctrl, and Alt keys) and then tap the key labeled with the function you want, finally releasing the Fn key. In Chapter 2, you did an exercise that showed you how to adjust the display settings on a laptop, but there are other options as well. For example, you might be able to adjust audio settings (as shown in Figure 3.6), enable and disable network settings, such as Wi-Fi or Bluetooth, put the laptop into sleep mode, or open menus within Windows.

FIGURE 3.6 Audio adjustment keys F7 (quieter), F8 (louder), and F9 (microphone mute)

From a usage standpoint, some people have trouble with the smaller keys and the fact that they're so close together. People with bigger hands or those who are used to typing on full-sized keyboards might find laptop keyboards a bit constricting.

Pointing Devices

Building a full-sized mouse into a laptop case just isn't feasible. The real estate is too valuable to waste on an accessory. Fortunately, laptops will often have one or more built-in devices to help you point to your heart's content. A few of these were covered in Chapter 2, but let's take a look at common laptop pointing devices here.

Trackball Many early laptops used trackballs as pointing devices. A *trackball* is essentially the same as a mouse turned upside down. The on-screen pointer moves in the same direction and at the same speed that you move the trackball with your thumb or fingers. They are cheap to produce but not very durable, so they're not as commonly used today.

Touchpad A *touchpad* is a device that has a pad of touch-sensitive material. The user draws with their finger on the touchpad, and the on-screen pointer follows the finger motions. Included with the touchpad are two buttons for left- or right-clicking (although with some touchpads, you can perform the functions of the left-click by tapping the touchpad. Macs will have one button).

Point Stick With the introduction of the ThinkPad series of laptops, IBM introduced a new feature known as the Touchpoint, generically known as a *point stick*. The point stick is a pointing device that uses a small rubber-tipped stick, usually right in the middle of the G, H, and B keys on the keyboard. When you push the point stick in a particular direction, the on-screen pointer goes in the same direction. The harder you push, the faster the on-screen pointer moves. The point stick allows fingertip control of the on-screen pointer, without the reliability problems associated with trackballs. One occasional problem with point sticks is that they do not return to center, causing the pointer to drift when not in use. Figure 3.7 shows a point stick and a touchpad on a laptop.

FIGURE 3.7 Point stick and touchpad on a laptop

Touchscreen *Touchscreens* are found on most laptops, except for low-end models, and are used extensively on smartphones and tablets. As the name implies, it's a video screen that you can touch, and the system senses it. It can be as simple as registering a click, like a mouse, or it can be more advanced such as capturing handwriting and saving it as a digital note.

Exploring Handheld and Mobile Devices

The large devices covered so far in this chapter provide the most computing power, largest displays, great gaming options, and best utility for workers and students. What they lack is upper-end portability. Sure, laptops are portable, but they can be heavy to lug around. Besides, have you ever tried to stuff one into your pocket?

If you're thinking about purchasing a smaller handheld computing device, a *tablet* or a *smartphone* are the two primary options. You'll find that the purpose for using each is slightly different. Tablets are larger and in some cases can serve as a laptop replacement. Smartphones are smaller and more portable, and it's really hard to do things such as take meeting notes on them. In terms of interacting with these devices, though, they're virtually identical. They use the same operating systems and have the same navigational features. Because they are so similar from an end-user standpoint, I am going to cover them together here. I'm also going to make one more executive decision here and refer to them collectively as *mobile devices*. Yes, there are other mobile devices, including tablets, but this shorthand saves you from having to read the words "tablets and smartphones" time and again.

In addition, there is a category of smaller mobile devices dedicated to special tasks such as playing games, augmenting reality, or creating a virtual reality environment. This section will cover those as well. Without further ado, let's start looking at mobile devices.

Comparing and Contrasting Mobile Devices

As noted earlier, there are a lot of similarities between different types of mobile devices. For example, if it's an Apple product, it will use some version of Apple's mobile operating system, iOS. If it's not, odds are that it will use some flavor of the Android OS. There are other mobile operating systems as well, but Android and iOS dominate the mobile market. Tablets and smartphones also, by and large, use the same apps as each other.

Tablets, smartphones, e-readers are listed in Tech+ exam objective 2.1 We will cover all of them in this section; tablets and smartphones will be frequently referenced. E-readers are specialized tablets and will be covered as well. Be sure to understand the similarities and differences between them all.

Here are some other things that mobile devices have in common:

They are not field-serviceable. If a computer that's laptop-sized or larger fails, a field technician can (most of the time) replace the failed component and get the system functioning. This generally isn't the case with mobile devices.

To be fair, many Android and other non-Apple devices allow the replacement of batteries and the use of removable memory cards as primary storage. With Apple products, though, even this basic level of access is removed. In an effort to produce a sleeker mobile phone, even Android devices have been developed without user access to the battery. But if any other component fails, it will probably be necessary to seek out an authorized repair facility and take or send your device to them for service. Attempting your own repairs can void any remaining warranty, and it can possibly render the device unusable. I'm not saying it can't be done, but it's not recommended.

Input methods are different. With mobile devices, space is at an absolute premium. There is no hardware keyboard (with rare exceptions and a hat-tip to the legacy BlackBerry, RIP 2022) and no mouse. You interact with the device using a touchscreen. I'll go into more depth on how to interact with a touchscreen in the "Using Mobile Devices" section later in this chapter.

There are two types of touchscreens to be aware of: resistive and capacitive. *Resistive touchscreens* respond to pressure, and they are highly accurate in detecting the position of the touch. These types of touchscreens require the use of a stylus or other hard object, such as a fingernail. *Capacitive touchscreens* are a little less accurate but more responsive. They respond to changes in electrical current; as such, the human fingertip works great as the facilitator of input.

Memory and storage are handled differently. Larger devices generally have two types of memory for data storage. The first is fast access but nonpersistent random access memory (RAM) for running applications, which loses its data if power is lost; the second is hard drive space for persistent, nonvolatile, long-term data storage. In smaller devices, there's not room for both.

Instead, mobile devices use solid-state memory for storage of both apps and data, as well as running the operating system and applications. As of the time of writing, there is a 1 TB version of the iPhone 16, but it's expensive. Most mobile devices will have 128 GB, 256 GB, or 512 GB. As such, storage space may be limited, and users might want to consider external (such as cloud) storage.

Now let's move on to the differences. First, tablets are larger than smartphones. Tablet screen sizes typically fall anywhere between about 7″ and 12.2″, although you can find much larger ones with 24″ displays as well. Because of the tablet's moderate screen size, you will find some users who are okay with running business applications, such as spreadsheets and presentations, on them. It becomes even easier if the user has a physical keyboard as an accessory.

Smartphones have a smaller screen size, generally less than 7″. This makes them poorly suited for business applications such as creating documents or spreadsheets, but they are the perfect size to carry around and read email, text, listen to music, or surf the Internet.

All smartphones come equipped with Wi-Fi, Bluetooth, and cellular capabilities. Tablets will have Wi-Fi and Bluetooth, but some do not come with cellular.

Real World Scenario

Is That a Tablet or a Smartphone?

Throughout the 1990s and early 2000s, miniaturization was the biggest trend in mobile phones. First there were brick designs, then flip phones, and then sliding phones—with each one getting smaller and smaller. Several popular movies and television shows made fun of the trend by showing characters using impossibly small devices, and some wondered if or when we would see the day when phones were simply a small microchip implanted inside a person's head.

Something funny happened on the road to cellular phone implants, though, and that was the smartphone. Smartphones made the device so much, well, smarter, than a regular phone. Among other things, they incorporated Internet access and video players, and users wanted to be able to see the content clearly. So instead of devices getting smaller, they started getting bigger.

At the same time, tablet computers were becoming more popular and smaller. It was inevitable that, at some point, a device would blur the line between smartphone and tablet, and that device was the phablet. Technically, a phablet was defined as a smartphone with a display size between 5″ and 7″.

From about 2011 to 2014, *phablet* was a hot buzzword in tech circles; in fact, Reuters called 2013 "The Year of the Phablet." The *New York Times* forecast that phablets would become the dominant computer device of the future. Fast-forward to today, and the term *phablet* isn't used at all; phones with screen sizes under 7″ are simply seen as large phones. It is possible though that screen sizes on phones have reached their maximum size. The last few releases of the iPhone and Samsung's popular Android phones have featured models between 6″ and 6.9″, but not larger. If there were consumer appetite for larger phones, surely the manufacturers would have made them by now.

Using Mobile Devices

Even if you are a holdout who doesn't own a smartphone or a tablet, odds are that you know someone who has one. Or maybe you know several people who own them, and they give you grief for not being part of the 21st century. Regardless of whether you own one, you need to understand how they work and how to set one up to get proper functionality.

To understand how mobile devices work, you need to know a bit about hardware, operating systems, and networking because they all come together in a small package. Hardware has already been covered in earlier chapters. Chapter 4, "Operating Systems," will further your knowledge on that topic, and Chapter 8 covers networking in depth. For now, I'll provide enough detail to help you know how to use and configure some key features. The focus is on three areas: specific usability features of mobile devices, setting up wireless network connections, and getting apps and synchronizing the device.

Using Mobile Device Interfaces

As noted earlier, the small size of mobile devices necessitated new ways of interaction, because traditional input devices such as the keyboard and mouse were far too large. The touchscreen and on-screen keyboard became the new tools for working with your device.

For the examples in this chapter, I am going to use iOS 17 on an iPhone as well as Android 13 on a Samsung phone. By the time you read this, both of these versions may be a few generations old. In newer versions of an OS, most of the options will stay in similar places but a few could move around. In the worst-case scenario that you can't find an option, an Internet search should help you out.

Before getting into the specifics of interacting with mobile devices, familiarize yourself with the home screen of the operating system. Figure 3.8 shows you a home screen in iOS 17 and Android 13.

FIGURE 3.8 Home screens for (a) iOS 17 and (b) Android 13 home screens

(a) (b)

With iOS, the default home screen is full of apps, and the one that you will use to set most configuration options will be Settings. Other apps will be on additional pages and can be accessed by swiping left or right.

In Android, the default is to show fewer icons, and there are three Navigation buttons at the bottom of the screen. They are, from left to right, Recents (the three bars), Home (the rounded square), and Back (the back arrow). You can get to the settings by swiping up from the home screen and then tapping the Settings icon—it's the one that looks like a gear.

Working With Mobile Device Touchscreens

When most users first experience a mobile device, there is a lot of uncertainty. There is no keyboard and no mouse. How do you possibly interact with this thing? Older iPhones had one button on the front (called the Home button), but that got axed with the iPhone X. Android devices classically have three virtual buttons on the home screen, but those too can be removed. New users need to get used to the functionality of a touchscreen in a hurry.

Mobile devices are built around a concept called *gesture-based interaction*, whereby users use their fingers and various movements to interact with their touchscreen. The good news is the device doesn't require complicated interpretive dance patterns to work, although it has sensors built in that could detect your dance movements if you wanted it to. The three gestures that you need to know are tap, swipe, and pinch. There is also a fourth closely related concept called *kinetics*.

Tap A tap of the finger is all it takes to get a lot done on a mobile device. It's a bit like clicking on a Mac or double-clicking on a PC. Tapping an icon will open that app. In this manner, your finger acts a lot like the mouse pointer does on a PC.

Swipe To swipe, you press your finger to the screen and then brush it in a direction. It's almost like the gesture of turning a page in a book. You will use this to move pages or scroll up or down. Swiping your finger up will scroll the page down, for example.

Pinch By placing two fingers apart and then pinching them together (while touching the screen, of course), you can zoom out. Placing two fingers together and then slowly spreading them apart will zoom in. (It's kind of a reverse pinch.) This feature doesn't work in all apps, but it is particularly helpful when looking at maps.

Kinetics *Kinetics* refers to the sense of motion. iPhones and other devices have an amazing array of kinetic sensors built in. For example, iPhones since the iPhone 6 have had a gyroscope, accelerometer, linear acceleration sensor, magnetometer, altitude sensor, and gravity sensor. These sensors let your device act like a GPS and compass, and they also detect movements such as tilting or shaking the device that many apps take advantage of.

Screen Orientation

One of the nice features of the gyroscope is that it can change the screen orientation from portrait to landscape depending on how you hold your device. This can be particularly helpful when using the on-screen keyboard to type. If you look at Figure 3.9, you'll see that it shows a new email in the Gmail app in portrait mode.

By keeping the screen facing you and rotating the device 90 degrees to the left or right, the phone automatically detects the rotation and switches to landscape mode, as shown in Figure 3.10.

The keys on the virtual keyboard are now a little larger, potentially making it easier to type. Some games also work better in landscape mode. Not all apps are built to use the gyroscope, so you won't get the rotation with everything.

FIGURE 3.9 Portrait mode

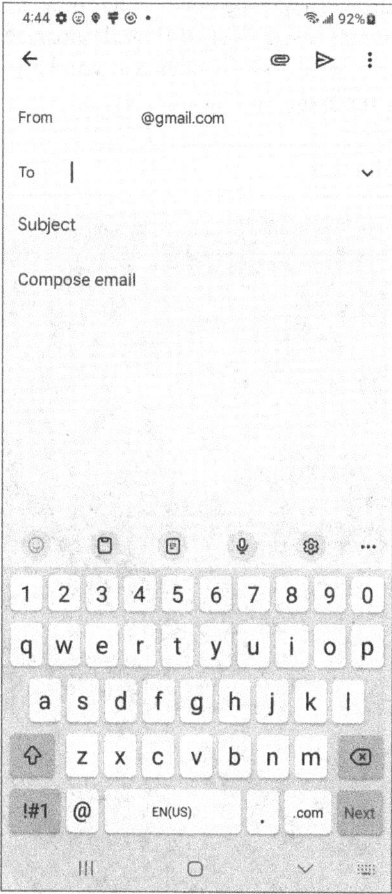

FIGURE 3.10 Landscape mode

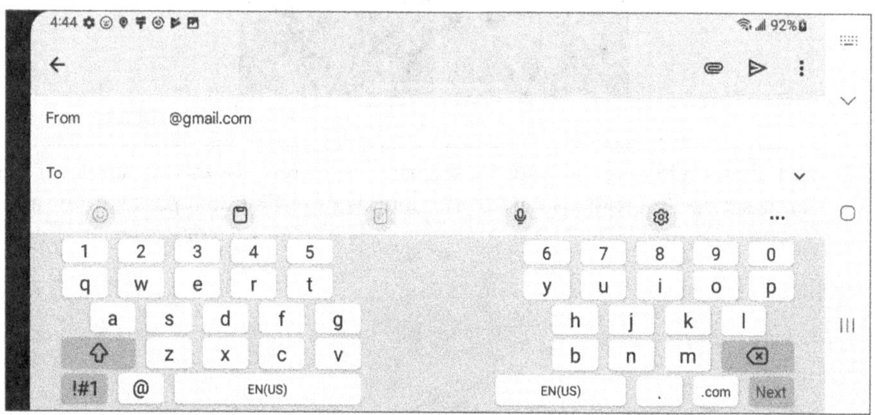

Locking and Security

One final feature of interacting with mobile devices that new users need to get used to is security. Mobile devices are much easier to steal than desktop computers, so it's important to secure the device. When you try to access the device, if you have set up the proper security, you will get a screen similar to the one in Figure 3.11.

FIGURE 3.11 iOS security lock

Figure 3.11 shows iOS, and the Android security lock screen looks very similar if you have a passcode set up. Android also gives you options of setting up a password or a

pattern lock based on a grid of nine dots, set up in a 3-by-3 matrix. Both operating systems support biometrics such as facial scanning to unlock as well. To use the device, you need to enter the correct password or have it scan your face. Some devices may support fingerprint scanning as well. Exercise 3.1 shows you how to change the security settings on iOS 17, and Exercise 3.2 does the same for Android 13.

EXERCISE 3.1

Changing Security Settings on iOS 17

1. Tap the Settings app to open it.
2. Scroll down to Face ID & Passcode (Figure 3.12) and tap it.

FIGURE 3.12 iPhone Settings

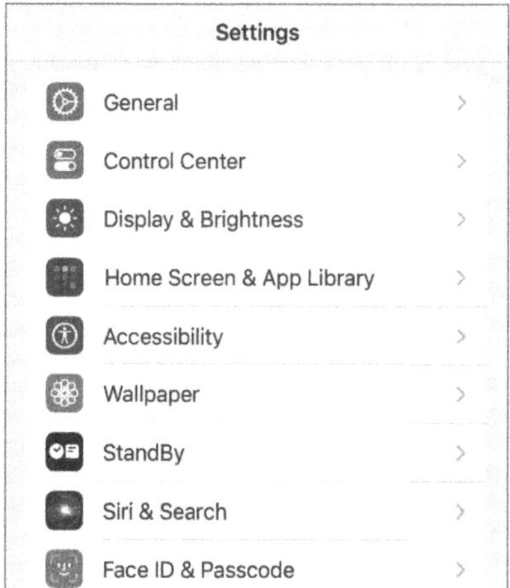

3. Enter your current passcode.
4. On the Face ID & Passcode screen (Figure 3.13), you can see the security settings. For example, you can choose which applications require Face ID, reset the Face ID, change the passcode, and select which apps can be accessed when locked (such as Siri, the personal assistant). Scroll down and tap Change Passcode to change your passcode.

EXERCISE 3.1 *(continued)*

FIGURE 3.13 Face ID & Passcode

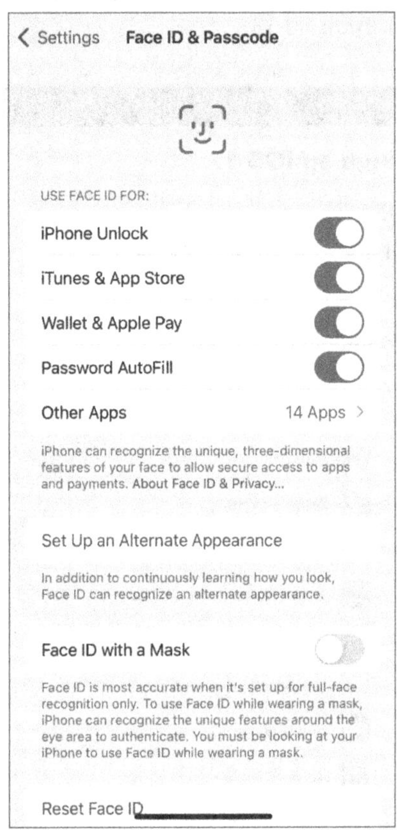

5. Enter your old passcode, and it will take you to the screen to enter your new passcode.
6. Enter your new passcode and tap Next.
7. Reenter your new passcode and tap Done.

EXERCISE 3.2

Changing Security Settings on Android 13

1. Tap the Settings app to open it.
2. Scroll down to Lock Screen (Figure 3.14) and tap it.

FIGURE 3.14 Android Settings

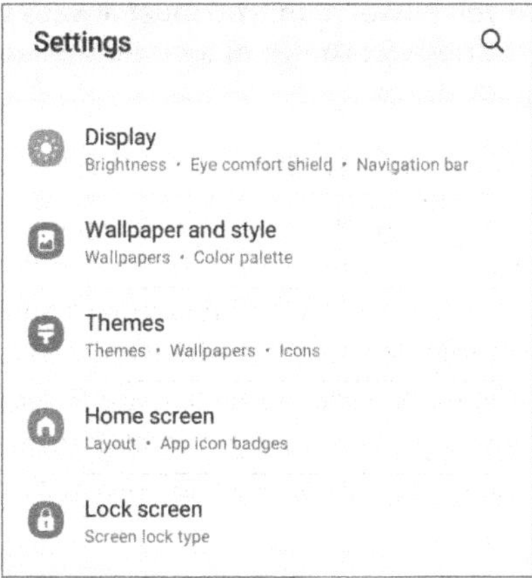

3. Tap Screen LockType.
4. Confirm your PIN.
5. In Screen LockType (Figure 3.15), tap the security type you want to enable.

FIGURE 3.15 Screen lock type

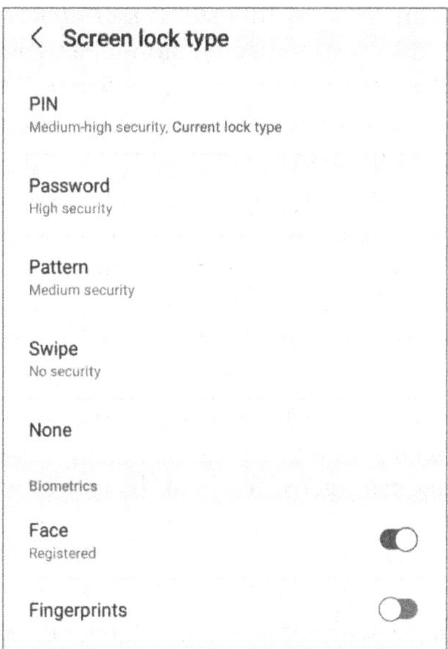

6. Enter the PIN, password, pattern, or follow the prompts to set up Face recognition.
7. If you entered a PIN, password, or pattern, tap Continue, enter it again, and then tap OK.

Even if you have enabled a biometric sensor on an iPhone or Android device, when you power it on, you must always type in the passcode (or password or pattern for Android) to access the device the first time.

Configuring Network Connections

The overall process to set up a mobile device is pretty straightforward. You buy it from a mobile provider, charge it with its USB cable, turn it on, and follow the prompts to configure it and get connected to your cellular provider. Manufacturers and wireless providers have spent a lot of time to make the setup process accessible and easy to navigate. When it comes to setting up wireless devices, the main areas on which you'll need to focus are the network connections that fall outside the scope of cellular connections. Still, there are a few cellular network terms you should be familiar with, so I'll start there. After that, I will cover Wi-Fi, Bluetooth, and Airplane mode.

Working With Cellular Networks

As I said in the introduction, connecting a smartphone or tablet to a cellular network has been made very easy, by design. Charge the phone, turn it on, and follow the prompts. You might need to go to the cellular carrier's website and set up an account and enter the phone's identifying information and choose your plan, but that's about it.

Mobile devices are identified by an *International Mobile Equipment Identity (IMEI)* number, which is a 15-digit serial number unique to each device. Further, each mobile device needs to have a small chip in it called a *subscriber identity module (SIM)* chip, which identifies the chip and links it to a specific mobile network. Each SIM card has a unique identifier called an *integrated circuit card identifier (ICCID)*, which is a 19- or 20-digit code. When setting up a phone on a cellular network, you may be asked to enter the IMEI and ICCID numbers. Usually these are printed on the box the phone came in, or they will be included in the documentation inside the box. On a working phone, you can look up your phone's identification numbers in Settings. In iOS it's under Settings ➢ General ➢ About, and scroll to the bottom under the ESIM section. In Android, you will find it in Settings ➢ About Phone ➢ Status Information and then tap either SIM Card Status or IMEI Information. Both OSs are shown in Figure 3.16, with iOS on the left and Android on the right.

On most Android phones, you can open the SIM compartment and change out the card to move from one cellular network to another. The SIM tray with a SIM card is shown in Figure 3.17. Notice there is an open microSD slot in the tray as well—this is about the limit of internal phone expandability. iPhones do not offer the luxury of a SIM tray. Apple really doesn't want people inside the case in any way, shape, or form.

Finally, some phones today are sold as *unlocked*, meaning they can participate in one of several different cellular networks without needing to have the SIM card replaced. Most people consider an unlocked phone to be better than a locked one because it offers flexibility of cellular providers. Cellular providers will of course want to convince you that locked phones are more secure and cheaper to operate. Know that if something goes wrong on an unlocked device, cellular providers are unlikely to provide technical support.

FIGURE 3.16 Identification numbers in (a) iOS and (b) Android

11:58

General About

Wi-Fi Address	28:02:2E:C8:23:AF
Bluetooth	28:02:2E:BA:09:E9
Modem Firmware	2.20.06
SEID	>
EID 890[redacted]26	
Carrier Lock	No SIM restrictions

ESIM

Network	Verizon
Carrier	Verizon 57.0
IMEI	35[redacted]6
ICCID	89[redacted]9

(a)

12:04 99%

Status information

SIM card status

IMEI information

IP address
fe80::9c2d:c3ff:fef6:d2a5
192.168.1.43
2600:2b00:7981:2c00:9c2d:c3ff:fef6:d2a5
2600:2b00:7981:2c00:59c7:1c45:853d:2955

Wi-Fi MAC address

Phone Wi-Fi MAC address
9C:39:28:18:F5:72

Bluetooth address
9C:39:28:18:F5:73

(b)

FIGURE 3.17 SIM tray and chip

Setting Up a Wi-Fi Connection

When you get a mobile device, you generally have a cellular connection to a provider such as AT&T, Verizon, T-Mobile, or others. Unless you have an unlimited plan, you pay for a certain amount of data each month. If you go over that amount, you will be charged extra—often, a lot extra. The other primary data connection that you can make is to a Wi-Fi network. When you are using Wi-Fi, you are not using your wireless data plan, so essentially your data is unlimited. If you're doing a lot of downloading, using a Wi-Fi connection can save you money, plus it's generally a lot faster than cellular. And as a bonus, you can use Wi-Fi calling for voice and video calls as well as texts over Wi-Fi instead of the cellular network. This can be incredibly handy if you're in a location with spotty cellular service.

The first thing to do when setting up a wireless connection is to verify that your device has wireless capabilities. If not, then this whole process won't work. Nearly all mobile devices support Wi-Fi, but you will want to confirm that yours does too.

After verifying that your device supports wireless, you want to turn on Wi-Fi. On the iPhone, tap Settings to open the Settings app (Figure 3.18). The second option down is Wi-Fi, and you can see that in this case it's turned off. Tap anywhere on the Wi-Fi line to open the Wi-Fi screen (Figure 3.19). There you see a slider bar to the right of Wi-Fi. Use your finger to tap it or slide it to the right into the On position (Figure 3.20). Once you do that, you will see the *security set identifiers (SSIDs)*, which are the network names, of networks in range under the heading Other Networks.

SSIDs will be covered in depth in Chapter 8.

FIGURE 3.18 iOS Settings

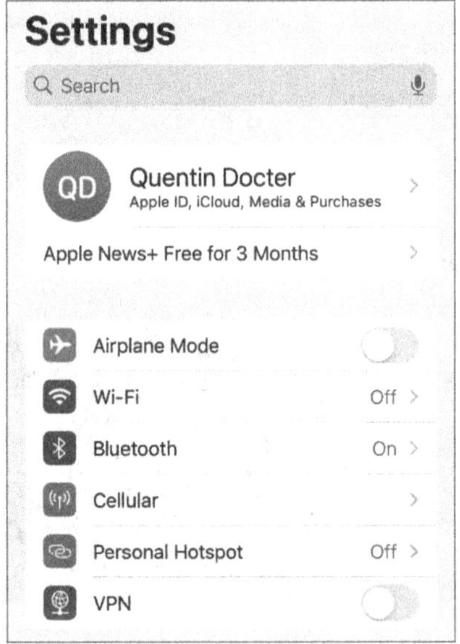

FIGURE 3.19 Wi-Fi is off.

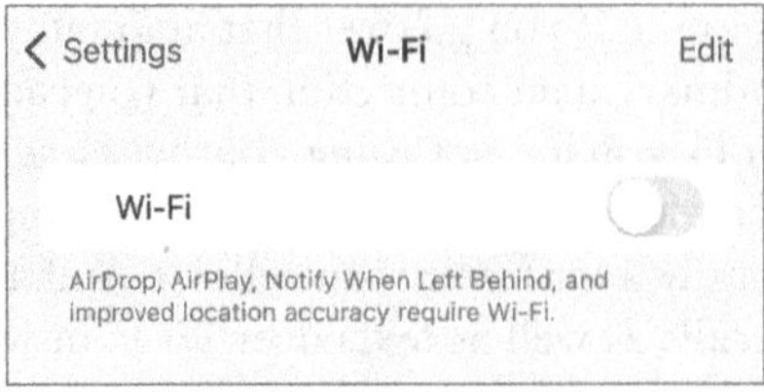

FIGURE 3.20 Wi-Fi is on, with available networks.

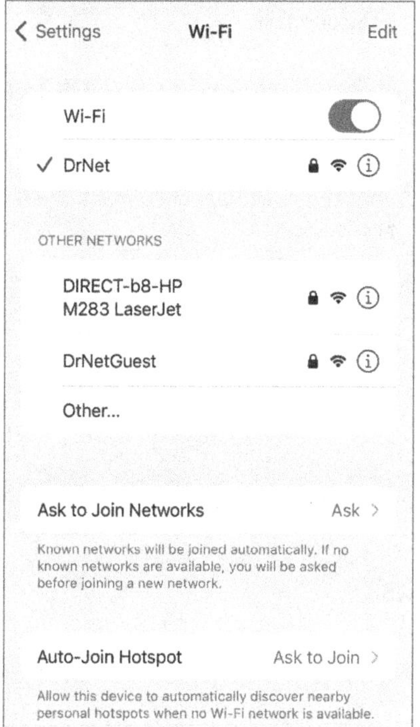

My phone is configured to join my network automatically (you can see that it's done so in Figure 3.20), but to join any other network, I would simply tap the SSID I want in the list of SSIDs. Networks with a padlock icon next to them are secured and require a password to join. Next to the padlock, you will see a signal strength indicator and an information button. The information button is where you configure options like auto-joining the network and TCP/IP protocol settings.

Once you enter the password and join the network, it will appear underneath Wi-Fi with a check mark next to it. The final step is to verify an Internet connection. To do this, go back to the home screen (swipe up once from the bottom edge) and open up Safari. Visit a website, and you are finished!

The process is similar on Android—open Settings ➢ Connections and you will see Wi-Fi as the first option (Figure 3.21). Tap on it to see additional available networks (Figure 3.22). To configure the current network, tap the gear to the right of the SSID (Figure 3.23). Once it's connected (it will say Connected under the SSID), verify Internet connectivity by opening Chrome.

FIGURE 3.21 Android connections

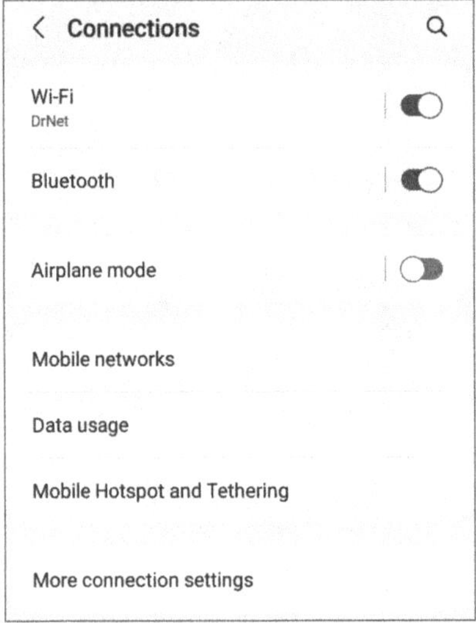

FIGURE 3.22 Wi-Fi networks

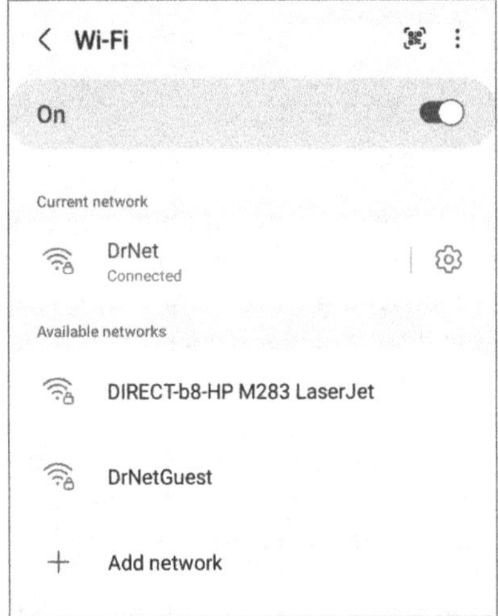

To summarize, the steps to set up a new Wi-Fi connection are:

1. Verify wireless capabilities.
2. Turn on Wi-Fi.
3. Locate or select the SSID.

FIGURE 3.23 Wi-Fi network configuration

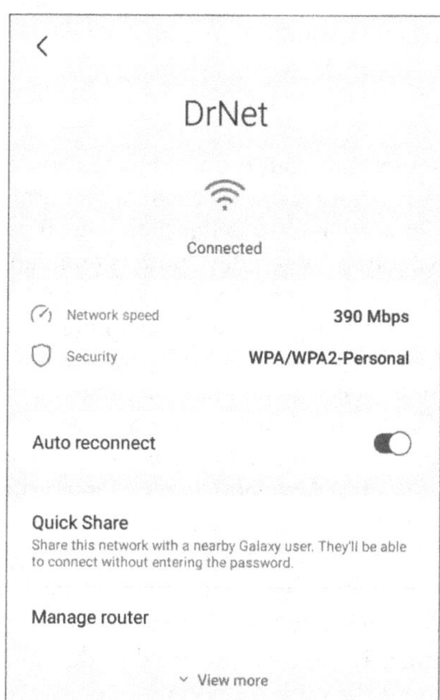

4. Enter the wireless password.
5. Verify the Internet connection.

Configuring Bluetooth

Bluetooth isn't a technology that you use for full-scale networking, but it works great for short-range connectivity with peripheral devices such as mice, keyboards, speakers, printers, and hands-free communication devices.

To enable two Bluetooth devices to communicate with each other, you need to work through a process called *Bluetooth pairing*. Essentially, it's a setup process that tells both devices that it's okay to communicate with one another. This process is required as an extra security step—you wouldn't want someone you don't know connecting to your Bluetooth-enabled phone in an airport and downloading your email or pictures!

The exact process for Bluetooth pairing will differ based on your mobile OS and the device to which you are connecting. In general, though, these are the steps:

1. Turn on the Bluetooth device.
2. Use your mobile device to locate and select the Bluetooth device.
3. Enter the Bluetooth device's passcode.
4. Confirm pairing on the Bluetooth device by pressing a button or a combination of buttons.

Bluetooth connections in iOS and Android use the same Settings app that manages Wi-Fi networks. Refer to Figure 3.18 for iOS and Figure 3.21 for Android to see Bluetooth listed under Wi-Fi. For specific instructions on how to pair your devices together, check the instructions for the Bluetooth device with which you are pairing.

Disable Bluetooth on your mobile devices unless you know that you are going to use it. There are two reasons. The first is that enabling Bluetooth will run down your battery faster than if it's disabled. The second is as a security precaution. When Bluetooth is enabled, you may be vulnerable to *bluejacking* or *bluesnarfing*. Bluejacking is the sending of (usually) harmless messages to your device via Bluetooth—think of it as Bluetooth spam. Bluesnarfing occurs when someone connects to your device without your knowledge and has access to all the data (pictures, contacts, emails, and so on) on your device. They can then hack your data or copy it to their device for later use. Manufacturers have enacted stricter security measures in the last few years and incidents such as these are declining. It's still better to be safe than sorry.

You can also perform data transfers between devices using Bluetooth by setting up an ad hoc (temporary) network. Most often this will be used to transfer pictures, videos, or contacts from one device to another. To do this, you need to download a Bluetooth sharing app from your device's app store and then pair the devices.

Using Airplane Mode

Airplane mode isn't as much about setting up connections as it is disconnecting them. Enabling Airplane mode instantly shuts off your wireless cellular connection (and your Bluetooth connection in Android). You can get to Airplane mode on an iPhone in a couple of different ways. One is to open Settings, and it's the first option listed (see Figure 3.24). When you tap it or slide it on, the words Airplane Mode will appear next to the Cellular option.

The other way is to access it from the Control Center. You can do this from both the lock screen and the home screen. Simply swipe your finger down from the top of the iPhone's touchscreen, and you will get the Control Center, similar to what's shown in Figure 3.25.

Tap the airplane icon in the upper-left corner to enable Airplane mode. The cellular icon will then switch from green (on) to gray (off). Notice that you also have a few other handy features in the Control Center, such as the ability to control music, adjust brightness or volume, turn on your flashlight, and use your calculator or camera.

Airplane mode in Android is under Settings ➢ Connections (see Figure 3.21). You can also get to it quickly in quick settings, shown in Figure 3.26. From the lock screen or home screen, swipe down twice to open it. Tap the airplane icon to active Airplane mode, and it will disable your cellular and Bluetooth connections.

FIGURE 3.24 Airplane mode on iOS 17

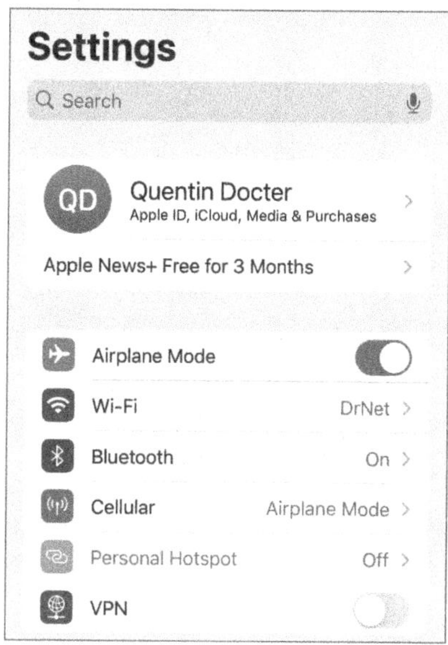

FIGURE 3.25 iPhone Control Center

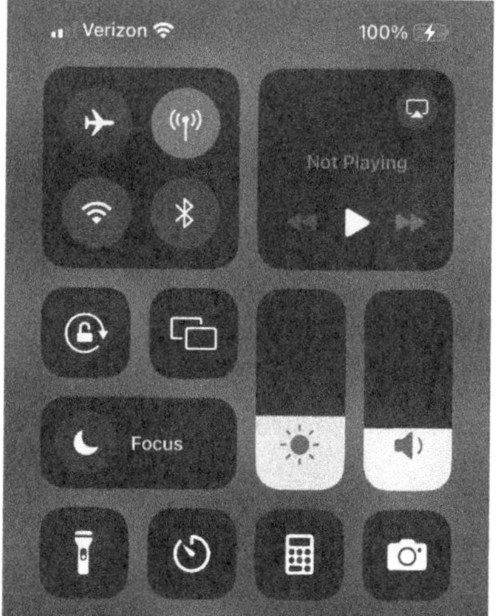

FIGURE 3.26 Android quick settings

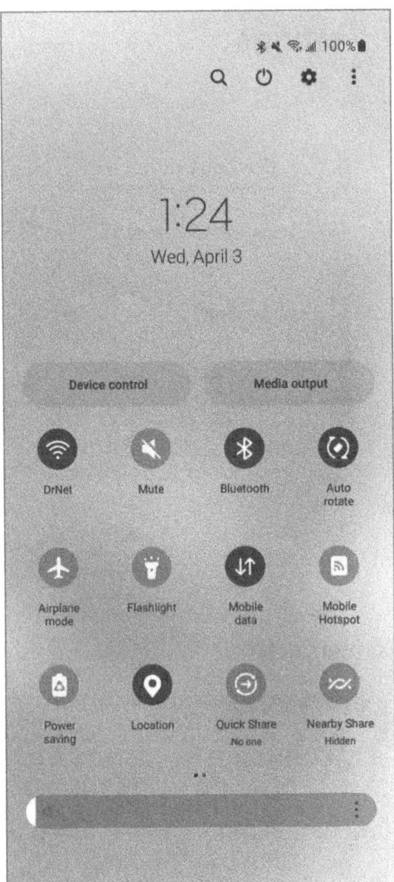

Getting Apps and Synchronizing

The two final concepts related to mobile devices help expand their functionality and protect your data. They are getting apps and synchronizing your device.

Getting Additional Apps

The first BlackBerry smartphones didn't have additional apps to download—you simply got what the manufacturer gave you. Newer devices came along that gave you the option to customize. Part of the reason BlackBerry declined so quickly was its slowness to adapt to that change. Now, downloading apps to mobile devices is a common thing for mobile users to do, whether it's to increase their productivity or maintain their sanity with a new distraction.

Each mobile platform has its own specific application store. Much like workstation apps are built for a specific OS, so are mobile apps. If you are using iOS, you get to the *Apple App*

Store by tapping the App Store icon on the home screen. The app will look similar to the one shown in Figure 3.27. There are multiple categories for free and paid apps and the ability to search for specific apps and update the ones currently on your device. The red badge over my initials in the upper-right corner conveniently reminds me that I have 14 installed apps with available updates.

FIGURE 3.27 Apple App Store

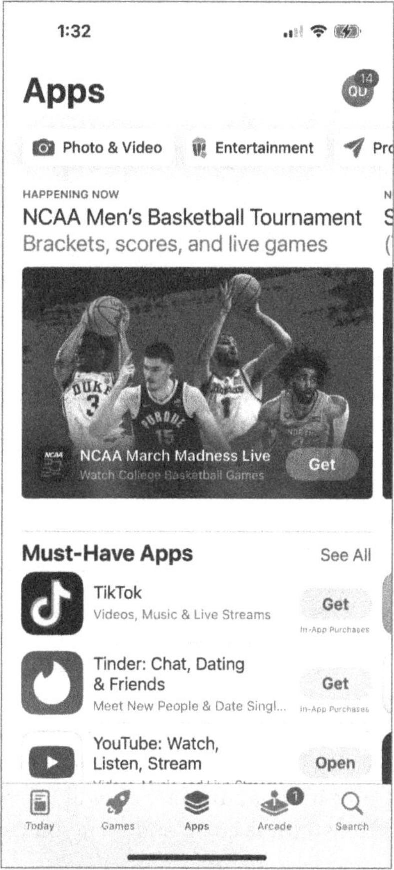

The *Google Play Store* is where to go for Android-based devices. You get to it by tapping the Play Store app from the home page. You will get a screen similar to the one shown in Figure 3.28. Here, you have categories to browse for apps, some popular apps from which to choose, and the ability to search for apps.

FIGURE 3.28 Google Play Store

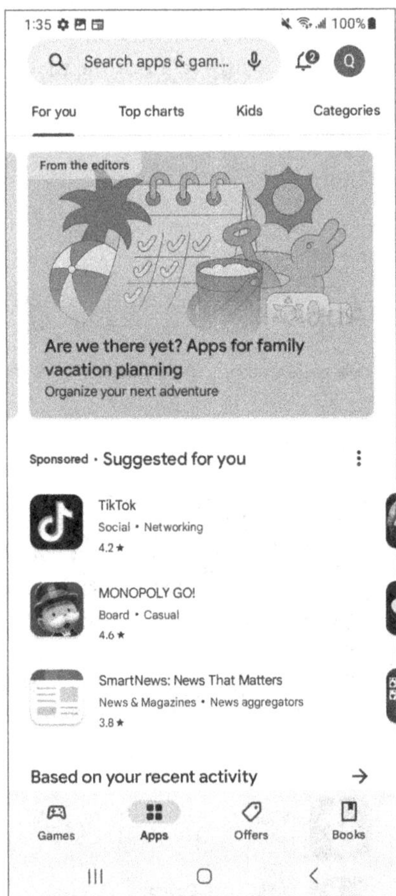

To install the app you want, tap it. You will be able to see more information on it, including what it does and reviews from other users. Then tap Install or Get. If apps have additional in-app purchases, or if it's not a free app, it will tell you (instead of the Install or Get button, it will have a button with the cost), and then you can make the decision whether or not to purchase it.

Real World Scenario

Avoiding Unpleasant and Expensive Surprises

The explosion of mobile devices has given billions of people instant access to data at their fingertips. What used to be friendly arguments with no provable answer now quickly turn into a chorus of "Just Google it!" Constant access has also led to some unpleasant side effects, though.

Either you have seen stories like this on the news, or maybe it's happened to you or someone you know. The exact details change, but the general premise goes like this: Joe or Jane user gets a bill from their mobile phone or credit card company with several hundreds or thousands of unexpected charges on it. Ultimately it gets traced back to their smartphone or tablet and the fact that the user unwittingly did something to rack up those huge costs. What happened?

It's usually one of a few things:

- Using too much data, if you don't have an unlimited plan
- Roaming charges (especially internationally)
- In-app purchases

When you register a mobile device with a provider, you will buy a data plan. Maybe you'll get only 5 GB of data per month, or maybe you'll get 20 GB. If you go over the allotted amount, however, the charge for extra data can be steep. Perhaps, under normal circumstances, you don't go over your data plan, but let's say that you go on vacation. While in the car or at your destination you choose to download some music, check email, and surf the web like you normally do. Only now you're using your minutes and data plan as opposed to using your Wi-Fi at home. You might not realize it at the time, but your idle surfing is costing you a lot of money.

If you're traveling internationally, the problem can be even worse. Check your plan to see what the provision is for traveling out of your home country. Some providers will automatically charge those minutes and that data as roaming, which will make it very expensive in a hurry.

The last one is in-app purchases. It might have been free to download the game and even to play it, but perhaps you can buy some gems or coins or something to level up even faster. Why wait around when you can become level 50 with just a few dollars? Maybe you have restraint when it comes to this, but maybe you don't. And maybe it's not you. A few years ago, one of my friends let her three-year-old son play Candy Crush Saga on her tablet while in the car. The next month, a bill came in for nearly $500 for in-app purchases. It wasn't what she considered money well spent.

So, how do you protect yourself against unexpected bills? First, be sure that you understand your wireless plan, including minutes, data maximums, and roaming charges. If you are going to travel, it might be worth it to increase your plan for a month or two as opposed to paying overuse fees.

Second, you can change the settings on your phone to potentially minimize the damage. In iOS 17, you can go to Settings ➢ Cellular to tell your phone how to behave, as shown in Figure 3.29. Turning off data roaming is a good way to avoid unexpected surprises. Notice at the bottom of Figure 3.29 it tells you how much cellular data and roaming has been used during the current billing period.

FIGURE 3.29 iOS 17 cellular data options

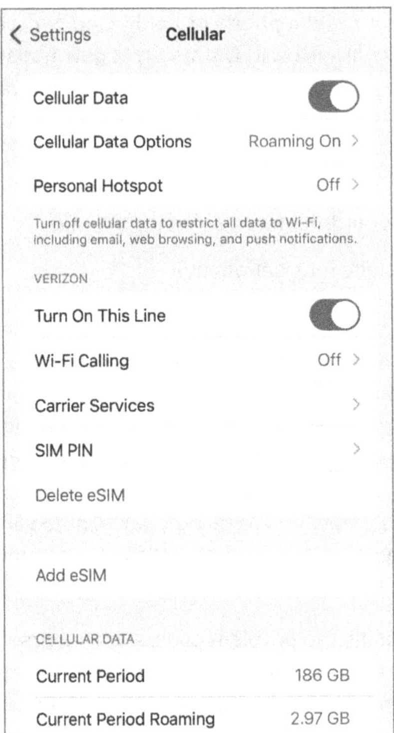

Android users can find cellular data options under Settings ➢ Connections (refer to Figure 3.21). Tap Mobile Networks to enable or disable roaming, shown in Figure 3.30, and tap Data Usage to allow Internet access through the mobile network and see current usage (Figure 3.31).

FIGURE 3.30 Android Mobile Networks

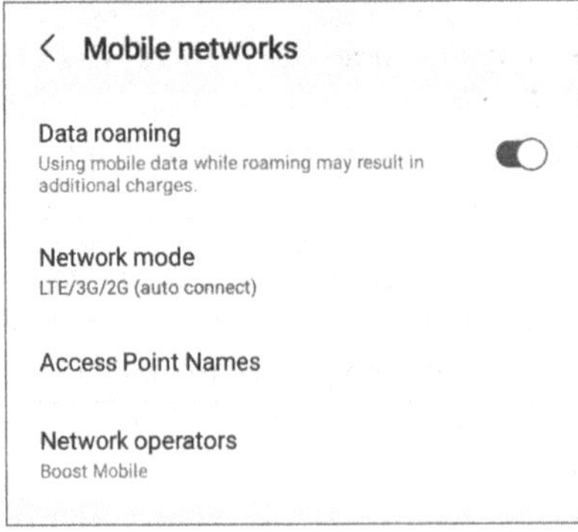

FIGURE 3.31 Android Data Usage

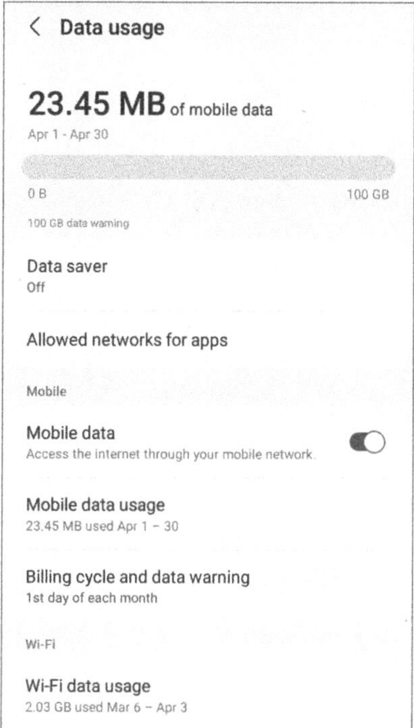

Finally, configure your app store account and apps so that new apps and in-app purchases require a password—and make sure your child or friends don't know it! (My friend: "Well, I guess he saw me type it in enough that he figured it out.") A few simple steps can potentially save you a lot of money; it's always a good idea to know how your device is being used and for what you are and are not required to pay.

Configuring Synchronization Options

Synchronizing your device has two benefits. The first is that you can access your files online or from your device. The second is that it provides a backup of your files in case you need to restore your device. Ideally, you'll never need to use the second option, but having backups of your important data is always important.

iPhones and iPads can sync to iCloud on the Internet or iTunes on a desktop or laptop computer. To use iCloud, manage all setup and configuration options through Settings ➢ *your account* ➢ iCloud, as shown in Figure 3.32.

FIGURE 3.32 iCloud configuration

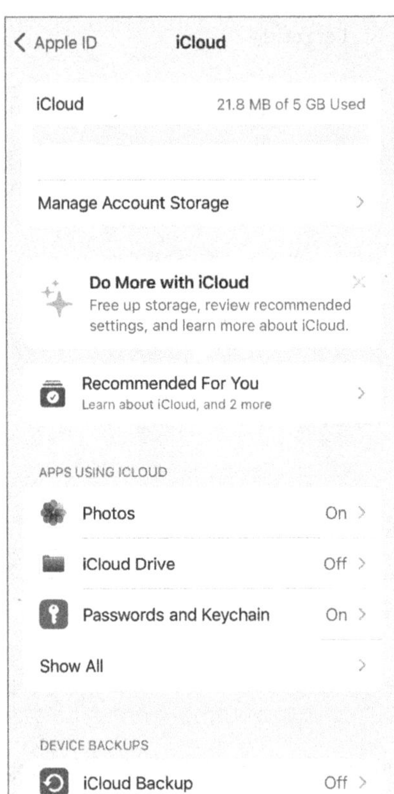

Figure 3.33 shows the sync summary of the iTunes app on a desktop computer. To get to this screen, you need to have the device plugged in. Then, click the icon that looks like a phone near the upper-left corner or in the top menu bar.

Within this app, you can see the summary or configure synchronization options for individual types of media or apps. You can also set the backup options to back up to iCloud or the local computer. The choice comes down to whatever is more convenient for you. There are additional options on this page, such as to sync automatically when the phone is connected and to sync over Wi-Fi.

Setting up sync is easy within Android as well. Go to Settings ➢ Accounts And Backup, as shown in Figure 3.34. Your options here will vary depending on your device; for this example, I tapped Back Up Data under Google Drive (Figure 3.35). Here you can see how much space you have used as well as configure what you want to back up. All of your data will be synced to Google Drive.

FIGURE 3.33 iTunes sync

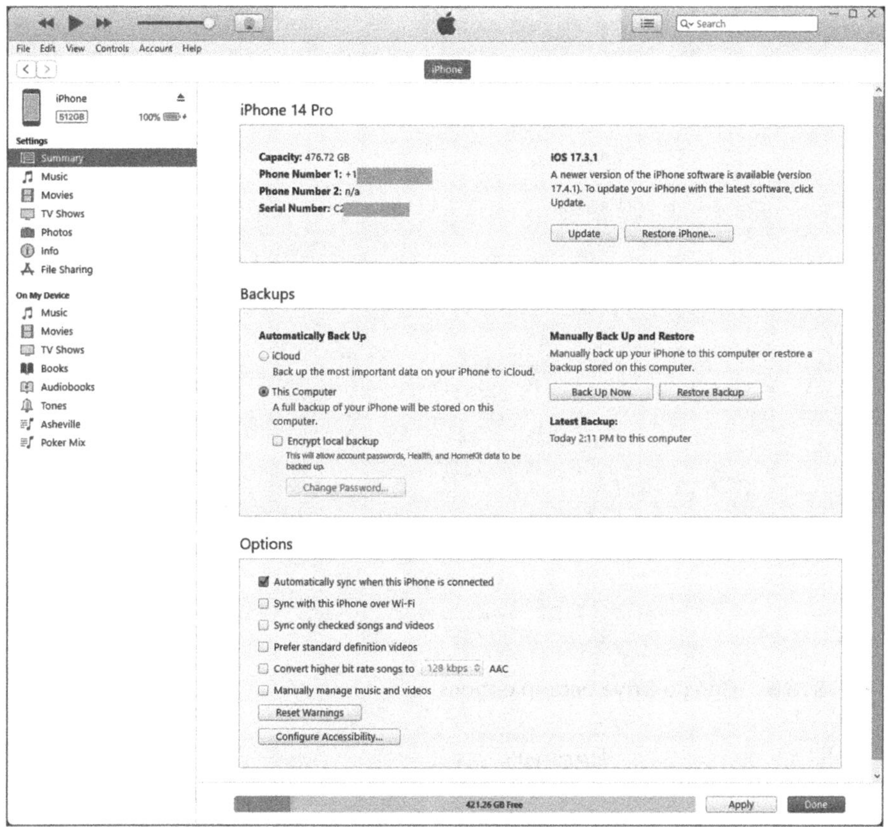

If you can't afford to (or don't want to) lose the pictures, videos, music, texts, or whatever else on your phone, be sure to back it up, regardless of the method you choose!

Exploring E-readers

An *e-reader* is a device similar to a tablet in size but optimized for reading digital books, magazines, and newspapers. The main characteristics that differentiate an e-reader from a tablet are the type of display, smaller onboard storage, and longer battery life.

Most e-readers use a technology called electrophoretic ink, or E Ink, which is a proprietary type of electronic paper. Although E Ink is available in color, many consider its best applications to be in grayscales or pure black and white. While e-readers might not look as fancy as tablets, there are two clear advantages of E Ink displays:

FIGURE 3.34 Accounts And Backup on Android

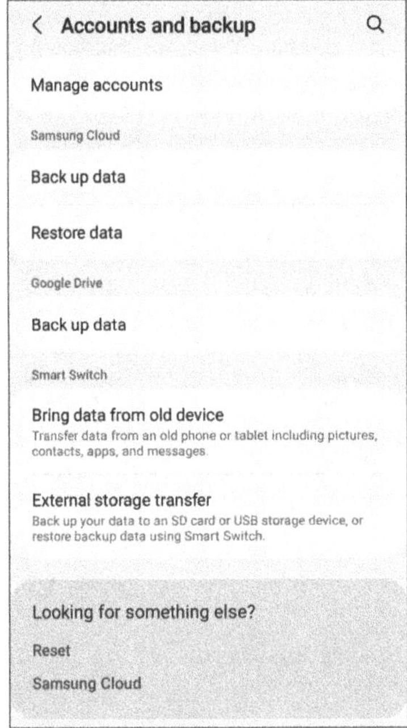

FIGURE 3.35 Google Drive backup options

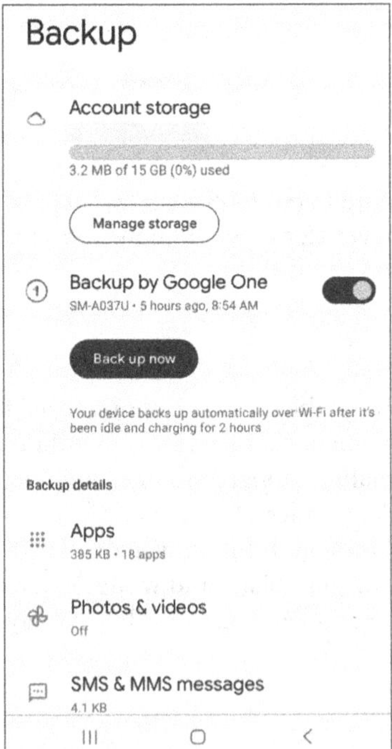

- Lower energy use than other LCD displays, which greatly prolongs battery life; many e-readers can go several weeks between charges.
- Much easier to read in bright conditions, such as sunlight.

Although the term *E Ink* is used to discuss a general technology, the term is a trademark of E Ink Holdings, Inc. (`www.eink.com`). E Ink is also marketed under the name Vizplex. Other competitors exist in this field, but Vizplex products lead the market.

The most popular e-reader is the Amazon Kindle, shown in Figure 3.36. Others include the Kobo Clara, Onyx Boox, and Barnes & Noble Nook. Specifications differ by manufacturer and model, but generally speaking, e-readers have a 6″ to 10″ touch screen, 8 GB to 64 GB storage, Wi-Fi connectivity (and maybe cellular as well), and weigh 6 oz to 8 oz. Some relatively common features are a built-in web browser, a backlight for reading in dim-light settings, and a microSD memory card reader. Most e-readers have a filesystem that allows users to store their titles in folders. (Kobo calls them shelves.) Users either subscribe to a service for a certain amount of monthly content, or they pay for each item that they choose to download.

FIGURE 3.36 A basic Kindle e-reader

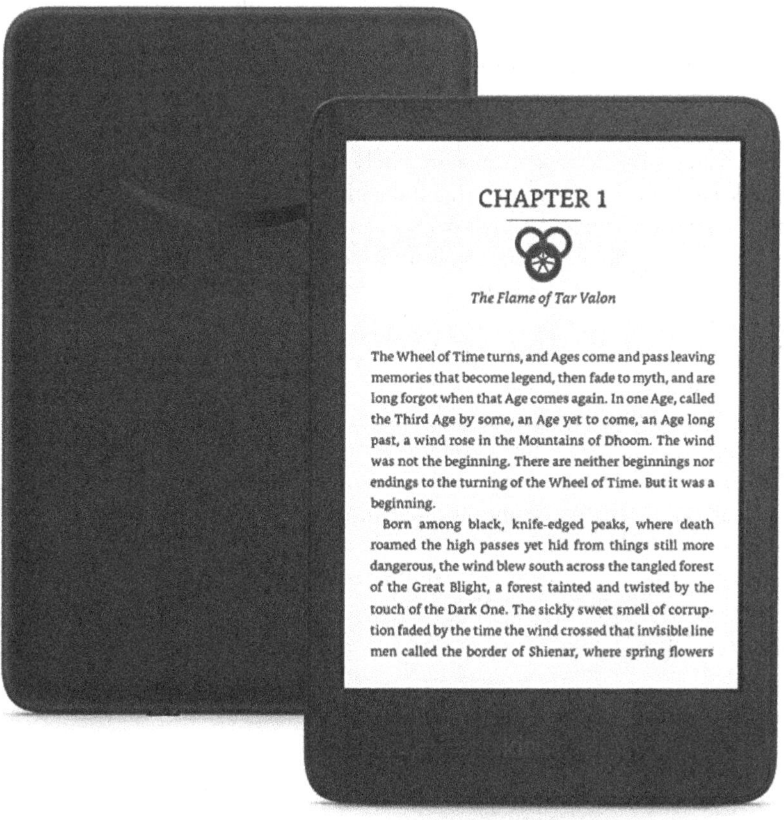

Based on market sales data, it would appear that the e-reader peak was in about 2011. Since then, sales have slowly declined, possibly due to the overlap between tablets and e-readers. Tablets with e-reader apps give the user much more flexibility than a simple e-reader. E-readers are much less expensive, though, and they fill a specific niche for those who read a lot.

Understanding Augmented and Virtual Reality

Without a doubt, augmented and virtual reality have been two of the hottest topics in computing technology in the 2020s. Advances in cloud technology have enabled both augmented and virtual reality to explode in popularity and enter mainstream lexicon. So what are the differences between the two, and what types of devices are needed to enable them? Let's take a look.

Augmented Reality

The idea behind *augmented reality* is that it, based on its name, enhances or modifies a user's current reality. It doesn't remove the user from reality, but rather adds something to it to help inform or entertain the user.

For example, let's say a person wearing eyeglasses with augmented reality is walking down the sidewalk in a busy traffic area and approaches an intersection. The augmented reality system may produce a warning on the inside of the glasses lens, where the person can read it, stating that this intersection is particularly dangerous and has a lot of vehicle-pedestrian accidents. Having been forewarned, the person can now exercise special care prior to crossing.

People who watch live sporting events are likely familiar with augmented reality too. Football broadcasts will show a yellow line indicating where the ball needs to go for a first down. Hockey games can track the puck with lines showing where it went from and to. In baseball games, a replay can show the angle and speed of a pitch or the path of a home run and how quickly it left the bat. All of these overlays on top of the game are examples of augmented reality.

And let's not forget gaming. Pokémon Go was released in 2016 and became incredibly popular. The idea was you would track down a Pokémon using a map on your phone. Once you got to the physical location you would hold your smartphone up, using its camera to identify the surroundings, "find" the Pokémon (it would appear on your screen), overlayed on the real background your camera lens was viewing (such as in Figure 3.37), and capture it for your collection. Of course, no mythical creature was ever physically present. Non-players would just see groups of people with their smartphones extended arms-length in front of their faces, wandering obliviously into cross-traffic. I sort of joke about the last part, but it did cause some problems, including traffic accidents and people venturing alone into secluded locations late at night.

FIGURE 3.37 Pokémon Go

Source: Delphotostock / Adobe Stock

Finally, there are social media and commerce applications. In social media, augmented reality filters can add features such as stars or flowers to your face or hair, distort your face shape or facial features into something more exotic, or even let you see what you would look like as a pickle. Companies use augmented reality too, to simulate you interacting with their products in the store, or aid in visualizing what a piece of furniture will look like in your room.

When you take the Tech+ exam, you should be able to explain augmented reality and virtual reality devices and their purposes.

For augmented reality to work, the end user typically doesn't need specialized, fancy hardware. All that's really required is a screen on which to project an image. The screen can be a smartphone, a television, eyeglasses, or a head's up display on the inside of a vehicle windshield. Some augmented reality experiences provide audio as well; speakers of some sort would be required in those situations.

Virtual Reality

As opposed to augmented reality, *virtual reality (VR)* creates an artificial environment for the user and completely immerses them in it. To experience VR, a user dons a pair of VR goggles or a *VR headset*, which displays images close to their eyes and blocks out all other light. The images create a 3D world which the user can navigate.

VR headsets got their start in 2012, when the newly formed Oculus company started a Kickstarter project to develop the Oculus VR. Early prototypes showed great promise, and in

2014 Facebook purchased Oculus. The Oculus Rift hit the markets in 2016 and was popular enough that Oculus had product shortages. Today, the most popular VR headsets include the Meta Quest, Apple Vision, Valve Index, ByteDance Pico, Sony PS VR, HP Reverb, and HTC Vive Pro. Figure 3.38 shows the Mega Quest 3 with its two handheld controllers.

FIGURE 3.38 Meta Quest 3

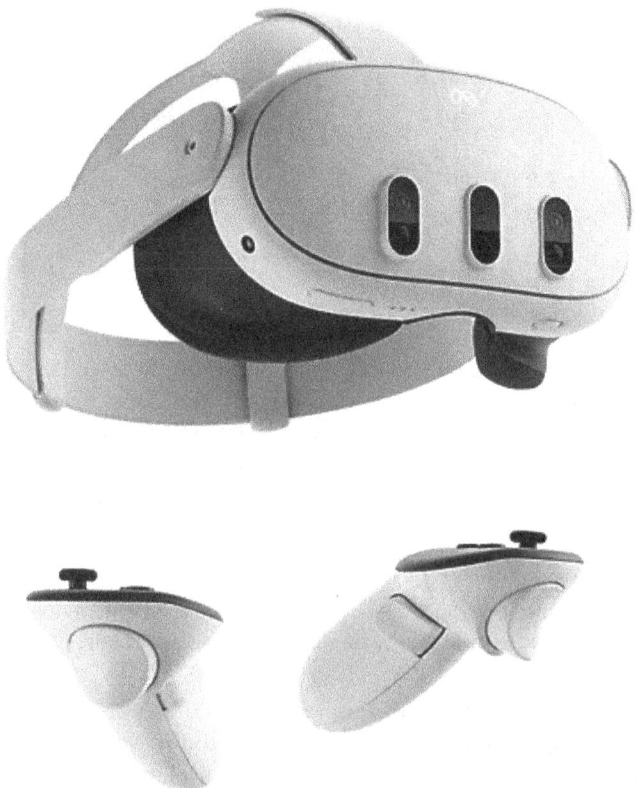

There are two common types of VR headsets—those that connect to a computer or gaming system, and those that use a smartphone as the screen. Computer-based headsets have a fairly high hardware requirement, mostly due to the intensive video processing that takes place. Table 3.2 shows the Meta Quest 3 specifications as an example.

The Quest 3 itself has two 4K OLED displays providing 2064 × 2208 resolution per eye at a 90 Hz refresh rate, a 110-degree field of view, 128 GB or 512 GB storage, and integrated headphones for 3D audio. It also has embedded sensors that allow for positional and rotational tracking, which can detect the position of a wearer's head within a millimeter. Nearly all systems also come with a handheld game controller or two to allow users to interact with the game.

TABLE 3.2 Meta Quest 3 hardware requirements

Component	Minimum	Recommended
Processor	Intel i5 / AMD Ryzen 5 1500x	Intel i7 / AMD Ryzen 7
Graphics Card	NVIDIA GeForce GTX 1070+ / AMD 400 Series+	NVIDIA RTX 20 series / AMD Radeon RX 6000 series
Memory	8 GB	16 GB DDR4
USB Ports	1x	1x USB-C
Operating System	Windows 10 or 11	Windows 10 or 11

Smartphone-based VR headsets are essentially a head strap with a phone carrier and blinders on the sides to block out light. Users snap their phone into the carrier, which they place on their head. It provides similar effects to a stand-alone headset, but the quality is generally regarded as inferior to PC- or gaming console–based systems.

Business applications are being developed for VR as well. For example, a store employee could use VR to navigate through shelves to learn the layout of a new store, or engineers can inspect their designs in three dimensions. Other applications, such as medical and other types of hands-on training, are easily within reach.

Exploring Gaming Consoles

Video games and computers enjoy a beautiful, symbiotic relationship. While it's true that video games wouldn't exist without some sort of computing device, the computer industry has definitely benefited from gaming. Game developers are constantly pushing the boundaries of technology, driving advances in video processing power and network speed. Gamers seek more realism, requiring not only better video but faster processors and giant caches of memory. Databases, spreadsheets, and other business applications are all important, but none fuel passion like video games do.

A *gaming console* is a computer with a single, specialized purpose: to play games. To facilitate this, consoles have a special input device, called a *controller*, as opposed to a traditional computer keyboard and mouse. Gaming consoles today also allow users to do things such as surf the web and play movies on Blu-ray or DVD, so really they're a multipurpose entertainment device. But don't be fooled—their primary function is to serve up a state-of-the-art gaming experience.

In the next two sections, I'll take you through a quick history of home video game consoles and then compare and contrast some current systems.

A Quick History of Gaming Consoles

As you learned in Chapter 2, the general-purpose computer has been around since the 1940s. So, perhaps it's a bit of a surprise to learn that gaming consoles didn't come into existence until the 1970s.

The first generation of home gaming consoles debuted in 1972 with the Magnavox Odyssey. It was a pretty simple device that used a home television for display (a practice that continues today), had very simple controllers with a few dials and a button, but didn't have any sound. Players would put a plastic overlay on the television screen for visuals and use their controllers to move a dot around on the screen (this was all monochrome, mind you) in some relationship to those visuals. Some games also used traditional board game components such as dice or play money. It might not sound like much, but it was quite the technological marvel.

Modeled after table tennis, Pong was the first home-based gaming console that went mainstream. Even today, it's considered a cult classic. Released for home use in 1975, it was monochrome and primitive. Figure 3.39 shows you what the game looked like. It featured two electronic paddles, a ball and a net, and the score at the top.

FIGURE 3.39 Pong

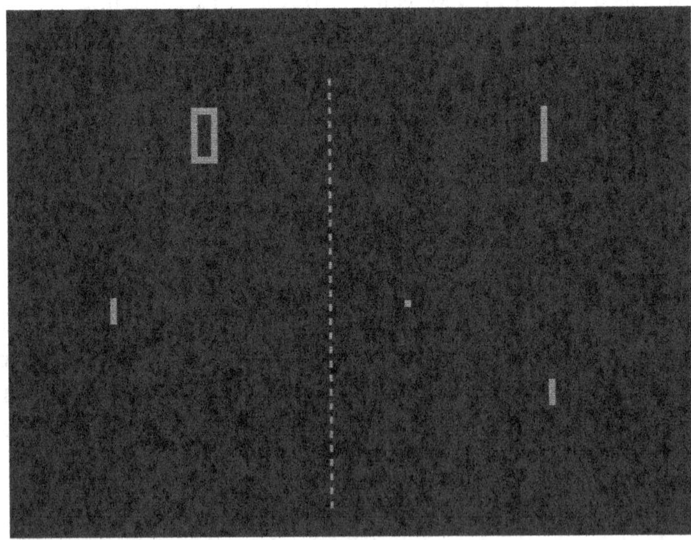

Source: Bumm13 / Wikimedia Commons / Public domain.

In the late 1970s and early 1980s, things really took off. Color graphics and sound were introduced. Controllers became more sophisticated, and games became more complex. Big names in the industry included Atari, ColecoVision, Nintendo, and Sega. The Nintendo Entertainment System, released in 1983, was the first incredibly popular console, selling nearly 62 million units. It was supported by an 8-bit processor, but it did not have any onboard RAM.

In the early 1990s, Nintendo was still the dominant player, although there were a large number of competitors. Sony released the PlayStation in 1994, and that quickly took over market dominance. After that, most competitors started dropping out. The next big entrant into the category was the Microsoft Xbox in 2001. The Nintendo Wii came out in 2006, which was novel because its controller could also detect player movements in three directions.

Current Gaming Consoles

Today, you will occasionally see off brands of video game consoles, but they are vastly inferior to the top ninth-generation consoles in the market. Really, there are three names to know: Sony, Microsoft, and Nintendo.

Gaming consoles are listed in Tech+ objective 2.1. Be able to explain some devices and their purposes.

Sony's PlayStation series and Microsoft's Xbox line battle it out for the action, adventure, and sports game market, but they both offer a variety of game types. Both of these units use a television as their display devices. The Nintendo Switch (released in 2017) is a smaller, handheld unit that has its own, smaller screen, but it can also be plugged into a television using an HDMI cord. Table 3.3 lists some of the performance characteristics of the latest consoles.

TABLE 3.3 Gaming console specifications

Component	PlayStation 5	Xbox Series X	Nintendo Switch OLED
CPU	3.5 GHz 8-core AMD Zen 2	3.8 GHz 8-core AMD Zen 2	1.267 GHz NVIDIA Tegra X1
GPU performance	10.28 teraflops	12 teraflops	1 teraflop
Display	N/A	N/A	7.0″ multitouch OLED touchscreen, 1280 × 720
RAM	16 GB	16 GB GDDR6	4 GB
Storage	825 GB SSD	1 TB NVMe SSD	64 GB SSD
Optical drive	4k Ultra HD Blu-ray	4K Ultra HD Blu-ray	N/A
Network	Gigabit Ethernet, Wi-Fi, Bluetooth	Gigabit Ethernet, Wi-Fi	Wi-Fi, Bluetooth
Ports	HDMI, 1x USB-C, 2x USB 3.1, 1x USB 2.0-A	HDMI, optical audio-out, 3x USB 3.1 Gen 1	HDMI, USB-C, microSD card, Switch game card
Weight	9.9lbs	9.8lbs	0.71lbs

Video Card Performance

It's common to see video card performance measured in terms of teraflops. A *teraflop* is one trillion floating-point operations per second. (*Flop* is shorthand for floating-point operations; it refers to how many math calculations can be done per second with floats, or real numbers that include decimals. *Floats* are covered more in-depth in Chapter 6, "Software Development.") Essentially, video game displays are composed of an array of polygons. Higher resolutions use more, smaller polygons in the same amount of space. A video card that's more powerful can move around more polygons faster than a less-powerful version.

You can see in Table 3.3 that the Switch has a lot less power, but remember, it's a handheld device with a built-in display similar to a large smartphone. The other two, as you can tell from their specifications, are as powerful as desktop computers.

Understanding the Internet of Things

Throughout this chapter, I've explained various types of computing devices that you will encounter. It's certainly not an exhaustive list. I'm sure that you can think of more types of devices, such as GPS systems, smartwatches, fitness monitors, and a host of others. What if we took it even one step further, though, and said that anything that uses power could be considered a device? Furthermore, all of those devices could be connected to each other and be in constant communication. That might sound amazing or terrifying or even a little bit of both. But that's what the Internet of Things promises to deliver.

The *Internet of Things (IoT)* is the network of devices that are able to communicate with each other and exchange data, and it's one of the hottest topics in computing today. The term *things* is rather loosely defined. A thing can be a hardware device, software, data, or even a service. It can be something like a jet engine, or it can be multiple sensors on the fan, motor, and cooling systems of that engine. The key is that these things are able to collect data and transmit it to other things. In this section on the IoT, I'll start with a quick history. Then, I'll talk about home and commercial applications and finish with potential issues.

A Brief History of the Internet of Things

The concept of IoT has been around for nearly four decades. Lore has it that the first "smart device" was a Coke machine on the campus of Carnegie Mellon University, in Pittsburgh, Pennsylvania, in 1982. The machine was outfitted with sensors that could detect when it needed to be refilled and when drinks were cold. While useful, it hardly sparked a technological revolution.

Throughout the next two decades, smart computer people wrote white papers about the possibilities and conducted limited experiments. But still, there was no revolution. The term

Internet of Things was coined in 1999, even though the concept was still relatively undeveloped. The idea was, if objects and people had sensors, computers could collect and store the information and possibly even make recommendations, such as refill the Coke machine!

In the 1990s, the most popular idea of how to implement the IoT was to embed a sensor, such as a *radio-frequency identification (RFID)* tag, in all produced items. Clearly there were some limitations to this approach. Embedding tags in all manufactured items could become incredibly expensive, and who would pay for it and why?

Fast-forward to around 2012, when the technological landscape had drastically changed. Devices had become smaller and less expensive to produce. Broadband Internet was common, and global cellular communications were nearly instantaneous. Technology was finally ready for the concept, and IoT started to take off.

IoT-enabled devices can communicate using a variety of methods, such as Wi-Fi, Bluetooth, near-field communication (NFC), networks over power lines, cellular, and satellite.

In 2024, it's estimated that there were between 15 billion to 17 billion IoT-enabled devices in the world. Estimates for growth vary, but some say that by 2030, that number could be between 30 billion and 50 billion. But what are all of these devices and what do they do? Let's explore some uses for IoT (besides the Coke machine).

Consumer Uses

Thus far, most IoT-enabled devices have been produced for consumer use. The concept seems pretty useful—multiple devices in your home are IoT-enabled, and you control them regardless of where you are. Did you go to work and forget to turn the lights off? No problem. You can do it from your phone. Did someone just ring your doorbell? See who it is and talk to them in real time through your phone as well.

Notice that I mentioned controlling devices from your phone twice now; let's dive into that a bit deeper. One option to control IoT devices would be for each device to have its own app—and indeed many of them do—and you have to open a dozen different apps to control 12 different devices. That would be frustrating at best, and the poor consumer experience would turn users off. Instead, IoT devices on a home network will all be controlled through a central coordinating device, which a user can access through one app on their smartphone.

In years past, companies would make dedicated devices solely intended to control IoT. Now, IoT control functions are built into home assistant devices to make life easier. The most popular *home assistants* are Amazon Echo (aka Alexa), Google Nest ("Hey, Google"), and Apple HomePod ("Hey, Siri"). They are voice-controlled devices that can help with a myriad of things, such as setting reminders, reading emails, playing music, and of course managing IoT devices. Some controllers look vaguely like a hockey puck that sits on your counter, and others have fancy touchscreen displays and can either sit on a counter with a stand or be mounted on a wall. They basically look like a small tablet computer. An Amazon Echo Hub is shown in Figure 3.40.

FIGURE 3.40 Amazon Echo Hub home assistant

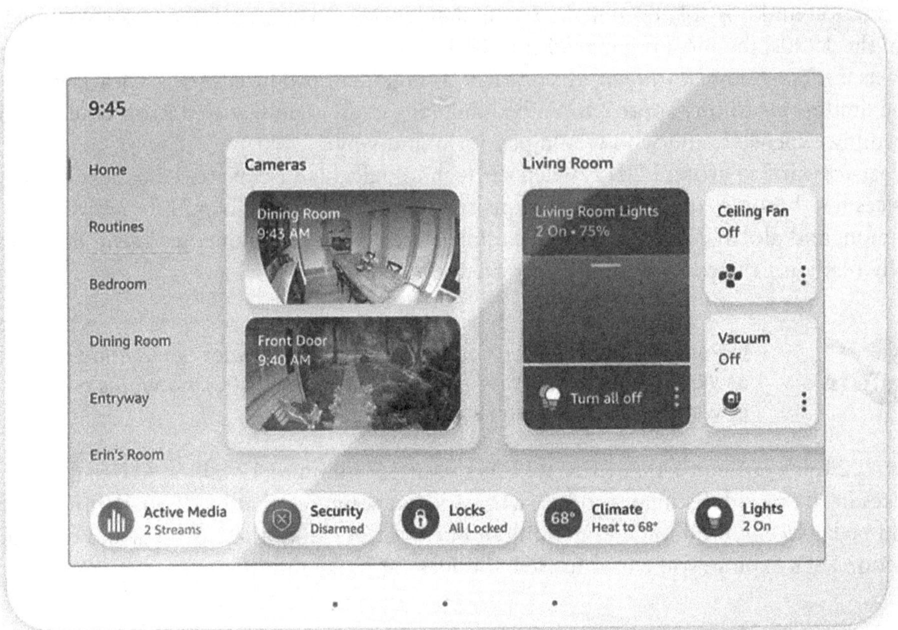

When purchasing an IoT device, one of the biggest considerations needs to be its compatibility with the controlling device. Let's take a look at a few specific examples of IoT devices.

Household Uses

Most of us have a lot of electronics in our home. We have televisions, computers, major appliances, and even toasters and blenders. Anything with electrical circuitry can be turned into a thing for the IoT and made into part of a "smart home" setup. If you can think of a use for a home automation device, odds are that one exists. Here are some IoT applications in use today:

Home Entertainment Systems Home entertainment is definitely the largest segment of IoT devices on the market today. Most new high-definition televisions are smart TVs with built-in wireless networking and the ability to connect to streaming services such as Netflix, Hulu, YouTube, or FuboTV. Other audio and video equipment will often have built-in networking and remote-control capabilities as well.

Not all smart TVs are really that smart, and large televisions are definitely not portable. For people who want to take their entertainment with them, there are streaming media devices. Examples include Roku, Amazon Fire, Apple TV, Chromecast, and NVIDIA

SHIELD. Some are small boxes, like the Roku Ultra, while others look like flash drives; all will have a remote control. Each has different strengths. For example, Amazon Prime customers will get a lot of free content from the Amazon Fire, and NVIDIA SHIELD has the best gaming package. If you're interested in one of these devices, it's best to do some research to see which one best fits your lifestyle and needs. Nearly all of these devices will have USB connections, and many of the box-type ones will also have a digital video connection such as HDMI. Figure 3.41 shows a Roku Ultra and Amazon Fire stick, both of which support 4K TV.

FIGURE 3.41 Roku Ultra and Amazon Fire

Heating and Cooling Programmable thermostats that allow you to set the temperature based on time and day have been around for more than 30 years. The next step in the evolution is a smart thermostat that's remotely accessible and that can do some basic learning based on the weather and your preferences. Figure 3.42 shows a smart thermostat. Popular brands include Google Nest, Amazon Smart, ecobee, LG, and Honeywell.

Home Appliances Do you want your refrigerator to tell you when you're out of milk? Or even better yet, do you want to have it automatically add milk to the grocery list on your smartphone? Perhaps your refrigerator can suggest a recipe based on the ingredients inside of it. Appliances like this exist today, and they are slowly becoming more popular. Other examples include smart washing machines, clothes dryers, and ovens.

Small appliances can be part of the IoT as well, if properly equipped. You could control your smart coffee maker (like the one in Figure 3.43) from bed, starting it when you get up in the morning. Even toasters or blenders can be made into smart devices. It will all depend on the consumer demand.

FIGURE 3.42 ecobee smart thermostat

FIGURE 3.43 Café smart coffee maker

Tech+ exam objective 2.1 lists quite a few IoT devices that you need to be able to explain the purposes of. The ones covered in this Household Uses section include home appliances, home automation devices such as thermostats, security systems, deadbolts/door locks, and video doorbells, IP security cameras, and streaming media devices. Of course, don't forget home assistants as well, which were covered earlier in the Consumer Uses section.

Security Systems While home entertainment is currently the biggest market for smart home devices, smart security systems is a massive market as well. Some systems require professional installation, whereas others are geared toward the do-it-yourself market. Many require a monitoring contract with a security company. Popular names include Ring, Vivint, Adobe Home Security, ADT Pulse, and SimpliSafe.

While specific components will vary, most systems have a combination of a *video doorbell* camera (such as Amazon Ring) and other *Internet Protocol (IP) security cameras*, deadbolts or door locks, motion sensors, gas and smoke detectors, garage door openers, lighting controls, a centralized management hub, and touchscreen panels. Of course, you are able to control them from your phone as well.

If you don't want to get an entire security system, you can buy systems to control the lights in your house. You can also get smart wall outlets that replace your existing ones, which enable you to turn devices plugged into them on or off, as well as monitor energy usage.

Other Consumer Uses

Smart home devices receive the most publicity, but consumer applications go beyond the home as well. A few other popular examples are modern vehicles and fitness-monitoring devices.

Vehicles, medical devices, exercise equipment, and wearable devices are subobjectives in exam objective 2.1. Be sure to understand the use of each type of device.

Modern Vehicles Thirty years ago, vehicles were entirely controlled through mechanical means. The engine powered the crankshaft, which provided torque to rotate the wheels. When you turned the steering wheel, a gear system turned the wheels in the proper direction. There were even these nifty little handles you could turn that would lower and raise the windows.

Not today. While there are clearly still some mechanical systems in vehicles—most still have gas engines, for example—the vehicles made today are controlled through an elaborate network of computers. These computers determine how much gas to give the engine based on how hard you press the accelerator, how far to turn the wheels when you crank the steering wheel, and how fast to slow down when you hit the brakes. They can even do smarter things, such as transfer power to certain wheels in slippery conditions, sense how hard it's raining to adjust the wiper speed, and warn you if there is a car in your blind spot. Many drivers love their GPS systems, and these are integrated too. Other new enhancements to vehicles include collision avoidance systems, adaptive cruise control, automated parallel parking, interactive video displays, and more.

While much of this innovation is great, it can make cars more expensive to fix if components in this network break. It can also make them susceptible to hackers, who could get in remotely through the GPS, entertainment, or communications systems.

Over the last few years, you've probably seen articles on self-driving cars that Uber, Google, Tesla, and others are working on. Set aside for a second the question of whether this a good development or not; this is only possible thanks to the Internet of Things.

Real World Scenario

Hacking Your Vehicle

Most modern vehicles are basically computer networks, and with their communications, navigation, and entertainment systems, they connect to the outside world. And ever since computer networks have existed, someone has tried to hack them. Vehicles are no exception.

While the odds of having your vehicle hacked are pretty low, the effects could be disastrous. Hackers could shut your engine off on the interstate or render your brakes inoperable.

Auto manufacturers are of course aware of the threats, and have taken steps to reduce the chances of a successful attack. Know that it's still a possibility, though. If you do an Internet search, you can find several articles related to vehicle hacking. One such example is `www.wired.com/2015/07/hackers-remotely-kill-jeep-highway`.

Fitness and Health Devices Fitness and health is a big industry, and making the devices IoT-compatible was just a matter of time. Initially, it was mostly the small, *wearable devices* such as fitness trackers that made it into the IoT. Popular brands included Fitbit, Garmin, Polar, Apple Watch, and Jawbone.

Then as the inevitable progress came, small wearable devices also took on functions of previously stand-alone medical devices, such as heart rate and blood sugar monitors. There's no sense in wearing two devices when one watch can count your steps and make sure your heart is beating properly, right?

The most recent development has been the creation of IoT-enabled exercise equipment. Adding smart capabilities and Wi-Fi connectivity to something like a treadmill that already had a display was a no-brainer. But newer, more inventive devices have popped up as well, such as smart exercise mirrors that display your workout program and monitor your movements to ensure you're doing them properly.

Protecting Your Information

With how important data security is, you are probably familiar with the term *personally identifiable information (PII)*. Companies that collect and store PII need to enact controls to ensure that your personal data is safe. As we all know, though, hackers do manage to compromise this information from time to time.

There's a subset of PII called *personal health information (PHI)*, which specifically governs the collection and protection of your personal health data. PHI is safeguarded in the United States under the *Health Insurance Portability and Accountability Act (HIPAA)* of 1996. Medical facilities and personnel need to take appropriate actions to keep health information private. Many other countries have similar laws. Fitness and health monitors are typically *not* subject to HIPAA nor are there PHI requirements. What this means for you is, when using IoT devices or apps that may collect your health information, it is your individual responsibility to protect it as appropriate.

Commercial Uses

Any number of industries can benefit from interconnected devices. If you are out and about, take a few minutes to just look around at the variety of equipment and electronics in use today. It's something that we rarely take the time to observe, but when you look for opportunities to embed sensors or other data collection components into things, you can find quite a few. This section explores examples for a few industries.

Medical Devices

The medical industry is full of equipment. If you've been to a hospital or clinic, the amount of machinery they have is pretty impressive. While there have been strides in interoperability, not all of the machines can talk to each other or react if something goes wrong.

Further, medical applications can be extended outside of the medical facility. Critical electronics such as pacemakers can be connected to a smart system, and patients can wear other devices that monitor their vital signs, such as heart rate and blood pressure. The readings can be transmitted back to an office and recorded and monitored. If something appears to be wrong, an application on the hospital computer can show an alert, notifying the medical professional of a problem. In this way, medical professionals can efficiently keep an eye on many people at once.

Manufacturing

Manufacturing plants have become heavily automated over the last few decades. Robots can do a lot of work, but historically, robots haven't been very smart. They do what they are programmed to do; if something goes wrong, they aren't able to adjust. For maintenance personnel, tracking down the problem can often be tedious and time-consuming. The IoT can greatly help here as it enables artificial intelligence (AI). You'll learn more about AI in Chapter 9.

Sensors built into machines can monitor production rates. If a component in the machine starts to wear down or fails, the technician will know immediately what to fix. Ideally, the technician will even be able to fix it before it breaks, because the technician can tell that the part is wearing down and will fail soon. Other sensors can be attached to pallets of raw materials or produced goods, enabling instantaneous tracking of the quantity and location of inventory. Finally, perhaps a manufacturing plant has several different lines of products. A smart system could increase or decrease production on the appropriate lines based on real-time customer demand.

Transportation

Earlier in this chapter, I mentioned self-driving personal vehicles. But what about self-driving semi-trucks? That's been done too. The first trip (that I know of) was completed in October 2016, with a self-driving truck delivering a trailer of beer on a 120-mile trip in Colorado. In early 2018, Embark, an autonomous trucking company, completed a 2,400-mile trip from California to Florida. There was a human driver on board, but the truck essentially completed the route on its own.

Another application could be in traffic signals. Have you ever waited at a red light for what seemed like forever, when there was no traffic coming from the cross direction? Some traffic signals do have sensors to detect the presence of cars, but not all do. If you take that one step further, sensors can monitor traffic to determine where there is congestion and then make recommendations to GPS systems to reroute vehicles onto a better path.

Finally, there are applications such as being able to set variable speed limits based on road conditions, electronic tolls, and safety and road assistance. Dozens of states use electronic toll collection systems. Users sign up and place a small transponder in or on their car. When they drive through the toll, a sensor records the vehicle's presence and bills the driver. Electronic toll systems are paired with IP cameras to detect those who attempt to cheat the system. Examples of road assistance apps include OnStar, HondaLink, Toyota Safety Connect, and Ford Sync.

Infrastructure

In 2007, an interstate bridge in Minnesota filled with rush-hour traffic collapsed, sending cars, trucks, and a school bus plunging into the river below. Thirteen people were killed, and 145 more were injured. This tragic event is a signal that infrastructure isn't permanent and that it needs to be repaired and upgraded periodically.

The IoT can help here too. Sensors can be built into concrete and metal structures, sending signals to a controller regarding the stress and strain they are under. Conditions can be monitored, and the appropriate repairs completed before another tragedy strikes. Sensors can be built into buildings in earthquake-prone areas to help assess damage and safety. In a similar way, IoT-enabled sensors can monitor railroad tracks, tunnels, and other transportation infrastructure to keep conditions safe and commerce moving.

Energy production and infrastructure can be monitored by IoT devices as well. Problems can be detected in power grids before they fail, and smart sensors can regulate power production and consumption for economic or environmental efficiency.

Finally, some cities are becoming smart cities using IoT. Through the use of sensors and apps that residents can download, cities can track traffic flows, improve air and water quality, and monitor power usage. Residents can get some interesting benefits, such as knowing if the neighborhood park is busy or being able to search for an open parking space downtown.

Potential Issues

As you've learned, the IoT has a tremendous amount of potential for revolutionizing how people interact with the world around them, as well as how devices interact with each other. All of this potential upside comes with its share of potential challenges and issues as well. That's what I'll cover here.

Standards and Governance

As with the development of most new technologies, there is not one specific standard or governing body for the Internet of Things. There are about a dozen different technical standards being worked on. Most of them focus on different aspects of IoT, but there is some overlap between standards as well as gaps where no standards exist. For example, organizations such as the U.S. Food and Drug Administration (FDA) are working on an identification system for medical devices; the Institute of Electrical and Electronics Engineers (IEEE), the Internet Engineering Task Force (IETF), and the Open Connectivity Foundation (OCF) are all working on standards for communications and data transmissions.

In the smart home space, devices produced by different companies might or might not follow similar standards, meaning that interoperability can be challenging. Some people suggest that governments should get involved to enforce standards, while others think that's the worst idea possible.

Generally speaking, standards have a way of working themselves out over time. If you're old enough to remember video tapes and VCRs, there was the VHS versus Beta debates. If not, your friend Google can help. More recently in video there was the high-definition optical disc format war between Blu-ray and HD DVD. VHS and Blu-ray were the winners, and the other standards disappeared from use. Ideally you didn't spend money on a Beta tape or HD DVD player. Other examples are easy to come by, such as FireWire versus USB, Bluetooth versus Wi-Fi, or Oculus Rift versus SteamVR in virtual reality. How IoT will turn out is anyone's guess, but one or two technologies will likely emerge as the winners.

Data Security and Privacy

Two of the reasons that governance can be such a hot topic are data security and user privacy. Stories about Random Company X suffering a data breach are all too common today. And let's face it, the purpose of many IoT-related devices is to collect information about you and your behaviors. That raises some huge security and privacy concerns.

Security Vulnerabilities Create Risk

The vast majority of adults today carry at least one electronic device on them at all times, whether it be their smartphone, a smartwatch, or a fitness monitor. Because of how common they are and the potential benefits, a lot of kids have smartphones and smartwatches as well. One benefit is that parents can track their child's location using convenient apps such as Life360, GPS Location Tracker, Canary, and mSpy. One unintended consequence is that means other people might be able to as well.

In October 2017, a security flaw was exposed in certain smartwatches specifically made for children. The flaw allowed hackers to identify the wearer's location, listen in on conversations, and even communicate directly with the wearer. For most parents, the thought of a stranger having this kind of ability is horrifying.

No breach was ever reported with these devices, but the possibility is unsettling.

Although security and privacy may seem like the same thing, there are differences. Data security specifically refers to ensuring that confidentiality, availability, and integrity are maintained. In other words, it can't be accessed by anyone who's not supposed to access it, it's available when needed, and it's accurate and reliable. Privacy is related to the appropriate use of data. When you provide data to a company, the purposes for which it can be used should be specified. Also, this means that companies to whom you are giving data can't sell that data to another company unless you've given prior approval. I'll talk a lot more about these concepts in Chapter 10, "Security Concepts and Threats."

The point is, companies can and are gathering a lot of information about you, and the more connected things become, the more data they will receive. This information can be worth a lot to a company, either for their own purposes or for selling the information to others. Some of their motives are relatively harmless (if not annoying), such as sending you marketing information. But if a hacker has information showing that your entire family's fitness trackers are on vacation halfway across the country, they could have entirely different intentions in mind.

When agreeing to give your data to a company, be sure to understand the purposes for which it can be used. For example, a smart home company may be able to sell all of the data it gathers about you to whomever it chooses. How much of your behavioral information are you comfortable with other people knowing?

Data Storage and Usage

IoT-enabled devices generate data—a lot of data. Because of the massive quantities of data generated, most of it gets stored in some sort of cloud-based solution. Again, this poses potential security risks.

For companies, the question becomes what do they do with all of that data? Just because they have petabytes of data doesn't mean it will do them any good. But of course, data can be incredibly valuable. Companies that figure out how to mine the data and translate it effectively into actionable insights will be ahead of the curve as compared to their competitors.

Summary

This chapter compared and contrasted several common computing devices and described their purposes. First, you learned about servers and workstations and the roles they play on a network. Next, you learned about laptops and special ways of interacting with them.

After that, I transitioned into smaller mobile devices such as smartphones, tablets, and e-readers, and how to interact with a device that doesn't have the traditional computer input methods. Examples include tapping, swiping, and pinching, as well as the kinetic sensors built into the devices. You also learned about screen orientation and locking and security. Configuring external connections is important on mobile devices too. Most come readily equipped to handle cellular connections. Beyond that, you can configure Wi-Fi connections, Bluetooth pairing, and synchronization. Airplane mode is used to turn external connections off.

Next, you learned about augmented reality and virtual reality systems and gaming consoles. Augmented reality supplements existing reality with overlays or information, and virtual reality creates an entirely new existence. Most of the new consoles on the market are as powerful as a desktop computer and offer a multifaceted entertainment experience.

The last part of the chapter covered one of the hottest topics in IT today, the Internet of Things. After a brief history, you learned about consumer and commercial applications and finished with some areas of potential concern about which you should remain aware.

Exam Essentials

Understand the role of servers and workstations. Servers exist to provide services to other devices on a network. Workstations are systems that workers use to accomplish daily tasks.

Understand the unique methods that you can use to interact with mobile devices. Examples include tapping, swiping, and pinching, as well as interacting through the use of built-in kinetic sensors.

Understand the differences between tablets and e-readers. Tablets are often larger and have multicolor displays. E-readers are designed specifically for reading books and often are black-and-white only.

Know how to configure external connections on mobile devices. Most connections are configured through the Settings app. Examples include Wi-Fi, Bluetooth, synchronization, and Airplane mode.

Know how to turn off cellular connections quickly on your mobile device. This is accomplished by enabling Airplane mode.

Know where to get new apps for mobile devices. For iOS devices, use the App Store icon on the home screen. Android devices use the Google Play Store icon on the home screen.

Know the differences between augmented and virtual reality and the systems they use. Augmented reality adds something to existing reality by displaying visuals or information on a screen. The screen can be a smartphone, watch, television, the inside of a vehicle windshield, or other display device. Virtual reality creates an alternate immersive reality and requires the use of a special headset.

Understand the purpose of a gaming console. Gaming consoles are primarily used to play video games, although most can connect to the Internet and play Blu-ray or DVD movies.

Know some common consumer applications of the IoT. Home-based applications include home automation devices such as thermostats and security systems, home appliances, entertainment systems, and streaming media devices. Other uses include smart cars and fitness trackers.

Know some common commercial uses for the IoT. Medical devices, manufacturing, transportation, and infrastructure all benefit from IoT-enabled technologies.

Chapter 3 Lab

You can find the answers in Appendix A.

IT professionals need to know how to use a variety of devices in order to help clients fix issues properly. Even if you're not pursuing an IT career, knowing how to work with different devices and their operating systems can help you easily navigate through problems when you encounter something unfamiliar to you. After all, users do the same types of tasks on nearly all computers, regardless of the size or OS. The trick is to figure out how to do it on a system with which you are not as familiar. This lab will have you install the BlueStacks emulator on your computer and familiarize yourself with the Android operating system.

To install BlueStacks, visit `www.bluestacks.com` and click the Download button. Follow the prompts to install it on your computer. It will not damage the other operating system or other software on your computer. Once installed, you should have a BlueStacks icon on your desktop. Use that shortcut to launch Andy. Here are some questions for you to answer:

1. There are three buttons in the top toolbar, just to the right of the BlueStacks App Player title. What are they called and what do they do?
2. What's the easiest way to do a Google search?
3. How do you see the apps installed on this virtual device?
4. Where do you configure accessibility options for users with disabilities?
5. How do you quickly enable Airplane mode?
6. How do you change the screen orientation?
7. Install a new app of your choice. Was it easy or difficult? How do you launch the app? How do you delete the app icon from your home page? Does it delete the app?

Review Questions

You can find the answers in Appendix B.

1. Using an Android phone, you want to scroll down. What do you do to accomplish this?
   - A. Swipe up
   - B. Swipe down
   - C. Pinch fingers together
   - D. Start with pinched fingers and separate them
2. For which of the following tasks are gaming consoles not used? (Choose two.)
   - A. Playing video games
   - B. Editing Word documents
   - C. Watching a DVD
   - D. Creating a spreadsheet
3. Which motion while using an iPhone allows you to zoom in on a map?
   - A. Tap
   - B. Double tap
   - C. Pinch
   - D. Reverse pinch
4. You want a device to hold files for several users to access on a network. What type of device do you need?
   - A. File console
   - B. Tablet
   - C. Server
   - D. Workstation
5. Rachel is using her iPad to view pictures. She turns the iPad 90 degrees and the image turns as well. Which sensor allowed this to happen?
   - A. Accelerometer
   - B. Magnetometer
   - C. Turnometer
   - D. Gyroscope
6. Which type of IoT device is used to control the temperature in a home?
   - A. Thermostat
   - B. Security sytem
   - C. Home appliance
   - D. Command center

7. Francis is trying to change the settings on his iPhone. He opens the Settings app. In order to see them better, he turns his phone 90 degrees but nothing happens. What is the most likely cause?
   - A. The gyroscope is broken.
   - B. The Settings app does not support rotation.
   - C. He needs to enable app rotation in Settings first.
   - D. He needs to turn off the device and turn it back on to reset the rotation feature.
8. What is the term used that refers to connecting two Bluetooth devices together for communications?
   - A. Synching
   - B. Netting
   - C. Pairing
   - D. Partnering
9. Agi has an iPhone with a biometric scanner enabled. What methods can she use to unlock her phone?
   - A. Fingerprint only
   - B. Passcode only
   - C. Fingerprint or passcode
   - D. Fingerprint, passcode, or iris scan
10. Which of the following is a required hardware device to use augmented reality?
    - A. AR headset
    - B. Earbuds/headphones
    - C. Smartphone
    - D. Display
11. Your friend recently got a new Android phone and comes over to your house. What app does your friend use to set up a Wi-Fi connection with your wireless router?
    - A. Wi-Fi
    - B. Settings
    - C. Networking
    - D. Connections
12. Which one of the following devices is likely to have the least amount of storage space?
    - A. Smartphone
    - B. Laptop
    - C. Workstation
    - D. Server

13. You are setting up a new Wi-Fi connection on your Android phone. What step do you take after turning on Wi-Fi?
    - **A.** Verify wireless capabilities.
    - **B.** Enter the wireless password.
    - **C.** Verify the Internet connection.
    - **D.** Locate SSID.

14. You want to enable backups of your new iPhone. Which two options do you have? (Choose two.)
    - **A.** iDrive
    - **B.** iCloud
    - **C.** iTunes
    - **D.** iBackup

15. A pacemaker is an example of what type of IoT device?
    - **A.** Medical device
    - **B.** Home appliance
    - **C.** Security system
    - **D.** IP camera

16. Which of the following accurately describes what Airplane mode does on an iPhone?
    - **A.** Turns off the Wi-Fi connection
    - **B.** Turns off the Bluetooth connection
    - **C.** Turns off the cellular connection
    - **D.** Turns off all wireless connections

17. Which IoT device is typically paired with security systems?
    - **A.** Home appliance
    - **B.** IP camera
    - **C.** Vehicle
    - **D.** Thermostat

18. You need to find a new productivity app for your Android-based tablet. Where should you look?
    - **A.** iTunes
    - **B.** Google Drive
    - **C.** Google Apps
    - **D.** Google Play

19. An Xbox Series X is an example of which type of device?
    A. Laptop
    B. Tablet
    C. Gaming console
    D. Server

20. Rebecca wants to get a copy of the newest game she heard about for her iPad. Where should she go to find and download it?
    A. iTunes
    B. iApps
    C. iPlay
    D. Google Play

Operating Systems

THE FOLLOWING COMPTIA TECH+ FC0-U71 EXAM OBJECTIVES ARE COVERED IN THIS CHAPTER:

✓ **3.0 Applications and Software**

✓ **3.1 Identify components of an OS.**

- Filesystem characteristics
    - Compression
    - Encryption
    - Types and extensions
- File management
    - Folders/directories
    - Permissions
    - Naming restrictions
- System applications and utilities
- Services
- Processes
- Drivers
- Interfaces
    - Console/command line
    - Graphical user interface (GUI)
    - File attributes and properties

✓ **3.2 Explain the purpose of operating systems.**

- Interface between applications and hardware
- Disk management
- Task and process management
- Application management

- Device management
- Access control
- OS types
  - Mobile Device
  - Desktop/workstation
  - Server
  - Embedded

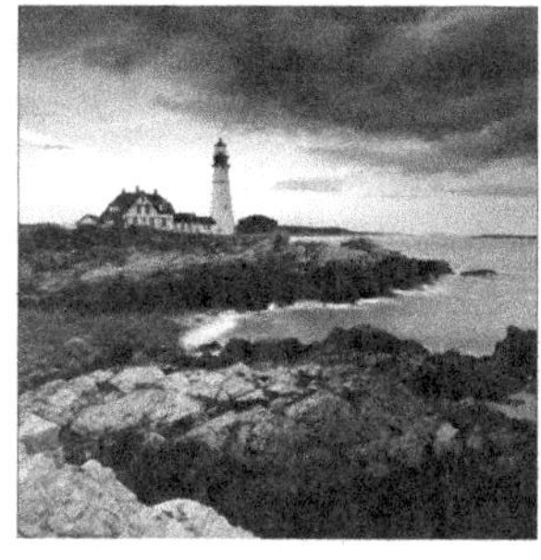

Computers are pretty much useless without software. A piece of hardware might just as well be used as a paperweight or doorstop unless you have an easy way to interface with it. Software provides that way. While there are many types of software, or programs, the most important application that you'll ever deal with is the operating system.

There are several types of operating systems on the market today, and each has its own unique functions and features. I'll cover four categories of important operating systems in this chapter. Even though they are all somewhat different and all complex, at the end of the day they all need to accomplish the same basic functions. I'll talk about what those functions are, types of operating systems, and a bit of history in the "Operating System Fundamentals" section of this chapter.

Finally, you need to know how to navigate through an operating system to make it work effectively for you. The "Managing an Operating System" section will give you an introduction to several interfaces and features of an operating system so that you know how to manage one. Then, you will learn how folders and files are structured, as well as how to manage that structure and execute programs. After reading this chapter, you should have a good fundamental understanding of what operating systems are and an appreciation for why they work the way they do.

Operating System Fundamentals

Before I begin discussing operating systems, it's important to take one step further back and talk about software in general. In computing, there are three major classifications of software that you will be dealing with: operating systems, applications, and drivers. Here's a description of each:

Operating System An *operating system (OS)* provides a consistent environment for other software to execute commands. Said another way, it provides an interface between applications and system hardware. The OS also gives users an interface with the computer so that they can send commands (input) and receive feedback or results (output). To do this, the OS must communicate with the computer hardware, as illustrated in Figure 4.1.

FIGURE 4.1 The operating system interacts with hardware.

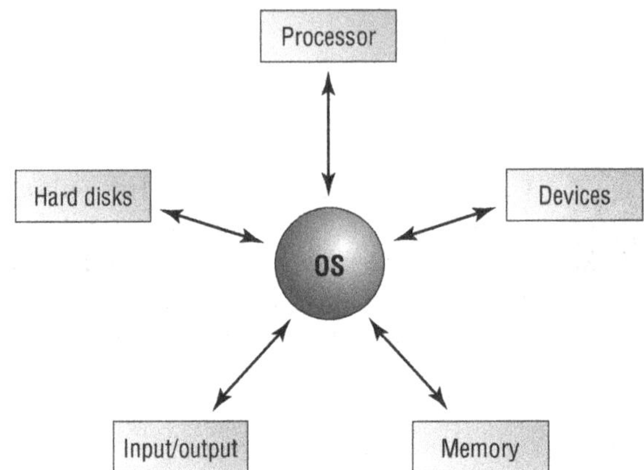

Once the OS has organized these basic resources, users can give the computer instructions through input devices (such as a keyboard or a mouse). Some of these commands are built into the OS, whereas others are issued through the use of applications. The OS becomes the center through which the system hardware, other software, and the user communicate; the rest of the components of the system work together through the OS, which coordinates their communication.

Application An *application* is a piece of software used to accomplish a particular task; it is written to supplement the commands available to a particular OS. Each application is specifically compiled (configured) for the OS on which it will run. Examples of applications include complex programs such as Microsoft Word and Google Chrome as well as simple programs such as a command-line file transfer program. I will cover applications in depth in Chapter 5, "Software Applications."

Driver A *driver* is an extremely specific application written for the purpose of instructing a particular OS on how to access a piece of hardware. Each hardware device, like a printer or network card, has unique features and configuration settings, and the driver allows the OS to understand properly how the hardware works and what it is able to do.

With those key software designations out of the way, let's take a trip back through time to understand where operating systems came from.

A Brief History of Operating Systems

First, I probably owe you a warning. You won't be quizzed on the history of operating systems on the CompTIA Tech+ exam. What you *will* be tested on is the basic functions of an operating system, the components of an operating system, and the different varieties on the market. The reason I want to take you through some history is that I believe it will give you some good perspective on *why* OSs do what they do and why there are so many, and perhaps some appreciation for them as well. So even though it won't be on the test, don't skip this part!

Pre-OS

Let's go back to the dawning of the computer age, about 1946. A few electronic "computers" had been developed by that time, and the U.S. government, in partnership with the University of Pennsylvania, announced the development of a machine named the Electronic Numerical Integrator and Computer (ENIAC). Like a lot of technology at the time, this one had the purpose of aiding the military. Among other projects, it helped calculate firing tables for artillery guns and also studied the feasibility of the nuclear bomb. It could do other things, though, and as such ENIAC is considered the first general-purpose electronic computer.

ENIAC was huge. Really huge. It was made up of nearly 18,000 vacuum tubes to go along with 70,000 resistors and 10,000 capacitors. It was 8 feet tall, 3 feet thick, and 100 feet long, weighing in at an impressive 27 tons. It consumed so much power that the joke was, when they turned it on, the power in the rest of Philadelphia dimmed. But it could run about 5,000 operations per second. Figure 4.2 shows a historical photo of this beast.

FIGURE 4.2 ENIAC

Source: Unknown author / U.S. Army Photo / Wikimedia Commons / Public domain.

In the introduction to this chapter, I said that hardware is useless without software, and ENIAC was no exception. It was "programmed" by switching out thousands of connections in the patch panel. Instructions on what the computer was supposed to do had to be written by hand and then transcribed to punch cards, which were fed into the machine. Output was produced on punch cards as well, which were fed into a separate IBM punch card reader to produce printed output. It could take a team of five technicians a week to program ENIAC, troubleshoot, find errors, and fix the problem so that the machine would produce the requested results. Clearly, improvements were needed.

By 1949, computers had memory. It wasn't much, and it was executed by using tubes filled with liquid mercury. Around the same time, other inventors were laying down the basic elements of programming languages. In 1952, the idea of reusable code (being able to run the same program multiple times with the same punch cards) surfaced. The assembler also appeared, which allowed programmers to write a command in a higher-level language, and it would be translated to assembly for the computer to take action.

Assembly code is a low-level programming language that corresponds to direct action that the computer needs to take. You'll learn more about this in Chapter 6, "Software Development."

These and other technological advancements started people on the path of developing the first operating system.

The Early Days

A group of IBM engineers put their heads together, and by 1954 they had developed the first computer programming language: Fortran. What Fortran allowed programmers to do was to create simple commands that told the computer (in assembly language) to execute several commands. It saved everyone a lot of time; simple programs could now be executed in just a few hours. Programmers started compiling multiple pieces of Fortran code together and sharing it with others, and the idea of a stable, consistent operating system started to gain traction.

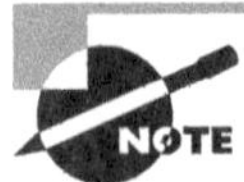

As old as it is, Fortran is still used today. Of course, revisions have been made over time to improve functionality. Fortran 2023 was released in November 2023.

Throughout the 1950s and 1960s, various companies (including IBM and Bell Labs) and universities (Massachusetts Institute of Technology, Manchester University, University of Michigan, University of California–Berkeley, and others) started developing their own compilations of code and giving them names. These were the first operating systems, and they were each designed to work with a specific model of computer.

Standardization

Operating systems of the time were slow and were not compatible with each other. In 1969, a group of engineers from Bell Labs came out with UNIX. By 1973, they had released the fourth edition of it, which had some big benefits. First, it was written in a newer programming language (called C), which was easier to deal with than Fortran. Second, it could work on different hardware platforms. Third, it was a lot faster than anything else on the market. By 1975, many universities (and their students) were using UNIX, and its growth spread quickly.

An interesting and hugely impactful note to the history of UNIX is that at the time, Bell Systems (which owned Bell Labs as well as the entire telephone infrastructure in the United States) was a regulated monopoly, so it couldn't get into the computer business. Therefore, since it couldn't make any money on UNIX, the company distributed it for free. Users were also free to make any modifications they wanted to the OS, which means that UNIX was *open source* code.

Open source versus commercial (closed-source/proprietary) code is still a matter of significant debate today. I'll get into that when I talk about different types of operating systems.

Through the late 1970s and early 1980s, operating systems were pretty basic. They had a command interpreter, the ability to load programs, and basic device drivers. That was until about 1981, when IBM introduced the first personal computer. With the IBM PC came the need for an easy-to-use operating system. The one that frequently got bundled with it? It was called MS-DOS, short for Microsoft Disk Operating System.

Pretty Pictures and Modern Operating Systems

Also, in 1981, Xerox introduced the Star workstation. It had the first window-based graphical user interface (GUI), mouse, and other conventions that we take for granted today like Internet access and email. But it never really got very popular. Figure 4.3 shows the basic interface, which feels strikingly familiar today.

FIGURE 4.3 The first PC graphical user interface

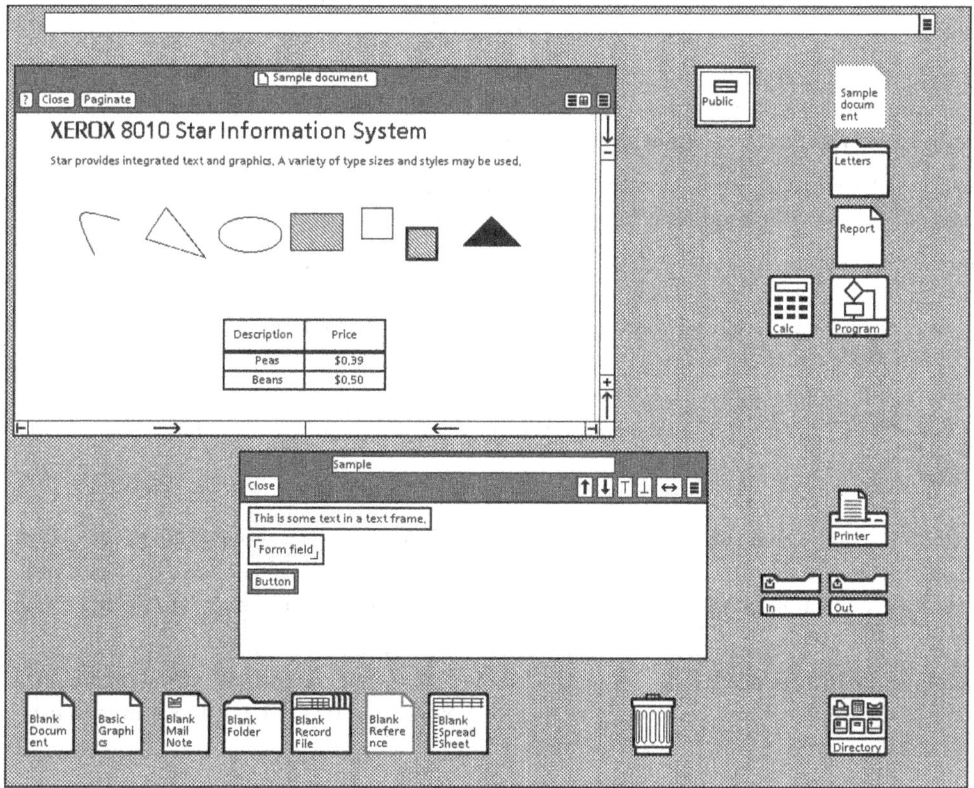

The Star interface was given the not-so-nice nickname WIMP— Windows, Icon, Mouse, Pointer—by its detractors. The nickname stuck around for future windows-based interfaces as well.

Apple licensed the operating system from Xerox, made some improvements, and introduced it on the Macintosh computer in 1984. It became immediately popular, and the world hasn't been the same since. (Apple was ahead of the curve even more than 40 years ago!) Up until this time, the only way you really interacted with your computer was with the keyboard, typing commands into what was called a *console* or *command line*, and all display was text-based. Not anymore. Graphical displays and windows were here to stay.

Microsoft tried (and failed) to popularize a graphical product until 1990, with its release of Windows 3.0. Even though it provided a graphical interface, Windows architecture was still mostly based on the very popular MS-DOS operating system.

Linux came along in 1991, written by Linus Torvalds. It has its foundations in UNIX and is open source, but not exactly like UNIX. All of the modern operating systems we use today have their foundations in UNIX or Xerox Star.

Basic Functions of Operating Systems

Before I get too far into our discussion of what modern operating systems are expected to do, it will be useful to define a few key terms. The following are some terms that you will come across as you study this chapter, and you should know them for computer literacy:

Kernel The central part of the operating system. It controls all actions of the OS, including input and output, which processes get to use the CPU and memory, and translating between hardware and software components in the computer.

Version A particular revision of a piece of software, normally described by a number that tells you how new the product is in relation to other versions of the product.

Source The actual code that defines how a piece of software works. Computer operating systems can be open source, meaning that the OS code can be examined and modified by anyone, or they can be closed source, meaning that only an owner or developer can modify or examine the code.

A word often used interchangeably with closed source is *proprietary*.

Shell A program that runs on top of the OS and allows the user to issue commands through a set of menus or other interface (which may be a text-based console or command line or a graphical interface). Shells make an OS easier to use by creating a relatively user-friendly interface.

Graphical User Interface (GUI) A method by which a person communicates with a computer using graphical images, icons, and methods other than text. GUIs allow a user to use a mouse, touchpad, or another mechanism (in addition to the keyboard) to interact with the computer to issue commands.

Cooperative Multitasking Computers appear to run multiple applications simultaneously, but in reality, they can focus on only one at a time. They're able to switch back and forth between programs so quickly that it appears that they are doing multiple things at once. Cooperative multitasking is a multitasking method that depends on the application itself to be responsible for using the processor and then freeing it for access by other applications. This is the way very early versions of Windows managed multiple applications. If any application locked up while using the processor, the application was unable to free the processor properly to do other tasks, and the entire system locked, usually forcing a reboot.

Preemptive Multitasking A multitasking method in which the OS allots each application a certain amount of processor time and then forcibly takes back control and gives another application or task access to the processor. This means that if an application crashes, the OS takes control of the processor away from the locked application and passes it on to the next application, which should be unaffected. Although unstable programs still lock, only the locked application will stall—not the entire system. This is what is used today in modern operating systems.

Multithreading The ability of a single application to have multiple requests (threads) in to the processor at one time. This results in faster application performance, because it allows a program to do many things at once.

Later on in this chapter in the "Process Management" section, you will learn about killing (stopping) processes using a tool called Task Manager. Here's a good place to introduce a few important terms and their distinctions. Any piece of software running on a computer runs as a *process*. A process will be an isolated program with its own memory space and other resources. Within a process, there will be one or more *threads* running. All of the threads within that process share the memory space that the process owns. How many threads run at once depends on how the programmers coded the app.

32-Bit An operating system that is 32-bit is one that not only can run on 32-bit processors but can also fully utilize the capabilities of the processor. While this may sound simple, the truth of the matter is that it took many years after the 32-bit processor became available before operating systems (which were 16-bit at the time) were able to utilize their features. Just as you cannot mix racecars with a country road, you cannot mix 64-bit software with 32-bit hardware.

64-Bit A 64-bit operating system is one that is written to utilize the instructions possible with 64-bit processors. Originally, these were more common with servers than desktops, but as prices have dropped, 64-bit processors are the standard for desktops and laptops as well, as are operating systems that will run on them. As mentioned earlier, you cannot mix 64-bit software with 32-bit hardware (but you can run most 32-bit software on 64-bit hardware).

With those terms in mind, let's look at the key functions of an operating system. The functions that you will examine in more depth in the upcoming sections are as follows:

- Interfacing between users and the hardware and coordinating between hardware components
- Provisioning an environment for the software to function
- Creating a structure for data management
- Monitoring system health and functionality

Coordinating Users and Hardware

Thank goodness we've moved beyond needing to spend an entire week manually moving connections around to just do a simple math problem. Even today, most people don't know how to tell the computer hardware (in assembly) to function, nor do they care to know how. We turn our computers on, and we expect that when we click something, it works, or when we press a key on the keyboard, that letter appears on our screen. The operating system coordinates all of that for us.

Most of us don't also really give much thought to the different types of hardware needed to execute what seem to be simple commands. If we open a document or a spreadsheet, it requires coordination of the mouse (or keyboard), motherboard, processor, memory, and hard drive. If that file is on another computer on the network, it also requires our network card. Again, the operating system manages all of this for us so that we don't have to think about it.

To talk to the hardware, operating systems use specialized programs called *device drivers*, or *drivers* for short. A driver tells the OS how to talk to the specific piece of hardware and how to use its features. If there is no driver for that OS, then the hardware will not be compatible with it.

Operating systems also keep us users in check. We're not allowed to perform any functions that would break the hardware, generally speaking. At a minimum, we're at least warned that what we are about to do will erase everything on our hard drive—are we sure that's what we want to do?

Another thing that OSs can do to help us silly people behave is to limit the resources that we are allowed to access. If you work for a company, you probably don't need to see everyone's salary information unless you're the boss or in the HR department. Many PC OSs allow for the creation of user accounts to manage who can get to what. This is done by assigning *permissions*—that is, specifying which users can access which files.

If you are the only person who uses your computer, user accounts and permissions aren't as big of a deal. But once you start getting into environments where more than one person is involved, they become important because permissions define who or what can access a file or resource. You'll learn how to create user accounts in the "Managing Features and Interfaces" section later in this chapter.

Providing an Environment for Software

I talked about how nice it is to have the operating system talk to the hardware for us. Similarly, the OS gives software applications one standard interface with which to work. Without an OS, each software application would need to know how to talk to each specific piece of hardware on the market—an impossible task for developers. So, the programmer creates a program that works with the OS, and then the OS figures out how to talk to the hardware.

Because each OS is created differently, though, applications are written for a specific OS and not compatible with different ones. For example, a game written for macOS won't work on a machine running Windows, or vice versa. Odds are that the developer will have a different version that works just fine on Windows. Within versions of an OS family, compatibility isn't generally as big of a problem as it is across OS types. If an app works on Windows 11, it will almost certainly run on Windows 10 or even Windows Vista as well. This isn't always true, and it starts becoming more problematic the farther apart generations of apps and operating systems become. For example, a game designed to run on Windows 95 (which is more than 30 years old) might not work *natively*—that is, without another program helping translate—in Windows 11.

Providing Structure for Data Management

Ideally, by now the idea that computers store data permanently shouldn't come as a shock to you. Data can be anything from files needed to run the OS to a spreadsheet with a work project to pictures and videos of a recent vacation. But how is it stored on the hard drive? Is it just a jumbled mess of bits? And if it were, then how do you easily find the data you need, when you need it?

In all actuality, the data stored on the hard drive does resemble a jumbled mess of bits. Fortunately, the OS comes to the rescue again by giving users a structured way to store and access those files and applications. OSs use a system of directories (often called *folders*) to store data in a hierarchical manner. It all starts with the root of the hard drive (typically C: on most PCs) and branches out from there; because of the branches, you might hear it called a *directory tree*. Thus, no matter where the data physically resides on the hard drive, the OS catalogs it in a logical manner so that you can always get to what you need—if you remember where you put it.

The "Managing Folder and File Structures" section later in this chapter covers this topic in significantly more detail.

Monitoring System Health and Functionality

Finally, OSs will monitor the health of your system's hardware, giving you an idea of how well (or not) it's performing. You can see how busy your CPU is or how quickly your hard drives retrieve data or how much data your network card is sending, all to understand how efficient your computer is. Monitoring system performance can also alert you if a component is starting to fail, if its performance starts to deteriorate rapidly.

Different OSs use different tools to monitor system health. In most versions of Windows, the utility is called Performance Monitor, and it's located in Windows Tools in Control Panel. In Figure 4.4, you can see processor performance on my computer.

FIGURE 4.4 Windows Performance Monitor

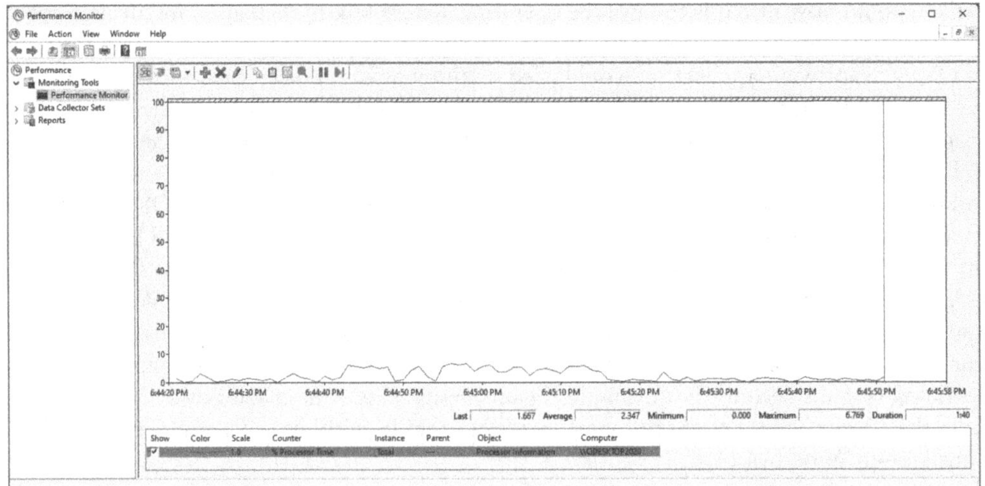

The small spikes in performance were when I opened a game and an Excel spreadsheet. But as you can see, my CPU isn't being taxed in any way. The vertical line moves across the screen to show current performance.

Most of the time, it's helpful to have context to decide whether or not the data that these tools produce indicates a problem. For example, if 20 percent of my memory is being used, is that good or bad? It's probably not a problem, unless I haven't changed anything and it used to be consistently at 10 percent. What administrators often do is to set up a *baseline* of performance for key hardware components (the CPU, memory, hard drive, and network) to know what normal performance looks like. Then, if the system is having issues, they can refer to the baseline to see how bad the issue really is.

The macOS performance tool is called Activity Monitor, and Ubuntu Linux's default one is System Monitor. Ubuntu is open source, so the user community has developed new fancier ones as well, such as Resources.

Configuring and using performance monitoring tools is beyond the scope of this book; just know that your operating system can perform these tasks for you.

Types of Operating Systems

You could literally spend a lifetime learning about all of the different types of operating systems in existence. There are OSs built specifically for servers, workstations, mobile devices, routers, home entertainment systems, and more. Within each of these designations, you'll find dozens if not hundreds or thousands of variants, each with its own unique features. Understanding it all is an interesting hobby for some and an absolute nightmare for others.

Fortunately, the CompTIA Tech+ exam doesn't ask you to memorize thousands of operating systems and their features. If they did, we would need several more books just to cover them. For this exam, you just need to know about four categories of OSs. For each category, I'll provide a quick background explaining the purpose of the category. Then, I will give you a few examples of operating systems within each category so that you can understand the similarities and differences between them.

On the Tech+ exam, you will need to "Explain the purpose of operating systems," per objective 3.2. This includes four OS types: mobile, desktop/workstation, server, and embedded. Be familiar with the major OSs in each category. That said, it's highly unlikely that you will get asked details about specific versions of any one OS, as is outlined in some of the upcoming tables. These details are provided to give you a flavor for the features introduced over the years.

Desktop/Workstation Operating Systems

Desktop/workstation operating systems are a perfect jumping-off point for us because they were the first operating systems in existence. When operating systems were first created, nobody specified that they were for a workstation—they were just operating systems. But they were designed to let users perform tasks on a single machine, which is essentially what a workstation does. Even a beast like ENIAC was essentially a workstation. Okay, maybe it was more like a giant calculator, but I'm going to call it a workstation anyway. It certainly wasn't a server or a mobile device.

Workstations are still abundant in today's computer world. Everyone's laptop or desktop computer at home is a workstation. On a network, the term *workstation* is synonymous with client computer, which again, is usually a laptop or desktop. In this section, I'll take you through four of the most important workstation OSs in the market.

Linux

Of the four OSs we're going to cover here, *Linux* is the least popular one for workstation installation. So why cover it first? Because it's easily the most influential. Linux was developed in 1991 by Linus Torvalds and is in many ways a derivative of UNIX.

First, I need to clarify one important thing: Linux isn't actually an operating system. Linux is a kernel, or the core of an operating system. To turn the kernel into a Linux-based OS, developers need to add other critical components such as daemons (services), a *shell*, shell utilities, a desktop environment (such as a *graphical user interface*), and desktop applications. The combination of all of these features is referred to as a *distribution*. There have been hundreds if not thousands of Linux distributions created.

Even though Linux is not technically an operating system, a lot of people still call it one. Here I'll do the same because it's a lot shorter than writing "the collection of Linux-based operating systems" every time I refer to it. Linux is also unique among our list of desktop OSs because it's the only one that's open source.

Most Linux distributions use what's called the *Bash shell*. Bash stands for Bourne-again shell, which was designed to replace an older commonly used shell called the Bourne shell. Bash is also the default shell of macOS.

Linux Versions

If you'll recall, *open source* means that anyone who wants to can modify the code, and many developers have decided to take that challenge. They can't change the kernel, which is what defines Linux, but they can change anything else they want in the distribution. One developer might add lots of services, whereas another might keep it lean and quick. Some versions are 32-bit, and others are 64-bit. Many distributions have a GUI, whereas others (mostly Slackware versions) have kept the default interface old-school, command-prompt-based. By some estimates, there are more than 600 current and well-known Linux distributions alive today. There are surely thousands more that are retired or unpublished. Like any proper OS, Linux distributions have names. Examples include Ubuntu Linux, Linux Mint, Debian, KDE, and Red Hat. Figure 4.5 shows the desktop of Lubuntu, which is in the Ubuntu family. (It's basically Ubuntu with a "lighter" and quicker desktop, designed to speed up performance.) You'll notice a similarity with other "Windows-like" desktops, complete with a Start-like button, folders, the ability to right-click to change desktop preferences, and similar menus to get to various applications and utilities.

FIGURE 4.5 Lubuntu desktop

Most Linux distributions in the wild today come from one of three families: Debian, Slackware, or RPM, which were popular Linux versions around 1993–1994. As is encouraged in the Linux community, developers took these versions, made changes, and redistributed them with different names. If you wanted to, you could take any existing version of Linux (except commercial ones), modify it, and call it whatever you like. Or, you could start from the ground up and develop your own, although that would take a considerable amount of work.

The website `www.linuxfromscratch.org` provides information on how to develop your own version of Linux, if the mood strikes you.

The vast majority of distributions are free of charge. The underpinning belief of the open source community is that software, particularly software that aids in educational or scientific endeavors, should be free. Commercial (nonfree) variants of Linux also exist, such as Red Hat Enterprise. In addition, several other OSs, such as Android and Chrome, are built upon a Linux foundation. You don't necessarily pay for those OSs, but they are bundled with devices that you do pay for, such as a smartphone or a Chromebook.

Distributions might or might not be backed by a corporation, which means that technical support for issues can be hit or miss. In most cases, you will need to rely on online support forums, such as `https://wiki.ubuntu.com` or `https://lubuntu.me/support`. Members in the community are generally pretty responsive when others have questions or need help, but again, it depends on the version.

Linux Usage

Linux is immensely popular on servers and Internet devices. In fact, you can safely say that the Internet runs on Linux. (Do a Google search on the words "The Internet runs on" and see what the autofill is!) Some estimates have the Linux share of the server market at 50 percent. But Linux is only installed on around 1–2 percent of all desktop and laptop computers. Why is that?

There are likely a few reasons. First, and most importantly, the vast majority of laptop and desktop PCs sold are bundled with a Windows-based OS. Related to that, considering the market share of Windows, most applications are written for that platform as well. There might or might not be a Linux version. Second, Linux has a bit of a reputation as being more technically challenging to run well—"geeky" if you will. This is based on its heritage as a UNIX derivative with a command-line interface, which probably turns off some users who might otherwise be interested in a free and efficient operating system.

For programmers or hardware developers, some version of Linux is generally the preferred choice. It has less overhead (lesser hardware requirements and usage) than other workstation OSs and is readily customizable for their needs. Even though it doesn't have a major installed base in the workstation market, Linux is an incredibly powerful OS that we really don't want to live without.

macOS

Apple introduced the Macintosh computer in 1984, and behind a massive marketing campaign it became popular. Its popularity can be attributed to the fact that it had an easy-to-use interface—the first popular WIMP interface. The OS on the first Mac was simply called System, or sometimes *System Software*. Apple developed System in-house, as a combination of its own previous OS (called the Lisa OS) and features from the Xerox OS.

macOS Versions

Early versions of System were relatively simple. They had an application called Finder, which allowed users to store and locate their files. One early challenge was that Finder created virtual folders for file storage, so those folders and files weren't visible in any program except for Finder. These early versions also could run only one application at a time.

Released in 1987, System 5 provided for cooperative multitasking with the MultiFinder application. This represented a big step forward for the OS. By then, files and folders were also integrated into the file system, so other applications could use them as well.

The next major version was System 7, which added some significant upgrades, including the following:

- Native support for virtual memory, so hard disk space could be used if the physical memory ran low.
- Built-in cooperative multitasking (as opposed to multitasking being done through an app).
- The first 32-bit OS widely available for workstations.
- A redesigned user interface.
- The Trash Can (for deleted files) was no longer emptied by default automatically at shut down.

System 7 was also the last version to use the "System" name. With update 7.6, Apple dropped the title and renamed it Mac OS.

Mac OS X was the tenth version of the Mac series of operating systems, and it marked a major departure from previous Mac OSs. In 2016, Apple renamed its operating system to *macOS*. This is in line with its other operating systems, such as iOS (which I will talk about later, in the "Mobile Operating Systems" section), tvOS, and watchOS. Before I get into the details, let's pause and review some of the major versions of the macOS to this point, as shown in Table 4.1.

Throughout the rest of this section, I am going to use "macOS" to refer to the family of Mac operating systems, unless I refer to a specific version.

TABLE 4.1 Selected macOS releases

Version	Year	Notes
System 1	1984	First widely popular GUI
System 2	1985	Introduces hierarchical file system
System 5	1987	Adds cooperative multitasking

Version	Year	Notes
System 7	1991	User interface redesign, virtual memory support, true 32-bit OS, and other enhancements
Mac OS 7.6	1997	Name change to make it easier for Apple to license OS to manufacturers of Mac clones
Mac OS X	1999	Major architecture change
OS X	2012	Name change
macOS	2016	Siri on the desktop, integrated Apple Pay, new Apple File System, better graphics capabilities (4K video, virtual reality), better integration with mobile OSs

The Mac clone market was short-lived—it lasted only about a year. Steve Jobs (one of the founders of Apple who was ousted by the board of directors in 1995) returned to Apple in August 1997, and one of his major goals was to shut down Mac clones. He succeeded in late 1997, right as Apple released Mac OS 8.

Mac OS X for servers was released in 1999, and the desktop version followed in the spring of 2001. OS X was a major departure from Apple's previous OSs, because it was UNIX-based. In fact, all of the most recent macOS versions are certified UNIX systems.

By the time OS X was released, Apple was in a challenging position. Windows was continuing to take market share, and Apple's OS interface was deemed a bit dated. OS X changed that with a new theme (layout) called Aqua. It's been updated several times, but the essence of Aqua still exists.

One of the interesting features of Mac operating systems is their naming. Since 2001, Mac OSs have gone through a number of revisions, each one adding new features. Each one is given a version number, but also a name. Apple named several versions after large cats and, since version 10.9, places in California. Table 4.2 shows you a few select versions of Mac OS X and macOS.

TABLE 4.2 macOS versions

Version	Year	Name	Notes
10.0	2001	Cheetah	First Mac OS X version. Panned by critics, loved by Mac enthusiasts. Aqua interface.
10.8	2012	Mountain Lion	Messages app replaced iChat. Apple commits to yearly OS release cycle.

TABLE 4.2 macOS versions *(continued)*

Version	Year	Name	Notes
10.12	2016	Sierra	Name changed to macOS. Siri on the desktop, integrated Apple Pay, new Apple File System, better graphics capabilities (4K video, virtual reality), better integration with mobile OSs.
11	2020	Big Sur	Moved away from 10.X naming. Updated the user interface.
14	2023	Sonoma	Revamped Widgets (mini apps on the desktop for quick access), the user lock screen, and screensaver/wallpaper integration.

At this point, Apple is committed to yearly updates of its OS, and it will give those upgrades for free to qualified users.

macOS Usage

The macOS has been preinstalled on every Mac ever made. And as mentioned earlier, there was a short period of time when Mac clones were made, and they had macOS as well. Today, you can buy any of several versions of a macOS on the Apple Store if you want and install it on a compatible system. macOS has a relatively low share of the workstation market—only about 4–5 percent of the install base. Most of this is because Apple has kept the OS mostly proprietary, whereas its main rival Windows has tried to be on every PC possible.

Macs tend to have very loyal users, and the general consensus is that if you're working on highly visual projects, Macs are the way to go. Macs also come with plenty of productivity software, but graphical applications are where Macs really shine.

As for using the interface, it's a lot like other WIMP interfaces out there. Figure 4.6 shows the Sonoma desktop. One difference versus some other interfaces is that Mac OS uses the dock, or the bar at the bottom of the desktop, for an easy way to activate icons of your favorite apps.

Windows

The Microsoft *Windows* family of operating systems has far and away the largest installed base in the laptop and desktop PC market. This might not come as a surprise to you, but it might actually be a little surprising considering the inauspicious start of the Windows OS. I'll get to that in a minute.

Windows has always been developed in-house by Microsoft, and it is seen as the flag bearer for closed-source software. Because of this and because Microsoft has a history of strong-arming competitors, the company has faced a significant amount of scorn from the open source community.

FIGURE 4.6 macOS Sonoma

Source: Sonoma screenshot / with permission from Apple.

Windows Versions

Let's get back to the bad start that Windows had. The first version, Windows 1.0, released in 1985, was nothing more than a somewhat graphical front-end to Microsoft's popular command-line MS-DOS operating system. Windows 2.0, released in 1987, didn't fare much better; Macintosh was clearly superior from a usability and aesthetics standpoint.

By the time Windows 3.0 rolled out in 1990, Microsoft and Apple were in a full-out battle with each other. Windows had copied, legally or not (depending on whom you talk to), a lot of the look and feel of Mac's System Software. In addition, Windows 3.0 supported cooperative multitasking and virtual memory. The Windows shell was called Program Manager, and it allowed users to navigate the system graphically to find files and to start applications. Upgrades to Windows 3.0 included Windows 3.1 and Windows for Workgroups 3.11. Figure 4.7 shows the Windows 3.11 Program Manager.

The next major revision came in August 1995: Windows 95. It replaced Program Manager with a shell based on Windows Explorer and added a new feature called the Start button, as shown in Figure 4.8. It had some 32-bit features, but it employed 16-bit features as well, so it wasn't a true 32-bit OS. By most accounts, what had already been an easy operating system to use just got easier. Windows 95 exploded in popularity. Windows Explorer remained the default shell for Windows for 17 years, until Windows 8 was released in 2012. (Now, what used to be Windows Explorer is called File Explorer.)

FIGURE 4.7 Windows 3.11 Program Manager

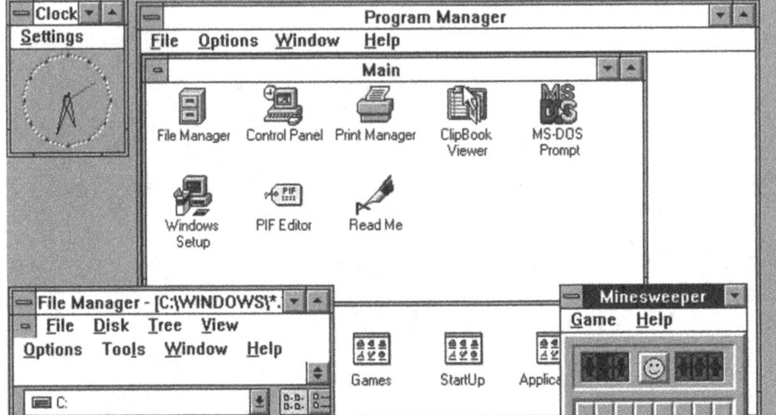

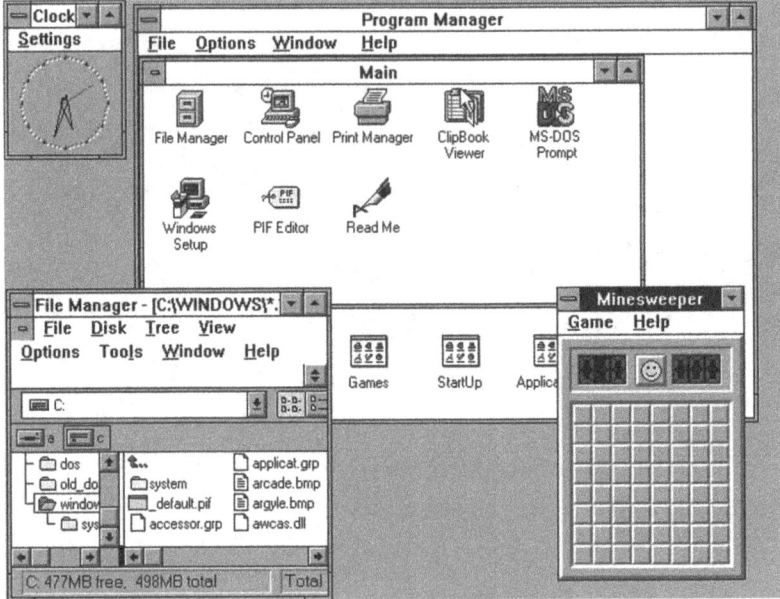

Source: Windows 3.11 Program Manager screenshot / with permission from Microsoft.

FIGURE 4.8 Windows 95 desktop

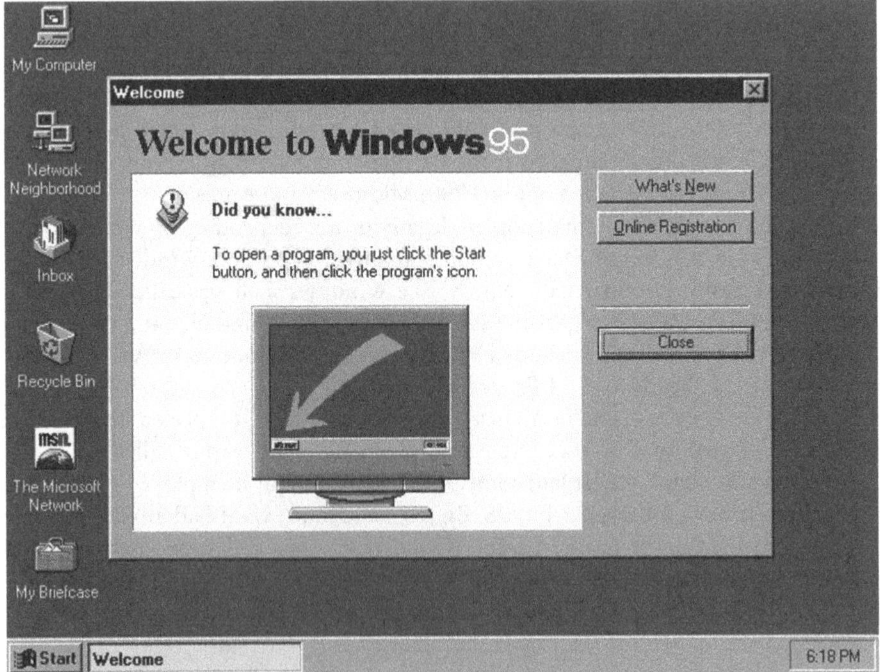

Source: Windows 95 desktop screenshot / with permission from Microsoft.

Around the same time, Microsoft was working on a server-based operating system called Windows NT. (NT stood for New Technology, although critics claimed it stood for "Nice Try.") Windows NT, using the 32-bit Windows NT kernel, was launched in 1993. At the time, of course, Microsoft was also busy working on Windows 95. Its goal was to unify the two operating systems into one platform, but that proved to be harder than it originally anticipated. Microsoft wouldn't be able to consolidate to one OS platform until Windows XP, which was released in 2001. XP was also the first version of Windows to come in a 64-bit version. From Windows XP on, all Microsoft OSs have used the Windows NT kernel.

Windows 8 was released in 2012, and it marked the most significant appearance change for Windows since 1995. Figure 4.9 shows the Windows Start screen, which replaces the Start button. It provides tiles for the user, originally called the "Metro" design but since changed to "Windows Store app," intended to allow for faster navigation to the items the user wants. It was also intended to look very similar to Windows Phone and is optimized for devices with touchscreen displays.

FIGURE 4.9 Windows 8.1 Start screen

Source: Windows 8.1 Start screen screenshot / with permission from Microsoft.

Unfortunately for Microsoft, Windows 8 did not achieve the commercial success it had anticipated. Critics complained about the lack of a Start button, noting that (at the time) very few desktops or laptops had touchscreens. Because of some of the issues, Microsoft announced a free upgrade to Windows 8.1, which placed the Start button back on the desktop.

Windows 10 (Microsoft skipped Windows 9) was launched in late 2015. Among other features, it kept the Start button, consolidated system settings into one place, added an area called Action Center to display notifications, and had a new web browser, Microsoft Edge.

The feature most people were excited about was Cortana, which is Microsoft's voice-activated personal assistant (think of Siri on the iPhone).

The most recent version (as of this writing) is Windows 11, released in 2021. It has a redesigned Start menu and taskbar, integrated widgets, better touch controls, and various quality-of-life upgrades. Windows 12 is projected for late 2024 or early 2025. Table 4.3 lists some key versions of Windows and associated features.

TABLE 4.3 Selected Windows versions

Version	Year	Notes
Windows 1.0	1985	A graphical interface for MS-DOS. Not widely received.
Windows 3.0	1990	The first serious competitor to Apple's graphical OS. Supported multitasking and virtual memory.
Windows 95	1995	Introduced the Start button.
Windows XP	2001	First Microsoft OS for home use with the Windows NT kernel. First 64-bit Microsoft OS version intended for home use.
Windows 7	2009	Available in 32- and 64-bit versions. Most popular desktop and laptop OS until Windows 10 launch in 2015.
Windows 8	2012	Originally removed the Start button (it returned in 8.1); optimized for touchscreen systems. Not as successful as Windows 7.
Windows 10	2015	Several major upgrades, including Cortana and better integration with mobile devices.
Windows 11	2021	Upgraded Start menu and taskbar, integrated widgets, better touch controls for touch-capable devices.

Windows Usage

In your travels in the IT world, you will see a lot of Windows because it is the most popular desktop and laptop OS worldwide. It has just over 80 percent of the laptop and desktop market. That is mostly because of Microsoft's desire to get it onto as many systems as possible. Whereas Apple has traditionally combined the hardware and OS as a package, for most of its existence Microsoft has not been in the hardware market. It produced an OS (and applications) and tried to make sure that it was bundled with every PC that shipped. The strategy has had some clear success.

As of early 2024, Windows 10 is still the most popular Windows-based OS out there, with about 70 percent of the installed base. Windows 11, despite it being a free upgrade to Windows 10 on machines that have the required hardware to support it, accounts for about 25 percent of the Windows installs. There are still some legacy Windows 7 installations and other random versions out there too.

ChromeOS

ChromeOS was developed by Google and launched in 2011. In many important ways, it's unlike any of the other OSs we've discussed so far. The guiding principle behind the design of ChromeOS is that it's supposed to be lightweight and perform the most common tasks users need today. And what's the most common thing that all of us do? Get on the Internet.

Google had its Chrome browser, and its original intent was to make an OS based on the browser alone. That's it. Several rounds of testing showed that it was close but not quite on target with the ideal user experience. So, Google went back to the drawing board and incorporated the Gentoo Linux kernel and package management system with Chrome. ChromeOS was born. Looking at the Chrome desktop in Figure 4.10, you'll see that it looks similar to Windows 11 and macOS, with a launcher in the lower center, a taskbar, and a status tray with a clock in the lower-right corner.

FIGURE 4.10 Google ChromeOS

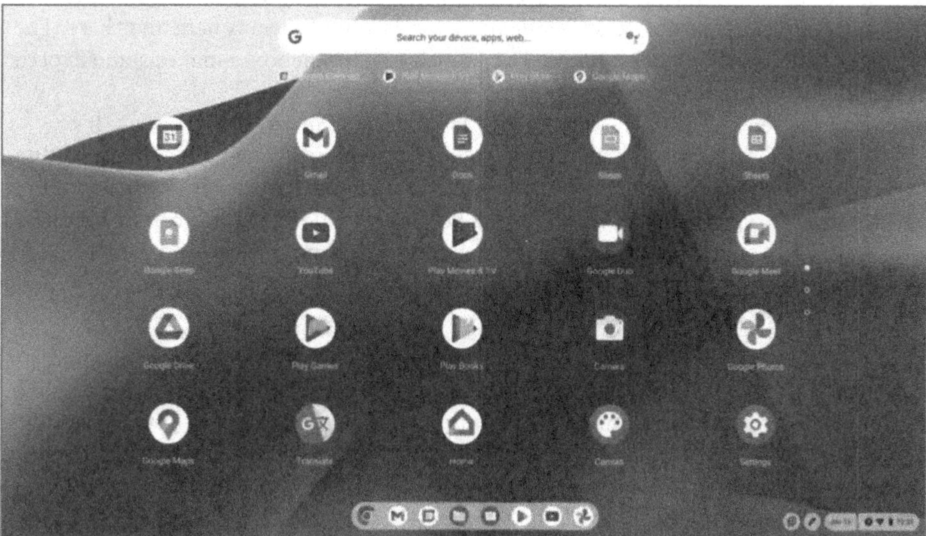

Source: ChromeOS desktop screenshot / with permission from Google.

What's particularly interesting about ChromeOS is that it stores little to nothing on the local computer. Everything is stored in the cloud.

ChromeOS Versions

ChromeOS doesn't have major version names as Microsoft or Apple OSs do, at least not yet. As Google publishes updates, the new version is automatically downloaded to the system with no user intervention needed. There are no compatibility issues to worry about because all of the apps themselves are stored on Google's cloud.

ChromeOS itself is available only on Chromebooks. ChromeOS Flex can be installed on any computer that has Windows or macOS. For what it's worth, the ChromeOS version released in April 2024 was 120.0.6099.304, and Chrome 124 was in beta testing. Not that anyone will quiz you on that.

ChromeOS Usage

ChromeOS was originally designed for small, portable computers called *netbooks*. Netbooks are like laptops, only smaller and very light. A netbook with Chrome is called a *Chromebook*. Netbooks have a processor, RAM, some ROM for storage, and a very, very small hard drive, typically SSD. Again, everything important is stored on the cloud. Occasionally, you will see desktop-type systems with ChromeOS as their operating system, called *Chromeboxes*. Regardless of your hardware platform, using ChromeOS requires an Internet connection because, again, everything is stored on the cloud.

Chromeboxes often do have hard drives. Google insists that these be SSD drives because of their speed, and they are usually very small, such as 16 GB.

Google claims that they do not intend for ChromeOS to be a replacement for traditional desktop and laptop OSs. They say that ChromeOS is for secondary systems, with which people typically surf the Internet, send email, and use a few applications here and there. The heavy lifting is still for other workstations. The launch of Chromeboxes makes some experts wonder if that's really the case.

ChromeOS has been one of the most popular OSs being sold in the last few years. It's a popular choice for elementary and high school students, and it does most of the things adults want a computer to do as well, which is surf the web, browse social media, and write email. They are also far less expensive than most laptops because they don't need as robust hardware to run. Choosing between the two often comes down to the features needed and price.

Server Operating Systems

Let's move on to server operating systems next because for the most part they are similar to workstation operating systems. Most companies that build both use an identical kernel and shell to keep the user experience similar between the two. In other words, if you know how to use a Windows-based workstation OS, you will easily find your way around a Windows Server installation. There will be some differences, of course, because servers need to do more than workstations.

Servers are in the business of providing resources to clients on a network. Workstations might need servers for security validation, access to files, or print capabilities. Server operating systems achieve many of these tasks by managing software modules called *services*, which I'll talk a lot more about in the "Managing Features and Interfaces" section later in this chapter. Server OSs are also optimized to handle multiple concurrent client connections over a network.

The major players in the server OS market are the same ones that are in the workstation OS market, with the exception of ChromeOS. Let's take a look at some details of three categories of server operating systems.

Linux-Based

As with Linux-based workstation OSs, there are a wide variety of Linux-based server OS distributions on the market. Overall, Linux-based servers have somewhere between a 10–20 percent market share, depending on who you ask.

One major difference is that server distributions are far more likely to be commercial, and therefore they cost money. After all, creating stable and secure OSs that can reliably serve your network isn't easy or cheap. Some big names in the marketplace are Red Hat Enterprise, SUSE Enterprise, Ubuntu Server, and Debian. Most are designed to be full enterprise-level servers, whereas others can be more specialized for tasks such as web server management.

One other name to know in the server OS market is FreeBSD. It's not Linux-based but rather is a direct descendant of BSD UNIX. My die-hard Linux-loving friends will probably take exception to me putting it in a Linux section, but for our purposes here, they're similar enough. There are two big differences to call out, though. First, FreeBSD is a complete OS, whereas you'll recall that Linux is just a kernel. Second, FreeBSD source code is even more open source than Linux. A lot of the FreeBSD code base is included in iOS and the PlayStation operating systems.

Mac-Based

Apple produced a server-based add-on to its macOS called, perhaps not surprisingly, macOS Server, that was discontinued in April 2022. To use it, you downloaded and installed it onto your existing Mac, and you were granted some server capabilities. It was inexpensive and billed itself as easy to use. Once installed, the macOS had a Server app that allowed the administrator to manage users and groups as well as services.

The target audience was small businesses, schools, and individuals. It had a very small installed base, which surely led to its demise. You're not likely to see it on a network of any substantial size.

Windows-Based

Windows NT 3.1 was Microsoft's first entrant into the server OS space in 1993. For many years, Windows-based servers lagged behind competitors in the marketplace, due partly to inferior technology but also owing to the perception that Microsoft wasn't a legitimate server software developer. As one administrator joked with me, "Windows NT is perfectly secure until you put a NIC in the machine." Ouch.

Over the years, Microsoft made improvements to its technology, and now Windows-based servers enjoy somewhere around 80–90 percent market share. It's easy for administrators to use Windows Server products because most of them are intimately familiar with Windows interfaces.

Microsoft no longer uses the Windows NT name but now names its server products Microsoft Server with the year that it was released. New versions have been coming out every four or five years. Versions you might see include Windows Server 2022, Windows Server 2019, Windows Server 2016, and even Windows 2000 Server. A new version typically arrives every three to four years, but most administrators are slow to upgrade.

You might find it strange that some companies still choose to use a server operating system that's more than 15 years old, like Windows Server 2008. Microsoft no longer supported it as of January 2020, so administrators could have some big challenges if they run into problems that they can't solve. Why doesn't the company just upgrade? There are three main reasons. First, with servers, the old adage of "If it's not broken, don't fix it" is gospel. If it's working well, there are few incentives to upgrade. Second, every time you upgrade a server, it requires a lot of time and energy for thorough testing, and most administrators just don't have that much time available. Third, tight budgets are also an issue—upgrading servers is not cheap. Consequently, you'll often see older operating systems in use on the server side than you will on the client side.

Mobile Operating Systems

As the name of this section implies, here I will be talking about operating systems specifically designed for mobile devices. You may recall that these OSs were touched upon in Chapter 3, "Computing Devices and the Internet of Things," as a necessary part of discussing iPhones, iPads, and Android device management. I promise to keep repetition to a minimum, though, and introduce you to new material here.

Apple iOS/iPadOS

Apple is one of the two major players in the mobile OS market with its iOS and iPadOS, running on the iPhone and iPad mobile platforms, respectively. Between those two devices, Apple has between 30 to 40 percent of the global smartphone and tablet market share. Figure 4.11 shows the home screen of iOS 17.

FIGURE 4.11 iOS 17 home screen

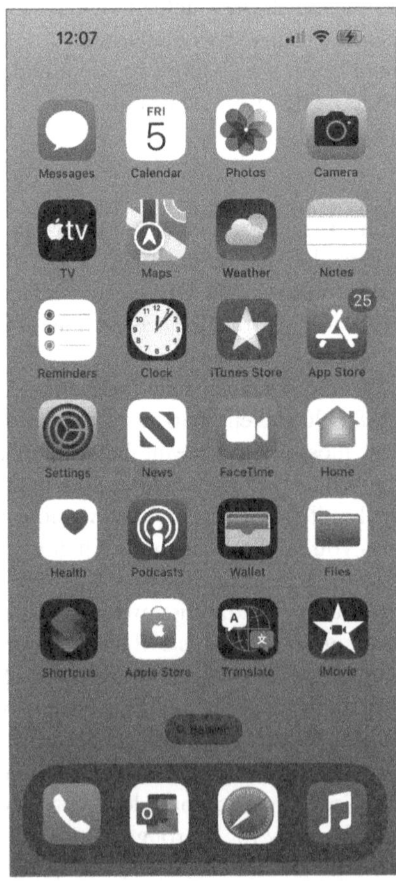

The *iOS* system is built on the same foundation as Apple's desktop OS. In fact, early marketing literature for the iPhone simply referred to the OS as a version of OS X. Later, it renamed it to iPhone OS, but after the introduction of the iPad, Apple went to the shortened iOS. Throughout their history, though, the workstation and mobile versions have been fairly different and not directly compatible with each other. Apps built for one would not work on the other; it's much more seamless today, and Apple is continually working to increase their compatibility.

The first generation was released in 2007 concurrently with the first iPhone. With this launch, Apple thrust itself into a very competitive mobile market, with a product that in many ways was considered inferior to the established players. Apple got one thing very right, though, and that was the user experience. The iPhone was the first popular phone to have a touchscreen that you could use with your fingers and not a stylus, and it used pinch-to-zoom and intuitive finger swipes to navigate the screen. It had only a few built-in apps (and no way to develop new ones) such as the Safari web browser and Maps, but it played music, videos, and movies, which you could get from the already-established iTunes store.

Apple releases newer versions with better features every year, often synchronized with the release of new hardware. With version 13 in 2019, Apple split its mobile OS into two, designating iPadOS specifically for tablets. This allowed for more features specific to that mobile platform. Table 4.4 highlights a few select versions and features.

TABLE 4.4 iOS versions and features

Version	Year	Selected features
iPhone OS 1	2007	First finger-based touchscreen, iTunes connectivity, Safari web browser, on-screen virtual keyboard
iPhone OS 2	2008	App Store for third-party apps, full email support for Microsoft Exchange
iOS 5	2011	Siri, iCloud, iMessage
iOS 7	2013	New visual interface, Control Center, iTunes Radio, biometric thumbprint scanner
iOS/iPadOS 13	2019	Split iOS and iPadOS, introduced dark mode
iOS/iPadOS 17	2023	New apps and customization options

Starting with the release of OS X Yosemite and continuing today, Apple is trying to make the experience between your workstation and your mobile device more seamless. Expect these efforts to continue until eventually the two platforms are basically seamless.

Apple also makes its own OS for the Apple Watch, called *watchOS*. It first launched in 2015, and like iOS it's updated once per year. The version numbers are not synchronized with iOS/iPadOS. For example, in 2023 when iOS 17 was released, the watchOS release was version 10.

Android

Along with Apple, Google is the other dominant player in the mobile market with its *Android* OS, with 60 to 70 percent share of the global mobile device market. If you look at the smartphone market alone, Android has far more users than Apple thanks to a bigger presence in Asia and Africa. (iOS owns a slight share advantage in Europe and North America.) Reputable sources claim that there are more Android installations than all other OSs in the world combined; as of 2024, it's estimated that there are nearly 4 billion active Android devices in the world, spread across 190 countries.

Android started off as its own company and was purchased by Google in 2005. Like Google's ChromeOS, Android is Linux-based. It's primarily installed on smartphones and tablets but also on specialized television, automobile, and wristwatch devices. It supports the use of similar touchscreen technology as Apple's iPhone. Figure 4.12 shows the Android 13 home screen.

FIGURE 4.12 Android 13 home screen

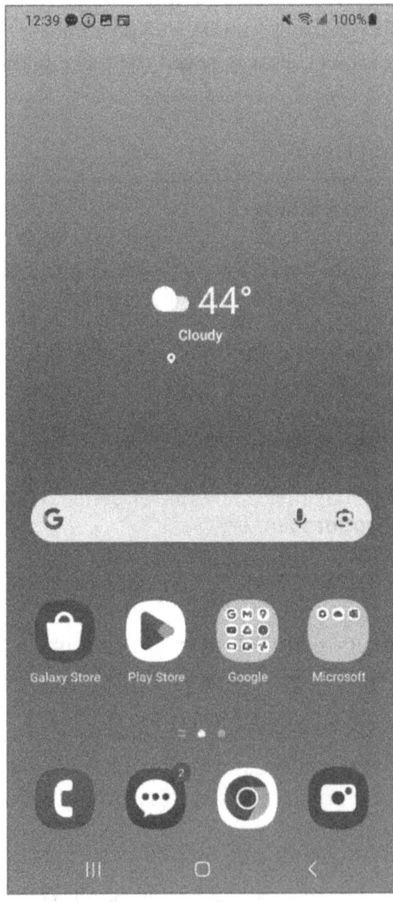

Android was slightly later to the market than iOS, with Android 1.0 launching in 2008. Since its launch, though, it has quickly grown in popularity and is the top smartphone platform, thanks in large part to it being available on devices from several manufacturers such as Samsung, LG, HTC, Sony, and Motorola, along with Google's own hardware. (Apple, much like it does with its macOS platform, restricts iOS to Apple hardware, which limits its potential install base.) Table 4.5 lists highlights of selected Android versions and features.

TABLE 4.5 Selected versions of Android OS

Version	Year	Name	Selected features
1.0	2008	(none)	Web browser, many Google apps, media player, Wi-Fi, and Bluetooth support.
1.5	2009	Cupcake	Widgets (mini apps that can be embedded in other apps and provide notifications), auto-rotation of screen.
6.0	2015	Marshmallow	Fingerprint reader support; Doze mode reduces CPU speed when screen is off to save battery life.
8.0	2017	Oreo	Major modular architecture change called Project Treble, adaptive icons, notification improvements.
13.0	2022	Tiramisu	Supports themed icons, reduced memory usage.
15.0	2024	Vanilla Ice Cream	Reintroduced lock screen widgets.

You'll notice that ever since version 1.5, Android versions have come with names of some sweet treat. In fact, all the way through version 9 (Android Pie) in 2018, the name was the primary reference and not the version number. In 2019 with the launch of Android 10 (Quince Tart), Google decided to put more emphasis on the version number rather than the sweet name.

Moving forward, Android appears to be positioned to maintain its significant market presence because of the multivendor support it receives.

Microsoft used to maintain mobile OSs, originally called Windows Phone OS and later rebranded as Windows Mobile. They never got much traction with iOS and Android entrenched in the market, so in 2017 Microsoft stopped producing a mobile OS.

Embedded Operating Systems

The final type of operating system that you need to know about is an *embedded operating system*. Embedded operating systems are designed to be small and efficient, typically only being responsible for a single task. The upside is that embedded OSs require very few hardware resources. The downside is there is little to no flexibility. For example, an embedded OS can run only one application, as opposed to multiple applications like the other OS types can run.

An example of an embedded operating system is *firmware*. Nearly all electronics devices have firmware of some type, which is responsible for managing that device's specific hardware. For example, a machine in an automobile factory may have firmware that dictates its precise movements to pick up a part and fit it into the right place on a car. That firmware is very specific to the machine, and it wouldn't be of any use on a different set of hardware. Firmware can also control very small devices, such as watches, fitness monitors, or children's toys. The firmware knows that if the user presses a button, it reacts by making a sound, displaying a menu, or doing whatever it was programmed to do.

Most firmware is put on a read-only memory (ROM) chip and is not designed to be upgraded. But as with the case of a system BIOS, some firmware can be upgraded by flashing it.

Managing an Operating System

Designers of operating systems go to great lengths to talk about how their OS is different and better than every other one on the market. Sure enough, if you look under the covers of each OS, you will see different methods of accomplishing similar tasks or different apps built in by default. The visual appearance is even more important, as programmers seem to try to out-design each other by creating fancy effects to catch your eye. A trip into the OS interface design world will introduce you to terms such as *skeuomorph*, dazzle you with color schemes, and amaze you with the moods that default system fonts generate.

As much as they try to differentiate themselves, it seems that most desktop operating systems since the launch of the Mac have looked, well, the same. Sure, there are differences, but the executional elements are all pretty similar. You have a desktop, a place to show you what's running, your system clock, and some sort of variation of a window. You'll run into some technical differences. For example, you can right-click a file to see its properties in Windows and most graphical versions of Linux, whereas to "right-click" with a Mac (which has only one mouse button) you hold down the Control key and click or turn on two-finger tapping in the trackpad preferences to right-click, as you would on a Chromebook with ChromeOS. But overall, using one desktop OS is very often like using any other OS.

Mobile operating systems have changed the game a bit because of their restricted real estate. But there again, the same concepts of how to open apps or swipe through screens remain relatively constant across systems.

The point is, learn how to use one OS, and it will be relatively easy for you to figure out how to use another. In this section, you are going to learn how to manage some of the key functions of operating systems, including using the correct interfaces. First, I will cover the topic of how to manage important OS features. Then, I'll look at managing file systems and permissions.

Most of the examples I use in the following sections will be from Windows because it has the largest market share. I will use examples from Windows 11, but recall that functionality across Windows versions will be similar. Again, if you learn the concepts, you can almost always figure out how to make things happen, even on an unfamiliar operating system. And if nothing else, the instructions are just an Internet search away.

Managing Features and Interfaces

Operating systems are the interface between the user, applications, and hardware. Knowing that high-level view is good, but what does it really mean? More importantly, as someone who needs to set up or configure an operating system to do those things, how do you do it?

As per exam objective 3.2, you should be able to explain how the operating system is an interface between applications and hardware.

Let's take a look first at some of the things an operating system needs to manage. In the previous paragraph, I mentioned users, applications, and hardware. Think of those as broad categories of things to manage, each of which can be broken down into more specific and tangible management tasks. While it's not a comprehensive list of everything an OS needs to manage, here are some of the specifics that you need to understand:

- User accounts
- Access control
- Applications
- Processes
- Services
- Devices
- Disk space
- Memory
- Files, folders, and permissions

The first two are related to users. Applications, processes, and services are software (application) related, and devices, disk space, and memory are all types of hardware. The last one, files, folders, and permissions, is a broad topic that warrants its own section, "Managing Folder and File Structures," later in this chapter. I'll cover each of the other eight items here, explaining the purpose of each as well as how to manage them in Windows.

User Account Management

A *user account* is an identity by which you're known when using the OS. Most OSs allow (or require) you to log in, identify yourself by your user account, and then adjust the system and user environment settings appropriately to match your user level and preferences. For example, your desktop background and available icons are linked to your user account.

Within most OSs are multiple levels of users, with each level having different security settings called *privileges*. (Privileges are grouped together into bundles called *permissions*.) This enables you to grant access to the system to someone whom perhaps you don't trust to have full access to it. For example, you might give a child permission to run applications on the system but not to make changes that affect other users, like changing system settings. Or, you might give the Finance group the ability to access a file whereas the Marketing group might be denied.

Three common levels of users are administrator, standard user (often just called *user*), and guest. In general, the administrator can do almost anything they want, the user can access files but not make system configuration changes, and the guest account has limited access. Figure 4.13 shows you the Accounts page in Windows 11, which is accessed via Start ➢ Settings ➢ Accounts. You can see that my account is an Administrator. To add additional accounts, I could click Family Or Other Users, depending on whether or not they are part of my Microsoft 365 family account. To add a user, Microsoft will want you to provide a verifiable email address or phone number for that person.

FIGURE 4.13 User accounts in Windows 11

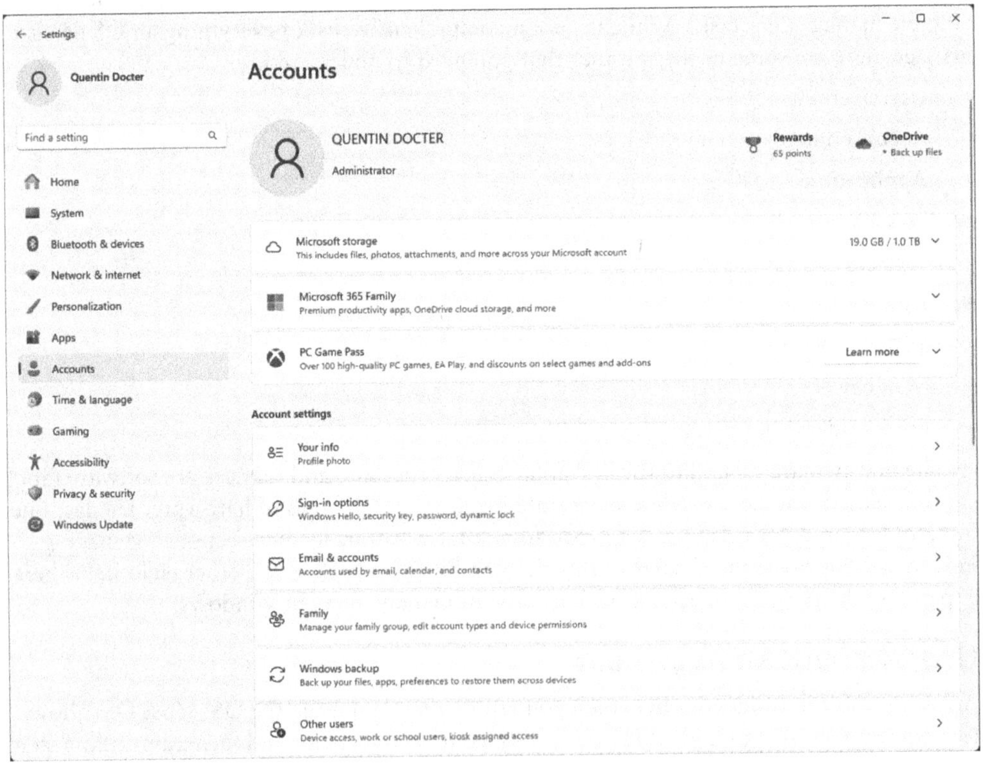

To see user accounts in Windows 10, click Start ➢ Settings (it looks like a gear) ➢ Accounts ➢ Family & Other People.

On a Mac, you have Standard and Administrator, and Sharing Only accounts available. Accounts are managed by going to the Apple menu ➢ System Settings, then clicking Users & Groups in the sidebar. The app is shown in Figure 4.14. Click the Add User button to add a new user. To manage account settings, click the information icon to the right of the username. There you can do things like make a user an administrator or impose parental controls.

FIGURE 4.14 Users & Groups in macOS

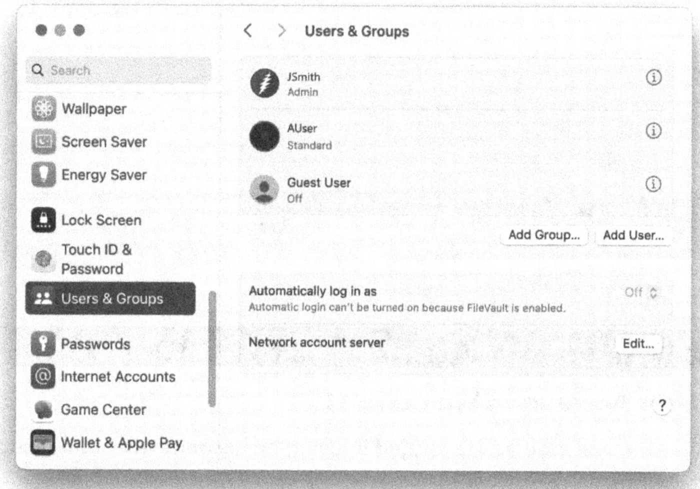

For Linux, the options available depend on the version you're using. Most versions offer some sort of Administrator, basic user, and guest or unprivileged account. In Linux and UNIX operating systems, the Administrator is often called `root` and may not be able to be renamed without altering system functionality. Figure 4.15 shows you the Lubuntu Linux User and Group setting screen, which is accessed via the Home Button (similar to the Start button in Windows) ➢ Preferences ➢ LXQt Settings ➢ Users And Groups. Adding a user is done with the Add button at the top of the window, and making changes to an account is done by highlighting it and clicking Properties.

No matter which account type and OS you choose, it's a good idea to password-protect it. The only exception to that is the Guest account on a Windows system. It usually doesn't have a password because by its nature it's accessible to the public. It's also a good idea to keep that account disabled unless you have a specific reason for enabling it. Exercise 4.1 has you create a user account in Windows 11.

FIGURE 4.15 Lubuntu user and group settings

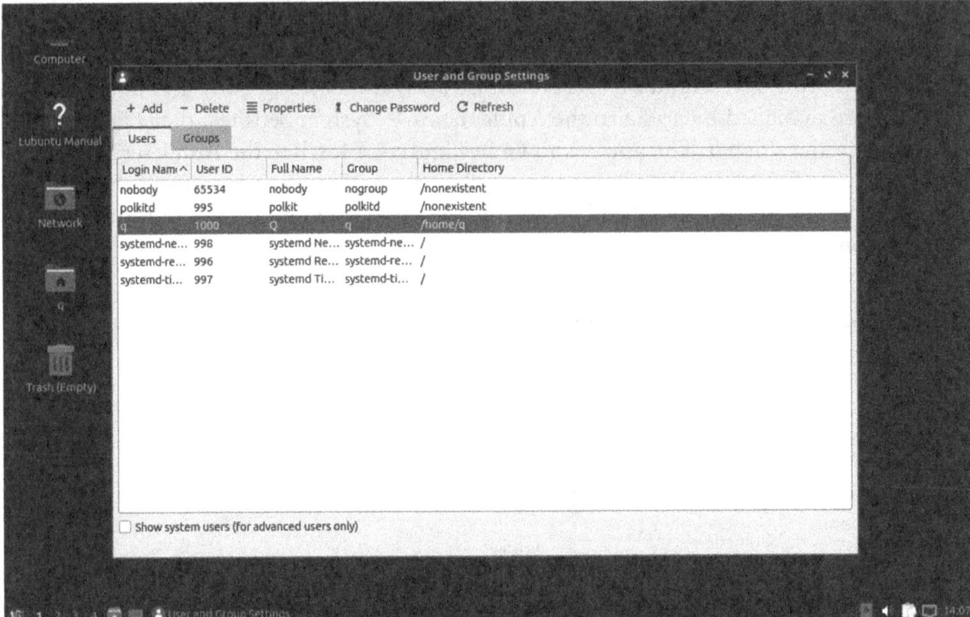

EXERCISE 4.1

Creating a User Account in Windows 11

1. In Windows 11, make sure you're logged in using an account with administrator privileges.
2. Click Start ➢ Settings (it looks like a gear).
3. Click Accounts.
4. Scroll down and click Other Users. You will see a screen similar to the one shown in Figure 4.16.
5. Click the Add Account button. A window will pop up asking how this person will sign in, and wants you to enter an email or phone. You can choose to enter a live email address or phone number here, but for this exercise click I Don't Have This Person's Sign-In Information.

   In this step Microsoft wants you to enter an email address for the person to sign in. This first started with Windows 10, and it's an effort to link the user seamlessly to Microsoft's cloud-based services. If you enter an email address and click Next, it will create the account. The first time that person logs in, they will get an email at that address and need to verify it.

FIGURE 4.16 Adding a user account

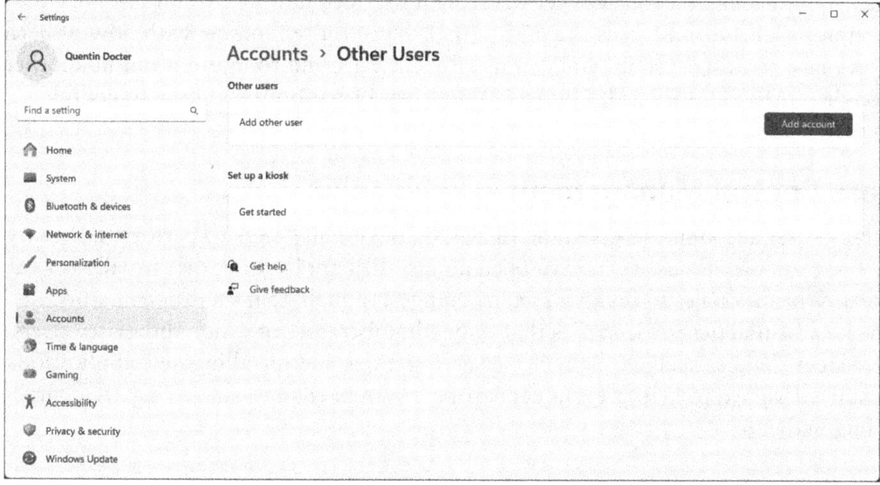

6. A Microsoft Create Account page will appear. You can create a Microsoft account here if you'd like. For this exercise, we'll keep going by clicking the Add A User Without A Microsoft Account link.

7. The next page will be the Create A User For This PC page, as shown in Figure 4.17. Enter a username and password, answer the three security questions that appear, and click Next.

FIGURE 4.17 Create a user

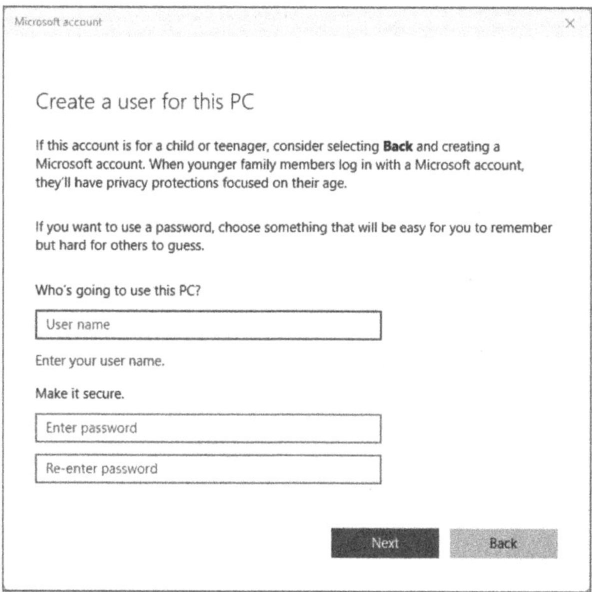

The user account name will now appear in Accounts ➢ Other Users.

Although the specific steps to create user accounts are different in each OS, the overall process is quite similar. (You will get to create a user account in Lubuntu at the end of this chapter's lab.) It reinforces the notion that once you're familiar with how to perform tasks in one operating system, you can usually click around to figure it out in another, or Google it. Moving forward, I will use Windows 11 to show you how to complete management tasks.

Access Control Management

By default, user accounts are given the right level of system access to perform necessary tasks. For example, if a user wants to open an installed application, that usually isn't a problem. When it comes to making system changes, though, that's a different story.

The idea behind *access control* is that only administrators or other authorized users can make system changes such as changing security settings and installing new applications or drivers. It's designed to help prevent catastrophic system changes, including accidentally installing malware.

Per Tech+ exam objective 3.2, you should be able to explain the purpose of access control in an operating system.

Microsoft implements Windows access control as User Account Control (UAC). With UAC, all programs or new tasks are run as if the user is using a standard user account. If the task tries to do something that requires elevated permissions, Windows sends a pop-up, similar to the one shown in Figure 4.18. If the account logged in has administrator access, the user can just click Yes to continue with the task. If not, the user will need to provide proper administrative credentials to continue.

FIGURE 4.18 User Account Control

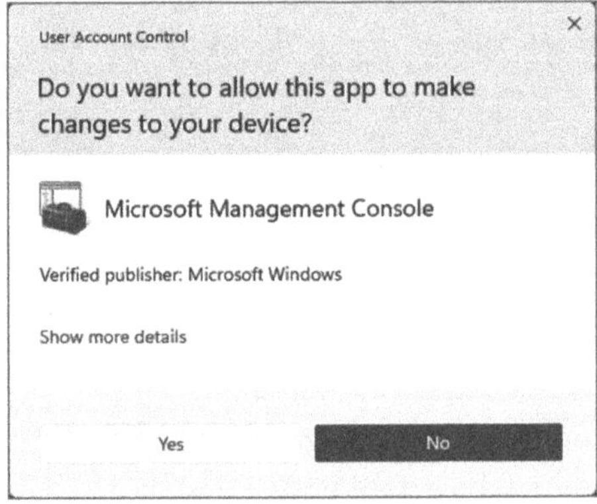

Windows UAC settings can be adjusted, although Microsoft does not recommend it. Keep that in mind as I show you how to do it in Exercise 4.2.

EXERCISE 4.2

Changing Windows User Account Control

1. Open Control Panel by typing **control** into the Windows search box and pressing Enter. Alternatively, type **user** or **uac** into the Windows search box and press Enter when Change User Account Control settings appears, and skip to step 5.
2. In the upper-right corner, adjust Control Panel to View By Small Icons.
3. Click User Accounts. (If you are viewing Control Panel by Category, you need to click User Accounts and then User Accounts again on the next screen.) This opens the Make Changes To Your User Account page, as shown in Figure 4.19.

FIGURE 4.19 Making changes to your user account

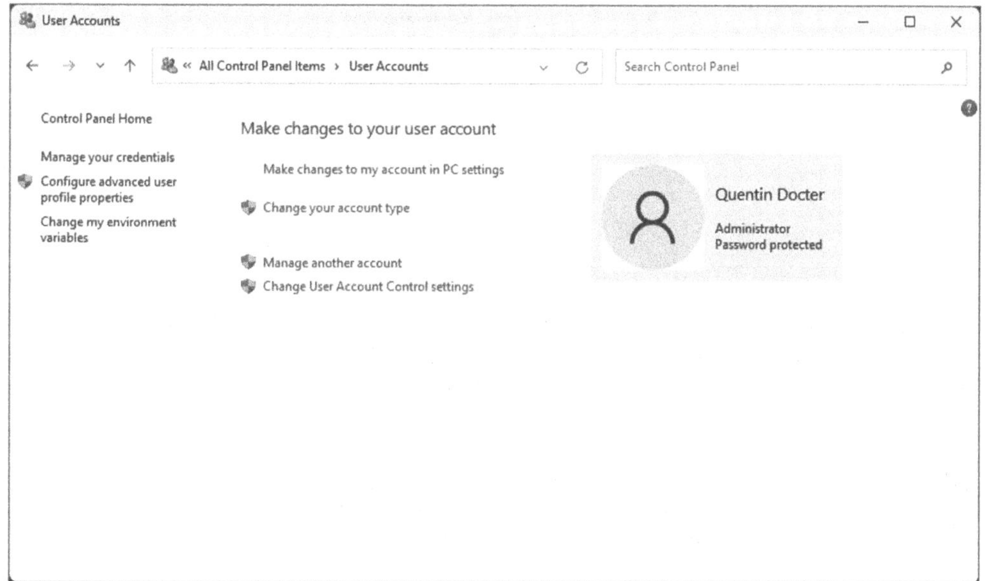

4. Click Change User Account Control Settings. You will get a window similar to the one shown in Figure 4.20.

EXERCISE 4.2 *(continued)*

FIGURE 4.20 User Account Control Settings

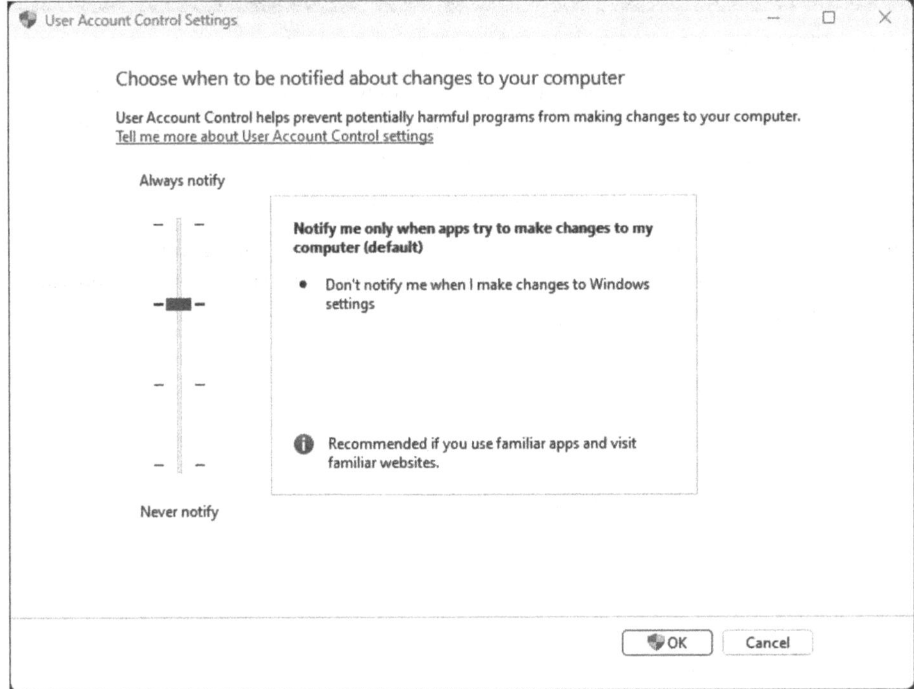

5. Adjust the slider bar to the four different security levels to see what UAC protects against. Choose your desired security level and then click OK to apply the changes.

Even if you are the only person using a computer, it's not a good idea to set UAC to Never Notify. This will help prevent accidental installation of malware when you browse the web.

Application Management

Without a doubt, applications make our computers more usable. Some aid our productivity while others entertain us or help keep our data safe. I'll talk in more depth about applications in Chapter 5. Within the operating system, administrators can install, modify, repair, update, or delete applications.

Application management is listed in Tech+ exam objective 3.2. Be able to explain its purpose.

When you install an application in Windows, it makes several system changes, including changes to a critical Windows database called the Registry. The *Windows Registry* maintains all system settings. Without it (or if it's messed up), Windows won't work. To uninstall, change, or repair an installed application properly, you should use the Programs And Features app in Control Panel, shown in Figure 4.21. To get to it, open Control Panel and click Programs And Features (if viewing by large or small icons) or Programs (if viewing by Category).

FIGURE 4.21 Programs And Features

Programs and Features

« All Control Panel Items › Programs and Features

Search Programs and Features

Control Panel Home

View installed updates

Turn Windows features on or off

Uninstall or change a program

To uninstall a program, select it from the list and then click Uninstall, Change, or Repair.

Organize ▾ Uninstall Change

Name	Publisher	Installed On	Size	Version
Into the Breach	GOG.com	8/24/2020	2.10 MB	1.2.24
LED Sync	EVGA	8/24/2020	7.03 MB	1.1.0
Microsoft 365 - en-us	Microsoft Corporation	4/4/2024		16.0.174
Microsoft Edge	Microsoft Corporation	3/28/2024		123.0.24
Microsoft Edge WebView2 Runtime	Microsoft Corporation	3/29/2024		123.0.24
Microsoft OneDrive	Microsoft Corporation	4/3/2024	308 MB	24.055.0
Microsoft Teams classic	Microsoft Corporation	4/1/2024	136 MB	1.7.00.7
Microsoft Update Health Tools	Microsoft Corporation	4/2/2024	1.02 MB	5.72.0.0
Microsoft Visual C++ 2008 Redistributable - x64 9.0.3...	Microsoft Corporation	2/20/2023	12.4 MB	9.0.3072
Microsoft Visual C++ 2008 Redistributable - x64 9.0.3...	Microsoft Corporation	11/22/2021	13.2 MB	9.0.3072
Microsoft Visual C++ 2008 Redistributable - x86 9.0.3...	Microsoft Corporation	8/23/2020	10.2 MB	9.0.3072
Microsoft Visual C++ 2008 Redistributable - x86 9.0.3...	Microsoft Corporation	11/22/2021	10.1 MB	9.0.3072

Microsoft Corporation Product version: 16.0.17425.20146

In the next section, we'll look at what to do when an application is not responding (aka locks up or hangs).

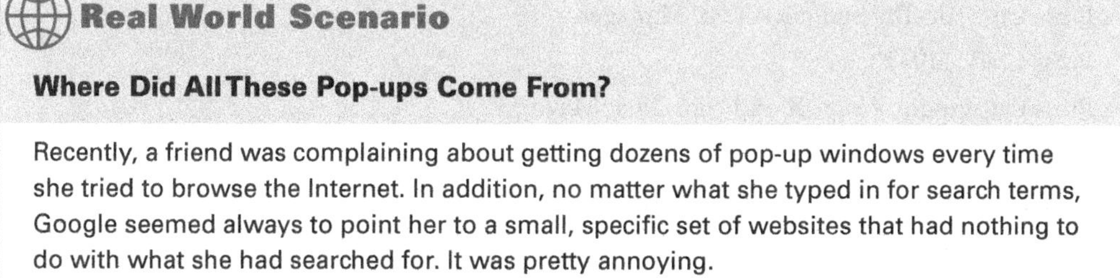

Real World Scenario

Where Did All These Pop-ups Come From?

Recently, a friend was complaining about getting dozens of pop-up windows every time she tried to browse the Internet. In addition, no matter what she typed in for search terms, Google seemed always to point her to a small, specific set of websites that had nothing to do with what she had searched for. It was pretty annoying.

Whenever something like this happens, you should always try to understand how long it's been happening and what has changed. A few weeks ago, she had downloaded a few free games for her small children to play. She couldn't remember for sure, but she thought the pop-ups started around the same time.

We opened Programs And Features and sorted the apps by install date. Sure enough, a few weeks ago a games package was installed. On the same date, two other applications were also installed, and she had no idea what they were.

The two additional apps were pretty simple adware that had been attached to the games. Fortunately, we were able to remove both of the adware applications, and the pop-ups and search redirection stopped.

Process Management

Nearly every program running on a computer is run as a *process*. This includes system operations, background tasks, and applications. The reason it's done this way is that it makes it easy to control who or what has access to various system resources at a very granular level. Imagine how many different things Windows does at once. If Windows were run as a single process, any little bit of it hanging up would cause the entire system to fail. With granular processes, one of them can fail but possibly not affect any other operations.

Tech+ exam objective 3.1, "Identify components of an OS," lists processes and system applications and utilities as subobjectives. Task and process management is also in objective 3.2. You should know what a process is and how to manage them.

Some people might think that if they have no applications open that "nothing" is running on their computer. That couldn't be further from the truth. The Task Manager utility helps you see everything that's running on a computer. You can get to Task Manager in several ways.

- Type **Task Manager** into the Windows search box and click it when it appears.
- Press Ctrl+Alt+Del and click Task Manager.
- Press Ctrl+Shift+Esc.
- Press the Windows key+X and click Task Manager.
- Right-click the taskbar and click Task Manager.

Regardless of how you choose to get there, Task Manager will look a lot like Figure 4.22.

FIGURE 4.22 Task Manager

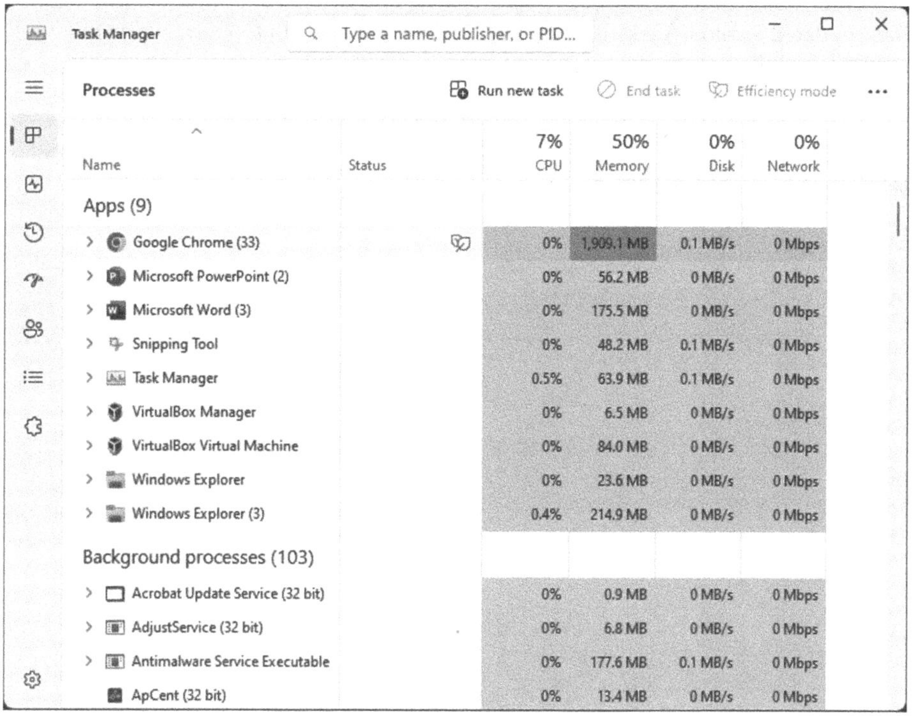

You can see in Figure 4.22 that I have nine different apps open and that there are 103 background processes running. If I scroll down further, I can also see that there are 97 Windows processes running. All of the background and Windows processes are part of a collection of *system applications and utilities*, so named because they are managed by the operating system. Task Manager tells me how much each app is consuming in terms of resources, which is very nice. If I have an app that's taking up way too much memory or is hogging the CPU, I can click it and then click End Task to shut it down. This is also known as *killing the process*.

It's not recommended that you kill processes if you're not sure what they do. I could safely kill Chrome or some of the other apps (although it will cause me to lose any unsaved data or work), but what about AdjustService? I'm not sure what it does, so I should probably just leave it alone. You can look up process names on the Internet to see what they do, if you're curious. In the worst-case scenario, if you kill something critical and Windows starts acting weird, a system reboot generally restores it and you'll be fine.

You can also schedule tasks to run at a certain time through the Task Scheduler app. To open it, type **Task Scheduler** in the Windows search box and then select it from the menu. It's shown in Figure 4.23. It's common to schedule tasks such as application update checks and system backups.

Figure 4.23 shows that my system has several active tasks scheduled. The highlighted one checks to ensure that my Google software is up-to-date, and if not, it will prompt me to install an updated version. Tasks include triggers that tell it when to start, actions that tell it what to do, conditions that might need to be present such as the system being idle, and various settings. Exercise 4.3 walks you through creating a task.

FIGURE 4.23 Task Scheduler

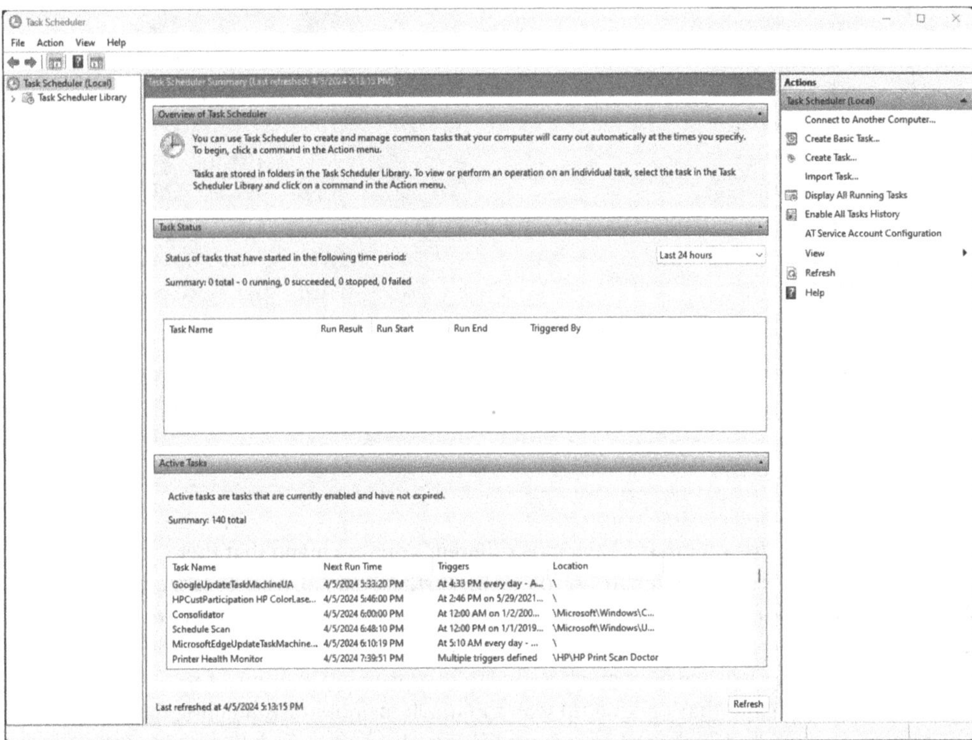

EXERCISE 4.3

Creating a Task with Task Scheduler

1. Open Task Scheduler by typing **Task Scheduler** into the Windows search box and pressing Enter or clicking it on the menu.
2. In the right pane of Task Scheduler, click Create Basic Task.

3. Give the task a name, and a description if you would like, as shown in Figure 4.24. Click Next.

FIGURE 4.24 Create a basic task

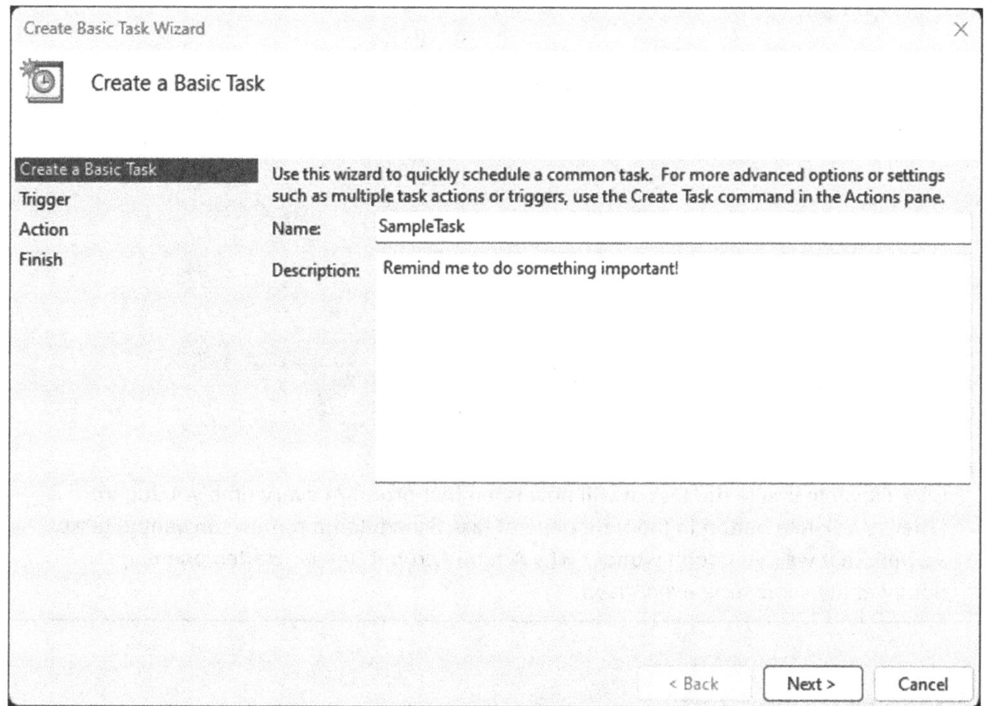

4. Create the trigger, stating when you want the task to start. If you choose any of the time-related options, you will be prompted on the next page for more details on when to trigger the task. Click When I Log On and then Next.
5. On the Action page, specify the action that you want it to take. In Windows 11, it can start a program. Older versions may also let you send an email or display a message. Choose Start A Program and click Next.
6. On the Start A Program page, use the Browse button to navigate to the location of the program you want to start, as shown in Figure 4.25. Click Next.

EXERCISE 4.3 *(continued)*

FIGURE 4.25 Starting a program

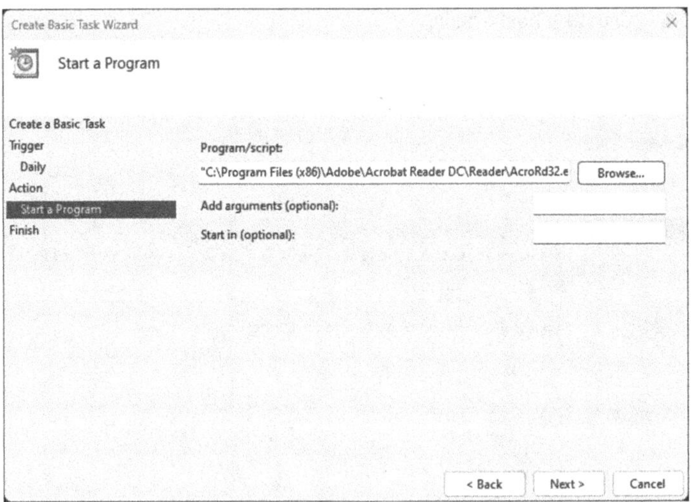

7. Click Finish to create the task. It will now open that program every time you log in. (There's a Delete button in the right pane of Task Scheduler to remove unwanted tasks as well. That way you don't wonder why Adobe Acrobat Reader started opening randomly at the same time every day.)

Service Management

Windows extends its functionality by using services. A *service* is a software package that provides additional features. For example, all printing requests are handled by a service called the Print Spooler, and a service called UserManager controls user accounts. A computer will have dozens of services running at one time. Some are always active, but many run quietly in the background, waiting for a specific trigger before springing into action.

Exam objective 3.1 wants you to be familiar with services as a component of an OS. Know what they are used for!

The easiest way to see the services on your computer is to use the Services tab of Task Manager (see Figure 4.26).

Much the same as processes, if I'm not sure what a service does, I'm probably not going to mess with it. If you do need to change the status of a service, though, right-click it, and you will have options to start, stop, or restart. You will also have the option of opening the Services management console (Figure 4.27), which provides more details on services on the computer. Services also allows you to start and stop services by using the buttons at the top of the window or by right-clicking the service you want to manage.

FIGURE 4.26 Services tab of Task Manager

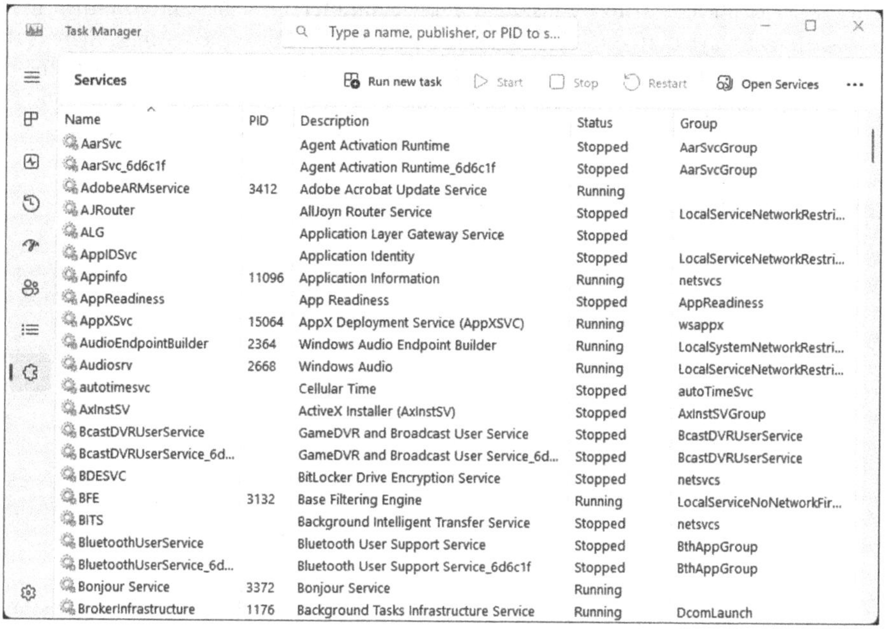

Task Manager | Type a name, publisher, or PID to s...

Services | Run new task | Start | Stop | Restart | Open Services | ...

Name	PID	Description	Status	Group
AarSvc		Agent Activation Runtime	Stopped	AarSvcGroup
AarSvc_6d6c1f		Agent Activation Runtime_6d6c1f	Stopped	AarSvcGroup
AdobeARMservice	3412	Adobe Acrobat Update Service	Running	
AJRouter		AllJoyn Router Service	Stopped	LocalServiceNetworkRestri...
ALG		Application Layer Gateway Service	Stopped	
AppIDSvc		Application Identity	Stopped	LocalServiceNetworkRestri...
Appinfo	11096	Application Information	Running	netsvcs
AppReadiness		App Readiness	Stopped	AppReadiness
AppXSvc	15064	AppX Deployment Service (AppXSVC)	Running	wsappx
AudioEndpointBuilder	2364	Windows Audio Endpoint Builder	Running	LocalSystemNetworkRestri...
Audiosrv	2668	Windows Audio	Running	LocalServiceNetworkRestri...
autotimesvc		Cellular Time	Stopped	autoTimeSvc
AxInstSV		ActiveX Installer (AxInstSV)	Stopped	AxInstSVGroup
BcastDVRUserService		GameDVR and Broadcast User Service	Stopped	BcastDVRUserService
BcastDVRUserService_6d...		GameDVR and Broadcast User Service_6d...	Stopped	BcastDVRUserService
BDESVC		BitLocker Drive Encryption Service	Stopped	netsvcs
BFE	3132	Base Filtering Engine	Running	LocalServiceNoNetworkFir...
BITS		Background Intelligent Transfer Service	Stopped	netsvcs
BluetoothUserService		Bluetooth User Support Service	Stopped	BthAppGroup
BluetoothUserService_6d...		Bluetooth User Support Service_6d6c1f	Stopped	BthAppGroup
Bonjour Service	3372	Bonjour Service	Running	
BrokerInfrastructure	1176	Background Tasks Infrastructure Service	Running	DcomLaunch

FIGURE 4.27 Services management console

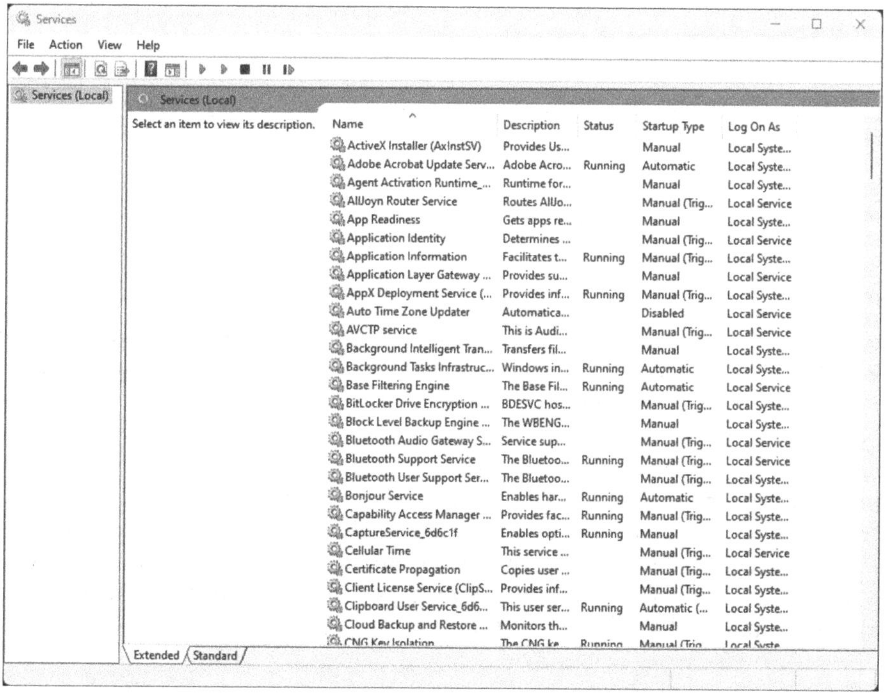

Services

File Action View Help

Services (Local)

Services (Local)

Select an item to view its description.

Name	Description	Status	Startup Type	Log On As
ActiveX Installer (AxInstSV)	Provides Us...		Manual	Local Syste...
Adobe Acrobat Update Serv...	Adobe Acro...	Running	Automatic	Local Syste...
Agent Activation Runtime_...	Runtime for...		Manual	Local Syste...
AllJoyn Router Service	Routes AllJo...		Manual (Trig...	Local Service
App Readiness	Gets apps re...		Manual	Local Syste...
Application Identity	Determines ...		Manual (Trig...	Local Service
Application Information	Facilitates t...	Running	Manual (Trig...	Local Syste...
Application Layer Gateway ...	Provides su...		Manual	Local Service
AppX Deployment Service (...	Provides inf...	Running	Manual (Trig...	Local Syste...
Auto Time Zone Updater	Automatica...		Disabled	Local Service
AVCTP service	This is Audi...		Manual (Trig...	Local Service
Background Intelligent Tran...	Transfers fil...		Manual	Local Syste...
Background Tasks Infrastruc...	Windows in...	Running	Automatic	Local Syste...
Base Filtering Engine	The Base Fil...	Running	Automatic	Local Service
BitLocker Drive Encryption ...	BDESVC hos...		Manual (Trig...	Local Syste...
Block Level Backup Engine ...	The WBENG...		Manual	Local Syste...
Bluetooth Audio Gateway S...	Service sup...		Manual (Trig...	Local Service
Bluetooth Support Service	The Bluetoo...	Running	Manual (Trig...	Local Service
Bluetooth User Support Ser...	The Bluetoo...		Manual (Trig...	Local Syste...
Bonjour Service	Enables har...	Running	Automatic	Local Syste...
Capability Access Manager ...	Provides fac...	Running	Manual (Trig...	Local Syste...
CaptureService_6d6c1f	Enables opti...	Running	Manual	Local Syste...
Cellular Time	This service ...		Manual (Trig...	Local Service
Certificate Propagation	Copies user ...		Manual (Trig...	Local Syste...
Client License Service (ClipS...	Provides inf...		Manual (Trig...	Local Syste...
Clipboard User Service_6d6...	This user ser...	Running	Automatic (...	Local Syste...
Cloud Backup and Restore ...	Monitors th...		Manual	Local Syste...
CNG Key Isolation	The CNG ke...	Running	Manual (Trig...	Local Syste...

Extended / Standard

Device Management

Windows refers to all the hardware installed in the computer as devices. In Windows 11, there are a few different ways that you can manage device settings. For basic settings, there is the Bluetooth & devices app. To get to it, click Start and then Settings. In Settings, click Bluetooth & Devices and you'll get a screen similar to the one shown in Figure 4.28. This is the place to go if you want to add a device, manage basic settings, or remove external peripherals.

FIGURE 4.28 Bluetooth & Devices in Windows Settings

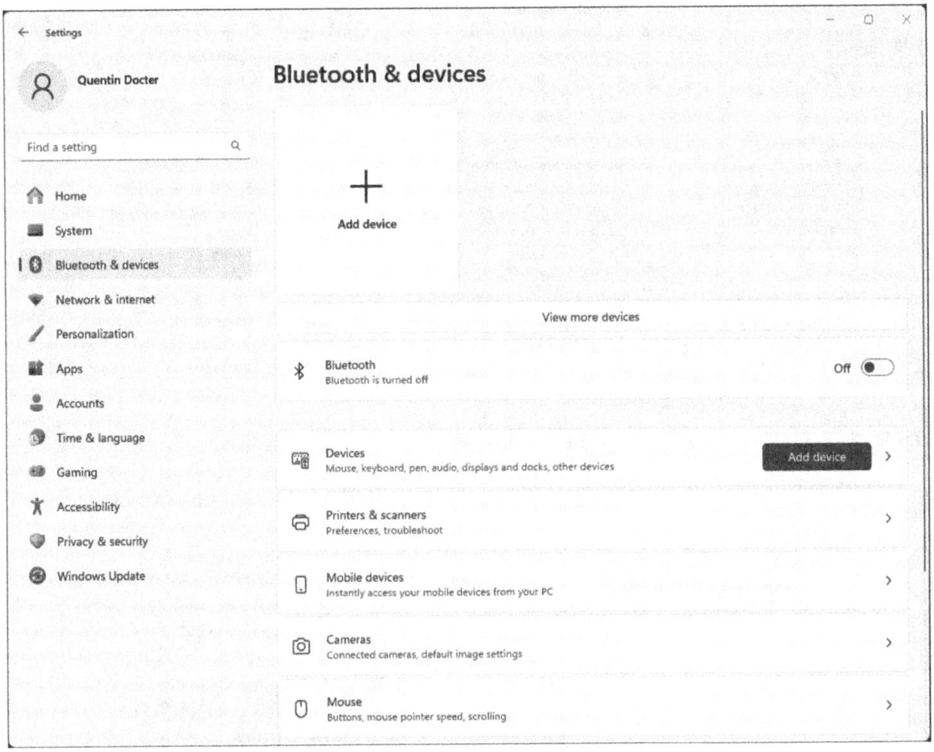

The more traditional hardware management interface is called Device Manager, shown in Figure 4.29. Device Manager is where to go if a device isn't being detected or isn't working properly. You can open it through Control Panel, by typing **Device Manager** in the Windows search bar, and by clicking it in the Quick Access menu (press Windows+X). In many instances, if there is a problem with the device, it will appear in this list with a yellow circle and an exclamation point over its icon. Here, you can also see driver details, install and update drivers, roll back a driver if a driver update fails, disable the device, or uninstall the device. (Remember, drivers are small software apps that tell the OS how to talk to the hardware device.) To get to these features, right-click a device, choose Properties, and then view the Driver tab, as shown in Figure 4.30.

FIGURE 4.29 Device Manager

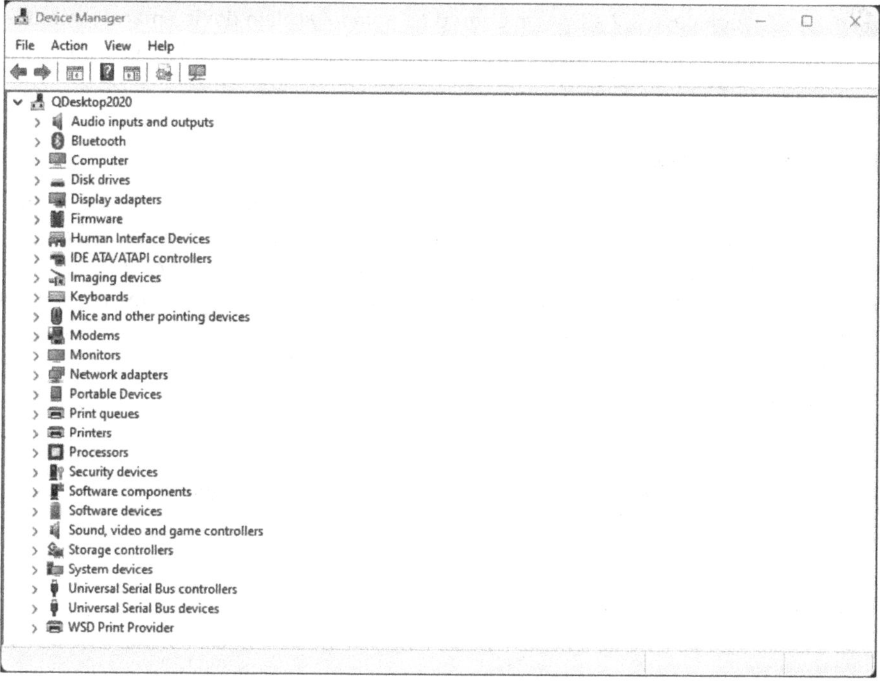

FIGURE 4.30 Driver details

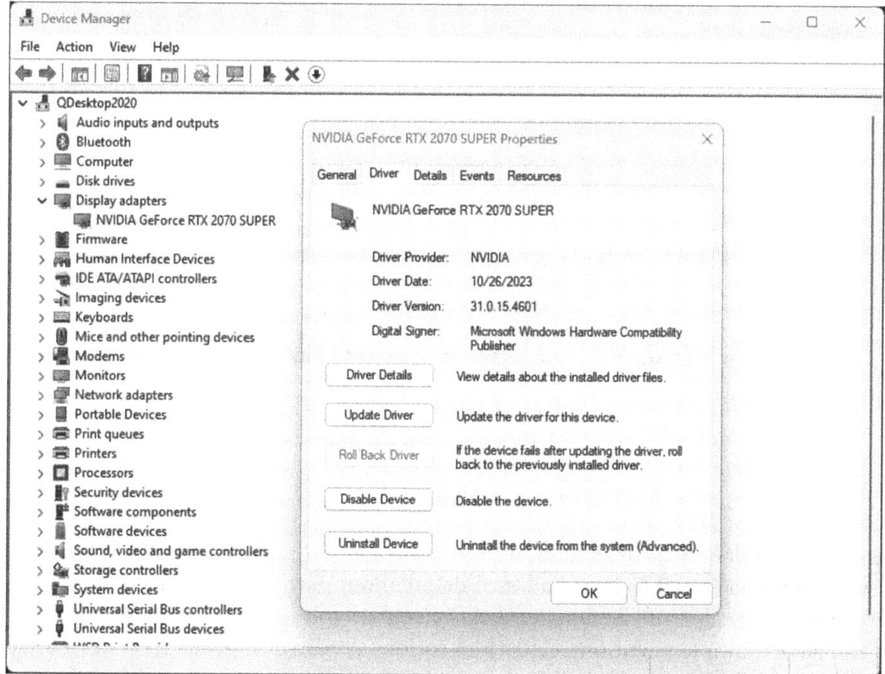

Tech+ exam objective 3.1 wants you to identify what a driver is, and objective 3.2 says you should be able to explain device management. Managing devices typically means installing or uninstalling them, or updating the driver if the device isn't working properly.

Disk Space Management

Having reliable, long-term storage of data is an important feature of desktop and laptop computers. You learned in Chapter 1, "Core Hardware Components," that hard drives are responsible for storing data. Windows manages disk space on these drives through a utility called Disk Management, shown in Figure 4.31. You can open Disk Management in many different ways, but one of the easiest ways is through the Quick Access menu (Windows+X). Disk Management doesn't care if the hard drive is HDD or SSD; it can manage either. In addition, removable media and optical drives will show up in the bottom pane.

Be sure you know how to explain what disk management is, as it's listed in exam objective 3.2.

FIGURE 4.31 Disk Management

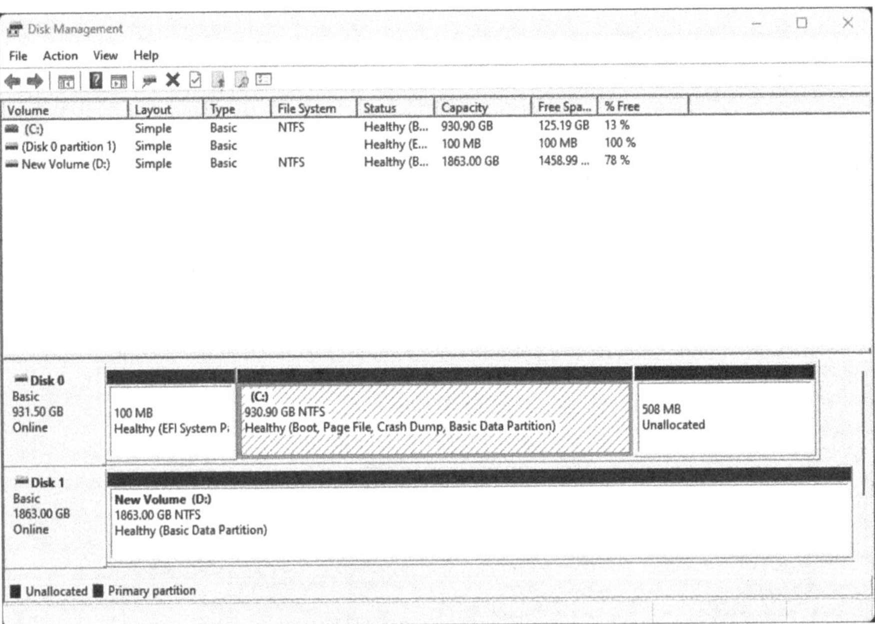

Before a hard drive can store data, it needs to be prepared. The first step is to create a partition. You won't need to know a lot of detail about partitions for the Tech+ exam, but think of them as walled-off sections of disk space that you intend to use for storage. A hard drive can have multiple partitions. After a partition is created, it needs to be formatted with a file system. I'll cover these concepts again in the "Managing Folder and File Structures" later in this chapter. Once a drive is partitioned and formatted, it's generally referred to as a volume, and it's ready to store data. Windows Disk Manager allows you to do these tasks.

Deleting a partition or formatting a volume will remove all data from that volume—be sure that's what you want to do before performing the task!

Using the Command Line

Windows and other operating systems provide beautiful visuals as the backdrop for the operating environment. The background, wallpaper, icons, color scheme, and all of those related objects are part of the *graphical user interface (GUI)*. By now, you have seen dozens of examples of several different operating systems' GUIs in action throughout this book and likely you're quite familiar with them in real life as well.

Before GUIs existed, though, early operating systems used a *command-line interface (CLI)*, usually shortened to *command line* and sometimes called a *console*. This was a text-based way of entering commands, opening applications, changing systems settings, and receiving output. It wasn't as sexy as GUIs are, but it got the job done. Today, you can still use the command line with many OSs. In fact, some old-school administrators actually prefer it.

Know how to identify a GUI and console/command line per Tech+ exam objective 3.1.

In Windows, it's easy to get to the command line, also called the command prompt. Simply type **cmd** into the Windows search box and press Enter. You will get a screen like the one shown in Figure 4.32. (By default the background will be black with white text, but I changed the color scheme to reverse that.)

FIGURE 4.32 Windows command prompt

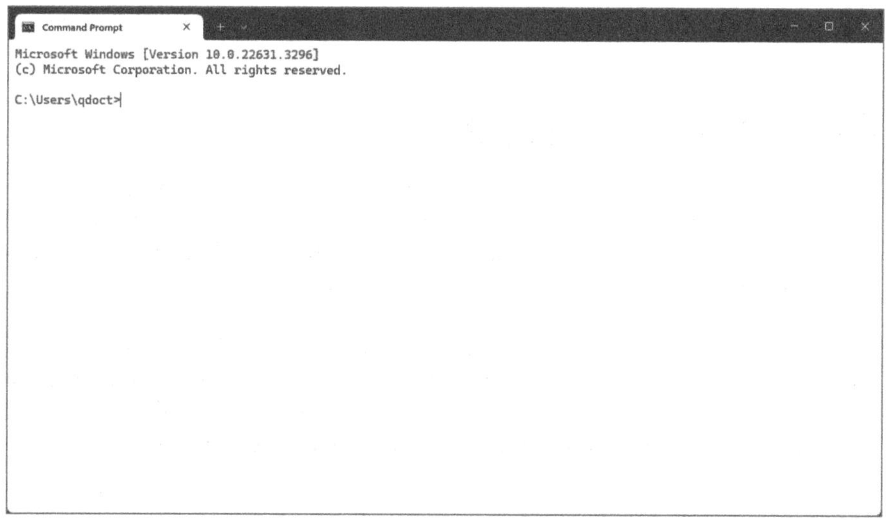

Staring at a blinking cursor with no clear idea on what to type in can be daunting. Know that at any time, you can type **help** and press Enter, and get a list of commands you can run, as shown in Figure 4.33. For help on a specific command, such as `attrib` (it lets you manage file attributes, which we will talk about in the "Viewing File Metadata" section later in this chapter) type **help attrib** and press Enter. To close the command prompt, type **exit** and press Enter. Sure, you could have clicked the X in the upper-right corner of the window, too, but the whole point was to use the command line!

FIGURE 4.33 Command prompt help

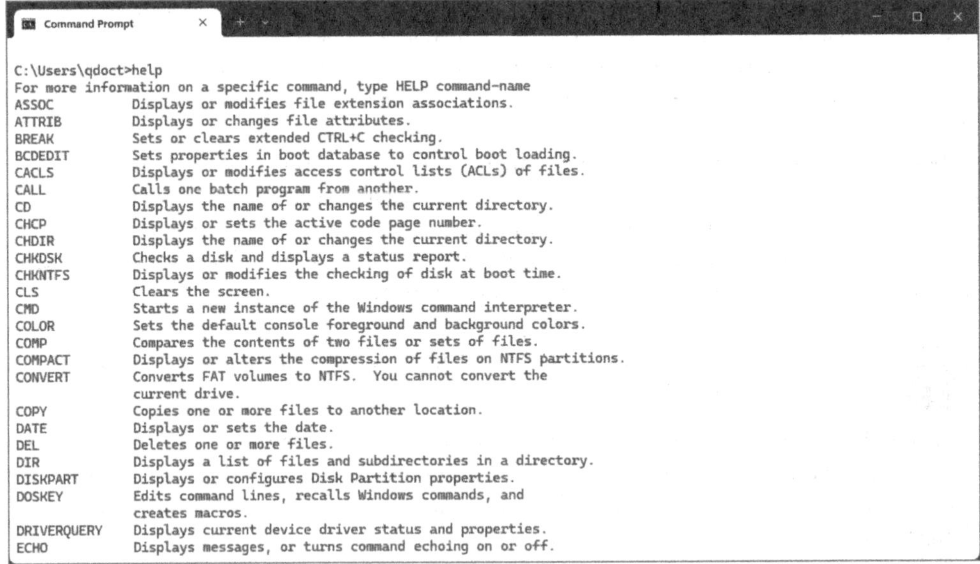

For now, that's all you need to know about the command line—simply how to identify it. Later in this chapter, in the "Viewing File Metadata" section, you will get the chance to play around with it a bit more.

Managing Folder and File Structures

We all like the fact that computers store our files for us; the hard drive takes care of that. What we like even more is the ability to find our files when we need them; the operating system takes care of that. Stored on the hard drive, the data is nothing but a very long string of 0s and 1s. The operating system makes sense of all this, knowing where one file ends and the next one begins.

Of course, what we see is far less complicated than that mess. We're used to seeing a file with a name we recognize and opening it to get to the information we want. Perhaps that file is located in a folder (also called a *directory*), which might be in another folder. But how does the computer take that mess of those 0s and 1s and make sense of it?

Let's start from the hard drive and work our way to a more granular level. When a hard drive comes from the factory, there is basically nothing on it. That might not come as a surprise to you. Before anything can be stored on that drive, someone needs to prepare it properly for storage.

The first step is to create what is called a *partition*. A partition is a logical area created on the drive for storage. Every hard drive needs at least one partition, but there can be more than one on a single hard drive if there is enough space. If you think of a partition in a room, it divides the room. A hard drive partition divides the physical disk into logical sections. If you create one partition, it will typically get the drive letter C:. Additional partitions will get subsequent drive letters.

Once the partition is (or multiple partitions are) created, you need to format the partition before it can receive data. Formatting lays down the tracks for data storage, based on the type of *file system* you choose. The partition created the giant space for storage, and the formatting lays down tracks and sectors that are the right size to store data. (The exact size depends on the size of the partition and the file system you use.) Once the file system is in place, you can install files on that drive.

An analogy a lot of people use is that of a house. The partition is the foundation of the house, and the formatting is the framing. The file system is the type of walls you put in. Once the house is framed and the walls are in, then you can store stuff in it.

File systems are responsible for managing the following:

Disk Space and File Access File systems organize the directories (folders) and files and keep track of their logical structure. When you save a new file to the disk, the file system determines where to put it physically on the disk. When you go to retrieve the data, the file system is responsible for finding it.

Filenames and Directories Some file systems have limitations on how long a filename can be or what characters can be used; some file systems are case sensitive, whereas others are not.

What's in a Name?

The old *file allocation table (FAT)* file system and MS-DOS influenced filenames for quite some time. In MS-DOS and FAT, filenames were limited to an 8.3 ("eight dot three") file-naming restriction, meaning that the filename itself could be no more than eight characters followed by a period and then a three-character *extension*.

(There were and are lots of other naming restrictions, too, such as prohibiting special characters like ?, &, %, @, \, or # appearing in a filename.)

The 8.3 naming convention forced you to be creative with filenames, because if you had something you wanted to call "Toys Western Division Profit Forecast for 2018," you might end up with something like `twdpf18.xls`. To someone not familiar with your work, that would look like gibberish.

The extension was, and is today, particularly important because it defines the *file type*. That is, it tells the operating system what program is needed for that type of file. For example, `.exe` is an executable file (meaning the OS runs the program located in the file), `.xls` is Microsoft Excel, and `.pdf` is an Adobe Portable Document Format file. When you double-click a PDF file, the OS has an association that tells it to open Adobe Reader and then the file you clicked. Extensions today aren't limited to three characters, but many still are, and all extensions need to be unique to the file type. For example, someone couldn't come along and create a new file type called a Pretty Darn Funny file and give it a `.pdf` extension, because `.pdf` already means something else. You can see (and change) the programs associated with file types in Windows 11 by opening the Choose Defaults By File Type app. Start typing **associate** into the Search box and it will appear. When you open it, you'll get a window like the one in Figure 4.34. If there is no default app, the OS will ask you which app you want to use to open the file.

FIGURE 4.34 App associations

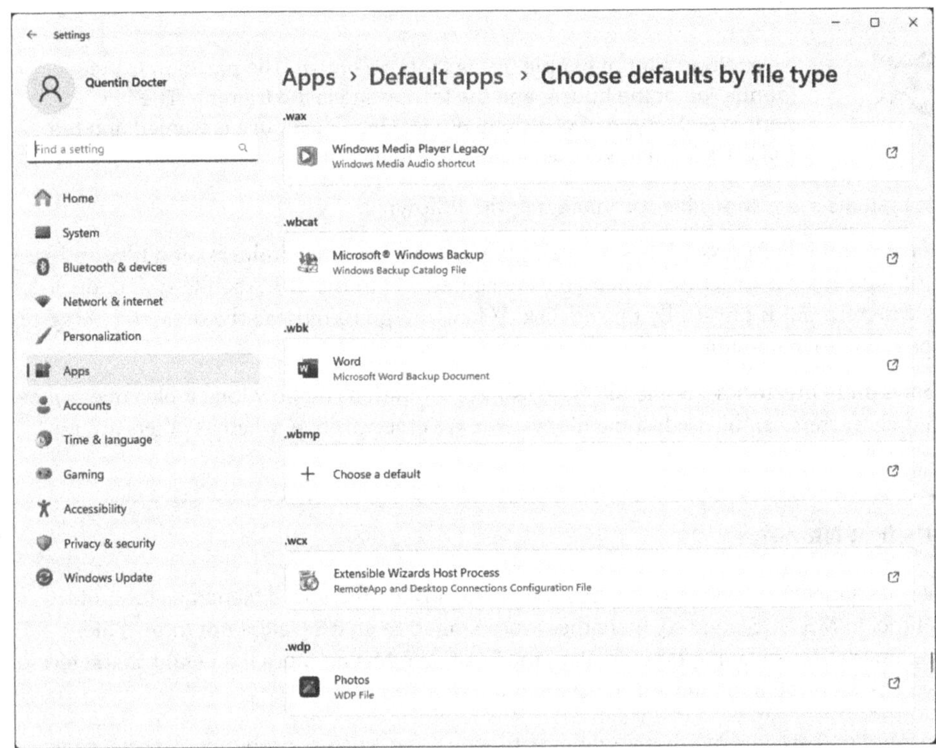

Directories are treated just like files in many OSs; files that are in the directory will just point to that directory as a parent. Directory systems can be flat, meaning that no other directories can be created in the parent directory, or hierarchical, meaning that several levels of directories can be placed inside each other.

File Metadata and Attributes Metadata is information such as the file's name, size, last time it was saved, and other attributes, such as read-only, hidden, or that the file has been changed since the last time it was backed up.

Some file systems also offer *compression* (making the file smaller to take up less disk space and then uncompressing the file when it's needed) and *encryption* (encoding the file so that only authorized users can read it).

As part of Tech+ exam objective 3.1, you may be expected to identify file system characteristics such as compression, encryption, and file types, extensions, and naming restrictions.

Security Most file systems have built-in security, which is referred to as its set of *permissions*. This allows an administrator or the creator of the file to permit some users to see the file and others to make changes to the file and yet prohibit others from accessing it altogether.

Journaling When a change is made to a file, the file system has two ways of managing it. One is to write the change directly to the drive and be done with it. The second is *journaling*, where the files changes are also written to a special file called a *journal*. Journaling results in a more fault-resistant file system. If the file system crashes or the computer unexpectedly loses power, journaled file systems are more likely to survive without errors.

Dozens of file systems have been created over the history of PCs, but only a handful are commonly used today. Most of the time, file systems are associated with a specific operating system. MS-DOS, for example, used File Allocation Table (FAT) as its default file system. Over the years, FAT was upgraded to FAT16 and FAT32, which provided additional functionality, such as larger maximum partition sizes. Since early versions of Windows ran on top of DOS, FAT also became associated with Windows. Table 4.6 gives you a list of some common and historical file systems.

TABLE 4.6 Common file systems

File system	Usual OS	Notes
File Allocation Table (FAT)	Windows	Obsolete, no security, no journaling, small max partition sizes; replaced by FAT16, FAT32, and NTFS.
New Technology File System (NTFS)	Windows	Default for Windows.
Apple File System (APFS)	macOS	Default for macOS and iOS since 2017; replaced older Hierarchical File System (HFS).
fourth extended file system (ext4)	Linux	Modern Linux file system, supports larger volumes; maximum of 64,000 subdirectories in a directory; replaced ext3.

TABLE 4.6 Common file systems *(continued)*

File system	Usual OS	Notes
Extended File System (XFS)	Linux	High-performance file system, supports large partitions.
Universal Disk Format (UDF)	n/a	Used for Blu-ray and DVDs.

If files are stored using a file system the OS doesn't recognize, the OS will not be able to read those files. In Exercise 4.4, you will look at metadata for your hard drive and begin a disk cleanup.

EXERCISE 4.4

Managing Storage Space in Windows

1. Open the Computer window. You can do this a few different ways. One way is to open File Explorer by pressing the Windows key+E and then clicking This PC in the left pane.
2. Find your C: drive, right-click it, and choose Properties. You will get a window similar to the one shown in Figure 4.35.

FIGURE 4.35 C: Properties

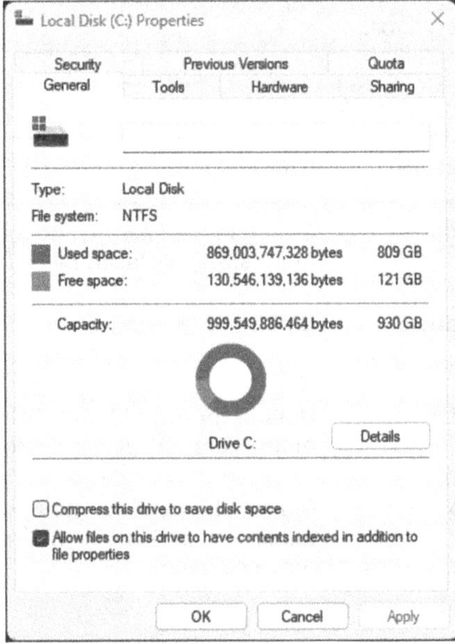

3. Identify the type of file system you have. If you run Windows, it's most likely NTFS.
4. Identify how much free hard disk space you have. Generally, you want to maintain at least 10 percent free space.
5. Notice at the bottom of the screen you have a check box to compress this drive. Doing so will free up disk space, but it will also slow down file access. If you click the Details button, it will show you how much file space is being taken up by different categories of files.
6. Close the Properties window.
7. Open the Disk Cleanup utility by typing **disk cleanup** into the Windows search box and pressing Enter. Choose C: and click OK.
8. See how much space you can free up by cleaning up your hard drive; Figure 4.36 shows an example.

FIGURE 4.36 Disk Cleanup

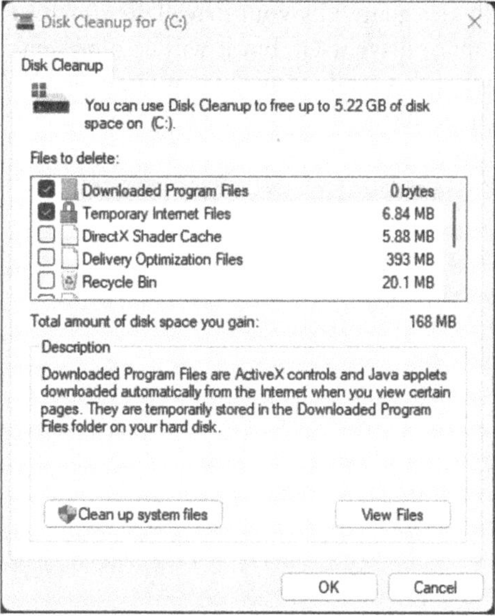

9. Check the boxes next to the types of files you want to clean up and click OK for it to begin. Otherwise, click Cancel.

Now that you understand how files are stored on the hard drive, let's get into specifics on managing a file structure within an operating system. First, I'll discuss how to navigate through a file structure. Then, I will talk about viewing file properties. Finally, I'll cover how to "do something" to a file.

Navigating a File Structure

While trying to think of a good way to define what a file is, I decided to ask Google, because Google knows everything. *File* can be used as a noun—a folder or box for holding loose papers that are typically arranged in a particular order for easy reference. It can also be a verb—to place (a document) in a cabinet, box, or folder. So, it seems that a "file" is where you put something, and "to file" is the act of putting that something somewhere. Thanks, Google!

Relating this to computers, we typically think of a *file* as a collection of information or data that has a name. Based on this definition, nearly everything stored on a computer is a file. Applications, documents, spreadsheets, pictures, even directories (or folders; I will use the term interchangeably) are files. Folders are just specialized files that organize other files.

Tech+ exam objective 3.1 says you should be able to identify the file management concepts of folders and directories.

Files are stored in directories, which can in turn be stored in other directories. Because of this structure, you will sometimes hear the file system called a *directory tree*. At the base of this tree is the root, typically designated by your drive letter, such as C:. That drive letter represents the partition on the hard drive itself, but it will be represented on the computer like any other folder. Let's see what this really looks like in Figure 4.37. To get there, press the Windows key+E to open File Explorer and then click This PC on the left side.

FIGURE 4.37 This PC window

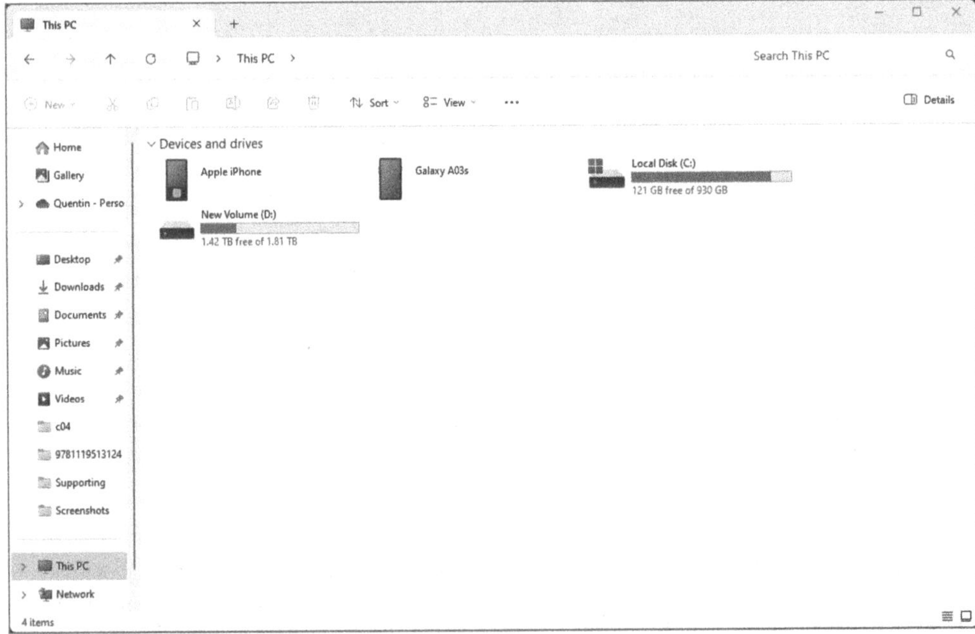

Among other things, you can see that my PC has two hard drives, C: and D:. From this view alone, it doesn't tell you for sure that there are two physical drives, I just happen to know that. It's possible that C: and D: could be on the same physical drive. For our purposes here, the distinction isn't important. When you double-click the C: drive, you get the first level of directories, as shown in Figure 4.38.

FIGURE 4.38 Directories in the C: drive

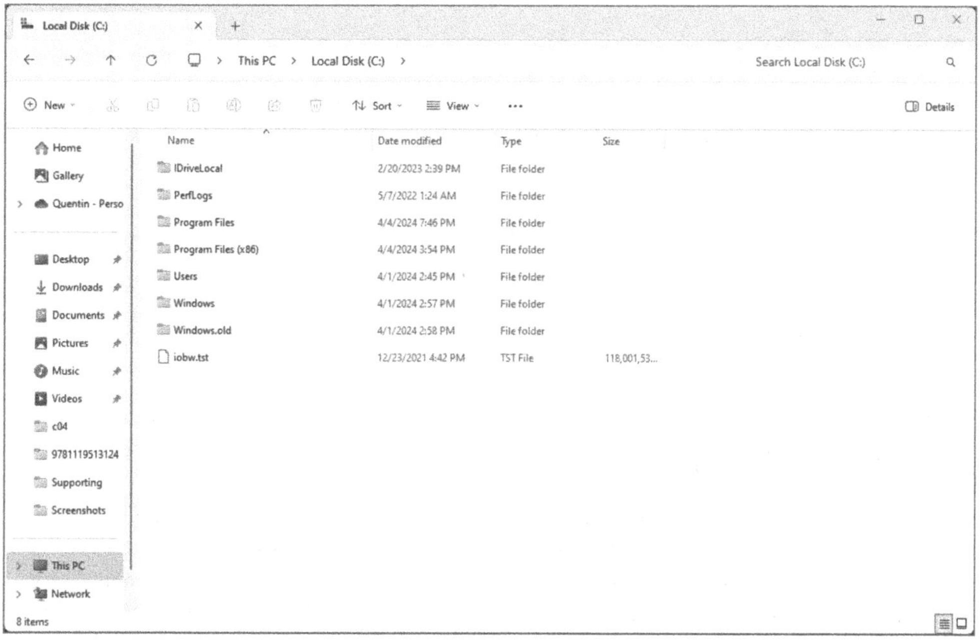

All the items that you see on the left in these figures, such as Desktop, Downloads, Documents, and Pictures, are also folders on the C: drive. If you click Documents and then another folder, you'll keep digging into further levels of folders. As you can see in Figure 4.39, I have highlighted a folder called `c04`.

And, if you want to know where you are in the directory tree, all you have to do is look at the address bar and it will tell you; it's at the top of Figure 4.39.

Using File Explorer, you can navigate to anywhere you want by double-clicking folders in the left pane. You can also click any of the directory names in the address bar (like the one at the top of Figure 4.39), and it will take you right to that directory. Clicking the little arrow to the right of the folder name in the address bar will let you go directly to any folder inside that folder.

You can also display the files in different ways, such as the filename only or more details. If you look at Figure 4.39, you will see a View menu at the top. Clicking that will let you change the way that files appear in the folder. You can choose a basic list, details, or various sizes of icons.

FIGURE 4.39 Several folders and files

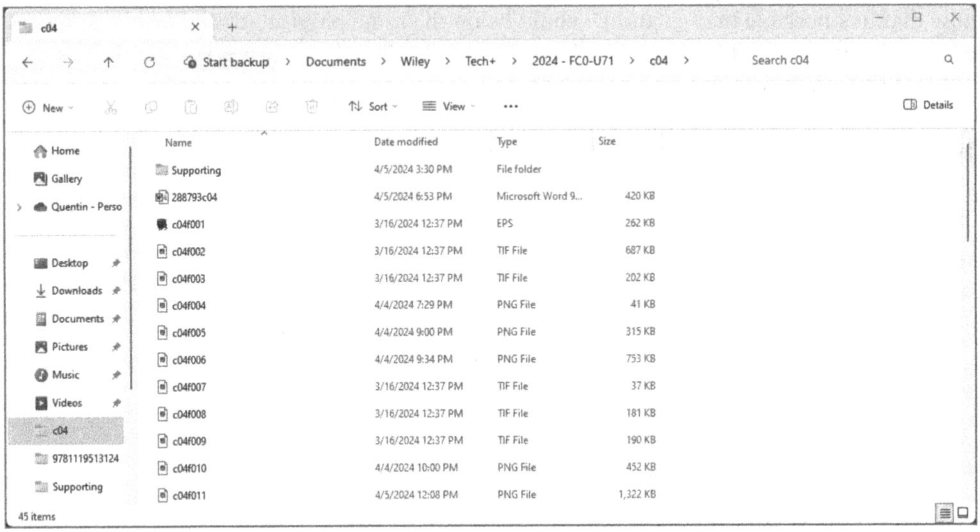

In Figure 4.39, you can see a small up arrow over the Name column. This shows how the files are sorted, with folders always first. Clicking Name again would sort the files in reverse alphabetical order. You can also sort by date modified, type, and size.

Finally, you can search for files or text in a file by using the Search box, which is in the upper-right corner of Figure 4.39. Type in the word you want to search for and press Enter or click the magnifying glass icon. It will search that folder, any files in that folder, and any subdirectories and files in that folder. You can configure the search to just look for filenames or to look in the files themselves or to look for specific file types, date modified, size, or author. There are lots of choices for you here. The results will pop up in the same window where the files are currently displayed.

Viewing File Metadata

While in File Explorer, you can also easily view the metadata for your file. This includes the size, security, and all sorts of other useful information. To get there, right-click the file (or folder), as shown in Figure 4.40, and choose Properties.

Remember the menu you see in Figure 4.40 because we will come back to it. For now, you should be looking at a window with your file properties, similar to the one shown in Figure 4.41.

In this window, you can see the name, type of file, location, size, creation and most recent modification dates, and check boxes to make the file read-only or hidden. Checking the Read-Only box will make it so that no one can make modifications to the file, and checking the Hidden box will hide it from view. Click the Security tab to see the security details of the file, like those shown in Figure 4.42.

FIGURE 4.40 Right-clicking a file

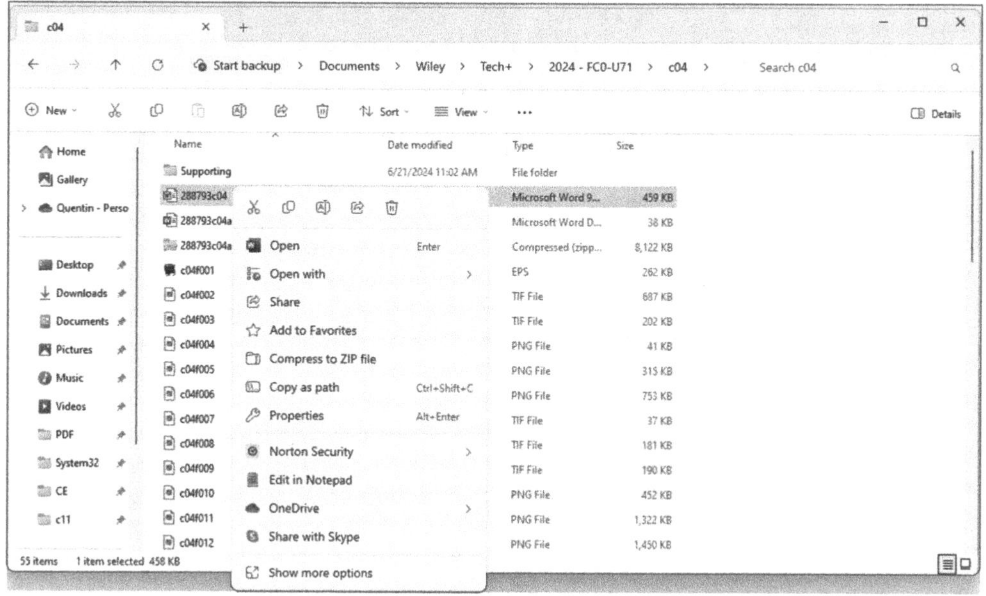

FIGURE 4.41 File properties

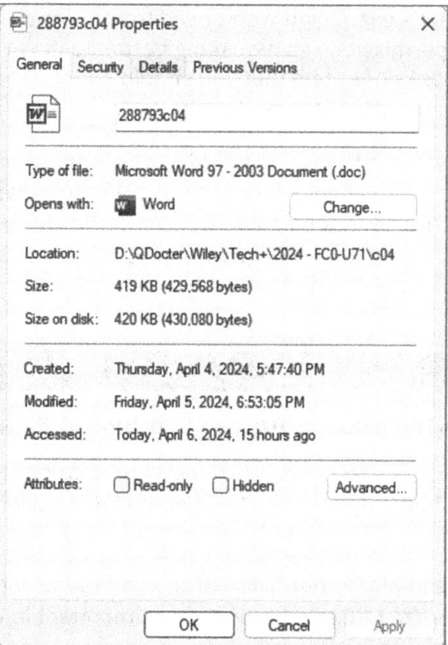

FIGURE 4.42 File security

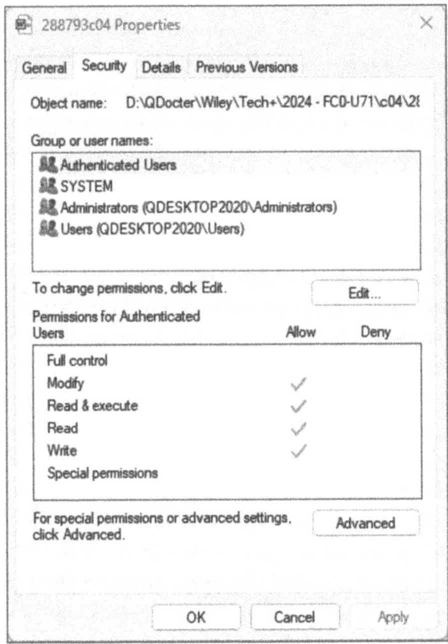

On the Tech+ exam, you won't need to know specifics about the different types of permissions shown in the bottom pane of Figure 4.42. However, objective 3.1 does state that you should understand the concepts of permissions, file attributes, and properties.

If you change permissions (read-only), the hidden attribute, or security on a file, it affects only that file. If you try to change it on a folder, Windows will prompt you. You can change it to affect only the folder and its contents or all subdirectories and their files as well. In Exercise 4.5 you get to manage file attributes through the Windows GUI and the command prompt.

EXERCISE 4.5

Modifying File Attributes and Using the Command Prompt

1. Open your C: in File Explorer by pressing Windows+E, clicking This PC in the left pane, and double-clicking C: in the right pane. (You should have a window similar to the one in Figure 4.38.)
2. In the right pane of File Explorer, right-click in an open space and choose New ➢ Folder. Name the folder **test**. (Capitalization is not important in Windows.)

3. Double-click `test` to open the folder.
4. In the right pane, it should say This folder Is Empty. Right-click in the open space below that and choose New ➢ Text Document. Name it **`text1`**. (It's an empty file, but that's fine for our purposes here.) Your Explorer window should look something like Figure 4.43.

FIGURE 4.43 Test folder with `text1` file

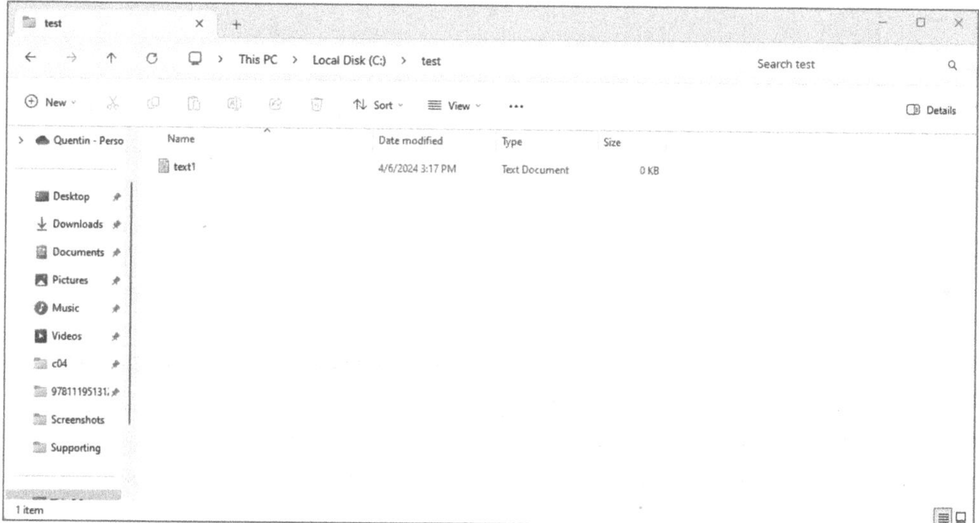

5. Right-click `text1` and choose Properties. Select the Read-Only check box, and click OK.
6. Right-click `text1` and choose Properties again. Confirm that the Read-Only box is checked, and click either OK or Cancel to close the box. Leave File Explorer open to this folder.
7. Open a command prompt by typing **cmd** into the Windows search box and pressing Enter.
8. Your command prompt should start with `C:\`. If not, type **c:** and press Enter to change it to the C: drive.
9. Type **`cd\ test`** and press Enter. The `cd` command is for change directory. Your prompt should now say `c:\test>`.
10. Type **`attrib text1.txt`** and press Enter. You will get a response like the one in Figure 4.44. Notice that there is an A and an R before the filename. This shows that the archive attribute is set (meaning that the current version of this file has not been backed up), and that the read-only attribute is set as well.
11. Type **`attrib -r text1.txt`** and press Enter. This removes the read-only attribute. (Conversely, `attrib +r` would set the attribute.)

EXERCISE 4.5 *(continued)*

FIGURE 4.44 File attributes in the command prompt

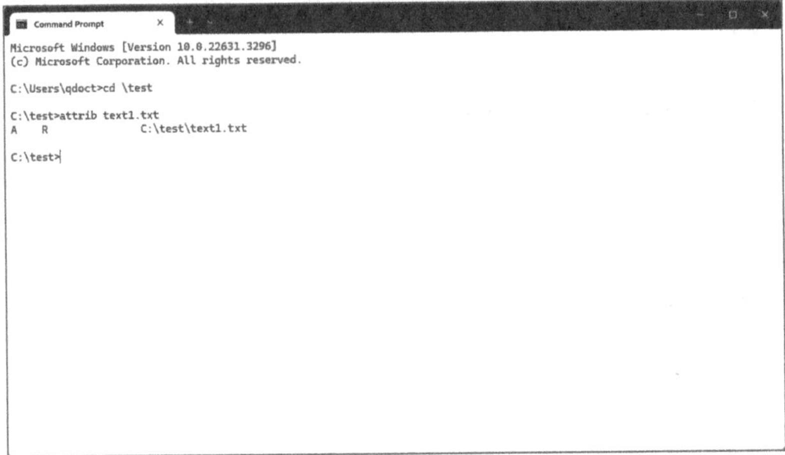

12. Type **`attrib text1.txt`** again and press Enter. You will get a response similar to the one in Figure 4.44, except the R should be gone.
13. Close the command prompt by typing **`exit`** and pressing Enter.
14. In File Explorer, right-click the `text1` file and choose Properties.
15. Notice that the Read-Only check box is now cleared!
16. (optional) Click the Advanced button. In the Advanced Attributes window (Figure 4.45), notice that the File Is Ready For Archiving option is checked. This corresponds to the A attribute we didn't change from the command prompt. Also notice that this is where you could compress or encrypt a file if desired.

FIGURE 4.45 Advanced attributes

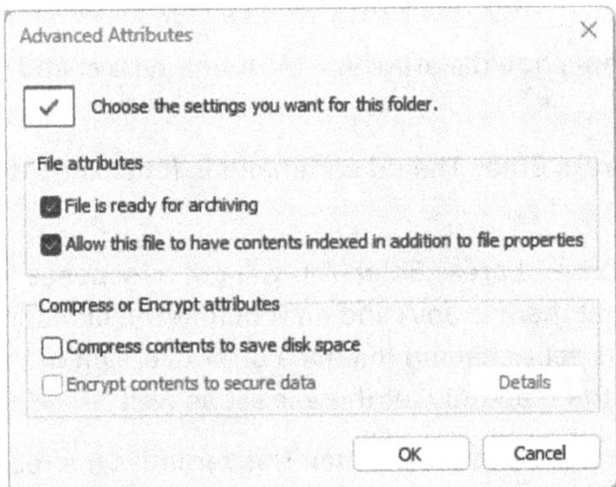

Don't delete the `test` folder just yet; you will use that in the next exercise.

Manipulating Files and Executing Programs

When I discussed file metadata, I right-clicked the file to get the menu as shown in Figure 4.40. You probably noticed that there were quite a few different options on the menu. Across the top there are buttons to cut, copy, rename, share, and delete. Then written out in text there are options to Open, Open with, Share, and others. You can see your computer might have more or less than mine, depending on the software you have installed. For example, since I have Norton Security, I have options to use that program on my context menu. The rest of what you see on that menu is pretty standard for Windows. Here are some of the key options for manipulating files about which you should be aware:

Open Opens the file in the default program for that file. Sometimes you will also have the option Open With, which allows you to specify the program you want to open the file. You can also open a file by double-clicking it.

Edit Opens the file in the default editor for that program. If it's a Word document, it will open Word just like the Open command will. For pictures, though, oftentimes you will have a different program to display the images versus edit the images.

Move Takes the file from one folder and moves it to another. The original file content does not change, but the location in the directory tree does. On the hard drive, the file does not actually move. The metadata just gets modified, associating it with the folder where you moved the file.

Copy Copies the file to the clipboard (a temporary storage space in Windows). If you want to place the file somewhere else, you need to paste it there. The original file is not changed in any way. If you paste the file somewhere else, the OS will create a new version of the file, with the same name, in the new location. It also creates an additional version of it on the hard drive. You can also copy a file (or multiple files) by highlighting it and then pressing Ctrl+C (holding down the Ctrl key and then pressing C once) on your keyboard.

Cut This is a lot like Copy, in the sense that it copies the file to the clipboard. To complete the transaction, you need to paste the file somewhere. The original file content does not change, but the location in the directory tree does. On the hard drive, the file does not actually move from one place to another. The metadata just gets modified, associating it with the folder where you pasted the file. You can also cut a file (or multiple files) by highlighting it and then pressing Ctrl+X on your keyboard.

Paste If you have something on your clipboard, it will paste the contents into wherever you executed the Paste command. If you cut and paste a file, the file does not physically move on the hard drive. It gets executed like a Move command. The keyboard shortcut for Paste is Ctrl+V.

Delete Removes the file from the directory it's in and moves it to the Recycle Bin (Windows) or Trash (macOS). It doesn't actually erase the file from the hard drive; it just changes the metadata to say it now belongs to the Recycle Bin or Trash directory. Emptying the Trash will erase it from the hard drive and free up disk space. You can also delete files by highlighting them and pressing the Del key on your keyboard.

Rename Changes the metadata for the file, giving it a new name. Functionally, it's very similar to Save As. You can't have more than one file with the same name in any directory.

In Windows 11, the right-click menu has been streamlined versus previous versions of Windows. To see the same list of options you would have seen in Windows 10, right-click and then choose Show More Options at the bottom of the list. Most of the choices will be the same between the two options screens, but the latter one will have a few more.

In NTFS, you can't change file metadata, such as renaming or moving, when the file is open. Other file systems such as ext3 and ext4 do not have this restriction.

Exercise 4.6 has you manipulate files on your computer. Well, folders, really, but remember that folders are files, too!

EXERCISE 4.6

Manipulating Files in Windows

1. Open File Explorer by pressing the Windows key+E. Navigate to the C: drive by clicking This PC in the left pane and then double-clicking C: in the right pane.

   Provided you didn't delete it, you should still see your `test` folder from Exercise 4.5.
2. Create a new folder by right-clicking in the right pane and choosing New ➢ Folder.
3. Name the new folder **happy**.
4. Right-click happy and choose Cut (it's the scissors icon). Notice how the folder icon looks more transparent.
5. Right-click text and choose Paste (it's the icon that looks like a clipboard). You could also open up `test` first and then right-click the right side and choose Paste, or just open `test` and press Ctrl+V.
6. Double-click `test`. The happy folder should now be in there.
7. Right-click happy and choose Copy.
8. Navigate back to your `Documents` folder and paste **happy** there. Now, you should have a happy folder in two locations.
9. Delete the happy folder by highlighting it, right-clicking, and choosing Delete. Leave the `test` folder for now.

We already talked about two ways to open a file, which are to right-click it and choose Open or simply to double-click it. If what you are double-clicking is an application, it will execute that program. Additionally, you can open a file or execute a program using the Start menu. Click Start, find the file or program in the list, and click it. Or type the name of the program into the Windows search box and press Enter.

There's one last way to open a file and that's to open a shortcut to the file or program. A *shortcut* is a file that points to the real file's location. Sometimes, you will hear it referred to as a *pointer file*. Normally, you will create these on your desktop to make it easier to access folders, files, or programs that you run a lot. The shortcut itself doesn't contain the data, so you can delete a shortcut and not lose any data. You can identify a shortcut because it has a small arrow as part of the icon. Exercise 4.7 walks you through creating a shortcut.

EXERCISE 4.7

Creating a Shortcut in Windows

1. Right-click an open area of your desktop and choose New ➢ Shortcut.
2. Click Browse, and a window will appear similar to the one shown in Figure 4.46.

FIGURE 4.46 Browsing for a folder or file

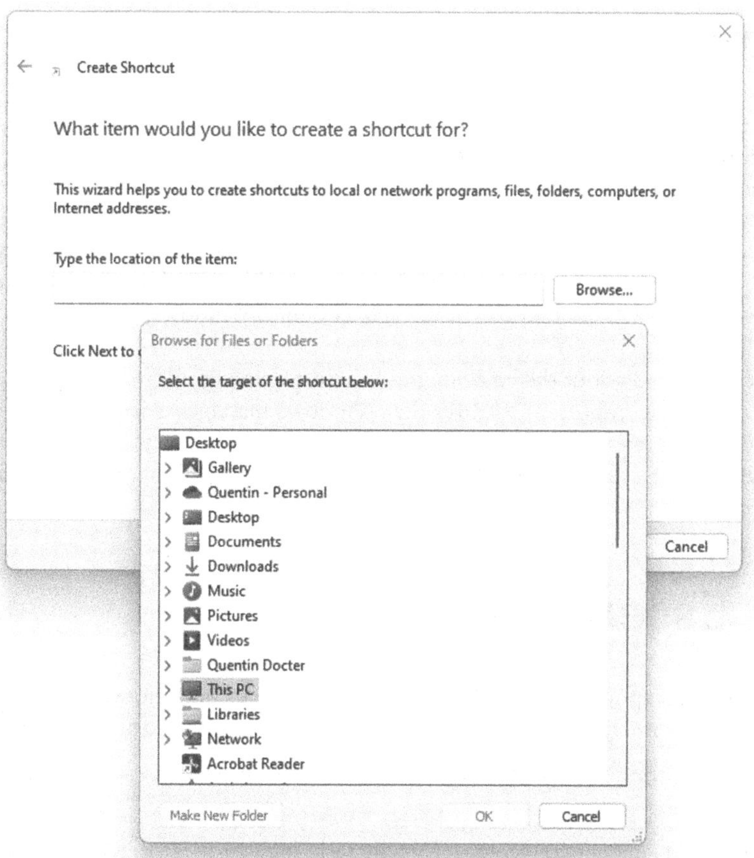

EXERCISE 4.7 *(continued)*

3. Find your `test` folder in the directory tree and click it. It will be under This PC > Local Disk (C:).
4. Highlight the `text1` file and click OK, and then click Next in the Create Shortcut window.
5. Type a name for your shortcut (if you want) and click Finish.
6. A new shortcut to the `text1` file will appear on your desktop. Notice that it has a small arrow in the lower-left corner, signifying that it's a shortcut. Double-click the shortcut and notice that it opens the file.
7. (Optional) Delete the shortcut if you want. Remember that deleting the shortcut will not delete the file itself!

Summary

In this chapter, we covered a wide variety of information about operating systems. First, I took you through a high-level history of operating systems so that you now have a better understanding of why they work the way they do. After that, we looked specifically at the basic functions that an OS performs.

Next, we moved into the types of operating systems. Specifically, we talked about four categories of OSs—workstation, server, mobile, and embedded. Within most categories, we covered the important OS families to know, such as Linux, Windows, macOS, Chrome, iOS, and Android.

After that, we talked about the basic methods used to manage an operating system. We started with examining important features that Windows manages, such as users, access control, applications, processes, services, devices, disk space, and memory. Then we finished by covering navigating the file structure, looking at file metadata, making changes to files, and executing programs.

Exam Essentials

Be able to identify components of an OS. The components include file system characteristics, file management, system applications and utilities, services, processes, drivers, and interfaces.

Know the characteristics of file systems. They include compression, encryption, and file types and extensions.

Understand file management concepts. They include folders/directories, permissions, and naming restrictions.

Understand how to use different OS interfaces. Be familiar with the console/command line as well as graphical user interfaces (GUIs). Know how to view file attributes and properties in these interfaces.

Be able to explain the purpose of operating systems. Operating systems are the interface between applications and hardware.

Understand features that operating systems need to manage. Operating systems manage disks, tasks and processes, applications, devices, and access control.

Know the four types of operating systems. The four types of operating systems are mobile device, workstation, server, and embedded.

Understand how files are stored on computers. Files are any items that have a filename. Files are stored in folders (or directories), which in turn can be stored in other folders on the hard drive.

Know how to view file properties. Metadata is part of a file's properties. In Windows, you can right-click the file and select Properties to view the metadata.

Chapter 4 Lab

You can find the answers in Appendix A.

Most people are familiar with Microsoft Windows because it's so popular. Not everyone is as familiar with Linux, though. In this lab, you are going to install Lubuntu on your machine. The goal is to familiarize yourself with another OS and to understand that other operating systems aren't scary or mysterious. They all do similar things; it's just a matter of figuring out how.

Historically, installing a second OS involved a relatively complicated process where you needed to dual-boot your computer. We're not going to do that here. You will use a technology called VirtualBox, which allows you to create a new virtual system on your hard drive and not affect your existing Windows installation. I promise you that this lab will not mess up Windows on your computer! And when you're finished, you can just uninstall VirtualBox, if you want, and nothing will have changed on your system.

The first two steps are for preparation. You need to download Oracle VirtualBox and a version of Lubuntu. Really, any version of Linux is fine; you will just have to slightly modify the download steps. Depending on your network speed, the download could take an hour or more.

1. Download Oracle VirtualBox from `www.virtualbox.org/wiki/Downloads`. Select VirtualBox For Windows Hosts, unless, of course, you have a Mac, and then you need the one for macOS hosts. Save it to your desktop for ease of access.
2. Download Lubuntu from `https://lubuntu.me/downloads`. Download the current release by clicking the button for Desktop 64-bit. As of this writing, the newest release is 23.10. It will download a zipped file with an `.iso` extension. You will need that ISO file later; it will essentially act as a bootable CD for your OS installation.

   Now you begin the installation of VirtualBox.

3. Double-click the VirtualBox icon. If you get a security warning, click the Run button. Then click Next on the Setup Wizard screen.
4. On the Custom Setup screen, click Next and then Next again. It will give you a warning about your network interfaces. Click Yes. (Your network connections will come back automatically.)
5. Click Install. The installation may take several minutes. (You might also need to clear another security warning box.)
6. Once the installation is complete, click Finish.

   It's time to configure VirtualBox.
7. You might get a VirtualBox warning telling you that an image file is not currently accessible. That's fine. Click Ignore. You should see a screen similar to the one shown in Figure 4.47.

FIGURE 4.47 VirtualBox preconfiguration

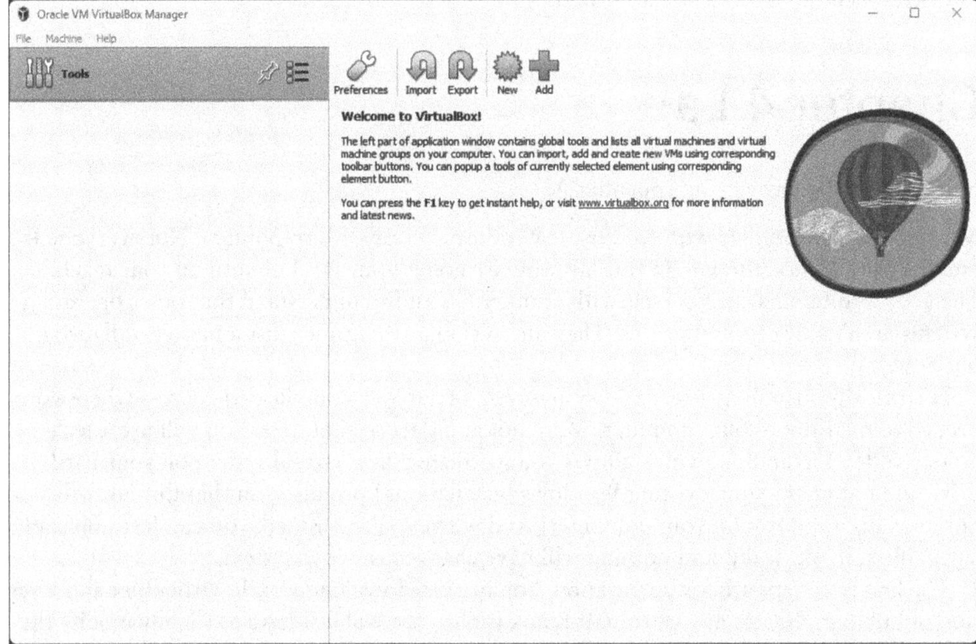

8. Click the blue New icon to create a new virtual machine. Give it a name. The Type and Version boxes aren't critical; they don't affect anything. If you type **Lubuntu** for a name, it will automatically set Type to Linux and Version to Ubuntu. Click Next.
9. In the Hardware window, click Next to accept the default base memory and processor allocation.
10. In the Virtual Hard Drive window, the default option is Create A Virtual Hard Disk Now. Leave that option selected and click Next. (If you were going to use this extensively, you would want to give the virtual machine more hard drive space than the default 10 GB.)

11. The Summary page appears with your choices. Click Finish. You should get a screen similar to the one shown in Figure 4.48.

FIGURE 4.48 VirtualBox with a virtual drive

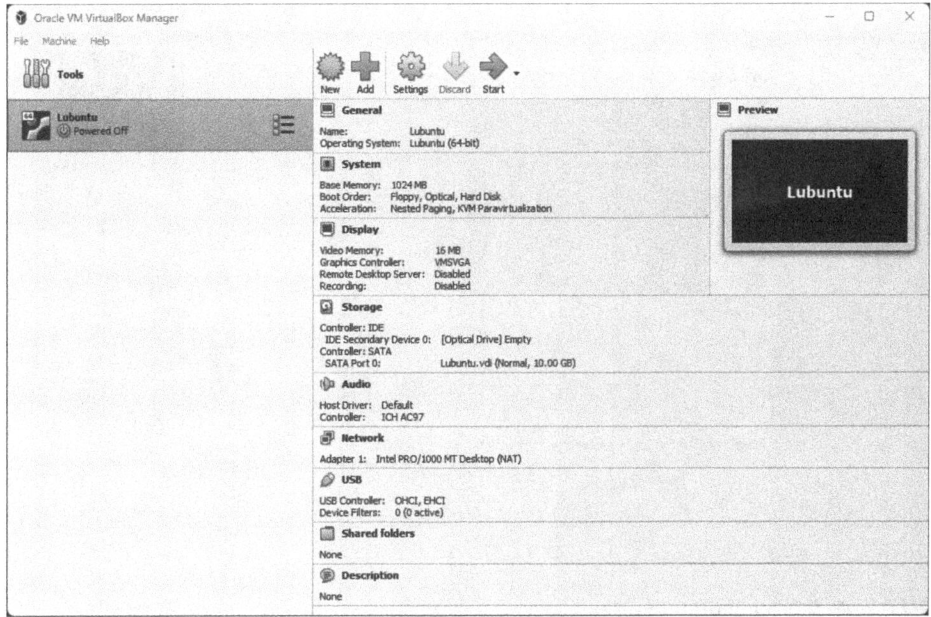

Great! You now have a virtual machine on your hard drive. Now you just need to put something, more specifically an OS, on it.

12. Click the Settings button.
13. In the Lubuntu – Settings window, click the Storage icon on the left.
14. Under one of your controllers, you should see something that looks like a disc icon that says Empty. It should look like Figure 4.49.
15. On the very right side of the window, you will have another disc icon with a little down arrow on it. Click that, and a menu will pop up. Select Choose/Create A Virtual Optical Disk.
16. The Optical Disk Selector window will appear. In this case, the Lubuntu ISO file is listed. If yours is not, you will need to navigate to the directory where you stored the `Lubuntu.iso` file that you downloaded. Highlight the file, and then click Choose.
17. Back on the Lubuntu – Settings dialog, your drive that was empty should now say Lubuntu. Click OK.
18. Now you are back to the Oracle VirtualBox Manager screen. With Lubuntu on the left highlighted, click the green Start arrow. This will boot into a live session of Lubuntu, like what you see in Figure 4.50.
19. Double-click the Install Lubuntu icon on the virtual desktop to begin installation.

FIGURE 4.49 Lubuntu – Settings dialog

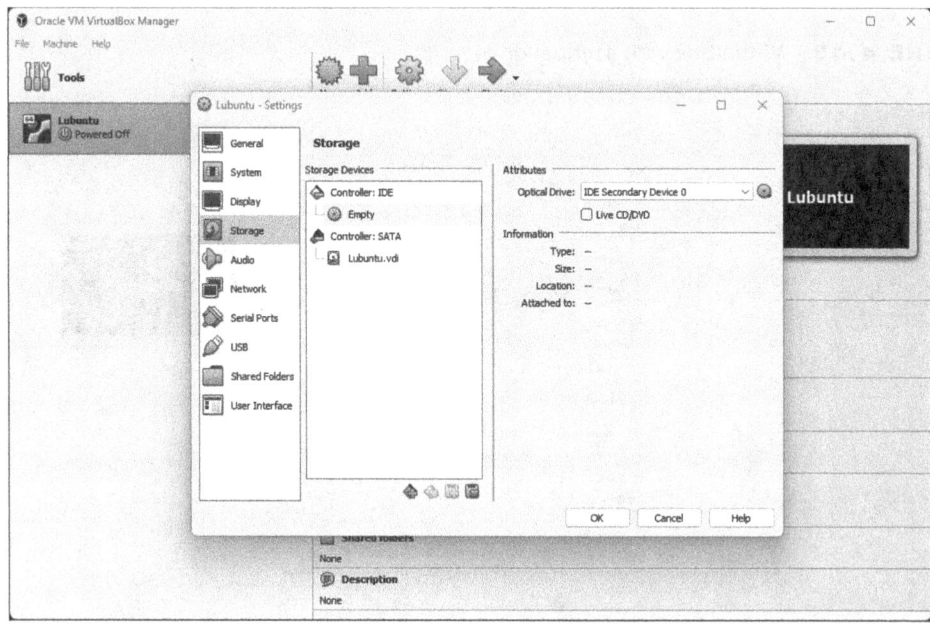

FIGURE 4.50 Lubuntu live session

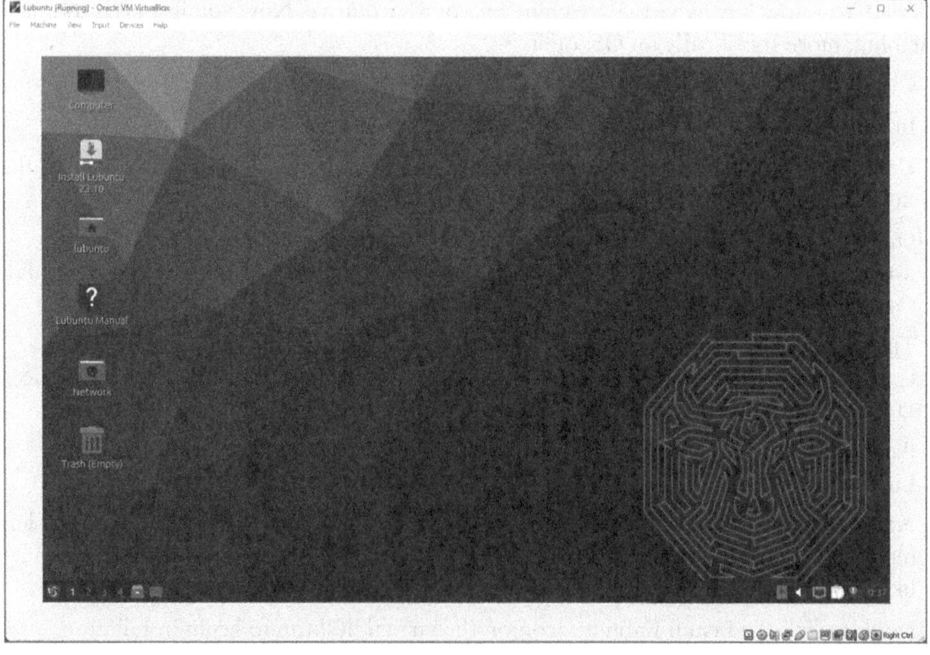

In step 18 after you press the green Start arrow, you might get an error message saying the operating system was not bootable. If that happens, use the drop-down box at the bottom of the error message to point to the ISO file again, and retry. It should work. If not, it's possible the ISO file is corrupted. You can download again, or try downloading a different distribution to make it work, starting back at step 12.

20. Choose a language, and click Next,
21. Choose a location and click Next.
22. Select a keyboard layout and click Next.
23. You will get to a screen similar to the one shown in Figure 4.51, which asks you for an installation type. It looks scary, but choose the Erase Disk option. This will install it on the virtual disk that you created earlier with VirtualBox, and it will *not* wipe out your entire hard drive. Click Next.

FIGURE 4.51 Installing Lubuntu

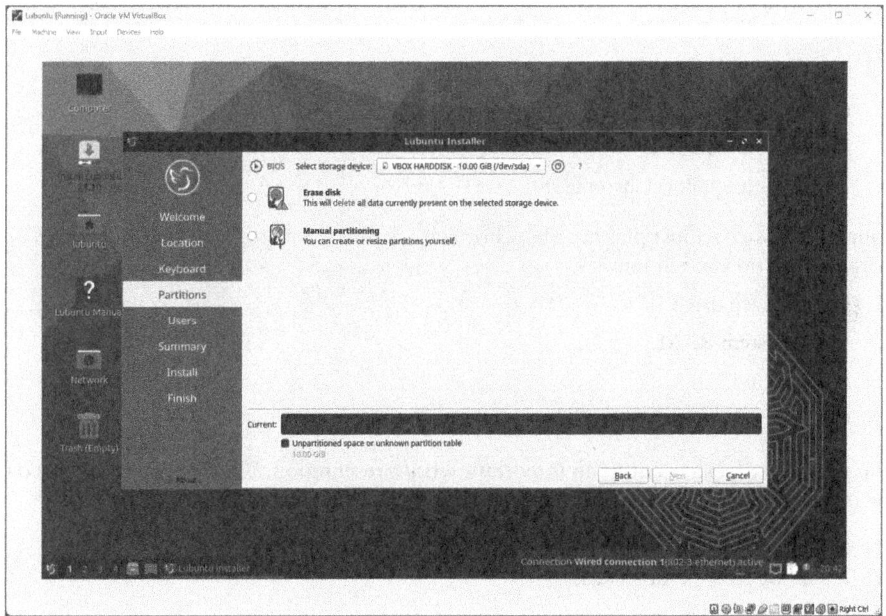

24. Continue with the installation process. When in doubt, choose the default and move to the next step.
25. When the installation is complete, check the Restart Now box and click Done.

Now that the installation is complete, play around in your new operating system! I strongly encourage you to go back through this chapter and do Exercises 4.1 and 4.4–4.7, but this time in Lubuntu. Also look for customization options to change your desktop wallpaper.

Review Questions

You can find the answers in Appendix B.

1. Which of the following is *not* a function of an operating system?
   - A. Interface between the user and the machine
   - B. Coordinate software applications
   - C. Coordinate hardware components
   - D. Monitor system health
2. Which of the following desktop operating systems can you freely modify if you choose?
   - A. macOS
   - B. iOS
   - C. Android
   - D. Linux
3. Peter, a friend of yours, has a piece of software that was written for macOS. Which of the following OSs will that software run on?
   - A. macOS only
   - B. macOS and Linux
   - C. macOS and ChromeOS
   - D. macOS, Linux, and ChromeOS
4. Your friend Michael just purchased a Chromebook and wants to know where his files are stored. What do you tell him?
   - A. On the hard drive.
   - B. In the system RAM.
   - C. In the cloud.
   - D. Chromebooks do not store files.
5. You just deleted a shortcut to an important work presentation. What happened to the data in the presentation?
   - A. Nothing.
   - B. It's in the Recycle Bin/Trash.
   - C. It's deleted.
   - D. It's in the recovery partition.
6. With which of the following file systems can you not rename a file when it's open?
   - A. ext3
   - B. ext4
   - C. APFS
   - D. NTFS

7. You are going to purchase a new iPhone. Which operating system will be installed on it?
   A. iOS
   B. OS X
   C. iPhone OS
   D. Android
   E. iDontKnow
8. Which of the following is an example of an embedded OS?
   A. Windows
   B. Firmware
   C. iOS
   D. Linux
9. Fred, a friend of yours, wants to host a website for his new company. Which type of OS should be on the computer hosting the website?
   A. Embedded
   B. Mobile
   C. Server
   D. Workstation
10. Which of the following is not a feature of a file system?
    A. Permissions
    B. Encryption
    C. Journaling
    D. Access control
11. Linux is defined as a _______________, which is also the core of an operating system.
    A. Distribution
    B. Version
    C. Kernel
    D. Shell
12. You need to kill a process in Windows. Which utility should you use?
    A. Task Manager
    B. Process Manager
    C. File Explorer
    D. Programs and Features

13. You just copied a file from the `Work` directory to the `Projects` directory on your Windows PC. What happened to the file on the hard drive?
   A. Nothing.
   B. The file was removed from the `Work` directory and placed in the `Projects` directory.
   C. The file was not moved, but a new pointer record was created associating the file with the `Projects` directory.
   D. The file was copied to a new location on the hard drive and was associated with the `Projects` directory.

14. Your hard drive is running low on space. Which of the following could help alleviate that situation?
   A. Compression
   B. Encryption
   C. Attribution
   D. Journaling

15. The combination of Linux-based files that gets released as a product is called what?
   A. Distribution
   B. Version
   C. Kernel
   D. Source

16. Which of the following items does Windows Task Manager allow you to manage? (Choose two.)
   A. Drivers
   B. Interfaces
   C. Processes
   D. Services

17. You need to prepare a brand-new replacement hard drive for storage. What is the first step needed to get it ready?
   A. Format the drive.
   B. Install an OS.
   C. Install a file system.
   D. Create a partition.

18. You need to update a Windows driver for a sound card. Which utility should you use?
   A. Device Manager
   B. Sound Card Manager
   C. Drivers app
   D. Control Panel

19. Which of the following would not be considered metadata for a spreadsheet file?
    - A. Read-only attribute
    - B. Calculations inside the file
    - C. Name of the file
    - D. File size
20. You want to keep a co-worker, Jerry, from accessing a file. What should you use to do this?
    - A. Permissions
    - B. Read-only
    - C. Archive
    - D. Compression

Software Applications

THE FOLLOWING COMPTIA TECH+ FC0-U71 EXAM OBJECTIVES ARE COVERED IN THIS CHAPTER:

✓ **3.0 Applications and Software**

✓ **3.3 Explain the purpose and proper use of software.**

- Productivity software
  - Word processing
  - Spreadsheet
  - Presentation
  - Visual diagramming
- Collaboration software
  - Email client
  - Conferencing
  - Online workspace
  - Document sharing
- Instant messaging software
- Web-browsing software
- Remote support software

✓ **3.4 Given a scenario, configure and use web browser features.**

- Private browsing
- Browser add-ons/extensions
  - Add
  - Remove
  - Enable/disable
- Caching/clearing cache
- Pop-up blockers

- Compatible browser for application(s)
- Profile synchronization
- Organizing features
    - Bookmarks
- Default search engine
- Password management
- Accessibility
- Appearance

✓ **6.0 Security**

✓ **6.2 Explain methods to secure devices and security best practices.**

- Securing devices (mobile/workstation)
    - Anti-malware
    - Firewall
    - Patching/updating
- Device use best practices
    - Licensing
        - Open source vs. proprietary
        - Subscription vs. one-time purchase vs. perpetual
        - Product keys and serial numbers
    - Software sources
        - Researching and validating legitimate sources
        - Original equipment manufacturer (OEM) websites vs. third-party websites
        - Application stores
    - Removal of software
        - Unwanted
        - Unnecessary
        - Malicious
    - Software piracy

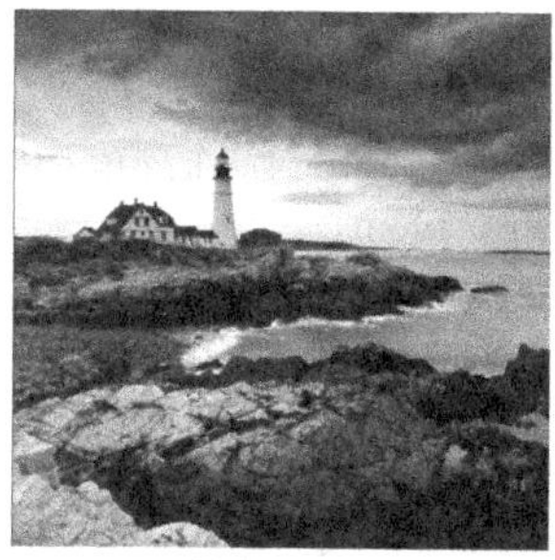

All of the hardware and the operating system in computers just provides a base for what you really want to do with computers, and that's to run software applications. You want your computer to help you do something—often a lot of somethings—such as writing a letter, creating a presentation, managing your taxes, or playing a game. Thanks to the myriad of software titles out there, you can do all of these things and even more, quite often doing more than one of them at one time.

Applications are the second major classification of software (after operating systems), and that is the focus of this chapter. Some of the topics that I will cover are application installation and management, licensing, and types of applications. Web browsers specifically will get a lot of ink because of their wide usage, unique configuration options, and potential security problems.

By the end of this chapter, you will be able to explain the purpose and use of software, configure and use a web browser, and explain methods to secure devices and security best practices. You will also be familiar with several types of software available for both business and personal use. Software truly makes that box of parts sitting in front of you useful, so let's begin!

Understanding Application Installation and Management

I'm going to go out on a not-so-shaky limb here and guess that you have used software before. If you have even touched a computer or a smartphone, then you have. And the fact that you are reading this book means that you're interested in computers, so it's an easy guess to get right. What you might not have done, though, is to take a step back and think about all of the things that need to happen for that application to run properly. All of those things fall under the category of software management.

Throughout this chapter, I will use the terms *software, application,* and *program* interchangeably.

Software management isn't too hard, as long as you follow a couple of basic rules—install and uninstall properly, patch/update as needed, and have the right licenses. If you do those things, you will have relatively few problems with the software on your computer. And if or when you have a scenario where you are having problems with an application, rebooting your computer or device often takes care of the issue. If the issue keeps coming back, uninstall and reinstall, and you should be back up and running with no problems.

In this section, I will cover best practices for software management. First, I will talk about the stuff you need to think about before installing an application, such as whether or not it will work with your OS and where you'll get it from. Then, I'll move on to the proper way to install and uninstall features of your operating system, applications, and drivers. Finally, I'll talk about updating or patching the software on your system.

Considerations for Installing Software

Before you buy any software, you need to make sure of a few critical things. The first is to figure out if the application works with your operating system, and the second is to figure out if your hardware is robust enough to support it. Then, decide where you will get the software from (the source) and determine the licensing requirements for that software and whether your intended use falls within those requirements.

Software Compatibility

Sometimes, you will find yourself staring at a web page, looking at the specifications for a new application, and wondering, "Will this work on my computer?" In the documentation for each application available for download or purchase, you'll find a "Minimum System Requirements" section. This usually includes a list of compatible OS versions, a minimum processor speed, a minimum amount of RAM, and the minimum required amount of hard disk space available. There may also be additional requirements, such as a particular display adapter, the amount of display adapter RAM, or a permanent Internet connection to use the software. An Internet search should provide all the information you need. Figure 5.1 shows the requirements page for a popular game. On this page you will find minimum and recommended requirements for all platforms this program is supported on, in this case a Windows-based PC and Mac.

Besides the generic minimum requirements, you would also be wise to research compatibility issues before spending a lot of money on an application. For example, some applications (particularly games) have known problems with certain display adapters.

When judging whether you have enough hard disk space, keep in mind that at least 10 to 15 percent of the hard disk space should be left empty to ensure best performance. Don't assume that if your hard disk has 1 GB of space left on it, you can install an application that requires 1 GB of space.

If your system barely meets the requirements in one or more aspects, the application may install but performance may suffer. For example, the application may crash frequently, run slowly, or have poor graphic or sound performance. It's always best to ensure you meet recommended requirements if possible.

FIGURE 5.1 System requirements

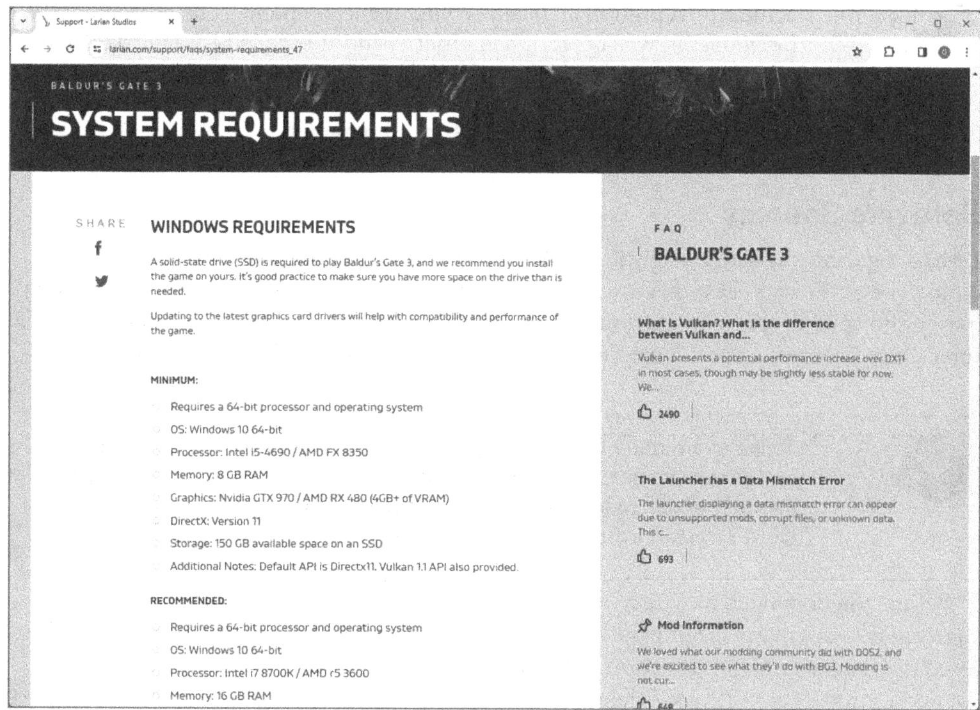

If you want to run an older application that is designed for a previous version of Windows, you may find the Compatibility Mode feature in Windows to be useful. This feature enables a newer version of Windows to mimic an older version selectively when it deals with an individual application. For example, an application may require a lower display resolution than Windows 11 provides; the Compatibility Mode feature can temporarily permit that lower resolution.

To start the Compatibility Mode troubleshooter in Windows 11, type **run programs** in the Windows search bar. The Start menu will show an app called Run Programs made for previous versions of Windows. Open it and you'll see the Program Compatibility Troubleshooter window. Click Next and follow the directions.

Some applications require an Internet connection to install them. Depending on the settings of your firewall software (such as Windows Defender Firewall), a warning may appear when the Setup program tries to access the Internet. In most cases, you can click a button to let the firewall know that it's okay to proceed.

For security purposes, it's good to have a firewall to help protect your computer. A firewall installed on your local computer, such as Windows Defender Firewall or Norton Internet Security, is called a *host-based firewall*. A *network-based firewall* is designed to protect multiple computers on a network. You will learn more about software-based firewalls in the "Software Firewalls" section later in this chapter.

Software Sources

Perhaps figuring out where you will get your software should come before checking compatibility—at the very least they would likely happen simultaneously. Sometimes you don't have a choice as to where to get your software, as it will only be available from the manufacturer's site. Other times you have choices, and as they say, choices have consequences.

Tech+ exam objective 6.2, "Explain methods to secure devices and security best practices," has software sources as a subobjective. For it, you should be able to explain researching and validating legitimate sources, OEM versus third-party websites, application stores, and software piracy.

Before you download any piece of software, be sure to do research and validate the source. There are many illegitimate sites masquerading as legitimate ones, peddling downloads that might or might not come with extra add-ons you weren't expecting. Three common software sources are original equipment manufacturer (OEM) websites, third-party websites, and application stores.

OEM Websites An *original equipment manufacturer (OEM) website* is one owned by the developer of the software. It's safe to say that software you get from an OEM website is legitimate and can be trusted, provided the developer is one that can be trusted.

Sometimes OEM developers have contracts with other parties and they will try to bundle services you might or might not want. For example, when you go to Adobe's site to download its reader, there is a selected check box for you to install McAfee Security Scan Plus (Figure 5.2). Providing this additional software isn't inherently good or bad as perhaps you already have security software or maybe you need it. The good news is they tell you about it up front and let you remove the option. Other software packages will have add-ons as options during installation. Only sketchy developers install software packages without your awareness and consent.

Third-Party Websites Many other websites besides the official Adobe one will let you download the Adobe Reader for free. Figure 5.3 shows the results of a Google search to download the reader.

FIGURE 5.2 Adobe reader download site

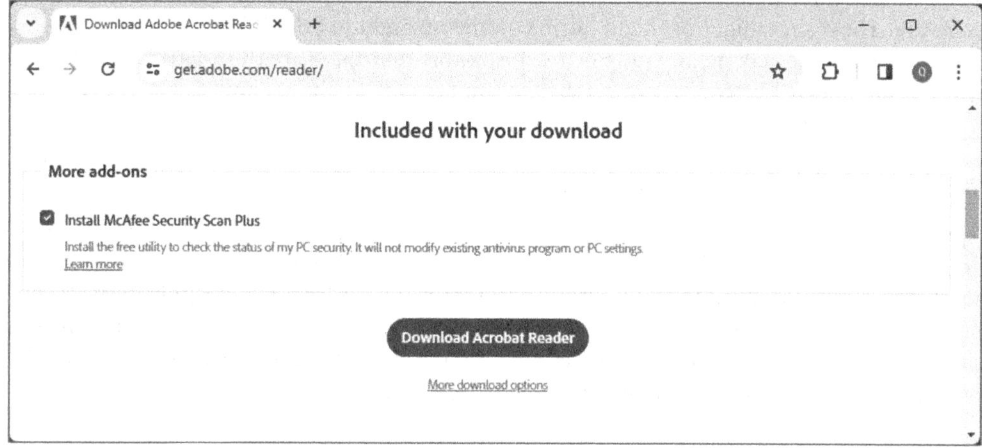

FIGURE 5.3 Third-party websites

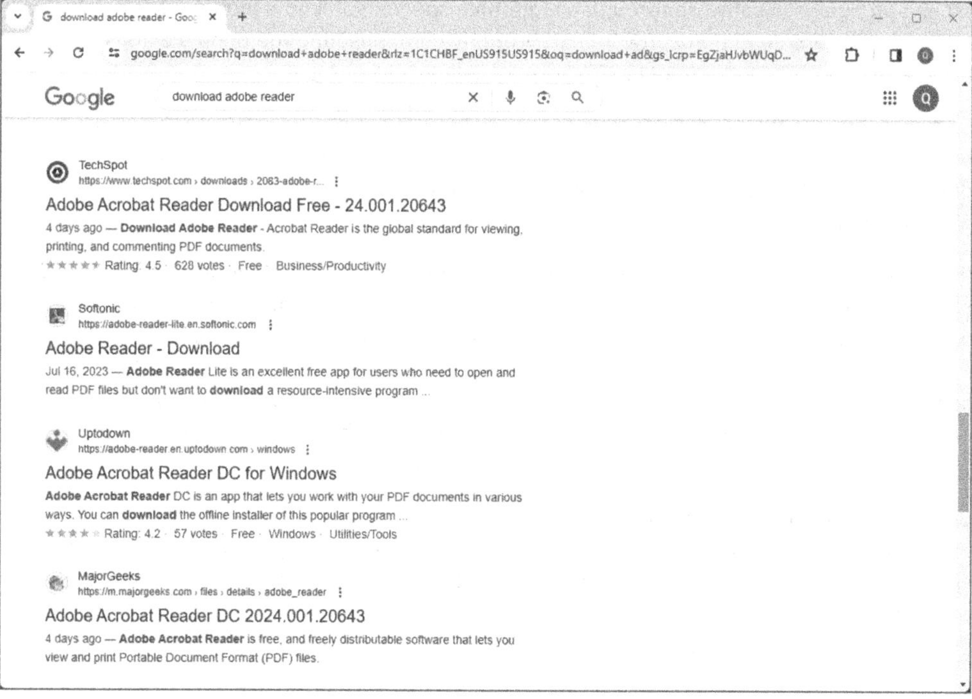

Look at the website addresses for each—none of them are from the `adobe.com` domain. They are called *third-party websites* because they don't belong to the original creator of the software. These sites might or might not be on the up and up; I don't know anything about them and I am not making any judgments. Just know that there are third-party websites that try to make it look like you're getting the file from the OEM site even though you aren't, and they might or might not be totally legitimate. The website names in Figure 5.3 make it pretty easy to tell they're not the Adobe site. Others will try to get tricky and come up with names like `adobe-download.com` or something that looks similar to the OEM site. Be vigilant.

Application Stores We talked about application stores in Chapter 3, "Computing Devices and the Internet of Things." There you learned about Apple's App Store and the Google Play store. These are considered the only legitimate sources of apps for devices running iOS/iPadOS and Android OS, respectively. Each store has a vetting process for apps and ones found there should operate on the appropriate devices without a problem. If developers are found to have practices that violate app store policies, they will be banned from the app stores.

Argh, Matey!

When you purchase software through a legitimate source, you know that you are getting a real and safe version of that software and properly compensating the people who worked to develop it. Another way to get software—illegally—is to pirate it.

Software piracy is the practice of making and distributing copies of software that is not properly licensed, and it's a huge business. Software developers have tried to crack down on it with things like online activations, but their best efforts have not stopped the phenomenon.

If you have pirated software on your computer at home, it's honestly highly unlikely that a big company like Microsoft will come after you. It would be expensive to try to track down one-off cases. I won't say it's impossible, though. One of my colleagues reports that he got a letter from his ISP showing the title of software he downloaded from a pirate website, complete with a warning of a $25,000 potential fine if he didn't stop. Regardless of whether or not you get caught, you do open yourself up to potential hackers and malware, because who knows how the software might have been modified.

Companies engaging in software piracy, intentionally or not, can be subject to massive fines in addition to the aforementioned hackers and malware. Mitigating the effects of software piracy costs companies hundreds of millions of dollars per year and can damage a company's reputation. The bottom line is, software piracy is illegal. Don't do it.

Software Licensing

When you pay for an application, you aren't actually buying the application. Instead, you're buying the right to use the application in a limited way as prescribed by the licensing agreement that comes with it. Most people don't read these licensing agreements closely, but suffice it to say that they're pretty slanted in favor of the software manufacturer.

Don't like the terms? Too bad. No negotiation is allowed. If you don't accept the *license agreement*, your only recourse is to return the software for a refund. (And good luck finding a vendor that will take back an opened box. Still, the software manufacturer is required to take it back and refund your money if you reject the licensing.)

A license agreement is also called an end-user license agreement (EULA).

Although the majority of applications that you acquire will probably be commercial products, there are a number of alternatives to commercial software sales. Here are some of the types of software you may encounter, and the first two typically don't require or use licenses:

Freeware *Freeware* is software that is completely free. On the small scale, you can get such software from download sites such as `https://download.cnet.com` or from the creator's personal website. Large companies like Google and Microsoft also sometimes offer products for free because it serves the company's interests to have lots of people using that software. Examples include Google Chrome and Microsoft Edge. Freeware doesn't include source code, and users aren't allowed to modify the application.

Open Source *Open source* software is freer than free: not only is the application free, but the source code (code used by programmers) is also shared to encourage others to contribute to the future development and improvement of the application. OSs such as Linux and applications such as Apache OpenOffice fit this category. Open source software can't be sold, although it can be bundled with commercial products that are sold. In addition, many open source software developers charge for technical support, which is how they make money.

Open source is the opposite of closed source. Closed-source programs are also called *proprietary* or *commercial* software.

Shareware *Shareware* is software that provides a free trial, with the expectation that you'll pay for it if you like it and decide to keep it. In some cases, a shareware version isn't the full product; in other cases, it expires after a certain amount of time. Some shareware provides a full and unlimited version, with payment requested on the honor system.

Proprietary Developers of *proprietary software* keep the code closed and own all aspects of the software. To use proprietary software, you almost always need to purchase a license. Licenses may specify that a single user can have the software, or there are a maximum number of users or devices allowed. For example, Microsoft 365 Family allows up to six people to use one subscription. And, in office or school environments, a *site license* may be in place stating that 100 or 1,000 users (or however many are negotiated) may use the software.

In terms of the software license itself, there are typically two options: *subscription* and *perpetual* (or *one-time*) licenses. In the olden days of software, perpetual licenses were the norm. In that model, you pay once for indefinite use of the software. Any updates or upgrades to the software might or might not be free of charge.

Many software manufacturers are moving to a subscription-based model rather than a one-time purchase model. Microsoft 365 is a great example of this, and antivirus software companies have used this model for years. Instead of paying for the software once and then "owning" it, the user subscribes and then has access to the software, typically for one year. Sometimes the app will be online (cloud-based), and at other times the user can install it locally. When the year is up, the user can subscribe again (and most software will conveniently sign you up for auto-billing) or lose access. One advantage of this is that you are always getting the newest features and updates of the software as part of the subscription cost.

Software licensing is part of Tech+ exam objective 6.2. You should be able to explain licensing in terms of open source versus proprietary, subscription versus one-time purchase versus perpetual licenses, and product keys and serial numbers.

When you buy any sort of commercial software, you will receive a *product key*, which you will need to enter during installation or the first time the application is opened. The product key might be emailed to you, or it could be located on the physical media if you got an installation disc. Figure 5.4 shows an example of a product key. It might be over 20 years old, but the format of product keys has largely remained the same since then.

FIGURE 5.4 Microsoft product key

Some apps come with a separate *serial number* that identifies the type and version of the software. (Others will use the terms product key and serial number interchangeably.) If you have separate product keys and serial numbers, the general rule of thumb is that the product key needs to be kept secret, whereas the serial number can be shared with others if needed, such as when talking to tech support for example.

Real World Scenario

How Do I Buy the Right Licenses?

After talking to your boss about software licenses, you decide to investigate the office productivity software on your department's computers. You are unable to find proper documentation that the correct software licenses were purchased, leading you to wonder whether the company has the right licenses. Your boss wants to avoid any potential legal issues and asks you to go buy enough copies of the latest version of Microsoft 365 for the 20 users in your department. What do you do?

One option is to go to the local computer store, load up 20 boxes of Office (if they have that many in stock), and trudge up to the cashier. A second option is to go to Microsoft's volume licensing site at `www.microsoft.com/en-us/licensing/product-licensing/office` to learn about purchasing multiple licenses. Microsoft will direct you to an authorized reseller so that you can purchase them; it will email you the list of license numbers to use when installing the software. Now you need just one physical (or downloaded) copy to perform the installation. Be sure to keep copies of the license numbers and receipts—that's the proof that you paid for the software!

Installing and Uninstalling Software

Software manufacturers have smartly made installing their products very easy. They understand that if the average user can't get the software onto their machine, then it won't get used and the company won't make money. Within an operating system, you might want to install additional OS features, applications, or drivers. Each requires a slightly different process, and I will cover them all here.

Collectively, the installation, maintenance, and removal of software is known as the *software management life cycle*.

Operating System Features

Most operating system features are installed during the initial installation of the OS. There are some optional features that perhaps not all users need, but you do. For example, if you need to run your Windows computer as a web server, you need a package called Internet Information Services. Clearly not everyone needs that, so it's not installed by default.

If you need to manage software that is already installed (and in this case, the OS is), you will do so through Control Panel. Exercise 5.1 walks you through how to do this in Windows 11.

EXERCISE 5.1

Installing and Uninstalling Operating System Features

1. Open the Windows Features app by typing **windows features** into the Windows search box (the Turn Windows Features On Or Off app will appear) and pressing Enter. You will see a window like the one shown in Figure 5.5.

   Optionally, you can get to the same app by opening Control Panel ➢ Programs And Features and in the left pane clicking Turn Windows Features On Or Off.

FIGURE 5.5 Turning Windows features on or off

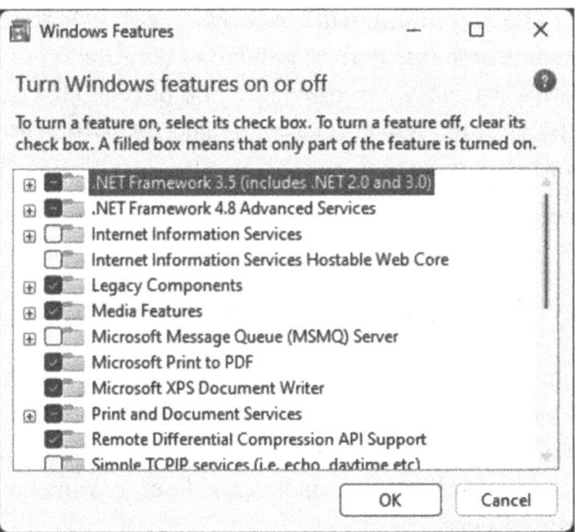

2. In this case, the Internet Information Services box is not checked, indicating that this component is not installed. To install it, select the option and click OK. Windows will search for the required files and install the feature. Once the process is complete, the message box will disappear.
3. To remove a feature, deselect the box and click OK. Windows will remove the files needed for that feature. Use this carefully, as it could affect the OS functionality.

Do not enable OS features unless you are sure you need them! Enabling unused and unnecessary features can potentially open security holes in your system, making it easier for a hacker to exploit your computer.

Applications

You will get applications on an optical disc or flash drive or from the Internet. Installing an application from a disc or flash drive is simple. For a disc, just pop it into the drive, and for a flash drive, insert it into the USB port, and the Setup program will generally start automatically. If it doesn't, go to File Explorer (press Windows+E) and double-click the drive icon for the drive. If that doesn't start the Setup program, it will open a list of files on that media; locate and double-click the one named Setup (or something similar).

You can also download and install applications. If you download an executable Setup file (usually it will have an `.exe` or `.msi` extension), you can double-click that file to start the setup routine.

Occasionally, an application you download may come in a compressed archive, such as a ZIP file. In such a case, you must extract the contents of the archive to a new folder on your hard disk and then run the Setup file from that new folder.

Applications are installed in similar ways regardless of your operating system. For example, many macOS applications come with an installer, similar to Windows. In other cases, you drag the program into the `Applications` folder. In either case, applications are often delivered in either a ZIP file or a disk image, designated with a `.dmg` file extension. Double-click either of these file types to access the program or installer. Exercise 5.2 gives you practice installing an application called 7-zip. You'll use 7-zip later in this chapter.

EXERCISE 5.2

Installing 7-Zip

1. Go to `www.7-zip.org/download.html`.
2. Click the Download link next to the file you want. For this exercise, I will download the EXE file for 64-bit Windows x64.
3. Save the file to your desktop (or other location).
4. Double-click the EXE file to begin installation.
5. Click the box to accept the license agreement and click Next.
6. Choose where to install the application (the defaults are fine) and then click Next.
7. Click Install to begin installation.
8. After installation is complete, click Finish to exit the installer.

If you want more practice installing applications, follow Exercise 5.3.

EXERCISE 5.3

Installing Free Applications

1. Go to `https://download.cnet.com`, and locate a freeware or shareware program that interests you.
2. Download the Setup file for the program.
3. Run the Setup file to install the application. If any problems come up, such as system permission or firewall issues, troubleshoot and solve them.

Regardless of the software you want to install, there are a few best practices to follow. When installing software, you should always do the following:

Read the instructions. Most people don't do this, and you'll find that the more a person knows about computers, the less likely it is they will follow this practice. I'm as guilty as anyone! Read the instructions to make sure you don't miss a step that could be crucial to the installation.

Read the agreements. Along with the instructions, read the licensing agreement. You might be surprised what you learn regarding how the software company can collect information on you and possibly sell it to their affiliates.

Be aware of advanced options. Usually the default options are fine. However, in some cases, you might want to change the directory where the software is installed. This will likely be in the advanced options. You might also be able to choose components to uninstall to save disk space or components to install to speed up the application. Sometimes things like security settings or app configuration preferences will be in the advanced options as well.

Registering and Activation

Registering software (that is, providing your contact information to the software maker) isn't always required. Nonetheless, software makers try to make you believe that it's in your best interest to do so. In actuality, it's a trade-off. Yes, companies want to collect your personal information for marketing purposes, and yes, they may sell it to a third party who might spam you with unwanted offers. However, if you register, you may be eligible for discounts on new versions, free updates, and other goodies.

Activating software is a different story—you have to do it. Either you will need to enter the product key before the app will work the first time, or it might work for a few times for free then ask you to activate. Some products, especially expensive ones that are frequently pirated, include *activation* features that lock the installed copy (by installation key code) to a particular PC so you can't use it on multiple PCs.

In a nutshell, here's how it works. The software company maintains an online database of all the installation key codes. When you install the software, you're prompted to activate it. (Usually you have 30 days to do so, or a certain number of uses, before it stops working.) The activation program examines the hardware on your system (processor, motherboard model, and so on), and it generates a code that describes the general state of the hardware. It then sends that code to the activation server online. If you try to activate the software on a different PC, the activation server compares the hardware code it has on file to the new one coming in, and if they're too different, it assumes that you're installing on a different PC and refuses to let you activate the software.

How is this code generated? Manufacturers are very cagey about that because releasing too much information may give hackers what they need to thwart the system. Generally, a small hardware change on a PC, such as a different network card or display adapter, won't be a problem. However, if you replace the motherboard, the software probably won't reactivate through the automated system.

Most of the manufacturers that use activation allow you to call to request an activation reset, and they won't give you any grief about it the first few times. But if you repeatedly call to request additional activation chances, they'll probably think that you're trying to get around the license agreement and won't let you reset the activation anymore.

Uninstalling Applications

Removing an application that you no longer want can free up disk space. In addition, if that application has a component that runs constantly in the background, removing the application can free up the memory that was previously occupied by that function.

Tech+ exam objective 6.2 wants you to know how to remove unwanted, unnecessary, and malicious software. In this section you will learn the basic steps. Malicious software can be more tricky; if the steps in this section don't work, additional mitigation steps are covered in the "Removing Malware" section later in this chapter.

For macOS users, unless the application specifically has a Remove folder/application, you can delete the application by dragging it to the trash. Also delete any ancillary folders or files associated with that application that may be stored in other locations, such as in the `Library/Application Support` folder. Doing so removes all application files and associated system resources.

With Windows 11, uninstallation is handled through one of two places:

- Control Panel ➢ Programs And Features
- Installed apps Settings program, accessed by typing **add or remove** into the Windows search box and pressing Enter

Either one will accomplish the same task, but the options are slightly different. Figure 5.6 shows you the Uninstall Or Change A Program window from the Programs And Features Control Panel. In it, you will see a list of installed programs. Find the application that you want to remove and highlight it. You should see an Uninstall option above the applications list. Click Uninstall and follow the prompts. Using this method is known as a *clean uninstallation*.

FIGURE 5.6 Uninstalling an application

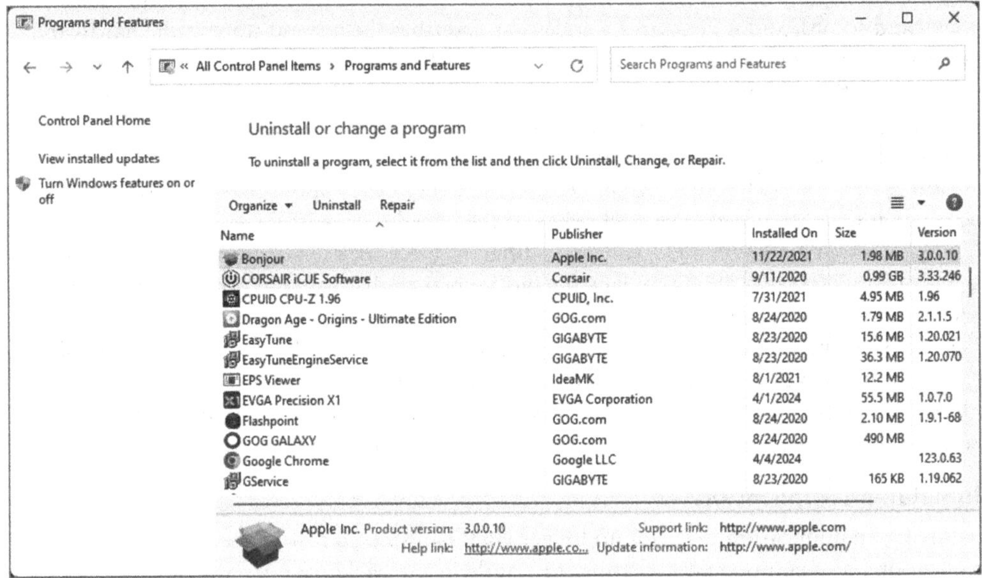

If you are using the Installed apps program instead (Figure 5.7), click on the more options menu to the right of the program name (it's the three horizontal dots) and choose Uninstall. Both of these apps let you see the software version of your apps, in case you need that for troubleshooting or to see if you're up-to-date.

FIGURE 5.7 Installed apps

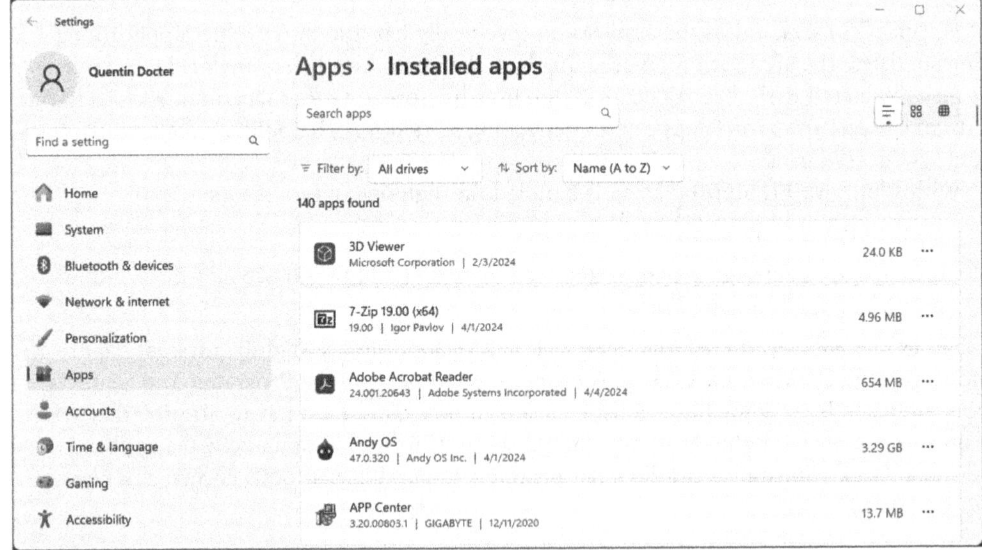

In Figure 5.6, you can see a Repair option next to Uninstall. If you have an application that is not working properly, you may be able to come here and repair it. If that doesn't work, you will probably need to uninstall and reinstall the program to get it to work properly.

During the uninstall process, you may be asked whether you want to keep certain data or configuration files. That's up to you. If you plan to reinstall the same application later (for example, if you're uninstalling to try to correct a problem rather than to get rid of the program entirely), you may want to save the configuration files. That's a double-edged sword, though, because if you're uninstalling to try to correct a problem, that problem could possibly be caused by one of those configuration files.

If for some reason you can't uninstall an application using the preferred clean method, you can remove it using a brute-force method that involves manually deleting the program's files and folders and perhaps manually editing the Windows Registry to remove the references to it. This is known as an unclean uninstallation.

An unclean uninstall isn't a good idea because the potential is great for accidentally deleting a file that is essential to some other application or making a change to the Registry that results in other problems. However, sometimes unclean uninstallations happen by accident. For example, you may accidentally delete the folder containing an application, or you may abort the standard Uninstall utility accidentally, resulting in a half-removed, unusable application that won't allow itself to be removed using the utility.

If you need to perform an unclean uninstallation for some reason, here are the basic steps for doing it:

1. Make sure that the application isn't running. If it has a background component, turn that off.
2. Delete the folder containing the program files. It's probably in the `C:\Program Files (x86)` folder.
3. Delete the program's icons or folders from the Start menu. To do so, open the Start menu, right-click the icon or folder, and choose Delete.
4. If you have enough information to know what to delete in the Registry, start the Registry Editor (type **`regedit`** into the Windows search box and press Enter) and make the needed changes.

It's not advisable to edit the Registry unless you know what you are looking for. Always be sure to back up the Registry before you edit it!

Drivers

As you learned in Chapter 4, "Operating Systems," a *driver*, also known as a *device driver*, is a piece of software written to tell the operating system how to communicate with a specific piece of hardware. This section serves as a reminder because drivers are critical. Without a driver, the piece of hardware will not function. Usually, the only time you think about drivers is when you install new hardware, such as a printer.

Most of the time when you connect your new hardware device and turn it on, your OS will recognize it and begin the driver installation process for you. Sometimes your OS will have a built-in driver that it can use. If not, it will ask you to provide one.

If you have to do it manually, installing a driver is often just like installing an application. Either it will come on a flash drive or optical disc, or, more likely, you will download it from the manufacturer's website. It will probably be an EXE file; double-click it and the installation process will begin.

Here are the basic steps to installing a driver:

1. Once you have connected and powered up the device, boot up the computer and wait for Windows to recognize the device.
2. Windows will pop up a screen indicating that it has detected new hardware and is installing it. If it does not have a driver, it will ask you for one. Provide the location of the flash drive, optical disc, or downloaded driver file.
3. Installation will finish.

If the new device isn't automatically detected, you can start the process manually by going to the Devices app. Click the Windows button and then Settings to make the Settings app appear. In the Settings window, click Bluetooth & Devices, as shown in Figure 5.8. Click either place where it says Add Device to begin the process.

FIGURE 5.8 Bluetooth & Devices window

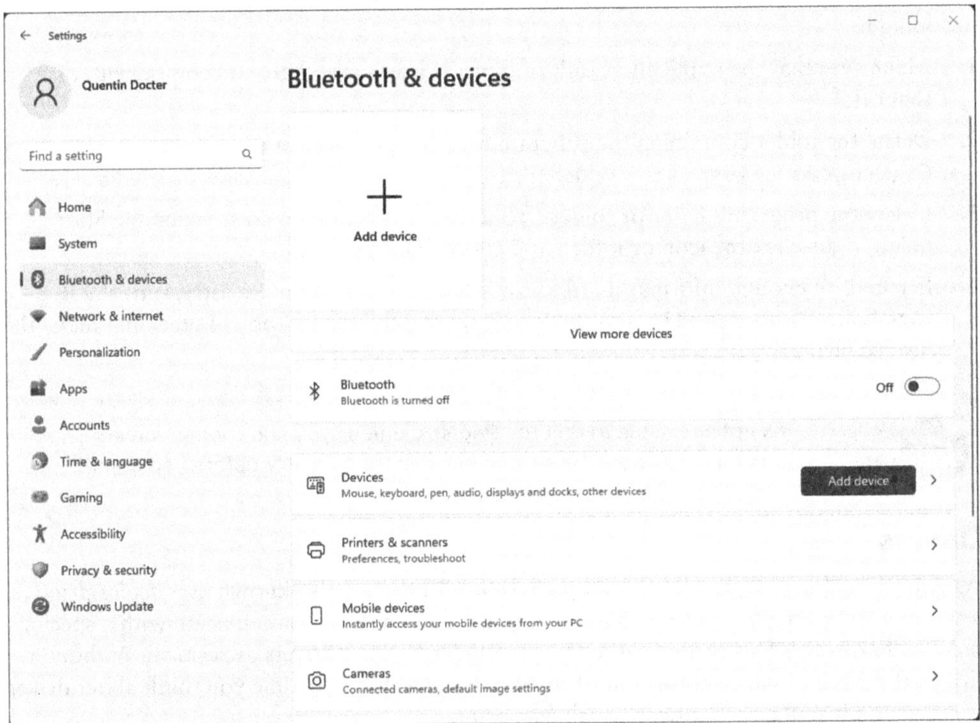

You will specify the type of device, and then Windows will ask you for the driver. Also remember that you can add and manage drivers through the Windows Device Manager (which is covered later in the "Updating Drivers" section).

Updating and Patching Software

Newer versions of existing software products are frequently released. These newer versions might fix known bugs with the application, whereas others will add functionality that didn't exist before. The frequency of version releases depends on the software manufacturer and the severity of the issue. If it's an update or a patch to solve an issue within the program, the manufacturer will provide that update for free.

In this section, you will look at updating and patching OSs, applications (including security software), and drivers. Here I will focus on how often you should update, scheduling of updates, and automatic updates.

Don't confuse updating with upgrading. Upgrading refers to replacing your current OS with a newer or more feature-rich release. For example, if you have Windows 10 and you install Windows 11 to replace it, that's an upgrade. It's also an upgrade if you go from a more basic to a more advanced version of the same OS, such as from Windows Home to Windows 11 Pro. On the other hand, if you apply a free patch from Microsoft that's designed to correct a problem or provide a minor enhancement, that's an update.

Updating and Patching Operating Systems

The OS is the platform on which everything else sits, so it's important that it be a stable and reliable platform.

Exam objective 6.2 wants you to explain methods to secure devices and security best practices. Patching/updating is part of that.

You don't always need to have the most recently released OS version, but you do need a version that's current enough so that all of the software that you want to use runs on it. Whatever version you use, you should make sure that all available security updates are applied to it to avoid problems due to viruses, worms, and other exploits.

Most OSs have an *automatic update* feature, which relieves users of the burden of remembering to look for and install updates. However, occasionally an update may cause a problem on some systems. For example, an update may have an incompatibility with a certain piece of hardware that you've installed, causing it to stop working, or an update may cause an older application to crash. For this reason, some network administrators prefer to keep control of updates themselves on all the PCs they support rather than enabling individual users to choose whether or not to download them; therefore, they may disable automatic updates on individual PCs.

In Windows, you control automatic updates via the *Windows Update* Settings app, as shown in Figure 5.9. You can manually check for updates, review update history, and more.

FIGURE 5.9 Windows Update

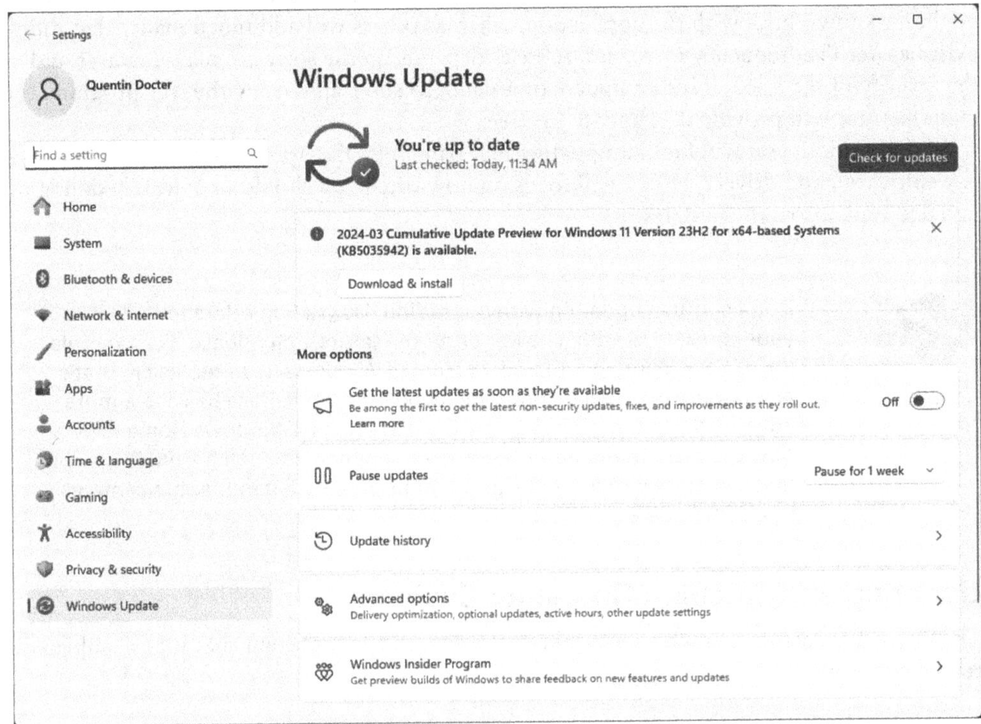

When you're installing updates, be aware that some updates require you to reboot the computer when they're finished installing. This can be an inconvenience if you're in the middle of an important project or have many open windows and applications. When an update requires a reboot, you can decline to restart until a more convenient time. If it's an update where a reboot is very important, the OS will remind you until you do it, letting you postpone the next reminder for a certain amount of time, from a few minutes to a few hours.

Although it may seem more convenient to avoid automatic updates because of that pesky restarting directive, there are risks associated with ignoring an available update. Some updates address critical security flaws. If you don't install updates promptly that are designed to protect your system, your PC may be vulnerable to security attacks from the Internet.

Windows Update (or Software Update in macOS) can also recommend and install updates for certain applications, especially those made by the same company as the OS. Also, depending on your hardware, it may be able to make updates for your hardware drivers available, such as a new version of a display-adapter driver or network-adapter driver. In Exercise 5.4 you will configure Windows Update.

EXERCISE 5.4

Configuring Windows Update

1. Open Windows Update. To find it, type **update** into the Windows search box and press Enter. Review whether there are any updates to be installed.
2. Click Update History. A list of the previously installed updates appears, like the one shown in Figure 5.10. Review this information, noting whether they were successful and the dates they were installed. You can click the link to get more information on the update. When you are finished reviewing, click the back arrow in the upper-left corner.

FIGURE 5.10 Windows Installed updates

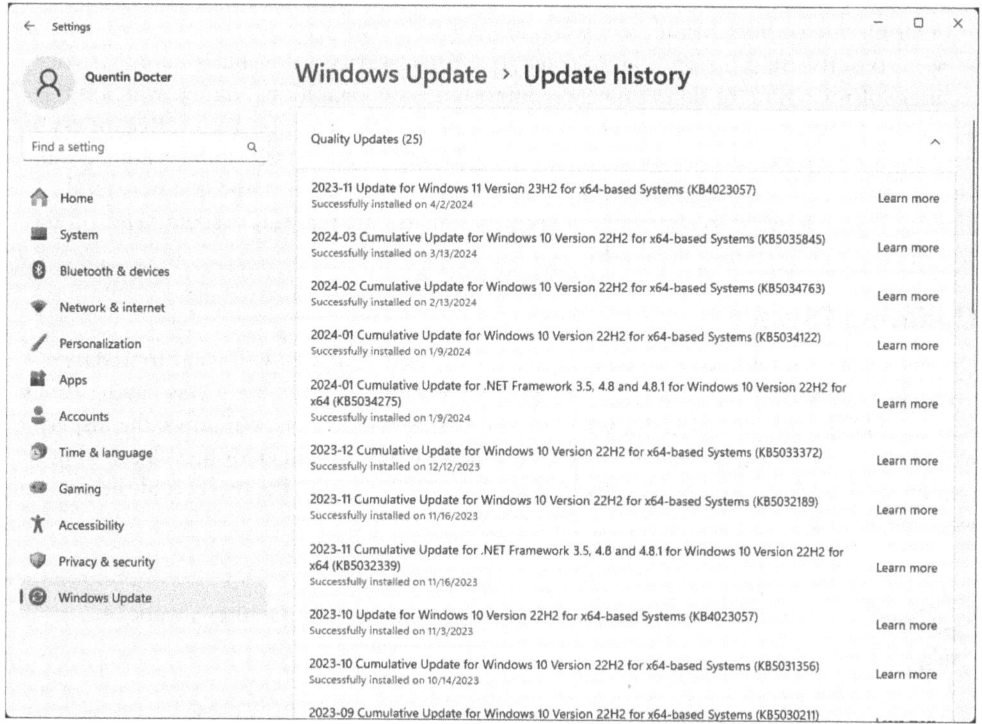

EXERCISE 5.4 *(continued)*

3. Click Advanced Options. This lets you choose options such as whether or not to receive updates for other Microsoft products, restart options, active hours (which is very handy), and additional options as well.
4. Click Active Hours. This lets you tell Windows when not to restart automatically, or at least to check with you before it does. Switch it from Automatically to Manually and set your desired times.
5. Close Windows Update.

Updating and Patching Applications

Updating or patching an application generally isn't as critical as the operating system, with the exception of your security software. As I mentioned in the previous section, Windows Update and other OS updating software can sometimes find updates for your applications as well. If not, the application manufacturer will release updates and patches as downloadable files on its website. You install these updates just like the application, with an EXE, MSI, ZIP, or other file you open to begin the installation.

Security software is the one major exception. You always want to make sure that your security software is up-to-date. Especially important is its definitions library, which is the database of known malware and what the software uses to detect problems. Regardless of the antivirus or other security program you have installed, automatic updates are a good idea. They keep you from forgetting and then ending up having not updated in several months. If you do want to control your security updates manually, it's recommended that you run them at least once per week.

Updating Drivers

Drivers also require infrequent updates. Usually the only time you will want to update a driver is if you are having problems with your hardware. For example, I was having issues with my video card. Occasionally, when I would resize windows in Windows, the display would freeze, go black, and then return to normal. I would see an error message stating that my display device driver had stopped responding. I updated the driver and the problem went away.

The best place to get drivers is always the manufacturer's website.

You can get to your device drivers to check for updates in a few different ways. One of the easiest ways in Windows is to open Device Manager (open the Quick Link menu by pressing Windows+X, or use Control Panel). Figure 5.11 shows Device Manager.

FIGURE 5.11 Device Manager

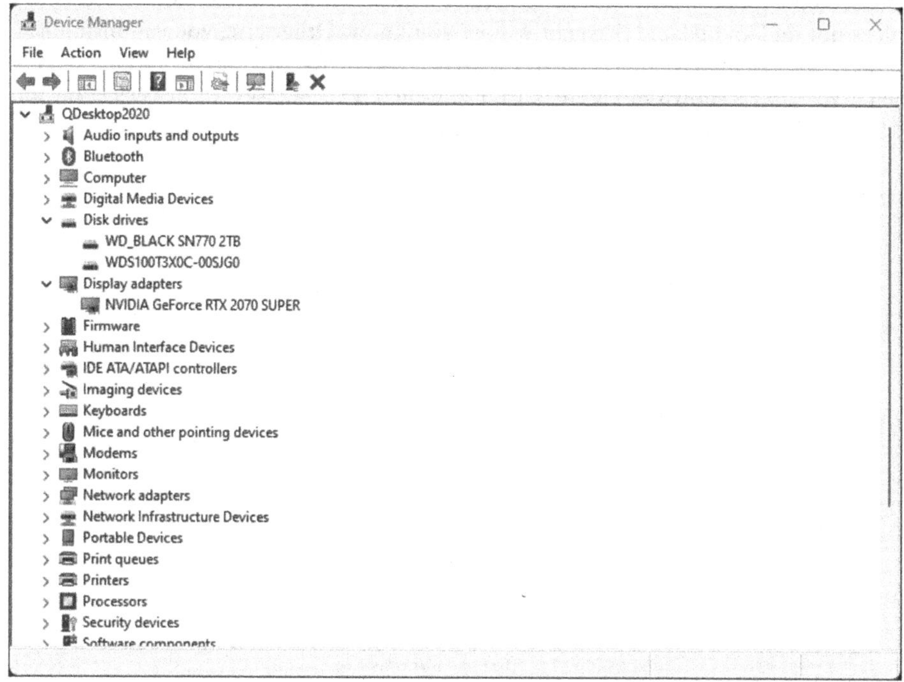

In Figure 5.11, you can see that I have expanded a few categories to show hardware devices. If you right-click any of the devices, you will get an option that says Update Driver. Click that and you will get a screen similar to the one shown in Figure 5.12.

FIGURE 5.12 Updating Drivers screen

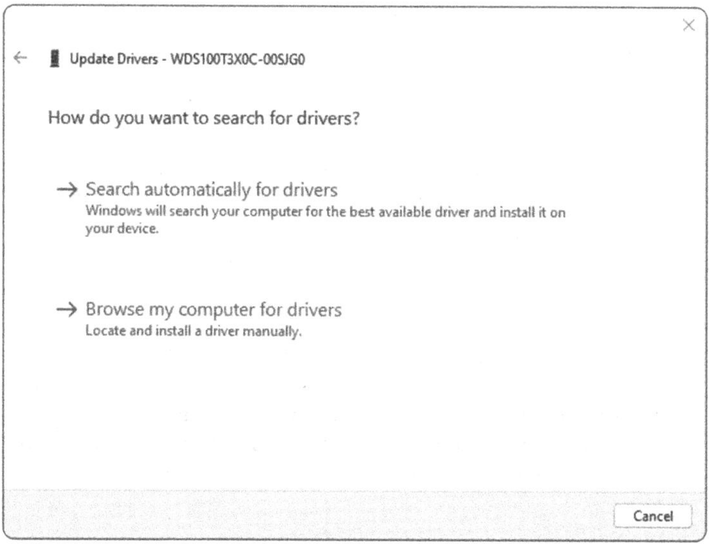

You can let Windows search the Internet for an updated driver, or you can point Windows to the location of a driver if you have downloaded one. If Windows searches for and does not find an updated driver, it will let you know. Otherwise, you can install it.

Another way to manage drivers is to right-click the device and choose Properties. Then go to the Driver tab, as shown in Figure 5.13. From there you can look at driver details, update the driver, roll back the driver, disable the device, or uninstall the driver.

FIGURE 5.13 Driver management

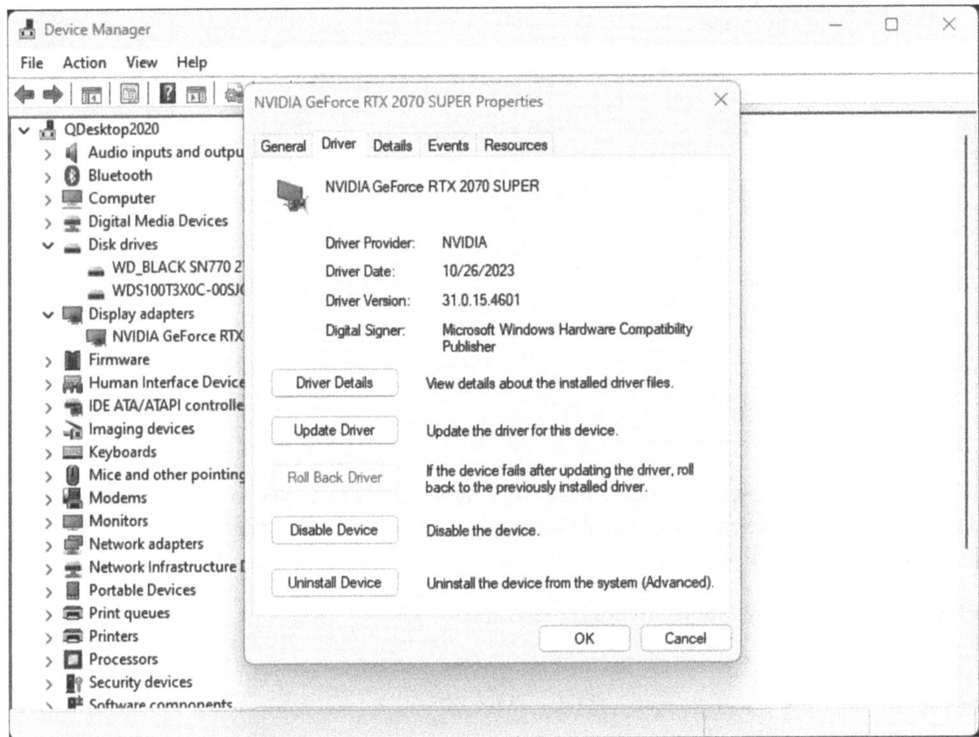

Occasionally, you will run into issues where you install a driver update and it causes more problems than you originally had. In situations such as this, you can roll back the driver. This basically uninstalls the current version of the driver and reinstalls the previous version. From there, you can continue to troubleshoot the situation as needed.

Some common device types and interfaces in Device Manager will have drivers that are 10+ years old. These are fine; there's been no need for the manufacturer to update it during that time. For devices such as video cards, printers, and other custom-installed components, having updated drivers is more important.

Exploring Common Application Types

There are a lot of different software applications in the world—a lot. I wouldn't even know where to begin if asked to count them. The good news is that if you want a piece of software that helps you accomplish a specific task, whether that task be productive or entertaining, you can probably find it. The Tech+ exam wants you to know about two groups of software—productivity and collaboration—as well as instant messaging, web browsing, and remote support software. Here I will place instant messaging and remote support into a third group called Utility software, with a few other key programs such as antimalware and software firewalls. Web browsers are widely used, have many custom options, and present such security risk that they're going to get their own section after this one. Let's start exploring software types.

File Extensions

Before getting into specific application types, let's take a minute to explore how operating systems know which files *are* applications. This was introduced in Chapter 4, but now is a perfect time for a refresher.

You're probably familiar with filenames on a computer. You might have a pretty good idea of what files like `AcroRD32.exe`, `resume.docx`, `finances.xlsx`, or `summervaca.jpg` are or what they contain. Part of that is probably because of the *file extension*, or the "dot whatever" part at the end. The file extension tells you a little about the file, and it tells the operating system what to do with the file.

The operating system knows that certain extensions are designed to execute a program directly—these are called *executables*. Table 5.1 lists some common executable file extensions that you should know.

TABLE 5.1 Common executable file extensions

Extension	Use
`.exe`	Short for "executable," it tells the OS to run the program. Most Windows desktop programs use this extension.
`.msi`	For installation and removal of software within Windows. Opening an MSI file actually launches `msiexec.exe`, which reads the MSI file and does what it says. MSI files use Windows Installer, so think of it as standing for "Microsoft Installation."
`.app`	Executes a program within macOS (as EXE does in Windows).
`.bat`	Batch file. Used to execute multiple commands from the Windows command prompt (`cmd.exe`) within one file.
`.scexe`	Self-extracting firmware updates that Hewlett-Packard (HP) produces, commonly associated with Linux machines.

Never open an executable file you are sent via email or with which you are otherwise unfamiliar. Doing so is a good way to spread viruses.

Based on Table 5.1, you can see that if you're in Windows and you double-click an icon named `excel.exe`, it will open Microsoft Excel, or `winword.exe` will open up Microsoft Word. What about files with different extensions? Why is it that if I double-click my `resume.docx` file, Word opens? (Not that we're complaining here, but how does the OS know to do that?) The OS keeps a list of known file extensions and associates them with specific applications. For example, if you open anything with a `.docx` extension, the OS knows that it needs to open Microsoft Word to read that file.

In Windows, you can use the Default Apps program to see and configure defaults for applications. Two ways to get to this app are by opening Control Panel ➢ Default Programs, or by typing **default** into the Windows search box and pressing Enter. It's organized alphabetically by app. To set a new default app for an extension, you could enter the type (such as `.asp`) into the Set A Default For A File Type Or Link Type window, and click Choose A Default. You will get a screen like the one in Figure 5.14 where you can choose from a list of apps or browse for an additional one.

FIGURE 5.14 Default Apps window

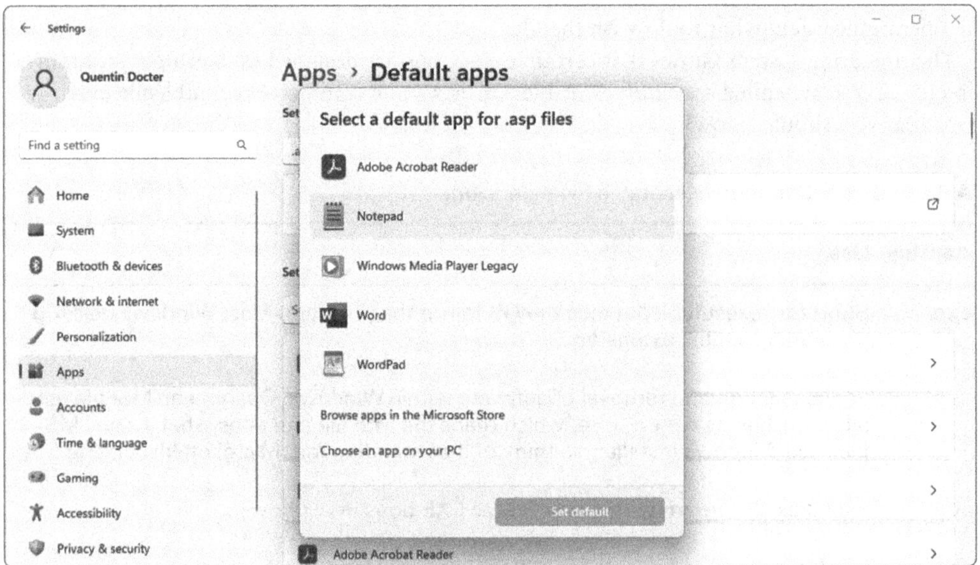

If you scroll almost all the way to the bottom of the Default Apps window, you will have the option Choose Defaults By File Type (or you can type **associate** into the Windows search box and press Enter). Click that option. This will give you a screen like the one in Figure 5.15 (I have scrolled down to the .d section). You can see that there are quite a few different file extensions associated with Microsoft Word! If you wanted to change the association, you would click the application and then choose a new one from a pop-up list. Where appropriate, I will talk more about specific file extensions and the applications with which they are associated throughout this section.

FIGURE 5.15 Choosing default apps by file type

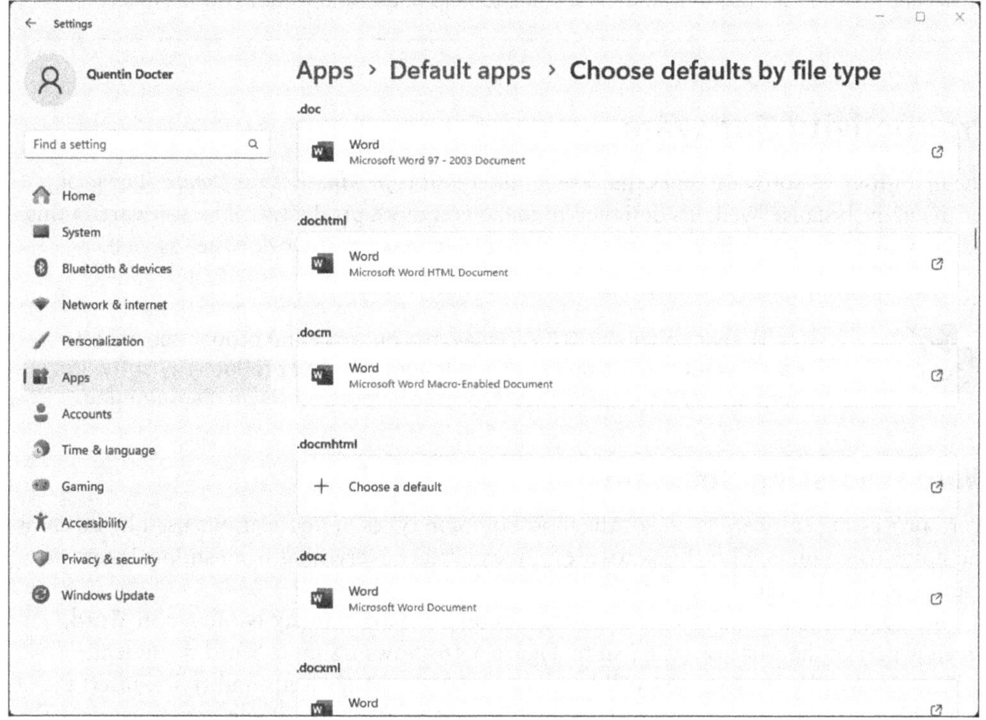

Real World Scenario

Not All Operating Systems Need File Extensions

After just telling you about file extensions and what OSs use them for, this topic might seem contradictory, but it's not. While most operating systems (and their associated filesystems) *use* file extensions, not all *require* file extensions.

There are two methods an operating system can use to determine what to do with a file as it's opened. The first, as you know, is through the use of file extensions. The second is by encoding the information within the file itself. When files are stored, some of the initial information in them is called a Multipurpose Internet Mail Extensions (MIME) type. Don't let the words *Internet* and *mail* throw you off—MIME is used for much more than that. Examples of MIME types include text/plain, application/msword, image/png, and audio/mpeg3.

Windows ignores MIME types and relies solely on the file extension. UNIX, Linux, and macOS read the MIME type when a file is opened, and that is how they determine which application to use to open the file. That said, most files on computers with these OSs will have extensions, mostly to provide compatibility in case the file ends up on a Windows box. In some cases, a file extension in macOS file can help if the MIME type is unclear. Web browsers and email clients also make use of MIME extensions to help determine what to do with files.

Productivity Software

The first group of software types that I will talk about is *productivity software*. The group gets its name because, well, it's designed to make you more productive. The software in this section will help you get more work done and ideally make that work easier as well.

Tech+ exam objective 3.3, "Explain the purpose and proper use of software," wants you to be familiar with four types of productivity software: word processing, spreadsheet, presentation, and visual diagramming.

Word Processing Software

Word processing software is one of the most common types of applications used by business and home users alike. With this software, you can create everything from simple letters or résumés to detailed reports and flyers.

The most popular word processing program on the market today is Microsoft Word, which is part of the Microsoft 365 suite. Figure 5.16 shows a simple Word document.

Within a word processor, you will have the ability to change fonts and styles; insert pictures, shapes, and tables; and manage many different facets of the document's appearance.

Of course, there are several other word processing programs, some of which are free and others that are not. Among the commercial offerings are Corel WordPerfect and Corel Write. Free options include Google Docs, AbiWord, Jarte, and LibreOffice. Each one has slightly different menus and features, but in general they all do the same thing. With features, sometimes you get what you pay for. In addition, the biggest issue you might run into is compatibility between formats. It's not guaranteed that a Microsoft Word document will be readable in WordPerfect or Jarte, or anything else for that matter. For the most part, you won't run into any problems with simpler documents, but more complicated files with unique features can pose problems. Compatibility can also be influenced by the format in which you save it. Simple text (`.txt`) files are more compatible across platforms than are files with the `.docx` extension. Table 5.2 lists some common file extensions for word processing software.

FIGURE 5.16 Word document

TABLE 5.2 Word processing file extensions

Extension	Use
`.txt`	Basic text file. Almost all word processors will open this, from the basic Notepad in Windows to Microsoft Word, and most other commercial and free apps as well. Generally, very few configuration options (such as fonts or inserting images) are available.
`.rtf`	Rich-text format. A fairly basic document format developed by Microsoft and generally more compatible than DOC files.
`.doc/.docx`	Microsoft Word files. DOCX files are newer and support more features than older DOC files.

The file extensions in Table 5.2 are only a few of the ones that exist in the wild—know that other extensions exist too. For example, WordPerfect typically uses the `.wpd` extension, AbiWord uses `.abw`, and OpenOffice can use several extensions, such as `.odt`, `.ott`, and `.sxw`.

Spreadsheet Software

Spreadsheets serve an important niche, which is to manage numbers and small quantities of data. They are almost as popular as word processing programs. In fact, most office "suites" of software bundle word processing and spreadsheet applications together, along with basic database and presentation software. Microsoft 365 includes Word (for documents) and Excel (for worksheets), and OpenOffice has Writer and Calc. Other versions include Quattro Pro, Google Sheets, and Gnumeric (for Windows and Linux). The `.xls` and `.xlsx` extensions are associated with Microsoft Excel; Figure 5.17 shows a basic Excel worksheet.

FIGURE 5.17 Microsoft Excel

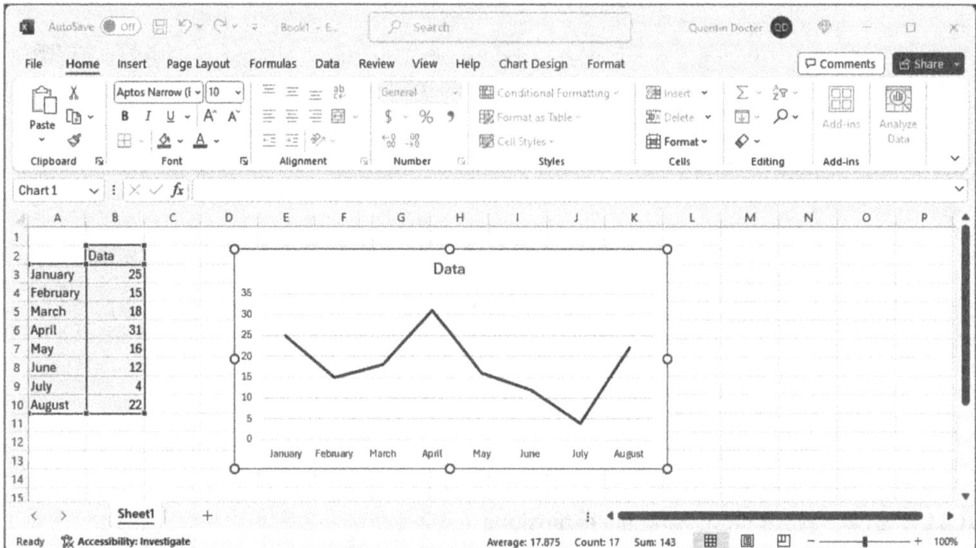

Spreadsheet software is mostly used for managing numbers or lists of data. You can have it do math for you using formulas, sort data, create visuals with charts and graphs, and perform relatively complex data manipulation tasks using macros. Some spreadsheet programs also have add-ins that let you do more complex analyses, such as correlations and regression analysis. If you have more sizable data management needs, then it's more efficient to use database software.

Databases are covered in depth in Chapter 7, "Database Fundamentals."

Presentation Software

You might find yourself in a situation where a meeting is coming up and you need to convey a message to a group of people. Presentation software is designed to help you do that by letting you put your ideas in slides so you can share a full-screen slide show from your computer.

Within your presentation, you can add text, graphs, charts, pictures, and shapes; embed videos for playback; and even create special effects such as having text fade in or out and adding sound. You can also set it up such that the slides transition after a set amount of time. Some people do this and set up a recording of the presentation to create what amounts to a presentation video to send to others.

As with other software types, you have plenty of presentation packages available, free and commercial, locally installed or web-based. Microsoft PowerPoint comes as part of Microsoft 365 and is a commonly used piece of presentation software. OpenOffice's equivalent is called Impress, there is Google Slides, and a popular macOS version is Keynote. Figure 5.18 shows you what editing a basic presentation in PowerPoint could look like. The `.ppt` and `.pptx` file extensions are associated with PowerPoint.

FIGURE 5.18 Microsoft PowerPoint

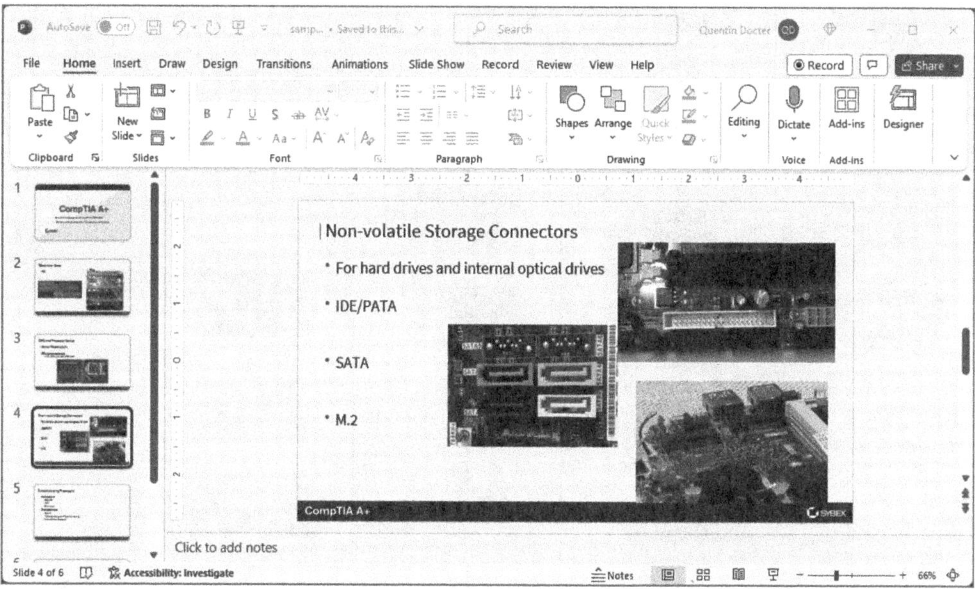

Visual Diagramming Software

They say that a picture is worth a thousand words. In some cases, visual diagrams can be worth 10,000 words. Some concepts simply need to be diagrammed. Visual diagramming software can help tremendously.

Examples in the business world include organization charts, flowcharts, and business processes. Technology examples include network diagrams, database structures, and data flow. These six examples just barely scratch the surface. Diagramming software can often create charts and graphs, as well as complicated schematic drawings such as floor plans or circuit paths. If you need to draw the relationship between multiple items or ideas, diagramming software is the way to go. Dozens of options exist in the marketplace. Some popular programs include SmartDraw, Microsoft Visio, Gliffy, Creately, and Lucidchart. Figure 5.19 shows an example of a diagram created with SmartDraw.

FIGURE 5.19 HR hiring process flowchart example

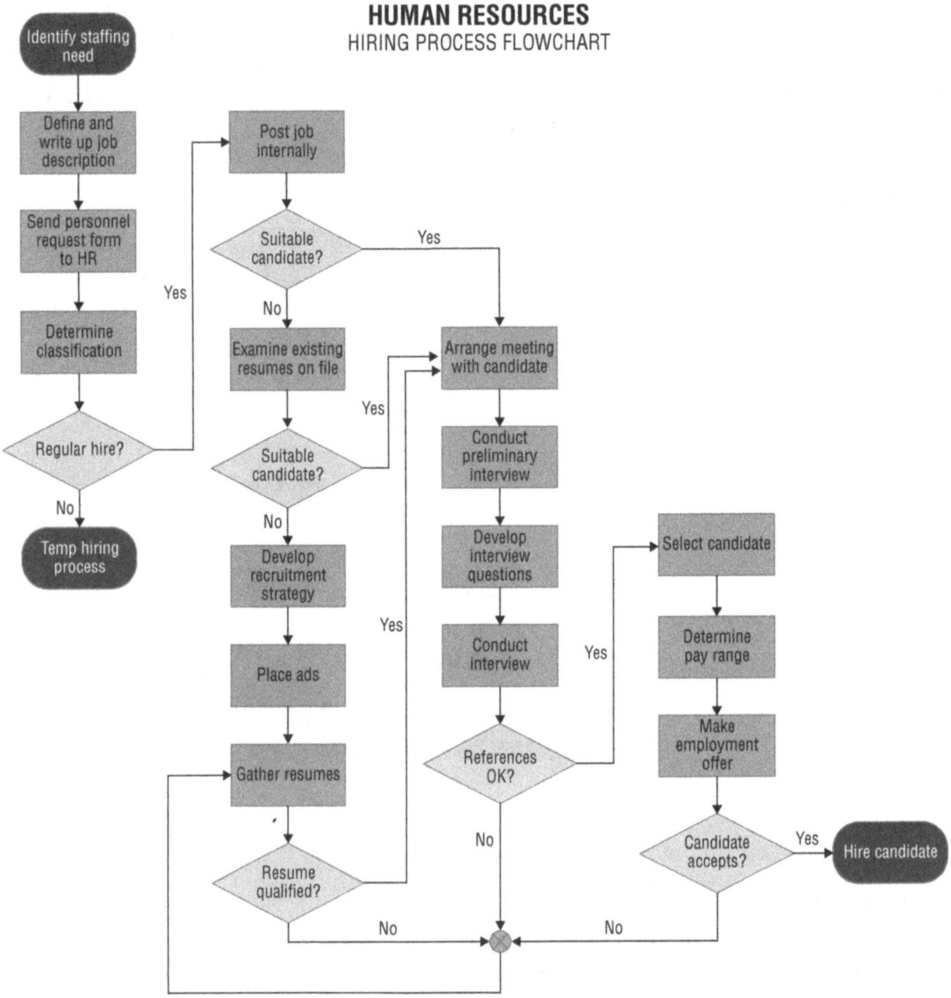

Real World Scenario

Which Software Should You Choose?

You are consulting for a friend who owns a small business with about 20 employees. She is in the process of standardizing all the software her employees use. They use a lot of productivity software, specifically presentation software, spreadsheets, and word processing applications. In addition, they quite often share the files with external agencies that collaborate on work with them. Your friend wants to keep costs down, but she also wants seamless integration with her external agencies. What should you advise her to choose?

You have probably three main choices: Microsoft 365, a free local option such as OpenOffice, or a cloud-based solution such as Google G Suite. All of them will provide the functionality that your friend's employees need, and odds are that the employees are already familiar with their shared features. The biggest concern might be sharing the files with external agencies. If the external agencies use Microsoft 365, then it will be much better for your friend's company to use it as well. If your friend is less concerned with occasional interoperability issues and more concerned about the bottom line, then free options might be a better alternative.

Present the three options along with pros and cons to your friend so that she can make the most informed decision possible.

Collaboration Software

The world is more interconnected today than it has ever been. If you work in an office environment, it's entirely possible that some or all members of your work team will be located in different cities or on different continents. No matter the situation, you still need to get work done effectively as a team, just as if you were sitting in the cubicles next to each other. That's where *collaboration software* comes into play.

The goal of collaboration software is to blur the lines between those who work right next to you and those who do not. It's sort of fitting then that most collaboration software applications blur the lines between the categories of collaboration software listed in the CompTIA Tech+ exam objectives. Said another way, one software package might be able to provide everything you need for collaboration, including email, working online, sharing and storing files, sharing screens, having videoconferences, and instant messaging each other. That said, I'll still cover each of the categories of collaboration software individually, mostly to address the specific goals of each type of software.

Tech+ exam objective 3.3 wants you to be familiar with four types of collaboration software: email client, conferencing, online workspace, and document sharing.

Email Client Software

Email is by far and away the most commonly used collaboration software today. The vast majority of people with computers or mobile devices use it daily. It's so prevalent that it can be a distraction for people; we could argue that it actually hurts productivity for some users. Regardless of whether you think you can't live without email or if you find the number of messages you get to be overwhelming, email is entrenched in our society.

To use email, you need an email client. Email clients let you send and receive messages, manage your contacts and calendar, and assign yourself tasks with deadlines, and they will give you reminders when you need to follow up on something.

Most businesses that use a commercial email client will choose Microsoft Outlook. There are dozens of other email clients that you can install locally on your computer, such as IBM Notes (formerly Lotus Notes), GNUMail, and Mozilla Thunderbird. If you have an email account through your company, university, or other organization, you will likely use one of these clients and connect to an email server managed by that organization.

If you use Outlook and Microsoft 365, they synchronize pretty well together. Formatting Outlook emails is similar to using Microsoft Word, because they use the same editor, and Outlook also links seamlessly with Microsoft Teams, which is its instant messaging and online collaboration software.

There are lots of free Internet email services that you can use as well. The most used is Gmail, but there is also Yahoo! Mail, AOL Mail, `Outlook.com`, and `Mail.com`. Each has different features and peculiarities. Most have the ability to use an instant messenger, link to your social media accounts, and work on your mobile device. Oftentimes, you also get presented with copious amounts of advertising. But they're free.

Conferencing Software

Three types of programs covered in the Tech+ exam objectives—conferencing, online workspace, and document sharing—are closely related to each other. In fact, most software that does one of these functions will do the others as well—and then some. It just depends on how you want to use the service.

Conferencing software can simply be for phone calls, but most incorporate a video component. Videoconferencing is making a call, like a telephone call, to a remote location using your computer. As the name implies, you and the other people on the call can use webcams to see each other, as opposed to just hearing their voices. This type of solution has obvious advantages, but it also means that you probably can't take calls lying around home in your pajamas anymore. Well, maybe you can—it depends on your coworkers!

The technology in this area has improved dramatically in recent years, with the goal of some of the higher-end videoconferencing suites to make you feel like you and the people on the other end of the line are actually in the same room. This has been termed *telepresence*. To make this seem like an authentic experience where everyone is in the same room, special videoconferencing rooms are set up. The rooms at both locations often have the same style of table and chairs and the same décor, including similar artwork and fake plants!

With most videoconferencing software packages, you have the ability to share what's on your screen. You can choose to share all applications or just one specific file. In addition, you will have options such as recording the session and allowing others to annotate your screen. Recordings can be played back later for people who couldn't make the conference or if you want to review comments made by someone on the call.

There are dozens of software solutions available for those who want videoconferencing. Microsoft Teams, Cisco WebEx, Zoom, and GoTo Meeting are the most popular commercial options. Free options include Skype, FaceTime, and Camfrog. The paid options usually have a quality of service (QoS) guarantee, whereas the free ones don't. The free ones might work fine one time and then be plagued by connection issues the next. In addition, the free ones are not as likely to have all the same features of their commercial counterparts.

One technology that is often seen along with videoconferencing is *Voice over Internet Protocol (VoIP)*. It isn't a specific software package but rather a group of technologies that work to deliver voice communications over the Internet or other data networks. VoIP can give you voice-only transmissions over network cables or video along with voice, all over the same network connection.

To see whether you are using VoIP, look at where the phone plugs in to the wall. Does it plug into a standard phone jack or a network jack? If it's the latter, you are probably using VoIP.

The biggest advantage of VoIP and teleconferencing is that they help reduce travel costs. Instead of paying to fly people to a remote location for a meeting, you can simply connect with your business partners in another location. Good teleconferencing systems are pretty expensive, but with the travel savings, the systems pay for themselves very quickly.

Online Workspace

Online workspace specifically means that multiple people can collaborate on (and make changes to) the same file at the same time. This usually involves sharing the screen of the file on which you are working with others, but it can also mean two users on different computers are editing the same file at the same time. Microsoft Teams is one of the leaders in this space, followed by Google Workspace.

Document Sharing and Storage

The lines between online workspace and document sharing are the most blurred, and as noted earlier, if an app does one it likely does the other. If you are working with colleagues in a different location, being able to access the files your team needs to work on quickly and easily is a big deal. Today, there are multiple cloud-based services that let you share and store documents online. Examples include Google Workspace, Microsoft OneDrive (part of the 365 bundle), Box, Dropbox, IDrive, and OpenDrive. Some are more geared toward businesses, others toward home users, and still others are best at online backups.

Here are some key features to look for when considering online document sharing and storage:

Storage and Upload Maximums How much data will the solution allow you to store, and what is the size limit on the files you upload? This might not be as big of a deal with a small team, but if you are considering a solution for an entire organization, size limits matter.

Backups Is the data backed up? And if so, how often? There would be nothing worse than to trust someone else to manage your data and then to lose it because it hasn't been backed up.

File Synchronization Can multiple people be in the file at the same time editing it? If not, that's a big deal. How does the system know, and what version does it keep? Also, some solutions allow you to keep a virtual copy of those files on your local system. Make sure that those are synchronized with the online versions.

File Encryption Are the online files encrypted when they are stored? They had better be. Storing plain-text data on a cloud-based resource is basically asking to have your data stolen. You will learn much more about encryption in Chapter 11, "Security Best Practices."

Maintained Servers Who owns and maintains the company's servers? Do they do it themselves or license it out to a third party such as Google? Companies that own their hardware have more control over that hardware and of course have a vested interest in making sure that it runs properly. There's nothing inherently wrong with a company that uses a third party such as Google to manage their cloud, but it does introduce one more player into the mix, which introduces more potential issues.

Security Mechanisms Can you set folder permissions and set different permissions for each folder? You should be able to. In addition, managing the security should be easy for anyone in your organization.

Mobile Platforms It should work with mobile devices, and most online storage and sharing systems do. Almost all online systems will synchronize with mobile devices as well.

Help and Support How accessible is their help and support system? Do they just have email support, or can you get live chat if you need it?

There isn't really a one-size-fits-all solution for all business situations. The best idea is to research the different options, weigh the pros and cons, and then choose the best one for your needs.

Utility Software

Many extra services that you can use on a computer are handy to have but are not necessarily ones that help you get your project done or communicate with others. These functions are managed by *utility software*. The programs in this section are not mandatory on any computer (although antimalware should be), but all of them are pretty useful.

Tech+ exam objective 3.3 wants you to be familiar with instant messaging and remote support software.

Instant Messaging

Instant messaging is sending a text note to another user in real time. If you do it on your phone, it's typically referred to as *texting*. Instant message (IM) software will keep a list of contacts that you have added. Some, such as Microsoft Teams, will synchronize with your Microsoft Outlook address book to make finding connections easier. Some IM programs are strictly for messaging, but many IM programs will also let you share your screen with those with whom who you are chatting and make audio/video calls as well.

There are dozens of IM applications, and most of them are free. In addition to Microsoft Teams, there are WhatsApp, WeChat, Facebook Messenger, Snapchat, Telegram, and others. The key is that the person with whom you want to chat needs to be on the same system; otherwise, you won't be able to connect.

Remote Support

If you've ever had to call technical support on any product for any reason, it can be frustrating trying to explain what the problem is. Maybe you're not familiar with the device or program, or perhaps you're intimidated by the fact that the person on the other end of the line is supposed to be an expert. In any case, talking to tech support isn't usually rated as people's favorite experiences.

From the support specialist's side, it can be frustrating as well. The user might not be able to accurately explain the problem or know when it started or what potential changes might have caused it. And people who are experiencing a problem with their device aren't generally in a great mood to begin with. Fortunately, there are remote support software packages available to help troubleshoot and resolve computer problems over the Internet.

With *remote support* software, a technician or other trained professional is able to access the user's device over the Internet and take control over the troubled device to help resolve the problem. It can be a huge time and stress saver for all involved parties. (Trust me, I did phone tech support for years before remote support software was a thing, and having it would have been a massive benefit.)

There are a few things you should look for in a remote support package. It should:

- Support multiple platforms, such as PC (Windows and macOS) and mobile devices.
- Offer file transfer and information sharing services, so the tech can download patches or other information as needed.
- Allow for screen recording or event logging to help isolate the problem or provide future training.
- Be easy to install and use.

Some of the top remote support software names include AnyDesk, BeyondTrust Remote Support, GoToMyPC, Splashtop, Windows Remote Desktop, and TeamViewer.

When the end user connects to the troubleshooter and the software is enabled, the tech will generally have to request control of the user's device, and the user will expressly grant it. Then, the tech can operate the remote device, through their own, as if they were actually sitting at or holding the remote device. While this is great, it can also be a potential security risk. Before giving someone control over your device, be sure that they are legitimate and authorized to perform repairs.

Antimalware

Malware is software that does harm to your computer. Why would software harm your computer? Well, the unfortunate reality is that there are bad people in this world. It's sad in a way because many people who are otherwise talented programmers choose to use their skills to harm others. It's reality, though, so you need to do what you can to protect your computer against malware.

Exam objective 6.2 wants you to explain methods to secure devices. Antimalware is included in that.

The term *malware* is really a grouping of different types of bad programs. I am sure that many of their names will be familiar to you, such as viruses, worms, spyware, and rootkits. I'll talk about each of these in more detail in Chapter 10, "Security Concepts and Threats," but for now I'll just cover how to keep them off your computer.

As the name of this section suggests, you use antimalware software to keep the malware off your machine. Some of the more popular programs in the antimalware arena are Symantec's Norton 360, McAfee Antivirus, AVG Antivirus, and Avast Antivirus. When choosing a software package, it's important to understand what it specifically protects against. Some apps protect against several types of threats, but others are specifically antivirus or antispyware packages. There's nothing wrong with those specialized products, as long as you're aware of the level of protection your computer has.

Just because you have antimalware installed does not mean that you are guaranteed to be virus or spyware free! Still, going without the antimalware software is very dangerous for computers with an Internet connection.

How Antimalware Works

Generally speaking, antimalware works by monitoring activity on your computer for any activity that appears suspicious. For example, an antivirus program is generally run in the background on a computer, and it examines all the file activity on that computer. When it detects suspicious activity, it notifies the user of a potential problem and asks the user what to do about it. Some antivirus programs can also make intelligent decisions about what to do. The process of running an antivirus program on a computer is known as *inoculating* the computer against a virus.

For a listing of most current viruses, refer to Symantec's Security Center at `www.broadcom.com/support/security-center`.

These programs have a database of known viruses and the symptoms each one causes. They look for those symptoms as well as signatures, or specific patterns of computer code, that could be suspicious.

Antivirus databases should be updated frequently. About once a week is good, although more often is better. Most antivirus programs will automatically update themselves if configured properly.

While a true antivirus program will scan for viruses, antimalware programs are a superset of virus scanners and will look for more than just traditional viruses, such as spyware, ransomware, and others. Microsoft OSs are the ones most affected by spyware, so Microsoft has developed Microsoft Defender starting with Windows 7 (now part of Windows Security) to combat the problem. Note that Windows Security is good at helping protect versus most types of malware, but leading security experts don't consider it to be a stand-alone solution. In other words, it's free and it does a fine job, so it's better than having nothing. But it's not as good as other programs out there. It's best to go with another option such as Norton, McAfee, or Malwarebytes.

Configuring Antimalware

After you install your software, you need to configure it. For the most part, the default settings for the antimalware program are going to be sufficient. The biggest thing will be to ensure that the software is set to update automatically. Figure 5.20 shows the main screen of Norton 360.

FIGURE 5.20 Norton 360

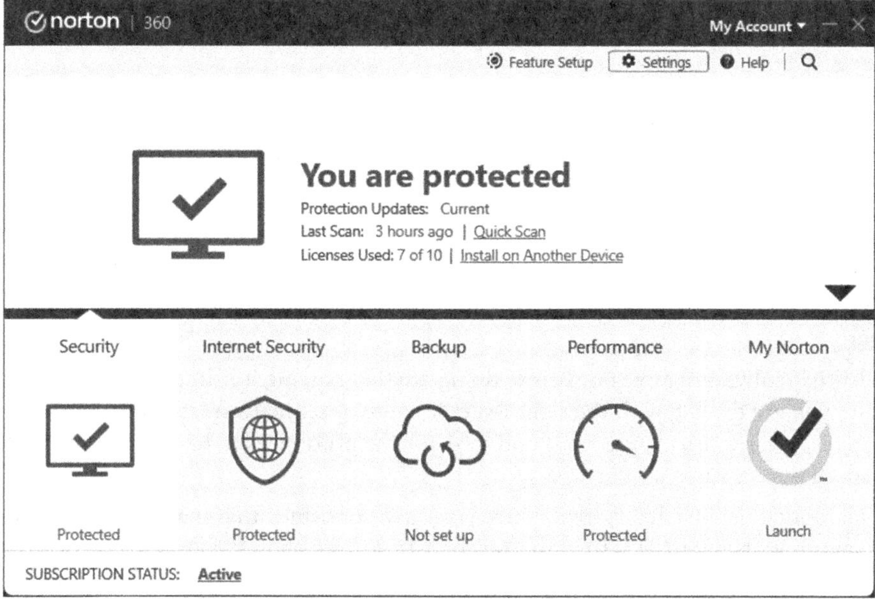

In Figure 5.20, you can see the security settings to turn on or off, as well as the ability to scan your system immediately or install on another device. To get to the configuration of updates in this software, I clicked Settings. It gave me the screen in Figure 5.21, and you can see that automatic updates are on.

FIGURE 5.21 Norton 360 settings

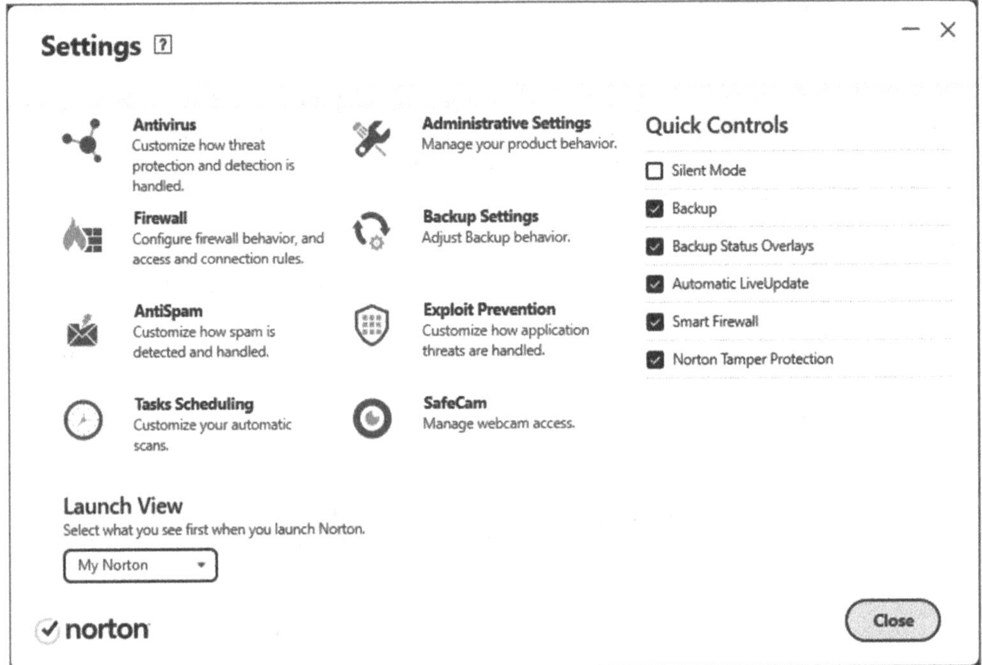

Removing Malware

If you think you have an infected computer, you will want to remove the malware. The following discussion presents the information you need to know for removing the bad software:

1. Identify malware symptoms. Before doing anything major, it is imperative first to be sure you are dealing with the right issue. If you suspect malware, then try to identify the type (spyware, virus, and so on) and look for the proof needed to substantiate that it is indeed the culprit.
2. Quarantine the infected system. Once you have confirmed that malware is at hand, then quarantine the infected system to prevent it from spreading the malware to other systems. Bear in mind that malware can spread any number of ways, including through a network connection, email, and so on. The quarantine needs to be complete to prevent any spread.

3. Remediate infected systems. The steps taken here depend on the type of malware with which you're dealing, but it should include updating antivirus software with the latest definitions and using the appropriate scan and removal techniques.
4. Schedule scans and updates. The odds of the system never being confronted by malware again are slim. To reduce the chances of it being infected again, schedule scans and updates to run regularly.
5. Educate the end user. Education should always be viewed as the final step. The end user needs to understand what led to the malware infestation and what to avoid, or look for, in the future to keep it from happening again.

Software Firewalls

A *firewall* is a hardware or software solution that serves as your network's security guard. They're probably the most important devices on networks connected to the Internet. Firewalls can protect you in two ways. They protect your network resources from hackers lurking in the dark corners of the Internet, and they can simultaneously prevent computers on your network from accessing undesirable content on the Internet. At a basic level, firewalls filter network traffic based on rules defined by the network administrator.

Antimalware software examines individual files for threats. Firewalls protect you from streams of network traffic that could be harmful to your computer.

Firewalls can be stand-alone "black boxes," software installed on a server or router, or some combination of hardware and software. In addition to the categorizations of hardware and software, there are two types of firewalls: network-based and host-based. A network-based firewall is designed to protect a whole network of computers and almost always is a hardware solution with software on it. Host-based firewalls protect only one computer and are almost always software solutions.

Exam objective 6.2 wants you to explain methods to secure devices. Firewalls are part of this objective.

How Firewalls Work

Most network-based firewalls have at least two network connections: one to the Internet, or *public side*, and one to the internal network, or *private side*. Some firewalls have a third network port for a second semi-internal network. This port is used to connect servers that can be considered both public and private, such as web and email servers. This intermediary network is known as a *screened subnet*. A screened subnet can also be configured as a space between two firewalls. Figure 5.22 shows two examples of screened subnets.

FIGURE 5.22 Two ways to configure a screened subnet

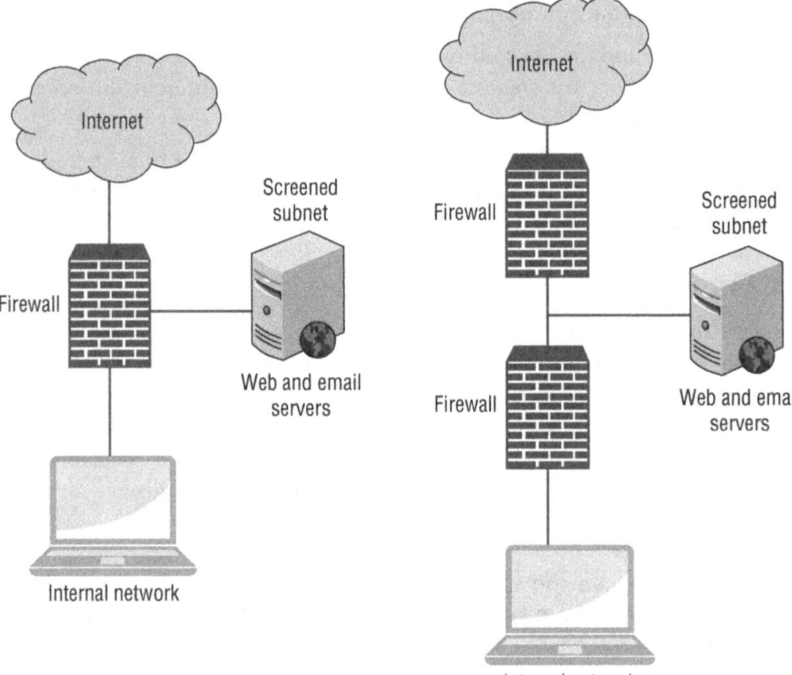

A firewall is configured to allow only packets (network data) that pass specific security restrictions to get through. By default, most firewalls are configured as default deny, which means that all traffic is blocked unless specifically authorized by the administrator. The basic method of configuring firewalls is to use an *access control list (ACL)*. The ACL is the set of rules that determines which traffic gets through the firewall and which traffic is blocked. ACLs are typically configured to block traffic by IP address, port number, domain name, or some combination of all three. Packets that meet the criteria in the ACL are passed through the firewall to their destination.

Enabling a Software Firewall

Windows comes with its own software firewall called Windows Defender Firewall. There are also numerous software firewalls on the market. Configuring Windows Defender Firewall is beyond the scope of the Tech+ exam. For now, know that turning on a firewall is a good thing to help protect your computer from hackers, and it should be turned on by default.

Windows Defender Firewall is found in Control Panel, or by typing **firewall** into the Windows search box. Figure 5.23 shows the screen where you enable Windows Defender Firewall.

FIGURE 5.23 Windows Defender Firewall

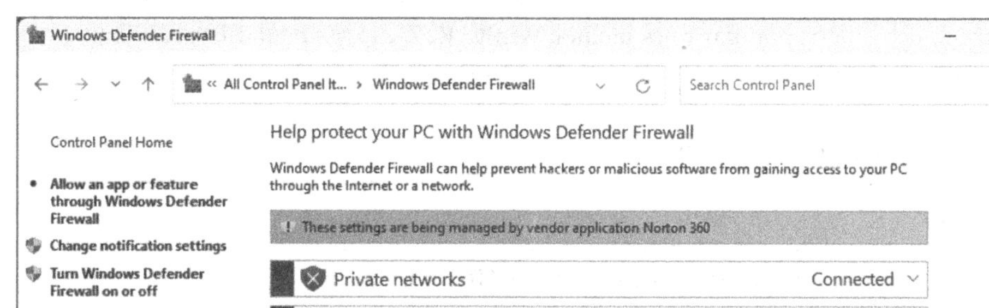

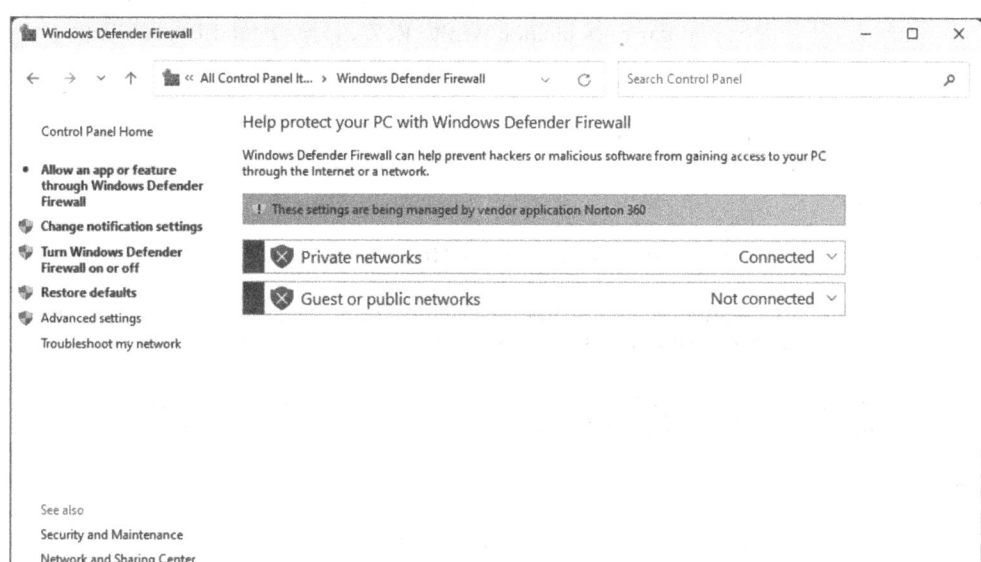

Some third-party security software, such as Norton 360, comes with its own software firewall. In cases where you have those types of programs installed, they will turn off Windows Defender Firewall automatically (as is the case in Figure 5.23).

Compression Software

You probably share files with other people quite a lot, and sometimes those files get really big—so big that they can clog up your email pipes and not make it through the server. At other times, you have 20 files that you want to share, but you really don't want to have to sit there and attach 20 separate files to an email. Compression software is the solution to both of these dilemmas.

Compressing a file is often called *zipping* a file, named after one of the compression file extensions, which is `.zip`.

Compression software removes redundant information within files and by doing so makes them smaller than their original size. You will see different levels of compression based on the type of file you are trying to compress. Text files and worksheets often compress quite a bit, whereas pictures don't usually see much of a size reduction. As noted earlier, compression software can also take multiple files and compress them into the same archive, which can be uncompressed later and the original files retrieved.

The gold standard in compression software for many years has been WinZip. It's a great program, but it's not free. Fortunately, Windows 11 has a free built-in compression utility. If you want to use others, popular ones include WinRAR, 7-Zip, gzip, and Express Zip. Table 5.3 lists common compression file formats and their use.

TABLE 5.3 File compression formats

Extension	Use
`.rar`	Compression format introduced by WinRAR program.
`.tar`	Short for tape archive, it's a format used in the UNIX and Linux environments. It's not compressed; a compressed TAR file would have the extension `.tar.gz`.
`.zip`	The most common compression format, supported by most compression software. Originally created by PKWARE, which makes the PKZIP program.
`.dmg`	macOS disk image files.
`.iso`	Disk image archive files for optical media, such as CD-ROMs.
`.7z`	Compression files generated by the 7-Zip program.
`.gz`	Compression files generated by the gzip program, which is mostly found on UNIX and Linux systems. gzip is the replacement for the `compress` utility.
`.jar`	Short for Java archive; similar in format to `.zip` files. Usually used to distribute software programmed in the Java language.

Earlier in Exercise 5.2, you downloaded and installed 7-zip. In Exercise 5.5, you will use 7-Zip to create an archive.

EXERCISE 5.5

Using 7-Zip to Create an Archive

1. In the Windows search box, type **7-zip** and press Enter. You will see a screen similar to the one shown in Figure 5.24. You can click any folder to navigate to it, or you can use the up folder arrow to the left of the location bar to move up one level.

FIGURE 5.24 7-Zip file manager

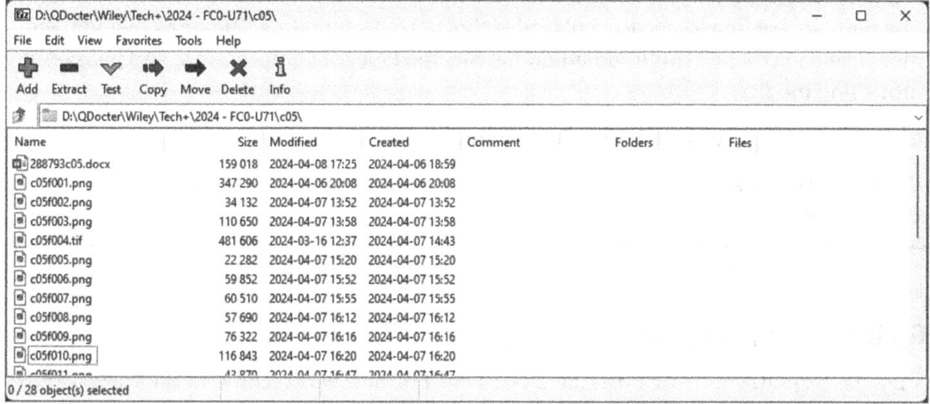

2. Navigate to a file or folder you want to add to the zipped archive, and click the green plus (Add) button. It will give you a screen similar to the one shown in Figure 5.25.

FIGURE 5.25 7-Zip archive options

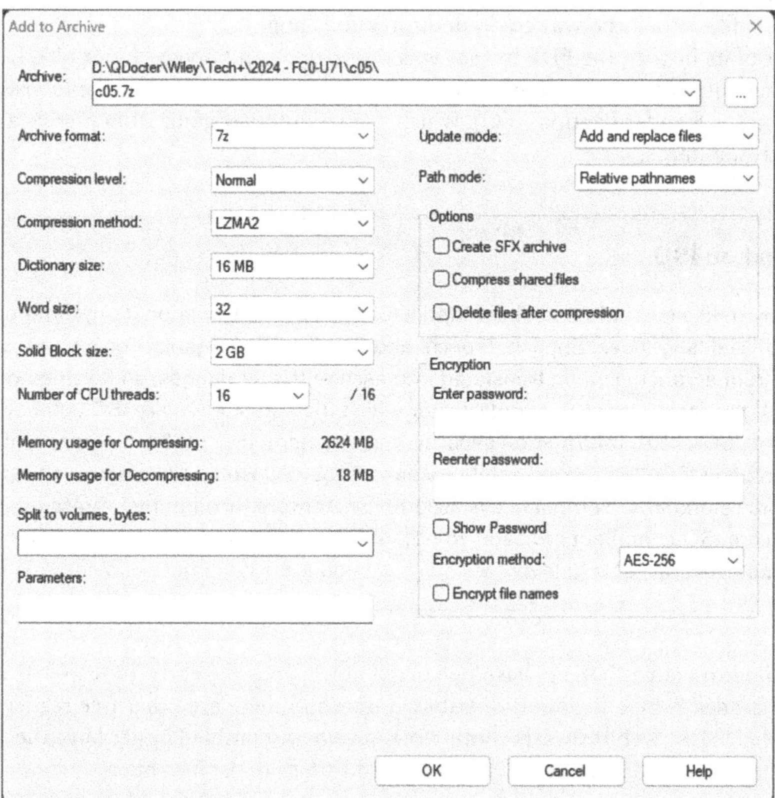

EXERCISE 5.5 *(continued)*

3. The defaults are fine to accept, but notice that you have options. The ones that you are most likely to use pertain to renaming the file, the level of compression, and password-protecting the file.
4. Click OK, and 7-Zip will create the file for you.
5. Compare the file with the `.7z` extension to the original or originals. How much smaller is it?

PDF Viewers and Creators

The PDF file format, short for Portable Document Format, was created in the early 1990s by software maker Adobe Systems. Adobe's goal was to create a document format that would work regardless of the user's computer platform, such as Windows, macOS, UNIX, or Linux. Instead of needing software such as Microsoft Word, which might or might not run on your computer, you needed a PDF reader, such as Adobe Reader (called Acrobat Reader back then), which could be installed on any OS. Usually, PDF files are documents, but they can be flyers, worksheets, presentations, or really anything you want them to be. Some organizations use PDF files as a basic way to do desktop publishing.

For most of its history, the PDF format was proprietary and owned by Adobe. In 2008, it decided to relinquish control and make it an open standard, managed by the International Organization for Standardization (ISO), which is a volunteer organization that establishes international standards.

Background on ISO

ISO might seem like it should be abbreviated IOS, but it's an international organization with three official languages: English, French, and Russian. The organization's name would require different acronyms when translated into each of the languages, so it settled on ISO. Some of the more common standards for which they are known are ISO 9000, quality management; ISO 27001, information security management; ISO 14000, environmental management; and ISO 22000, food safety management. ISO isn't a policing organization, so it can't enforce standards. Compliance is accomplished more through peer pressure; showing that you are ISO-compliant indicates to potential business partners that you take quality (or information security, or whatever) seriously, so you are a legitimate business partner.

The method to read a PDF file hasn't changed much since the early 1990s—you still need a PDF reader. Adobe Reader is distributed free, and there are other free readers on the market as well. Most web browsers (both workstation and mobile) either have the ability to read PDF files natively or have a downloadable add-on to make it happen.

One of the nice features of PDF files is that normally when you distribute them, they are read-only. Other people can't modify the files unless they have PDF-editing software, and even then, you can set passwords to protect the file's contents. Another cool feature is that you can enable the PDF file for people to edit certain parts of it. For example, say you are distributing a form to clients and you want them to enter their name and address, as well as choose from several options in which they might be interested (by checking boxes). You could create a PDF file that lets users edit those fields but not the rest of the document.

To create or edit a PDF file, you need special software called a PDF creator. The most popular creator is Adobe Acrobat, and several versions are available. You will also find numerous free PDF converters online that will take existing documents and convert them for you. Others will convert PDF back to a format such as DOC or DOCX, but usually you need to pay for software that does this. Finally, Microsoft Office 2010 and newer have a feature that lets you generate a PDF file directly from the application. As shown in Figure 5.26, if in Microsoft 365 you go to the File menu and navigate to Save As, you have the option to choose the PDF format. You can also usually choose to save as a PDF when you print a file. On macOS, the print dialog allows you to Save As a PDF. Figure 5.27 shows what a PDF file looks like inside the viewer.

FIGURE 5.26 Creating a PDF file from Office 365

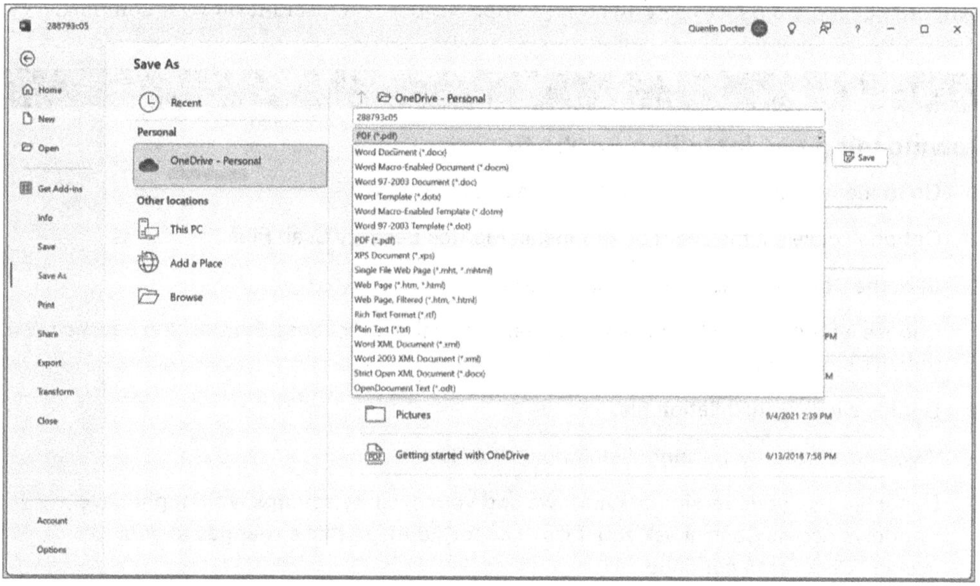

FIGURE 5.27 Viewing a PDF file

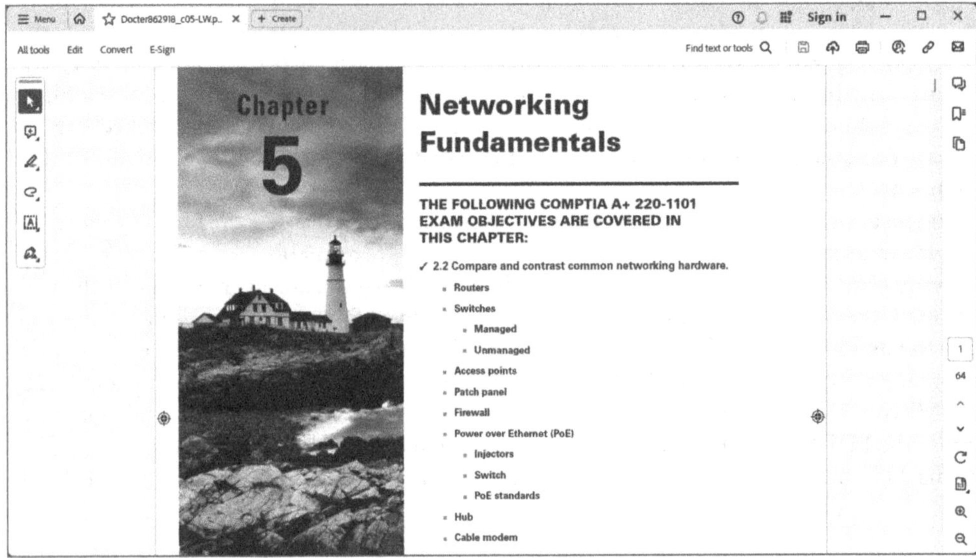

PDF viewers are commonly used, and there's no reason not to have one installed on your computer. Exercise 5.6 has you download Adobe Reader and install it on your computer.

EXERCISE 5.6

Downloading and Installing Adobe Reader

1. Go to the website `https://get.adobe.com/reader`.
2. Optional: deselect the check box to install McAfee Security Scan Plus.
3. Click the Download Acrobat Reader button.
4. Choose where to save the installation file. (Many times, I choose the Desktop because then it's easy to find.)
5. Double-click the installation file.
6. If you get a security warning dialog box, click Run.
7. Depending on your version of Windows and your security settings, you might have Windows Access Control ask you if it's okay for Adobe to make changes to your system. Click Yes to continue.
8. Follow the Adobe Reader installation procedure.
9. When it's complete, you will have an icon on your desktop to launch Reader.

Using Web Browsers

It's safe to say that nearly all computer users interact with a web browser on a daily basis. Accessing the Internet is commonplace from a variety of mobile devices as well as laptop and desktop computers. While it's nice to have a connection to the rest of the world, that connection can also be used by unscrupulous people as a gateway into your world. Proper configuration and use of web browsers can help reduce the risks of contracting malware or accidentally releasing personal information.

In this section, I'll cover some standard browser configuration methods, basic browser security, and private browsing. These topics are closely related to security concepts and risks, so I'll talk about some of them in more detail in Chapter 11.

Configuring Web Browsers

There's a certain amount of preparation that you can take before browsing the Internet, which will make your experience safer. Even if you have never done it before, it's a good idea to review the settings for these items on your system. In addition, you should periodically perform maintenance to ensure that these settings are still correct and that everything is properly updated. All of the settings that you are going to learn about are managed in your web browser. The most common PC-based browser is Google Chrome (which is also the Android default), so I will primarily use the desktop version of that to show examples. Safari (the iOS/iPadOS default) and Microsoft Edge (Windows default) are the second and third, so I will sprinkle in a few examples here and there. Other browsers include Mozilla Firefox, Vivaldi, and Opera.

Tech+ exam objective 3.4, "Given a scenario, configure and use web browser features," has 11 separate subobjectives. There is a lot to know about using web browsers! In this configuration section, you will learn about:

- Browser add-ons/extensions (adding, removing, and enabling and disabling)
- Compatible browser for applications
- Profile synchronization
- Organizing features such as bookmarks
- Default search engine
- Accessibility
- Appearance

In addition, there are a few other configuration topics covered because test objective or not, they are important to understand.

Fortunately, most browser configuration options are managed through the same menu. Laptop and desktop users who primarily utilize Chrome and Edge click an icon in the upper-right corner that has three dots—it's called the More button. Chrome's dots are vertical (Figure 5.28), whereas Edge's are horizontal. It's highly recommended you familiarize yourself with these menus; I'll refer back to them several times in this section.

FIGURE 5.28 (a) Chrome and (b) Edge options menus

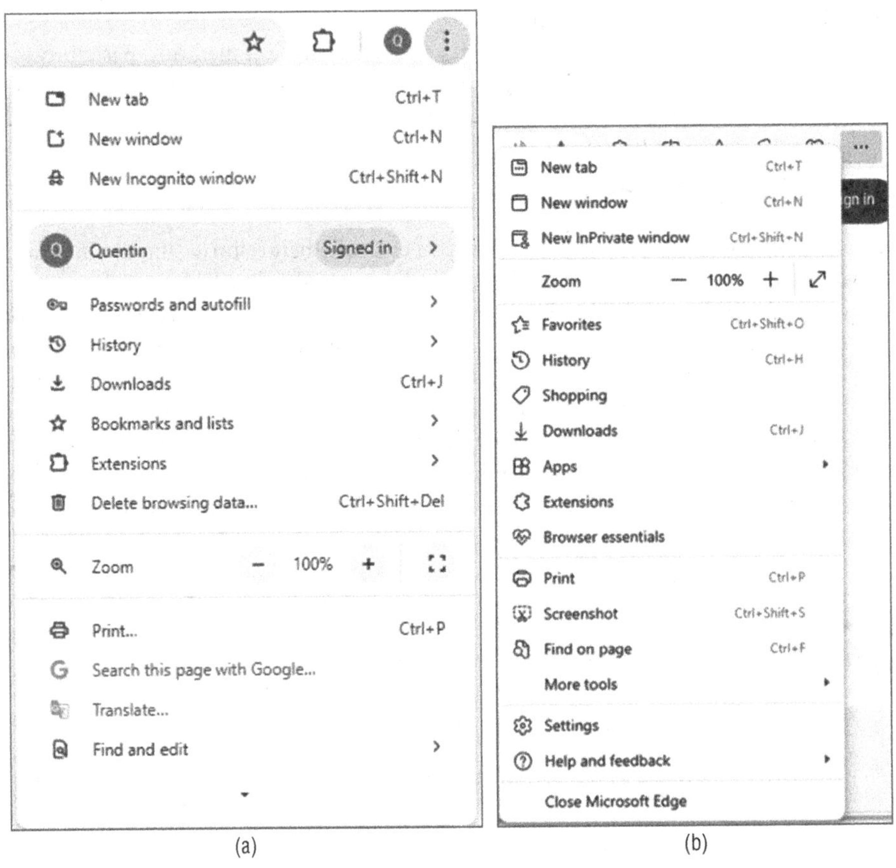

Both browsers have relatively similar menus, which makes it convenient to find the option you're seeking. And if worse comes to worst, you can always click around in the browser until you find the option you need. Mobile Safari users on an iPhone or iPad can find browser configuration options in Settings ➢ Safari. Android users will find Chrome options in Settings ➢ Apps ➢ Chrome. Both are shown in Figure 5.29.

FIGURE 5.29 (a) Safari and (b) mobile Chrome options menus

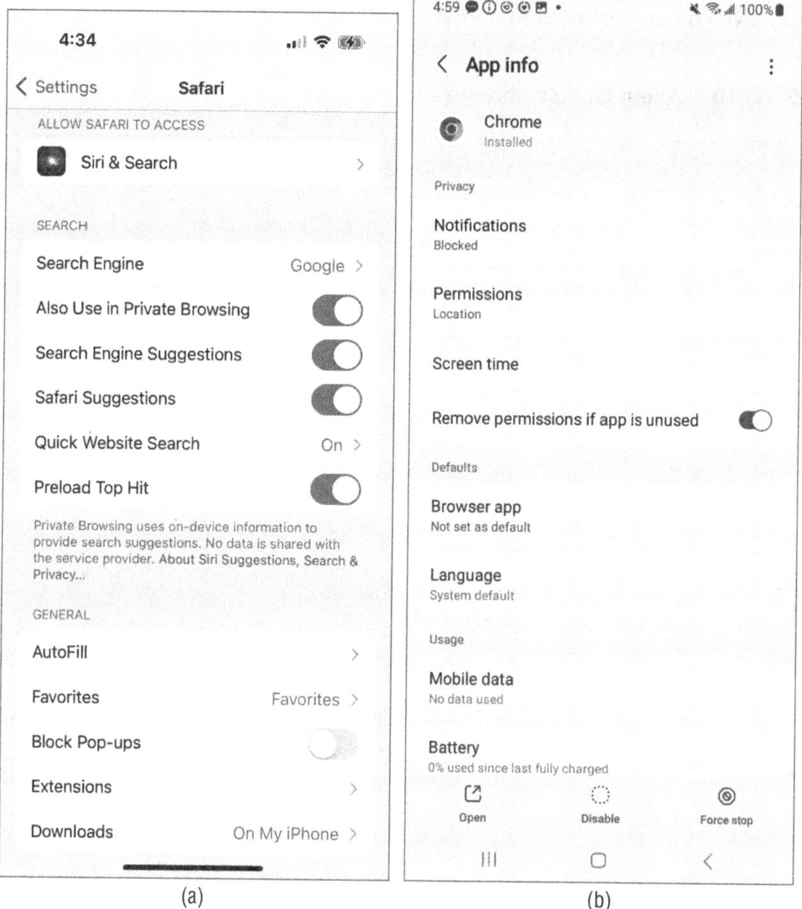

Managing Internet Browser Versions

The first thing for you to do is to make sure that the web browser you are using is the most current version available. Older versions, called *legacy browsers*, may have security holes or fewer features that can protect you as you browse the web. In addition, older browsers might not be compatible with some web applications. The good news is, updating a browser is pretty easy.

To see the version of your browser, click the More button. In Chrome, click Help ➢ About Google Chrome (Figure 5.30). Edge hides its version just a bit. Click More ➢ Settings. Then, in the upper-left corner click the Settings menu (the three horizontal lines) and then About Microsoft Edge. You'll see in Figure 5.31 that by going to this option, it automatically started to update Edge. In either browser, if it's not up-to-date, it will tell you so here and give you an option to update it now.

FIGURE 5.30 About Google Chrome

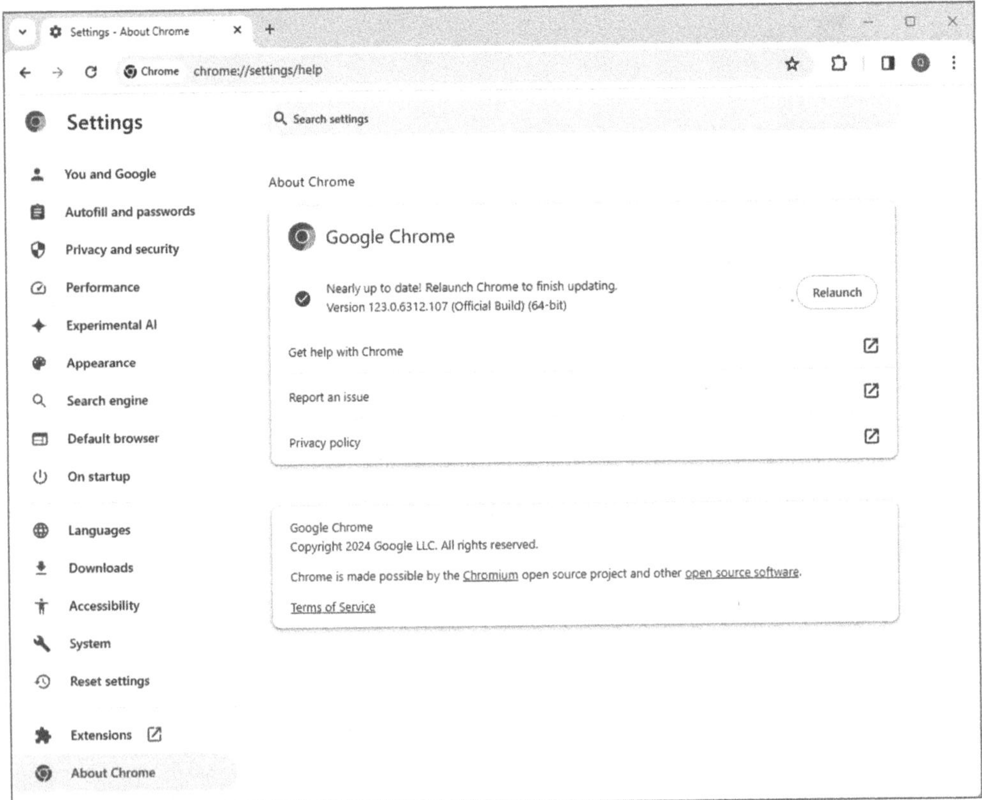

FIGURE 5.31 Microsoft Edge version

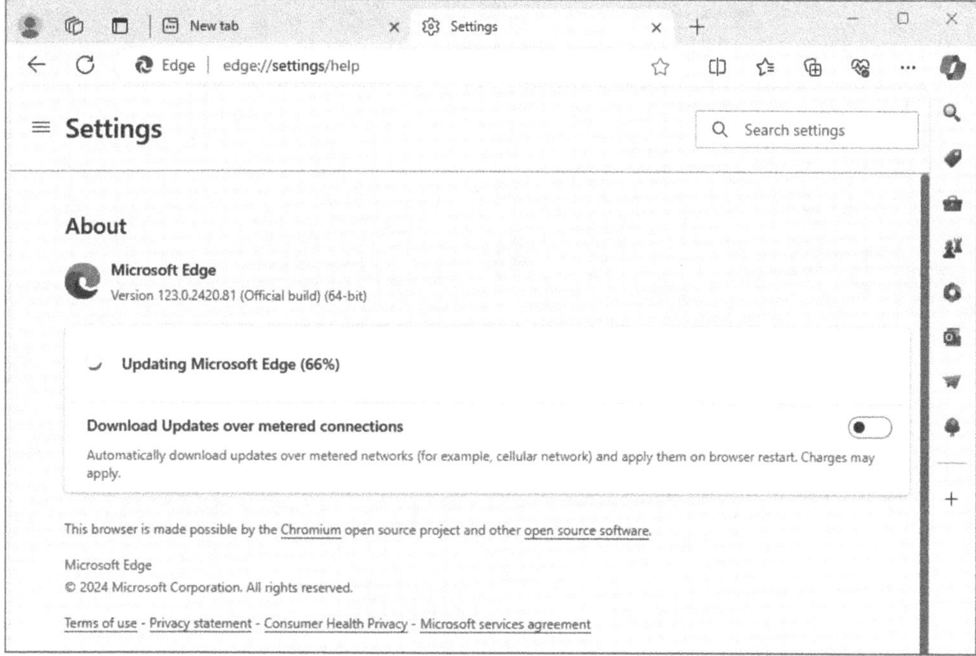

Managing Add-Ons and Extensions

Web browsers have a wide array of capabilities by default, but sometimes you want to add in an extra feature or enhance existing features. This is done through an *add-on* or an *extension*. The difference between the two is open to interpretation—it kind of depends on who you ask. Theoretically, an add-on provides a new feature to a browser, whereas an extension simply improves upon an existing feature. Practically speaking, though, they basically do the same thing and are managed in the same way.

In Chrome there are two ways to manage add-ons/extensions. The first is to click the Extensions icon near the upper-right corner. It looks like a puzzle piece and is just to the right of the address bar. The second is to click More ➢ Settings ➢ Extensions. Either way you will get the Extensions screen like the one in Figure 5.32. This browser has three extensions installed. To enable or disable an extension, use the slider in the lower-right corner of the extension's information box. There's also a handy Remove button if you want to get rid of it. For more information on any extension, click Details. This will show you the version, the size, what it does, and give you various configuration options.

Managing extensions in Edge is similar. Look for a puzzle piece icon to the right of the address bar. If the browser doesn't have any extensions, the piece might not be there. If that's the case, go to More ➢ Settings and look for Extensions there.

FIGURE 5.32 Chrome add-ons/extensions

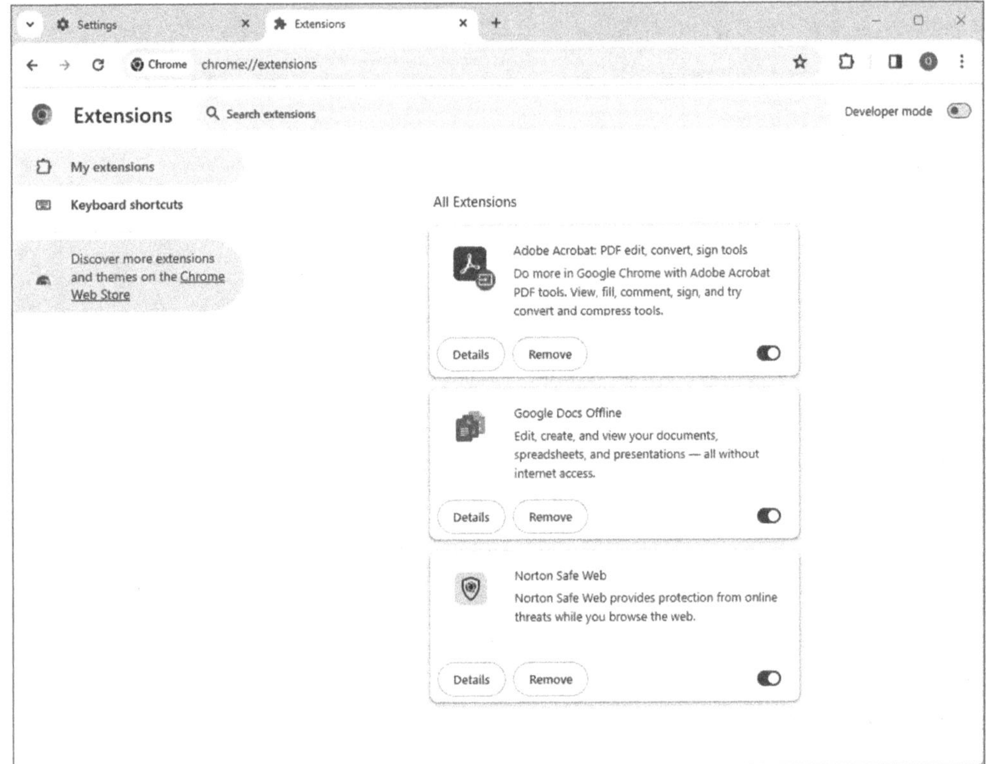

Getting more extensions can also be done in two ways. First, when you install some apps (such as Adobe Acrobat or Norton 360), it will ask you if you want to install a browser extension. Easy enough. Second, you can go to an app store to get them. In Figure 5.32, notice on the left that there's a link to the Chrome Web Store. Edge will have a similar option, and you can browse through extension apps. On a mobile device, you can get additional extensions through the appropriate app store.

All plug-ins or extensions that affect Internet browsing should appear in the browser settings, so you can disable them if you want. Some suspicious add-ons won't show up there, which makes them a little more inconvenient to remove. These items should show up in your installed programs in Control Panel. To disable (or better yet uninstall) these, go to Control Panel ➢ Programs And Features, or type **uninstall** into the Windows search box to open the Installed Apps window. Find the app in the list and remove it.

Synchronizing Profiles

For users who operate multiple devices, it's a major convenience to have the same settings on each system, such as bookmarks, autofill, extensions, and browsing history. This is done through *profile synchronization*. It requires the user to have an account through which they can log into the browser—for example, a Gmail account for Chrome or a Microsoft 360 account for Edge—and then to enable synchronization. Then, the synchronized browser settings will be stored in the cloud for access on any device the user logs into.

In Chrome, go to More ➢ Settings ➢ You And Google (Figure 5.33) to turn on synchronization. If it's already enabled, you can get to it other ways too, such as by clicking the More menu, then your username. Once sync has been enabled, you have multiple configuration options, many of which are shown in Figure 5.34.

FIGURE 5.33 You and Google

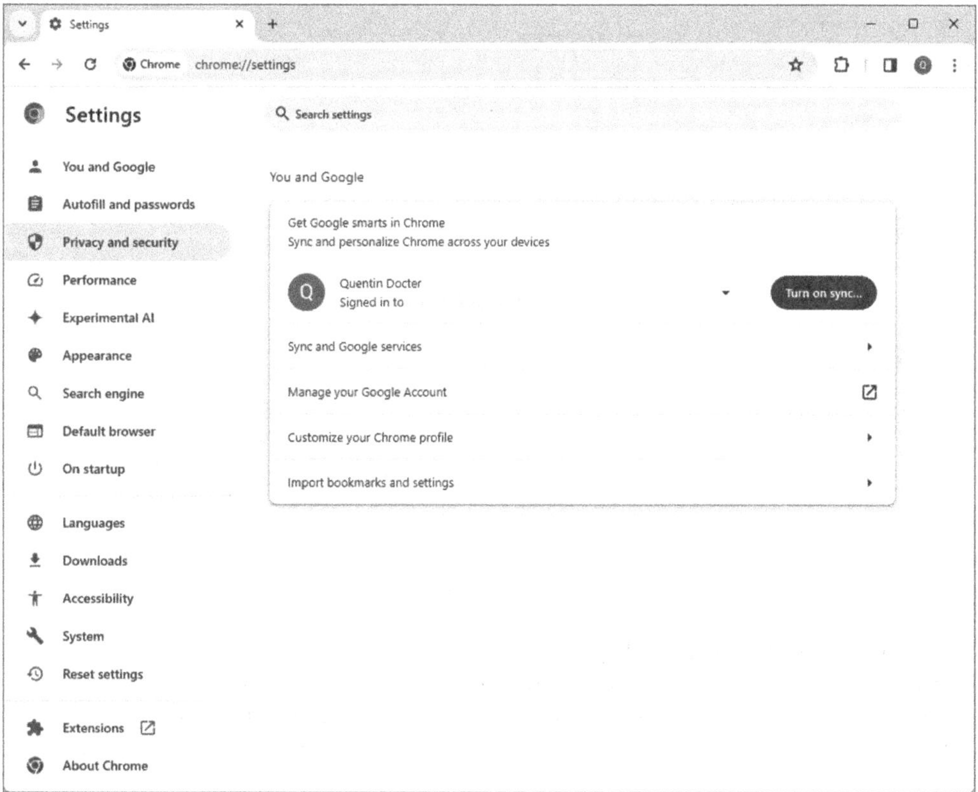

FIGURE 5.34 Synchronization options

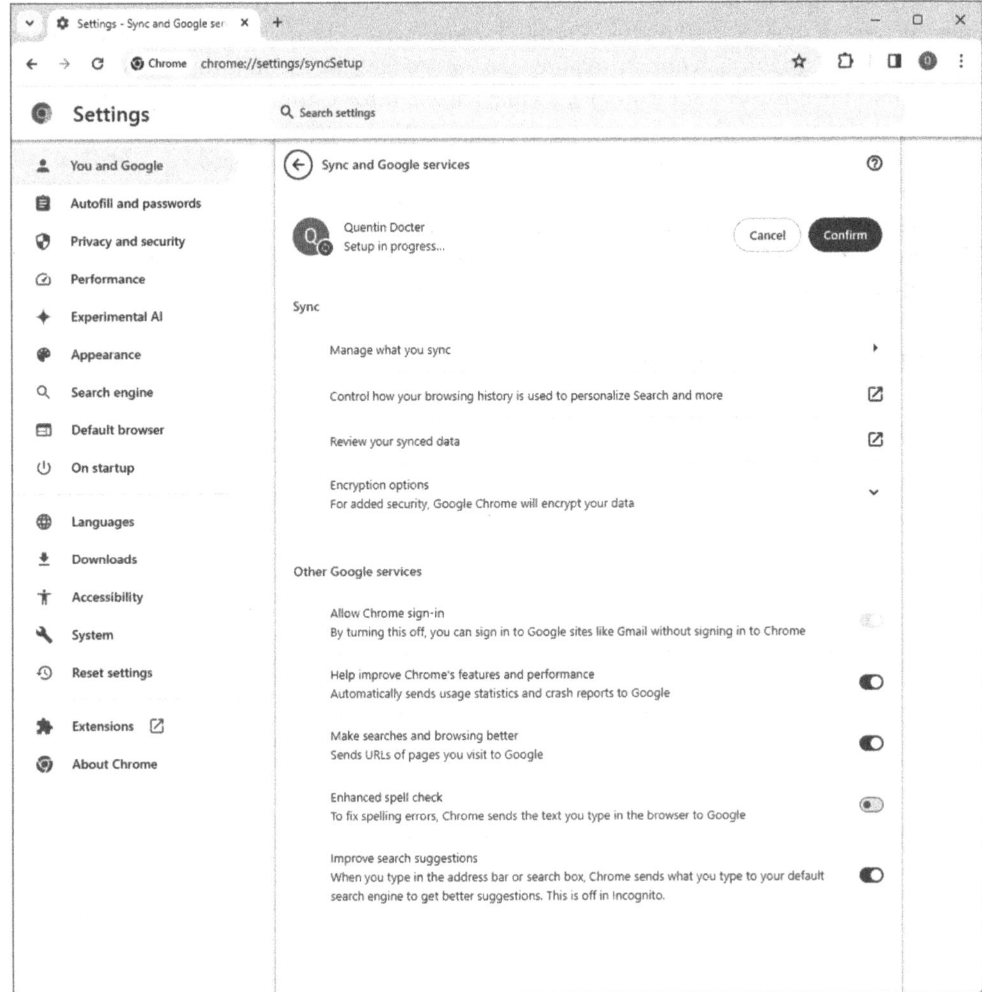

Perhaps the most important of these options is Manage What You Sync, shown in Figure 5.35. While it's easy for you to sync everything, you might want to choose to leave some options out if you use public computers or those accessed by others often. For example, addresses and payment methods might be good ones to leave out in those cases.

FIGURE 5.35 Manage What You Sync

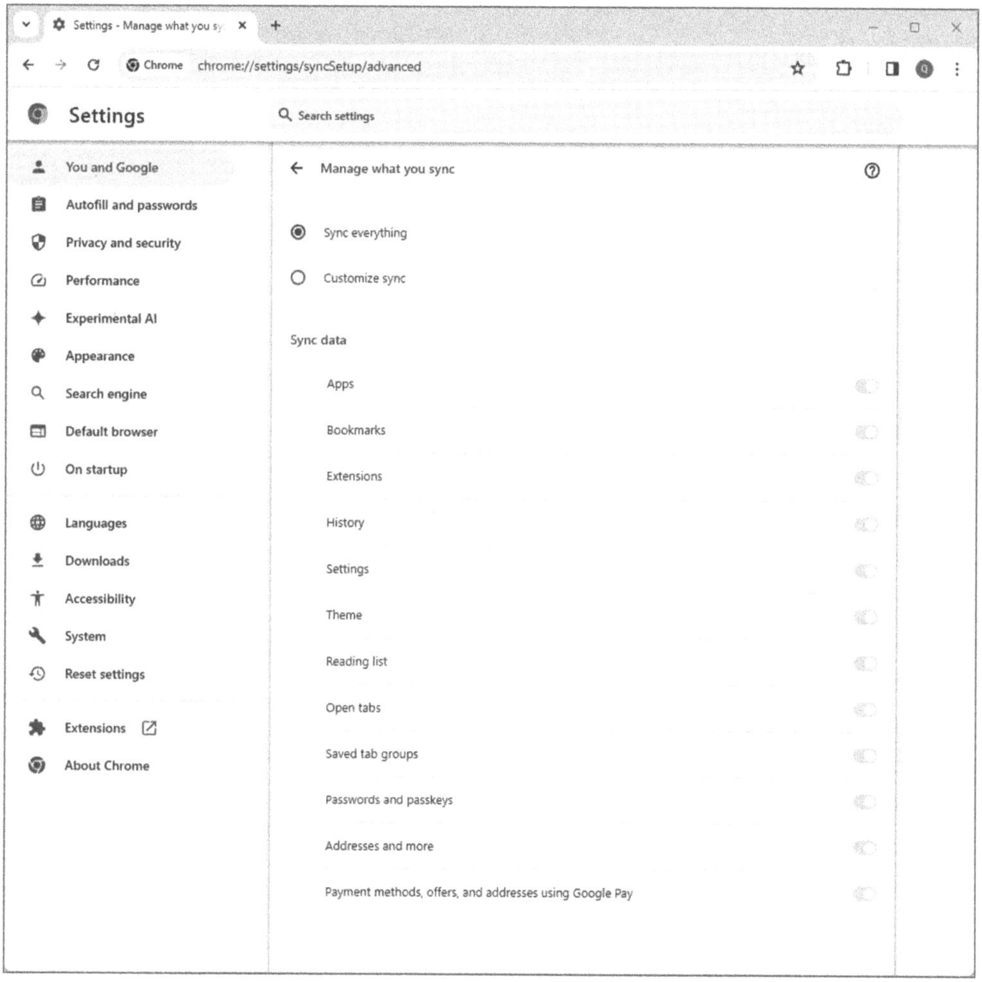

NOTE Edge users can manage synchronization through More ➢ Settings ➢ Profiles (Figure 5.36). In Safari it's under Settings ➢ Username ➢ iCloud. On an Android device, open Chrome, go to More ➢ Settings ➢ Sync.

FIGURE 5.36 Edge sync settings

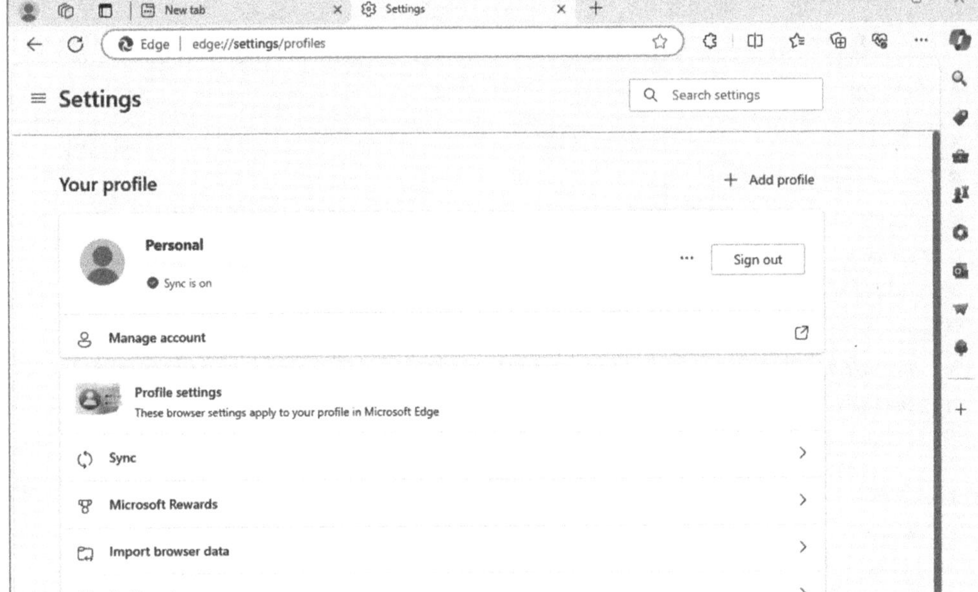

Using Organizing Features

Have you ever visited a website you really liked, closed the browser tab, and then in the future couldn't remember the name of the site to go back to it? Many of us have; after all, there are a lot of websites out there. To help easily navigate to websites you like, you can create *bookmarks* (called *Favorites* in Edge).

A bookmark is simply a link to favorite or frequently viewed websites. Adding them is easy; simply navigate to a website, and click the star to the right of the address in the address bar (Figure 5.37).

When you create a bookmark, you can give it a name, and place it into a folder of bookmarks as well. Of course, if you turn on sync, you will be able to access this bookmark from any device. To access a bookmark in Chrome, open a new tab (Figure 5.38), click the Bookmarks folder, and then navigate to the bookmark you want. In Edge, open a new tab and click the Favorites icon (it looks like a star flying in) to open Favorites, as in Figure 5.39.

FIGURE 5.37 Creating a bookmark

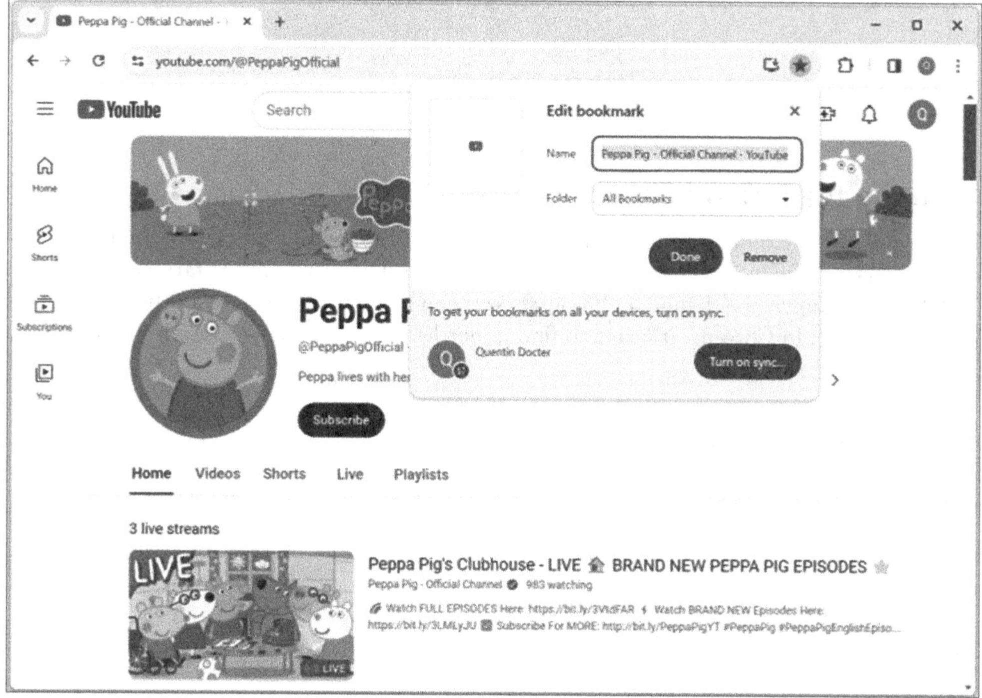

FIGURE 5.38 Chrome new tab with Bookmarks folder

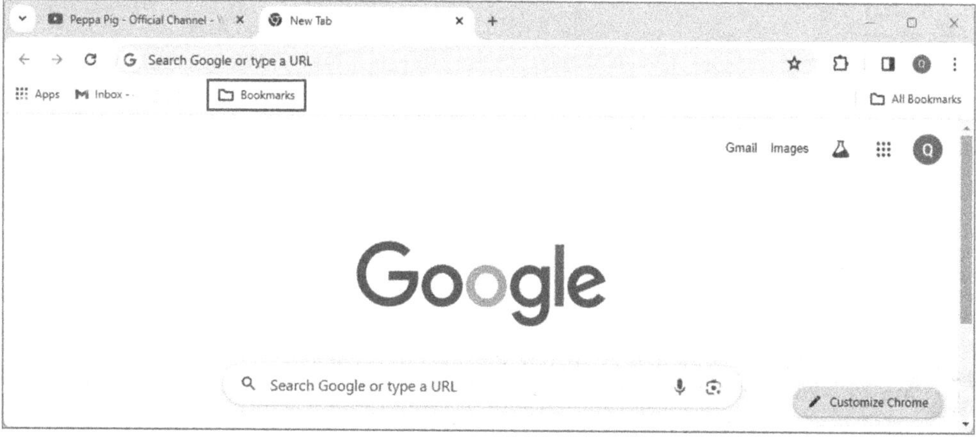

FIGURE 5.39 Edge new tab with favorites

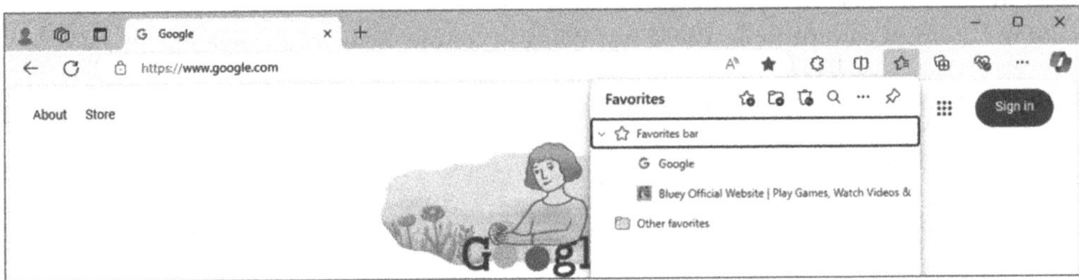

Changing the Default Search Engine

When you type something into the address bar of the browser and press Enter, it will use the *default search engine* to find an answer or website for you. Chrome and Safari use Google and Edge uses Bing as the defaults. Of course, you can change them to use a different one if you would like. In Chrome, it's easy to find under More ➢ Settings ➢ Search Engine (Figure 5.40).

FIGURE 5.40 Chrome search engine

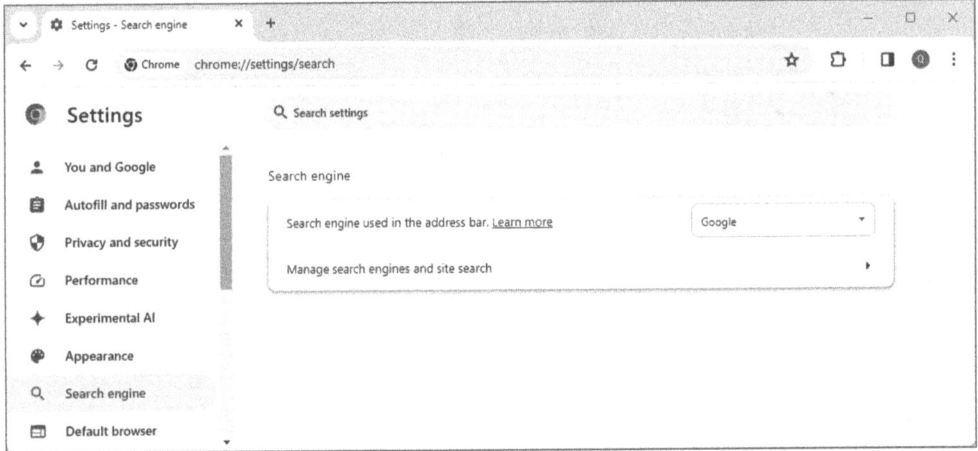

In Edge it's a little more buried. Go to More ➢ Settings ➢ Privacy, Search, And Services, and scroll all the way to the bottom and click Address Bar And Search. Safari users can find it in Settings ➢ Safari.

For the Windows 11 search box, the default search engine is Bing. The only way to change it is to install a third-party utility. As always, install third-party utilities at your own risk!

Enabling Accessibility

Some users may have a hard time reading websites due to small fonts, confusing images, or the text color not being different enough from the background. Browsers provide *accessibility* features for those who would otherwise have problems reading the browser's content.

To enable accessibility in Chrome, go to More ➢ Settings ➢ Accessibility, as shown in Figure 5.41. Here there are some basic options such as live captioning and highlighting text if the mouse stops on it (called a focused object). There are far more accessibility options than what's shown in Figure 5.41, and those are obtained by clicking the Add Accessibility Features link. In the Chrome Web Store, there are apps that will read websites aloud, change fonts and contrasts to make reading easier or reduce eyestrain, boost the volume, reduce clutter, translate, and perform a host of other tasks. Edge users will find accessibility under More ➢ Settings ➢ Accessibility.

FIGURE 5.41 Chrome accessibility options

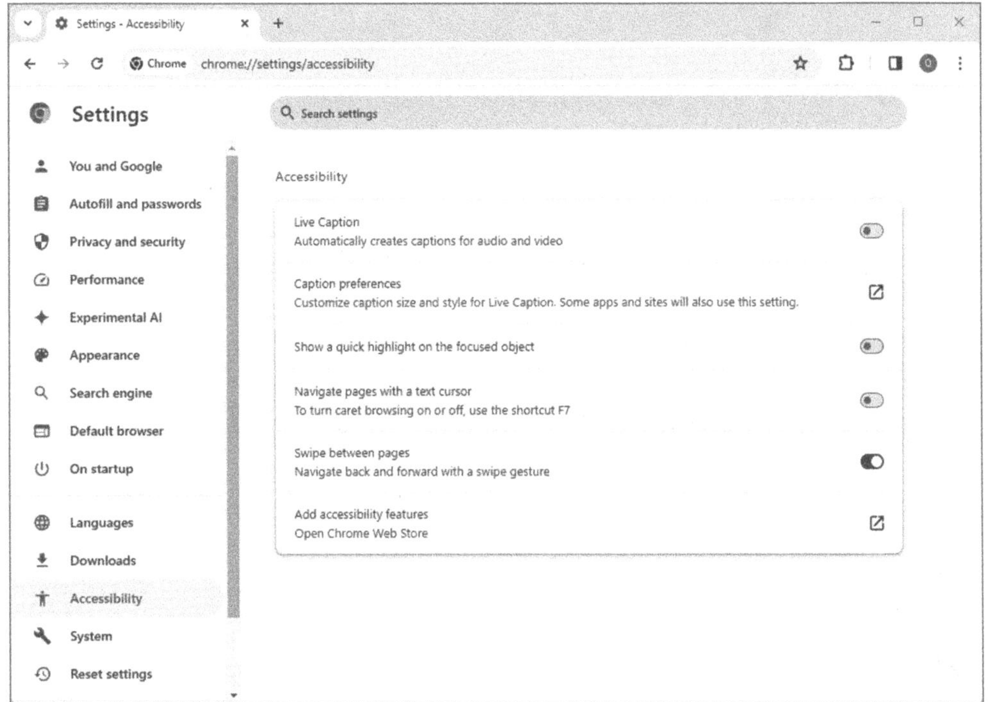

Configuring Appearance

Users can configure their browser's appearance in a number of ways to customize their browsing experience. Figure 5.42 gives you a sense of the available appearance options, such as color scheme (themes), light and dark mode, bookmarks, font options, and page zoom. Edge users will find these settings in More ➢ Settings ➢ Appearance; this is one area where Edge has a lot more options than Chrome does.

FIGURE 5.42 Chrome appearance settings

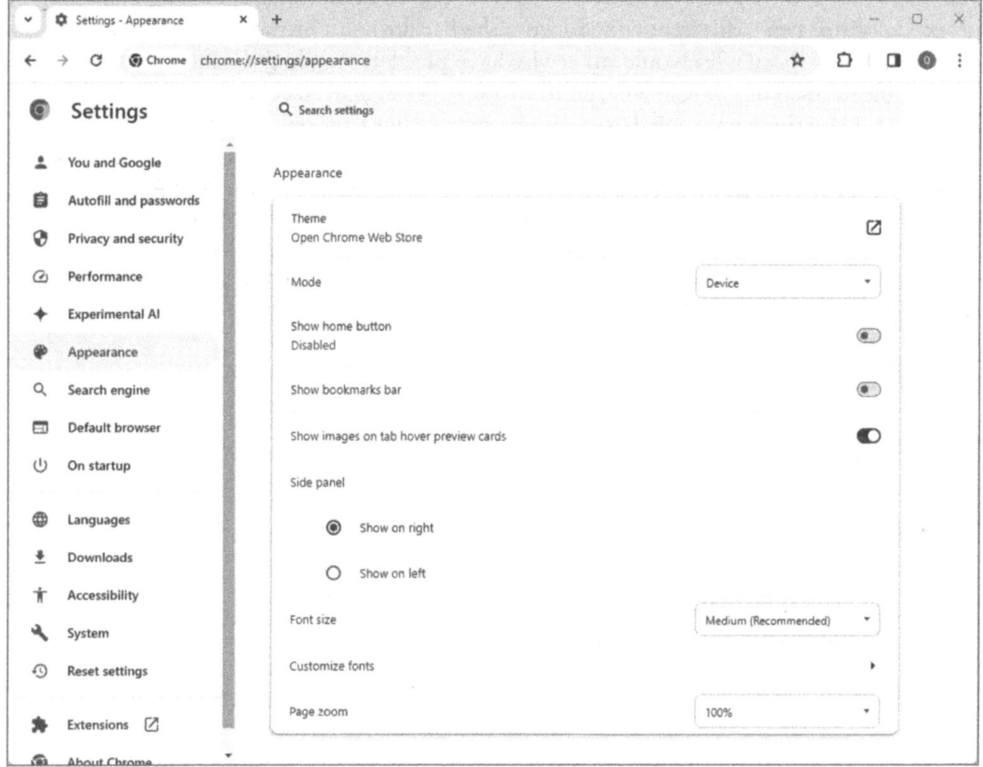

Understanding Basic Browser Security

Incorrect security settings in your web browser can result in a variety of security risks, such as running content on your computer that you don't want to be executed. Fortunately, in most browsers, it's pretty easy to configure security settings. Here, I'll go over cookies and the cache, pop-up blockers, and password management.

Tech+ exam objective 3.4 wants you to be able to configure and use web browser features, including caching/clearing cache, pop-up blockers, and password management. All three are related to browser security.

Managing Cookies and Cache

Since what seems like the beginning of the Internet, there have been people wanting to understand users' browsing behaviors. Mostly, it's been an effort to monetize browsing data. For example, if you visit websites and perform web searches about running shoes, a shoe store or shoe manufacturer would want to make sure you get their ads, whereas they probably don't want to advertise to a non-runner. Of course, they are willing to pay for that information because it helps them generate more sales. And also of course, the company collecting the data is more than happy to make money by selling it. All they needed was a tracking mechanism, and the cookie was born.

A *cookie* is a plain-text file that a web page (or an ad on a web page) stores on your hard disk for tracking purposes. A cookie can tell an advertiser that you've previously viewed a certain ad, for example, or can keep track of the items in your shopping cart on an e-commerce site.

Cookies are harmless 99.99 percent of the time, and they can actually perform useful functions that you want, such as remembering your preferences when you return to an oft-visited website. However, two risks are involved with cookies. One is a privacy threat; a cookie can deliver personally identifiable information to a website. The other is a security threat; a virus or Trojan horse may copy a stored password from a cookie and deliver it to someone who can then steal your login information for a site to commit identity theft or some other type of fraud.

Because of privacy concerns, cookies are going away by the end of 2024. Instead, advertisers will need to rely on things such as users voluntarily providing an email address and contextual advertising (e.g., putting ads on a web page based on the content of that site) to better attract potential customers. Even though cookies are going away, as of this writing, browsers still have options to manage them. And managing them is related to an exam objective—the cache and clearing the cache.

A *cache* is a temporary storage area. In browsers, the cache is used to maintain a list of websites you've visited in the past, called the *history*; store cookies (at least until they are fully depreciated); and hold temporary Internet files. In Exercise 5.7 you will look at and clear your cache in Chrome.

EXERCISE 5.7

Managing Cache in Chrome

1. Open Chrome.
2. Click the More button and then choose Settings.
3. In the menu on the left, choose Privacy And Security. Your screen will look like the one in Figure 5.43. There are several important topics on this page.

EXERCISE 5.7 *(continued)*

FIGURE 5.43 Chrome privacy and security

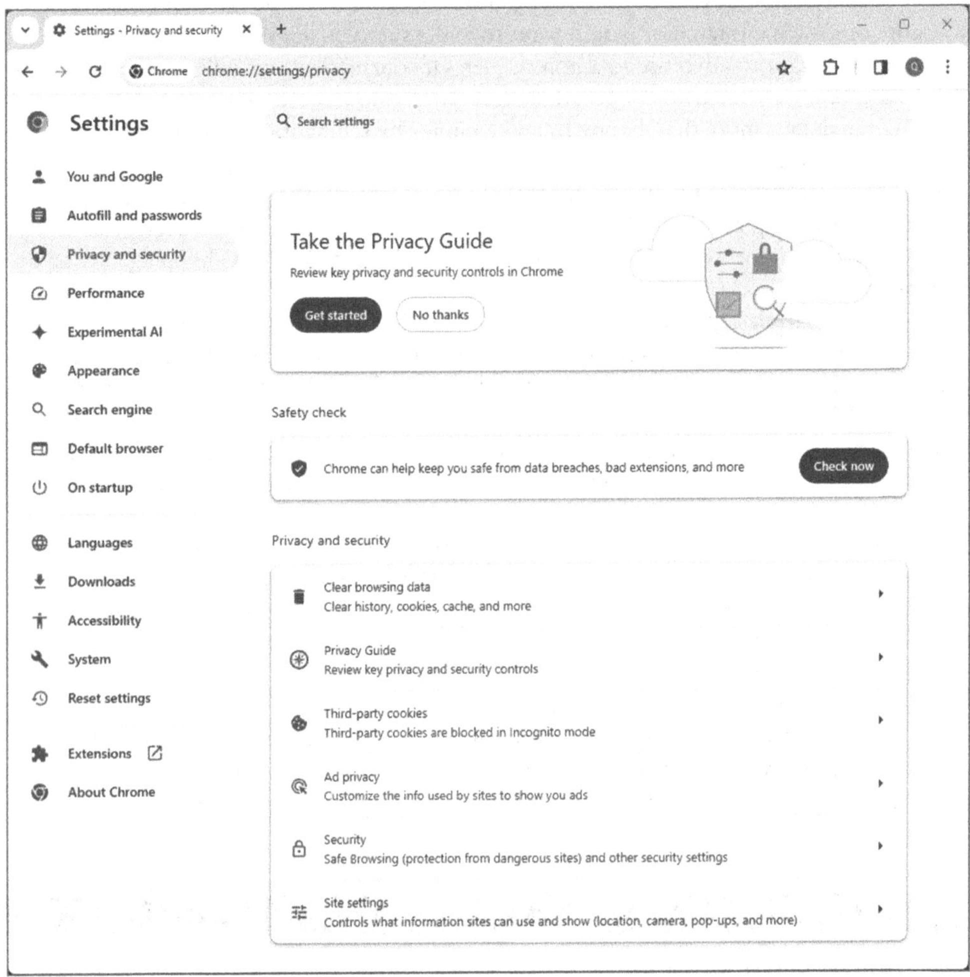

4. Click Clear Browsing Data. You will see a pop-up window like the one in Figure 5.44.

FIGURE 5.44 Clear Browsing Data

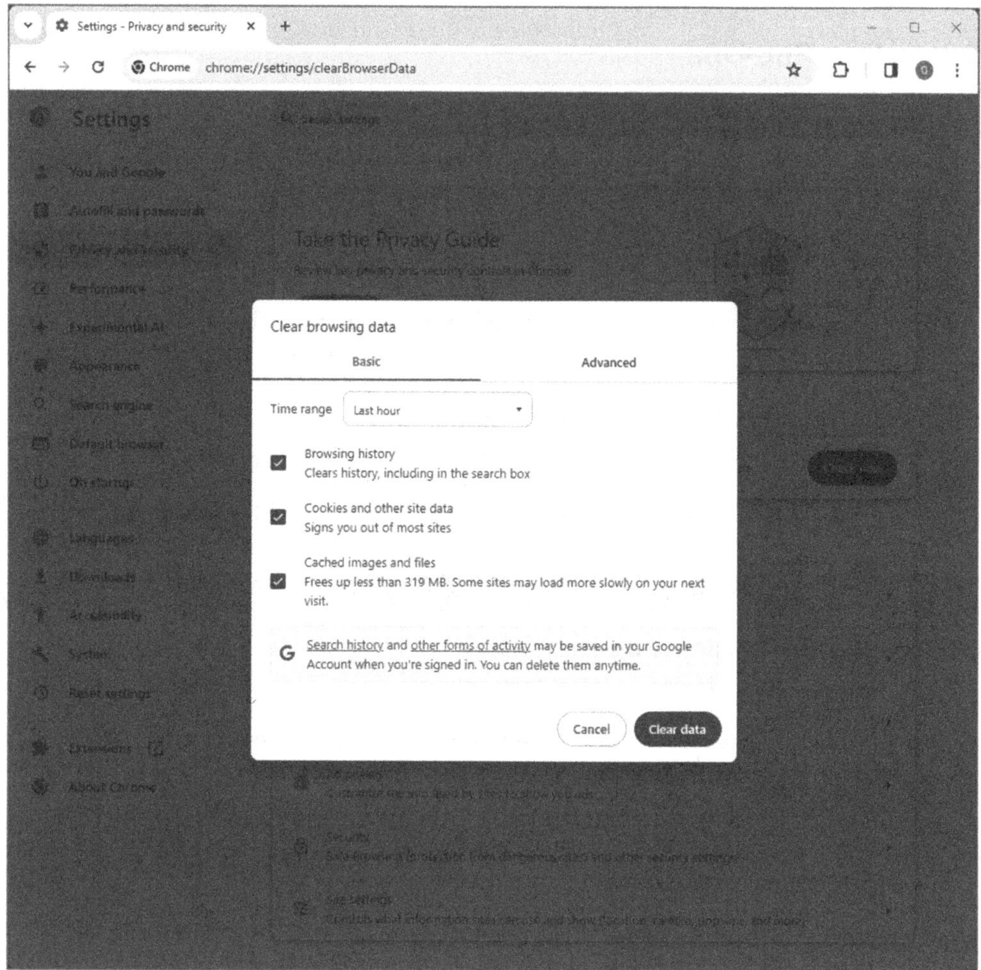

5. (Optional) Click the Advanced tab at the top to see a more detailed list of items stored in the cache.
6. On either the Basic or the Advanced tab, select the check boxes for the items you want to clear, and then click Clear Data.
7. Close Chrome.

Edge users can manage the cache in More ➢ Settings ➢ Privacy, Search, And Services. Cookies are managed in More ➢ Settings ➢ Cookies And Site Permissions.

Controlling Pop-Ups

A *pop-up* is an extra, usually small browser window that appears automatically when you display a certain web page or click a certain button on a page. Pop-ups can serve useful functions, such as displaying the amount of time you've been logged in at a public Wi-Fi location that charges you by the minute or by displaying details for you to download a file you want. However, pop-ups are more often used to display advertisements or fake dialog boxes that trick you into doing something you really don't want to do, such as branching to another company's website.

Your web browser most likely has a pop-up blocker built into it that is enabled by default. You can enable it or disable it, and in some cases, you can configure it to be more or less aggressive about blocking pop-ups. Not all browsers' pop-up blockers are very effective, though; sometimes they can miss certain pop-up types. Third-party pop-up blocker extensions are also available and are often more effective than the web browser blockers. Exercise 5.8 shows you how to configure Chrome's pop-up blocker. Edge's settings are configured in Settings ➢ Cookies And Site Permissions ➢ Pop-ups And Redirects.

EXERCISE 5.8

Configuring the Chrome Pop-Up Blocker

1. Open Chrome.
2. Go to Settings ➢ Privacy And Security ➢ Site Settings. If your browser has recently blocked a pop-up, notification, or redirect attempt, it will appear in the Recent Activity section.
3. Scroll to the bottom of the page and click Pop-ups And Redirects. That will take you to a screen like the one in Figure 5.45.
4. Notice that by default, the option to not allow sites to send pop-ups or use redirects is selected. It's best to leave it that way.
5. If you wanted to add a specific site that's allowed to send pop-ups, you can click the Add button next to "Allowed to send pop-ups and use redirects." Notice in this example that the `www.ups.com` site has been added.

   Why might you want to allow a site to send pop-ups? Some websites have built-in functionality, such as a security box or notification window, that requires the use of pop-ups. Let's say you visit a site that requires a pop-up. When you click a link that activates the pop-up, you'll get a message in the browser saying that it blocked a pop-up from the site. At that time, depending on your security settings, you may be able to tell it to allow the pop-up and also add the site to your list of allowed sites for pop-ups. Or, it might just say the pop-up is blocked and give you no recourse. If it's the latter, you will need to change your browser security settings to be less restrictive.

FIGURE 5.45 Pop-ups and redirects

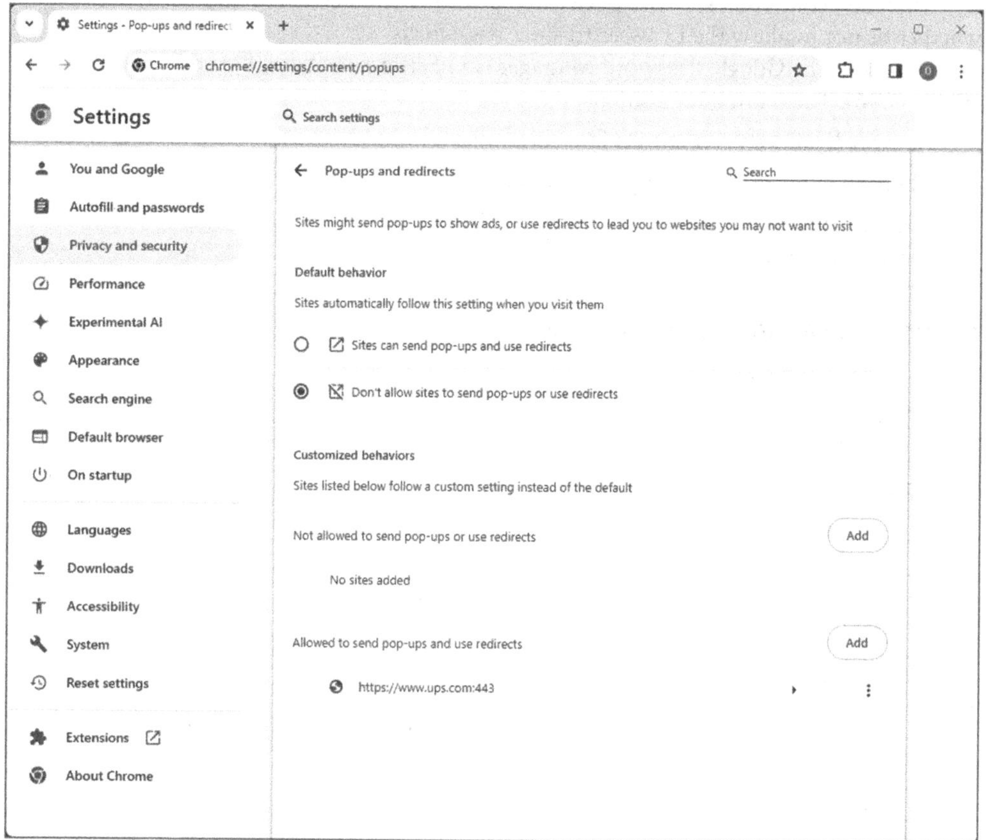

6. Close Chrome.

Managing Passwords

A lot of websites require a user to enter a username and password. Perhaps it's an e-commerce site, or maybe it's a site that requires the user to log in to their subscription to read content. Web browsers will store passwords for different sites the user visits so they don't need to log in every time. This service is known as a *password manager*. Windows has a password manager called Credential Manager, and macOS has one called Keychain that can handle both OS and web credentials. In addition, third-party password managers exist that can manage far more than just website passwords.

While password managers can be a time-saving convenience, they can also pose a security risk if someone else uses your device. Keep the pros and cons in mind when deciding whether or not to allow the browser to store passwords.

In Chrome, the Google Password Manager is in Settings ➢ Autofill And Passwords (Figure 5.46). There are three sections:

- Passwords shows you the sites for which a password is stored.
- Checkup will check for compromised, unique, and weak passwords.
- Settings has key features such as whether the browser offers to save passwords, automatic sign-in, and others.

FIGURE 5.46 Google Password Manager

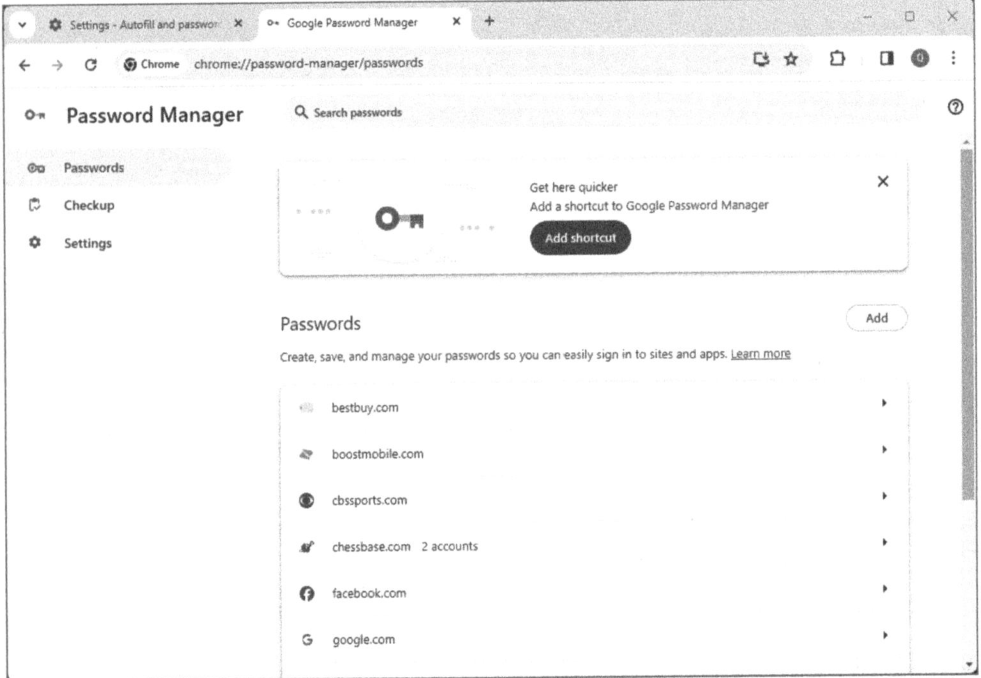

Edge password management is done through Microsoft Wallet and is in Settings ➢ Profiles ➢ Passwords (Figure 5.47).

FIGURE 5.47 Microsoft Wallet

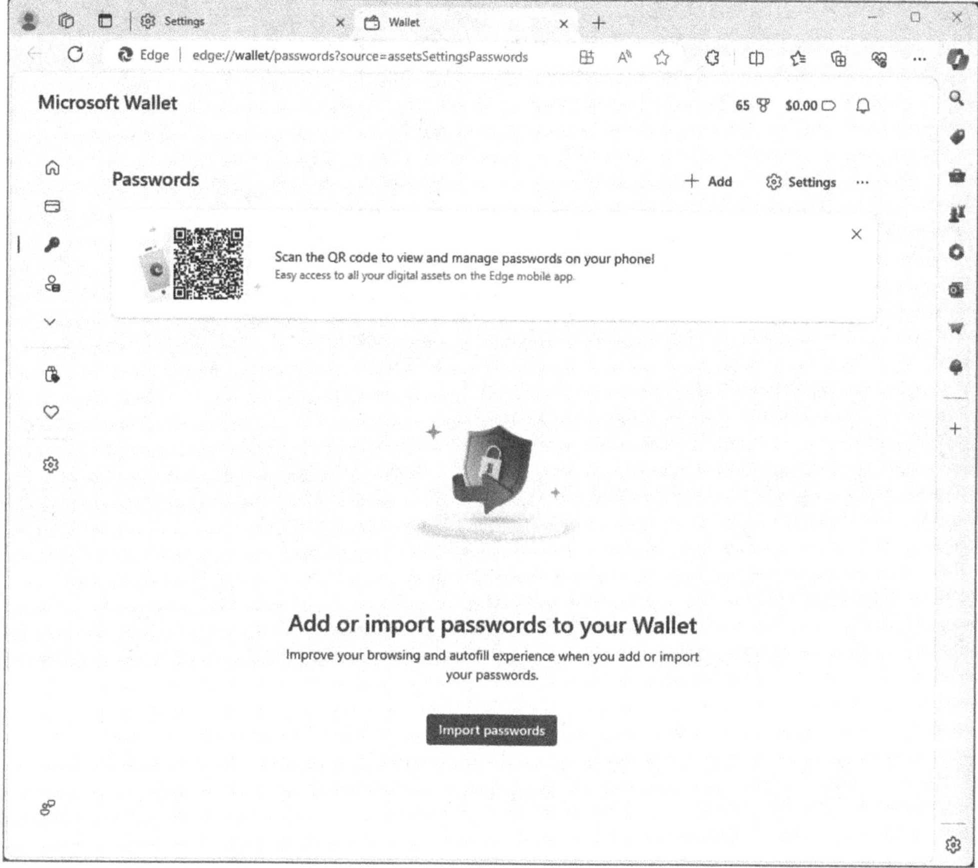

Private Browsing

If you want to protect your privacy while surfing the Internet (or perhaps feel like a super-secret spy), you can use the undercover features of your browser. Chrome calls it Incognito, and Microsoft Edge calls it InPrivate browsing. They are both instances of *private browsing*, which lets a user browse the Internet without leaving the typical traces of their identity.

When you start a private session, none of the history is stored, regardless of your browser's normal history settings. No passwords and login information are stored, and no cookies or temporary Internet files are kept. This mode is useful when you're visiting a site where safety may be questionable because in this mode Chrome and Edge won't permit the website to affect your computer in any way.

To open an Incognito window, open Chrome and then click More ➢ New Incognito Window, or press Ctrl+Shift+N. A new window will appear similar to the one shown in Figure 5.48. Chrome puts an icon that looks like a spy in the upper-right corner of the browser window.

FIGURE 5.48 Incognito browsing

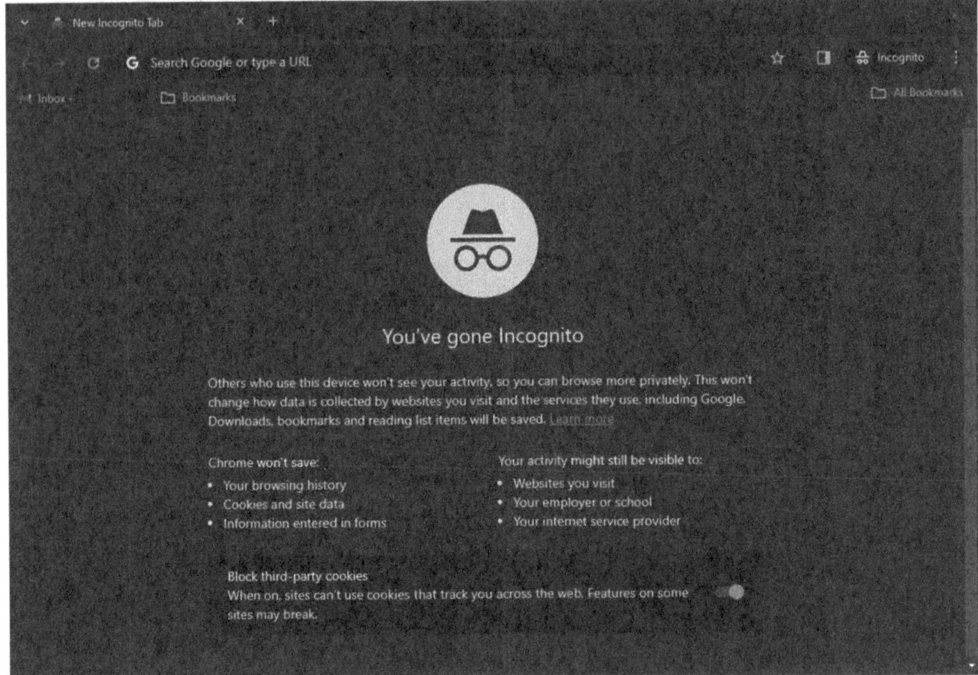

To turn on InPrivate Browsing in Edge, click More ➢ New InPrivate Window. A new Edge window opens (Figure 5.49), along with a message letting you know that InPrivate Browsing is enabled, and an indicator appears in the upper-left corner. Close the browser window when you're finished.

Summary

In this chapter, we covered a wide range of information on software applications. We started with software management best practices. Key topics included researching sources, installing software, licensing requirements, and uninstalling. Updating and patching operating systems, applications, and drivers is part of software management as well.

Following that, you learned about different classifications of software. The first was productivity software, which helps you get your job done. Examples include word processing, spreadsheets, presentation software, and visual diagramming software. Collaboration software was discussed next, and this includes email clients, conferencing, online workspace, and document sharing. The third category was utility software, which includes the important antimalware and firewall software apps, as well as instant messaging, remote support, compression programs, and PDF readers.

FIGURE 5.49 InPrivate Browsing

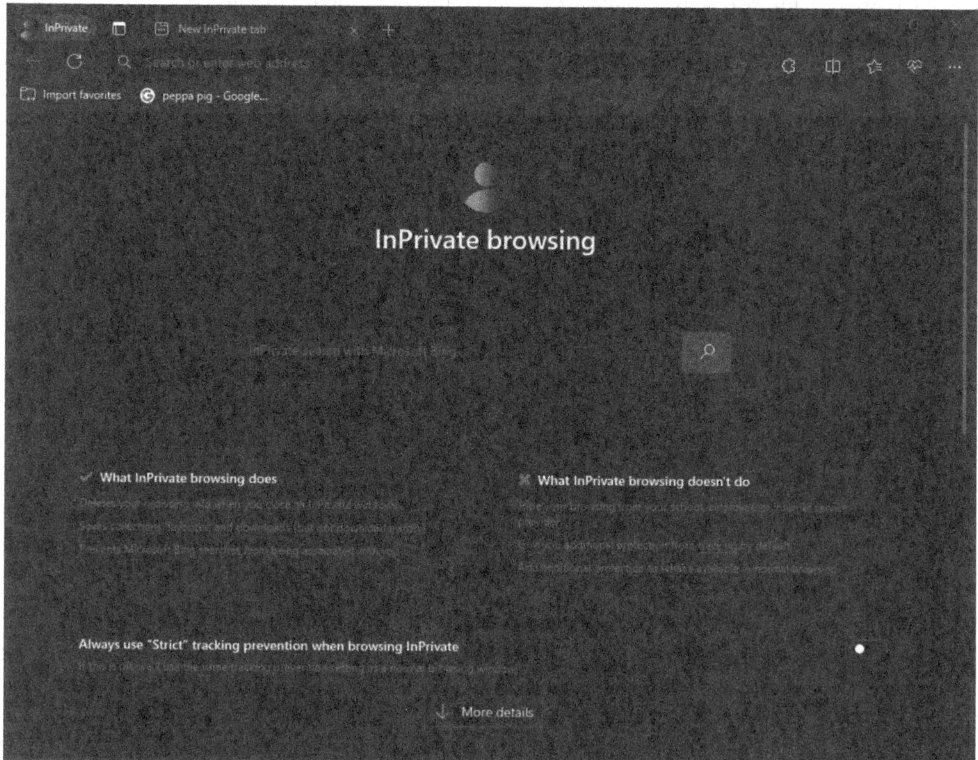

The last section focused on configuring and using web browsers. You looked at configuration options such as ensuring the most recent version; managing add-ons and extensions; using profile synchronization; configuring organizing features such as bookmarks; and setting the default search engine, accessibility, and appearance. Then I covered some basic security principles such as the cache, pop-up blockers, and password management, finishing up with private browsing.

Exam Essentials

Know executable file extensions. Executable file extensions include `.exe`, `.msi`, `.app`, `.bat`, and `.scexe`.

Be able to name examples of productivity software. Productivity software includes word processing, spreadsheets, presentation software, visual diagramming software, and web browsers.

Be able to give examples of collaboration software. Collaboration software includes email clients, conferencing software, online workspace, and document storage.

Know some examples of utility software. Utility software includes antimalware, software firewalls, instant messaging, remote support, compression utilities, and PDF readers.

Understand licensing and activation processes. Software that you purchase comes with a license to use it, which defines how you can use the software and how many people can use it. Some software packages require you to activate them before they will work, linking that software to your computer.

Understand open source versus proprietary software. Open source is free to use and you can modify the code. Proprietary software generally needs to be purchased and the code can't be modified.

Know the difference between subscription, one-time purchase, and perpetual licenses. One-time purchase means you pay once for the software and it's yours to use. The terms one-time and perpetual are interchangeable. A subscription needs to be renewed periodically, typically every year.

Understand the difference between OEM and third-party websites. An OEM website is one owned by the software developer. A third-party website is not owned by the software developer, but may allow you to download their software.

Know how to install and uninstall applications. Installing applications is typically done by double-clicking the EXE or other installation file or by inserting removable media and letting it autorun. Software manager tools within your OS are generally used to uninstall applications.

Know how to configure and use web browsers. You should know how to clear the cache, disable pop-ups, configure add-ons and extensions, synchronize profiles, set the default search engine, and enable private browsing.

Chapter 5 Lab

You can find the answers in Appendix A.

Chapter 5 introduced a lot of software concepts that are good to know and some that are absolutely critical to the safety of your computer. For this lab, you are going to do two separate activities.

First, you should familiarize yourself with software that you have not used before. Most people are familiar with Microsoft 365, but not everyone has seen a competing office suite. So, for the first part of the lab, go to `www.libreoffice.org` and download LibreOffice. Install it and open it. In particular, play with Writer and Calc, or whichever Microsoft 365 equivalent you are most familiar with. Can you find what you need in the menus? Also, if you have a DOC or an XLS file, see whether you can open it in LibreOffice. Does it work like it's supposed to?

For the second part of your lab, you need to make sure your computer is secure and up-to-date on its important patches. Here are some steps you can take:

1. If you don't have antivirus or antimalware software, install some! Options are suggested in the chapter, and you can also do a Google search for recommended options from reputable sources.
2. If you do have antivirus software, open it up and see when it last updated its definitions. It should be within the last week. If not, update them.
3. Make sure that your OS is scheduled to receive automatic updates. Perhaps you have a good reason why you might not want them installed automatically, but for the most part, installing automatically is the best bet.

Review Questions

You can find the answers in Appendix B.

1. A user calls to tell you that every time he browses the Internet, multiple browser windows keep appearing on his screen even though he has not opened them. In this scenario, what should you do to fix the problem?
   - **A.** Deactivate client-side scripting.
   - **B.** Clear the cache.
   - **C.** Disable browser extensions.
   - **D.** Configure a pop-up blocker.
2. Rose opens her software application and gets a message stating that she has only 16 more uses of the product available. Given this scenario, what is her best course of action to use it more than 16 additional times?
   - **A.** Activate the software.
   - **B.** Register the software.
   - **C.** Uninstall and reinstall the software.
   - **D.** No longer close the application.
3. You are visiting a website to order a product, but you keep seeing old information that you know is outdated. Which of the following will most likely fix the problem?
   - **A.** Deactivate client-side scripting.
   - **B.** Disable browser exensions.
   - **C.** Clear the cache.
   - **D.** Configure proxy settings.
4. You have just purchased licensed software and want to install it. Which of the following are you required to enter to install this software?
   - **A.** Your name and contact information
   - **B.** The product key
   - **C.** The serial number of your processor
   - **D.** None of the above
5. You are setting up a technical support help desk for a new app. What type of software should you get to help the technicians fix problems more effectively?
   - **A.** Remote support
   - **B.** Instant messaging
   - **C.** Document sharing
   - **D.** Visual diagramming

6. John wants to download a PC-based software package made by Company X. He sees that he can get the software for free from a dozen different websites on the Internet. What advice would you give John?
   - A. Download the software from any of the sites because it should all be the same.
   - B. Download the software only from the Company X website.
   - C. Disable his pop-up blocker and download the software from the site promising the fastest download speed.
   - D. Look on the Apple Store to find the package and download it.
7. A user wants to have the same browser color scheme, security settings, and favorite website list available from any computer they log in to. What should be enabled?
   - A. Profile synchronization
   - B. Bookmarks
   - C. Accessibility
   - D. Compatible browser for applications
8. Word processing, spreadsheets, and presentation software are examples of what?
   - A. Productivity software
   - B. Collaboration software
   - C. Utility software
   - D. Operating system add-ins
9. Which of the following types of software licenses requires the user to pay yearly?
   - A. Proprietary
   - B. Perpetual
   - C. Subscription
   - D. Recurring
10. What software is designed to let the OS talk to hardware?
    - A. Driver
    - B. Application
    - C. Patch
    - D. Virtual
11. You need to set up software for five users on a network. They all need to have access to and edit the same Excel files. Which is the best type of software for them to use?
    - A. Project management software
    - B. Online workspace
    - C. Conferencing software
    - D. Document sharing

12. When thinking of software compatibility, which two factors matter most? (Choose two.)
    - A. If the software will work with other software on the computer
    - B. If the software will work with the operating system
    - C. If the minimum hardware requirements are met
    - D. If the software comes with automatic updates

13. You have just plugged in a new HP printer to your Mac. You can't find a printer driver. What should you do given the circumstances?
    - A. Use the default HP printer driver for macOS.
    - B. Visit Apple's website to download the printer driver.
    - C. Visit HP's website to download the printer driver.
    - D. Run Software Update to install the printer driver automatically.

14. A company employee has limited eyesight and needs the web browser to be set up with high-contrast colors to make it easier to read. What type of feature is this?
    - A. Accessibility
    - B. Profile synchronization
    - C. Compatibility
    - D. Scripting

15. Which of the following is not a configurable web browser feature?
    - A. Private browsing
    - B. Profile synchronization
    - C. Pop-up blocker
    - D. Browser kernel

16. You just installed an antivirus program on your laptop computer. Given a scenario in which you want to maintain proper levels of security, how often should you update the software?
    - A. At least once a week
    - B. At least once a month
    - C. At least once a year
    - D. Only when a new virus is discovered

17. Which of the following does not require users to pay for the software?
    - A. Proprietary software
    - B. Open source software
    - C. Concurrent license
    - D. Single use

18. Your boss calls you on the phone while he is trying to install software. It is telling him that he needs a product key. Where should you tell him to look for it? (Choose two.)
    - A. On the package the installation media came in
    - B. In an email from the manufacturer
    - C. On the screen in the Options menu
    - D. In Windows Update

19. You want to visit a web page and make sure that the website does not steal any information about your identity. In that scenario, which of the following should you use?
    - A. Script blocker
    - B. Invalid certificate
    - C. Disabled extensions
    - D. Private browsing

20. You are trying to enter registration information into a website. When you click the Submit button, nothing happens. You try again and still nothing. What is the most likely cause of this problem?
    - A. Default search engine
    - B. Pop-up blocker
    - C. Disabled browser extension
    - D. Invalid certificate

Software Development

THE FOLLOWING COMPTIA TECH+ FC0-U71 EXAM OBJECTIVES ARE COVERED IN THIS CHAPTER:

✓ **1.0 IT Concepts and Terminology**

✓ **1.2 Identify notational systems.**

- Binary
- Hexadecimal
- Decimal
- Octal

✓ **4.0 Software Development Concepts**

✓ **4.1 Compare and contrast programming language categories.**

- Interpreted
  - Scripting languages
  - Markup languages
- Compiled programming languages
- Query languages
  - Assembly languages

✓ **4.2 Identify fundamental data types and their characteristics.**

- Char
- Strings
- Numbers
  - Integers
  - Floats
- Boolean

✓ **4.3 Explain the purpose and use of programming concepts.**

- Identifiers
  - Variables
  - Constants
- Arrays
- Functions
- Objects
  - Properties
  - Attributes
  - Methods

✓ **4.4 Identify programming organizational techniques and logic concepts.**

- Organizational techniques
  - Pseudocode concepts
  - Object-oriented methods
  - Comments and documentation
  - Flow chart concepts
    - Sequence
- Logic concepts
  - Branching
  - Looping

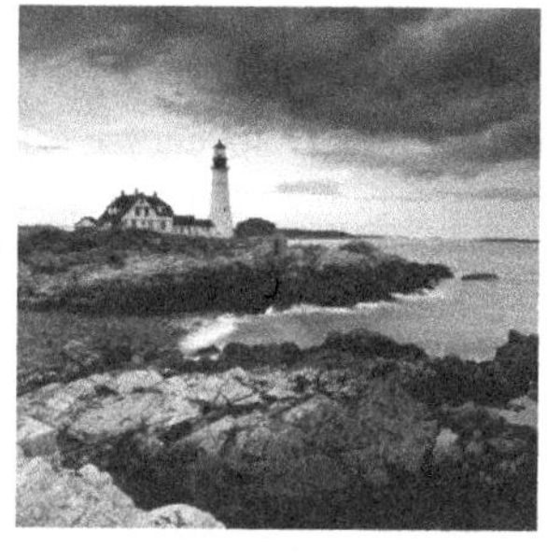

It's easy to imagine the creators of ENIAC or other early computers looking at each other and saying, "There has to be an easier way." They had created what was (at the time) an engineering marvel—an automated computer that could do thousands of mathematical operations per second. It was significantly faster than any human at doing math, but there was a problem. The developers had to tell the computer what to do, and that "programming" process could take weeks for a team of engineers to create and debug. Any change in the program, even a simple one such as telling it to subtract instead of add, took hours of changes and testing. And if they had a different math equation altogether, it required the creation of an entirely new program. There had to be an easier way.

Fast-forward to today, and it's impossible to count the number of software titles in existence. From operating systems to productivity software to games to—you name it—the breadth and depth of available programs would blow the minds of those early computer pioneers. One thing hasn't changed, though: people still need to tell computers what to do. Computers can't independently think for themselves. Perhaps that will change (for better or worse) with advances in artificial intelligence, but for now computers need instructions, and those instructions are delivered via preprogrammed software packages. It is the easier way.

This chapter gives you an overview of foundational software development concepts. It's not intended to turn you into a programmer—one chapter could not do that task justice. Rather, at the end of this chapter, you will understand the basics of different programming languages as well as some concepts and techniques that programmers use to make their jobs easier. If you find these topics interesting and want to pursue a path that includes programming, there are ample courses, books, and online materials to help you get there.

Exploring Programming Languages

All of the software that you use today, whether it's on your smartphone, a workstation, or a cloud-based app, was created by a programmer. More than likely, it was created by a team of them. Small and simple programs might have only a few hundred lines of code, whereas an elaborate program like Windows 11 reportedly has about 50 million lines of code. Now, most developers will tell you that lines of code are a terrible measure for anything—the goal is to get the desired functionality with as little code as possible—but the Windows 11 statistic underscores the complexity of some applications.

I use the terms *programmers, developers,* and *coders* interchangeably in this chapter.

Just as there are a large number of software titles on the market, numerous programming languages exist. Each language has its own grammar and syntax, much like the rules of English are different from the rules of Spanish. Software developers typically specialize in one or two languages but have a basic foundational understanding of the popular ones in the marketplace. For example, a coder might identify as a C++ programmer but also know a scripting language like JavaScript. Because of the similarities between language concepts, the coder can look at code from an unfamiliar language and generally understand what it does.

In this section, you will learn about four categories of programming languages: assembly, compiled, interpreted, and query.

Tech+ exam objective 4.1 wants you to compare and contrast programming language categories. These include assembly, compiled, interpreted (scripting and markup), and query languages.

Assembly Language

Any programmer writing code is telling the computer—specifically, the processor—what to do. *Assembly language* is the lowest level of code in which people can write. That is, it allows the developer to provide instructions directly to the hardware. It got its name because after it's created, it's translated into executable machine code by a program called an *assembler*.

Assembly code is specific to processor architectures. A program written for a 64-bit Intel chip will look different than one written for an ARM chip, even if the functionality is identical.

Originally developed in 1947 at the University of London, assembly was the primary programming language used for quite some time. Operating systems such as IBM's PC DOS and programs like the Lotus 1-2-3 spreadsheet software were coded in assembly, as well as some console-based video games. In the 1980s, higher-level languages overtook assembly in popularity.

Even though it doesn't dominate the landscape, assembly is still used today because it has some advantages over higher-level languages. It can be faster. It's also used for direct hardware access, such as in the system BIOS, with device drivers, and in customized embedded systems. It's also used for the *reverse engineering* (deconstructing so one can understand its design and purpose) of code. Translating high-level code into assembly is fairly straightforward, but trying to disassemble code into a higher-level language might not be. On the downside, some virus programmers like it because it's closer to the hardware.

Understanding Notational Systems

Before I get into how assembly works or what it looks like, it's important to take a step back and think about how computers work. Computers only understand the *binary notational system*—1s and 0s. Everything that a computer does is based on those two digits—that's really profound. When you're playing a game, surfing the web, or chatting with a friend using your computer, it's just a tremendously long string of 1s and 0s. Recall from Chapter 1, "Core Hardware Components," the basic organizational structure of these 1s and 0s. One digit (either a 1 or a 0) is a bit, and eight digits form a byte.

There are a lot of real-life practical examples of binary systems. Take light switches, for example. Ignoring dimmable lighting for a minute, a conventional light switch is in one of two distinct states, either on (1) or off (0). This is binary, also known as "base-2" because there are two distinct values.

Humans are far more used to counting in base-10, which is the *decimal notational system*. In decimal, the numbers 0 through 9 are used. To show the number that's one larger than 9, a second digit is added in front of it and reset the rightmost digit to 0. This is just a complicated way of telling you something you already know, which is 9 + 1 = 10.

Binary math works much the same way. The binary value 1 equals a decimal value of 1. If you add 1 + 1 in binary, what happens? The 1 can't increase to 2, because only 1s and 0s are allowed. So, the 1 resets to a 0, and a second digit is added in front of it. Thus, in binary, 1 + 1 = 10. Then, 10 + 1 = 11, and 11 + 1 = 100. If you're not accustomed to looking at binary, this can be a bit confusing!

Now think about the structure of a byte, which is 8 bits long. If you want to convert binary to decimal, then the bit's position in the byte determines its value. Table 6.1 illustrates what I mean.

TABLE 6.1 Converting binary to decimal

Position	8	7	6	5	4	3	2	1
Bit	1	1	1	1	1	1	1	1
Base	2^7	2^6	2^5	2^4	2^3	2^2	2^1	2^0
Value	128	64	32	16	8	4	2	1

If the bit is set to 1, it has the value shown in the value row. If it's set to 0, then its value is 0. Using the example from a few paragraphs ago, you can now see how binary 100 equals a decimal 4. The binary number 10010001 is 128 + 16 + 1 = 145 in decimal. Using 1 byte, decimal values between 0 and 255 can be represented.

It's unlikely that you will be asked to perform binary-to-decimal conversion on the Tech+ exam. It's a good concept to understand, though, and it's material to understanding how assembly works!

To take things one step further, there's a third system used commonly in programming, which is the *hexadecimal notational system*, or base-16. You'll also see it referred to as *hex*. In hex, the numbers 0 to 9 are used, just like in decimal. However, the letters A to F are used to represent decimal numbers 10 through 15. So, in hex, F + 1 = 10. Finally, there is *octal*. Octal is base-8. Digits 0–7 are valid, and then it starts over again. Octal isn't used very much, whereas hex and decimal are used a lot. Binary is the underpinning of them all.

Aren't notational systems fun? The key when dealing with numbers in programming is to understand clearly which notational system you're supposed to be using. Exercise 6.1 will give you some practice converting between the three systems. This is very similar to Exercise 1.1 that you did back in Chapter 1, but having familiarity with these systems is important.

EXERCISE 6.1

Converting Between Decimal and Other Numbering Systems

1. In Windows 11, open the Calculator application by typing **calc** into the Windows search box and pressing Enter.

2. Click the Calculator menu button (upper-left corner), and choose Programmer to switch to Programmer view, as shown in Figure 6.1. Notice on the left that there is a mark next to the Dec option because it's set to decimal.

FIGURE 6.1 Calculator in Programmer view

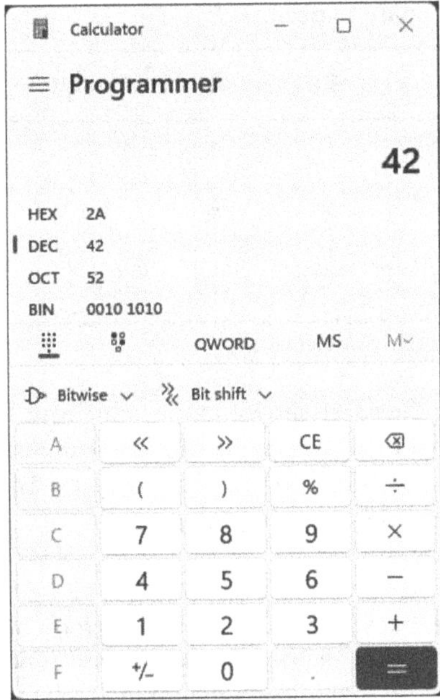

3. Enter the number **42**.

4. Notice that the calculator shows you the hexadecimal (HEX), decimal (DEC), octal (OCT), and binary (BIN) conversions of the number. They are 2A, 42, 52, and 0010 1010,

respectively. If you have an older version of Calculator, you will need to click the radio buttons next to these options to perform the conversion.

5. Now enter the number **9893**. Notice that in binary, 2 bytes (16 bits) worth of bits are displayed, and there are four hex characters used.

6. Experiment with other numbers. What would your birth date look like in binary or hex? Close the calculator when you are finished.

Some programming languages will use the prefix `0x` in front of a number to indicate that it's in hexadecimal. For example, you might see something like `0x16FE`. That just means the hex number 16FE. Other languages will use an `h` suffix, so it would be written as `16FEh`.

Tech+ exam objective 1.2, "Identify notational systems," lists binary, decimal, hexadecimal, and octal as subobjectives. Be able to identify each one.

Binary, decimal, and hex work great for representing numbers, but what about letters and special characters? There are notational systems for these as well. The first is *American Standard Code for Information Interchange (ASCII)*, which is pronounced *ask-e*. ASCII codes represent text and special characters on computers and telecommunications equipment. The standard ASCII codes use 7 bits to store information, which provides for only 128 characters. Therefore, standard ASCII only has enough space to represent standard English (Latin) uppercase and lowercase letters, numbers 0 to 9, a few dozen special characters, and (now obsolete) codes called *control codes*. Table 6.2 shows you a small sample of ASCII codes. You can find the full table at `www.asciitable.com`.

TABLE 6.2 Sample ASCII codes

Dec	Hex	HTML	Character
33	21	!	!
56	38	8	8
78	4E	N	N
79	4F	O	O
110	6E	n	n

Covering only the Latin alphabet isn't very globally inclusive, so a superset of ASCII was created called *Unicode*. The current version of Unicode supports 136,755 characters across 139 language scripts and several character sets. Unicode has several standards. UTF-8 uses 8 bits and is identical to ASCII. UTF-16 uses 16 bits (allowing for 65,536 characters, covering what's known as the Basic Multilingual Plane) and is the most common standard in use today. UTF-32 allows for coverage of the full set of characters. The Unicode table is at `https://symbl.cc/en/unicode-table`.

Working with Assembly

Coding in assembly is not for the faint of heart. As I mentioned earlier, you need to know the version specific to the processor's platform. In addition, you need to know how memory segmentation works and how processor codes will respond in protected and unprotected memory environments. There's more to it than those few criteria, but suffice to say it's challenging work.

Let's start with a simple example, remembering that all computers understand are 1s and 0s. Say that you have a 32-bit Intel processor and want to move a simple 8-bit number into a memory register. The binary code to tell the processor to move data is `10110`, followed by a 3-bit memory register identifier. For this example, you'll use the lowest part of the accumulator register (you won't need to know this for the exam), which is noted as AL. The code for this register is `000`. Finally, you need to tell the CPU the number that you want to move into this register—you'll use 42 (which in binary is 101010). Therefore in binary, the command looks like this:

```
10110000 00101010
```

The literal translation of these 16 digits is "move data" (10110) "into memory register AL" (000) "of value 42" (00101010). Again, please understand that you don't need to know this for the exam. This is just an example to show you how the sausage is made. Looking at this, it blows my mind that something like the Internet actually works!

The previous example is not very user friendly or easy to remember. Using decimal to hex conversion, you can simplify it to the following:

```
B0 2A
```

Again, that literally means, "Move into memory register AL the number 42." It's still not very user friendly. To help ease the challenge, assembly developers have created mnemonic codes to help programmers remember commands. For example, the command `MOV` (short for move) is a mnemonic to replace the binary or hex code. So, the command can now be written as follows:

```
MOV AL, 2Ah    ;Move the number 42 (2A hex) into AL
```

You'll notice a few things here. The first is that the command `MOV AL` ("move data into memory register AL") is much easier to remember than the binary code, and it makes more sense in human terms than does `B0`. The second is that I added some real words after a semicolon. Most languages allow coders the ability to add comments that are not processed. In assembly, anything on a line after a semicolon is considered a comment and ignored by the processor. The comment is intended for a human to read and understand. You or I didn't write the original code, but now we can look at it and say, "Ahhh, yes! That's what the original programmer was trying to do!" (We might not know why, but . . . whatever.)

Remember the concept of comments, because "comments and documentation" are subobjectives under exam objective 4.4, "Identify programming organizational techniques and logic concepts." Comments are a form of documentation—that is, putting into plain words what the code is intended to do.

So, to summarize the basic structure of a line of code, it contains processor instructions ("do this"), directives (defining data elements or giving the processor specific ways of performing the task), data, and optional comments. This is pretty much true for all programming languages, although the structure and syntax will vary.

As I wrap up this section on assembly, I want to leave you with one small gift. A tradition in pretty much every programming class is that the first program you are taught to write is how to display "Hello, world!" on the screen. The way to create this friendly greeting varies based on the language, so when I cover various languages, I am going to show you what it looks like or have you do it. The intent isn't to have you memorize the code or learn to program but to give you a feel for what the code looks like for an actual application. So, without further ado, here is "Hello, world!" in all of its assembly glory:

```
section .text
    global _start      ;must be declared for linker (ld)

_start:                ;tells linker entry point
    mov edx,len        ;message length
        mov ecx,msg    ;message to write
        mov ebx,1      ;file descriptor
        mov eax,4      ;system call
        int 0x80       ;call kernel

section .data
msg db 'Hello, world!', 0xa          ;the message!
len equ $ - msg                      ;length of the string
```

When the code is assembled and executed, it will display the following on the screen:

```
Hello, world!
```

In the Tech+ exam objectives, assembly is listed as a subobjective of query languages. In reality the two are very different—assembly is not a subset of query. Remember that assembly is the lowest-level language possible; it's closest to the processor.

Compiled Languages

Trying to program everything in assembly would be tedious at best, so high-level languages have replaced assembly as the most commonly used ones in software development today. Compiled and interpreted languages allow for shorter command sequences. You will see this in action later when we look at subsequent versions of "Hello, world!"

When creating a new application, the developer must decide between a compiled language and an interpreted language. A *compiled programming language* is one that requires the use of a *compiler* to translate it into machine code. Creating and using a program using a compiled language consists of three steps:

1. Write the application in a programming language, such as Java or C++. This is called the *source code.*
2. Use a complier to translate the source code into machine code. Most software development applications have a compiler.
3. Execute the program file, which (in Windows) usually has an `.exe` extension.

There are dozens of compiled languages a programmer can choose from, but unless there is a specific need, the programmer is likely going to go with one of the more common ones. In days past, the choices might have been Fortran, BASIC, or Pascal. Now, Java, C, C++ (pronounced C plus plus), and C# (pronounced C sharp) are the most popular. The Linux and Windows kernels are written in C. The rest of Windows is written mostly in C++, with a bit of custom assembly thrown in for good measure.

Let's take a look at the source code for "Hello, world!" in Java, which is one of the most popular programming languages in use today:

```
public class HelloWorld {
    public static void main(String[] args) {
        // Prints "Hello, world!" in the terminal window.
        System.out.println("Hello, world!");
    }
}
```

Compare and contrast the Java code to assembly. A few things might jump out. First, the program is a lot shorter. Second, the syntax is different. Java uses braces (the { and }) to indicate code blocks. Notice that for every open brace, there is a corresponding close brace. Single-line comments in Java are preceded with two slashes (//) instead of a semicolon. Even little things—assembly uses single quotes around the words that you want to print while Java uses double quotes—are different. As for the rest of the context, don't worry about understanding it all right now. Again, the point is to just get a feel for what some basic code looks like.

The next stop on your tour of compiled languages is C++. Let's look at source code for your new favorite program:

```
// Header file
#include<iostream>

using namespace std;

// the main function is where the program execution begins
int main()
{
    // the message to the world
    cout<<"Hello, world!";

    return 0;
}
```

There are a few similarities to Java. C++ and Java are both derivatives of the C language, so it makes sense that they would share some features. For example, comments start with two slashes, and braces are present to create blocks of code. Other things that you might have noticed are that both use a `main` function, double quotes for text, and a semicolon to end a statement.

Finally, take a look at the same program written in C#. C# is also a derivative of C, so some of this code might start to look familiar to you:

```
using System;

namespace HelloWorld
{
    Class Program
    {
        // the main function - also known as a method
        Static void Main(string[] args)
        {
            // the message to the world
            Console.WriteLine("Hello, world!");
            Console.ReadLine();
        }
    }
}
```

The indentation used in programming, in most cases, does not affect the functionality of the program. It's there to make it easier for the developer (or other people looking at the code) to read. In the C# example, the indentation makes it easy to see that there are three open braces and three corresponding close braces. Again, for the Tech+ exam, don't worry about being able to read or write code in a specific language. These examples are intended to give you a flavor for what a few common languages look like.

Tools of the Trade

In this section you were introduced to the topic of a compiler, which is the tool that translates the code into machine code. A programmer could write code in just about any text editor, send it off to the compiler, and let it do its thing. That seems kind of barbaric by today's standards. Instead, most programmers use a tool called an *integrated development environment (IDE)*, which is a software package that contains a code editor, compiler, and debugger to help resolve problems all in one. IDEs help programmers work more efficiently because everything they need is in one place. In addition, IDEs have features like syntax highlighting and an autofill-like solution to help the developer along. Some of the most popular IDEs are Visual Studio Code, Visual Studio, and Eclipse.

Interpreted Languages

The second major classification of modern, high-level programming languages is interpreted languages. With an *interpreted programming language*, each line of code is read by an interpreter every time the program is executed. Contrast this with compiled languages, in which the source code is compiled once and then executed any number of times.

An interpreter and a compiler essentially do the same thing—they take high-level source code and translate it into low-level machine code. They differ a bit in how they perform their job, however. Table 6.3 outlines some of the key differences.

TABLE 6.3 Interpreter vs. compiler

Task	Interpreter	Compiler
Translating source code	One statement at a time	Entire program at once
Executing programs	By the interpreter	Creates an executable file (usually `.exe` file extension)
Analyzing source code	Faster	Slower
Executing code	Slower	Faster
Using memory	Lower	Higher
Debugging	Easier	Harder

Debugging interpreted code is easier because the source code is read line by line. If the interpreter gets to a line that is written incorrectly, it stops there and generates an error. A compiler will read all of the code, and if something is wrong somewhere, it will generate an error.

Some compilers will give you a clue as to the location of the problem, but troubleshooting a compiled language is usually more challenging than troubleshooting an interpreted language.

There are two types of interpreted languages you need to be familiar with: markup languages and scripting languages.

Markup Languages

A *markup language* is a language that programmers can use to annotate—or *mark up*—text to tell the computer how to process or manipulate the text. You might be familiar with markups in other walks of life. For example, have you ever used a highlighter or pencil to mark text in a book, such as a school book? That's an example of markup, because you are highlighting something important. To create a markup language, there needs to be a codified set of rules telling the processor what to do with the marked-up text when it encounters it.

There are multiple classes of markup languages, but the most common application of them is in the creation of web pages. *Hypertext Markup Language (HTML)* is the language in which most web pages are created. HTML allows web developers to format web pages. It's sort of a joke among developers that if you know HTML, all that means is that you're good at drawing boxes. HTML does allow you to do that in order to lay out a web page, but HTML developers can do much more than just draw boxes! The current version is HTML5 (HTML6 may reach us in 2025–2027), but you'll see it referred to simply as HTML.

HTML is a bit unique among languages in that the pages that contain it are stored on a server, and the pages themselves are downloaded to a client and then processed by specialized software—the web browser. This might sound complicated, but it's quite likely you're familiar with the process. Said differently, a user opens a web browser and visits a website. The site sends the page to the browser, which interprets the language and displays it properly.

Another common markup language is Extensible Markup Language (XML).

HTML works by using tags to signify instructions for the browser. Tags take this format:

```
<TAG> (something) </TAG>
```

Generally speaking, all tags have an opening tag <> and a closing tag </>. For example, to tell the browser to bold the word penguin, the web page would read `<b> penguin <b>`. Tags enable the developer to control all elements of the text, such as where the text should appear on the screen, in what font it should it appear, the color of the text, and all other features related to its style. Tags are also used to create tables, place images properly, set background colors, and include links to other web pages.

Remember the "Hello, world!" program? You get to create a simple web page displaying this text in Exercise 6.2.

EXERCISE 6.2

Creating "Hello, World!" in HTML

1. Open Notepad (or another text editor). You can open Notepad by typing the word **note** into the Windows search bar and clicking Notepad when it appears.

2. Type the following code in the text editor:

```
<html>
<header><title>Tab title</title></header>
<body>
Hello, world!
</body>
</html>
```

3. Save the file to your desktop as **`hello.html`**.

4. Double-click the `hello.html` file. It should open in your browser and look something like Figure 6.2.

FIGURE 6.2 Hello, world!

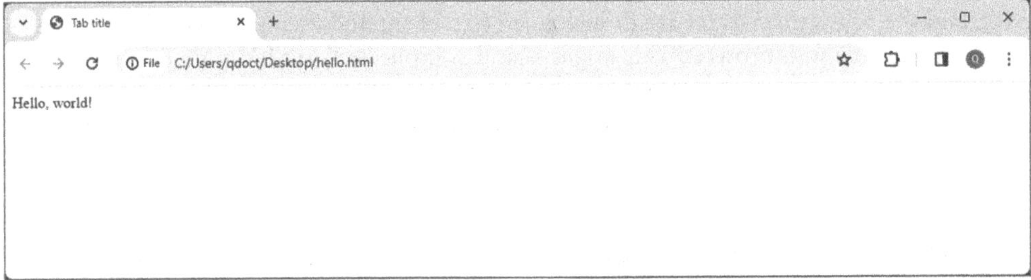

5. Go back to your `hello.html` file in the text editor. (If you closed it, right-click, select Open With ➢ Choose Another App and select Notepad.)

6. Change the line that says `Hello, world!` to the following:

```
<b><i>Hello, world!</b></i>
```

7. Save the file.

8. Open `hello.html` again in a web browser. Notice the change in the text.

9. Open the file in the text editor again, and change the `<body>` line to the following:

```
<body bgcolor="#DDEA11">
```

10. Save the file.

11. Open `hello.html` again in a web browser. What change do you see? (The words should be bold and italic, and the background color of the page should be green.)

In Exercise 6.2, step 9, the code DDEA11 is a hexadecimal code to indicate color. The first two characters are for red, the second two are for green, and the third two are for blue. For example, 00FF00 is true green, and 0000FF is true blue. Learning about hex was important! You can play around with hex color codes on several different websites, such as www.color-hex.com.

Scripting Languages

The second category of interpreted languages is *scripting languages*. For much of the history of computers, operating system interfaces were a simple command prompt, and only one task could be executed at a time. Scripting languages came along and were used for executing a list of tasks. One of the earlier common scripting languages was the Bourne Again shell (Bash), which also happened to be a popular command interface (or shell) for UNIX-based operating systems. Essentially, someone could create a file that contained multiple actions to perform and then execute the file.

Scripting languages today have evolved a great deal, but for the most part are still designed to create simple programs that execute a list of tasks or get data from a dataset. Their advantage is that they're less code-intensive than the compiled language counterparts; you can get more done with less code. In addition, modern scripting languages support the use of objects, variables, and functions, which I'll talk about in the "Understanding Programming Concepts and Techniques" section later in this chapter. Some of the most popular scripting languages are JavaScript (JS), Visual Basic (VB) Script, PHP, Perl, PowerShell, and Python.

Perhaps the most common use of scripting languages is to execute tasks from within a web page written in HTML. Remember that a markup language is designed to present and format information—it doesn't really "do" anything else like execute a program. So, developers will insert a script to execute the tasks they need the website to perform. Here's an example, with some code you have seen before:

```
<html>
<header><title>Tab title</title></header>
<body>

  <script>
    alert('Hello, world!');
  </script>

</body>
</html>
```

When you execute this web page, you will see something like Figure 6.3.

FIGURE 6.3 "Hello, world!" JavaScript alert

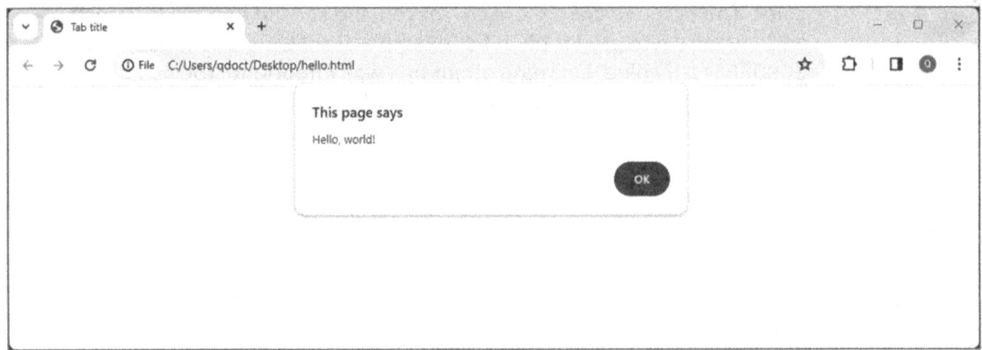

Notice that an alert box pops up, because the `alert` method was used. You can get the message to appear in the browser window by using `document.write('Hello, world!');` instead. One question you might have is, how did the browser know that it's reading JavaScript and not some other script? The `<script>` tag tells HTML that a script is coming; by default, HTML assumes that it's JavaScript.

The syntax for Python is even simpler. All that's needed is the following:

```
print("Hello, world!")
```

As I've said before, don't worry about memorizing the code or specific methods. Know a few examples of scripting languages, and remember that they are usually short, don't need a compiler, and typically execute a list of tasks.

Query Languages

Of the four language categories, query languages are the most unlike the others. The term *query* is synonymous with question, and a *query language* is specialized to ask questions. Specifically, query languages are designed to retrieve data from databases. The most common query language, by far, is Structured Query Language (SQL). Another example is the Lightweight Directory Access Protocol (LDAP), which is designed to query directory services such as Microsoft's Active Directory.

Active Directory is beyond the scope of this book, but essentially it's the database on a Microsoft server that stores all of the information about users and security.

Basic SQL syntax is straightforward. To ask the database for data, a `SELECT` statement is used, followed by the specifics of what you want and where you want it from. Queries often follow a structure like this:

```
SELECT column_name
FROM table_name
WHERE condition
```

While the basic syntax is relatively simple, it can get a lot more complicated. SQL allows for insertion of data into tables, joining data from multiple tables, and several different types of operators, such as finding the minimum and maximum, counting, finding averages, and summing values. Interfacing with databases is covered in more detail in Chapter 7, "Database Fundamentals."

Real World Scenario

One Is the Loneliest Number

Throughout this chapter, I've talked about different categories of programming languages and what they are used for. In the real world, most programs actually use code from multiple languages to complement each other's functionality. Some languages are simply better at certain tasks than others.

For example, as mentioned earlier, Windows 11 uses three languages: The kernel is written in C, most of the code is in C++, and some custom Intel assembly is also included. If any application needs to get data from a database, it's most likely using SQL in addition to the language in which it was coded. Websites use HTML and most likely a scripting language, such as JavaScript or Python. YouTube uses both JavaScript and Python.

Using a single language for a program seems to be more of the exception than the norm. If you want to get into coding, it's good to have proficiency in multiple languages to expand your effectiveness.

Understanding Programming Concepts and Techniques

A programmer's goal is to get a computer to do what they want it to do. Think just a minute about the variety of things that different programs do. Operating systems are massive and complex and perform thousands of different tasks, from accepting input and providing output to managing and monitoring devices to establishing connections to remote computers. Each of these tasks is handled by different parts of the program, so you can see why Windows reportedly has 50 million lines of code. Even relatively simple programs can easily contain several thousands of lines.

One of the ways that programmers can simplify their work is to reuse sections of code. For example, imagine that a program needs to perform a mathematical calculation. The developer would write code for it. Later in the program, if the same calculation is needed, the programmer can simply reference the previous section of code as opposed to needing to rewrite the whole thing. Many programs are kind of like Frankenstein in nature. Blocks of code perform specific tasks, and the developer figures out how to stitch them all together into a finished product. Sometimes it's elegant, sometimes it's ugly, and sometimes it's a bit of each.

In this section, you will learn about concepts that developers use to make their tasks easier. First up is programming logic. This refers to what the program does and includes topics such as logic components, data types, and identifiers. Then you will learn about organizational techniques such as flowcharts, pseudocode, containers, functions, and objects.

Programming Logic

Processors perform math and logic operations, so it figures that all programs are made up of logic and arithmetic. For example, processors can add or subtract numbers or compare two values to each other and determine an action to take based on the result. Essentially, the job of the programmer is to tell the processor what to do based on the results of a logic puzzle.

The two main ways that programs perform logic are branching and looping.

Tech+ exam objective 4.4, "Identify programming organizational techniques and logic concepts," calls out branching and looping as specific techniques you should be able to identify.

Branching

People use a lot of *branching* logic in their daily lives. For example, if you're driving a car, your brain probably follows a simple process when it comes to traffic lights. If the light is red, you stop. From a programmatic standpoint, this is represented as a simple `if... then` statement. If a certain condition exists (red light), then take a specific action (stop the car). "But, wait!" you might say. "What if the light is green?" The logic then used is called `if... then, else`. If the light is red, stop, else go. This is an example with only one choice to make based on two discrete conditions. Branching can handle many more conditions as well.

For example, most traffic lights have an amber light too, telling you to slow down because a red light is imminent. The processor now needs to take an action based on one of three conditions. You can tell it to do that by using `else if` statements. Here's an example:

```
if light = red, then stop
    else if light = green, then go
    else if light = amber, then slow down
```

This pseudocode isn't for a real programming language, but it illustrates how the logic works. Computers, as you know, deal only in data and not stoplights. Instead of comparing the colors of a stoplight, a processor compares two different pieces of data. Table 6.4 lists common data types with which you need to be familiar.

Tech+ exam objective 4.2, "Identify fundamental data types and their characteristics," lists char, strings, numbers (integers and floats), and Boolean as subobjectives. Be sure you understand what each one is used for!

TABLE 6.4 Common data types

Type	Explanation	Examples
Char	One character, such as a UTF-16 or UTF-32 character	A or a
String	Zero or more characters	"This is a string" and "S0 is th1$."
Integer	Whole number with no decimal point	5 or 500000
Floats	Any number with a decimal place	5.2 or 5.000001
Boolean	A true or false condition, usually represented by a 1 (true) or 0 (false)	1 or 0

There can be some overlap between the definitions, meaning that some data could appear to be multiple data types. For example, a *string* can consist of only one character, making it look like a *char*. Numbers designated as *floats* might not have a decimal place, whereas an *integer* definitely does not have any decimal places. A *Boolean data type* is always true or false; if its output is represented as a 1 or 0, it could look like an integer. Regardless of what it looks like, the data type is what it was defined to be within a program.

Boolean values are particularly important because they often directly control computer logic. If the processor compares two values and based on the condition, the result is true (e.g., is random integer 1 greater than random integer 2), then the program will follow a specific path. If false (random integer 1 is not greater than random integer 2), then the program will go down a different path.

Here's another example using `if, else if` statements, this time comparing integers. Assume that you're creating a program that needs to categorize people based on their age. If the person is younger than 13, they are a child. Anyone younger than 20 is a teen, younger than 65 is an adult, and older than 65 is a senior. What would that logic look like? It could look something like this:

```
if age < 13, then category "Child"
    else if age < 20, then category "Teen"
    else if age < 65, then category "Adult"
    else category "Senior"
```

Based on an input to the program, the person will be categorized appropriately.

There's one other concept to introduce here, and it's that of *identifiers*, or names assigned to a program element. In the example of age classification, the numbers defining the categories are set. A set or predefined number like this is called a *constant*. As you might imagine based on its name, this means that it doesn't change. The other type of identifier is a *variable*, which simply means that it can change.

Identifiers (variables and constants) are in Tech+ exam objective 4.3, "Explain the purpose and use of programming concepts." Be sure to understand how they are used.

Imagine a scenario where instead of putting people into a category based on their age, the program is designed to determine who is older. The age values of two people will be entered, and the program is supposed to say if person 1 is older than person 2. Since the ages of the people are not predetermined, they are variable. The logic could look something like this:

```
if age (person 1) > age (person 2), then "Older"
    else if age (person 1) = age (person 2), then "Same"
    else "Younger"
```

Variables can also change throughout a program. For example, think of a program designed to count sums of money. A variable can be defined early in the program to accept the first input. Then, when the second amount of money is input (again, a variable amount), the program adds the two values together and uses the sum as a third variable.

Branching logic statements are used to compare variables and constants to other variables and constants and can be used across different data types. The Boolean output of the comparison (true or false) is used to determine the path that the program takes. Branches are good for simple logical comparisons, but more complicated activities might require different logic.

Looping

As its name implies, *looping* logic is circular rather than linear like branching logic. At the center of looping is the `while` statement. Looping is useful for monitoring a state within a program, and then invoking an action when that state changes. Think back to the simple stoplight example given earlier. In human terms, the logic can basically be, "While the stoplight is red, stop; otherwise, go." While the light is red, you keep repeating the loop until the condition changes, and once it changes, you take a different action.

You can also use looping for a counting function—for example, `while x < 10 is true, count x + 1`. This pseudocode example uses a few concepts you've learned in this chapter, such as variables (`x`) and Boolean (`true`).

Loops can be powerful tools, but they can also be problematic. If not coded properly, the program can end up in an infinite `do while` loop. (Sometimes you hear people say that they don't want to get stuck in a "do loop," and this is where that reference comes from.) An example would be using a loop to count but then neglecting to tell it when to stop. To avoid this, the developer must ensure that they provide proper exit conditions for the loop.

Loops and branches can (and often are) used together to perform more complex operations.

Organizing Code

Earlier in this chapter, I mentioned that programs often have a Frankenstein feel to them. This is because when programmers sit down to write code, they think about it in terms of the tasks to be done and what it takes to accomplish those tasks. This compartmentalization is one of the key organizing principles that developers follow. Breaking something like Windows down into manageable chunks lets the developer focus on exactly what is needed for a small, discrete task rather than feeling overwhelmed by the enormity of it all.

As you can imagine, organizing the code is important, but it's also important for the developer to be organized outside of the code; that is, to lay out a blueprint of how the program will function so the developer can construct it or to have people on the team build various parts of it. The following sections cover different organizational concepts.

Flowcharts

A *flowchart* is a visual representation of a program that uses boxes to represent the logic. Flowcharts are critical in the software development process. They should be created before the code is developed, much like blueprints should be drawn before building a house. They help the developers visualize the flow of the program, making it easier to plan out the sections of code needed.

Flowcharts show the order of operations within a program, including where data input is needed as well as decisions to be made and the logic choices. Different shapes are used to indicate different components. For example, a rectangle is used to indicate a process, whereas a diamond is used to show a decision point.

A *sequence* and flowchart both contain logical steps for the app to perform. The big difference is that, generally speaking, sequences require multiple steps to perform a specific action, whereas flowcharts are related to a specific task. Both terms are part of exam objective 4.4, and you should be able to identify a flowchart and a sequence.

There are various flowchart software packages on the market, and you can also use Microsoft Word or PowerPoint to create simple ones. Figure 6.4 shows a simple flowchart for a program designed to find the smallest of three values.

Pseudocode

True to its name, *pseudocode* is literally fake code. It's fake in the sense that it's not read by the processor and has no effect on the functioning of the program. It can be helpful to people trying to read the code, however.

I've used the term a few times in this chapter already, in describing examples of logic. The pseudocode I wrote wouldn't be recognized by any interpreter or compiler, but it was intended for ease of reading and understanding. Another example of pseudocode is for comments in programs. Comments can be used to describe the purpose of a line or block of code or to show a mathematical formula that might be incredibly complicated and hence harder to read in the actual code.

FIGURE 6.4 Flowchart

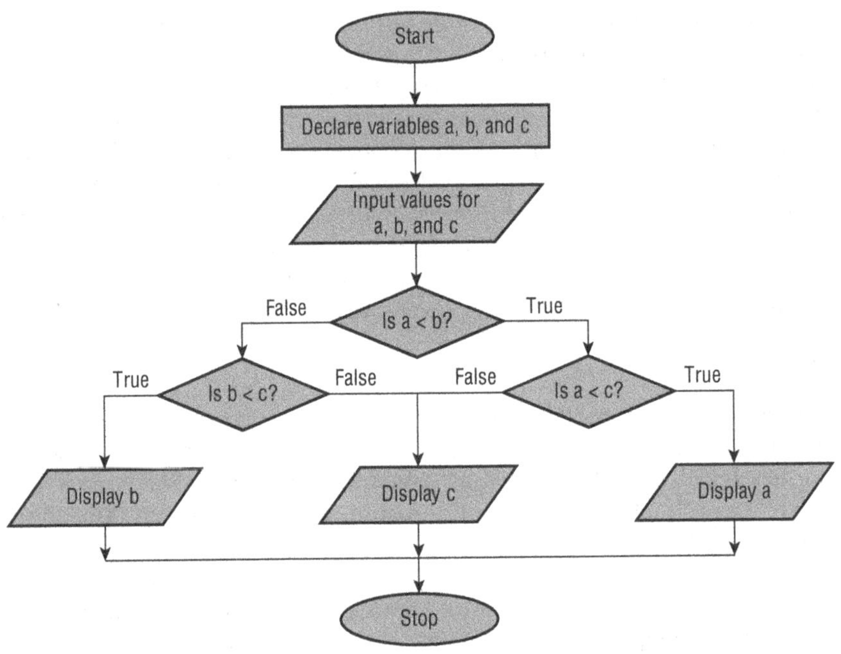

A joke among programmers is that some modern scripting languages, like Python, use such simple syntax that you could write a Python script in pseudocode and it would still work.

Pseudocode can be particularly helpful in situations where a team of programmers is responsible for one program. It can be challenging for a developer who didn't write the code to figure out what's wrong if there's a problem. Having well-annotated code can help the troubleshooter understand what the original developer intended when creating the code.

Pseudocode concepts are part of exam objective 4.4. Be able to explain its purpose and where it's used.

Containers

In real life, containers hold things—in computer programming, they do the same thing. Earlier in this chapter you learned about variables, which are values that can change based on different input or conditions within a program. When developers define a variable, they're allowed to specify only one value for that variable. Using *containers*, multiple values of similar types can be grouped together and accessed at the same time. There are two types of containers you should be aware of: arrays and vectors.

Arrays are part of exam objective 4.3. Be able to explain their purpose and where they are used.

An *array* is simply a list of values. There are a couple of key defining factors to an array. First, all of the elements in an array must be of the same data type. Second, the array is predefined in size and does not change.

A *vector* also holds a list of values. However, the values do not need to be of the same data type, and vectors can be dynamically allocated, meaning that they can shrink or grow as the program requires. Otherwise, vectors behave very similarly to arrays (in the sense that they store values and allow for their retrieval). Because vectors are dynamically sized, they are far more versatile than arrays and are the preferred container type.

Functions

Developers often employ sections of reusable code, and that is what *functions* are. When a particular set of instructions is needed, a function block can be created to accomplish the task. Whenever that task is needed, the program references that function. Functions are generally designed to take input, transform it somehow, and deliver output.

Functions are part of exam objective 4.3. Be able to explain their purpose and where they are used.

Functions are linear in nature, meaning that they take input, process it, and then deliver output. It's not to say they can't have looping logic in them but rather that the function starts at the beginning of the code block and finishes at the end, handing off to another process.

Here's an analogy to help illustrate how functions work—the command prompt on older operating systems. The command prompt just waits for user input. The computer won't perform any other tasks while it sits and waits, and it has an indefinite supply of patience (unless, of course, it loses power). A user enters a command, and then the computer springs into action. It performs one or more tasks based on the command. Maybe it opens a file, changes permissions on a folder, or creates a network connection with a server. It completes that task, perhaps produces some output, and then gives the user another command prompt. It's then ready for another task, and it will be patient.

Objects

Since I just provided an analogy for how functions work, it's a good time to do the same for objects. As you're probably aware, modern operating systems do not provide a simple command prompt for input. In fact, the graphical user interface (GUI) of an operating system has dozens of ways in which you can "enter" into functionality with it. There are icons on the screen, some sort of launcher like the Start button, more icons on the taskbar, and a clock and random items in the system tray. You can click any of them and make something happen, or you can right-click the screen and make something happen too. Even better, you can click multiple items and have several processes running at once. (Okay, technically, only one process ever runs at a time, but they switch back and forth so quickly that it appears to us like they all run at the same time.)

Objects (and their properties, attributes, and methods) are part of exam objective 4.3. And object-oriented methods are part of organizational techniques in objective 4.4. Be able to explain their purposes and where they are used.

How does this analogy relate to an object? In a few ways. First, each item on your desktop with which you can interact is considered its own object, each with its own set of properties and attributes. Second, thinking of the GUI, you can begin interacting with it at any number of entry points and stop interacting with it at any number of places as well. There isn't just one specific entry and exit point.

Now that you have a rough idea of how objects work, here's the definition: *Objects* are collections of attributes, properties, and methods that can be queried or called upon to perform a task. Said differently, an object can be a variable, function, method, or data structure that can be referenced.

Objects have properties and attributes. The words are synonyms, but there are differences. The term *properties* describes the characteristics of the object, and *attributes* refers to additional information about an object. As a specific example, people have a property called *height*. However, height can be expressed in several different ways, such as 5′8″, 173 centimeters, or 1.73 meters, depending on the attribute used.

Properties and attributes are used in different ways in coding. First, a property can be different data types, such as a string, integer, or Boolean. Properties of an object can be modified through code. Attributes only have the data type of string and can't be changed. If you attempt to modify the value of an attribute and then ask to display the attribute's value, the program will return the default value.

If the terms properties and attributes are confusing to you, know that you're not alone. Asking for the difference between them is a challenging question—even for experienced programmers!

When referring to *methods*, think of them like functions for objects. They are ways to organize several tasks together to perform an operation.

Real World Scenario

Objects and Classes and Methods, Oh My!

A major feature of object-oriented programming (OOP) languages such as Java, C++, C#, Python, PHP, Perl, and Ruby is the use of objects. As you learned earlier, an object is a collection of properties and attributes.

In most OOP languages, objects consist of three things:

- *Identity,* which is the name of the object
- *State,* which is represented by attributes and reflects properties of the object
- *Behavior,* which determines the response of the object and is represented by methods

For example, let's say that a dog is an object. The dog has an identity, which is its name. In theory, you can use the name of the dog to interact with it. (I say in theory, because the dog may choose to ignore you.) The dog has a state, such as its breed, height, color, and coat length, and it has behaviors such as eating, playing, sleeping, and barking. Multiple behaviors can be called from a method. For example, playing and barking might belong to a method called "fun time."

OOP languages also use the concept of classes. A class is the blueprint for objects—it describes an object's state and behaviors. In computer terms, the class describes what the object can hold or do. To create an object, you need a class from which to create it.

Any introduction to objects needs to include the mention of classes, so now you know!

Summary

In this chapter, you learned about software development concepts. To begin, you explored four categories of programming languages. The first was assembly, which is a low-level language that is used to access hardware directly. While learning about assembly, you also learned about notational systems such as binary, hexadecimal, decimal, octal, ASCII, and Unicode. The second grouping was compiled languages. Compiled languages are high-level languages that require a use of a compiler. Examples include Java and C++. The third grouping was interpreted languages, which do not require a compiler. Interpreted languages include markup languages and scripting languages. The fourth group was query languages, which are used to retrieve data from a database.

Next, you learned about programming concepts and techniques. The first concept was programming logic, and it focused on branching and looping. You also learned about common data types, such as char, strings, integers, floats, and Boolean. After that, the chapter finished by discussing organizational topics such as flowcharts, pseudocode, containers, functions, and objects.

Exam Essentials

Know the five notational systems. Binary (base-2), decimal (base-10), octal (base-8), and hexadecimal (base-16) are the numerical notational systems. Numbers, letters, and symbols can be represented using ASCII or Unicode, which is a superset of ASCII.

Know the five fundamental data types. The five data types are char, which is one character; string, which is zero or more characters; integer, which is a number with no decimals; floats, which are numbers with decimals; and Boolean, which is a true/false data type.

Understand the difference between compiled languages and interpreted languages. Compiled languages require a compiler for the source code and are compiled once and run many times. Interpreted languages do not require a compiler and are interpreted every time the program is executed.

Be able to give some examples of interpreted languages. Markup languages include HTML and XML. Scripting languages include JavaScript, Visual Basic (VB) Script, Python, PHP, and Perl.

Know what a query language does. Query languages interact with databases to retrieve or insert data. Most of the time they are used to retrieve data.

Know which programming language is best for direct hardware access. For direct hardware access, a low-level programming language such as assembly is the best.

Understand what pseudocode and flowcharts are used for. Pseudocode is most often used to annotate the code with comments to make it easier for people to read. Flowcharts help organize the code and plan out a program.

Understand how to interpret branching and looping logic. Branching logic makes use of `if, then, else` statements. Looping logic uses `while` statements.

Know the difference between the two types of identifiers. Constants are a predefined value and do not change, whereas variables can change.

Know the difference between the two types of containers. Arrays are fixed length and must contain the same data type. Vectors can be dynamically sized and can contain data of different data types.

Understand what functions and methods are used for. Functions and methods are used to group lines of code or tasks together.

Know what objects are. Objects are collections of attributes, properties, and methods that can be queried or called upon to perform a task.

Chapter 6 Lab

You can find the answers in Appendix A.

If you want to become a programmer, you will need to study one or more languages. You have a variety of options available, including online materials, in-person classes, and study guides. While this chapter certainly didn't teach you everything you need to know to become a programmer, you did learn some concepts and a bit about how to read and understand code. For this lab, you will look at a few different websites and see how their code was constructed.

Open the website `www.youtube.com` in Chrome or Edge. To view the source code in Chrome, right-click the page, and choose View Page Source. In Edge, press the F12 key to show the code. (Or, you can click the More menu—the three horizontal dots in the upper-right corner—and click More Tools ➢ Developer Tools.)

Here are some questions for you:

1. In what language is the page written?
2. What organizational techniques do you see?
3. Do you see any branching or looping logic?
4. Does the page use functions at all?
5. Which scripting languages are used on the home page?
6. Find a string of text. Can you find where that string is on the web page?
7. Can you find any instances of where a background color is set?

Repeat the lab with a different website of your choice, just to see the similarities and differences between how the developers coded it.

Review Questions

You can find the answers in Appendix B.

1. Which of the following numbers is written in hexadecimal format?
   A. 100101
   B. 3268
   C. 18AF
   D. 100101.11

2. Which of the following terms describe concepts related to breaking code into smaller, repeatable sections? (Choose two.)
   A. Functions
   B. Variables
   C. Containers
   D. Methods
   E. Objects

3. Which of the following are examples of object-oriented programming languages? (Choose two.)
   A. Java
   B. XML
   C. Python
   D. C
   E. SQL

4. Which of the following statements is true regarding arrays and vectors?
   A. Arrays contain one data type and are dynamic in length. Vectors can have multiple data types and are fixed in length.
   B. Arrays can have multiple data types and are fixed in length. Vectors have one data type and are dynamic in length.
   C. Arrays can have multiple data types and are dynamic in length. Vectors have one data type and are fixed in length.
   D. Arrays contain one data type and are fixed in length. Vectors can have multiple data types and dynamic length.

5. A developer needs to use a code designation for non-English letters. Which notational system does the developer need to use?
   A. ASCII
   B. Unicode
   C. International
   D. Strings

6. Which of the following are examples of interpreted languages? (Choose two.)
   - A. Compiled
   - B. Query
   - C. Scripted
   - D. Markup

7. What type of high-level programming language is translated into machine code once and then executed many times?
   - A. Compiled
   - B. Scripted
   - C. Scripting
   - D. Markup

8. A programmer wants to write code that directly accesses the computer's hardware. Which is the best type of language for the programmer to use?
   - A. Complied
   - B. Query
   - C. Interpreted
   - D. Assembly

9. Interpret the following logic. For data input on someone who is 20 years old, which category will they fall into?

```
if age < 13, then category "Child"
       else if age < 20, then category "Teen"
       else if age < 65, then category "Adult"
       else category "Senior"
```

   - A. Child
   - B. Teen
   - C. Adult
   - D. Senior

10. A programmer is writing a program that needs to accept an input of someone's name. What type of variable should the programmer create?
    - A. Char
    - B. String
    - C. Float
    - D. Unicode

11. Looping logic makes use of which of the following statements?

    A. `while`

    B. `when`

    C. `loop`

    D. `if`

12. In object-oriented programming, which of the following are integral parts of objects? (Choose two.)

    A. Arrays

    B. Properties

    C. Attributes

    D. Variables

13. A program shows the number 11010.11. Which data type is this?

    A. Binary

    B. Boolean

    C. Integer

    D. Float

14. You have created an array that can hold 15 items, all of the integer data type. You want to add a 16th integer. Which of the following is the best approach to doing this?

    A. Add it to the existing array.

    B. Create a separate variable for the 16th integer.

    C. Convert the integers to floats and add the 16th integer.

    D. Create a vector and replace the array with it.

15. What type of programming language is designed to retrieve data from a database?

    A. Query

    B. Assembly

    C. Interpreted

    D. Compiled

16. Interpret the following logic. A law enforcement agency has received data indicating that there are 10 current threats to public safety. What should the threat level be?

```
if threats < 3, then level "Green"
    else if threats < 6, then level "Yellow"
    else if threats < 9, then level "Orange"
    else if threats < 12, then level "Red"
    else level "Emergency"
```

    A. Green

    B. Yellow

    C. Orange

    D. Red

    E. Emergency

17. Which of the following is an example of a markup language?
    A. SQL
    B. XML
    C. Python
    D. Java

18. You want to understand the sequence of a program, from start to finish. Which of the following is the best to use for this purpose?
    A. Pseudocode
    B. Function
    C. Flowchart
    D. Object

19. Which of the following programming language types is the lowest-level language?
    A. Interpreted
    B. Compiled
    C. Query
    D. Assembly

20. Flowcharts depict which one of the following?
    A. Programs
    B. Objects
    C. Functions
    D. Identifiers

Database Fundamentals

THE FOLLOWING COMPTIA TECH+ FC0-U71 EXAM OBJECTIVES ARE COVERED IN THIS CHAPTER:

✓ **5.0 Data and Database Fundamentals**

✓ **5.2 Explain database concepts and the purpose of a database.**

- Database uses
  - Create
  - Import/input
  - Query
  - Reports
- Flat file vs. database
  - Multiple concurrent users
  - Scalability
  - Speed
  - Variety of data
- Database records
- Storage
  - Data persistence
- Data availability
  - Cloud vs. local
  - Online vs. offline

✓ **5.3 Compare and contrast various database structures.**

- Structured vs. semistructured vs. non-structured
- Relational databases
  - Schema
  - Tables
    - Rows/records
    - Fields/columns
      - Primary key
      - Foreign key
    - Constraints
- Non-relational databases
  - Key/value databases
  - Document databases

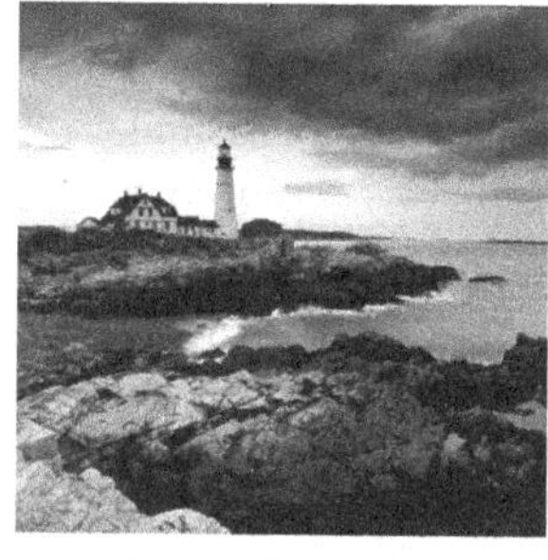

"Data is the new oil." You might have heard that phrase or one similar to it such as, "Data is the new currency" or "Data is the new bacon." The person who coined the last phrase clearly rates bacon highly—perhaps a bit too much—but the point remains the same: in today's world, data is an incredibly valuable commodity.

An entire service industry has been built upon storing and managing data. Some companies have business models revolving around acquiring and selling data to other interested companies. And, of course, you can't forget about data analysis and modeling. Companies have so much data today that they often don't know what to do with it. So, they employ teams of data scientists and analysts to mine the data, looking for a brilliant insight to unleash their company's growth.

All of this data needs to be stored somewhere, and that somewhere is a database. This chapter introduces you to database fundamentals. Much like Chapter 6, "Software Development," this chapter won't teach you everything there is to know—that can take years of study—but it will give you a fundamental understanding of why databases are used, the different types of databases, and how to work with databases. If this is a topic that interests you, dive deeper! Database administration can be a lucrative career path for those who are interested in it.

Understanding Databases

If someone asked you what a database does, you would probably answer, "It stores data." You'd be absolutely correct. There are many different types of databases out there for different situations, but they definitely all store data. The differences are in how they store it and, more importantly, how a user extracts data from the database.

Databases are used in a variety of business settings. Banks, online retailers, government agencies, nonprofits, and even bloggers use databases to store data that's important to them or their customers. Databases can be stored on local workstations (e.g., Microsoft Access), stored on servers (e.g., Oracle, Microsoft SQL Server, or MySQL), or accessed via the cloud (e.g., Amazon Web Services, Microsoft Azure, or Google Cloud Platform). There isn't a one-size-fits-all solution, and it might take some investigation to find the right solution for the situation. Regardless, though, the concepts of storage and access are pretty consistent across platforms.

This section starts off with exploring database concepts and structures so you know when to use a database and why, as well as various types of databases. After that, you will learn how to work with a database, including adding, accessing, and removing data.

Exploring Database Concepts and Structures

When most people think of a database, they often think about a list with columns similar to an Excel worksheet, like the one shown in Figure 7.1. Each column has a certain type of data, such as an identifier, name, phone number, or email address. Other sheets might have data such as a date, part number, amount, product description, and so on. One difference is that in a database, the structure shown in Figure 7.1 would be called a *table* (instead of a *worksheet*). Otherwise, a basic database with a flat structure looks a lot like something you could see in Excel.

FIGURE 7.1 Simple data in a worksheet

	A	B	C	D	E	F	G
1	ID	Last	First	Phone	Email		
2	C1	Smith	Joe	(123) 456-7890	joesmith@fakeemail.com		
3	C2	Larson	Jane	(123) 456-7891	janesmith@notreal.com		
4	C3	Hernandez	Maria	(111) 234-5678	mh123@notreal.com		
5	C4	Calderon	Juan	(112) 345-6789	juanc@fakeemail.com		
6	C5	White	Michael	(113) 456-7890	mcwhite@notreal.com		
7	C6	Jefferson	Mary	(124) 123-4567	maryj@fakeemail.com		
8							

In fact, you can import data from Excel into a database application, such as Access, and it will look similar. As you can see in Figure 7.2, there isn't much difference in the data, other than the formatting of the phone number (which isn't a big deal).

FIGURE 7.2 Simple data in Access

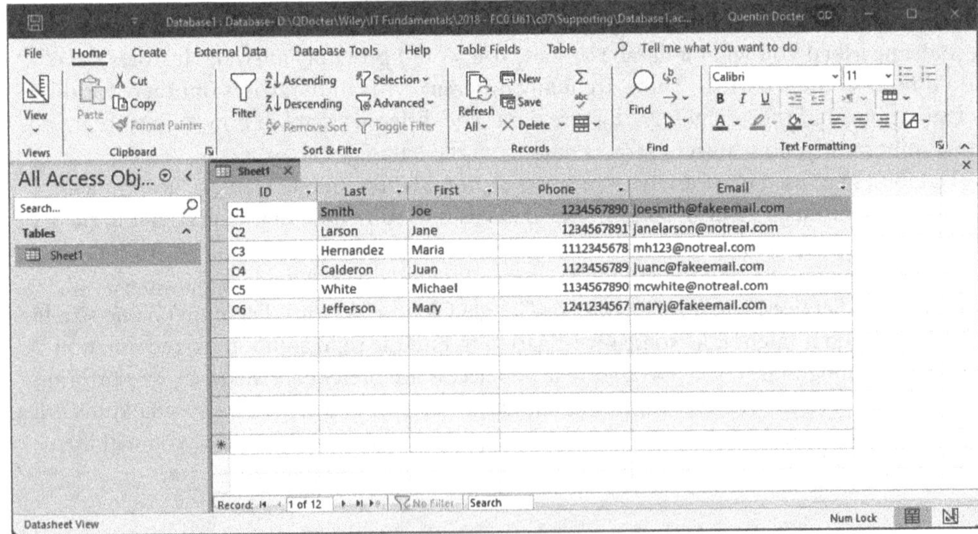

The Excel example shown in Figure 7.1 is what's known as a *flat file*. It's called that because the data has two dimensions, rows and columns. Databases don't need to have a flat structure—and in fact most don't—which is one of their advantages over spreadsheet software. This allows databases to manage far more complicated relationships between data points than spreadsheets can.

For example, say you have a list of part numbers, their descriptions, and their costs. You also have a list of customers. A customer buys a part, and you need to charge them and update your inventory. With a database, you could have two tables: one for customers and the other for inventory. The two tables could be linked together by the commonality of the part numbers that the customer has purchased. This is something a flat file cannot provide, at least not without some real heartburn for the data entry person.

When to Use Databases

You've already seen one example of when using a database makes more sense than using flat files, but let's explore some more.

Tech+ exam objective 5.2, "Explain database concepts and the purpose of a database," has several subobjectives covered here related to database advantages versus flat files. They include multiple concurrent users, scalability, speed, variety of data, number of database records, storage and data persistence, and data availability, such as if it's stored in the cloud or on a local PC.

Multiple Concurrent Users If you need to have multiple concurrent users accessing data, you need a database. Flat files don't do well when several people try to access them at once. In the vast majority of cases, one user might be able to write to the file, but all users will be limited to a read-only copy. This is because of how record locks are employed by flat files versus databases.

When a user tries to write to a flat file, the whole file is locked until the function executes. Databases generally lock only on a record level (or individual line of data), so multiple people can actively use the database at one time.

Some data collaboration software packages will let multiple users "edit" a spreadsheet at the same time. This is a bit of sleight of hand. The collaboration software provides for the functionality by essentially holding multiple copies of the spreadsheet, tracking the changes, and then writing the changes based on a time stamp. The spreadsheet software isn't aware that multiple people are editing it.

Scalability In a flat file, performance degrades as the number of users grows or the number of data points increases. Flat files are meant to be single-user instances, even if several users may be able to access them at one time.

Database servers such as Microsoft SQL Server and Oracle are extremely scalable, allowing access to hundreds or tens of thousands of users at a time. Enterprise versions of database software also allow databases to stretch between on-site servers and the cloud, with the most recent data being available on-site.

Microsoft SQL Server allows for a maximum of 32,767 concurrent connections.

Speed Similar to scalability, databases are much faster than flat files at processing and accessing large amounts of data. Database software is very memory intensive, so having plenty of RAM in a database server is critical. Also, speed can be increased by placing databases and their log files on SSDs rather than HDDs. Admittedly, finding large enough SSDs can be an issue for large databases, but the speed difference helps.

Variety of Data Spreadsheets are great at storing numbers and text, but have you ever tried to store images in them? Or how about entire text files in one cell? And even if you did, how would you know what was in that embedded file? Databases can store virtually any type of data and make it available quickly when searching for it.

Number of Records Excel worksheets are limited to no more than 1,048,576 rows and 16,384 columns. In addition, one cell can't contain more than 32,767 characters. While this might sound like a lot, think about large organizations. Does Amazon serve more than one million customers? Probably so—just this week. How about the U.S. Internal Revenue Service? The IRS needs to keep track of the Social Security numbers of roughly 350 million living Americans and many more deceased ones too. A spreadsheet just isn't going to cut it.

Data Persistence Users expect their data to be stored indefinitely, and this is what is meant by *data persistence*. Spreadsheets and databases both write data to hard drives, so by definition, both possess this trait. However, imagine a situation where you are entering data and the computer loses power. If you were editing a spreadsheet, all changes since the last file save are gone. With a database, all changes are essentially saved after each cell of data is edited. Furthermore, databases log changes in separate log files. If something happens to corrupt the data, the log files can be used to re-create the missing or corrupted data. Therefore, databases have much better data persistence than do spreadsheets.

Data Availability Flat files are meant to be stored on a local computer. This limits the number of people who can access them. Databases can be stored on a local computer, called *offline storage*, but they can also be stored on a server or in the cloud to enable broad access, called *online storage*. Each of these options enhances *data availability*, which means data is available to all users at any time of day and regardless of location. You will learn more about the cloud in Chapter 9, "Cloud Computing and Artificial Intelligence."

Security Databases provide much more granular security than do spreadsheets. With a spreadsheet, either a user can open the file and read all of its contents or the user can't. By using databases, users might be able to access specific columns or rows of data but not see anything else. For example, a customer might be able to look up all of their orders in the database, but they won't be able to see orders from other customers.

Relational Databases

Relational databases are an example of *structured data*. A *relational database* is predictable and organized, with tables containing columns and rows of text or numerical data. Data in a relational database must conform to specific rules as specified in the schema, and generally speaking, data is easy to search for and access.

All databases are managed by a *database management system (DBMS)*, and relational databases use a *relational database management system (RDBMS)*. The DBMS (or RDBMS) ensures data integrity by enforcing the following principles:

- No duplicate rows are allowed.
- Column values must not be arrays or repeating groups of data.
- Where data is not present, null values are used.

It's important to discuss the null value in more detail. A null value means the absence of data, not a value of 0. In a relational database, a 0 equals a 0, but a null value does not equal 0. In addition, a null value is not considered equal to another null value. They are just treated as missing data points.

The following sections discuss some relational database concepts with which you should be familiar.

Tech+ exam objective 5.3 is "Compare and contrast various database structures." You should understand structured databases, which includes relational databases. Within relational databases, be able to explain the following: schema, tables, rows/records, fields/columns, primary key, foreign key, and constraints.

Schema

The rules and structure of the database are called its *schema*. It defines the tables, forms, reports, queries, data types allowed, and pretty much everything else about the database.

There are two types of schemas in relational databases: the logical schema and the physical schema. The *logical schema* outlines the structure of the database, such as the tables and their fields (columns), and relationships between tables. Logical schemas can be created by almost any visual diagramming software package or even in a spreadsheet. Figure 7.3 shows an example of what a logical schema might look like at a university.

In Figure 7.3, you can see that there are four tables. Why would an administrator set it up this way? One of the key principles to setting up a database is to secure the data and make it available only to those who need it. At the same time, it should be easily accessible to users with proper access. In the example of this fictitious university, a student may log into the system and see their personal data, courses for which they are registered, and the instructors' names. But they have no reason to see an instructor's personal information unless the instructor provides it. Someone in the registrar's office can add new courses without seeing personally identifiable information about a student. And instructors can be set up to see the names of the students in their course, but not the student's contact information or credits or GPA. Databases are usually modular to make it easier to allow or restrict access to specific data.

FIGURE 7.3 Logical relational database schema

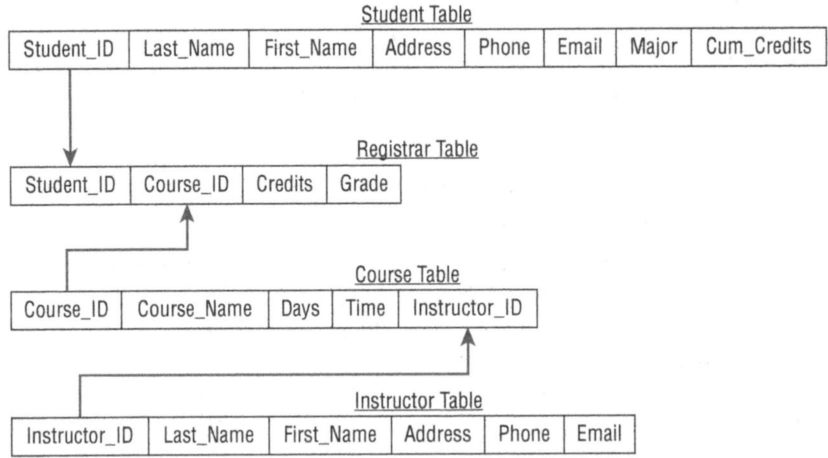

The *physical schema* is the actual tables, columns, and relationships created in the RDBMS. Many database management tools have a process for creating a physical schema based on a logical schema, or the physical schema can be created manually. Regardless, the logical schema should exist first—it's always best to plan a database out on paper before implementing it, so you can catch any potential issues while they're still easy to fix.

Any changes made to the physical schema should also be reflected in the logical schema.

Tables

These are what look like worksheets and contain data. One database can (and often does) have multiple tables. Each row in a table is called a *record*. If you want to link multiple tables together, you need to structure the data in such a way that it makes it easy to identify which records belong with each other, such as by using a customer identifier.

Fields

Columns in a table are called *fields*. Fields contain a single data type for all records. For example, a field could contain a phone number, cost, or other numerical data, or a name, product description, or other text data. A database wouldn't be designed in such a way that a field contains a part number for one record and a cost for another. Those need to be two separate fields. This is because when databases are queried, the user is looking for a specific type of data. It needs to be in the correct field!

For a table in a database to be relational, it must have a primary key. In fact, its creation is mandatory when a table is created. A *primary key* is one or more fields whose data is used to identify a record uniquely. The following must be true for primary keys:

- The data in the combination of columns must be unique. (For example, if a database uses `first_name` and `last_name` fields together as the primary key, one person can have the name Joe Smith, and one person can be Jane Smith. But a second Jane Smith would not be allowed.)
- No values in the column can be blank or null.

Usually, data such as a customer ID is used as the primary key—most administrators prefer to use as few fields as possible for the primary key. Phone numbers and names can be used as well, but care must be taken to ensure that the primary key of each record is unique. Primary keys for tables are stored in an index, which enforces the uniqueness requirement.

Tables may also have a foreign key. A *foreign key* is one or more columns in a table that refers to the primary key in another table. Foreign keys are not required, and they don't need to be officially designated in the RBDMS (although they can be defined by the administrator in the index). Take a look at Figure 7.4, which shows the same logical schema as in Figure 7.3, with the addition of icons to indicate primary keys.

Remember that fields, primary key, and foreign key are important terms in Tech+ exam objective 5.3!

FIGURE 7.4 Logical schema with primary keys

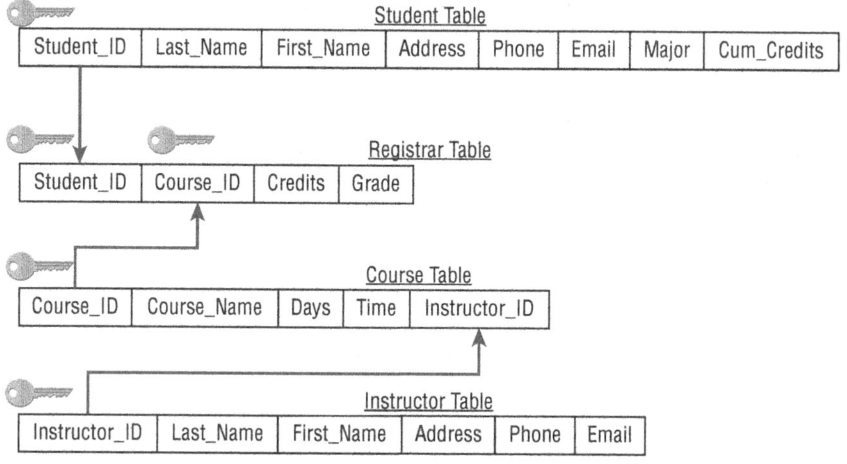

In Figure 7.4, the `Instructor_ID` field in Course Table is a foreign key because it refers to a primary key in Instructor Table. Foreign keys can contain duplicate values and null values, and there are no limits to the number of foreign keys in a table.

Even though foreign keys are much more flexible than primary keys, some RDBMS programs allow administrators to create *constraints* on foreign keys. Constraints are limitations that prevent someone from taking an action that would cause major problems within the database. For example, constraints can prevent someone from doing the following:

- *Entering a value that isn't found in the linked table's primary key.* If this were to happen, the record in the second table wouldn't be able to reference a record in the first table, which could cause problems.
- *Changing the foreign key value to a value that doesn't exist in the linked table's primary key.* This is for the same reason as the last bullet point.
- *Deleting rows from the primary key table, which would create an orphan record.* This is kind of the opposite of the first two, but it would have the same effect of having a record in the second table without a corresponding record in the first table.

Constraints can also be placed on fields to limit the type of data that may be entered into the field. For example, if a field is set to accept integers only, users will not be allowed to enter text data. This serves to increase reliability and accuracy of data in a database.

Table 7.1 summarizes the differences between primary and foreign keys.

TABLE 7.1 Primary and foreign keys

Detail	Primary key	Foreign key
Required	Yes	No
Number allowed per table	One	No limit
Automatically indexed	Yes	No
Duplicate values allowed	No	Yes
Null values allowed	No	Yes
Function	Uniquely identify records in a table	Refer to records in primary key table

Forms

Forms are how data is entered into and often viewed from your database. You don't need forms to have a database, but they make database management a lot easier. For example, you can have one form that lets customer service agents enter new client information, and another form that lets a manager review all new clients entered in the last week.

Queries

Queries are the real power of databases. They let you mine your data to find the specific information that you need. If you have a database with millions of records, queries are the only realistic way that you will find anything useful.

Reports

Reports are generated to answer specific questions. For example, a manager could have an automatic report that generates the list of new clients in the last week, as opposed to viewing the list in a form. Think of them as preformed queries.

You should be able to explain key database concepts, per exam objective 5.2. The database uses you need to remember are that users can create or import/input data, and also run queries and reports.

Macros and Modules

Macros and *modules* let you add functionality to your database. For example, if you want to do a monthly cleanup of all records older than a certain date, you can automate that by creating a module. For anything that you would have to run manually, you can probably create a macro to make the process faster.

Nonrelational Databases

Relational databases are great for holding structured data, but not all data fits into a nice, clean structure with rows and columns. Two other types of data that people need are nonstructured and semi-structured. These types of data can be housed in nonrelational databases. Before diving into the types of nonrelational databases, it's important to understand the key features of nonstructured and semi-structured data.

For the exam, you need to know two different types of nonrelational databases: semi-structured and nonstructured. Also be able to explain what key-value databases and document databases are. These are all outlined in exam objective 5.3.

Nonstructured Data

Most data in the world—80 percent by some professional estimates—is nonstructured data. Examples of *nonstructured data* include pictures, videos, web pages, emails, documents, texts, and social media. Realize that this data has structure within itself. For example, emails have a sender and receiver, a subject line, and a message body. The data is considered unstructured because it doesn't fit neatly into a database.

Here's a good analogy to help think about dealing with unstructured data: imagine you have a file folder on your computer. In that folder, you've placed photos from a vacation, emails, work history, school transcripts, text messages, all of your social media content, and X-ray images from a medical procedure you underwent a few years ago. That folder is now your "database," and the content in it is your data. You can see that the data has no structure, but there may be interesting links between different pieces of it. It will be quite challenging to find those links, though, considering all of the different data types included.

Nonstructured data is often referred to as *unstructured* data.

Semi-Structured Data

As its name implies, semi-structured data fits somewhere in between structured and nonstructured data. Specifically, *semi-structured data* is generally thought of as unstructured data that has been tagged with metadata. *Metadata* is literally data about data.

Take the vacation photos and X-ray images from the unstructured data folder, for example. Both of them are images, which are just collections of pixels—how would they be included in a search? In a semi-structured world, tags of metadata could be associated with the pictures to provide some context (maybe the date they were taken, the location, or even some more specific information such as it included a hand). Granted, the hand picture could be either from a vacation or an X-ray, but at least you've got something to go on. Emails can be tagged too by listing the sender and the recipient, time, and date. Going back to the messy unstructured data folder example, you can probably think of ways to include metadata for each type of data mentioned.

By using metadata, the unstructured data suddenly has some structure. The data still doesn't fit neatly into a rows-and-columns database, but you can at least start to query it.

A sizable portion of unstructured data has some sort of metadata associated with it, blurring the lines between the two types of data. In some circles, you'll hear debates on whether unstructured data is still a relevant term. Regardless of which side of the debate you take, just know that if it has metadata, it's semi-structured. And yes, there is some gray area when it comes to defining semi-structured versus nonstructured data.

Document Databases

While structured databases definitely have their place in the world, they're not known for their flexibility. A popular type of nonrelational database is a document database. In a *document database*, each record and its associated data is considered a document. Said differently, a picture and the 15 keywords someone used to describe it, along with the date it was taken, location, and photographer, can all be combined into the same document.

Structured Query Language (SQL) is a critical component of relational databases. When nonrelational databases started gaining popularity in the early 2000s, the term "NoSQL" was coined to designate that these databases were different. For some, the term represents a rebellion against the rigid structure of relational databases. For others, NoSQL means "not only SQL," because their products allow for the comingling of unstructured and structured data.

When SQL is used to access a nonrelational database such as a document database, it's an example of programmatic access.

A few cool features of document databases are that each document is considered to be a completely independent unit, and documents don't all need to have exactly the same types of information. If one document has a picture associated with it and another doesn't, it's no big deal—they can still reside in the same document database. This allows for the easy storage of unstructured data of any type. The structure also makes it easy to store parts of the database on different servers—all objects are independent from each other, so while a singular object is stored in one location, other objects don't need to be in the same place. There is no assumed relationship between different objects.

Document databases do need to have the ability to index all of the available metadata, and they need to have robust search engines to mine the data available. Examples of NoSQL document database software include MongoDB, Amazon DynamoDB, and Couchbase.

Key-Value Databases

A second major classification of NoSQL databases is the key-value database. In a *key-value database*, data is represented as a collection of key-value pairs. Key-value databases manage associative arrays of data, also known as a *dictionary*, which is a collection of objects or records. Each object or record can have one or more fields, much like a relational database has fields containing data. Records are stored and retrieved by using the key that identifies them.

Each key is allowed to exist only once in a given collection. A key is an arbitrary string of characters. It can be a filename or a URL or random characters, but it must be unique. The value can be any kind of data, including a picture, file, number, data string, or really anything else. Values are stored as blobs, meaning that they don't confirm to a schema.

Key/value databases are also known as key-value stores.

Some popular key-value databases are Redis, Amazon DynamoDB (it's a multimodel DBMS), Memcached, Microsoft Azure Cosmos DB, and Oracle NoSQL.

Understanding Big Data

A hot topic in business and computing circles is big data. Big data is defined as extremely large datasets that can be analyzed to identify patterns or trends. While it's true that most big datasets are large, perhaps a more defining characteristic is that they are incredibly complex, bringing together structured and unstructured data from a myriad of sources. The big challenge, then, is what to do with big data.

Companies have hired scores of data scientists to write algorithms to mine data, searching for the next insight to drive their business. Other companies specialize in collecting data for their data lakes, which are large banks of raw data waiting to be analyzed or processed. In many cases, these companies are looking for consumer behaviors—what did they buy, how often did they buy it, and what drove them to make the purchase? Did they view a particular advertisement exactly four hours before the purchase? Does that even matter? Or what do we know about the likelihood of someone purchasing a certain brand of car based on their social media likes that have nothing to do with cars? Again, does that even matter? Odds are that someone, somewhere, knows the answer to that question.

More and more data is being collected all of the time, from the aforementioned social media habits to IoT devices to drones taking pictures of everything—there certainly isn't a shortage of data. The big question, without a doubt, is what will companies or governments do with all of it? If data truly is the new currency (or the new bacon), how will these massive and complex datasets be put to good use? Or will they simply be massive sets of data with no identifiable purpose? Companies and governments are investing heavily in using it, but where big data goes from here is anyone's guess. Stay tuned to find out!

Working With Databases

Having a database is great, but it won't do you much good unless you know how to get data into it and pull data from it. Databases can storge huge amounts of data, so it needs to be as easy as possible to both input and extract the needed information.

This section on working with databases does not specifically link to any current Tech+ exam objectives, so in that sense you can consider it optional. You're highly encouraged to read through and understand this section as it has real-world applicability.

There are several ways to access a database, including the following:

Manual Access This means going directly into the tables of a database to view or change data. If the user wants to view or change a few cells, this isn't usually much of a problem. If several thousands or millions of cells need to change, that's a totally different story. Figure 7.5 shows a table from a sample Microsoft Access database. The table contains orders. A user could click a cell (just like in a spreadsheet) and change the data.

FIGURE 7.5 Microsoft Access table

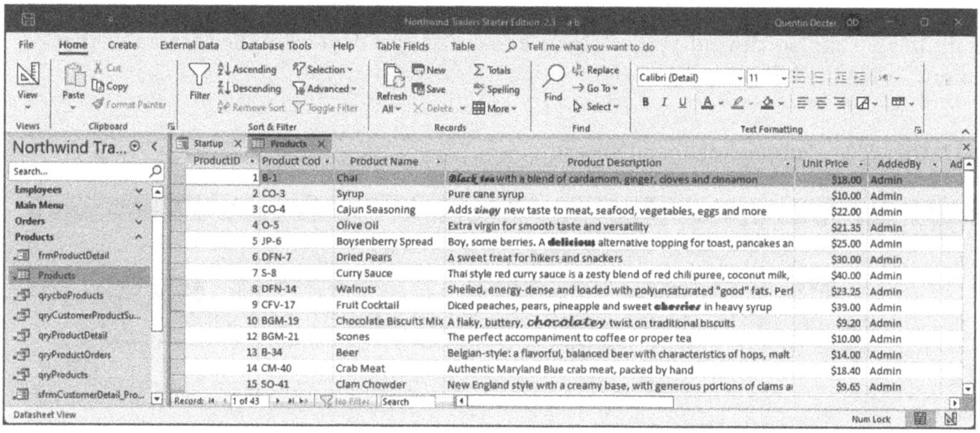

Microsoft Access comes with a sample database for a fictitious company called Northwind Traders. Figure 7.5 shows the Products table from that database. The sample database is free to use and playing around with it can help cement some of the concepts you've learned in this chapter.

Direct Access Some people use the term *direct access* as a synonym for manual access, whereas others differentiate the access types. The other usage of direct access generally refers to accessing the database tables directly across a network connection. Most often, this is done with an application programming interface (API), Open Database Connectivity (ODBC), or Java Database Connectivity (JDBC) link. The remote computer establishes a link between itself and the table with one of these methods and then has direct access to the data tables.

APIs generally return formatted data, whereas ODBC and JDBC connections return raw or unformatted data.

Programmatic Access By definition, this means accessing the data through a program or a programming method. SQL is a common programming language used to work with data in databases. This concept can also be extended. For example, a program might use an ODBC connection to connect to a database and then retrieve data from the database using SQL.

User Interface and Utility Access Instead of accessing the database manually, users can use a graphical interface or utility. The interface or utility could be built into the database program or specifically developed to access the data. For example, many database software packages include forms, which are simple graphical interfaces that let users enter or manage data without directly touching the table. A form could exist to enter new products, with all of the required fields, without the user needing to open the table. Figure 7.6 shows a product details form from Northwind Traders. Notice that it shows data from the same table that you saw in Figure 7.5.

FIGURE 7.6 Form in Microsoft Access

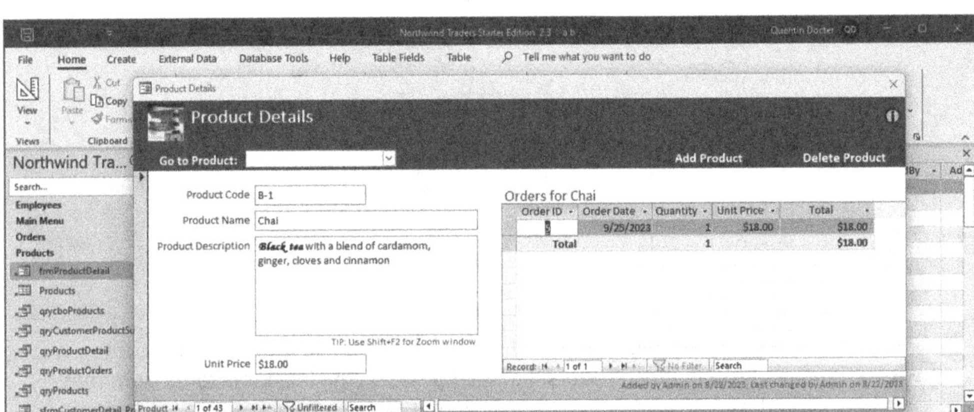

As another example, a developer could create a web-based user interface to allow a customer to sign up for information. The data would be entered into a database by the user interface. This is prevalent on the Internet.

Databases can also be accessed via query and report builders. Queries and reports are big enough topics to deserve their own section—they are covered in the "Extracting Data" section later in this chapter.

Regardless of how you choose to access a database, you need to ensure that the right security measures are in place. The next section will focus on permissions, and then you'll learn how to create a database, manage data, extract data, and back up a database.

Understanding Database Permissions

When creating a database or table, it's critical to ensure that the right security is implemented. Databases can contain vital information—personally identifiable information or critical business data—that needs to be protected. Leaving a database open to potential attackers is not good policy.

Different DBMSs will implement permissions (also called *privileges*) in different ways, but in general, there are three different classifications:

- *Server permissions* affect the entire server. These would typically be granted to an administrator account. Sometimes you will hear these referred to as *global permissions* because they apply to all databases on that server.
- *Database permissions* apply to one database and all objects within the database. These can be global as well, if they are applied to all databases on a server.
- *Object permissions* will affect specific database objects, such as tables, views, forms, indexes, and macros or modules.

Permissions are hierarchical in nature. If a permission is established on a database, then by default it applies to all tables in the database. If a permission is set on a table, it applies to all objects that are part of that table.

Permissions can be assigned to individual user accounts, but in general, that is an incredibly inefficient way to manage security. Instead, assign permissions to groups (called *roles*) and use predefined database role types.

For example, there are typically one or more server-wide administrator roles on most DBMSs. That level of access should be closely guarded and granted only to those users who absolutely need it.

Database roles have less scope than server-wide roles. For granting access or setting specific privileges to databases, this is generally the appropriate role level to use. Table 7.2 lists some specific database roles.

TABLE 7.2 Predefined database roles

Role	Access level
`db_owner`	Full access (read, write, delete, back up)
`db_datareader`	Read data
`db_datawriter`	Add, delete, or modify data
`db_bckupoperator`	Back up the database
`db_denydatareader`	Can't view data
`db_denydatawriter`	Can't add, delete, or modify data

There's an additional database role called Public, and every user added to the database is automatically added to the Public role. When a user hasn't been granted or denied specific permissions to a database or object, the user inherits permissions granted to Public. By default, Public can view the database—this could potentially be a major security hole. Most security experts recommend not using Public but rather creating a role for those who need access and then assigning users to that group instead.

Permissions can be managed programmatically with the `grant`, deny, and `revoke` commands in the DBMS. The `grant` command grants permissions to users or roles, and deny explicitly denies permissions. The `revoke` command removes previously granted or denied permissions. If there is a conflict, such as a user account has been granted a permission but a role the user belongs to has been denied a permission, the deny will override the grant. An explicit deny will always override all other permissions.

Creating and Managing a Database

As apparent as it may seem, the first step in using a database is creating the database. After the database is created, you can create one or more tables within the database, as well as other objects such as indexes, forms, macros, and queries. Earlier in this chapter, you learned about several database access methods. Throughout the next few sections on working with databases, I am going to explain commands that you can use to work with data and relational databases, as well as include graphical examples from Microsoft Access.

Before creating a database that you intend to use for an actual purpose, be sure to map out the logical schema.

Creating a Database

The SQL command to create a database is `CREATE`. This command can be used to create both databases and tables. Here's the syntax for using it to create a database:

```
CREATE DATABASE database_name;
```

Simple enough, right? When entered into the SQL server, a database is created. For example, to create a database named StudentData, you would enter **`CREATE DATABASE StudentData;`**. Be sure to pick a database name that does not already exist on the server. Also, don't forget that you need to have administrative privileges on the SQL Server instance to execute this command. Once you have created the database, you can verify that it was created by using the `SHOW DATABASES;` command, which will list all databases on the server.

If you want to learn more about SQL and SQL commands, there are a ton of resources online. One example is `https://learnsql.com/blog/sql-server-cheat-sheet`.

The `CREATE` command is also used to create tables in databases. Here is the syntax:

```
CREATE TABLE table_name (column1 datatype, column2 datatype, ...);
```

You don't need to define columns and data types, but it can be convenient to do so when you create the table. There are dozens of different data types, and they differ based on the database implementation you're using. The good news is that you don't need to memorize a long list of data types right now. Here's an example, creating a table with four columns:

```
CREATE TABLE Student (Student_ID int, Last_Name varchar(255), First_Name
varchar(255), Address varchar(255));
```

This command creates the first four columns of a table named `Student`. The first column contains the student identifier, which is an integer data type. The next three columns are strings that can be up to 255 characters each. This follows the logical schema shown back in Figure 7.4.

If you forget to create the column during table creation or are working with an existing table, managing columns is done with the `ALTER` command. You can use `ALTER` to add, delete, and modify columns. Here is the syntax for the three alternatives:

```
ALTER TABLE table_name ADD column_name datatype;
ALTER TABLE table_name DROP COLUMN column_name;
ALTER TABLE table_name ALTER COLUMN column_name datatype;
```

Some SQL implementations use a different argument for altering columns. Instead of `ALTER COLUMN` *`column_name`*, you might see `MODIFY COLUMN` *`column_name`* or `MODIFY` *`column_name`*. Don't get hung up on the syntax differences; just know that all three could be valid.

Exercise 7.1 walks you through creating a database and tables in Microsoft Access.

EXERCISE 7.1

Creating a Database and Tables in Microsoft Access

1. Open Microsoft Access. In the Windows search box, type **Access** and press Enter. You will see a screen similar to the one shown in Figure 7.7. This screen shows several templates with preformatted tables from which you can choose, or you can open a blank database.

EXERCISE 7.1 *(continued)*

FIGURE 7.7 Microsoft Access

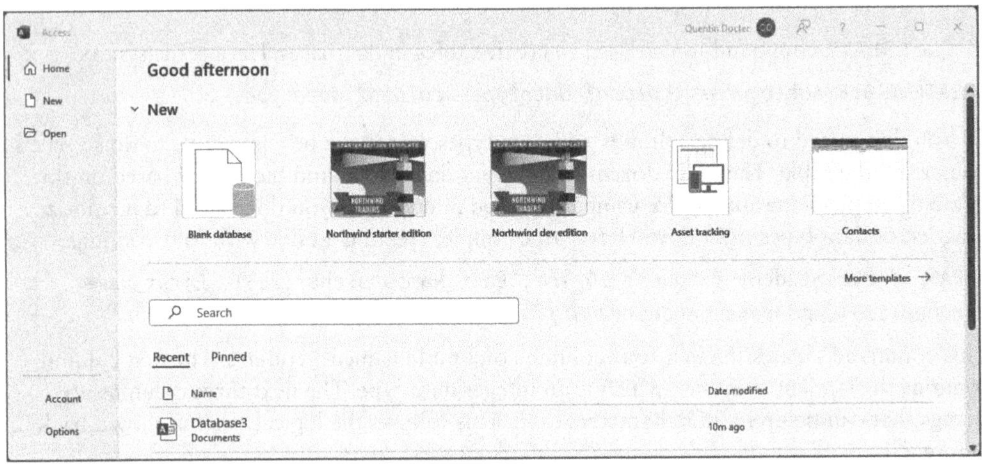

2. Click Blank Database. In the Blank Database pop-up window, specify the filename, such as `MyDatabase`, and then click Create. A new database will appear, like the one shown in Figure 7.8. Notice that Access automatically created a table called Table1.

FIGURE 7.8 Empty database

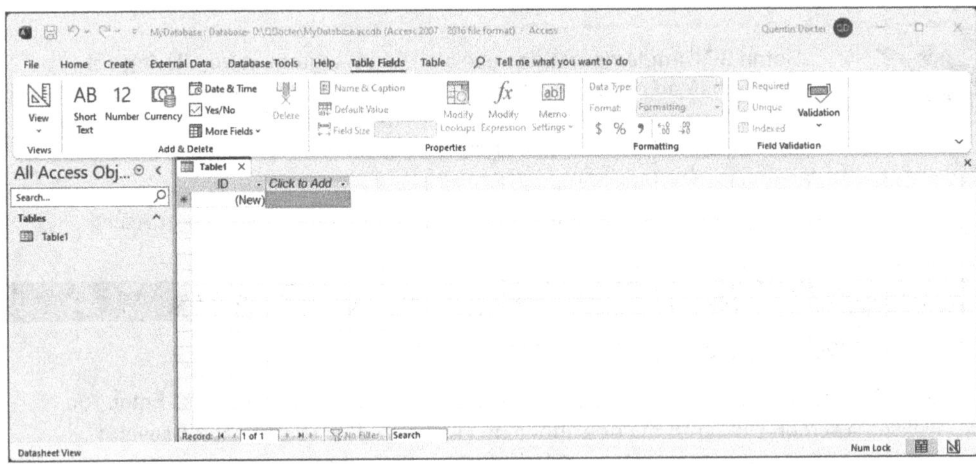

3. The first column in the database is labeled ID. Right-click the field cell, and choose Rename Field. Name it `Student_ID`. You can also rename the field by double-clicking it and entering a new name.

4. Add a new field by clicking the ClickTo Add field to the right of Student_ID. A pop-up menu will ask you to choose the data type, such as short text, number, or yes/no. Click ShortText. Access automatically names the field `Field1`. Change the name to **`Last_Name`**.

5. Create a new table by choosing Create ➢ Table. You will now see two tables in the left-side navigation and two tabs for tables, like you see in Figure 7.9.

FIGURE 7.9 Two tables

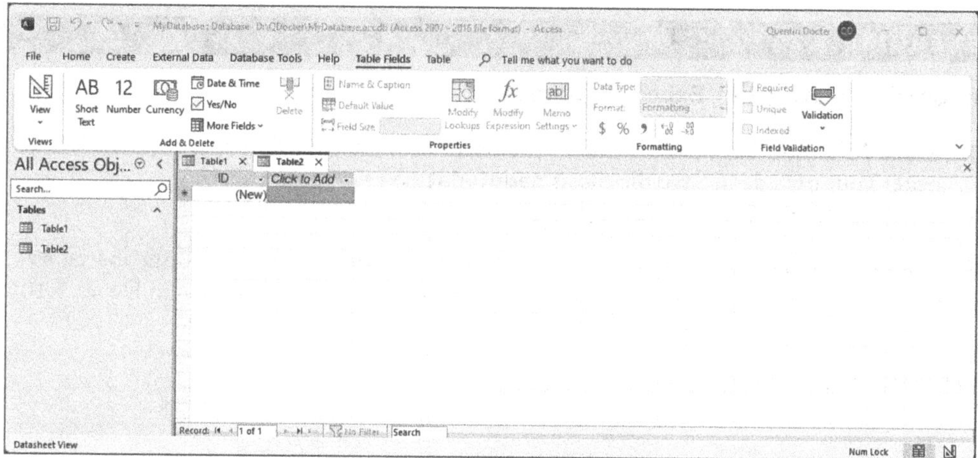

6. To navigate between tables, click the tab for the table that you want to see. Otherwise, double-click the table name in the left pane. Right-click Table1 in the left pane and click Rename. What happens?

7. In the top navigation, right-click Table1 and choose Close.

8. In the left navigation, right-click Table1 and choose Rename. Rename the table to **`Students`**.

Importing and Inputting Data

A blank database isn't the most useful creation. Once you've created a database, the next step is to either import or input data. Inputting data manually isn't difficult—it's basically done the same way as entering data into a spreadsheet. Click the cell, enter the value, and move on. One difference is that some fields may be constrained to certain types. For example, if you set a field type as a number and then try to enter letters into a record for that field, the DBMS won't accept it.

Importing data from an existing source can save a lot of time compared to manually entering it. Many DBMSs let you import data from a command line using the `LOAD DATA INFILE` command. Here's an example:

```
LOAD DATA INFILE 'sample.csv' INTO TABLE Students FIELDS TERMINATED BY ',';
```

This command loads data from the `sample.csv` file into the `Students` table, and it lets the DBMS know that fields in the file are separated by commas. Importing data using a DBMSs GUI is much easier, though. Exercise 7.2 shows you how to import data from Excel into Access.

EXERCISE 7.2

Importing Data from Excel to Access

1. Open Microsoft Excel, and create a worksheet with the data shown in Figure 7.1. Or, enter your own data. Save the file as **`sampledata.xlsx`**. Close Excel.
2. Open the Access database that you created in Exercise 7.1.
3. On the External Data tab, in the Import & Link section, choose New Data Source ➢ From File ➢ Excel. The Get External Data window will open, as shown in Figure 7.10.

FIGURE 7.10 Get External Data window

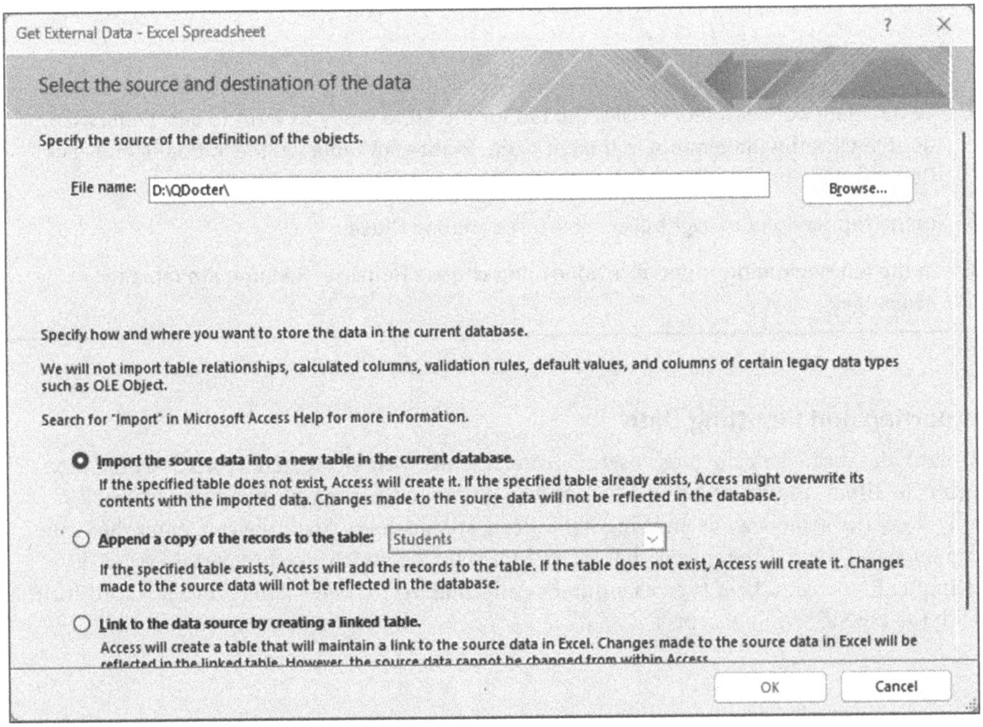

4. Browse to the location where you saved your `sampledata.xlsx` file. Choose how and where you want to import the data. Notice that you can import to a new table, append the data to an existing table, or link to a table. Select Import The Source Data Into A New Table In The Current Database and click OK.
5. On the Import Spreadsheet Wizard screen, choose the worksheet or worksheets you want to import. For this exercise, choose Sheet1. Click Next.
6. On the Import Spreadsheet Wizard screen, select First Row Contains Column Headings and then click Next.
7. The Import Spreadsheet Wizard will now ask you to specify information about each of the fields that you are importing. For the Indexed Field Option for the ID column, select Yes (No Duplicates). Examine the other fields and configure them as you would like. Click Next.
8. The Import Spreadsheet Wizard will now let you select a primary key. Access will add it itself, or you can choose your own. Click Choose My Own Primary Key, and set it to the ID field. Click Next.
9. Name the new table **`Customers`** and click Finish.
10. (Optional) Save the import steps if you'd like and click Close.
11. Notice the new `Customers` table in your database, as shown in Figure 7.11.

FIGURE 7.11 Imported Customers table

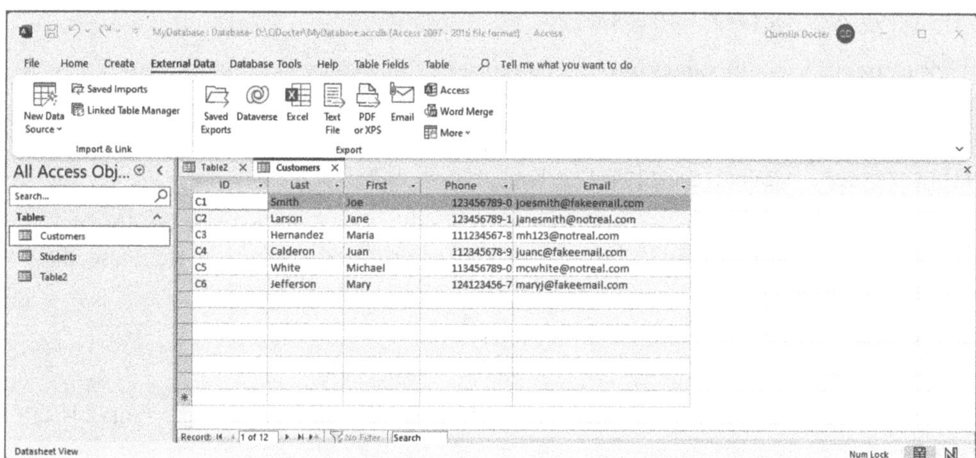

12. In the example shown in Figure 7.11, the phone number formatting doesn't look quite right. Click the Phone field. Then on the Table Fields tab, in the Formatting heading, click Format and set it to General Number. This will remove the strange formatting.

Dropping Databases and Tables

Sometimes you need to delete tables or databases, and in database terms this is known as *dropping*. The DROP commands for dropping a database and dropping a table are shown here:

```
DROP DATABASE database_name;
DROP TABLE table_name;
```

It might go without saying, but be careful with these commands! Dropping a database or table will completely remove all data in that database or table. Unless you have a backup, it's gone.

In Access, you can delete a table by right-clicking it in the left navigation pane and choosing Delete. To delete an Access database, close it, find the filename, and delete it from Windows File Explorer.

Manipulating Data

You need to be aware of the four commands that are frequently used to manipulate data in a relational database: SELECT, INSERT, UPDATE, and DELETE. The SELECT command is core to queries, which I am going to cover in the next section, "Extracting Data."

The INSERT command is used to insert records into an existing table. The syntax is as follows:

```
INSERT INTO table_name (column1, column2, column3...)
VALUES (value1, value2, value3...);
```

For example, to insert values into the Customers table you created in Exercise 7.2, you could use the following command:

```
INSERT INTO Customers (Last, First, Phone, Email)
VALUES (Brown, Robert, 5551234567, bobbyb@notreal.com);
```

If you intend to insert data into all columns of a table, you don't need to specify the column names. Just be sure that all of the values are in the correct order. In that case, the syntax would look like this:

```
INSERT INTO Customers
VALUES (Brown, Robert, 5551234567, bobbyb@notreal.com);
```

The UPDATE command is used to update existing data in the database. The syntax is as follows:

```
UPDATE table_name
SET column1 = value1, column2 = value2, ...
WHERE condition;
```

Here's an example, using the Customers table again:

```
UPDATE Customers
SET Last = Johnson, Phone = 9876543210
WHERE ID='C1';
```

The `WHERE` clause in the `UPDATE` command is particularly important to pay attention to. If not specified, the `UPDATE` command will update all data in the database for the specified columns. Said differently, if you don't want all of the customers to have the last name Johnson, use the `WHERE` clause!

Finally, there is the `DELETE` command. You can probably guess what it does—deletes records—so let's move on to the context:

```
DELETE FROM table_name
WHERE condition;
```

So, to delete all customers with the last name of Smith, you would use the following:

```
DELETE FROM Customers
WHERE Last='Smith';
```

As with the `UPDATE` command, be sure to include the `WHERE` clause. Otherwise, all data will be deleted from the table.

Extracting Data

The true utility of a database comes from being able to do something with all the data contained within it. If a database has only a few hundred records in one table, it can be relatively easy to sift through the table and find the information you want. But if the database has millions of records and multiple tables, the sifting becomes much more difficult. Two primary methods exist to extract data from a database: queries and reports.

Queries use the `SELECT` command to identify and display the data the user needs. The basic syntax of a simple query is straightforward—just specify the columns and table name:

```
SELECT column1, column2, ...
FROM table_name;
```

For example, you could run a query against the `Customers` table with the following command:

```
SELECT Last, First
FROM Customers;
```

This will return the last and first names of all six entries in the `Customers` table. It's useful but not so practical if there are a significant number of records. To help, the `SELECT` command is usually augmented by the use of operators and clauses to refine the results. Some of the more common operators are `WHERE`, `AND`, `OR`, and `NOT`, and a helpful clause is `ORDER BY`. Here's some syntax for a more complicated query:

```
SELECT column1, column2, ...
FROM table_name
WHERE condition1 AND condition2 AND condition3
ORDER BY column1;
```

Let's say you have a customer database with 50,000 records. You want to see the names, addresses, and phone numbers of all customers with the last name Smith who live in

Anytown. You want the results sorted by phone number. The query could look something like this:

```
SELECT Last_name First_name, Address, Phone
FROM Customers
WHERE Last_name='Smith' AND City='Anytown'
ORDER BY Phone;
```

An asterisk (*) can be used as a wildcard in SQL statements to mean "everything." For example, you could use **SELECT * FROM Customers WHERE...**to return all fields from the database that meet the specified criteria.

Basic SQL queries can be pretty easy to write, but they can also get incredibly convoluted in a hurry. Complex queries pulling data from several columns that span multiple tables using numerous conditions as well as joins or unions can easily span multiple pages.

One limitation of queries is that they return raw, unformatted data in columns and rows like a spreadsheet—they aren't very pretty. For nicely formatted results, reports are used. A report is essentially a query that's been formatted to make them look like a finished product. Access has a built-in report generator, but a lot of DBMSs don't. For those, you need to use a third-party reporting tool such as Crystal Reports.

Reporting doesn't just make pretty reports and forms—it can also produce different visuals, such as a pie chart of total inventory or a report of inventory owned in dollars. Given enough data, reporting can even be taken further to show business intelligence (BI). Business intelligence can help you purchase more of a certain item so that you don't run out by using trend analysis to show visually inventory on hand versus how often it's sold.

Backing Up Databases

Data loss can be catastrophic. When I first started in the IT industry, I was on a support call where the user had just suffered a failed hard drive. The user was a doctoral student, and the only copy of his dissertation was on that drive. Several years' worth of hard work was gone. There are also statistics out there showing how big of a problem data loss is for small companies. A 2023 article claims that 60 percent of small businesses that lose data will shut down within six months. That's similar to a 2011 report by the accounting firm PricewaterhouseCoopers that showed that 70 percent of small firms that experienced a major data loss would be out of business within a year. The solution is simple: Back up your data! And preferably, store the backups in the cloud or elsewhere off-site.

There are two recommended ways to back up data from a database. The first is to do a database dump, and the second is to run a backup. The difference between a database dump and backup isn't much. A *database dump* is a one-time logical backup of a database. It exports the schema, tables, views, and the data. A backup as executed through a backup program is a physical backup. Not only can it be scheduled and repeating, it also backs up everything a data dump does plus the physical structures of the database (indexes, control files, archive logs, and data files). Database backup programs are capable of backing up the database while it's open and users are accessing it.

Restoring the data is where the biggest difference is seen. Imagine a situation where the database is completely lost. With a data dump, a new database would need to be created, followed by restoring the data from the dump. An actual backup could restore the entire database without needing to create a new database to house the data.

Data dumps can also be used to export data from one database and import it into another. However, most DBMS tools have specific export and import utilities for this purpose.

Figure 7.12 shows where to back up a database in Access (it's in File ➢ Save As). Back up early and back up often—it could save your bacon.

FIGURE 7.12 Backing up a database

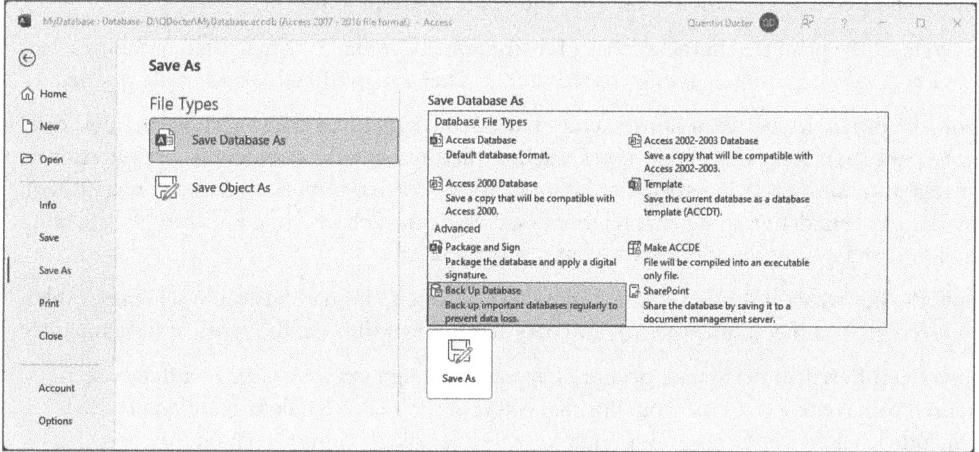

Summary

This chapter discussed database fundamentals. First, you learned about database concepts and structures. You learned the differences between flat files and databases and when to use a database instead of a flat file. Then you learned about structured, semi-structured, and nonstructured data in the context of relational and nonrelational databases. Relational databases have a consistent structure of rows (records) and columns (fields) and use schemas and tables. Two types of nonrelational databases are document databases and key-value databases.

Next, you learned how to work with a database. Databases are created, data is imported or inputted, and then queries and reports can be run. Users and administrators access databases using several different types of access, including direct, manual, programmatic, user interfaces, utilities, and query and report builders. Commands used to manage tables and databases are `CREATE`, `ALTER`, and `DROP`, whereas commands to manage data in a database are `SELECT`, `INSERT`, `DELETE`, and `UPDATE`. Finally, you learned how to prevent catastrophic data loss by using database dumps and backups.

Exam Essentials

Understand database uses. Databases are used to manage data. Specifically, you can create, import/input, query, and run reports on data.

Know when to use a database instead of a flat file. Databases are better when there are multiple concurrent users, large quantities of data, multiple varieties of data, and speed, scalability, data persistence, data availability, and security are of concern.

Understand the primary characteristics of a structured database. Structured databases use rows (records) and columns (fields) to store data. They are predictable and easily queried.

Know the difference between nonstructured and semi-structured data. Nonstructured data can be data from several different types, such as pictures, emails, documents, presentations, and text and numbers. Semi-structured data is nonstructured data that has been tagged with metadata to help define some characteristics of the data, such as when a picture was taken, by whom, and a brief description of what's in the picture.

Know the key structures in a relational database. Relational databases use schemas, tables, rows (records), and columns (fields), and may have constraints on the types of data included.

Know the differences between a primary key and a foreign key. A table in a database is required to have one (and only one) primary key, and it's used to identify unique records in the table. There can be several foreign keys. Primary keys cannot contain null or blank values.

Know the two types of nonrelational databases. The two types of nonrelational databases are document databases and key-value databases.

Chapter 7 Lab

You can find the answers in Appendix A.

Creating your own database can take a lot of time and effort. Fortunately, if you have Microsoft Access, there are free sample databases that you can use to practice the skills learned in Chapter 7. The purpose of this lab is to get you more comfortable with a relatively simple database, including tables, forms, and queries. Use this time to play around—the data is not for a real company, so you can do whatever you want to it with no repercussions!

The sample database you will use in this lab is called Northwind. Most versions of Access have Northwind available as a template when you open Access. If not, you will need to search for it. To find Northwind, you will need to search for it. Here's how to install it:

1. Open Microsoft Access.
2. In the Search For Online Templates bar at the top of the page, type **`Northwind`** and press Enter.
3. The Northwind sample will appear in the search results. Click it.
4. A window will pop up explaining what Northwind is, like the one shown in Figure 7.13. Provide a filename (if desired) and click Create.

FIGURE 7.13 Installing Northwind

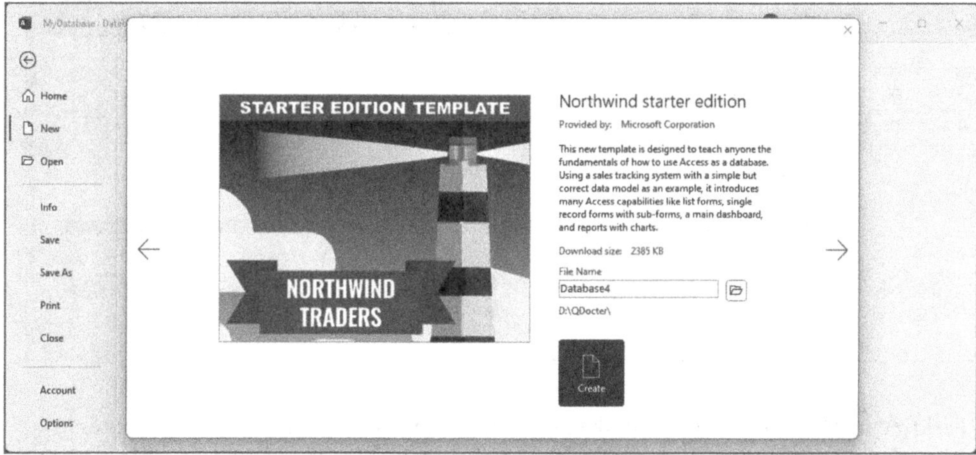

5. When Access opens the database, you might get a security warning across the top of the page. If so, click Enable Content.
6. On the login page, enter your first and last name and job title (or make one up) and click Add Me.

Now that you have logged in, it's time to explore the Northwind database. On the left is the navigation pane. In it you will see several categories of forms, tables, queries, reports, and other objects. Click Customers to expand the category. You will see three different types of objects—they have different icons. The first is a table called `Customers`. Double-click it, and the table opens in the right pane. The second type is a form. In this database, the forms are conveniently named with a `frm` prefix. The third type is a query, which is named starting with `qry`. If you open a query, you can right-click its tab in the right pane, and click SQL View to see the query in SQL.

In the left pane, double-click the Customer Details form. It will open a window showing a customer's information (see Figure 7.14). Using this form, someone could modify the information for a customer, which will be saved to a table. To enter information for a new customer, click Save and New in the top menu bar of the Customer Details form. Feel free to do it if you'd like!

FIGURE 7.14 Customer details

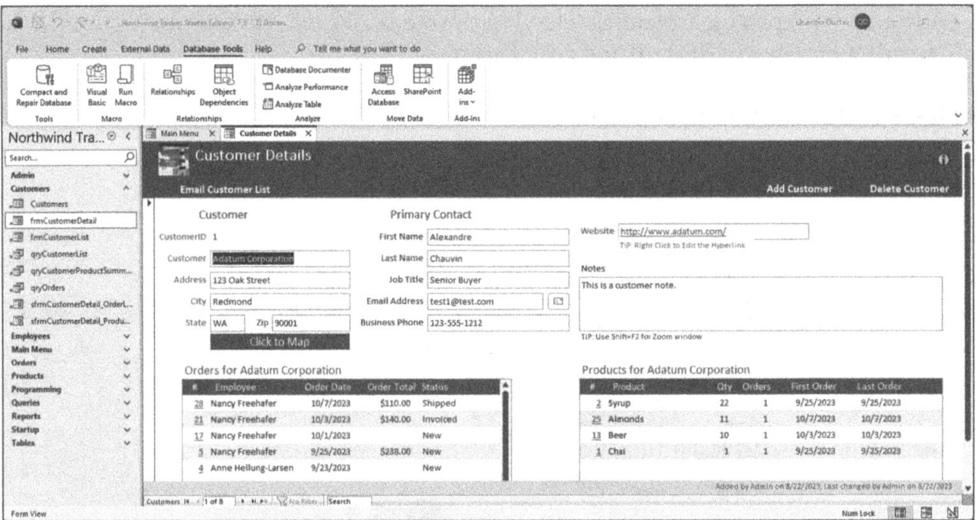

Feel free to click whatever you'd like now. I recommend spending about 30 minutes looking around, familiarizing yourself with the objects and data available. For example, if you find data in a form, see whether you can track down in which table or tables that data is housed. Here are some specific questions for you to explore. (Ideally Microsoft doesn't change the data in the template!)

1. Who is the Sales Coordinator for Northwind Traders?
2. How many orders has Woodgrove Bank placed, and how much have they spent?
3. How many units of coffee did Northwind sell?
4. What were the three items that Northwind sold the most?
5. Who was responsible for order 48?

Review Questions

You can find the answers in Appendix B.

1. You have an address book for a small business with contact information for about 100 clients. The address book is used by two people. Which solution should you use to store the data?
   - A. Spreadsheet
   - B. Relational database
   - C. Word processing software
   - D. Nonrelational database
2. A database developer is working on generating queries. If the developer needs to ensure that the output of the query has data persistence, to where should the data be written?
   - A. RAM
   - B. Cachè
   - C. SSD
   - D. CPU
3. Which of the following consists of columns and rows of numerical or text data?
   - A. Document database
   - B. Key-value database
   - C. Database dump
   - D. Relational database
4. Joe creates a database. What does he need to do next to make it usable?
   - A. Enable permissions
   - B. Import data
   - C. Run queries
   - D. Create forms
5. A user, Ann, is granted permissions to access a database. What is this an example of?
   - A. Data collection
   - B. Data manipulation
   - C. Direct/manual access
   - D. Data definition

6. A medical office needs to create a solution to manage patient records. They have about 10,000 patients and eight staff; they want to include notes from medical professionals, emails to and from patients, and images such as x-rays. What should they create?
   A. Spreadsheet
   B. Relational database
   C. Nonrelational database
   D. Primary key
7. You have created a relational database. Which of the following elements uniquely identifies a record in the database?
   A. Primary key
   B. Foreign key
   C. Schema
   D. Field
8. Mary, an administrator, creates a field and designates it to hold integer data. Joe, a user, tries to enter his name in the field, but it doesn't let him save the data. What is this an example of?
   A. Schema rules
   B. Primary key
   C. Foreign key
   D. Constraints
9. Rachel, a database administrator, has created a database for her website. It contains pictures of vacations that people have uploaded. In the database, pictures have associated information about who uploaded them and the date. What is this an example of?
   A. Semi-structured data
   B. Nonstructured data
   C. Structured data
   D. Schema definition
10. Peter is accessing a database using a JDBC connection. Which of the following terms best describes the type of access he is using?
    A. Direct/manual access
    B. Programmatic access
    C. User interface/utility access
    D. Query/report builder

11. Oscar's user account has been granted permissions to view a database. Nathan then uses the `deny` command in an attempt to deny Oscar the ability to view the database and applies it to a group to which Oscar belongs. Which of the following statements is true?
    - **A.** Oscar will still be able to view the database because a grant overrides a deny.
    - **B.** Oscar will no longer be able to view the database because a deny overrides a grant.
    - **C.** Oscar will no longer be able to view the database, because the deny cancels the grant, giving Oscar no specific permissions.
    - **D.** Oscar will still be able to view the database because granted permissions must be removed with the `revoke` command.
12. A school has a database with four tables, but it needs a fifth table. Which command is used to accomplish this task?
    - **A.** `INSERT`
    - **B.** `UPDATE`
    - **C.** `CREATE`
    - **D.** `ALTER`
13. Michael, an administrator, needs to add a column to an existing table. Which command should he use?
    - **A.** `INSERT`
    - **B.** `UPDATE`
    - **C.** `CREATE`
    - **D.** `ALTER`
14. Laura, your manager, instructs you to remove a table from a database permanently. Which command should you use?
    - **A.** `DELETE`
    - **B.** `REMOVE`
    - **C.** `DROP`
    - **D.** `ALTER`
15. Which of the following statements most accurately describes what a primary key refers to?
    - **A.** A schema in a database
    - **B.** A table in a schema
    - **C.** A field in a table
    - **D.** A record in a table
16. Kate, a database administrator, needs to add records into a database. Which command should she use?
    - **A.** `CREATE`
    - **B.** `INSERT`
    - **C.** `ALTER`
    - **D.** `UPDATE`

17. Henry wants to understand which of his customers has purchased part number BB8. Which command should he use?
    A. `QUERY`
    B. `FIND`
    C. `SEARCH`
    D. `SELECT`

18. George needs to remove a customer's information completely from a table. Which command should he use?
    A. `DELETE`
    B. `DROP`
    C. `ALTER`
    D. `UPDATE`

19. Which of the following descriptions best describes the type of structure that stores values as blobs?
    A. Relational database
    B. Nonrelational database
    C. Document database
    D. Key-value database

20. An employee at your office just got married and changed their last name. Which command do you use to change their last name in the employee database?
    A. `EDIT`
    B. `MODIFY`
    C. `ALTER`
    D. `UPDATE`

Networking Concepts and Technologies

THE FOLLOWING COMPTIA TECH+ FC0-U71 EXAM OBJECTIVES ARE COVERED IN THIS CHAPTER:

✓ **1.0 IT Concepts and Terminology**

✓ **1.3 Compare and contrast common units of measure.**

- Throughput unit
  - Bits per second (bps)
  - Kilobits per second (Kbps)
  - Megabits per second (Mbps)
  - Gigabits per second (Gbps)
  - Terabytes per second (Tbps)

✓ **2.0 Infrastructure**

✓ **2.3 Compare and contrast storage types.**

- Local network storage
  - Network-attached storage (NAS)
  - File server
  - Cloud storage service

✓ **2.7 Compare and contrast common internet service types.**

- Fiber optic
- Cable
- Digital subscriber line (DSL)
- Wireless
  - RF
  - Satellite
  - Cellular

✓ **2.8 Identify basic networking concepts.**

- Basics of network communication
- Network identifiers
  - IP address
  - Media access control (MAC) address
  - Ports
- Basic network services
  - Secure web browsing
  - File transfer
  - Email
- Networking devices
  - Modem
  - Router
  - Switch
  - Access point
  - Firewall
- Networking models
  - Client/server
  - Peer-to-peer
- Local area network (LAN)
- Wide area network (WAN)

✓ **2.9 Explain the basic capabilities of a small wireless network.**

- 802.11n/ac/ax
  - Speed considerations
  - Interference and attenuation factors
- **Older vs. newer standards**
- **Band options**
  - 2.4GHz
  - 5GHz
  - 6GHz

✓ **6.0 Security**

✓ **6.5 Given a scenario, configure security settings for a small wireless network.**

- Changing the service set identifier (SSID)
- Changing the default password
- Encrypted vs. unencrypted
    - Open
    - Pre-shared key
    - Wireless Protected Access (WPA)
    - Wireless Protected Access 2 (WPA2)
    - Wireless Protected Access 3 (WPA3)

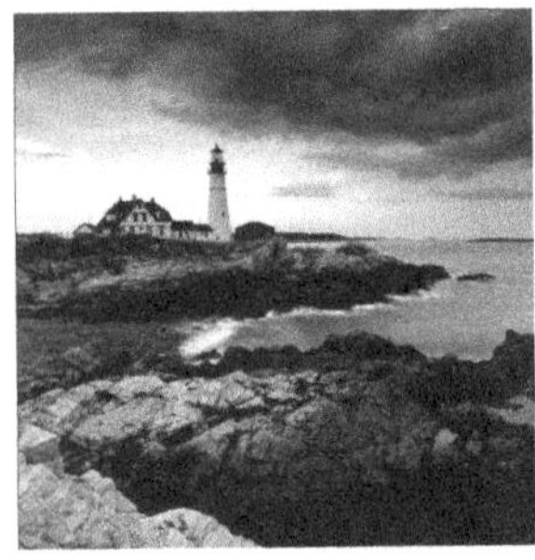

It seems like nearly everyone is on the Internet these days. Media used to be restricted to desktop and laptop computers but is now accessible by small handheld devices such as smartphones and even smartwatches. This chapter is called "Networking Concepts and Technologies," but it could just as easily be called "Getting on the Internet."

Now, to be fair, this chapter is about setting up a small network for your *small office/home office (SOHO)* environment, which means it's about connecting computers to each other and not just the Internet. It just happens that many of us get twitchy when we have to go more than a few hours without getting our update on what's going on in the world.

To start off this chapter, I'll cover network connection types and features. If you're new to networking, this will be a good primer for you to understand the different types of connections that you can make both within a network and when connecting your network to the outside world. As part of that discussion, I'll compare and contrast the different types of connections so that you can make the best decision possible for your needs.

The second major section of this chapter will discuss key networking concepts. This includes devices to make the network function, protocols and addressing, and the basics of data transmission.

The third major section of this chapter will focus on setting up a small wireless network. First, I'll show you some key steps to take in order to set up and configure the network. I will then take that base of information and dive into securing the network. All of this is designed to give you what you really want: a reliable connection to other computers (and the Internet!).

Exploring Connection Types and Features

There are a lot of analogies that we can make between humans and computers. You've already heard analogies for hardware, such as the motherboard being the nervous system of a computer and the processor the brain. These comparisons continue when it comes to connecting computers together.

For people to communicate with one another, they need to be connected somehow. It used to be that people needed to be in the same physical location to speak to each other. Then, technology improved, and by 1876 people could say things like, "Mr. Watson, come here. I want to see you," into a little box with wires sticking out of it, and other people could hear them in the next room. That technology worked well enough, but then humans figured out how to communicate via radio waves. Today, humans are so advanced as a species that when some apparently crazy individual walks down the street seemingly talking loudly to himself, he might actually be talking to a good friend halfway around the world by using a small wireless device in his ear. The line between insanity and technology-enabled has blurred a bit possibly, but that's not the point of this section.

The point is that computers need to be connected to each other to communicate as well. The same also holds true for our other mobile electronic devices. The first computer networks relied on wired physical connections, and technology has evolved to provide relatively high-speed wireless communications as well.

There are several available options when it comes to connecting devices together. These options fall into two major buckets: wired and wireless. In the next two sections, I am going to cover these in terms of connections that you might make to the external world (that is, the Internet) and then connections that you might make on an internal network.

There are two reasons for organizing the chapter this way. First, later in this chapter you will learn how to set up and configure a small wireless network using a SOHO router. The assumption is that you're setting up a network because you will have computers (or mobile devices) connected to this router, and you will also have this router connected to the rest of the world. It's hard to know how to make these connections without the right background. Second, wired and wireless technologies have different pros and cons, which make some better suited for external connections than for internal connections, and vice versa.

Finally, you also need to think about the future. When choosing a connection type, think not only about what your needs are today but also what they could be in two or three years. There is no sense in going overboard and buying a top-of-the-line solution if it's not needed, but you do want to plan for expansion if that's a possibility.

The goal is that by the end of this section, you will be able to make informed decisions on which type of connection is best for any situation.

Choosing External Network Connections

By "external" connection, I really mean "Internet" connection because that's the most common connection type, by a significant margin. Historically, Internet connections were always wired and could be broadly broken into two categories: dial-up and broadband, such as DSL or cable Internet. Now with 5G and other technologies, a wireless connection can be viable for Internet use as well. Each has pros and cons but the major factors to weigh are throughput and cost.

Your Internet connection will give you online service through an *Internet service provider (ISP)*. The type of service that you want will often determine your ISP choices. For example, if you want cable Internet, your choices are limited to your local cable companies and a few national providers. I'll outline some of the features of each type of service and discuss why you might or might not want a specific connection type based on the situation.

Dial-up/POTS

One of the oldest ways of communicating with ISPs and remote networks is through dial-up connections. Although this is still possible, dial-up is rarely used anymore because of the prevalence of broadband options. In addition, dial-up is painfully slow because of limitations on modem speed, which tops out at 56 Kbps. (The U.S. Federal Communications

Commission [FCC] actually limits download speeds to 53 Kbps, so there was never any sense in modem manufacturers trying to exceed this threshold.) Dial-up uses modems that operate over regular phone lines—that is, the *plain old telephone service (POTS)*—and cannot compare to speeds possible with broadband. In 2000, about 74 percent of American households used dial-up Internet connections. By 2021 that number had dropped to about 0.1 percent. Most of the people who still use dial-up do it because high-speed access isn't available where they live.

The biggest advantage to dial-up is that it's cheap and relatively easy to configure. The only hardware that you need is a modem and a phone cable. You dial into a server (such as an ISP's server), provide a username and a password, and you're on the Internet.

Companies also have the option to grant users dial-up access to their networks. As with Internet connections, this option used to be a lot more popular than it is today. Microsoft offers a server-side product to facilitate this called Remote Access Service (RAS), as do many other companies. Today, you might still hear people talking about connecting remotely to your company's network as "remote access."

It seems that dial-up is considered to be a relic from the Stone Age of Internet access. But these are some reasons why it might be the right solution:

- The only hardware it requires is a modem and a phone cord.
- It's relatively easy to set up and configure.
- It's the cheapest online solution (usually $10 to $20 per month).
- You can use it wherever there is phone service, which is just about everywhere.

Of course, there are reasons why a dial-up connection might not be appropriate. The big one is speed. If you need to download files or have substantial data requirements, dial-up is probably too slow. In addition, with limited bandwidth, it's really good only for one computer. It *is* possible to share a dial-up Internet connection by using software tools, but it's also possible to push a stalled car up a muddy hill. Neither option sounds like much fun.

Reviewing Throughput Speeds

In Chapter 2, "Peripherals and Connectors," you were introduced to throughput units as part of Tech+ exam objective 1.3, "Compare and contrast common units of measure." Here's a reminder of that concept.

The most basic measure of throughput is in bits per second (bps)—that is, how many bits are transmitted across the network media (or wireless connection) any given second. Each of the following designations increases that speed by 1000 times:

- Kilobits per second (Kbps)
- Megabits per second (Mbps)
- Gigabits per second (Gbps)
- Terabits per second (Tbps)

So, Kbps is 1,000 bps, Mbps is one million bits per second, Gbps is one trillion bits per second, and Tbps is one quadrillion bits per second. Note that in the exam objectives, the Tbps acronym is spelled out as *Terabytes per second*. Any abbreviation of bits will use a lowercase *b*, whereas bytes will always be abbreviated with an uppercase *B*.

DSL

One of the two most popular broadband choices for home use is *digital subscriber line (DSL)*. It utilizes existing phone lines and provides fairly reliable high-speed access. To use DSL, you need a DSL modem (see Figure 8.1) and a network card in your computer. The ISP usually provides the DSL modem (the one shown in Figure 8.1 is also a router), but you can also purchase them in a variety of electronics stores. You use a network cable with an RJ45 connector to plug your network card into the DSL modem (see Figure 8.2) and use the phone cord to plug the DSL modem into the phone outlet.

FIGURE 8.1 A DSL modem

FIGURE 8.2 The back of the DSL modem

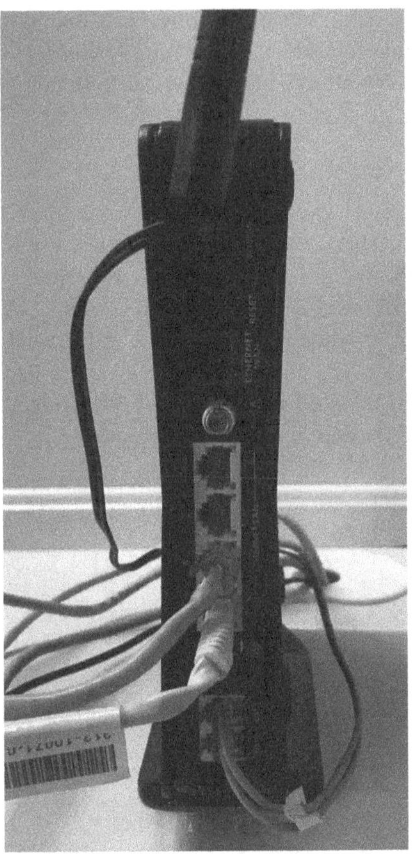

Instead of plugging your computer directly into the DSL modem, you can plug your computer into a router (such as a wireless router) and then plug the router into the DSL modem. This allows multiple devices to use the DSL connection.

There are actually several different forms of DSL, including *high bit-rate DSL (HDSL)*, *very high bit-rate DSL (VDSL)*, *rate-adaptive DSL (RADSL)*, *symmetric DSL (SDSL)*, and *asymmetric DSL (ADSL)*. The most popular in-home form of DSL is ADSL. It's asymmetrical because it supports download speeds that are faster than upload speeds. Dividing up the total available bandwidth this way makes sense because most Internet traffic is downloaded, not uploaded. Imagine a 10-lane highway. If you knew that 8 out of 10 cars that drove on the highway went south, wouldn't you make 8 lanes southbound and only 2 lanes northbound? That is essentially what ADSL does.

ADSL and voice communications can work at the same time over the phone line because they use different frequencies on the same wire.

The first ADSL standard was approved in 1998 and offered maximum download speeds of 8 Mbps and upload speeds of 1 Mbps. Today, you will see telephone companies offer maximum DSL download speeds of around 30 Mbps with 5 Mbps uploads. The speed you actually get will vary depending on a lot of factors, including the distance you are from the phone company's equipment.

You will probably see Internet providers offering broadband speeds of 1 Gbps or faster, and they might call it DSL. Technically, though, speeds that fast are fiber-optic connections, which are covered later. Over the last few years, the lines between DSL and fiber-optic Internet have blurred considerably. It used to be that you ordered one or the other. Today, it's more common to order a broadband speed and the provider figures out if they will give it to you via traditional copper wires (DSL) or fiber-optic. It usually depends simply upon which type of cable is run to the curb in front of your residence. While most existing homes have copper cabling run to them, not all have fiber. DSL providers are replacing copper with fiber, but it will take a while for all of the old copper lines to be replaced. Conversely, new construction might have fiber-optic cabling but no copper. Ultimately, the DSL provider will tell you what speeds are available to you based on the wiring type available at your location.

One major advantage that DSL providers tout is that with DSL you do not share bandwidth with other customers, whereas that may not be true with cable modems.

To summarize, here are some advantages to using DSL:

- It's *much* faster than dial-up.
- Your bandwidth is not shared with other users.
- It's generally very reliable (depending on your ISP).

There are some potential disadvantages of using DSL:

- DSL may not be available in your area. There are distance limitations as to how far away from the phone company's central office you can be to get DSL. Usually this isn't a problem in metro areas, but it could be a problem in rural areas.
- DSL requires more hardware than dial-up: a network card, a network cable, a DSL modem, a phone cord, and line filters for each phone in the home. And you usually pay a monthly rental fee for the DSL modem.
- The cost is higher. Lower-speed packages often start off at around $30 to $40 per month, but the ones advertised with great data rates can easily run you $100 a month or more.
- If you are in a house or building with older wiring, the older phone lines may not be able to support the full speed for which you were paying.

That said, DSL is a popular choice for both small businesses and home users. If it's available, it's easy to get the phone company to bundle your service with your landline and bill you at the same time. Often, you'll also get a package discount for having multiple services. Most important, you can hook up the DSL modem to your router or wireless router and share the Internet connection among several computers.

To see whether DSL is available in your area, go to `www.dslreports.com`. You can also talk to your local telephone service provider.

With many people using their mobile phones as their home phones and landlines slowly fading into history, you may wonder whether this causes a problem if you want DSL. Not really. Many phone providers will provide you DSL without a landline (called *naked DSL*). Of course, you are going to have to pay a surcharge for the use of the phone line if you don't already use one.

Tech+ exam objective 2.7, "Compare and contrast common internet service types," wants you to be familiar with DSL, cable, and fiber-optic wired connectivity.

Cable

The other half of the popular home-broadband duet is the *cable modem*. These provide high-speed Internet access through your cable service, much like DSL does over phone lines. You plug your computer into the cable modem using a standard Ethernet cable, just as you would plug into a DSL modem. The only difference is that the other connection goes into a cable TV jack instead of the phone jack. Cable Internet provides broadband Internet access via a specification known as Data Over Cable Service Internet Specification (DOCSIS). Anyone who can get a cable TV connection should be able to get the service.

As advertised, cable Internet connections are generally faster than DSL connections. While cable is generally regarded as faster than DSL, a big caveat to these speeds is that they are not guaranteed, and they can vary. And again, with many phone companies not really differentiating between DSL and fiber-optic, it can be difficult to understand exactly what you're comparing.

One of the reasons that speeds may vary is that you are sharing available bandwidth within your distribution network. The size of the network varies, but it is usually between 100 and 2,000 customers. Some of them may have cable modems too, and access can be slower during peak usage times. Another reason is that cable companies make liberal use of bandwidth throttling. If you read the fine print on some of their packages that promise the fast speeds, one of the technical details is that they boost your download speed for the first 10 MB or 20 MB of a file transfer, and then they throttle your speed back down to your normal rate.

It may seem as though I am a bit negative about cable modems, but you need to understand exactly what you are getting. In practice, the speeds of cable modems are pretty comparable to those of DSL. Both have pros and cons when it comes to reliability and speed of service, but most of that varies by service provider and isn't necessarily reflective of the technology. When it comes right down to it, the choice you make between DSL and cable (if both are available in your area) may depend on which company offers the best package deal: phone and DSL through your telephone company or cable TV and cable modem from your cable provider.

To summarize, here are the advantages to using cable:

- It's *much* faster than dial-up, and it can be faster than DSL (particularly for uploads).
- You're not required to have or use a telephone landline.
- It's generally very reliable (depending on your ISP).

As with anything else, there are possible disadvantages to using cable.

- Cable may not be available in your area. In metro areas this normally isn't a problem, but it could be in rural areas.
- Cable requires more hardware than dial-up: a network card, a network cable, and a cable modem. Most ISPs will charge you a one-time fee or a monthly lease fee for the cable modem.
- Your bandwidth is shared with everyone on your network segment, usually a neighborhood-sized group of homes. Everyone shares the available bandwidth. During peak times, your access speed may slow down.
- The cost is higher. Lower-speed packages often start off at around $20 to $30 per month, but the ones they advertise with the great data rates can easily run you $100 a month or more.

Cable modems can be connected directly to a computer, but they can also be connected to a router or wireless router just like a DSL modem. Therefore, you can share an Internet connection over a cable modem.

For detailed information about broadband Internet availability and performance, check out `www.highspeedinternet.com`.

Fiber-Optic Internet

Fiber-optic cable is pretty impressive with the speed and bandwidth it delivers. For nearly all of fiber-optic cable's existence, it's been used mostly for high-speed telecommunications and for network backbones. This is because it is much more expensive than copper to install and operate. The cables themselves are pricier, and so is the hardware at the end of the cables.

Technology follows this inevitable path of getting cheaper the longer it exists, and fiber is really starting to embrace its destiny. Many telephone and media companies offer fiber-optic Internet connections for home subscribers.

An example of one such option is Fios, offered by Verizon. It offers *Fiber-to-the-Home (FTTH)* service, which means that the cables are 100 percent fiber from their data centers to your home. As of this writing, the fastest speeds offered were 2.3 Gbps download and 1.5 Gbps upload. That means you could download a two-hour HD movie in just about 25 seconds. That's ridiculous.

Are there any downsides to a fiber Internet connection? Really only two come to mind. The first is availability. It's more limited than cable or DSL, although phone companies are rapidly installing fiber throughout the country. More rural areas will likely be the last to see it. The second is price. That great fast connection can cost you about $200 a month.

Wireless Internet

The four Internet service types covered so far are all wired options. In some cases, wired isn't an option. Perhaps someone lives on a mountainside without wired choices, or maybe someone simply wants the convenience of not being tethered to a location for Internet. The next three options covered are wireless.

The wireless Internet options you need to know for exam objective 2.7 are satellite, cellular, and radio frequency (RF).

Satellite

One type of broadband Internet connection that does not get much fanfare is satellite Internet. *Satellite Internet* is not much like any other type of broadband connection. Instead of a cabled connection, it uses a satellite dish to receive data from an orbiting satellite and relay station that is connected to the Internet. Satellite connections are typically a little slower than wired broadband connections, often maxing out at around 150 Mbps download and 3 Mbps upload.

The need for a satellite dish and the reliance on its technology are one of the major drawbacks to satellite Internet. People who own satellite dishes will tell you that there are occasional problems due to weather and satellite alignment. You must keep the satellite dish aimed precisely at the satellite or your signal strength (and thus your connection reliability and speed) will suffer. Plus, cloudy or stormy days can cause interference with the signal, especially if there are high winds that could blow the satellite dish out of alignment. Receivers are typically small satellite dishes (like the ones used for DIRECTV or Dish Network) but can also be portable satellite modems (modems the size of a briefcase) or portable satellite phones.

Satellite Internet is often referred to as *line-of-sight* wireless because it does require a clear line of sight between the user and the transmitter.

Another drawback to satellite technology is the delay (also called *connection delay*), or *latency*. The delay occurs because of the length of time required to transmit the data and receive a response via the satellite. This delay (between 250 and 350 milliseconds) comes from the time it takes the data to travel the approximately 35,000 kilometers into space and return. To compare it with other types of broadband signals, cable and DSL have a delay between the customer and an ISP of 10 to 30 milliseconds. With standard web and email traffic, this delay, while slightly annoying, is acceptable. However, with technologies like VoIP and live Internet gaming, the delay is intolerable.

Online gamers are especially sensitive to latency. They often refer to it as *ping time*. The higher the ping time (in milliseconds), the worse the response time in the game. It sometimes means the difference between winning and losing an online game.

Finally, installation can be tricky. When installing a satellite system, you need to ensure that the satellite dish on the ground is pointed at precisely the right spot in the sky to ensure line of sight. This can be tricky to do if you're not trained, but some have a utility that helps you see how close you are to being right on (you're getting warmer . . . warmer . . .).

Of course, satellite also has advantages or no one would use it. First, satellite connections are incredibly useful when you are in an area where it's difficult or impossible to run a cable or if your Internet access needs are mobile and cellular data rates just don't cut it.

The second advantage is due to the nature of the connection. This type of connection is called *point-to-multipoint* because one satellite can provide a signal to a number of receivers simultaneously. It's used in a variety of applications from telecommunications and handheld GPSs to television and radio broadcasts and a host of others.

Real World Scenario

All in the Name of Entertainment

As a teenager, I worked for a local television station during the summer. Each summer, the television station would broadcast a Senior PGA golf tournament that was held at a nearby mountain course.

Before the tournament, the crew would spend three days setting up the control truck, cameras, and link back to the station. (It was a network with TV cameras instead of workstations!) Because of the remote location, the crew had to set up a satellite uplink to get the signals back to civilization. From the control truck, a transmitter was pointed at a relay station on the side of the mountain, which in turn was pointed at a satellite orbiting the earth. It took a team of four engineers to get it set up. Two engineers would stay at the truck, and two others would board ATVs and journey up the remote mountainside. Once in position, they would set up the relay station, which looked a lot like a keg of beer with a few antennas. The engineers at the truck would adjust their directional microwave transmitter until the relay station received a strong signal. Then the engineers on the mountainside would perform the arduous task of pointing their transmitter at the satellite.

It was a long and tedious process, and that's really the point of the story. Satellite was the *only* option available to complete the network, but satellite networks can be a challenge to set up and configure.

Cellular (Cellular Networking)

Cellular Internet connections were for years relegated to serving only one mobile device, because connection speeds were limited. Now with fifth generation (5G) cellular available, speeds are good enough that cellular can be considered a legitimate wireless Internet option.

5G started to become available in early 2019, replacing the earlier fourth generation (4G) standard, which of course replaced third-generation (3G) cellular in about 2011. If you've learned anything so far from this book, it might be that newer generations of technology are always faster than older ones, and cellular is no different. 3G technology was limited to about 500 Kbps downloads, and 4G enhancements over time increased that to a respectable 100 Mbps. With 5G, users can currently get up to 1 Gbps downloads, and major cellular providers are always looking for ways to increase that.

The sixth generation (6G) of cellular networking is currently under development, with standardization expected sometime between 2025 and 2029. Experts in the field suggest it will become commercially available around the year 2030.

Because 5G is so fast, many users choose to connect laptops or similar devices to the Internet through their smartphones or cellular-enabled tablets. This is called using the smartphone as a *mobile hotspot*. Once enabled on the smartphone, the laptop makes a Wi-Fi connection to the phone and then has Internet access. In iOS, a hotspot is enabled in Settings ➢ Personal Hotspot, as shown in Figure 8.3a. Toggle the Allow Others To Join option on, and then enter the password on the device that needs access. Android users can find the hotspot option in Settings ➢ Connections ➢ Mobile Hotspot And Tethering ➢ Mobile Hotspot (Figure 8.3b). Once enabled, the password and security settings are customized by tapping Configure.

Before enabling a phone as a hotspot, be sure to understand if the wireless plan supports it and under what conditions. Hotspot usage can quickly consume significant amounts of data and you don't want to be hit with surprise charges!

Radio Frequency Internet

Wireless *radio frequency (RF) broadband Internet* access is one of the newest options for home Internet. Cellular providers might offer it as "cellular home Internet" or "fixed wireless" plans. Typically, the service provider uses a transmitter, similar to a cell tower (but much less powerful), to broadcast a signal. At the receiving end, customers need a radio receiver and wireless antenna. The receiver plugs into a router or computer just like a cable or DSL modem. Cellular providers will note that it might not be available in all areas.

FIGURE 8.3 iOS (a) and Android (b) hotspot configuration

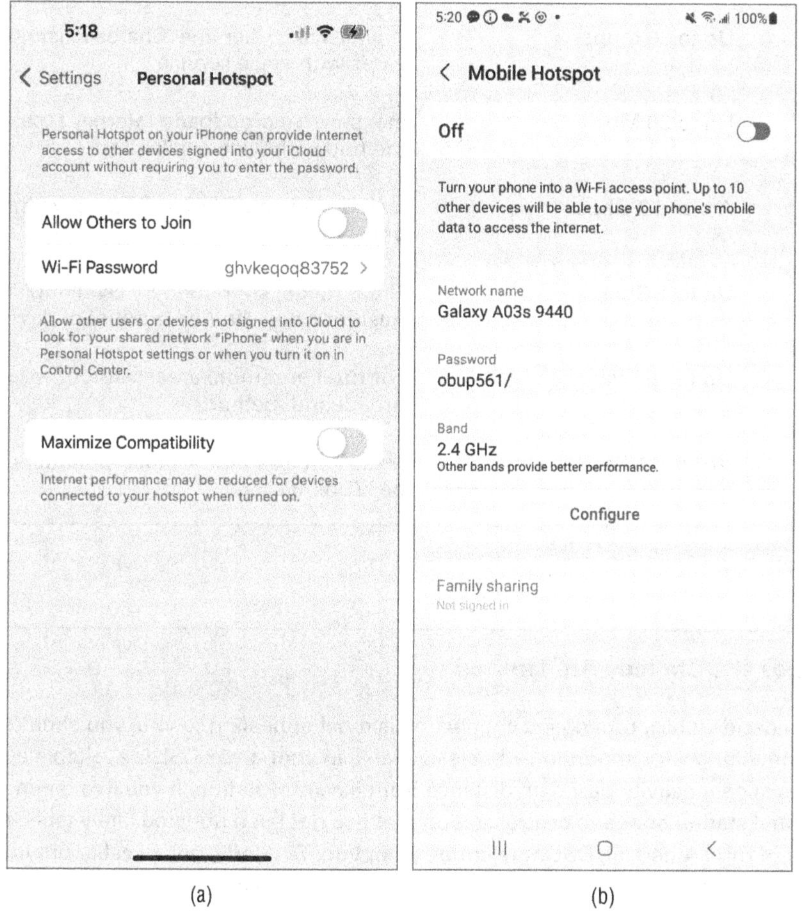

Radio frequency Internet speed is similar to cellular Internet. The maximum will depend on the technology at play, so a 5G fixed wireless connection will give the user up to about 1 Gbps. The cost generally starts off at around $40–$60 per month, and you may get a discount if you bundle your cellular service with it.

Table 8.1 summarizes the connection types that you have just learned. In Exercise 8.1, you will scout out the Internet connection options in your area.

TABLE 8.1 Common Internet connection types and speeds

Designation	Maximum download speed	Description
Dial-up	Up to 56 Kbps	Plain old telephone service. A regular analog phone line.
DSL	Up to 30 Mbps	Digital subscriber line. Shares existing phone wires with voice service.
Cable	Up to 50 Mbps	Inexpensive broadband Internet access method with wide availability.
Fiber-optic	Around 2 Gbps	Incredibly fast and more expensive than DSL or cable.
Cellular	Up to 1 Gbps	Great range; supported by cellular providers. Best for a very limited number of devices.
Satellite	Up to 150 Mbps	For rural or remote areas without wired broadband methods.
Radio frequency	Around 1 Gbps	Fixed wireless from cellular providers. May be 5G or 4G.

Sometimes the Choices Are Limited

Before you decide which broadband connection is most appealing to you, you should also factor in something very important: what is available in your area? DSL is available at different rates of connectivity based on distance from a central station. If you live far enough from a central station or near a central station that has not been updated lately (such as in the middle of rural America), DSL may not be an option. Similarly, not all cable providers are willing to take the steps necessary to run a connection in all situations.

Make certain that you know the available options—not just the technological options—before you spend too much time determining what is best for you.

EXERCISE 8.1

Pricing Internet Connectivity

If you're unsure which websites to visit to perform this exercise, visit `www.highspeedinternet.com` to see who offers service in your area.

1. Visit the website for a telephone provider in your area, and see what offers are available for DSL. What is the most basic package that you can get, and what does it cost? What is the fastest package that you can get, and what does it cost?
2. Visit the website for a cable television provider in your area, and see what offers are available for cable Internet. What is the most basic package that you can get, and what does it cost? What is the fastest package that you can get, and what does it cost?
3. Visit the website for a satellite Internet provider. If you're not familiar with one, `www.hughesnet.com` is a popular provider. What is the fastest package that you can get, and what does it cost?
4. (Optional) Can you find a dial-up ISP in your area? How much does it cost?

Choosing Internal Network Connections

Along with deciding how your computers will get to the outside world, you need to think about how your computers will communicate with each other on your internal network. The choices you make will depend on the speed you need, distance and security requirements, and cost involved with installation and maintenance. It may also depend some on the abilities of the installer. You may feel comfortable replacing copper cables but not so much when it comes to fiber-optic. Your choices for internal connections can be lumped into two groups: wired and wireless.

Many networks today are a hybrid of wired and wireless connections. Understand the fundamentals of how each works separately; then you can understand how they work together. Every wireless connection eventually connects back to a wired network point somehow.

Wired Network Connections

Wired connections form the backbone of nearly every network in existence. Even as wireless becomes more popular, the importance of wired connections remains strong. In general, wired networks are faster and more secure than their wireless counterparts.

When it comes to choosing a wired network connection type, you need to think about speed, distance, and cost. Your two choices are *unshielded twisted pair (UTP)*, which is copper and transmits using electrical pulses, and *fiber-optic*, which is made of glass or plastic and transmits using light. You'll run one of the two (or maybe a combination of the two), with UTP being by far the most popular choice. The most common configuration when you use either of these is to connect all computers to a central connectivity device, such as a *switch*. If you're using a wireless router with some wired ports, that works too.

The first question you need to ask yourself is, "How fast does this network need to be?" For home networks, the 1 Gbps provided by UTP running Gigabit Ethernet is probably sufficient. If you have higher throughput requirements, then you can start looking into faster standards (10–40 Gbps).

What Is Ethernet?

Ethernet is a standard for wired computer network communications, as defined by the Institute of Electrical and Electronics Engineers (IEEE) 802.3 specification. It specifies that only one computer can talk on a wired network at one time; a computer will listen on the network cable, and if it doesn't hear any traffic, it will transmit. If two or more computers attempt to talk at once, the network packets will collide, and no communication will get to its destination. The sending computers will detect this, wait a short random amount of time, and then resend their data. This whole process is called *Carrier Sense Multiple Access with Collision Detection (CSMA/CD)*.

In 1990, the Ethernet specification called for transmissions of 10 Mbps over twisted-pair copper cable. At the time, the cable standard was Category 3 (Cat 3) UTP. By 1991, a standard was developed for Cat 5 cable, and it could handle speeds of 100 Mbps. (They increased the number of twists per foot in the cable.) The Ethernet standard was updated to account for this faster speed and was called Fast Ethernet.

The Cat 5e (enhanced) cable standard was introduced in 2001 and could handle speeds of 1 Gbps, so running Ethernet over Cat 5e became known as Gigabit Ethernet. Cat 6a came along in 2008, supporting speeds of 10 Gbps (10-Gigabit Ethernet). The most current version is Cat 8. It was ratified in 2016 and supports speeds up to 40 Gbps at up to 30 meters or 10 Gbps at up to 100 meters. It will be used mostly in server rooms for the foreseeable future.

In the real world, you'll hear people ask if you have an Ethernet cable, which is typically synonymous with the words *network cable* and *twisted-pair cable*. Most of the time, people don't differentiate between the standards, assuming that you just have Cat 5e or better. It's usually a good assumption, considering it's hard to find anything older. If you know that you're running 10-Gig E, then you might want to specify at least a Cat 6a cable.

When referring to UTP cable types, there is no consensus on how to abbreviate category names. For example, you will see Cat 8, Cat-8, CAT 8, and CAT-8 all used. None of them are right or wrong, and it makes no difference in the cable's performance.

The second question is then, "What is the maximum distance I'll need to run any one cable?" In most office environments, you can configure your network in such a way that 100 meters will get you from any connectivity device to the end user. If you need to go longer than that, you'll definitely need fiber for that connection unless you want to mess with signal repeaters.

As you're thinking about what type of cable to use, also consider the hardware that you'll need. If you are going to run fiber to the desktop, you'll need fiber network cards, routers, and switches. If you are running UTP, you'll need network cards, routers, and switches with RJ45 connectors. If you're going to run gigabit, all of your devices will need to support it.

The third question to ask yourself is, "How big of a deal is security?" Most of the time, the answer lies somewhere between "very" and "extremely"! Copper cable is pretty secure, but it does emit a signal that can be intercepted, meaning that people can tap into your transmissions (hence the term *wiretap*). Fiber-optic cables are immune to wiretapping. Normally, this isn't a big deal because copper cables don't exactly broadcast your data all over as a wireless connection does. But if security is of the utmost concern, then fiber is the way to go.

Fourth, "Is there a lot of electrical interference in the area?" Transmissions across a copper cable can be ravaged by the effects of *electromagnetic interference (EMI)*, which is interference from objects like motors, power cables, microwave ovens, and fluorescent lights. The effects include shortened distances that electrical signals can travel or lower transmission speeds. Fiber is immune to those effects.

Finally, ask yourself about cost. Fiber cables and hardware are more expensive than their copper counterparts. Table 8.2 summarizes your cable choices and provides characteristics of each.

Understand that the costs shown in Table 8.2 are approximate and are for illustrative purposes only. The cost for this equipment in your area may differ. Fiber has gotten considerably cheaper in the last 10 to 15 years, but it's still far more expensive than copper.

Fiber-optic cabling has some obvious advantages over copper, but as you can see, it may be prohibitively expensive to run fiber to the desktop. What a lot of organizations will do is to use fiber sparingly, where it is needed the most, and then run copper to the desktop. Fiber will be used in the server room and perhaps between floors of a building as well as any place where a very long cable run is needed.

TABLE 8.2 Cable types and characteristics

Characteristics	Twisted-pair	Fiber-optic
Transmission rate	Cat 5e: 1 Gbps Cat 6a: 10 Gbps Cat 8: 40 Gbps	100 Mbps to 100 Gbps
Maximum length	100 meters (328 feet) for up to 10 Gbps 30 meters (100 feet) for 40 Gbps	~100 kilometers (62 miles)
Flexibility	Very flexible	Fair
Ease of installation	Very easy	Difficult
Connector	RJ45	Special (SC, ST, and others)
Interference (security)	Susceptible	Not susceptible
Overall cost	Inexpensive	Expensive
NIC cost	1 Gbps: $25–$40 10 Gbps+: $70 and up	$50–$150; easily $600–$800 for server NICs
10-foot cable cost	Cat 6/6a: $8–$15 Cat 8: $10–$20	Depends on mode and connector type, but generally $15–$30
8-port switch cost	10/100 Mbps: $30–$50 1 Gbps: $70–$400 10 Gbps: $200–$800	$350 and up

Wireless Network Connections

People love wireless networks for one major reason: convenience. Wireless connections enable a sense of freedom in users. They're not stuck to their desk—they can work from anywhere! (I'm not sure if this is actually a good thing.) Wireless isn't as fast, and it tends to be a bit more expensive than wired copper networks, but the convenience factor far outweighs these drawbacks.

Wireless LAN (WLAN)

When thinking about using wireless for network communications, the only real technology option available today for a *wireless local area network (WLAN)* is IEEE 802.11. Bluetooth and infrared (which I'll cover in just a bit) can help mobile devices communicate, but they aren't designed for full WLAN use. Your choice becomes which 802.11 standard you want to use. Table 8.3 summarizes the different standards.

Tech+ exam objective 2.9, "Explain the basic capabilities of a small wireless network," focuses on Wi-Fi standards and specifications. You should be the most familiar with 802.11n/ac/ax, and understand basic speed differences and interference and attenuation factors. Also be familiar with the older standards, and understand implications of different frequency band options.

TABLE 8.3 802.11 standards

Standard	Generation name	Year	Frequency	Maximum data rate	Indoor range	Outdoor range
a		1999	5 GHz	54 Mbps	35 m	120 m
b		1999	2.4 GHz	11 Mbps	40 m	140 m
g		2003	2.4 GHz	54 Mbps	40 m	140 m
n		2008	2.4/5 GHz	600 Mbps	70 m	250 m
ac	Wi-Fi 5	2014	5 GHz	3500 Mbps	35 m	120 m
ax	Wi-Fi 6	2019	2.4/5 GHz	9600 Mbps	70 m	250 m
ax	Wi-Fi 6E	2021	6 GHz	9600 Mbps	15 m	15 m
be	Wi-Fi 7	2024	2.4/5/6 GHz	46 Gbps	30 m	100 m

Not So Fast . . .

The maximum data rates and distances shown in Table 8.3 are theoretical maximums and should be taken with a large grain of salt. They're estimates based on testing in ideal conditions. First, the distance from the wireless access point to your device makes a huge difference because wireless suffers from *attenuation* (the weakening of signals) more than wired signals. For example, Wi-Fi 5 users will only get the maximum data rate at a range of up to about 5 meters from the access point. At about 20 meters, the data rate is cut in half, and it just gets worse from there. Also keep in mind that's for a clear, unobstructed signal.

Attenuation effects can't be overstated as it affects all forms of wireless communication. At higher frequencies, the maximum distance becomes shorter and attenuation problems are magnified. For example, Wi-Fi 6E, which operates at the highest licensed Wi-Fi frequency of 6 GHz, has a maximum range of about 15 meters, and some users even report losing connection if devices lose line of sight. Granted, Wi-Fi 6E routers have the option to fall back to lower frequencies to maintain longer connections, but the speed will be slower.

As a second example of the effects of frequency on distance, consider terrestrial AM radio. In the United States, AM radio is regulated between 540 kHz and 1700 kHz. During the daytime, the maximum range is about 162 kilometers (100 miles). At night, AM radio signals can bounce off the atmosphere and reach three times as far. AM radio signals interfering with each other became such a problem that in 1934 the FCC made a law that AM radio stations must decrease their power at night as to decrease their signal range or cease broadcasting altogether.

Second, *interference* from other electronics and obstructions will lower the data rate. Radio frequency interference (RFI) from communications devices will degrade the signal. Microwave ovens and electrical motors are notoriously harsh on wireless signals. Solid objects, especially concrete block walls and steel, cut down on range as well.

Third, wireless bandwidth is shared among all devices connecting on that wireless network. Real-world testing shows that Wi-Fi 5 devices usually deliver between 300 Mbps and 1.7 Gbps, and Wi-Fi 6 will range from 600 Mbps to 4.8 Gbps.

New generation Wi-Fi speeds are still incredibly fast. Just don't be too disappointed if the wireless performance you're expecting isn't quite as great as advertised!

So, how do you choose which one is right for your situation? You can apply the same thinking that you would do for a wired network in that you need to consider speed, distance, security, and cost. Generally speaking, though, with wireless it's best to start with the most robust technology and work your way backward.

Security concerns on wireless networks are similar regardless of your choice. Since you're broadcasting network signals through air, there will always be some security concerns. It really comes down to speed and cost.

In today's environment, it's silly to consider anything older than 802.11n, and good luck finding hardware that old anyway. Deciding that you are going to install an 802.11g/n network from the ground up at this point is a bit like saying you are going to build a mud house in Manhattan. You could, but why?

Earlier in the "Wired Network Connections" section you learned what Ethernet is, and it's based on the CDMA/CD access method. Wireless 802.11 networks use a similar method to access the network medium (in this case, air), called Carrier Sense Multiple Access with Collision Avoidance (CSMA/CA). The inner workings of these access methods is well beyond the scope of the Tech+ exam, but it's interesting stuff to know.

That brings you to your most likely choices: 802.11ac (Wi-Fi 5) and 802.11ax (Wi-Fi 6/6E). Devices are plentiful and are backward compatible with the previous versions, provided they broadcast on the same frequency. (Many routers are labeled *dual-band*, which means that they support multiple frequencies, such as 5 GHz and 2.4 GHz.) It will come down to cost. In Exercise 8.2, you will go shopping for Wi-Fi gear to understand the cost differences.

To summarize this section and explicitly bring it back to exam objectives, remember the following:

- The three newest standards, from oldest to newest, are 802.11n, 802.11ac (Wi-Fi 5), and 802.11ax (Wi-Fi 6). As standards get newer, they provide faster speeds. Wi-Fi 7 is out but is not currently listed in the Tech+ Exam objectives.
- As a rule of thumb, higher frequencies (e.g., 6 GHz versus 2.4 GHz) will have higher throughput rates, but shorter distances and are more susceptible to attenuation.
- Interference from other devices broadcasting on the same frequency as a Wi-Fi network and natural signal attenuation will shorten maximum distances.

EXERCISE 8.2

The Cost of Networking

1. Visit the website for an electronics store. If you're unfamiliar with any, try `www.bestbuy.com` or `www.newegg.com`.
2. Find a Wi-Fi 6 wireless router. How much is it?
3. Find an older standard. See if you can find an 802.11n one. (Probably not, except for maybe on eBay.) If not, go for Wi-Fi 5. How much is it?
4. Now price out wireless network cards. Find one supporting different standards. How much difference is there?

Bluetooth

Bluetooth is not designed to be a WLAN but rather a *wireless personal area network (WPAN)*. In other words, it's not the right technology to use if you want to set up a wireless network for your office. It is, however, a great technology to use if you have wireless devices with which you want your computer to be able to communicate. Examples include smartphones, mice, keyboards, headsets, speakers, and printers.

Every laptop comes with built-in Wi-Fi capabilities, and most come Bluetooth-enabled. Desktops don't always have it built in, though. To use Bluetooth devices, you might need to add an adapter, such as the one shown in Figure 8.4.

FIGURE 8.4 Bluetooth USB adapter

Almost all smartphones and other mobile devices today support Bluetooth.

Bluetooth devices can belong to one of three classes. Most mobile Bluetooth devices are Class 2 devices, which have a maximum range of 10 meters.

Like some of the 802.11X standards, Bluetooth uses the unlicensed 2.4 GHz range for communication. To avoid interference, Bluetooth can "signal hop" at different frequencies to avoid conflicts with devices using other technologies in the area. Thanks to technology improvements, interference with Wi-Fi is unlikely, but it can still occur.

One of the unusual features of Bluetooth networks is their temporary and informal nature. With Wi-Fi, you need a central communication point, such as a wireless access point or router. Bluetooth networks are formed on an ad hoc basis, meaning that whenever two Bluetooth devices get close enough to each other, they can communicate directly with each other. This dynamically created network is called a *piconet*. A Bluetooth-enabled device can communicate with up to seven other devices in one piconet.

Infrared

Infrared (IR) waves have been around since the beginning of time. They are longer than light waves but shorter than microwaves. The most common use of infrared technology is the television remote control, although infrared is also used in night-vision goggles and medical and scientific imaging.

In 1993, the *Infrared Data Association (IrDA)* was formed as a technical consortium to support "interoperable, low-cost infrared data interconnection standards that support a walk-up, point-to-point user model." The key terms here are *walk-up* and *point-to-point*, meaning that you need to be at very close range to use infrared, and it's designed for one-to-one communication. Infrared requires line of sight, and generally speaking, the two devices need to be pointed at each other to work. If you point your remote away from the television, how well does it work?

You can find more information on the IrDA standard at the organization's website: `www.irda.org`.

Some laptops and mobile devices have a built-in infrared port, which is a small, dark square of plastic, usually black or dark red. For easy access, infrared ports are located on the front or side of devices that have them. Figure 8.5 shows an example of an infrared port on a laptop.

FIGURE 8.5 Infrared port

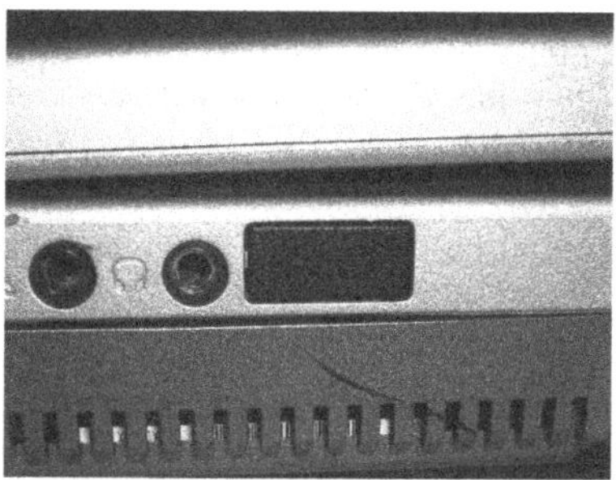

Current IrDA specifications allow transmission of data up to 1 Gbps. Because infrared does not use radio waves, there are no concerns of interference or signal conflicts. Atmospheric conditions can play a role in disrupting infrared waves, but considering that the maximum functional range of an IrDA device is about 1 meter, weather is not likely to cause you any problems.

Security is not much of an issue with infrared. The maximum range is about 1 meter with an angle of about 30 degrees, and the signal does not go through walls, so hacking prospects are limited. If someone is making an attempt to intercept an infrared signal, it's going to be pretty obvious. The data is directional, and you choose when and where to send it.

Different Infrared Technologies

You might have read the 1-meter distance limitation regarding infrared and thought, "But my television remote works at longer distances than that"—and you are right. Television and other consumer electronics remote controls are not governed by IrDA. They use a different infrared technology, based on the RC-5 protocol developed by Philips in the late 1980s. The maximum functional distance of these remote controls is about 15–20 feet, depending on the device.

Computer communications standards using infrared are managed by IrDA, and the maximum distance is about 1 meter. There are methods that IR manufacturers can use to modify this, but the general specification guarantees data rates at only 1 meter.

Understanding Network Connectivity Essentials

The ultimate goal of this chapter is to teach you how to set up your own small wireless network successfully. To do it right and really understand what you're doing, it's important to know some critical details. After all, there's a difference between plugging in a box and having it work and being able to make it work if things don't quite go smoothly.

In the first section of this chapter, you learned how to connect your computers physically to the Internet, as well as to each other via cables or wireless connections. That's the first part. But now that they're connected to each other, *how* do they communicate? That's just as important, and that's what I'll cover here in the second part.

The "how" has two components. The first is the hardware involved, and the second is by using a protocol, which is the communication language. In the next section, you will learn about some common networking devices used to connect computers to each other. Then, the following sections will teach you the basics of networking protocols and TCP/IP, which is the language that most computers speak when they talk to each other on a network. Finally, this section will finish with a discussion of network storage concepts.

Common Networking Devices

It seems like devices on a network do a lot of talking to each other. Users tell their computers to connect to the Internet, send jobs to printers, and spam co-workers who are 5 feet away with emails. All of this happens even though the sending and receiving devices aren't directly connected to each other. Instead, they use connectivity devices to manage the communication. In this section, we'll talk about some of those connectivity devices, as well as a few other important devices to know.

Tech+ exam objective 2.8, "Identify basic networking concepts," wants you to be familiar with several networking devices. They are modems, switches, access points, routers, and firewalls.

Modem

Chapter 1, "Core Hardware Components," covered modems, so I won't repeat too much here. Here's a quick refresher: modems are used to connect to a network via telephone lines. They do that by converting digital signals from a computer into analog signals that can be transmitted over phone lines and back again. As you learned earlier in this chapter, modems are dreadfully slow by today's standards and essentially obsolete.

Switch

A *switch* is the network connectivity device at the center of most networks. You might hear some people call them hubs, but a hub is a similar device that's not quite as good as a switch. They often look similar to hubs, so it's easy to confuse them. There are big performance differences, though. Hubs pass along all traffic, but switches examine the header (beginning portion) of the incoming data packet and forward it properly to the right port and only to that port. (Only one device is plugged into each port.) This greatly reduces overhead and thus improves performance because there is essentially a virtual connection between sender and receiver.

When taking about switches and other connectivity devices, I will refer to ports. Those are literally the physical holes the network cable plugs into on the device. Later in this chapter you will learn about ports in relation to TCP/IP communications (and they are an exam objective)—those are logical in nature and entirely different. Don't let the terminology mess you up!

Nearly every hub or switch that you will see has one or more status indicator lights on it. If there is a connection to a port of the switch, a light either above the connector or on an LED panel elsewhere on the device will light up. If traffic is crossing the port, the light may flash, or there may be a secondary light that will light up. Many devices can also detect a problem in the connection. If a normal connection produces a green light, a bad connection might produce an amber one. Figure 8.6 shows a basic eight-port switch.

FIGURE 8.6 Eight-port switch

Switches direct traffic based on the destination computer's *Media Access Control (MAC)* address, which is its physical address built into the network card.

Access Point

An access point is any point that allows a user on to a network. The term is commonly used in reference to a *wireless access point*, which lets users connect to your network via an 802.11 technology. Wireless access points may connect to other wireless access points or wireless routers, but eventually they connect back to a wired connection with the rest of the network. Wireless access points look nearly identical to wireless routers and provide central connectivity like wireless routers, but they don't have nearly as many features.

Router

A *router* is a highly intelligent network connectivity device that can connect multiple network types to each other. Routers use routing tables to store network addresses and route packets based on the best path available.

Routers are much more advanced than switches. One of the big differences between the two is that while switches direct traffic based on the physical MAC address, routers use the logical IP address to make decisions. (I'll cover MAC and IP addresses in more depth later in this chapter.) Routers are also capable of connecting more devices to each other than switches can do. Figure 8.7 shows you how routers and switches might work together on a network.

FIGURE 8.7 Sample network with routers and switches

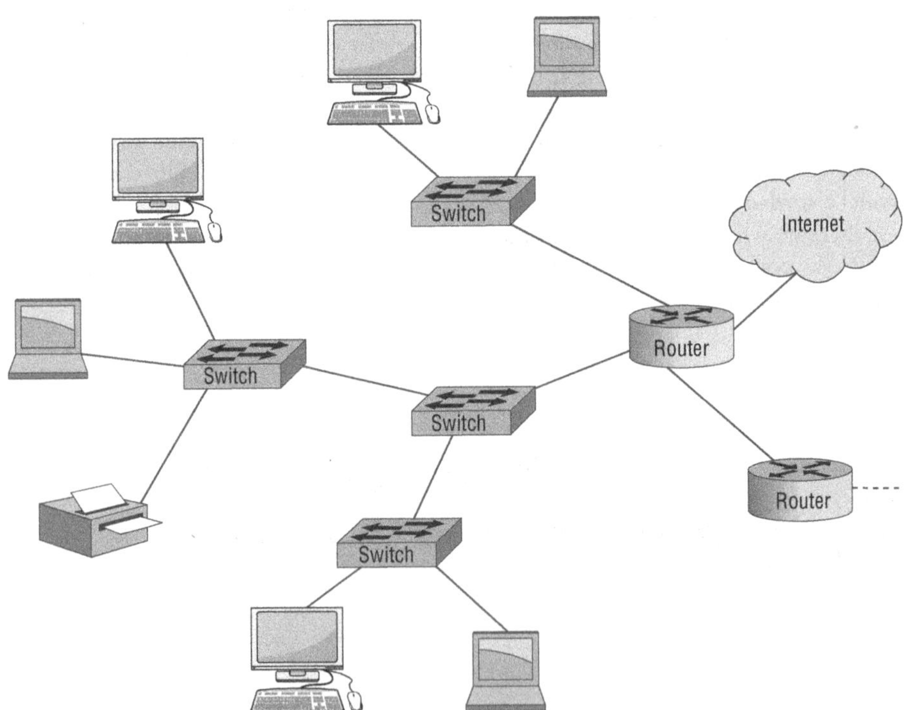

Figure 8.7 depicts a wired network, but it could just as easily show a wireless one. Instead of switches, there would be wireless access points. The routers could be wired or wireless, but remember that all connections lead back to wired ones at some point.

Wireless routers are common in homes and offices. Physically, they look like wireless access points. Figure 8.8 shows the back of a wireless router with four wired ports. Functionally, wireless routers work just like their wired cousins.

FIGURE 8.8 A wireless router

Firewall

Firewalls were initially covered in Chapter 5, "Software Applications." They are incredibly important devices for network security, though—they're gatekeepers that can help thwart hackers and malware. Here's a review:

Firewalls filter network traffic. Firewalls filter inbound and outbound network traffic based on rules defined by the administrator. That list of rules is called an *access control list (ACL)*. By default, most firewalls are configured as default deny, which means that all traffic is blocked unless specifically authorized by the administrator.

Firewalls can be software-based, hardware-based, or a combination of both. Firewalls can be stand-alone "black boxes," software installed on a server or router, or some combination of hardware and software. Many routers have firewall capabilities.

There are two types of firewalls: network-based and host-based. A network-based firewall is designed to protect a whole network of computers and almost always is a hardware solution with software on it. Host-based firewalls protect only one computer and are almost always software solutions. Windows comes with a built-in software firewall called Windows Firewall, also known as Microsoft Defender Firewall.

Network-based firewalls separate public versus private networks and can also create a screened subnet. Most network-based firewalls have at least two network connections: one to the Internet, or public side, and one to the internal network, or private side. Some firewalls have a third network port for a second semi-internal network. This port is used to connect servers that can be considered both public and private, such as web and email servers. This intermediary network is known as a *screened subnet*. A screened subnet can also be configured as a space between two firewalls.

Real World Scenario

Understanding LANs and WANs

When talking with others about networks, you're certain to hear the acronyms LAN and WAN. What do they mean?

A *local area network (LAN)* is a small network, usually confined to one office or building. While you need at least two devices to count it as a network, there's no hard and fast limit to the number of devices allowed on a LAN. Devices will be connected to each other with switches, hubs, and access points. A LAN might or might not have a router and might or might not be connected to the Internet.

A *wide area network (WAN)*, as its name implies, is larger. Think of it as two or more LANs connected to each other. A WAN configuration is usually spread across multiple geographical areas and certainly requires the use of a router. WAN locations are generally connected to each other using a dedicated connection. Historically, WAN connections were much slower than LAN connections. While this is still mostly true today, WAN connections have gotten much faster thanks to broadband and fiber-optic Internet.

Sometimes the lines between the two get a little blurry. And to make things even more confusing, there are other network designations such as a *metropolitan area network (MAN)*, which encompasses a town or city. The network depicted in Figure 8.7 would most likely be considered a WAN, but it depends on a few things. First, where are the network segments located? If they are all co-located, it's more likely a LAN. Second, what is the connection speed between the network segments? If it's a fast connection, say, faster than broadband, it's probably a LAN as well. If the network segments are in different places and connected via broadband or something slower, it's a WAN.

There are different management considerations for each. For example, if you have a LAN, do you want to use a router to connect to the Internet or another network? And with a WAN, you need to worry about securing the connections between sites. For now, though, just be able to classify a network based on the location of the site or sites and the speed of the connection between them.

Be sure to understand the difference between a LAN and a WAN, as they are part of Tech+ exam objective 2.8.

Networking Protocol Basics

Networking protocols are a lot like human languages in that they are the language that computers speak when talking to each other. Technically speaking, a *protocol* is a set of rules that govern communications. If computers don't speak the same language, they won't be able to talk to each other. To complicate matters, there are dozens of different languages that computers can use. Just like humans, computers can understand and use multiple languages. Imagine that you are on the street and someone comes up to you and speaks in Spanish. If you know Spanish, you will likely reply in kind. It doesn't matter if both of you know English as well because you've already established that you can communicate. On the other hand, it's going to be a pretty quick conversation if you don't know Spanish. This same concept applies to computers that are trying to communicate. They must have a network protocol in common for the conversation to be successful.

Throughout the years, hundreds of network protocols have been developed. As the advent of networking exploded, various companies developed their own networking hardware, software, and proprietary protocols. Although a few achieved long-term success, most have faded into oblivion. The one protocol suite that has sustained is TCP/IP. While it has some structural plusses such as its modularity, it didn't necessarily succeed because it was inherently superior to other protocols. It succeeded because it is the protocol of the Internet.

This is why I focus on TCP/IP. It is the protocol used on the Internet, but it's also the protocol used by the vast majority of home and business networks today. I'll start by taking a quick look at the history of TCP/IP, the model on which it's based, and a few of the common protocols you'll hear about. Then, I'll spend some time on IP addressing, which is essential for proper communication. This chapter will give you the foundation you need to understand it well and set up your own network.

For a more detailed discussion of networking protocols and TCP/IP, read the *CompTIA A+ Complete Study Guide* by Quentin Docter and Jon Buhagiar (Sybex, 2022). The A+ certification is a great one to get after you pass your CompTIA Tech+ exam!

TCP/IP Essentials

Every computer protocol that's created needs to accomplish a specific set of tasks for communication to be successful. To give some structure to these tasks, theoretical networking models were developed in the 1970s. TCP/IP's structure is based on a model created by the U.S. Department of Defense: the *Department of Defense (DoD) model*. The DoD model has four layers that specify the tasks that need to happen: Process/Application, Host-to-Host, Internet, and Network Access.

The *Transmission Control Protocol/Internet Protocol (TCP/IP) suite* is based on the DoD's theoretical model. While the protocol suite is named after two of its hardest-working protocols, Transmission Control Protocol (TCP) and Internet Protocol (IP), TCP/IP actually contains dozens of protocols working together to help computers communicate with one another. Figure 8.9 shows the DoD model's four layers and some of the TCP/IP protocols that correspond to those layers.

FIGURE 8.9 DoD model and the TCP/IP protocol suite

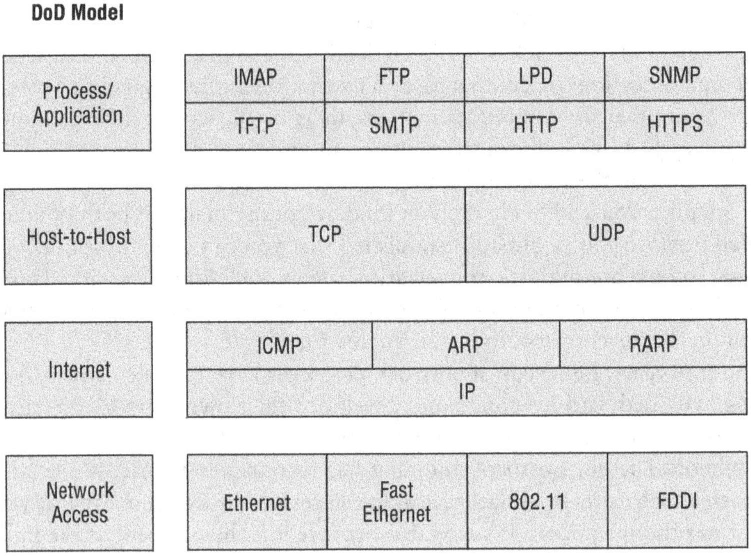

DoD Model

Layer	Protocols			
Process/ Application	IMAP	FTP	LPD	SNMP
	TFTP	SMTP	HTTP	HTTPS
Host-to-Host	TCP		UDP	
Internet	ICMP	ARP	RARP	
	IP			
Network Access	Ethernet	Fast Ethernet	802.11	FDDI

Don't feel the need to memorize the components of the TCP/IP suite—yet. When you move on to more advanced exams, more detailed knowledge will be required.

Think of TCP/IP as a puzzle. You need one item from each layer to make the puzzle fit together. The majority of TCP/IP protocols are located at the Process/Application layer. You might already be familiar with a few of these, such as *Hypertext Transfer Protocol (HTTP)*, *Hypertext Transfer Protocol Secure (HTTPS)*, *File Transfer Protocol (FTP)*, *Post Office Protocol 3 (POP3)*, *Internet Message Access Protocol (IMAP)*, and *Simple Mail Transfer Protocol (SMTP)*.

At the Host-to-Host layer, there are only two protocols: TCP and User Datagram Protocol (UDP). Most applications will use one or the other to transmit data, although some can use both but will do so for different tasks.

The most important protocol at the Internet layer is IP. This is the backbone of TCP/IP. Other protocols at this layer work in conjunction with IP, such as Internet Control Message Protocol (ICMP) and Address Resolution Protocol (ARP).

You'll notice that the Network Access layer doesn't have any protocols per se. This layer describes the type of network access method you are using, such as Ethernet, Wi-Fi, or others.

Basic Network Services and Protocols

If you've used the Internet, you've used HTTPS. Websites using the HTTPS protocol have `https://` at the front of their addresses. Most of the time the browser hides it for simplicity. HTTPS replaced the older, unsecure HTTP, which did not encrypt data as it went back and forth between the web server and client's browser. HTTPS does encrypt data in transit and makes things such as entering passwords or financial information into a website secure.

If you download a file from a site, it might redirect you to a server dedicated to file downloads. Its website would possibly start with `ftp://` because FTP is specifically designed for file downloads.

POP3, IMAP, and SMTP are all email protocols. POP3 and IMAP are used to receive (download) email, and SMTP is used to send email.

Many times a basic network service such as downloading a file will share the name of the protocol that is used, as is the case with FTP. You might have FTP client software, and FTP is the protocol it uses. Another example is email client software that might tell you to connect to a POP3 server or SMTP server. Those servers, as you might expect based on their names, use the POP3 or SMTP protocols to communicate with their clients to transfer email over the network.

Understand basic network services such as secure web browsing, file transfers, and email because they are part of Tech+ exam objective 2.8.

Understanding IP Addressing

To communicate on a TCP/IP network, each device needs to have a unique address, which is called an *IP address*. Any device with an IP address is referred to as a *host*. This can include servers, workstations, printers, and routers. If you can assign it an IP address, it's a host.

The material here focuses on the version of IP addresses called IPv4. There is a newer standard called IPv6, which will be covered shortly. Both are currently used. Assume people are talking about IPv4 when they say "IP address" unless they specify IPv6.

An IP address is a 32-bit hierarchical address that identifies a host on the network. It's typically written in dotted-decimal notation, such as 192.168.10.55. Each of the numbers in this example represents 8 bits (or 1 byte) of the address, also known as an *octet*. The same address written in binary (how the computer thinks about it) would be 11000000 10101000 00001010 00110111. As you can see, the dotted-decimal version is a much more convenient way to write these numbers! The addresses are said to be hierarchical, as opposed to "flat," because the numbers at the beginning of the address identify groups of computers that belong to the same network. Because of the hierarchical address structure, you're able to do really cool things like route packets between local networks and on the Internet.

IP addresses are logical addresses that can be changed. Remember also that every network card has a physical MAC address that does not change. MAC addresses are not used in a hierarchical fashion.

A great example of hierarchical addressing is your street address. Let's say that you live in Apartment 4B on 123 Main Street, Anytown, Kansas, USA. If someone sent you a letter via snail mail, the hierarchy of your address would help the postal service and carrier deliver it to the right place. First and broadest is USA. Kansas helps narrow it down a bit, and Anytown narrows it down more. Eventually they get to your street, the right number on your street, and then the right apartment. If the address space were flat (for example, Kansas didn't mean anything more specific than Main Street), or you could name your state anything you wanted to, it would be really hard to get the letter to the right spot.

Take this analogy back to IP addresses. They're set up to organize networks logically to make delivery between them possible and then to identify an individual node within a network. If this structure weren't in place, a huge, multinetwork space like the Internet wouldn't be possible. It would simply be too unwieldy to manage.

Each IP address is made up of two components: the *network ID* and the *host ID*. The network portion of the address always comes before the host portion. Because of the way IP addresses are structured, the network portion does not have to be a specific fixed length. In other words, some computers will use 8 of the 32 bits for the network portion and the other 24 for the host portion, while other computers might use 24 bits for the network portion and the remaining 8 bits for the host portion. Here are a few rules that you should know about when working with IP addresses:

- All host addresses on a network must be unique.
- On a routed network (such as the Internet), all network addresses must be unique as well.
- Neither the network ID nor the host ID can be set to all 0s. A host ID portion of all 0s means "this network."
- Neither the network ID nor the host ID can be set to all 1s. A host ID portion of all 1s means "all hosts on this network," commonly known as a broadcast address.

Computers are able to differentiate where the network ID ends and the host address begins through the use of a *subnet mask*. This is a value written just like an IP address and may look something like 255.255.255.0. Any bit that is set to a 1 in the subnet mask makes the corresponding bit in the IP address part of the network ID. The rest will be the host ID. The number 255 is the highest number you will ever see in IP addressing, and it means that all bits in the octet are set to 1.

Here's an example based on two numbers I have used in this chapter. Look at the IP address of 192.168.10.55. Assume that the subnet mask in use with this address is 255.255.255.0. This indicates that the first three octets are the network portion of the address and the last octet is the host portion. Said another way, the network ID is 192.168.10, and the unique host ID is 55.

All of this is important to know because it governs how computers communicate. If a computer wants to send a message to another computer on the same network, it just spits the message out on the wire (or wireless) and the other computer receives it. If the destination is on a different network (as determined by the network address), then the router comes into play. The sender will forward the message to the router to send to the destination. In this case, your router is called a *default gateway*. It's basically the door from your network to the outside world.

All of this TCP/IP stuff can get a little heady. On more advanced CompTIA exams, such as A+ and Network+, you will need to know how to determine the network and host portions of the address based on a given subnet mask. You shouldn't be asked this on Tech+, though. For now, the key things to remember are:

- To communicate using TCP/IP, each computer is required to have an IP address and a correct subnet mask.
- Each IP address on a network must be unique.
- If you want to connect your network to other networks (such as the Internet), a default gateway is also required.

TCP/IP Ports

In the previous section, you learned that an IP address identifies a unique host on a TCP/IP network. Knowing the right IP address is just part of the equation, however. To complete communication between two hosts, an additional identifier called a *port* (or *port number*) is used. Ports are based on the Process/Application layer protocol used.

TCP/IP applications combine the host's IP address with the port number in order to communicate. This combination is known as a *socket*.

A good analogy for understanding port numbers is to think of cable or satellite television. In this analogy, the IP address is your house. The cable company needs to know where to send the data. But once the data is in your house, which channel are you going to receive it on? If you want sports, that might be on one channel, but weather is on a different channel, and the cooking show is on yet another. Those channels are analogous to ports. You know that if you want a cooking show, you need to turn to channel 923 (or whatever). Similarly, a client computer on a network knows that if it needs to ask a question in HTTPS, it needs to do it on port 443.

There are 65,536 ports numbered from 0 to 65535. Ports 0 through 1023 are called the well-known ports and are assigned to commonly used services, and 1024 through 49151 are called the registered ports. Anything from 49152 to 65535 is free to be used by application vendors. Fortunately, you don't need to memorize them all. Table 8.4 lists a few network services (the ones in the Tech+ exam objectives), associated protocols, and port numbers used.

TABLE 8.4 Common port numbers

Service	Protocol	Port
Web browsing (not secure)	HTTP	80
Secure web browsing	HTTPS	443
File transfer	FTP	20, 21
Email (sending)	SMTP	25
Email (receiving)	POP3	110
Email (receiving)	IMAP4	143

A complete list of registered port numbers can be found at `www.iana.org`.

For the Tech+ exam, be sure to understand the following, as they are part of exam objective 2.8:

- IP address (It's a logical address and can be changed.)
- MAC address (It's a physical address built into the NIC and can't be changed.)
- Ports (They are like a channel within TCP/IP to identify a service.)

Quick Intro to IPv6

IPv4 was originally developed in 1973. Considering how fast technology evolves, it's pretty amazing to think that the protocol still enjoys immense popularity over 50 years later. There are a few problems with IPv4, though. One is that we ran out of available network addresses, and the other is that TCP/IP can be somewhat tricky to configure (I'm pointing at you, subnet masks).

IPv4 has 32 bits of addressing space, which allows for nearly 4.3 billion addresses! So how could we run out of addresses? With the way it's structured, only about 250 million of those addresses are actually usable, and all of those are pretty much spoken for.

A new version of TCP/IP has been developed, and it's called IPv6. Instead of a 32-bit address, it uses 128-bit addresses. That provides for 3.4×10^{38} addresses, which theoretically should be more than enough that they will never run out globally. (Famous last words, right?) Figure 8.10 shows an example of an IPv6 address.

FIGURE 8.10 IPv6 address

```
2001:0db8:3c4d:0012:0000:0000:1234:56ab
______________|_____|__________________
Global prefix   Subnet      Interface ID
```

IPv6 also includes, as standard features, many optional but useful IPv4 ones. While the addresses may be more difficult to remember, the automatic configuration and enhanced flexibility make the new version sparkle compared to the old one. Best of all, it's backward compatible with and can run on the computer at the same time as IPv4, so networks can migrate to IPv6 without a complete restructure. Figure 8.11 brings this section to a close by showing you a sample output from the `ipconfig /all` command. In it, you can see examples of an IPv4 address and subnet mask, MAC address (labeled physical address), and IPv6 address.

FIGURE 8.11 `ipconfig /all` output

```
Command Prompt

Wireless LAN adapter Wi-Fi:

   Connection-specific DNS Suffix  . : zoomtown.com
   Description . . . . . . . . . . . : Intel(R) Wireless-AC 9462
   Physical Address. . . . . . . . . : AC-67-5D-F5-85-C5
   DHCP Enabled. . . . . . . . . . . : Yes
   Autoconfiguration Enabled . . . . : Yes
   IPv6 Address. . . . . . . . . . . : 2600:2b00:7981:2c00:50e0:6cd8:a50e:8f27(Preferred)
   Link-local IPv6 Address . . . . . : fe80::4b22:f923:6dce:ac8e%4(Preferred)
   IPv4 Address. . . . . . . . . . . : 192.168.1.81(Preferred)
   Subnet Mask . . . . . . . . . . . : 255.255.255.0
   Lease Obtained. . . . . . . . . . : Tuesday, April 9, 2024 11:15:40 PM
   Lease Expires . . . . . . . . . . : Saturday, April 27, 2024 5:06:17 PM
   Default Gateway . . . . . . . . . : fe80::c641:1eff:fe3f:8cbb%4
                                       192.168.1.1
   DHCP Server . . . . . . . . . . . : 192.168.1.1
   DHCPv6 IAID . . . . . . . . . . . : 61630301
   DHCPv6 Client DUID. . . . . . . . : 00-01-00-01-26-D5-50-04-18-C0-4D-29-3E-E6
   DNS Servers . . . . . . . . . . . : 2600:2b00:7981:2c00:c641:1eff:fe3f:8cbb
                                       192.168.1.1
   NetBIOS over Tcpip. . . . . . . . : Enabled
   Connection-specific DNS Suffix Search List :
                                       zoomtown.com

C:\Users\qdoct>
```

DHCP and DNS

Two critical TCP/IP services about which you need to be aware are *Dynamic Host Configuration Protocol (DHCP)* and *Domain Name System (DNS)*. Both are services that are typically installed on a server (or in the case of DHCP, a router), and both provide key functionality to network clients. I'll talk about them now because they're important compo nents of TCP/IP, and you will see them come up when you configure your router.

DHCP servers are configured to provide IP configuration information automatically to clients. The following configuration information is typically provided:

- IP address
- Subnet mask
- Default gateway
- DNS server address

DHCP servers can provide a lot more than the items on this list, but those are the most common.

The alternative to DHCP is for an administrator to enter in the IP configuration information manually on each host. This is called *static IP addressing*, and it is administratively intensive as compared to DHCP's dynamic addressing.

DNS has one function on the network, and that is to resolve hostnames (or URLs) to IP addresses. This sounds simple enough, but it has profound implications.

Think about using the Internet. You open your browser, and in the address bar you type the *uniform resource locator (URL)* of your favorite website, something like `www.google.com`, and press Enter. The first question your computer asks is, "Who is that?" (Remember, computers understand only 0s and 1s.) Your machine requires an IP address to connect to the website. The DNS server provides the answer, "That is 72.14.205.104." Now that your computer knows the address of the website you want, it's able to traverse the Internet to connect to it.

Each DNS server has a database where it stores hostname-to-IP-address pairs. If the DNS server does not know the address of the host you are seeking, it has the ability to query other DNS servers to help answer the request.

Think about the implications of that for just a minute. We all probably use Google several times a day, but in all honesty how many of us know its IP address? It's certainly not something that we are likely to have memorized. Much less, how could you possibly memorize the IP addresses of all of the websites you visit? Because of DNS, it's easy to find resources. Whether you want to find Coca-Cola, Toyota, `Amazon.com`, or thousands of other companies, it's usually pretty easy to figure out how. Type in the name with a `.com` on the end of it and you're usually right. The only reason why this is successful is that DNS is there to perform resolution of that name to the corresponding IP address.

DNS works the same way on an intranet (a local network not attached to the Internet) as it does on the Internet. The only difference is that instead of helping you find `www.google.com`, it may help you find Jenny's print server or Joe's file server. From a client-side perspective, all you need to do is to configure the host with the address of a legitimate DNS server and you should be good to go.

Real World Scenario

How to Get from Point A to Point B on a Network

Understanding the basics of network communication is important. I've already hit a few of the key points in this chapter, but it's time to tie them all together.

Imagine a scenario where a laptop user connected to the Internet just pressed Send on an email to a friend. It's a pretty common occurrence, right? Well, what happens next?

Based on the software used (an email client), the laptop knows that it needs to send the message to the email server. And, the email software has been configured with the name of the email server: `mail.wiley.com`. An IP address is needed, so the laptop looks in its TCP/IP configuration information for the address of a DNS server. It then sends a message to the DNS server asking for the IP address to `mail.wiley.com`. The DNS server responds with an address, and the laptop can send the message.

Let's take a more granular look at what happens next. The next thing that the laptop needs to decide is whether the mail server is on the same network as the laptop. It does this by looking at its IP address and subnet mask to determine its network address. It then looks at the destination address with its (the sender's) subnet mask. If the network addresses are the same, the message will get sent out on the local network. If not, then the message will get sent to the default gateway, the router, for transmission to the next network. Usually this is to the Internet.

The message does not get sent all in one piece, though. The message will be broken down into smaller chunks called *packets*. A packet has a couple of main sections: a header and the data. The header contains, among other things, the sending and destination IP addresses and the protocol being used. When the router receives the packet, it sends it on to the next router based on the destination IP address. The packet will bounce from router to router until it gets to the network where the mail server is located. Once the mail server receives all of the packets, it reassembles the message.

(Technically speaking, packets are broken into even smaller chunks called *frames*, and then frames are broken down and sent across the wired or wireless connection as individual bits. The receiving device reassembles the bits into frames and frames into packets. But that is way more detail than you need to remember for the Tech+ exam!)

The process sounds complicated, and it really is. It's pretty amazing that the Internet works at all, much less as smoothly as it does! If you're curious to see how many routers (hops) it takes to get from your computer to a website you like, use the trace route (`tracert`) command, shown in Figure 8.12. In this example, I traced the route to `Amazon.com`. For my computer to talk to Amazon, the packet went through 17 hops. You can see how long each hop took in milliseconds, as well as the name or address of the router it went through. The lines with asterisks are routers where the owner set it up to not return an IP address or name.

FIGURE 8.12 `tracert` output

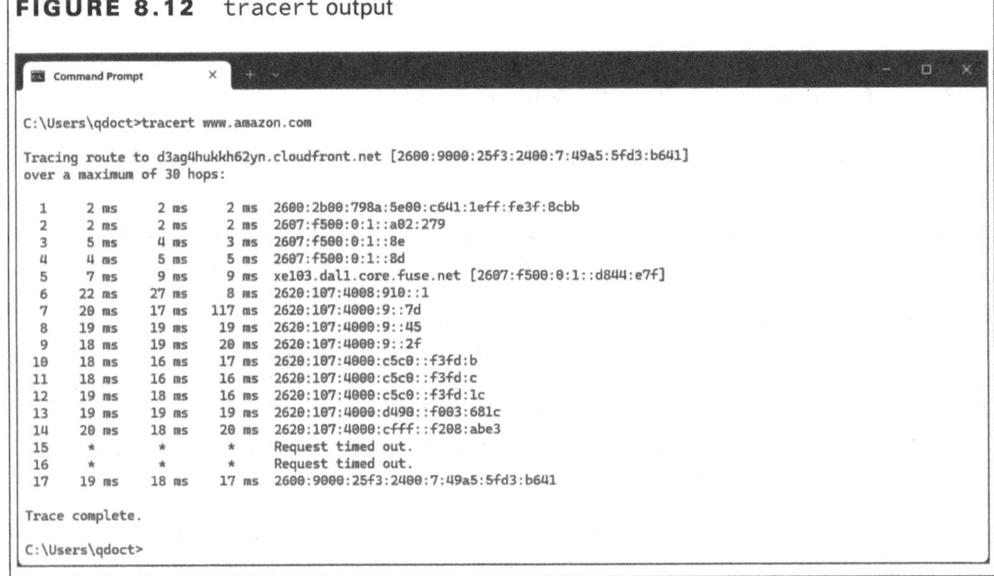
Command Prompt
C:\Users\qdoct>tracert www.amazon.com
Tracing route to d3ag4hukkh62yn.cloudfront.net [2600:9000:25f3:2400:7:49a5:5fd3:b641]
over a maximum of 30 hops:
1 2 ms 2 ms 2 ms 2600:2b00:798a:5e00:c641:1eff:fe3f:8cbb
2 2 ms 2 ms 2 ms 2607:f500:0:1::a02:279
3 5 ms 4 ms 3 ms 2607:f500:0:1::8e
4 4 ms 5 ms 5 ms 2607:f500:0:1::8d
5 7 ms 9 ms 9 ms xe103.dal1.core.fuse.net [2607:f500:0:1::d844:e7f]
6 22 ms 27 ms 8 ms 2620:107:4008:910::1
7 20 ms 17 ms 117 ms 2620:107:4000:9::7d
8 19 ms 19 ms 19 ms 2620:107:4000:9::45
9 18 ms 19 ms 20 ms 2620:107:4000:9::2f
10 18 ms 16 ms 17 ms 2620:107:4000:c5c0::f3fd:b
11 18 ms 16 ms 16 ms 2620:107:4000:c5c0::f3fd:c
12 19 ms 18 ms 16 ms 2620:107:4000:c5c0::f3fd:1c
13 19 ms 19 ms 19 ms 2620:107:4000:d490::f003:681c
14 20 ms 18 ms 20 ms 2620:107:4000:cfff::f208:abe3
15 * * * Request timed out.
16 * * * Request timed out.
17 19 ms 18 ms 17 ms 2600:9000:25f3:2400:7:49a5:5fd3:b641
Trace complete.
C:\Users\qdoct>

In Exercise 8.3, you will find your computer's IP configuration information.

EXERCISE 8.3

Finding Your IP Configuration Information in Windows

1. In the Windows search bar, type **`cmd`** and press Enter. This will open a Command Prompt.
2. At the prompt, type **`ipconfig`** and press Enter. This will display the IP configuration information for your computer. Can you find your IP address, subnet mask, and (optional) default gateway?

   The link-local address shown is an IPv6 address, which is written in hexadecimal.
3. At the prompt, type **`ipconfig /all`** and press Enter. This will show you much more information, including the address of your DHCP and DNS servers, if you have them.
4. Type **`exit`** and press Enter to close the Command Prompt.

NOTE

To get IP configuration in macOS, open the terminal by pressing Cmd+spacebar and typing **`terminal`**. At the prompt, type **`ifconfig`**. The `ifconfig` command also works in Linux, as does the `ip` command.

Network Storage Options

Joining a computer to a network provides it with many more storage options than it would have on its own. There are several scenarios in which more storage is desirable. One common one is for mobile devices with limited space—storing data in the cloud can be a tremendous help. Another is for laptop users with small SSDs. A third is when multiple users need to access data, making it impractical to store on someone's local drive. In this section, you'll learn about network storage types, including file servers, network-attached storage (NAS), and cloud storage service.

Tech+ exam objective 2.3 is "Compare and contrast storage types." Ones you need to know are file server, network-attached storage (NAS), and cloud storage.

Local Network Storage Types

There are two types of local network storage with which you need to be familiar. The first is a file server, and the second is NAS.

File Server

A *file server* is a server computer that is specialized to store user files. It can be a dedicated or nondedicated server. The primary hardware requirement for a file server is lots of hard drive space. Oftentimes, file servers will have multiple optical drives as well.

Since we're on the subject of servers, now is as good a time as any to remind you about two networking models you need to be familiar with as part of exam objective 2.8. They are client/server and peer-to-peer. In a *client/server network*, some computers are designated as servers whereas others are clients (also called workstations). Client/server models have the advantages of centralized security and resources, but the disadvantage of requiring more administration. A *peer-to-peer network* is one in which no servers exist, and all hosts are considered equals. Peer-to-peer networks, sometimes called *workgroups*, are only practical to manage for up to about 10 computers.

Network-Attached Storage

A *network-attached storage (NAS)* device takes hard drive storage to the next level. Based on its name, you can probably guess that it's attached to the network, which it is, but that's just the beginning. First, take a look at a simple NAS device in Figure 8.13.

FIGURE 8.13 NETGEAR NAS device

Source: PJ / Wikimedia Commons / CC BY-SA 3.0.

Figure 8.13 shows is a self-enclosed unit that can hold up to four hard drives. Some hold more; some hold less. Nicer NAS systems will allow you to hot-swap hard drives, meaning that if one fails, you can remove it and replace it without shutting the NAS down. Most NAS systems will also offer *Redundant Array of Independent Disks (RAID)* configurations for you with very little intervention required. RAID is a form of fault tolerance, which means it can help protect against data loss in the event of a single drive failure. In addition to the hardware, the NAS device contains its own operating system, meaning that it acts like its own file server. In most cases, you can plug it in, do some very minor configuration, and have instant storage space on your network.

As far as connectivity goes, NAS devices typically connect directly to the network, and that is how all of the network users access the storage space. NAS systems will also connect to a PC through a USB port, but that is primarily so you can use that PC to run the configuration software for the NAS. If you are running a small office and need additional local centralized storage, a NAS system is a good way to go.

Accessing a NAS server over the network will generally be slower than having an external hard drive on your computer. The advantage is that if you have multiple users on a network, everyone can easily get to it.

Cloud Storage Services

Storage is the area in which cloud computing got its start. The idea is simple—you store files just like you would on a hard drive but with two major advantages. One, you don't need to buy the hardware, and two, users can access the files regardless of where they are physically located. You can have users in the United States, China, and Germany, and all of them have access via their web browser. In that respect, cloud storage is much easier to configure than a file server or NAS.

You will learn more about cloud computing in Chapter 9, "Cloud Computing and Artificial Intelligence."

There is no shortage of cloud-based storage providers on the market today. Each one offers slightly different features. Most of them will offer limited storage for free and premium services for more data-heavy users or organizations. Table 8.5 shows you a comparison of some personal plans from the more well-known providers. Please note that this table is for illustrative purposes only, as the data limits and cost can change. Most of these providers offer business plans with very high or unlimited storage as well for an additional fee.

TABLE 8.5 Cloud provider personal plans

Service	Free	Premium	Cost per year
Dropbox	2 GB	3TB	$199
Apple iCloud	5 GB	50 GB, 200 GB, or 2TB	$12, $36, or $120
Box	10 GB	100 GB	$120
Microsoft OneDrive (part of Microsoft 365)	5 GB	100 GB or 1TB	$20 or $70
Google Drive	15 GB	100 GB or 2TB	$20 or $100

Which one should you choose? If you want extra features such as web-based applications, then Google or Microsoft is probably the best choice. If you just need data storage, then Box or Dropbox might be a better option.

Nearly all client OSs will work with any of the cloud-based storage providers, with the exception of Linux, which natively works only with Dropbox.

Most cloud storage providers offer synchronization to the desktop, which makes it so that you have a folder on your computer, just as if it were on your hard drive. And importantly, that folder will always have the most current edition of the files stored in the cloud and be automatically backed up.

Accessing the sites is done through your web browser or an app you download. Once you are in the site, managing your files is much like managing them on your local computer. In Figure 8.14, you can see the Google Drive interface, with four folders and two files in it.

FIGURE 8.14 Google Drive

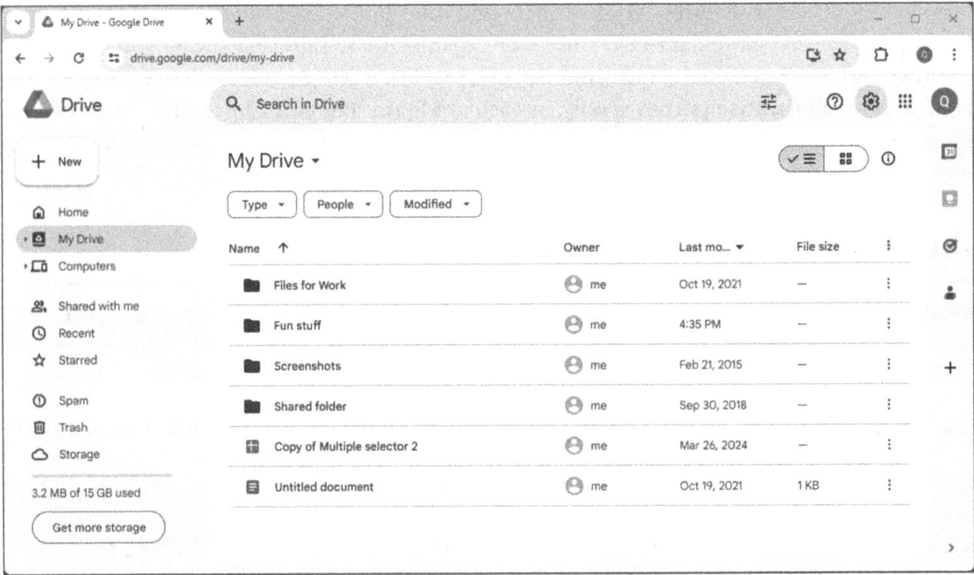

You have a few options to share a folder with another user. The easiest way to do this is to right-click the folder and choose Share ➢ Share. You'll be asked to enter their name or email address and indicate whether they can view or edit the file (see Figure 8.15).

FIGURE 8.15 Sharing a folder on Google Drive

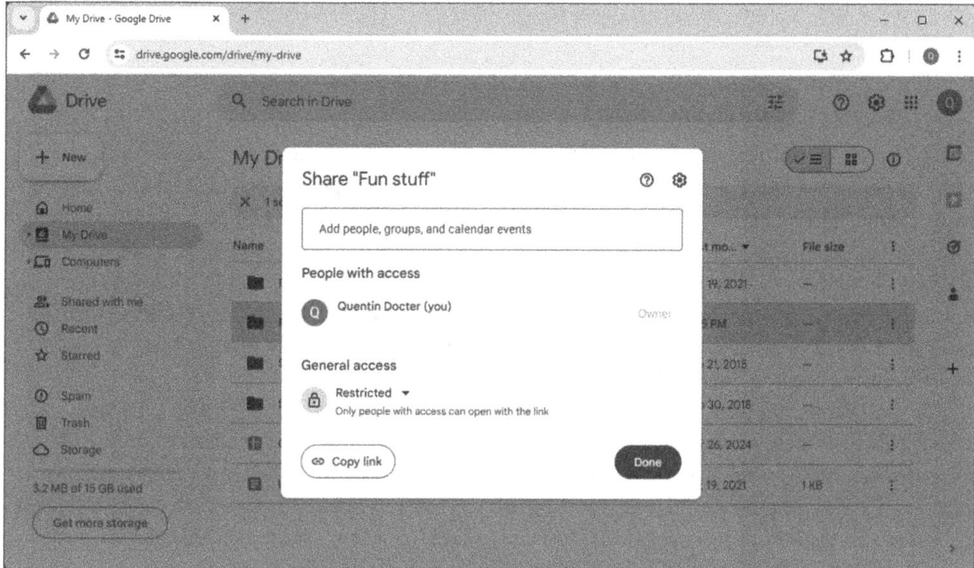

Setting Up a Small Wireless Network

Finally, the part you have been waiting for! This is the section where I will show you how to configure a router for your small wireless network. The exam objectives mention small wireless networks; most of the routers you buy today for small office home office (SOHO) use are wireless but also have about four wired ports. Plugging your computer into one of those ports makes you wired, but you still use the router to get to the Internet as a wireless client would.

Each wireless router manufacturer uses different software, but you can usually configure their parameters with a web-based configuration utility or downloadable app. While the software is convenient, you still need to know which options to configure and how those configurations will affect users on your networks. The items that require configuration depend on the choices you make about your wireless network. I will divide this part into three sections: basic configuration, security options, and additional services.

Basic Configuration

The Wi-Fi Alliance (`www.wi-fi.org`) is the authoritative expert in the field of wireless LANs. It lists five critical keys to setting up a secured wireless router:

1. Change the router's SSID.
2. Change the administrator username and password. Make sure that it's a strong password.

3. Enable WPA3, WPA2 Personal, or the highest level of security the router supports.
4. Choose a high-quality security passphrase. Make it different from the administrator password!
5. From the clients, select WPA3 (or security that matches your router's setting) and enter the security passphrase to connect.

This list has a few new acronyms in it, and I'll define each of them in just a minute. To set up the Linksys router, you need to download the Linksys app. Open the app and follow the directions. They have tried to make it as easy as possible for users to set up wireless networks without the help of a technician. If you need step-by-step directions for a router, you will likely be able to find them on the manufacturer's website as well. After it's set up, you can administer the router from the app or from a browser by typing in the IP address of the default gateway. For the examples in this section, I am going to show images from a Linksys MR9000, because that's what I have.

Before we start changing settings, first take a look at the home page for the Linksys Smart Wi-Fi software, as shown in Figure 8.16. The SSID is shown as well as some other basic parameters. Options are changed by using the menu on the left. For a comparison, Figure 8.17 shows the home page of the Linksys app. All menu options are accessed from the hamburger menu icon in the upper-left corner. The rest of the examples in this section will feature the browser version.

FIGURE 8.16 Linksys Smart Wi-Fi

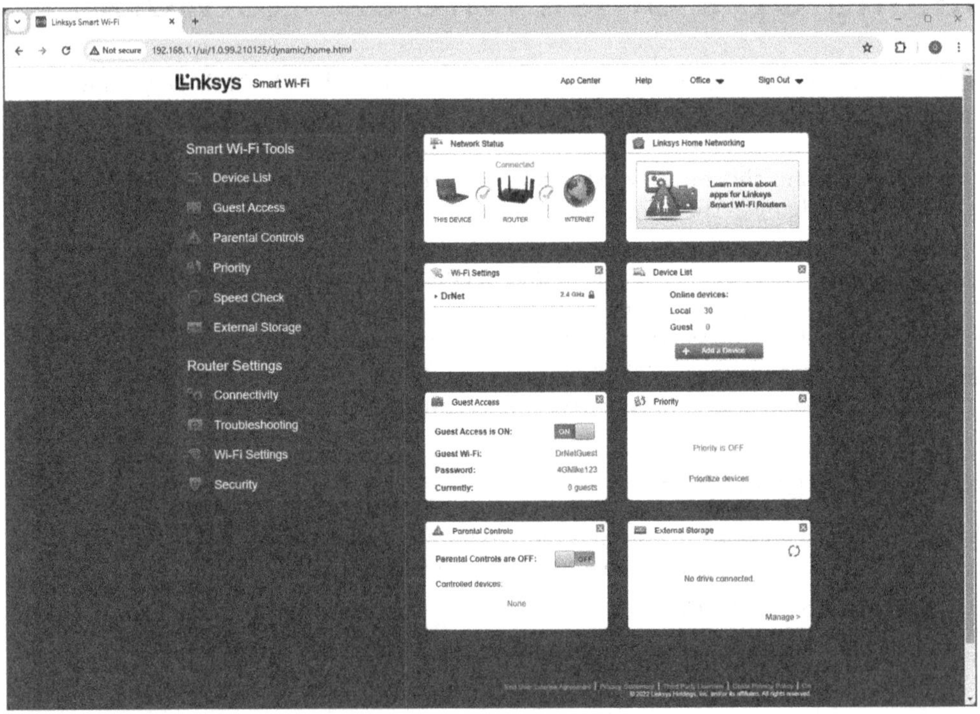

FIGURE 8.17 Linksys app home page

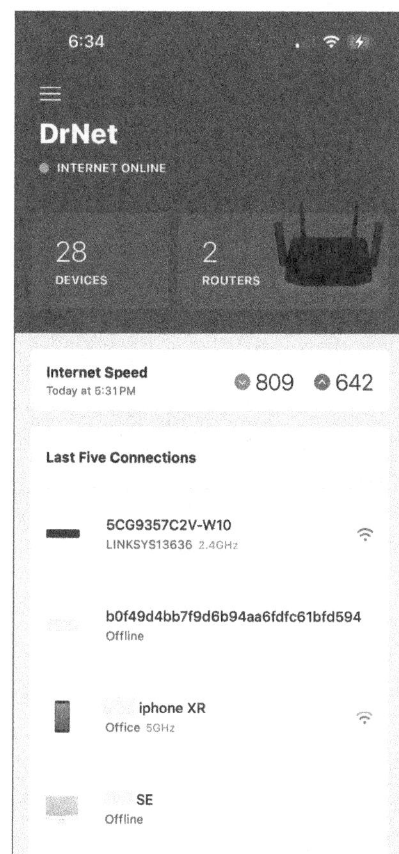

Changing the SSID

The parameter that you will configure first is the *service set identifier (SSID)*, which is your wireless network name. An SSID is a unique name given to the wireless network. All hardware that is to participate on the network must be configured to use the same SSID. When you are connecting clients to a wireless network, all available wireless networks will be listed by their SSIDs.

The SSID in Linksys Smart Wi-Fi is changed from the Wi-Fi Settings menu (Figure 8.18). The default network name will likely be the brand name of the router followed by some random numbers, such as Linksys03451. You need to change the default to something more memorable.

FIGURE 8.18 Wi-Fi Settings

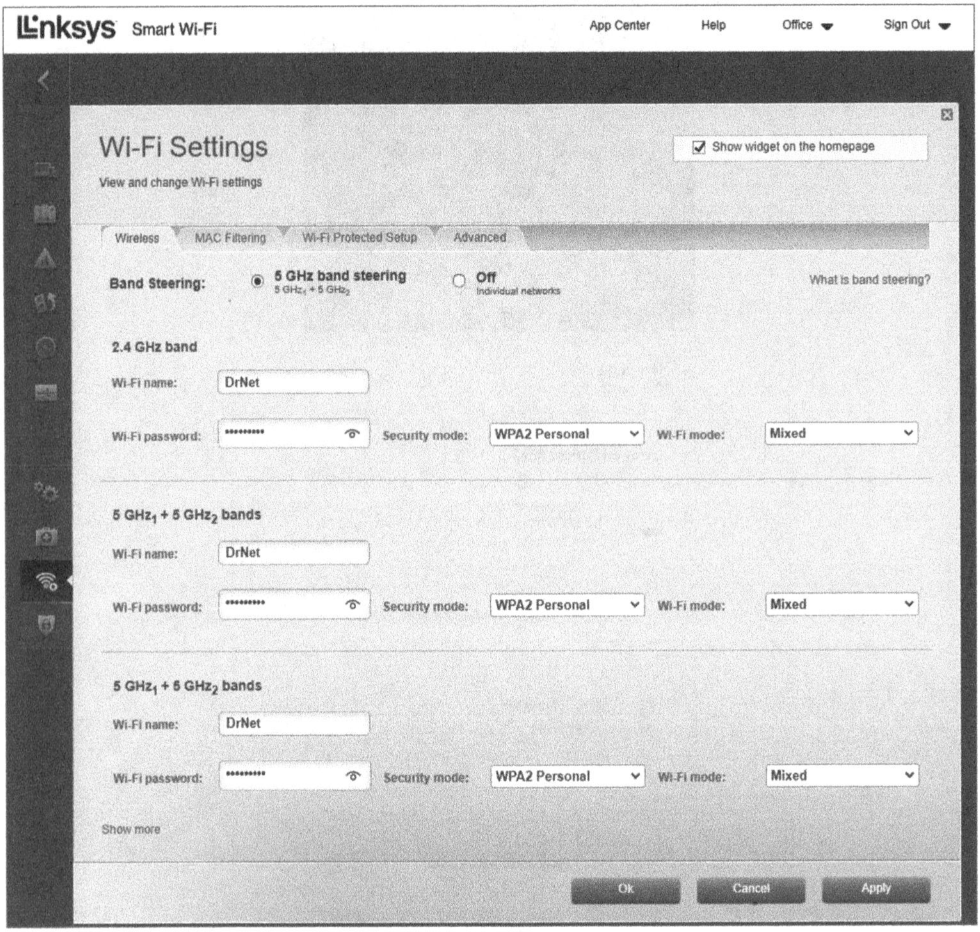

For better security, you should set your network name to something that doesn't identify to whom it belongs. This keeps potential hackers from coming after you personally or possibly being able to guess your password based on information about you. I am probably setting a bad example in Figure 8.18 by naming my network something close to my last name.

This router has the option to change SSIDs for different bands. To change any of them, click in the box next to Wi-Fi Name and type in the new name.

Changing the Administrator Username and Password

Keeping the administrator name and password away from users or potential hackers is of utmost importance. The username should be difficult to guess and not linked to your name or other user account names you have, and the password should be very secure.

In Linksys's case, the username will be based off the email address used to create the account. The password is changed from the Connectivity menu shown in Figure 8.19. Notice also that this page is where the firmware updates are configured. Always keep the firmware up-to-date to help protect the network!

FIGURE 8.19 Connectivity settings

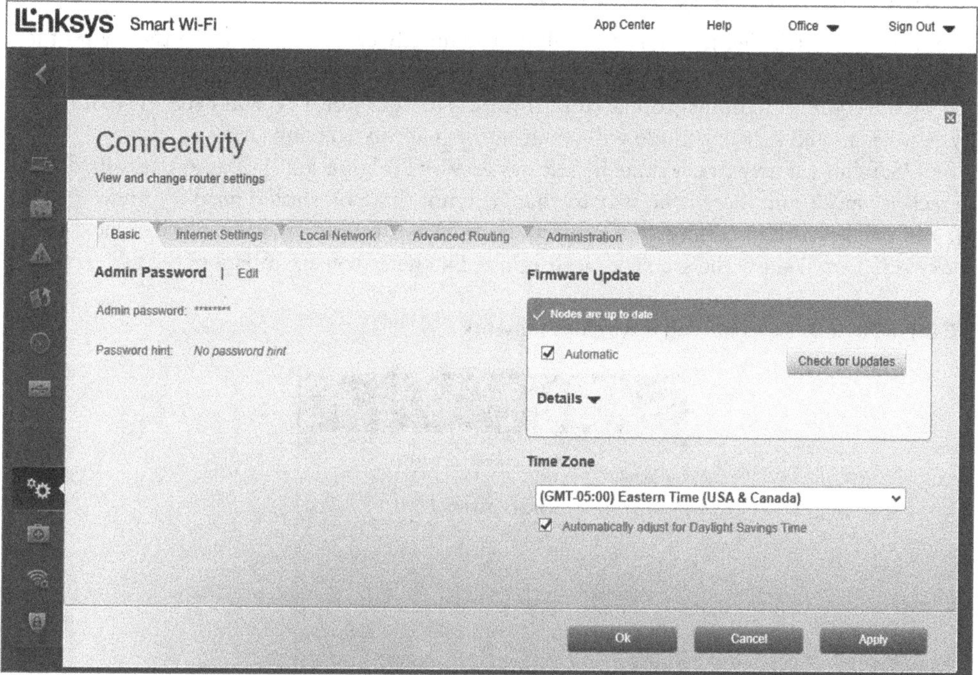

If you forget your wireless router's administrator password, you won't be able to make any configuration changes. Wireless routers have a recessed reset button on them, usually on the bottom or the back. You may need a pen or a paperclip to be able to push it. Push that button in and hold it for about 20 to 30 seconds. The router's lights will flash several times, and it will reset to factory settings. Then, launch your configuration utility to set up the router again.

Enabling the Best Security

Security modes are configured by SSID and done from the Wi-Fi settings tab (refer to Figure 8.18). You might recall from the "Basic Configuration" section earlier in this chapter that the recommendation is WPA3, WPA2, or the highest security setting possible. On this router, the two options for encryption are WPA2 Personal and Open, so WPA2 is the best choice. You will learn about encryption options in the upcoming "Wireless Router Security" section. Having an open, unencrypted wireless network is never a good idea.

Choosing a High-Quality Passphrase

When users attempt to join the network, they need to enter the passphrase. In the Linksys software Wi-Fi settings (Figure 8.18 again), it's labeled Wi-Fi Password. To change it, click in the box and type the new password. It should be different than the administrator password and challenging to guess.

Connecting Clients to the Network

To join the network, clients will need to find or manually enter the SSID and then enter the appropriate passphrase. Most client OSs today will automatically detect the security mode used by the router and adjust to match it. If the client does not, you will need to set it manually. A mismatched security mode will result in the inability to connect.

In iOS, joining a network is done in Settings ➢ Wi-Fi (Figure 8.20). It automatically detects the security mode and there is no way to change it, not that you should need to. Android users will join the network in Settings ➢ Connections ➢ Wi-Fi. Tapping the Settings icon next to the network SSID will show the security mode in use, like what you see in Figure 8.21.

FIGURE 8.20 iOS joining a wireless network

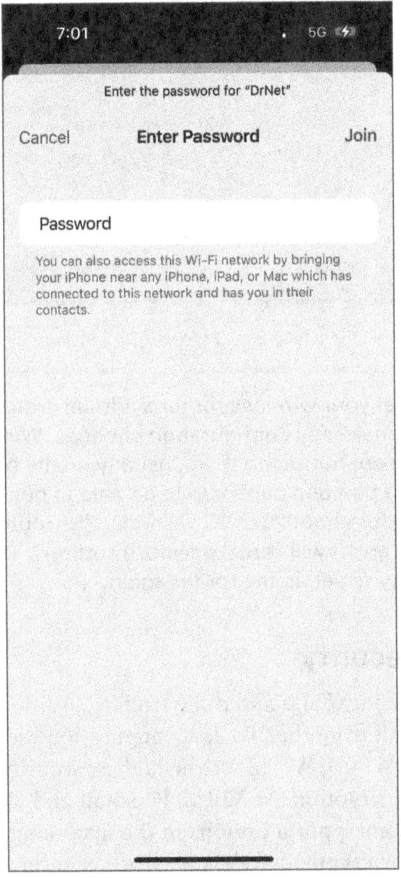

FIGURE 8.21 Android Wi-Fi settings

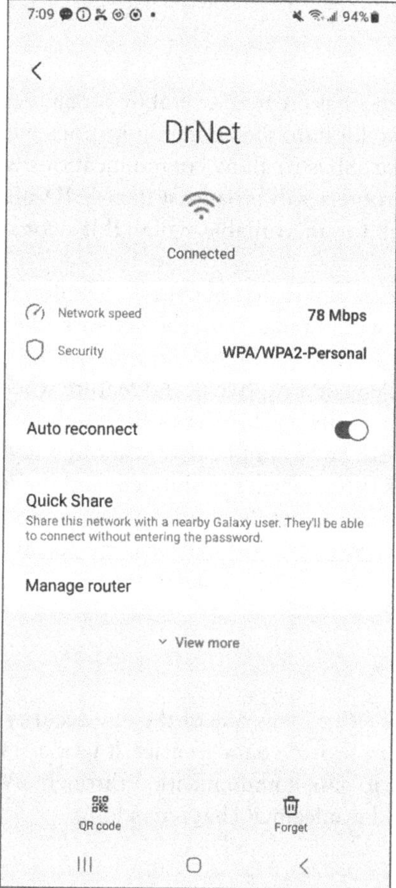

Once the client is connected to the network, verify Internet connectivity. Do this by opening the browser of your choice and seeing whether you can get to a website such as `www.google.com`.

Tech+ exam objective 6.5, "Given a scenario, configure security settings for a small wireless network," wants you to know about changing the SSID and default passwords.

Wireless Router Security

By their very nature, wireless routers are less secure than their wired counterparts. The fact that their signals travel through the air makes them a little harder to contain. The best way to help protect network data while it's being transmitted is to use wireless encryption.

While you can create an open network connection, it's recommended that instead you use one of the encryption methods outlined in this section.

Open Portals

The growth of wireless systems has created several opportunities for attackers. These systems are relatively new, they use well-established communications mechanisms, and they're easily intercepted. Wi-Fi routers use SSIDs to allow communications with a specific access point. Because by default wireless routers will broadcast their SSID, all someone with a wireless client needs to do is to search for an available signal. If it's not secured, they can connect within a few seconds.

The advantage of an open portal is that potential users don't need to enter a password. If the goal is to let everyone within range onto the network, then an open portal is the way to go.

Some administrators implement a captive portal feature when using open portals. A *captive portal* is a welcome page notifying the user of the conditions of the network, including which behaviors are permitted. For example, they will often say something to the effect that hacking and other malicious behaviors are prohibited, and the user assumes responsibility for their own security. Of course, a sternly worded message won't keep those with bad intent from doing bad things, but it can (in theory) absolve the portal owner from any liability.

The point is, open portals pose security risks to the network and to users on the network. Use them with caution.

WEP

Wired Equivalency Protocol (WEP) was one of the first security standards for wireless devices. WEP encrypts data to provide data security. It uses a static key (password); the client needs to know the right key to gain communication through a WEP-enabled device. The keys are commonly 10, 26, or 58 hexadecimal characters long.

You may see the use of the notation WEP.*x*, which refers to the key size; 64-bit and 128-bit are the most widely used, and 256-bit keys are supported by some vendors (WEP.64, WEP.128, and WEP.256). WEP.64 uses a 10-character key. WEP.128 uses 26 characters, and WEP.256 uses 58.

The protocol has always been under scrutiny for not being as secure as initially intended. WEP is vulnerable because of the nature of static keys and weaknesses in the encryption algorithms. These weaknesses allow the algorithm potentially to be cracked in a very short amount of time—no more than two or three minutes. This makes WEP one of the more vulnerable protocols available for security.

Because of security weaknesses and the availability of newer protocols, WEP is not used widely. It's still better than nothing, though, and it does an adequate job of keeping casual snoops at bay. But if you have any other options, it's best to avoid WEP.

WPA

Wi-Fi Protected Access (WPA) is an improvement on WEP that was first available in 1999 but did not see widespread acceptance until around 2003. Once it became widely available, the Wi-Fi Alliance recommended that networks no longer use WEP in favor of WPA.

This standard was the first to implement some of the features defined in the IEEE 802.11i security specification. Most notable among them was the use of the *Temporal Key Integrity Protocol (TKIP)*. Whereas WEP used a static 64- or 128-bit key, TKIP uses a 128-bit dynamic per-packet key. It generates a new key for each packet sent. WPA also introduced message integrity checking.

When WPA was introduced to the market, it was intended to be a temporary solution to wireless security. The provisions of 802.11i had already been drafted, and a standard that employed all of the security recommendations was in development. The upgraded standard would eventually be known as WPA2.

WPA2

Even though their names might make you assume that WPA and WPA2 are very similar, they are quite different in structure. *Wi-Fi Protected Access 2 (WPA2)* is a huge improvement over WEP and WPA. As mentioned earlier, WPA2 implements all of the required elements of the 802.11i security standard. Most notably, it uses Counter Mode CBC-MAC Protocol (CCMP), which is a protocol based on the *Advanced Encryption Standard (AES)* security algorithm. CCMP was created to address the shortcomings of TKIP, so consequently it's much stronger than TKIP. Typical WPA2 security keys are 128 bits long.

The terms CCMP and AES tend to be interchangeable in common parlance. You might also see it written as AES-CCMP.

Since 2006, wireless devices have been required to support WPA2 to be certified as Wi-Fi compliant. WPA2 provides strong encryption and data protection, although it can be somewhat susceptible to brute-force attacks, where passwords are rapidly guessed until the right one is found.

Both WPA and WPA2 can use an authentication mode called *preshared key (PSK)*, in which a security key is generated by the server (or router) and shared with all clients on the network. In Wi-Fi, PSK is in use anytime the "personal" suffix is added, for example, "WPA2 Personal" like you saw in Figure 8.18. This is in contrast to the more secure WPA2 Enterprise, where each user or device gets individualized security credentials to join the network. As long as the WPA2 passphrase is kept confidential, it's very secure.

WPA3

The newest and best wireless encryption standard is *Wi-Fi Protected Access 3 (WPA3)*, introduced in 2018. It uses AES-CCMP like WPA2 as well as the more advanced AES Galois/Counter Mode Protection (AES-GCMP) standard. It supports security keys of 128 bits and 256 bits in length.

One major improvement over WPA2 is the replacement of PSK with a more secure method called Simultaneous Authentication of Equals (SAE), also known as the Dragonfly Key Exchange. SAE basically works by generating unique security codes every time the device connects and authenticates (logs in) to the router, rather than using the same passcode every time.

Exam objective 6.5 specifies that you should know Wi-Fi encryption options such as an open network, preshared key, WPA, WPA2, and WPA3. I threw a lot of acronyms and detail at you in describing each of these, and it's very likely way more than you will need to know for the Tech+ exam. Focus on understanding that open networks are unsecure, and that WPA3 is better than WPA2, which is better than WPA. Also know the basic workings of PSK, in that the same passphrase (or passcode) is used by all clients.

Additional Wireless Router Services

Wireless routers offer many more services than I've been able to cover to this point, and most of them are out of the scope of Tech+ exam training. Still, there are a few items mentioned earlier in this book that I want to cover while on the subject.

Guest Access

Clients who access your wireless network can see other clients on the network and access their resources that are shared. If you have clients who need Internet access but you don't want them to see the rest of the network, you can let them on as guests.

As a security precaution, leave your guest network disabled unless you have a specific reason to enable it.

Guest clients will need to know the SSID of your guest network as well as the password. Of course, make sure this password is different than the other ones you have configured so far. If you look back at Figure 8.16, you can see the guest network configuration on my router. Notice that the password is displayed in plain text. Clicking any of the links in the Guest Access box, or clicking the Guest Access icon in the left menu, will bring up the Guest Access window (Figure 8.22), where you can change the settings.

FIGURE 8.22 Guest network configuration

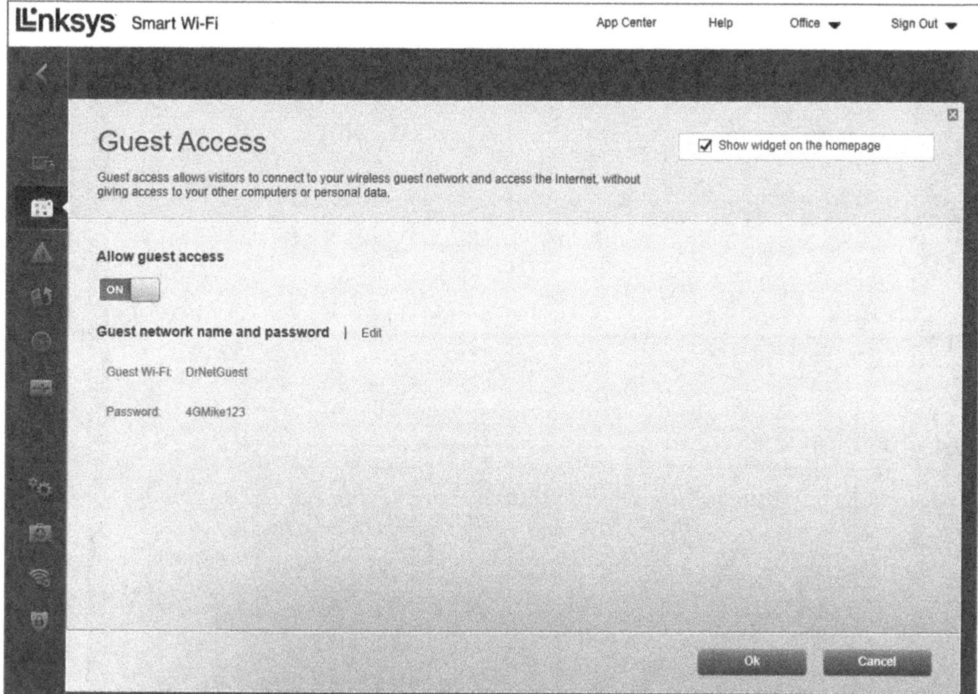

DHCP

Earlier in this chapter, I talked about DHCP and how it automatically configures your clients with IP addresses. This router has it enabled (see Figure 8.23), and you can see some of the configuration options. For the most part, you won't need to change any of these, unless perhaps you want to allow more than the default of 50 clients onto your network. Odds are if you have that many clients, you will need a second wireless access point to handle the traffic.

Firewall

Software firewall functionality was detailed in Chapter 5. A router is often used as a hardware firewall to protect several computers. Figure 8.24 shows you the Security section of the router's configuration, which allows you to set up your firewall rules.

FIGURE 8.23 DHCP configuration

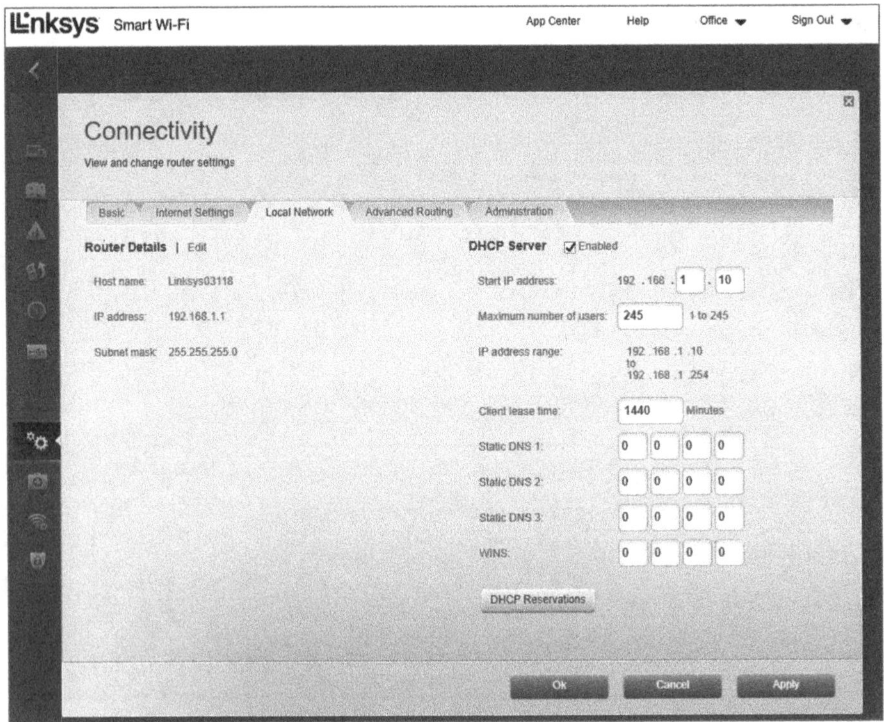

FIGURE 8.24 Firewall settings

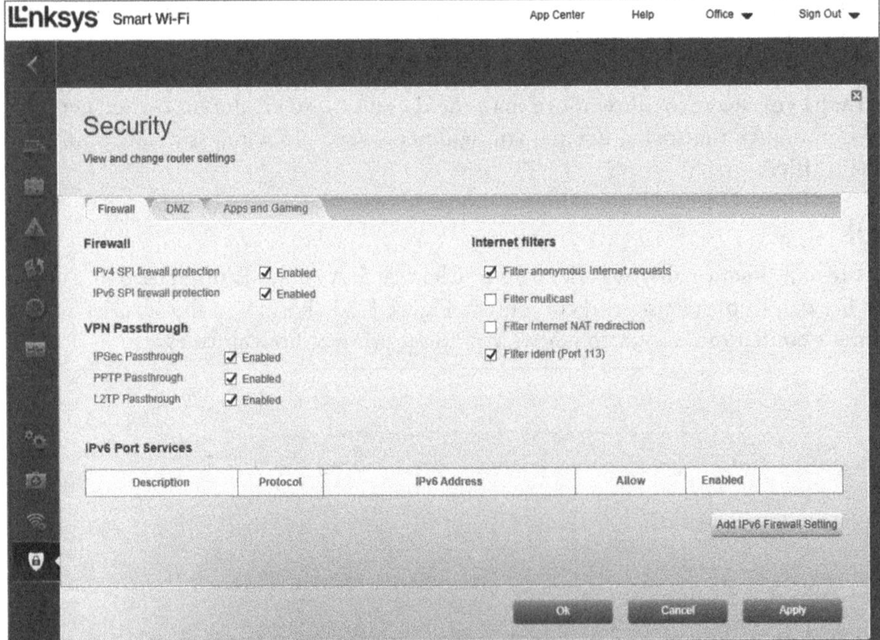

On these three security tabs, you can set an Internet access policy and block protocols such as HTTPS, FTP, and others. Other security options are under Parental Controls, which allows you to block websites by URL and limit Internet access times, as shown in Figure 8.25.

FIGURE 8.25 Parental controls

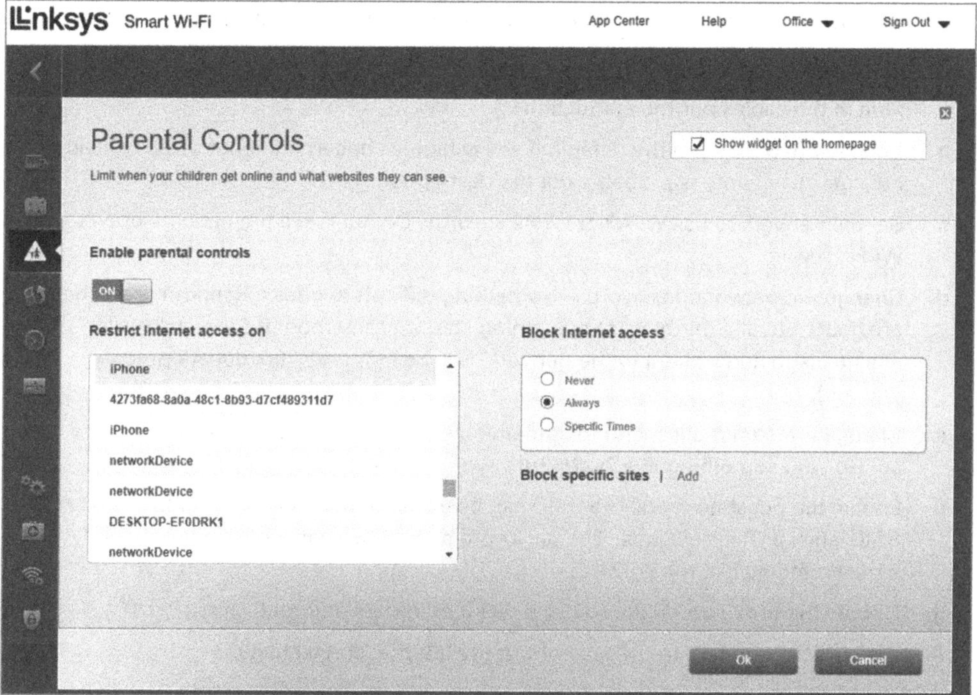

Real World Scenario

Configuring a Small Office Network

You are helping a friend who is opening a small tax preparation firm. She needs to set up an office network for five users. Her office will need Internet access, and because she is dealing with confidential financial information, security is a big concern.

When clients come into the office, some bring their laptops to help the tax preparer find all of the documentation needed. The clients may need Internet access for this. What steps should you take to help her configure a network in the most appropriate way?

Answers can vary somewhat, but here are some recommended steps:

1. Contact the local phone company and the local cable company to see what the best deal is for Internet access and set up an account. Once the DSL or cable modem arrives, begin the network setup.
2. While you are waiting for the modem, purchase a wireless router. It's generally best to get the most current technology, so 802.11ac or 802.11ax is the best choice.
3. Set up the wireless router:
   a. Plug in the cables per the instructions.
   b. Change the SSID from the default. If she is highly concerned about security, using her company name is probably not the best option.
   c. Set the network to use WPA3 or WPA2 security. Do not leave the network open to Wi-Fi access!
   d. Change the network password to something difficult to guess. Random characters are good, but she might want something she can remember if for some reason she needs to add a client to the network. Maybe Tx$pr4y2 (Tax dollars prep for you too).
   e. Change the admin password to something equally difficult to guess, if not more so. Go with something like 7ygH$2p*.
   f. Enable the guest network. The SSID can be easier to use than the regular network SSID, such as TaxPrepGuest. The password should be challenging but not overly so—something like tpg$2024.
   g. Update the firmware on the router or set it to update automatically.
4. Add the client computers to the network. Verify Internet connectivity.
5. Using your laptop, verify that the guest network works and that you are able to get on the Internet using it.

Summary

This chapter provided an in-depth discussion of networking concepts. You started off by learning about the connection types and features of each. For example, external connections to the Internet are almost always broadband today, and the most popular choices are fiber-optic, DSL, and cable Internet. For internal networking, you have two primary choices: wired and wireless. Wireless networking really means Wi-Fi, which is based on the IEEE 802.11 standard. Other wireless connection types include Bluetooth and infrared, but those are specialized connection types not intended for full-scale networking.

The next topic was networking essentials, starting with important devices such as modems, switches, access points, routers, and firewalls. You then learned about protocols and in particular the most important protocol used today, TCP/IP. You learned about IP addresses, subnet masks, and default gateways. In addition, you learned about DHCP and DNS. The section finished with a discussion of network storage options.

This chapter concluded with a detailed look at how to set up and configure a wireless router enabling a wireless network. Important facets included changing the SSID, setting up the best security possible, and making sure that clients can access the Internet.

Exam Essentials

Know what the three network storage types are. The three types are a file server, NAS, and the cloud.

Remember common designations for network throughput units. From slowest to fastest, they are bits per second (bps), kilobits per second (Kbps), megabits per second (Mbps), gigabits per second (Gbps), and terabits per second (Tbps). The exam objectives say Terabytes per second is Tbps, but any acronym using bytes will have an uppercase *B*.

Understand what the common options are for Internet access. Options include dial-up, DSL, cable modems, fiber-optic Internet, satellite, cellular, and radio frequency.

Know the two types of internal network connections and pros and cons of each. The two choices are wired and wireless. Wired is more secure and faster, but wireless is popular because of its vastly superior mobility.

Know what five networking devices do. Modems are used to connect computers via telephone lines. Switches connect computers in a LAN. Access points are used in wireless networks to provide connectivity. Routers connect networks to each other, and firewalls are security appliances that can block network traffic.

Understand two networking models. They are client/server, where some computers are designated as servers and others as clients or workstations, and peer-to-peer, where all computers are treated as equals.

Know the difference between a LAN and a WAN. A local area network (LAN) is typically confined to a small area. A wide area network (WAN) is usually geographically dispersed and connected via broadband networking.

Know which IP configuration options are required. To communicate on a network, every host needs an IP address and a subnet mask. If you want to get on the Internet, you also need a default gateway (such as a wireless router).

Understand what DHCP and DNS do for you. DHCP automatically assigns TCP/IP configuration information to clients. DNS resolves user-friendly hostnames such as `www.google.com` to an IP address.

Understand three types of network identifiers. IP addresses are logical addresses and can be changed. MAC addresses are physical addresses built into the network card and cannot be changed. Ports are like an extension of the IP address that identify which protocol is being used.

Know the best wireless security options. WPA3 is the best, followed by WPA2, WPA, and as a minimum, WEP.

Understand three basic network services and what six related key network protocols do. HTTP and HTTPS are used on the Internet; HTTPS is secure. FTP is for file transfers. POP3 and IMAP are protocols used to retrieve (download) email from a mail server. SMTP is used to send emails.

Understand the 802.11 standards, speed limitations, and interference and attenuation factors. The standards are 802.11a/b/g/n/ac/ax. 802.11ax is the newest and fastest. Distance, radio frequency interference, and physical obstacles are factors that will cause signals to attenuate faster.

Know the three bands that Wi-Fi uses. They are 2.4 GHz, 5 GHz, and 6 GHz. Generally speaking, the higher the band number, the more data throughput it can support, but it will also cover shorter distances due to higher attenuation and risk of interference.

Given a scenario, configure small network security settings. In addition to changing the SSID and default passwords, remember the difference between open (unencrypted) networks and those encrypted by some version of WPA.

Chapter 8 Lab

You can find the answers in Appendix A.

The Chapter 8 lab has two parts to it. In Part 1, you will set up your own secure network. In Part 2, you will see how well others around you have done.

Part 1: Setting Up Your Wireless Router

1. Plug in your router per the manufacturer's instructions, and configure the connection to your Internet device (if applicable).
2. Run the setup routine.
3. Set your SSID.
4. Set security to the strongest available option.
5. Change the wireless password to something that is challenging to guess.
6. Change the administrator password to something that's even harder to guess.
7. Connect your client computer to the network.
8. Verify Internet access.
9. Update the firmware; set the firmware to update automatically if you like.

Part 2: Testing Your Neighbors

In this part, you will check to see how well your neighbors have set up their wireless networks.

1. Open the list of available networks on your client computer (or mobile device). How many do you see available?

   If you live in a densely populated area, especially an apartment or condominium, you will probably have a really long list of available networks.

2. How many of those networks are unsecured?
3. Don't try to connect to neighbors' unsecured networks. One big reason why is that it's illegal. Another reason is that it could expose your computer to potential threats on that unsecured network.

Review Questions

You can find the answers in Appendix B.

1. You are configuring a computer to participate on a TCP/IP network. Which of the following are mandatory? (Choose two.)
   - **A.** IP address
   - **B.** Default gateway
   - **C.** DHCP server
   - **D.** Subnet mask
2. Which one of the following types of network connections can give you the highest data transfer rates?
   - **A.** T1
   - **B.** DSL
   - **C.** ISDN
   - **D.** Cellular
3. You are configuring a wireless network with six computers and no dedicated administrator. Which networking model is most appropriate?
   - **A.** LAN
   - **B.** WAN
   - **C.** Peer-to-peer
   - **D.** Client-server
4. You have a scenario where you need to disable the guest network on your wireless router. You try to log in, but your password does not work. After several attempts, you realize that you forgot your password. What can you do?
   - **A.** Use the password reset option in your router configuration utility.
   - **B.** Unplug the router and plug it back in.
   - **C.** Use the default password of admin.
   - **D.** Hold the reset button down for 30 seconds to reset the router.
5. Your company has a remote office on a cruise ship that sails across the ocean. Which type of Internet service is likely the best choice?
   - **A.** Fiber-optic
   - **B.** Satellite
   - **C.** Cellular
   - **D.** RF

6. This question refers to the scenario at the end of the chapter, in "Configuring a Small Office Network." When connecting client computers to the network, what password do they need to enter?

   A. `tpg$2015`

   B. `7ygH$2p*`

   C. `Tx$pr4y2`

   D. No password is required.

7. Your friend Maria asks you which router feature helps secure against malicious network traffic. What do you tell her?

   A. DNS

   B. DHCP

   C. Firewall

   D. DSL

8. Which of the following is true about TCP/IP ports?

   A. It's based on the protocol being used.

   B. It's the network address of the host.

   C. It will differ based on the MAC address.

   D. It will differ based on the networking model used.

9. Your friend Michael is setting up a wireless network and asks you which security option he should choose to make the network the most secure. What do you suggest?

   A. WEP

   B. WPA

   C. WPA2

   D. Open

10. Which of the following connectivity options gives you the best mobility?

    A. Cellular

    B. Wireless

    C. Wired

    D. Broadband

11. You need to set up a wireless network. Which standard will give you the highest speed?

    A. 802.11a

    B. 802.11ac

    C. 802.11g

    D. 802.11n

12. Which of the following Wi-Fi band options will cover the shortest distance?
    - A. 6 GHz
    - B. 5 GHz
    - C. 2.4 GHz
    - D. 1180 kHz
13. Which one of these connection types has the longest delay?
    - A. Wireless
    - B. Infrared
    - C. Wired
    - D. Cellular
14. Which networking device is designed to connect networks to each other?
    - A. Switch
    - B. Router
    - C. Firewall
    - D. Access point
15. Which network protocol is designed specifically for uploading and downloading files?
    - A. HTTPS
    - B. POP3
    - C. SMTP
    - D. FTP
16. You are connecting to an email server to download email. Which of the following protocols is your computer most likely using? (Choose two.)
    - A. HTTPS
    - B. POP3
    - C. SMTP
    - D. IMAP
17. What command would you use in macOS to determine your TCP/IP configuration information?
    - A. `ifconfig`
    - B. `ipconfig`
    - C. `ipinfo`
    - D. `tcpipconfig`

18. By definition, what is an SSID?
    A. A wireless network name
    B. A wireless network security protocol
    C. A wireless network security password
    D. A wireless network authentication method

19. When configuring a wireless router, which of the following should you always do? (Choose two.)
    A. Enable DHCP.
    B. Change the SSID.
    C. Change the admin password.
    D. Configure the firewall.

20. This question refers to the scenario at the end of the chapter. Your friend wants the tax prep agents to be able to let clients connect their wireless devices to the network. Which password should she tell the agents to give to clients?
    A. `7ygH$2p*`
    B. `tpg$2015`
    C. `Tx$pr4y2`
    D. No password is required.

Cloud Computing and Artificial Intelligence

THE FOLLOWING COMPTIA TECH+ FC0-U71 EXAM OBJECTIVES ARE COVERED IN THIS CHAPTER:

✓ **2.0 Infrastructure**

✓ **2.6 Compare and contrast virtualization and cloud technologies.**

- Virtualization
  - Hypervisor
  - Guest operating system (OS)
- Cloud concepts
  - Platform as a Service (PaaS)
  - Infrastructure as a Service (IaaS)
  - Software as a Service (SaaS)
- Deployment models
  - On premises
  - Cloud
  - Hybrid

✓ **3.0 Applications and Software**

✓ **3.5 Identify common uses of artificial intelligence (AI).**

- AI chatbots
- AI assistants
- Generative AI
  - AI-generated code
  - AI-generated content
- AI predictions and suggestions

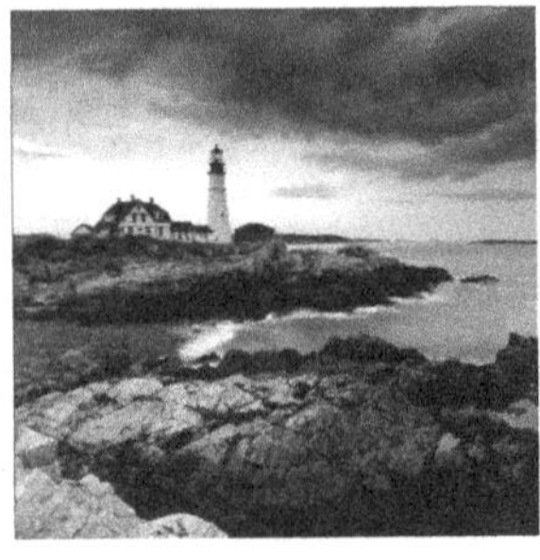

For those of us who are interested in technology, watching the trends and evolution within the computer industry can be fascinating. Some are short-lived and quickly forgotten, such as the Iomega Zip drive that was going to revolutionize portable storage and replace the floppy drive. It lasted about five years in the late 1990s before it, too, was made obsolete by newer technology in rewritable CD-ROMs and USB flash drives.

Others have a far longer arc and make lasting impacts decades after their introduction. This list could easily include dozens of technologies that you're probably familiar with. A few examples include fast broadband Internet access (which replaced dial-up), gigabit Wi-Fi (reducing the dependence upon cables), and the multicore processor, which was a major revolution in the early 2000s and whose limits are still being stretched today by hardware engineers.

Part of the intriguing aspect of tech trends is how new technology moves concepts from the theoretical drawing board to the palms of our hands. One of my favorite examples comes from a comic strip about a high-tech detective named Dick Tracy that debuted in the United States in 1931. Dick Tracy had a wristwatch that enabled two-way communication between himself and the police headquarters—technology that was decades ahead of its time. Today, we of course know the device as a smartwatch, and a combination of miniaturization of components, improvements in display technology, and enhanced cellular networking standards were all required to make it possible.

New technologies also cause the spontaneous creation of entirely new industries. Cloud computing is a great example. Networking enhancements, scalable computing power, and data storage improvements aided in the industry getting off the ground. And in turn, cloud computing has enabled advancements such as big data analysis and artificial intelligence.

This chapter focuses on two newer (but still hot) technology trends—cloud computing and artificial intelligence. Although they are newer, they have both already made profound impacts upon our world and will likely continue to do so for at least the next decade. After that, who knows? Maybe they will continue to dominate the "new trend" space, or perhaps they will be replaced entirely by a newer idea that as of now has just been scribbled on a whiteboard in a lab somewhere. In either case, it will be fascinating to watch.

Understanding Virtualization and Cloud Computing

Throughout most of the history of computers, the relationship between the physical computer and the operating system was relatively straightforward. That is, one operating system could be run on a single computer at a time. There was a one-to-one relationship between hardware and software. For the most part, this has served users pretty well, but there are some cases where it's limiting.

For instance, imagine that there is a Windows-based workstation being used by an applications programmer. The programmer has been asked to code an app that works in Linux, macOS, or anything other than Windows. When the programmer needs to test the app to see how well it works, what do they do? Traditionally, they would need to configure this system to dual-boot—that is, have multiple OSs installed, but every time the programmer needs to use the other OS, they must reboot the computer and choose it from the boot menu. It's hardly fast or efficient. The programmer's company could purchase a second system, but that quickly starts to get expensive when there are multiple users with similar needs.

Similar challenges can arise on the server side. Imagine that the machine in question is being asked to run Windows Server and Linux at the same time. In the traditional computing model, we have a problem because only one OS can run at a time. Each OS is built to think it completely controls the hardware resources in the computer. So, if the requirement is to have a Windows-based file server and a Linux-based Apache web server, there's a problem. Two physical computers are needed.

This is where virtualization comes in. The term virtualization is defined as creating virtual (rather than actual) versions of something. In computer jargon, it means creating virtual environments where "computers" can operate. I use quotation marks around the word computers because they don't need to be physical computers in the traditional sense. Virtualization is often used to let multiple OSs (or multiple instances of the same OS) run on one physical machine at the same time. Yes, they are still bound by the physical characteristics of the machine on which they reside, but virtualization breaks down the traditional one-to-one relationship between a physical set of hardware and an OS.

Virtualization has been around in the computer industry since 1967, but it has only recently exploded in popularity thanks to widely available high-speed Internet access.

Virtual Machines

I have already hit on the major feature of virtualization, which is breaking down that one-to-one hardware and software barrier. The virtualized version of a computer is appropriately called a *virtual machine (VM)*. Thanks to VMs, it is becoming far less common to need dual-boot machines today than in the past. In addition, VMs make technology like the cloud possible. A cloud provider can have one incredibly powerful server that is running five instances of an OS for client use, and each client is able to act as if it had its own individual server. On the flip side, cloud providers are able to pool resources from multiple physical servers into what appears to be one system to the client, effectively giving clients unlimited processing or storage capabilities (assuming, of course, that the provider doesn't physically run out of hardware!).

When running multiple virtual OSs, each virtual OS can be powered on or off individually without affecting the host OS or other virtual OSs.

The underlying purpose of all of this is to save money. Cloud providers can achieve economies of scale because adding clients doesn't necessarily require the purchase of additional hardware. Clients don't have to pay for hardware (or the electricity to keep the hardware cool) and can pay only for the services they use. End users, in the workstation example I provided earlier, can have multiple environments to use without needing to buy additional hardware as well.

Two virtualization components you need to be familiar with are the hypervisor and the guest operating system.

The Hypervisor

The key enabler for virtualization is a piece of software called the *hypervisor*, also known as a virtual machine manager (VMM). The hypervisor software allows multiple operating systems to share the same host, and it also manages the physical resource allocation to those virtual OSs. As illustrated in Figure 9.1, there are two types of hypervisors: Type 1 and Type 2.

Tech+ exam objective 2.6, "Compare and contrast virtualization and cloud technologies," lists two virtualization subobjectives. They are hypervisor (the type isn't specified) and guest operating system. Be familiar with both concepts for the exam! Remember for the exam that Unlike Type 2 hypervisors, type 1 hypervisors interact directly with hardware.

FIGURE 9.1 Type 1 and Type 2 hypervisors

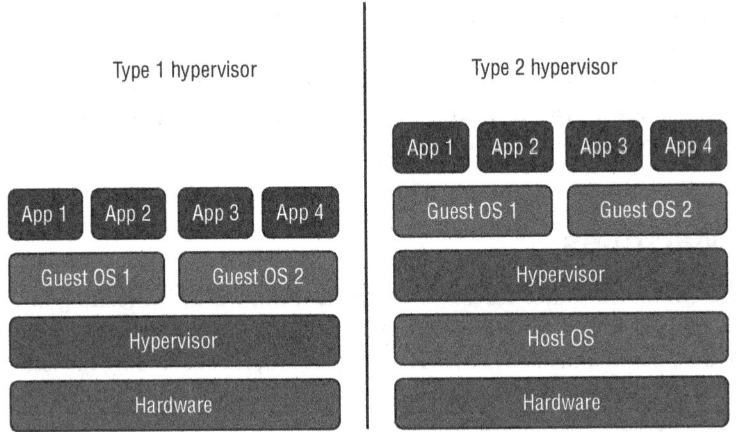

A Type 1 hypervisor interacts directly with (or "sits on") the hardware, and because of this, it's sometimes referred to as a *bare-metal hypervisor*. In this instance, the hypervisor is basically the operating system for the physical machine. This setup is most commonly used for server-side virtualization, because the hypervisor itself typically has very low hardware requirements to support its own functions. Type 1 is generally considered to have better performance than Type 2, simply because there is no host OS involved and the system is dedicated to supporting virtualization. Virtual (guest) OSs are run within the hypervisor, and the virtual OSs are completely independent of each other. Examples of Type 1 hypervisors include Microsoft Hyper-V, VMware ESXi, and Citrix XenServer.

A Type 2 hypervisor sits on top of an existing operating system, called the host OS. This is most commonly used in client-side virtualization, where multiple OSs are managed on the client machine as opposed to on a server. An example of this would be a Windows user who wants to run Linux at the same time as Windows. The user could install a hypervisor and then install Linux in the hypervisor and run both OSs concurrently and independently. The downsides of Type 2 are that the host OS consumes resources such as processor time and memory, and a host OS failure means that the guest OSs fail as well. Examples of Type 2 hypervisors include Microsoft Virtual PC, Oracle VirtualBox, VMware Workstation, and KVM.

Exercise 9.1 shows you how to enable Hyper-V within Windows 11.

EXERCISE 9.1

Enabling Hyper-V in Windows 11

To enable Microsoft Hyper-V, perform the following steps:

1. Check for minimum system requirements:
   - Windows 11 Pro or Enterprise
   - 64-bit processor with Second-Level Address Translation (SLAT)
   - BIOS-level virtualization support enabled
   - 4 GB of RAM or more
2. If requirements are met, then start the Windows Features app by typing **windows features** into the Windows search box and pressing Enter.
3. Select Hyper-V, as shown in Figure 9.2, and click OK.

FIGURE 9.2 Enabling Hyper-V

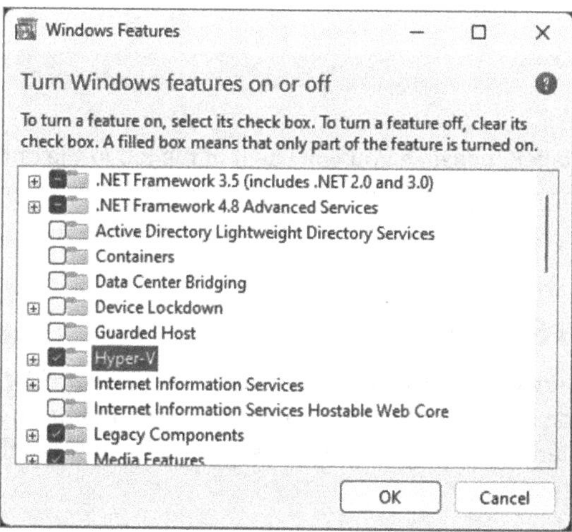

EXERCISE 9.1 *(continued)*

4. When prompted, restart your computer to finish the installation.
5. After rebooting, you can open Hyper-V Manager by typing **hyper** in the Windows search box and pressing Enter. The Hyper-V Manager is shown in Figure 9.3.

FIGURE 9.3 Microsoft Hyper-V Manager

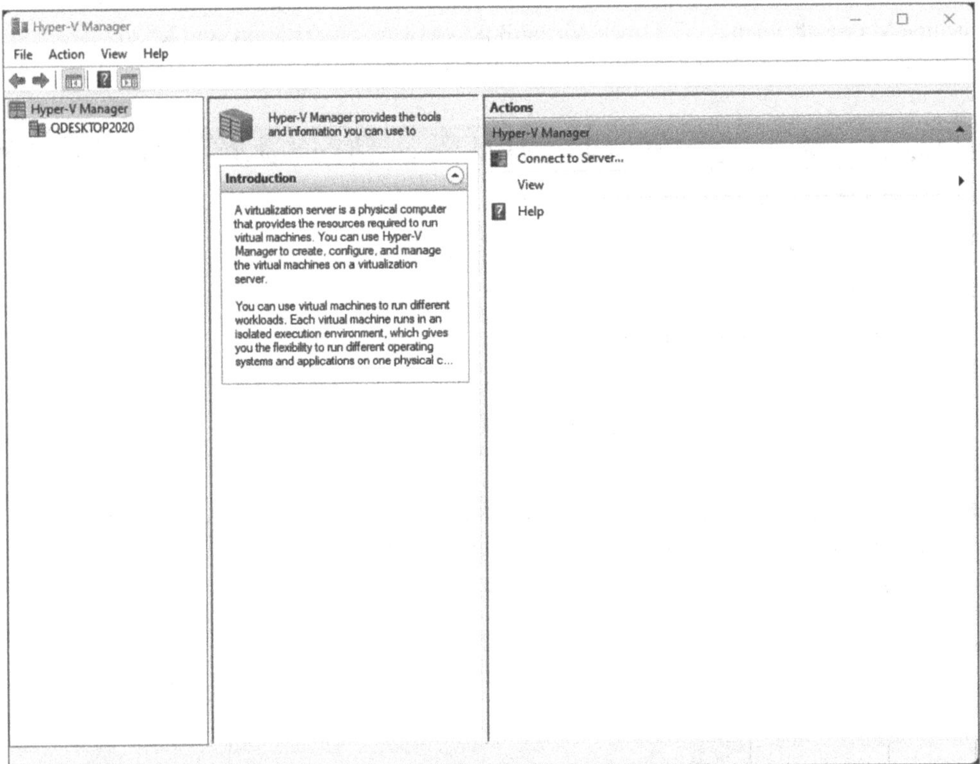

6. Leave Hyper-V installed, because you will use it in the lab at the end of the chapter.

Guest Operating Systems

As introduced in the previous section, the *guest operating system (OS)* is the operating system that is run inside the virtual machine. There are few limitations on the guest OS; it can be the same or different than the host OS. As long as it has enough resources to run properly, it should be fine.

If you've read this book straight through, you're already familiar with virtualization and guest OSs. In Chapter 4, "Operating Systems," you installed Oracle VirtualBox and Lubuntu inside it. As a reminder (or in case you haven't read Chapter 4 yet), Figure 9.4 shows Lubuntu running inside Oracle VirtualBox, with the Windows 11 desktop in the background.

FIGURE 9.4 Lubuntu guest OS

Each has its own desktop, icons, "Start" button, and hardware resources it manages. Neither interferes with the other. Of course, since Windows is the host OS, if it were to crash then Lubuntu would as well, but otherwise they essentially ignore each other. To Windows, VirtualBox is just another app.

Other Virtual Terms to Know

A few pages on virtual machines is a good primer of the technology, but it barely scratches the surface of what there is to know. If virtual machines and cloud computing are interesting to you, a career can definitely be made out of designing and managing them.

For the Tech+ exam, objective 2.6 lists the critical concepts you need to understand for the test. However, the Tech+ Acronym List has a few terms in it you should know as well that aren't explicitly called out in the objectives. The terms are as follows:

- *vCPU*—Virtual central processing unit
- *vHDD*—Virtual hard disk drive
- *vNIC*—Virtual network interface card
- *vRAM*—Virtual random access memory

You are already familiar with the physical versions of these hardware components. The virtual ones function exactly the same way. Instead of having a dedicated physical CPU or network card (or hard drive or RAM) though, the client OS uses virtual ones. When the client OS communicates with another computer, it sends packets to its vNIC. The vNIC is linked to one or more physical network cards. Those sent packets will make it to a physical NIC to go out on the network, but that NIC might be shared with a dozen other virtual machines or it might be one of three NICs shared with a dozen other virtual machines. The exact configuration is obscured to the client and in the end it doesn't really matter, as long as the communication works.

Cloud Computing

You hear the term a lot today—*the cloud*. What exactly is the cloud? The way it's named, and it's probably due to the word *the* at the beginning, it sounds like it's one giant, fluffy, magical entity that does everything you could ever want a computer to do. Only it's not quite that big, fluffy, or magical, and it's not even one thing. Its name comes from the fact that the technology is Internet-based; in most computer literature, the Internet is represented by a graphic that looks like a cloud.

Cloud computing is a method by which you access remote servers to store files or run applications for you. There isn't one cloud but hundreds of commercial clouds in existence today. Many of them are owned by big companies, such as Microsoft, Google, HP, Apple, and Amazon. Basically, they set up the hardware and/or software for you on their network, and then you use it.

Using the cloud sounds pretty simple, and in most cases it is. From the administrator's side, though, things can be a little trickier. Cloud computing relies upon virtualization. There might be one physical server that virtually hosts cloud servers for a dozen companies, or there might be several physical servers working together as one logical server. From the end user's side, the idea of a physical machine versus a virtual machine doesn't even come into play, because it's all handled behind the scenes.

There are many advantages to cloud computing—as you learned earlier in this chapter the most important ones revolve around money. Using the cloud is often cheaper than the alternative. Plus, if there is a hardware failure within the cloud, the provider handles it. If the cloud is set up right, the client won't even know that a failure occurred. Other advantages of cloud computing include fast scalability for clients and ease of access to resources regardless of location.

The biggest downside of the cloud has been security. The company's data is stored on someone else's server (off-premises), and company employees are sending it back and forth via the Internet. Cloud providers have dramatically increased their security over the last several years, but this can still be an issue, especially if the data is highly sensitive material or *personally identifiable information (PII)*. Also, some companies don't like the fact that they don't own the assets. Table 9.1 summarizes some pros and cons to using cloud computing. We'll get into more details on each in the following sections.

TABLE 9.1 Cloud computing pros and cons

Pro	Con
Lower cost	Long-term fixed contracts can end up costing more than expected.
Easily scalable	Hard to move from one provider to another.
Can access data from anywhere	Requires Internet.
Data protected from on-site disaster	Lack of total control.
Security and privacy	Security and privacy.

PII is data about a person that could be used to uniquely identify them, such as their name or email address. This and other privacy fundamentals are covered in Chapter 10, "Security Concepts and Threats."

Security and privacy is listed as both a pro and a con in Table 9.1, and you might wonder how it can be both. For small companies that can't afford dedicated IT support or security experts, cloud providers can offer superior security options. However, because of the nature of cloud storage—it is almost always stored and accessed across the Internet—new security problems could arise. For instance, although Internet data transmissions are encrypted to cloud sites, encryption is not impossible to hack. And someone could have their password hacked that renders security mechanisms ineffective. Finally, a third-party company (hopefully a trusted and reputable one) is managing the data, which introduces additional possibilities for security breaches.

Now let's dive into the types of services clouds provide, the types of clouds, and cloud-specific terms with which you should be familiar.

Cloud Services

Cloud providers sell everything "as a service." The type of service is named for the highest level of technology provided. Common levels from lowest to highest are:

- Infrastructure ("virtual hardware")
- Software development tools
- Applications

For example, if computing and storage is the highest level, the client will purchase Infrastructure as a Service. If applications are involved, it will be Software as a Service. Nearly everything that can be digitized can be provided as a service. Let's take a look at details within the three most common types of services offered by cloud providers, from the ground up:

Infrastructure as a Service Let's say that a company needs extra network capacity, including processing power, storage, and networking services (such as firewalls) but doesn't have the money to buy more network hardware. Instead, it can purchase *Infrastructure as a Service (IaaS)*, which is a lot like paying for utilities—the client pays for what it uses. Of the three major cloud services, IaaS requires the most network management expertise from the client. In an IaaS setup, the client provides and manages the software.

Platform as a Service *Platform as a Service (PaaS)* adds a layer to IaaS that includes software development tools such as runtime environments. (A runtime environment is the software and hardware infrastructure that supports running a type of code. It's used to give applications access to memory and other resources.) Because of this, it can be very helpful to software developers; the vendor manages the various hardware platforms. This frees up the software developer to focus on building their application and scaling it. The best PaaS solutions allow for the client to export their developed programs and run them in an environment other than where they were developed. Examples of PaaS include Google App Engine, Microsoft Azure, Red Hat OpenShift, Amazon Web Services (AWS) Elastic Beanstalk, Engine Yard, and Heroku.

Software as a Service (SaaS) The highest of these three levels of service is *Software as a Service (SaaS)*, which handles the task of managing software and its deployment, and includes the platform and infrastructure as well. This is the one with which you are probably most familiar, because it's the model used by Google Docs, Microsoft 365, and even storage solutions such as Dropbox. The advantage of this model is to cut costs for software ownership and management; clients typically sign up for subscriptions to use the software and can renew as needed.

Figure 9.5 shows examples of these three types of services. SaaS is the same as the Application layer shown in the figure.

FIGURE 9.5 Common cloud service levels

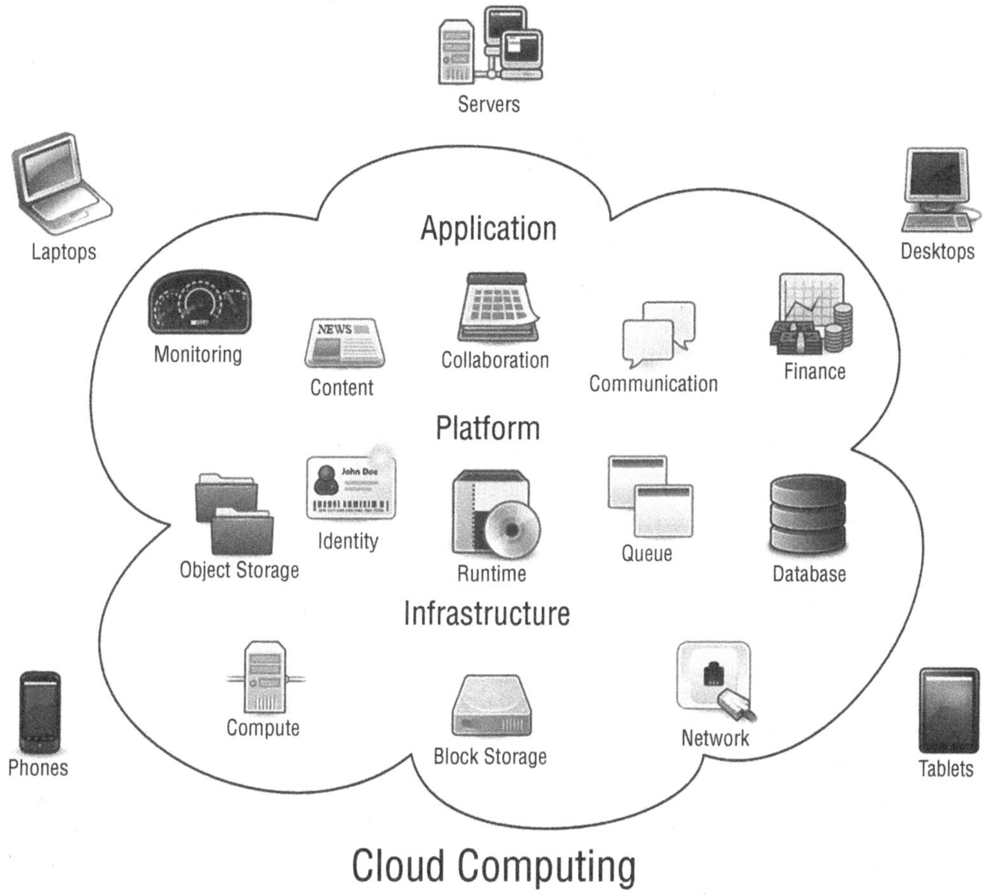

Servers
Laptops
Desktops
Application
Monitoring
Content
Collaboration
Communication
Finance
Platform
Object Storage
Identity
Runtime
Queue
Database
Infrastructure
Compute
Block Storage
Network
Phones
Tablets
Cloud Computing

Source: Sam Johnston / Wikimedia / CC BY SA 3.0.

Although not included in the Tech+ objectives, the following other service levels also exist:

- *Hardware as a Service (HaaS),* which is similar to IaaS but is more likely related specifically to data storage
- *Communications as a Service (CaaS),* which provides things like voice over IP (VoIP), instant messaging, and video collaboration
- *Network as a Service (NaaS),* which provides network infrastructure

- *Desktop as a Service (DaaS)*, which provides virtual desktops so that users with multiple devices or platforms can have a similar desktop experience across all systems
- *Data as a Service (also DaaS)*, which provides for multiple sources of data in a mash-up
- *Business Processes as a Service (BPaaS)*, which provides business processes such as payroll, IT help desk, or other services
- *Anything/everything as a Service (XaaS)*, which is a combination of the services already discussed

The level of responsibility between the provider and the client is specified in the contract. It should be very clear which party has responsibility for specific elements, should anything go awry.

Exam objective 2.6 lists PaaS, IaaS, and SaaS as the types of clouds to know. It lists on-premises and hybrid clouds as objectives as well.

Types of Clouds

Running a cloud is not restricted to big companies offering services over the Internet. Companies can purchase virtualization software to set up individual clouds within their own network. That type of setup is referred to as a *private cloud* or an *on-premises cloud*. Running a private cloud pretty much eliminates many of the features that companies want from the cloud, such as rapid scalability and eliminating the need to purchase and manage computer assets. The big advantage, though, is that it allows the company to control its own security within the cloud.

The traditional type of cloud that usually comes to mind is a *public cloud*, like the ones operated by the third-party companies I mentioned earlier. These clouds offer the best in scalability, reliability, flexibility, geographical independence, and cost-effectiveness. Whatever the client wants, the client gets. For example, if the client needs more resources, it simply scales up and uses more. Of course, the client will also pay more, but that's part of the deal.

Some clients have chosen to combine public and private clouds into a *hybrid cloud*. This gives the client the great features of a public cloud while simultaneously allowing for the storage of more sensitive information on the private cloud. It's the best of both worlds.

The last type of cloud to discuss is a *community cloud*. These are created when multiple organizations with common interests combine to create a cloud. In a sense, it's like a public cloud but with better security. The clients know who the other clients are and, in theory, can trust them more than they could trust random people on the Internet. The economies of scale and flexibility won't be as great as with a public cloud, but that's the trade-off for better security.

Important Cloud Characteristics

To finish the discussion on cloud computing, let's take a look at what *exactly* the cloud is supposed to provide. The National Institute of Standards and Technology (NIST), a group within the U.S. Department of Commerce, has defined the following five essential characteristics of cloud computing:

On-Demand Self-Service This is one of the cloud's best features from an end user's standpoint. With on-demand self-service, users can access additional storage, processing, and capabilities automatically, without requiring intervention from the service provider.

Broad Network Access This means that cloud capabilities are accessible over the network by different types of clients, such as workstations, laptops, tablets, smartphones, and other mobile devices, using common access software such as web browsers. The ability for users to get the data they want, when they want, and how they want is sometimes referred to as *ubiquitous access*.

Resource Pooling The idea of *resource pooling* means that the provider's resources are seen as one large pool that can be divided up among clients as needed, and each client pays for the fraction of those resources they use. Clients should be able to access additional resources as needed, even though the client may not be aware of where the resources are physically located. Typical pooled resources include network bandwidth, storage, processing power, and memory.

With the exception of private clouds, all cloud types use resource pooling or shared resources. In a private cloud, one company controls all the resources.

Rapid Elasticity We've talked about the ability to scale up resources as needed, and that is elasticity. In most cases, clients can get more resources instantly (or at least very quickly), and that is called *rapid elasticity*. For the client, this is a great feature because they can scale up without needing to purchase, install, and configure new hardware. Elasticity can also work backward; if fewer resources are required, the client may be able to scale down and pay less without needing to sell hardware. You will hear some subscriptions with built-in elasticity referred to as *pay-as-you-grow services*.

Measured Service Most cloud providers track clients' usage and then charge them for the services used. This type of setup is called *metered service* or *measured service*. Resource usage is monitored by the provider and reported to the client in a transparent fashion.

In addition to those characteristics, two more important ones are file synchronization and high availability. *File synchronization* is straightforward enough—it makes sure that the most current copy is on the cloud as well as on a local device. If changes are made to one, the other copy gets updated accordingly. *High availability* refers to uninterrupted and responsive service. When I say uninterrupted, though, I should probably clarify that by saying it's *mostly* uninterrupted. The level of uptime guaranteed by the cloud service provider (CSP) will be specified in a document called the service level agreement (SLA).

Service availability is measured in terms of "nines," or how many nines of uptime the provider guarantees. For example, "three nines" means that the service will be available 99.9 percent of the time, whereas "four nines" will be up 99.99 percent of the time. More nines means more money, and different aspects of your service contract might require different levels of uptime. For example, a critical medical records database might need more guaranteed uptime than would a word processing application. The level of service you should get depends on how much risk your company is willing to take on and the trade-off with cost. Table 9.2 shows how much downtime is acceptable based on the number of nines of guaranteed uptime.

TABLE 9.2 Availability downtime

Availability	Downtime per year	Downtime per day
Three nines (99.9%)	8.77 hours	1.44 minutes
Four nines (99.99%)	52.6 minutes	8.64 seconds
Five nines (99.999%)	5.26 minutes	864 milliseconds
Six nines (99.9999%)	31.56 seconds	86.4 milliseconds

Guaranteeing that services will be available with the possible exception of less than one second per day seems pretty impressive, as is the case with five nines. You might see other combinations, too, such as "four nines five," which translates into 99.995 percent availability, or no more than 4.32 seconds of downtime per day. The majority of CSPs will provide at least three nines or three nines five.

Exploring Artificial Intelligence

Artificial Intelligence (AI) is the hottest topic in IT right now and for good reason. The goal for many AI developers is to create machines that think independently and creatively like humans. It could have a tremendous impact on learning and productivity, along the scale of what the Internet or the Industrial Revolution did for humanity. At the same time, AI could pose risks that we as a species don't know how to manage.

When a lot of people think about AI, they imagine self-aware robots—and that could be good or bad depending on their perspective. On the bright side, those robots could do work that is dangerous for humans or that we don't want to do. Or perhaps if self-driving vehicles become the norm, the number of traffic accidents and injuries could dramatically decrease. One negative possibility is that AI robots could, in theory, take jobs from people, and consequently, there is a massive rise in unemployment and poverty. This same concern was raised when industrial robotics was an emerging trend in the 1980s and 1990s. Certainly, robots have taken a lot of jobs, particularly in manufacturing, but they have helped keep production costs down and created new jobs, such as technicians to fix the robots.

Although science fiction writers have laid out a number of positive and negative possibilities about self-aware machines for us, we're not anywhere close to those situations yet. The reality of what AI is and where it's going is likely far more muted than the extremes in someone's imagination. Still, the potential implications of this technology should not be underestimated.

With that picture in mind, let's take a look at what AI is and how it works, and then examine some current applications of it. Odds are you are already familiar with many examples of AI, and you might not even realize it.

How AI Works

To best understand how AI works, take into consideration how computers have traditionally operated. At a basic level there is a collection of hardware components. A computer programmer creates an app that has the hardware complete a specific task or tasks. The computer program knows that if it gets certain input, it does *X* or *Y* task and produces output. This basic computing model is illustrated in Figure 9.6.

FIGURE 9.6 Basic computing model

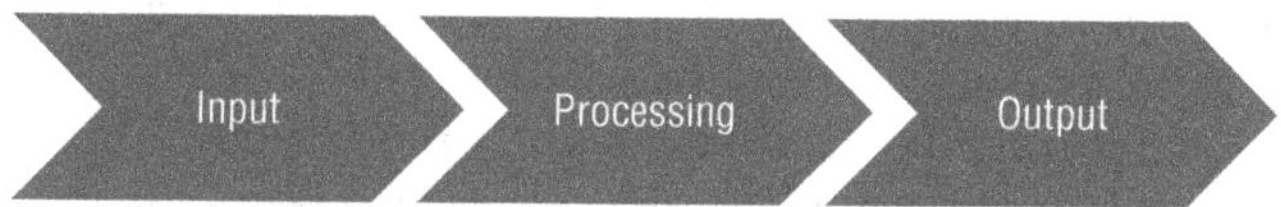

Now, in reality of course it's far more complex than that, because there can be multiple inputs, the output can be used as input into the original process or a different process, or the app might have multiple logical paths it can take depending on the input. Software is pretty complicated. The key things to take away are that it's an algorithm developed by a person and it's linear in the sense that there's a defined start, process, and end. (An *algorithm* is a process used for solving a problem or completing a task.) It does what it's programmed to do.

Imagine a situation where a program is created to scan millions of images and identify and count people wearing green shirts. Ignoring some of the complexities for the moment—such as what shade of green, long-sleeve or short-sleeve, what about sweaters?—the program will do what it's told and give the user an answer. Maybe it says there are 3,000 people wearing green shirts. To determine how accurate the program is, someone would need to manually examine the pictures, count them, and come up with a number themselves. If the app is found to be lacking the necessary accuracy, the developer needs to edit the code with updates and run the entire process again to see what the new count is. At best it's tedious and time-consuming.

This is where AI comes into play. A person still needs to program the algorithm telling the software how to properly identify people wearing green shirts. The big difference, though, is that the program gets feedback on how accurate it is and then can adjust on its own to improve its performance. This is the "intelligence" part of AI; a simplified version of its computing model is shown in Figure 9.7.

FIGURE 9.7 Basic AI computing model

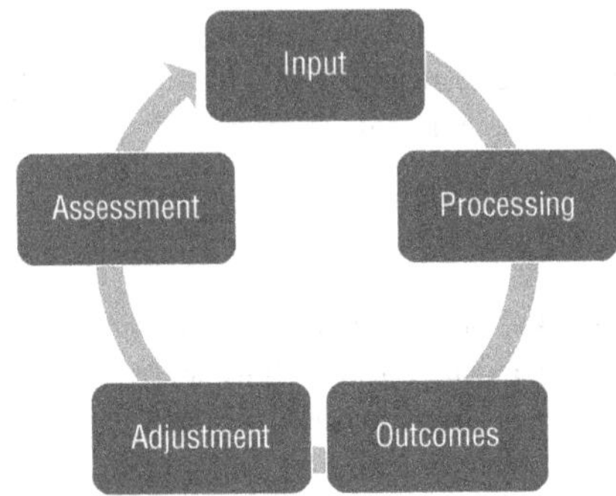

Looking at Figure 9.7, you can see that there are two new aspects versus the basic computing model in Figure 9.6: adjustments and assessments. The developer programs the app in such a way that when provided with feedback on past performance, it can learn how well or poorly it did on a previous assessment and adjust as needed.

If we go back to the green shirt example, let's say that on the first pass it identifies 3,000 people, but the developer knows that there are really 10,000 people. Examples would be provided to the AI showing it where it was incorrect; it would learn from that and incorporate that learning into its next round of scanning the images. It might take several rounds of adjustments and assessments, with the ultimate goal of getting as accurate as possible. This adjustment and assessment process is referred to as *training the model*. Once the model is trained on the initial dataset to a certain level of accuracy, it can be used with confidence to evaluate new datasets.

How the Cloud Enables AI

In the chapter introduction, I mentioned that cloud computing and AI are related, but how?

Cloud computing has enabled AI by providing scalable and accessible computing power to process large datasets and complex algorithms required for AI tasks. Through cloud services, users can access the necessary computational resources and storage capabilities without the need to invest in expensive hardware infrastructure. This accessibility has democratized AI by allowing a wider range of users to leverage advanced machine learning and deep learning technologies for various applications.

The previous paragraph was written by a free online AI tool—a paragraph written by cloud-enabled AI on how the cloud has enabled AI. How meta is that? It's an example of generative AI, where you give the AI a prompt and it will generate non-copyrighted content based on what you asked it to do. (I will cover generative AI more in the next section.) While the paragraph is good, generative AI at this point is usually better at coming up with general content, and it's not as good at providing specific details. The rest of the book is written without the help of AI.

Types of AI

The use of AI has expanded exponentially in the last decade or so, and now there are several disciplines within AI focused on different tasks. Depending on whom you ask, you will find anywhere from five to 12 different disciplines of artificial intelligence. Some of them overlap with other areas of AI, while others will be totally unique. Here is a glimpse into some of the different types of AI in use today:

Machine Learning Defined as teaching computers to learn from experience, or teaching computers to learn like humans do, *machine learning (ML)* is the core of AI. Several techniques are used in machine learning. Most of the time, the AI is fed a series of tagged stimuli in what's known as *supervised learning*. For example, it's fed pictures of people and a tag (metadata that describes what's important) indicating if the person is or is not wearing a green shirt. From these examples, the algorithm is trained to identify people wearing green shirts.

Another example is *reinforced learning*, where the AI is subjected to rewards for making a correct decision or a punishment for making an incorrect one. Finally, there is *deep learning*, which incorporates multiple layers of algorithms in an attempt to simulate the behavior of the human brain. Deep learning is usually employed when the AI is asked to synthesize insights from large unstructured datasets.

Natural Language Processing When an AI is trained to understand written or spoken human languages, it's using *natural language processing (NLP)*. If you have ever tried to learn a second language, you might grasp how complicated it is to teach a computer how to do so as well. One immediate example that might come to mind is an AI assistant such as Alexa, Siri, or Google Assistant. You'll learn more about these and other NLP examples in the next section.

Neural Networks Neural networks are machine learning programs designed to make decisions like how the human brain would. Neural networks and deep learning are terms often used interchangeably. As implied by the name, a neural network consists of several nodes linked together, each of which will specialize in a different task or part of the process. There is an input layer or function, the hidden neural network of one or more additional layers, and finally an output layer. Input is taken, passed from one node to another as needed, and eventually make it to the output layer. Most of the time, each node in the hidden layer is enabled to learn independently on its own. Figure 9.8 illustrates a neural network.

FIGURE 9.8 A neural network

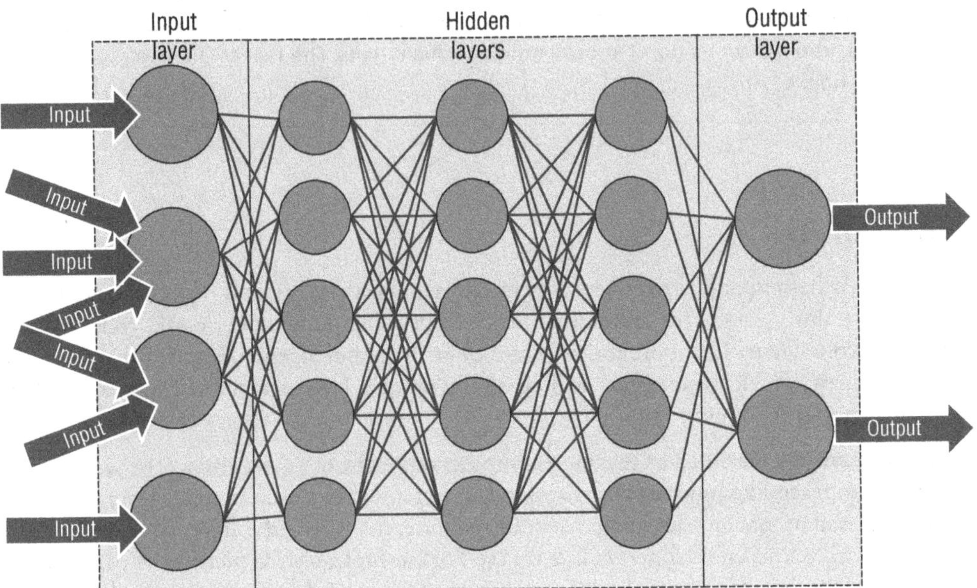

Robotics *Robotics* is the science of designing and building physical machines to perform automated tasks. It's different from AI, but AI can definitely play a role in robotics. A simple example of AI in robotics is a manufacturing machine that can learn to adjust if a part is misaligned or isn't fastening properly. The robot may have capabilities to adjust and fix the problem or notify a person to resolve the issue. A more complex example is the field of creating humanoid robots capable of performing feats of agility and strength based on conditions that might change. For instance, Boston Dynamics' Atlas program does exactly this. If you're interested in learning more, visit `https://bostondynamics.com/atlas`.

Computer Vision Combining machine learning and neural networks, *computer vision* trains computers to understand and interpret digital images and videos. Going back to our green shirt example, this is the technology that would be behind such a program. Computer vision can also be used in conjunction with security systems, identifying potential security incidents as they happen and also using facial recognition software to identify people who may have previously committed a crime.

The highest soccer league in England, the Premier League, uses computer vision in a few different ways. One is the video assistant referees (VAR) system, which helps determine whether a goal is valid. It can detect in near-real time if the ball crossed the goal line and is capable of measuring accurately within a few millimeters. Another is for security. At some matches, facial recognition is used to spot known criminals or those previously banned from matches due to bad behavior as they attempt to enter the stadium. Such potential spectators are denied entrance or met by law enforcement, depending on the situation. Of course, these types of systems also bring up potential privacy issues. The goal here isn't to make a judgment one way or another, but simply to provide examples of how the technology is currently used.

Expert Systems One final example of AI disciplines is expert systems, in which a computer is trained to mimic someone who is an expert in a field of study. The goal of the system is to make decisions about a situation the same way an expert would. Most of the time, expert systems are used in a way to supplement human experts rather than replace them.

The six disciplines outlined here give you an idea of how AI is being developed, but the field is changing all the time as new avenues of application are pursued. Next, let's take a look at three categories of common uses of AI today: conversational, generative, and predictive.

Tech+ exam objective 3.5, "Identify common uses of artificial intelligence (AI)," wants you to understand the following:

- AI chatbots and assistants (which are conversational AI)
- Generative AI, including AI-generated code and AI-generated content
- AI predictions and suggestions

Be familiar with these before you sit for the exam!

Conversational AI

Having conversations with others is something most of us do in our daily lives. Some of us might find it easier to do so than others, but it's a skill with which most of us have some level of proficiency. Conversations can of course be voice-based or they can be text-based, depending on the situation. Voice and text conversations will follow slightly different rules, even if they're in the same language. For example, when speaking, one doesn't call out punctuation. A pause may indicate the end of a sentence, and raising ones voice slightly usually signals a question. Someone *could* say "period" at the end of each of their verbal sentences. Doing so once might provide emphasis, but if they did it at the end of each sentence it would lose all meaning and get tiresome in a hurry. Writing is an entirely different story. Although punctuation in texting can be informal, a two-page email written with no punctuation would be very challenging to get through.

Through the advances of AI, computers can now conduct verbal and text-based conversations with people or with each other. Specifically, conversational AI is enabled through a combination of NLP and machine learning. Two common applications of this are AI chatbots and AI assistants. The line between the two is fuzzy. Generally speaking, *AI chatbots* are automated response systems designed to respond to specific questions or comments on a given topic. *AI assistants* are automated response systems as well but can handle a broader range of topics or questions.

AI Chatbots

If you have ever called into a company, and an automated voice on the other end says something like, "please tell me the reason you are calling," or "please say your account number," that is a chatbot. Based on the reason you state, it might route you to a specific department. Or once you provide your account number and verify your identity, it will tell you your account balance and payment due date. Either of those tasks is relatively narrow in scope. If you call your credit card company and ask to talk about avocados, the AI probably won't know what to do with that.

AI chatbots are online too on company websites. See Figure 9.9 for an example from a local auto dealership. Sorry if this next piece of information is shocking to you, but Alice isn't a real person. She's an AI chatbot. At the bottom of the figure it shows that the chatbot is powered by FordDirect, which is a marketing company based out of Michigan that uses AI to help Ford dealers market better to its potential customers. If, during the conversation with the chatbot, you seem like a strong enough lead, you will be transferred to a live salesperson who will be happy to help you.

FIGURE 9.9 Chatbot on a website

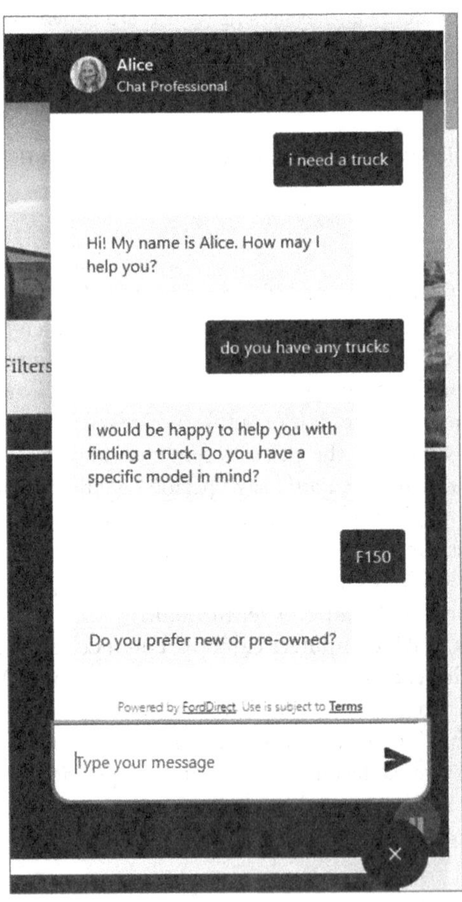

AI Assistants

Like AI chatbots, AI assistants are designed to have conversations and provide responses to questions. Odds are you are familiar with this technology, because it's common today with the use of Amazon's Alexa, Apple's Siri, Google Assistant, and Samsung's Bixby all being general, all-purpose AI assistants. You can ask them to look up something online, play music, send messages, set timers, provide directions, get notifications, and a bunch of other things. Based on the broad range of prompts these assistants can respond to, they are considered more complex than AI chatbots.

Along with the general AI assistants, there are ones designed for specific purposes such as financial advice and management, travel help, work help (scheduling meetings, handling email, organizing notes, managing projects, etc.), and writing. Some AI assistants are free, while others require a usage fee.

Generative AI

The realm of *generative AI* focuses on creating content, including text, images, or videos. One of the more famous generative AI platforms right now is ChatGPT, but there are dozens of options available online. To use generative AI, you go the website and enter a prompt where asked. The prompt is a sentence describing the type of content you want. Figure 9.10 shows an example from ChatGPT. I asked it, "who is the best soccer player ever?," and it provided an answer.

FIGURE 9.10 ChatGPT

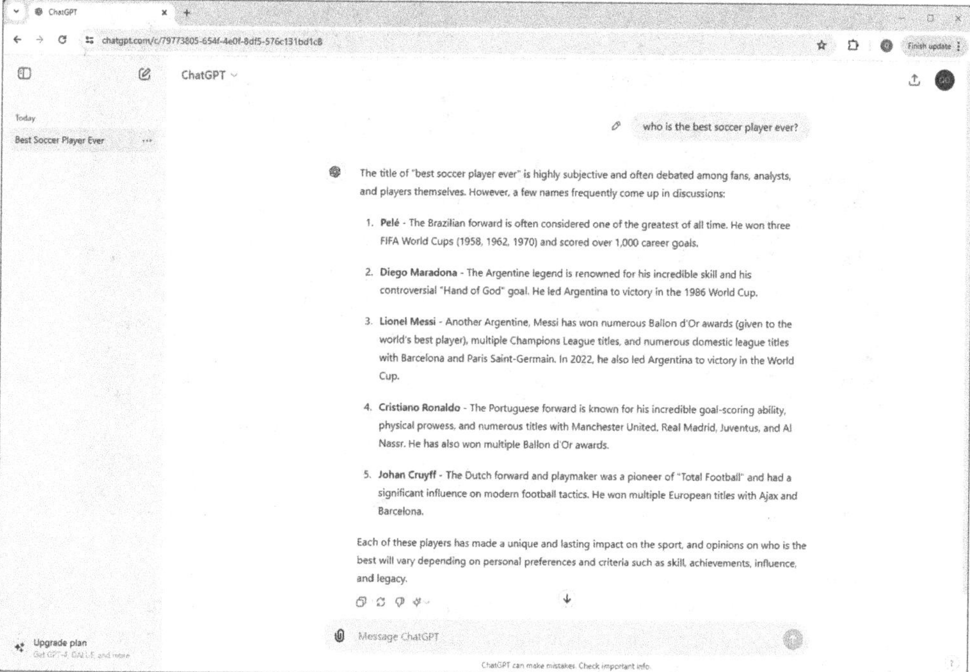

The two major classifications in the Tech+ exam objectives are *AI-generated content* and *AI-generated code*. AI-generated content can take many text forms, such as prose, poetry, and educational or training materials. It can also be visual content, such as artwork, company logos, or even basic videos. When seeking out an AI tool for a project, be sure to look for one that specializes in the type of content you need. Craiyon, for example, generates AI art. You can see output from the site when asked to create a BBQ company logo in Figure 9.11. If you subscribe to AI sites, you can often take output and then add additional prompts to refine it. For example, you could take a logo you liked from Figure 9.11 and tell the AI to make it have more smoke or less green or a happier-looking pig—whatever you wanted.

FIGURE 9.11 Craiyon AI art

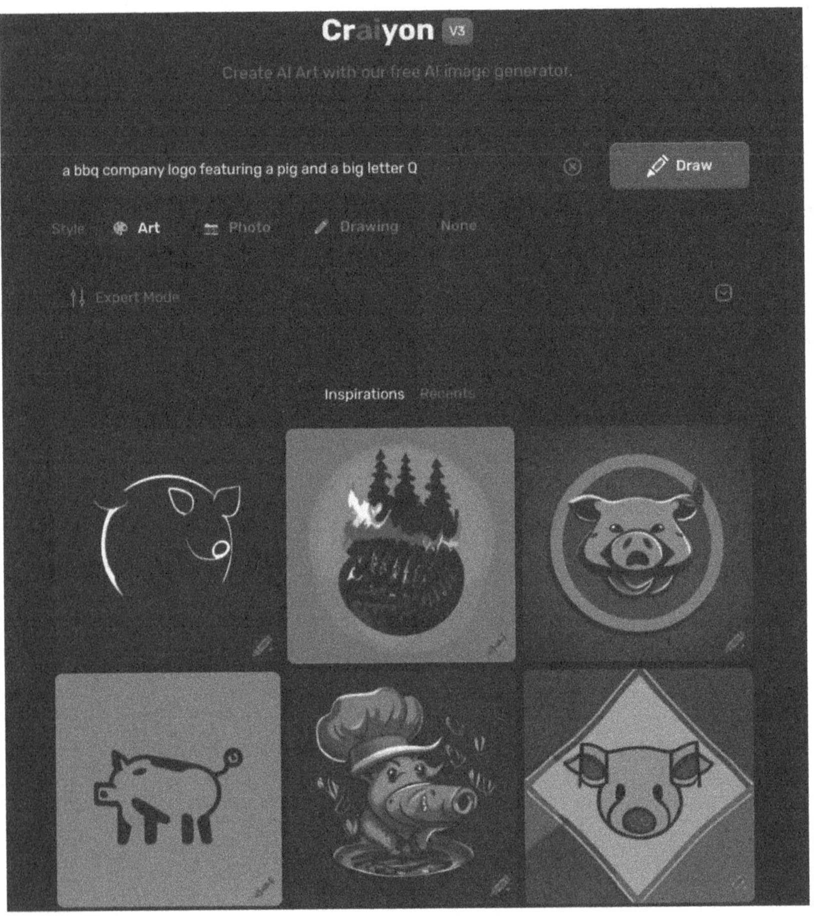

AI-generated code writes computer code in the language specified. AIs can write in common languages such as C++, R, Java, JavaScript, Python, and Lisp, among others. Much like generating AI content, the user provides information at the prompt telling the AI what the code should do. The code might not be perfect, and you shouldn't expect it to be able to write entire programs for you. It will, however, be useful as a starting point for a developer. Other AIs can analyze code and perform error checks if a developer is running into issues they are unsure how to resolve. Exercise 9.2 introduces you to using generative AI.

Real World Scenario

When AI Got Dumber

One of the most fascinating aspects of AI is its ability to learn, adapt, and get better at tasks. As the AI ingests feedback and additional data, it should become better at whatever tasks it's given. But what if the AI instead becomes . . . dumber?

This phenomenon was observed in 2023 when ChatGPT was found to get worse at certain tasks over a period of several months. For example, when asked to solve math problems or answer medical licensing exam questions, ChatGPT performed worse in June than it did in March of that year. And this isn't picking on ChatGPT, either. Other generative AIs have occasionally shown similar behaviors. How does that happen?

The answer is *AI drift*. Technically speaking, AI drift is when the model behaves in an unpredictable or unexpected way. Drift can indicate a small error somewhere in the AI code, often unintentionally caused by trying to optimize or fix another area of the AI. Or it could mean that the AI is learning from incorrect data. In practical terms, the AI ingests bad or incorrect data, doesn't realize the data is bad, and then incorporates the bad data into its models. It would be akin to feeding an AI dozens of articles claiming the sky was red and then asking it to write a story about the sky. Without knowing better, the AI would write about a brilliant red sky. Garbage in, garbage out.

AI developers can combat drift a few ways. One is to ensure that all data sources are checked and cross-referenced. This can be especially challenging when the AI learns from user input, which isn't controlled by the developer. Another is to occasionally purge the model and start over or have a cycle where the model is intentionally retrained with data that's known to be correct. Finally, the model can incorporate adaptive techniques that use feedback loops from the developer or trusted sources.

There are two morals of this story. The first is that while there have been tremendous advancements in AI, it's not perfect. The second is simple—don't always blindly trust AI-generated results to be 100 percent correct.

EXERCISE 9.2

Using Generative AI

1. Open your web browser.
2. In the address bar, type **`chatgpt.com`** and press Enter.

EXERCISE 9.2 *(continued)*

3. On the ChatGPT website, you will notice an entry field at the bottom of the page that says "Message ChatGPT." This is where you enter your prompt.

   Notice just below the prompt it has a warning of sorts, telling you that ChatGPT can make mistakes and to check important info.

4. Ask ChatGPT to do something for you. For example, you can ask it to name the 10 best movies ever, or tell you about a famous person or location. The world is your oyster.

5. Repeat step 4 as many times as you would like.

   This is the free version of ChatGPT, so you don't have a lot of options. Paid versions of this AI and others let you enter multiple prompts and refine results.

6. Close the browser window when you are done.

Predictive AI

Predictive AI uses machine learning to predict behaviors and anticipate future events. Like some of the other forms of AI you've already learned about, you probably have experienced predictive AI and might not have realized it. For example, autocorrect and word suggestions on your smartphone are an example of predictive AI. Another very common example is typing in words in your web browser's address bar. If you look at Figure 9.12, it shows predictive AI filling in the query "how do I." Apparently, common questions include taking screenshots and getting a passport. As of this writing, the northern lights were visible in much of the United States (an uncommon occurrence in most places), so that was a topical prediction.

FIGURE 9.12 Predictive AI suggestions

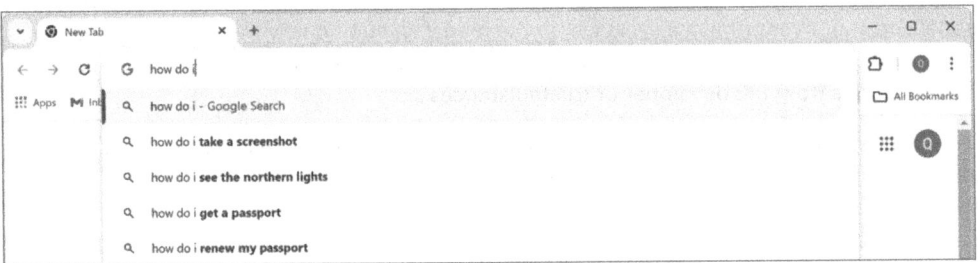

Predictive AI is used a lot in shopping environments as well. If you shop online, doubtless you've seen something like, "If you like this product, you'll want to buy these five other things too!" That's predictive AI in action, based on the behaviors of other shoppers who might have similar interests to yours. Unfortunately, the AI isn't smart enough to *stop* recommending something after you've purchased it. Someday it will be.

Whenever there is a large dataset with past behavior, predictive AI can be used to anticipate future behavior. This can be applied to financial data such as forecasting or fraud protection, healthcare, insurance, entertainment, and dozens of other things. The model needs to be developed and validated, and then used to attempt to predict the future.

Summary

This chapter covered two newer major technologies in IT: cloud computing and artificial intelligence. First, you learned about cloud computing. The cloud is a fancy term for saying that virtual hardware or software you're using is Internet-based rather than local to you. Cloud technology uses virtualization, which is enabled by a hypervisor that hosts a guest operating system. Clouds can be deployed on-premises or in the cloud, or some combination of the two. All cloud capacity is sold "as a service," such as Infrastructure as a Service, Platform as a Service, or Software as a Service.

The scale provided by cloud computing has enabled technologies such as artificial intelligence. AI is when computers are programmed to learn and adapt, with the intent to mimic human learning and behavior. There are several types of AIs. Common ones for commercial use include conversational AIs like chatbots and AI assistants, generative AI such as ChatGPT and others, and predictive AI, which includes autocorrect and online shopping suggestions.

Exam Essentials

Understand what a hypervisor is. The hypervisor is software that allows multiple operating systems to share the same host, and it also manages the physical resource allocation to those virtual OSs.

Know what a guest operating system is. A guest operating system is one that resides in a hypervisor and controls only the resources allocated to it.

Understand the differences between IaaS, PaaS, and SaaS. Infrastructure as a Service gives the user access to virtual hardware. Platform as a Service adds software development tools. Software as a Service includes apps as well, such as Google Docs or Microsoft 365.

Know where and how clouds can be deployed. Clouds can be on-premises (in the location that the company owns), in the cloud (over the Internet), or some sort of hybrid between the two.

Know where and how AI chatbots are used. AI chatbots are used extensively in customer service, both phone-based and online. They can answer basic questions related to a specific subject and help users navigate a company's systems. They can retrieve information (such as a credit card balance or payment information) as well as pass the customer along to a real human if needed.

Know what an AI assistant is. Examples of AI assistants are Alexa, Siri, and Google Assistant. They are general conversational AIs that can answer a broad range of questions, play music, set reminders, and perform other duties.

Understand two types of generative AI. Two classifications of generative AI are AI-generated code and AI-generated content. AI-generated code is computer programming code created by the AI. Content can be words or graphics, based on the AI used.

Understand examples of AI predictions and suggestions. Some examples include autocorrect, filling in queries in web browsers and other places where users seek information, and shopping suggestions.

Chapter 9 Lab

You can find the answers in Appendix A.

In this lab, you will create a new virtual machine using Microsoft Hyper-V. In order to do this lab, you first need to complete Exercise 9.1 and install Microsoft Hyper-V.

1. Open Microsoft Hyper-V manager by typing **Hyper** in the Windows search bar and pressing Enter.
2. In the left pane, click your computer name.
3. In the row of options at the top, click Action ➢ New ➢ Virtual Machine. This will open the New Virtual Machine Wizard shown in Figure 9.13.

FIGURE 9.13 New Virtual Machine Wizard

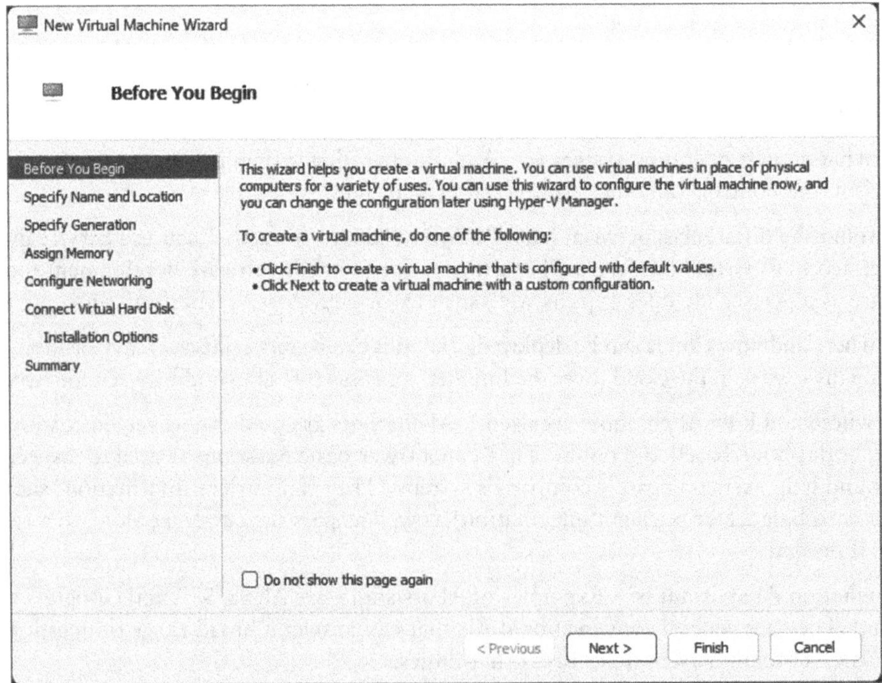

4. Notice in Figure 9.13 that you can click Finish to create a virtual machine with default values, or click Next to create one with a custom configuration.
5. For purposes of this lab, click Finish to create a virtual machine with default values.

Now that you have created a virtual machine, answer the following questions.

1. How do you turn on the virtual machine?
2. By default, how much memory is allocated to the virtual machine?

Start the virtual machine. (I won't tell you how here because it would give you the answer to question 1.) After starting it, attempt to connect to the virtual machine.

3. How do you connect to the virtual machine?
4. What is the result of trying to connect to the virtual machine?
5. Why did that happen?

In Chapter 4, you previously installed a virtual machine operating system into a hypervisor. Because of that, we won't repeat the exercise here, so consider the rest of this lab optional. However, if you still have the Lubuntu ISO file on your computer (or you want to download it again), you can install it in the Hyper-V hypervisor as well. To do so, you would:

1. Right-click the virtual machine and go to Settings.
2. In the Hardware list, under IDE Controller 1, click DVD Drive.
3. In the right pane under Media, click Image File and browse to the location of the ISO file.
4. Follow the installation instructions.

Once it's installed, when you try to connect to the virtual machine, it will start Lubuntu instead of giving you the boot error you encountered when you tried to connect earlier.

Review Questions

You can find the answers in Appendix B.

1. On your Windows 11 computer, you can run macOS in a smaller window without affecting Windows. What is macOS called in this instance?
   A. Hypervisor
   B. On-premises
   C. Virtualization
   D. Guest OS
2. What is the name of the software that allows you to install a second OS on your computer without needing to dual-boot?
   A. Hypervisor
   B. Virtualization
   C. Hybrid
   D. Guest OS
3. What is the difference between a Type 1 and a Type 2 hypervisor?
   A. Type 1 sits on top of a host OS and Type 2 directly on the hardware.
   B. Type 1 sits directly on the hardware, and Type 2 sits on top of a host OS.
   C. Type 1 sits directly on the hardware, and Type 2 sits on top of a guest OS.
   D. Type 1 sits on top of a guest OS and Type 2 directly on the hardware.
4. What is required to run client-side virtualization?
   A. Type 1 hypervisor
   B. Type 2 hypervisor
   C. Type 1 or Type 2 hypervisor
   D. Virtualization server
5. A guest OS needs to communicate with a server on the network. What does the guest OS use to send the network packets?
   A. NIC
   B. CPU
   C. vCPU
   D. vNIC

6. Your company uses cloud services provided by Amazon and also has a few cloud-based storage servers in the building. What type of deployment model is this?
   - A. On-premises
   - B. Cloud
   - C. Hybrid
   - D. Unable to determine

7. Your company buys cloud services and it includes Gmail and other Google apps. What type of service does your company purchase?
   - A. PaaS
   - B. IaaS
   - C. GaaS
   - D. SaaS

8. Which of the following is the highest level of cloud services you can purchase?
   - A. PaaS
   - B. IaaS
   - C. SaaS
   - D. They are all the same level.

9. You need to purchase the lowest level of cloud services possible to enable programmers on your team to have development tools. Which level of service should you purchase?
   - A. PaaS
   - B. IaaS
   - C. SaaS
   - D. GaaS

10. The ability to get additional cloud resources without intervention from the cloud provider is called what?
    - A. Measured service
    - B. High availablity
    - C. Resource pooling
    - D. Rapid elasticity

11. Ensuring that cloud clients receive uninterrupted services is known as what?
    - A. Measured service
    - B. High availability
    - C. Broad network access
    - D. Virtualization

12. Your company just signed a contract with Amazon to use the Amazon Web Services cloud. What type of deployment model is that?
    A. On-premises
    B. Public
    C. Private
    D. Hybrid
13. A virtual router and network infrastructure can be provided as part of which of the following cloud service levels? (Choose all that apply.)
    A. SaaS
    B. PaaS
    C. IaaS
    D. None of the above
14. You visit the website for your bank. A window pops up with text showing a customer service representative asking you if they can help. What is this an example of?
    A. AI assistant
    B. Generative AI
    C. Predictive AI
    D. AI chatbot
15. Amazon's Alexa and Siri are examples of which type of AI?
    A. AI assistant
    B. Generative AI
    C. Predictive AI
    D. AI chatbot
16. Which branch of AI is focused on understanding written or spoken language?
    A. ML
    B. NLP
    C. Neural networks
    D. Expert systems
17. Which of the following is an example of generative AI?
    A. Amazon Alexa
    B. Customer service pop-up window on a website
    C. ChatGPT
    D. Autocorrect on a smartphone

18. If a computer programmer needs sample code from which to write a program, what type of AI can provide it?
    - **A.** AI chatbot
    - **B.** AI assistant
    - **C.** Generative AI
    - **D.** Predictive AI

19. You are shopping online and search for a product. As you close the product window, another window pops up showing you a similar item. What type of AI is this an example of?
    - **A.** AI chatbot
    - **B.** AI assistant
    - **C.** Generative AI
    - **D.** Predictive AI

20. A rock band wants to design a new logo to boost their image. What type of AI should they use for this?
    - **A.** AI chatbot
    - **B.** AI assistant
    - **C.** Generative AI
    - **D.** Predictive and suggestions AI

Security Concepts and Threats

THE FOLLOWING COMPTIA TECH+ FC0-U71 EXAM OBJECTIVES ARE COVERED IN THIS CHAPTER:

✓ **5.0 Data and Database Fundamentals**

✓ **5.1 Explain the value of data and information.**

- Data and information as an asset
  - Critical vs. non-critical data
- Data-driven business decisions
  - Data capture and collection
  - Data correlation
  - Meaningful reporting
- Data monetization
- Data analytics
- Big Data

✓ **6.0 Security**

✓ **6.1 Explain fundamental security concepts and frameworks.**

- Confidentiality, integrity, and availability
- Privacy
  - Social networking sites
  - Email
  - File sharing
  - Instant messaging
  - Personally identifiable information (PII)
  - Government regulations (e.g., General Data Protection Regulations [GDPR])
  - Cookie consent

- Authentication, authorization, accounting, and non-repudiation concepts
    - Authentication
        - Single factor
        - Multifactor
        - Single sign-on
    - Authorization
        - Permissions
            - Administrator vs. user accounts
        - Least privilege model
    - Accounting
        - Logs
        - Location tracking
        - Web browser history

In an ideal world, computer security systems let in the right people and applications without any hassle and keep out the wrong people and applications. The world isn't ideal, though, and computer security certainly isn't either. There are two extremes to access. The first is that you can open everything up and let anyone access anything. While this is simple, it's not secure. The other extreme is to lock everything down tight. It's secure, but it kind of defeats the purpose of having a network—you want to be able to share resources with others. It follows then that effective computer security is a constant balance between safety and convenience.

The fact that you have to open up your systems to allow others to access resources has an inherent flaw, which is that opening can allow people who shouldn't have access to try to get in anyway. Those people might be simply curious, or they could be serious criminals who want to steal data or damage businesses. Either way, they're out there, and they're writing malware and trying to get unauthorized access to computer networks right now. In the world of computer security, paranoia is a good thing. You don't need to be part of the tinfoil hat–wearing brigade, but a healthy dose of wariness can save you a lot of grief.

In this chapter, you'll learn about the many types of threats to safety, security, and privacy, because what you don't know *can* hurt you. I am going to break the chapter into three sections. First, I will talk about the people making threats and what they are after. What are they trying to do and why? Second, I'll cover three key facets of security—confidentiality, integrity, and availability. Finally, I'll show you a framework for controlling access to resources. Throughout this chapter, I will also talk about some mitigation techniques, although most of those will be covered in Chapter 11, "Security Best Practices."

Understanding Hackers and Motives

Hacking refers to a variety of computer crimes that involve gaining unauthorized access to a computer system or its data, usually with the intent to steal private information from, or causing harm or embarrassment to, the rightful owner.

The word *hacker* also has a benign meaning, referring to a computer expert who is thoroughly familiar with, and enthusiastic about, the inner workings of a computer system. This meaning is older, but the newer meaning, which associates the term *hacker* with criminal activities, is now more prevalent.

Some examples of hacking are as follows:

- Stealing passwords or personal information
- Gaining remote access to a server or an operating system
- Logging in locally and stealing data
- Changing a website's content
- Gaining access to the contents of a database (perhaps one that contains passwords or credit card information)
- Surreptitiously analyzing network traffic
- Installing software designed to cause harm or steal data
- Creating a condition in which a computer or network no longer works well
- Modifying existing software so that it no longer performs as it should or so that it secretly does harmful things in addition to its usual activity

Much of this chapter is devoted to helping you understand how hackers target computer systems to gain access or cause damage. If hackers can gain access to certain system files, for example, they may be able to retrieve the administrator password for the system. To prevent this type of attack, you might use BIOS-level security to prevent a PC from booting from a disk other than its hard drive.

Wireless networks are great for users, but they also can open up huge security holes in our networks. Hackers may try to connect to your wireless network looking for computers or data that isn't protected. To prevent this type of attack, you can employ wireless networking security techniques, which I introduced in Chapter 8, "Networking Concepts and Technologies," such as WPA2 and WPA3.

Or perhaps a hacker might take advantage of open network ports to access a computer remotely. Firewalls can help guard against this type of attack. Finally, hackers might install software on your computer that causes damage or causes additional security breaches. The trick is to get you to install it for them without knowing! Antimalware software can help out in some of these cases, and safe web browsing and emailing practices can thwart others.

What is the goal of the hacker, though? Most criminal hackers generally want to make money from their exploits or cause damage to businesses or individuals. The bigger impact they can have, the better. Hackers know that data or information is often the most valuable asset that a company owns. After all, data is the new oil, right? And with nearly everything being digitized today, there are plenty of targets for hackers to pursue. Here are four specific areas that hackers might find appetizing:

Data and Information as an Asset Companies and individuals have data that can be valuable to someone looking to make money. Two classifications of data are *critical data* and *noncritical data*. Critical data is the stuff that is worth money for both legitimate and illegitimate purposes. It includes things like usernames, passwords, and account information. It can also include intellectual property (IP), digital products, physical product plans, financial documents, social security numbers, telephone numbers, and email addresses. Critical data must be protected at all times. Noncritical data is stuff that if it's lost or hacked, it's not a tragedy.

A text from your friends telling you when a party is, or a copy of a new recipe you want to try might be noncritical. If a hacker gets into your phone and reads or deletes either one, that is definitely spiteful but it probably won't make them any money.

Data as a Driver of Business Decisions It's impossible to overemphasize how much companies use data to make decisions. Chapter 7, "Database Fundamentals," talked about how many companies have massive data repositories detailing their customers, products, and services. This requires the company to capture and collect data from customers, websites, or other places and then use data correlation to find meaningful patterns within it. All of that data is, or at least could be, worth huge amounts of dollars to that company or its competitors.

In addition, some companies use data for reporting their business performance. *Meaningful reporting* refers to the process of translating data into insights and action for an audience. These reports could be used by management to make multimillion-dollar strategic decisions. Imagine what would happen if the data is missing or incorrect. It could cause the company to fail. Finally, some companies, such as healthcare providers, are required to report on the meaningful use of data to be compliant with government regulations. Again, having the data stolen, destroyed, or compromised could cause serious problems.

Data correlation refers to relationships between points of data. For example, if a product's price increases and so do the total sales for the company, those two data points are positively correlated because they increase together. However, if the price increase results in lower units sold, those two data points are negatively correlated because as one increases, the other decreases. If two data points don't seem to exhibit a pattern, then they are not correlated.

Correlation does not imply causation. That is, just because two data points move together does not necessarily mean that one causes the other.

Data Monetization Companies use data to make money—this process is called *data monetization*. Some use the data to improve their products or find and retain customers. Others, such as Google and social media sites, sell their data to advertisers who want to reach potential customers. It makes sense then that a hacker might figure they can steal the data and sell it as well.

Data Analytics and Big Data *Data analytics* and Big Data are closely related. As noted earlier, companies capture and collect massive amounts of data about their products and customers. They might also employ entire teams whose job it is to analyze the data, find meaningful patterns, and then determine new or better courses of action to grow the business. This is what data analysts do.

Big Data is a newer term within data analytics. It refers to large, unstructured databases and the suite of tools needed to analyze and visualize that data. The objective is the same, though, which is to find meaningful patterns within the data that can be monetized.

Tech+ exam objective 5.1, "Explain the value of data and information," lists the following which you should be familiar with:

- Data and information as an asset (critical vs. noncritical data)
- Data-driven business decisions, including data capture and collection, data correlation, and meaningful reporting
- Data monetization
- Data analytics
- Big Data

Because of the great value of these resources, it's paramount that companies invest in the security to protect them. The challenge is daunting, as it seems that hackers are always one step ahead of everyone else. Know that you're not alone in this fight. There are companies and tools out there to help you protect what's rightfully yours. Being aware of potential threats is a great first step in mitigating them.

Real World Scenario

Different Motivations

There are various factions within the hacking community, and they are motivated by different goals. As I mentioned earlier, some are motivated by money or the thrill of causing damage, whereas others have political aims. Over the last decade or so, major hacks made news headlines, such as the following:

- Optus—a hack in 2022 exposed the names, birth dates, and addresses of more than 9 million customers.
- Marriott—in 2020, had a hack where information on 5.2 million guests was stolen.
- Dubsmash was hacked in 2018, exposing account information, including usernames and passwords, of nearly 173 million users.
- Facebook revealed hacking in 2018 as it related to the 2016 U.S. presidential election.
- Equifax, the credit bureau, in 2017.
- Uber in 2016.
- Yahoo, in 2013 (but not discovered until 2016).

I could go on, but one could literally write an entire book on recent hacks. The prevalence of such activities has caused some major news publications to ask, tongue in cheek, who *hasn't* reported a breach? (To be fair, most major businesses have not been hacked—yet.)

Others are motivated by the challenge of getting into a system that is hard to penetrate—literally, just so they can say they did it and gain the admiration of fellow hackers. These hackers may leave clues as to their attack for the hacked network administrators to find along with helpful suggestions on how to breach the hole they exploited. Still others are interested in doing damage to organizations whose views differ from their own—in a sense, they want to make their own political statement.

In fact, within many professional hacking circles, the idea of hacking for monetary gain is frowned upon. You won't find these groups trying to steal credit card data—that type of petty criminality is beneath them. They are oftentimes more motivated by moral or political beliefs and trying to expose organizations that they consider dishonest or unethical. The WikiLeaks group qualifies here. Its self-reported profile is that it is an "international, non-profit journalistic organization which publishes secret information, news leaks, and classified media from anonymous sources." Organizations that have had their information published by WikiLeaks definitely call them hackers, but clearly WikiLeaks sees itself in a much more altruistic light.

Understanding Security Threats

If you are a security guard at a bank, your job is to keep your eyes open for anything that might be suspicious. Certainly you would watch for anyone entering the bank wearing a ski mask. Sometimes, it feels easy to identify threats, but of course that's not always the case. It's even harder in the computer world, because the threat could be on the other side of the world and you don't even know it exists.

In this section, I am going to show you a variety of security threats. To categorize the threats, I'll use a common information security framework that focuses on confidentiality, integrity, and availability, known as the *CIA triad* (see Figure 10.1). After those three, I include a section on privacy expectations and another that covers specific software-based security threats in depth. The software-based threats might not be specific exam objectives, but they are real-world threats about which you need to be familiar. As you read about them, you'll see how they relate to the areas of confidentiality, integrity, and availability.

FIGURE 10.1 The CIA triad

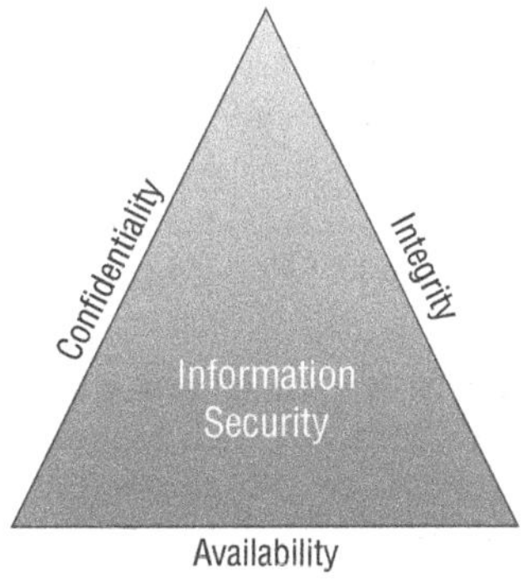

Each type of threat poses different problems and therefore requires its own mitigation techniques. I will talk some about mitigation here, but the more in-depth conversation on preventing and dealing with threats will occur in Chapter 11. The primary goal in this section is to raise awareness so that you have an idea of what to look out for.

Confidentiality Concerns

When a user provides personal information, such as a credit card number, Social Security number, or medical information, they have an expectation that other people who aren't supposed to see that information won't see the data. This is *confidentiality*—ensuring that private information stays that way. It's an expectation when entering data into websites (at least those using HTTPS), filling out a form to mail, or talking to a customer service representative over the phone.

Companies have an obligation to ensure confidentiality. There have been too many examples in the news over the last several years where data breaches have exposed usernames, passwords, and credit card data. Users become rightfully upset when this happens. Attacks on confidentiality can include snooping, eavesdropping, wiretapping, social engineering, and dumpster diving.

Tech+ exam objective 6.1, "Explain fundamental security concepts and frameworks," lists confidentiality, integrity, and availability as the first subobjective. At a minimum you should be able to define what those three terms mean. The specific confidentiality concerns listed here, such as snooping, eavesdropping, and wiretapping, are not specific exam objectives but serve as great examples to help you understand how these threats manifest themselves in the real world.

Snooping

Network administrators have some really cool tools to help them maintain good operations and troubleshoot problems. One of those tools is a protocol analyzer (sometimes called a *sniffer*, which is the name of a popular tool originally made by Network General, now NETSCOUT). A *protocol analyzer* lets administrators capture network traffic and analyze its contents. There are wired and wireless protocol analyzers. The risk is that sniffers can theoretically be used by people who shouldn't have access to network data as well. This type of attack is called *snooping*, and it is sometimes called *sniffing*.

In a snooping attack, the attacker captures network traffic and then looks for key pieces of information. On most network systems, usernames and passwords are encrypted, and those will be hard to crack. But there could be additional useful information gathered.

On wireless networks, it's critical to enable strong encryption such as WPA2 or WPA3. Without it, data sent through the air will not be encrypted, and it will be an easy target for someone with a sniffer within range of the network.

Eavesdropping

Many office environments today are open, meaning that it's practically impossible to *not* hear others' conversations. *Eavesdropping* is often a low-tech attack method in which the attacker simply listens to a conversation to glean key information. Perhaps a co-worker is reading off a credit card number or verifying their date of birth over the phone. Of course, this threat is more acute in public places such as coffee shops and airport waiting areas. Anyone within ear-shot has access to that information and could potentially use it with malicious intent.

Eavesdropping can also involve more high-tech methods, such as video cameras and microphones to listen in on conversations.

Wiretapping

Back in the days before wireless communications were everywhere, *wiretapping* was a literal term—the attacker would have to tap into the physical wire on which the communication traveled. This was often done by placing a monitoring device, colloquially known as a *bug*, in someone's phone (to be specific, their land line). Today, the definition of wiretapping necessarily needs to be a little broader—it's the unauthorized monitoring of communications between two parties. Wiretapping can still be done over land lines and network cables, but also over cellular, Wi-Fi, or other wireless connections.

Social Engineering

Hackers are more sophisticated today than they were 10 years ago, but then again, so are network administrators. Because most of today's system admins have secured their networks well enough to make it pretty tough for an outsider to gain access, hackers have decided to try an easier route to gain information: they just ask the network's users for it.

These are relatively low-tech attacks and are more akin to con jobs, so it's relatively astounding how often they're successful. If someone randomly called you up and said, "Give me your bank account number," there's no way you would provide it. At least I hope not! But if that same someone calls you up and pretends to be a co-worker in a remote office with your company, who really needs help and has a plausible story, then things might be different. These types of attacks are called social engineering.

Social engineering is a process in which an attacker attempts to acquire information about you or your network and system by social means, such as talking to people in the organization. This isn't a new concept—people have been trying to defraud others for centuries. A social engineering attack may occur over the phone, by email, or even in person. The intent is to acquire sensitive information, such as the following:

- User IDs and passwords
- Preferred email addresses
- Telephone numbers and physical addresses
- Personal information, such as date and location of birth, maiden name, or mother's maiden name
- Other information that can help them guess passwords, such as the school you attended, your favorite sports team, or your favorite type of music

Social engineering works because the personal touch is often the hardest for people to resist and because the individuals concerned are normally very good at encouraging you to reveal personal information. It's more difficult when you're unsure if they're genuine—it's unpleasant to mistrust everyone.

Here's how it might work over the phone. Let's say you get a call at your desk at work from "Joe" in IT. He says he's noticed some unusual activity on your network account and wants to check it out, but for security purposes, he needs your permission first. So, he proceeds to confirm your login, and then he tells you that he needs to enter your password into the network tracker. He asks, "What's your password?" What do you do? To protect yourself from this one, all you need to do is confirm *his* information and verify it with your IT department *before* you give him any of your data. Just because "Joe" knows your login doesn't mean he's on the up-and-up.

In fact, if you ever get a call from someone whom you're unsure of, start asking questions: "Who did you say you are? What department? Oh—who is your manager? You know I am kind of busy right now, at what number can I call you back?" Many times, once you start asking questions, the person at the other end will figure you're not worth the trouble and will hang up. But even if "Joe" hangs up on you, you should still report the call to IT or security.

How did Joe get your login and telephone number? Maybe he did some network reconnaissance and found a company phone directory on the web. Even if it isn't published, maybe Joe did some earlier homework by calling one of your co-workers and, pretending to be a colleague at another site, asked for your phone number. But what about the username? On most networks, your username is the same as your email address, because that makes things easier for your administrator. This means that knowing that information is probably just a good guess on the attacker's part. Maybe Joe the hacker has gotten an email from someone at your company and knows what your email format is, and he may have some other information to help him figure out your network login. And even if the number on your caller ID when Joe called was an internal phone number, it doesn't mean a thing—hackers have software that can allow them to spoof phone numbers.

Exercise 10.1 gives you some good ways to test others on how likely they are to be susceptible to a social engineering attack. The steps are suggestions for tests; you may need to modify them slightly to be appropriate at your workplace. Before proceeding, make certain your manager or security department knows that you're conducting such a test and approves of it.

EXERCISE 10.1

Testing Social Engineering

1. Call the receptionist from an outside line when the sales manager is at lunch. Tell them that you're a new salesperson, that you didn't write down the username and password that the sales manager gave you last week, and that you need to get a file from the email system for a presentation tomorrow. Do they direct you to the appropriate person or attempt to help you receive the file?

2. Call the human resources department from an outside line. Don't give your real name, but instead say that you're a vendor who has been working with this company for years. You'd like a copy of the employee phone list to be emailed to you, if possible. Do they agree to send you the list, which would contain information that could be used to try to guess usernames and passwords?
3. Pick a user at random. Call them and identify yourself as someone who does work with the company. Tell them that you're supposed to have some new software ready for them by next week and that you need to know their password to finish configuring it. Do they do the right thing?

The best defense against any social engineering attack is education. Make certain that the employees of your company would know how to react to the requests presented here.

The golden rule is don't ever give any of your information or anyone else's to anyone whom you're not absolutely sure should have it. And if they are someone who should have it, they probably already do and shouldn't be contacting you for it!

The social engineering examples so far have been phone-based, but they are more commonly done over email or instant messaging.

Phishing

Phishing is a form of social engineering in which someone uses email to ask you for a piece of information that they are missing by making it look as if it is a legitimate request. The email will often look like it comes from an official source, such as a bank, and it will contain some basic information like your name.

These types of messages often state that there is a problem with your account or access privileges. You will be told to click a link to correct the problem. After you click the link—which goes to a site other than the bank's—you are asked for your username, password, account information, and so on. The person instigating the phishing can then use this information to access the legitimate account.

One of the best countermeasures to phishing is simply to mouse over the Click Here link and read the URL. Almost every time the URL is an adaptation of the legitimate URL as opposed to a link to the real thing.

Two other forms of phishing to be aware of are *spear phishing* and *whaling*, and they are very similar in nature. With spear phishing, the attacker uses information that the target would be less likely to question because it appears to be coming from a trusted source. Suppose, for example, a user receives a message that appears to be from their spouse and it says to click here to see a fun video of their children from last Christmas. Because it appears far more likely to be a legitimate message, it cuts through the user's standard defenses like a spear, and the likelihood that they would click the link is higher. Generating the attack requires much more work on the part of the attacker, and it often involves using information from contact lists, friend lists from social media sites, and so on.

Whaling is nothing more than phishing, or spear phishing, for so-called "big" users, thus the reference to the ocean's largest creatures. Instead of sending out a To Whom It May Concern message to thousands of users, the whaler identifies one person from whom they can gain all of the data they want—usually a manager or business owner—and targets the phishing campaign at them.

The only preventive measure in dealing with social engineering attacks is to educate your users and staff never to give out passwords and user IDs over the phone or via email or to anyone who isn't positively verified as being who they say they are.

Shoulder Surfing

One form of social engineering is known as *shoulder surfing*, and it involves nothing more than watching someone when they enter their sensitive data. They can see you entering a password, typing in a credit card number, or entering any other pertinent information. This is a visual version of eavesdropping.

The best defense against this type of attack is simply to survey your environment before entering personal data. It might also help to orient your screen such that people walking by can't easily see it. If it's impossible to hide the monitor adequately from unauthorized lookers, and if the data on the screen is highly confidential, you may find a screen filter useful. A screen filter (also called a *privacy screen*) directs the light from the display at a restricted angle so that anyone who isn't viewing it straight on won't be able to read it clearly. An example made by `StarTech.com` is shown in Figure 10.2. Many modern laptops have a Function key that can toggle a built-in digital privacy screen on or off as well.

FIGURE 10.2 Laptop privacy screen

Source: StarTech.com

It's common courtesy when someone else is typing in a password to make an obvious effort to look away.

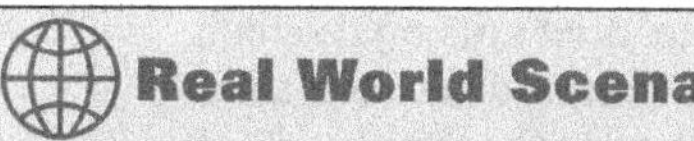

Real World Scenario

Don't Make It Too Easy

As a teenager, before I got into IT, I was a clerk in a retail store. The company had just opened up a new store, and the store manager, Robert, asked me to come with him to look at an area of the store. During this time, he needed to check something on our computer system (which was new to all of us), so he went to one of the terminals and logged in.

When he typed in his password, I did not make an obvious effort to look away (I didn't know the common courtesy tip yet), but I wasn't exactly trying to look at what he typed either. I basically just saw his arm movements, and I knew from previous experience that he typed with the index finger on each hand only. What I semi-observed was three slowly typed letters, left-right-left, followed by a pause, and three rapid left-hand keystrokes.

After we took care of our task, I got to thinking about the situation and quickly realized that he had given me his password—it was his first name! I never did anything with that information, but imagine the access I might have had to the system! I am quite certain that I would have been able to view information that I had no business seeing, had I tried.

There are two big problems in this scenario. First, he clearly was not practicing good password selection (which I'll talk about in detail in Chapter 11), especially considering his level of importance in our company. Second, I should have made the attempt to avoid shoulder surfing. The moral of the story is don't make it too easy for others to hack in on your behalf. Make sure you choose tough passwords, and also make sure that you are aware of your surroundings when entering sensitive information.

Dumpster Diving

Although it might sound like a made-up term from Wall Street takeover movies, *dumpster diving* is a real thing. It is pretty much what it sounds like—people can go through the dumpster, or your garbage, and steal information. In many places there are laws that prohibit such behavior, but we're talking about people who generally ignore such inconveniences anyway.

The best way to avoid being a victim of dumpster diving is not to throw away anything that can cause you problems later. Be sure to shred all papers in a good shredder. When disposing of media such as hard drives or flash drives, reformatting isn't enough to ensure that the data can't be read again. Damaging the drive physically and then taking it to a recycling center is a better way to go. I've seen some professionals recommend opening the case of hard drives and drilling through the platters to make them completely useless. Whether or not you choose to go that far is up to you. Regardless, ruining the device beyond repair isn't a terrible idea, and you should always recycle old computer parts to dispose of them properly.

Before recycling a hard drive or other storage media, it's always best to use a utility designed to wipe them clean of data. Just erasing the files or formatting the media isn't enough. The gold standard is called a DoD wipe, because it meets U.S. Department of Defense standards.

Integrity Concerns

When users access data, they have the expectation that the data is correct and from a valid source. For example, someone logging into a credit card company's website expects that it's really that company and that the information they see regarding the charges to their account is valid. Likewise, if a customer checks the inventory of a supplier before placing an order, they expect the data to be accurate. In information security, *integrity* means that the data is accurate and consistent and from the indicated source. Four threats to data integrity are on-path attacks, replay attacks, impersonation, and unauthorized information alteration.

Remember that integrity is part of Tech+ exam objective 6.1. As with the confidentiality section, the types of threats below aren't specifically called out in the objectives but give you good examples of what data integrity means. And who knows, they might show up on the exam anyway!

On-path Attack

In an *on-path attack* (formerly known as a *man-in-the-middle* attack), someone secretly places something (such as a piece of software or a rogue router) between a server and the client, and neither party is aware of it. The on-path software intercepts data and then sends the information back and forth as if nothing is wrong. Both the client and the server respond to the rogue, each thinking that it's communicating with a legitimate system. Usually this type of attack is accomplished via some form of wiretapping.

The attacker can be trying to do one of two things. First, the on-path software may be recording information for someone to view later, which is more of a confidentiality concern. However, the attacker might also modify the data, which is an integrity concern.

The popularity of wireless networks has increased the number of targets for on-path attackers. It's no longer necessary to connect to the wire, so a malicious rogue can be outside of the building intercepting packets, altering them, and sending them on. A common solution to this problem is to enforce a secure wireless authentication protocol such as WPA2 or WPA3.

Replay Attack

In a *replay attack*, the attacker captures information from a sender with the intent of using it later (said differently, replaying the message). This type of attack can be an extension of snooping or wiretapping.

For example, say that a rogue agent has captured transmissions from a client computer logging into a network. The rogue can then later attempt to replay the message to the server in an effort to gain unauthorized access.

Impersonation

As discussed earlier, it's a lot easier to pull off a social engineering attack if the victim trusts the person they think is sending the message. After all, if Joe from IT says he needs my email password to save all of my email from being deleted, it must be a big deal, right? Joe seems pretty legit. But what if the person seeking the information really isn't Joe? It could be someone pretending to be Joe, which is a form of *impersonation*—pretending to be someone or something that you are not.

Impersonation is all too easy to do and very common today. I already used a social engineering example, but it's easy to spoof (that is, fake) IP addresses and phone numbers too. I usually get three or more spam phone calls every day, each with a different phone number so it's practically impossible to block them. The computers spoofing the phone number are even smart enough to use a fake number with my area code and the same first three digits of my phone number so it looks like a local call, increasing the odds that I might answer.

The same thing can happen on computer networks as well, except that a server doesn't think to not answer the call and let it go to voicemail. The server will respond to what it thinks is a legitimate IP address, and the attacker is on the way to achieving their goals.

Unauthorized Information Alteration

Once into a system, an attacker can change information in an attempt to damage a business or person. Many times, this involves altering data within a database. If a company lost its entire client list, it could be in huge trouble. Or, if a client is looking for a part and sees that it's out of stock (when it really isn't), perhaps they will order from a different supplier.

Unauthorized information alteration is an attack that can also come from internal sources. After all, employees already know where the information is—they don't have to hunt for it—and many times they already have legitimate access. A disgruntled employee could seek to damage the company, or perhaps another employee might try to do something like sneak a pay raise through the HR system.

Availability Concerns

Some attackers want to steal data, while others simply want to make it so that no one can access the data. When people go to a website like `Amazon.com`, they expect that the site is working and they can purchase something. If the site is down, it's pretty hard for Amazon to make money. The final pillar of the CIA triad is *availability*, which means that the data is accessible when the user needs it. Availability concerns can be broken into two types of causes: denying service and hardware issues.

As the final pillar of the CIA triad, availability is part of Tech+ exam objective 6.1. You know the routine by now—the following examples aren't explicitly listed in the exam objectives but are very good to know, both for real-world awareness and in case they appear on the exam anyway.

Denying Service

There are a number of ways to try to keep users from accessing the data or network they need. One example is to flood a server with a multitude of illegitimate connection requests—more than it can handle—so that it's unable to respond to legitimate requests. This type of attack is referred to as a *denial of service (DoS)*. Any time a service is denied, it is considered a *service outage*. If an administrator detects a DoS attack, one mitigating step is to use the firewall to shut down incoming connection requests from the attacking IP address. Unfortunately, hackers have a way around this too. They can command several dozens or hundreds of infected systems across the Internet (often called *zombies* or *bots*) and execute a *distributed denial of service (DDoS)*. These are significantly harder to shut down and generally cause the site to be down for a longer period of time than a standard DoS attack.

DoS attacks aren't aimed solely at web servers, although they are the most common target. Wireless networks can also be hit with DoS attacks by an attacker jamming the wireless frequency so that no legitimate traffic can get through. In cases such as this, the only real mitigation technique is to find the offending signal and shut it down.

The final cause of service denial is a *power outage*. In most cases, hackers don't go after power grids, but it is possible. Most causes of a power outage are far more benign, such as a widespread power failure or a natural disaster. To help deal with power outages, use an *uninterruptable power supply (UPS)*—you read about these in Chapter 2, "Peripherals and Connectors"—which is a battery backup that a server plugs into. A UPS will generally keep the server running for 15 minutes to an hour or more, which won't keep an online company in business, but it will let the administrator power down the server gracefully.

Hardware Concerns

Organizations lose millions of dollars in equipment every year through thefts and damage. Therefore, it's important to secure your computer hardware physically in whatever environment you place it.

Hardware Damage

Within your own company's offices, solutions for securing computers and peripherals focus mainly on securing the environment overall, rather than on securing an individual piece of hardware. For example, some possible measures include the following:

- Requiring a security keycard for access to the office area
- Having a professional security presence in large organizations
- Keeping doors and windows locked
- Being prepared to challenge anyone who isn't normally a part of your work environment

Physically securing your area prevents two types of problems: hardware damage and hardware theft (covered in the next section). If an attacker can get to your computer with a hammer, it doesn't matter how good your firewall is or if you are using the latest and most secure encryption technology. That person can do some damage, causing *destruction* and *hardware failure*.

Hardware damage can also be inadvertent. For example, one company I used to work for was having roof repairs done. The workers left it unfinished over the weekend, when there happened to be an unusually heavy rainstorm. The roof leaked and water flooded into the server room, causing tens of thousands of dollars in damage.

Hardware Theft

The risk of hardware theft varies with the environment, of course. Leaving a laptop unattended at an airport is a very different matter from leaving it unattended in your own office when you go to lunch.

When traveling with a laptop or other portable technology device, the emphasis should be placed on the physical security of the individual device. Here are some pointers:

- Know where the device is at all times—preferably within arm's reach or at least in your sight.
- Don't leave the device unattended, even for a minute.
- Carry the device in an unconventional bag, rather than an expensive-looking laptop bag.
- Install an alarm that beeps if your device gets more than a certain distance away from a transponder that you keep close to you (such as on your keychain or belt).

Mobile devices such as smartphones are even easier for a thief to walk away with. The principles for these devices are the same as other mobile devices, but you need to be even more astute in your defense. It's best to never set your phone down at all.

If you aren't in a secured area (and even if you are), it may be appropriate to use locks and other devices that physically attach the hardware to a desk or other fixed object in order to prevent it from "walking away." There are various types of locks, cages, and racks designed to make it difficult for someone to remove a computer from its location.

Most laptops have a K-slot, which is short for Kensington security slot. Kensington is a company that makes a type of lock that fits into that slot. The lock is then attached to a security cable, and the other end of is bolted to the wall or furniture. The locks are secured with either a key or a combination. Figure 10.3 shows an example of a security cable attached to a K-slot on a laptop.

FIGURE 10.3 A laptop security cable

Services are available, such as Absolute Home & Office, that can track stolen hardware and disable a stolen computer remotely so the data that resides on it won't be compromised. Absolute Home & Office functionality comes preinstalled in the BIOS of many major brand-name laptop computers, including Dell, Lenovo, HP, Toshiba, and others. The tracking ability comes free with the computer, but you must pay to install and use the service. You can learn more about this software at `https://homeoffice.absolute.com`. In addition, many smartphones and tablets have built-in "kill switches" that permanently disable the device in the event that it is stolen.

Privacy Expectations

The Internet is an integrated part of our daily lives. We send emails and texts, buy items, perform banking, and do a host of other activities online. Most of the time we don't think about data *privacy*, which is the ability to control how our personal data is collected, stored, and used. Most of us sort of assume that our information is private, but that could be a faulty assumption. In fact, a measure of paranoia is healthy when it comes to sharing your information online. Let's take a look at different aspects of data privacy.

The privacy section of Tech+ exam objective 6.1 is long, because it's such an important topic. Be able to explain privacy as it relates to social networking sites, email, file sharing, instant messaging, and cookie consent. Also be familiar with privacy laws such as those regulating PII, like GDPR in the European Union (EU).

Rules and Regulations

In most countries, a user's personal information is protected by law. Companies and governmental organizations have a legal responsibility to protect the private information they collect, store, and use. Laws differ by country, including what is considered personal information and how the information should be protected. If someone wants to steal your credit card number, though, for example, it's probable that they're not concerned with such laws. Same for those who hack large companies for lists of usernames and account numbers. Still, the regulations are important incentives for companies to do their best to protect personal information.

The type of user information that needs to be protected is generally referred to as *personally identifiable information (PII)*. PII is defined as information that can be used to identify an individual, and includes but is not limited to:

- First and last name (when combined with other information)
- Identifiers such as Social Security number (SSN), driver's license number, passport number, taxpayer identification number, patient number, financial account number, or credit card number

- Physical address, email address, and phone number
- Biometric data, including fingerprints, voice signatures, medical images, or photographs
- Any information that when combined with other information can be used to identify an individual, including but not limited to date and place of birth, religion, employment information, educational history, medical records, and financial information

In the United States, PII is protected under the Privacy Act of 1974. It prohibits the disclosure of PII without the written consent of the individual, with some limited exceptions, such as if the information is needed pertaining to law enforcement. Some U.S. states have laws regarding PII protection as well, such as the California Consumer Privacy Act (CCPA) of 2018.

There are different categories of PII. For example, medical records are referred to as personal health information (PHI) and are regulated in the United States under the Health Insurance Portability and Accountability Act (HIPAA) of 1996. Credit card and financial information is referred to as payment card industry (PCI) information and includes credit card and bank account numbers, expiration dates, security codes, and cardholder names.

In the European Union (EU), data privacy is governed by the *General Data Protection Regulation (GDPR)* law, passed in 2018. As of this writing, it's considered the strongest personal privacy and security law in the world. It protects all people in the EU, regardless of who they do business with. So, for example, if an EU citizen is dealing with a U.S.-based company, the U.S.-based company must protect that citizen's data in compliance with GDPR.

GDPR emphasizes individual consent and limitations to PII use. Individuals must unambiguously consent to their personal information being collected and used, such as by voluntarily providing an email address. And when the information is used, it must be used for legitimate purposes specified when the individual provided consent and only for the duration specified. Failure to comply with GDPR can result in massive fines. For more information, visit `https://gdpr.eu`.

Think of PII from two angles—the individual and a company that collects the data. As an individual, you should have an expectation that your personal data stays private, although reality tells us that this expectation shouldn't be ironclad. You do need to be careful. From the side of the company collecting the data, you need to do everything in your power to secure the data, such as using secure data centers and data encryption when transmitting data. The specifics on how to do this are beyond the scope of the Tech+ exam, but know that data security experts are always in high demand if that's a career path that interests you.

Social Networking Sites

People join social networking sites with the intent of sharing information with others. That might seem to conflict with protecting the privacy of one's information, and in some cases that's true. There is still an expectation of *some* privacy, though, when visiting these sites. Social media companies are expected to not share your private information with others without your consent. But if *you* share your private information with the world, that's on you.

In fact, there are social media accounts created for the sole purpose of mocking those who post pictures of their credit or debit card online, because that's a really, really bad idea.

Within the various social media platforms, there are security settings where users can control their privacy to some extent. For example, Snapchat, Instagram, and Facebook all have account settings where you can make either your entire account or certain posts public or private. If your goal is to be a social media influencer with millions of followers or if the account represents a company or a celebrity, then leaving it public is logical. Then, when others want to see, follow, or be a friend of the account, they can search for and find it. If instead you just want friends or family to see your posts, it's best to make the account private to increase your privacy.

Email and Instant Messaging

In the Tech+ exam objectives, email and instant messaging (IM) are listed separately. Many email apps are integrated with messaging apps, too, so it makes sense to combine them here because they're treated very similarly.

Unlike social media, which is intended to be a one-to-many sharing platform, email and instant messaging is designed to be inherently more private. Sure, you can email or message groups of people, but most of the time the intended recipient list is more limited than it is in social media. Commercial email and messaging packages such as Gmail, Outlook, Zoho, and others have a fundamental responsibility to protect your emails and messages from getting into the wrong hands.

As with everything, there are caveats to email and IM privacy. First, if you are using company-provided email or messaging, that company can likely read and archive your messages as it sees fit, considering the message to be company property. Your employer can't legally access your private email accounts, though, unless the information is stored on a device owned by the employer. Regardless, it's best to not use company email or IM to write messages you don't want to become public. At many companies, they have "the headline test." Don't put into email or IM anything you wouldn't want to see in the headlines of a national newspaper. Second, private email and IMs can be subpoenaed if there is reason to believe it's been used in conjunction with criminal activity. So, if you're going to commit crimes, it's best to not email your friends about it.

In the United States, the Stored Communications Act (SCA) generally prohibits emails, IMs, and text messages from disclosure in civil subpoenas. It's probably still best to not press your luck, though!

File Sharing Sites

File sharing websites have an obligation to protect data as well as the personal information of users who store data on them. Considering that many file sharing sites are used by companies, the consequences of unintended data breaches could be catastrophic. The good news is that most commercial file sharing sites use encryption for both data transit and data storage. It's recommended to always use sites that do so. Here are a few tips to help ensure privacy and security when using file sharing sites:

Password-protect files. The file sharing site will of course require a login from those trying to access your file, and you need to take the step to specify which users can access a file. By password-protecting sensitive files, another layer of security is added.

Use multifactor authentication. Multifactor authentication requires something beyond a simple username and password to log in, such as an access code. (Multifactor authentication is covered in depth later in this chapter, in the "Authentication" section.)

Avoid using public Wi-Fi to access file sharing sites. Public or unencrypted Wi-Fi networks present large security holes. Wait until you can get to a private network or use a virtual private network (VPN) to access the site. VPNs are covered in Chapter 11.

Use expiration dates for shared file links. When you share the file with others, it will send them a link to the file within your folder. Set an expiration date so the file isn't shared in perpetuity.

Always use updated file sharing software. As you learned in Chapter 5, "Software Applications," outdated software can lead to security vulnerabilities. Be sure to update file sharing client software and use the most current version.

Cookies and Consent

In Chapter 5, you were introduced to *cookies*, which are small files downloaded from websites onto your personal device for tracking purposes. There are actually two kinds of cookies used: first-party cookies and third-party cookies.

A *first-party cookie* is one that holds your information for a single website. These are generally considered helpful because they store things like your username so the website recognizes you when you visit again. They can also remember preferences if you have certain options configured on that site. A *third-party cookie* is one that tracks your identity and traffic across websites. They are used by advertisers to send you ads based on what they think your interests are. In the past, websites would download cookies to a user's device unannounced and without consent.

With regulations such as GDPR and California's CCPA, third-party cookies came under increased scrutiny. Google originally announced it would phase out third-party cookies in 2020, but that decision was postponed. Then in 2023, Google announced that it would eliminate the use of third-party cookies by the end of 2024. This is a big deal, because Google Chrome has about 60 percent of the global browser market share. Other web browsers beat Google to the finish line, with Apple Safari blocking all cookies by default and Mozilla Firefox doing the same with third-party cookies. Microsoft Edge lets you change security settings to block all third-party cookies as well.

The upshot to all of this is that now when you visit websites, they will not automatically download any third-party cookies to your device. The website must get *cookie consent*, that is, permission from the end user to download the cookie. First-party cookies may be exempt if the cookie is determined to be critical to the website's functionality, such as if it remembers your username. Noncritical first-party cookies cannot be automatically downloaded either, though. Instead, most websites will prompt you with their cookie policy and ask for your consent to download them, as shown in Figure 10.4. (Figure 10.4 also has a chatbot on the right side—remember those from Chapter 9, "Cloud Computing and Artificial Intelligence"?) The end result, per consumer privacy protection groups, is enhanced privacy for the world's Internet users.

FIGURE 10.4 Cookie consent

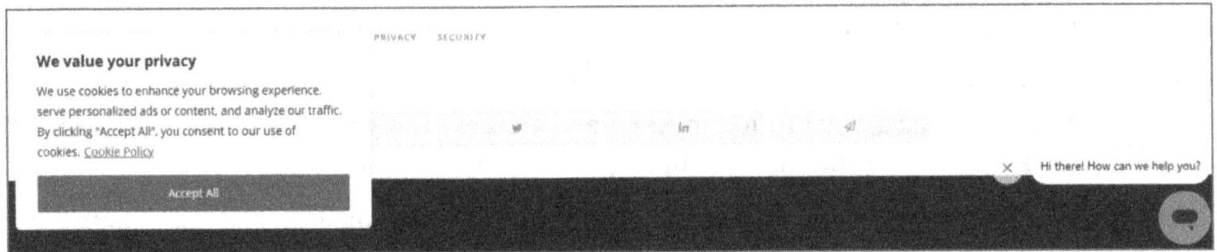

Software-Based Security Threats

Software-based threats are by far the widest-ranging group of security threats you need to worry about. It seems that the creators of malicious software applications have no shortage of imagination. The broad term for software designed to do harm to your computer is *malware*, and it covers anything that has been installed on anyone's computer without their intent and designed solely to cause mischief. In the realm of malware, here are most of the categories about which you need to be aware:

Exploits These take advantage of flaws in the OS or an application.

Viruses These are used to cause damage and/or disruption.

Worms These are used to transmit malware.

Trojan Horses These are applications that mask their true intent.

Adware These are used to display unwanted advertisements.

Spyware These are used to report on your computer and possibly steal data.

Ransomware These are used to extract payments from the infected user.

Rootkits These conceal themselves on the host OS, allowing for full-control access of the computer at a later date.

Backdoors These open ports or other routes into your system.

Keyloggers These record every keystroke and then use that data for identity theft.

In the following sections, you'll learn more about each of these malware types. In addition, you will learn about spam and password cracking. The last two don't technically qualify as malware because most of the time they're not software installed on an unsuspecting user's computer. They are horribly annoying, though, so they deserve to be covered here as well. As you read about each type of threat, think about how it would directly affect information security. Would it compromise confidentiality, integrity, or availability, or some combination of the three?

OS and Application Exploits

All OSs and applications have potential vulnerabilities that criminals can exploit. A *vulnerability* exists when flaws in the programming create the potential for misuse, an attacker is aware of the flaw, and a tool or technique that the attacker can use to exploit that vulnerability for malicious purposes is readily available. When criminals use a vulnerability to attack a system, it's called an *exploit*.

Although some OSs are considered to be more secure than others, the reality is that all OSs have weaknesses that, when discovered, are exploited. To guard against exploits, operating systems have mechanisms to update and patch themselves automatically as programmers become aware of vulnerabilities. That's why it's important to download and install all available updates for your OS promptly. Refer to Chapter 5 for details on Windows Update.

Real World Scenario

My Mac Is Safe from Viruses, Right?

A common misperception among computer users is that Windows is the only operating system that is vulnerable to viruses or other malware attacks. It's not true.

macOS, Linux, Android, and iOS systems aren't immune to malware attacks, but Windows systems do run a greater risk of infection. There are two reasons for this. The first is that some hackers have an axe to grind against Microsoft, so that's who they target. The second and biggest reason, though, is because of the popularity of Windows. It's by far the most widely used laptop and desktop OS, so any financial gain a criminal might get from malware would be maximized by targeting Windows systems.

Applications can also be exploited, although it happens less frequently because an application is a smaller and less-appealing target to a criminal. Widely used applications such as Microsoft Office are most often the targets of application exploit attempts. The best way to avoid software exploits is to ensure that the latest updates and patches are installed.

Viruses

A *virus* is computer code that inserts itself into an executable file. When that file is run, the virus's code executes along with the application's code. The virus hides itself inside its host file, so it's not obvious that it's there. A virus's code can cause all manner of mischief, from annoying but harmless things such as displaying a message to really destructive things such as deleting all files of a certain type or causing your OS to stop working. Most viruses also have a self-replicating component that causes them to spread from one executable file to another. This usually happens via RAM. When the infected file executes, the virus code is copied into RAM, and from there it can attach itself to other executable files.

Many other types of malware are often called viruses as well, even though they are not because they don't hide themselves in executable code. Instead, they may be worms or Trojan horses, which will be explained in later sections.

Viruses can be classified as polymorphic, stealth, retrovirus, multipartite, armored, companion, phage, and macro viruses. Each type of virus has a different attack strategy and different consequences.

Estimates for losses due to viruses are in the billions of dollars. These losses include financial loss as well as lost productivity.

The following sections introduce the symptoms of a virus infection and explain how a virus works. You'll also see how a virus is transmitted through a network and look at a few hoaxes.

Symptoms of a Virus/Malware Infection

Many viruses will announce that you're infected as soon as they gain access to your system. They may take control of your system and flash annoying messages on your screen or destroy your hard disk. When this occurs, you'll know that you're a victim. Other viruses will cause your system to slow down, cause files to disappear from your computer, or take over your disk space.

You should look for some of the following symptoms when determining whether a malware or virus infection has occurred:

- The programs on your system start to load more slowly. This happens because the virus is spreading to other files in your system or is taking over system resources.
- Unusual files appear on your hard drive, or files start to disappear from your system. Many viruses delete key files in your system to render it inoperable.
- Program sizes change from the installed versions. This occurs because the virus is attaching itself to these programs on your disk.
- Your browser, word processing application, or other software begins to exhibit unusual operating characteristics. Screens or menus may change.
- The system mysteriously shuts itself down or starts itself up and does a great deal of unanticipated disk activity.
- You mysteriously lose access to a disk drive or other system resources. The virus has changed the settings on a device to make it unusable.
- Your system suddenly doesn't reboot or gives unexpected error messages during startup.

This list is by no means comprehensive. What is an absolute, however, is the fact that you should immediately quarantine the infected system. It is imperative that you do all you can to contain the virus and keep it from spreading to other users or other computers if you are on a network.

How Viruses Work

A virus, in most cases, tries to accomplish one of two things: render your system inoperable or spread to other systems. Many viruses will spread to other systems given the chance and then render your system unusable. This is common with many of the newer viruses.

If your system is infected, the virus may try to attach itself to every file in your system and spread each time you send a file or document to other users. Figure 10.5 shows a virus spreading from an infected system either through a network or by removable media such as a flash drive. When you give removable media to another user or put it into another system, you then infect that system with the virus.

FIGURE 10.5 Virus spreading from an infected system

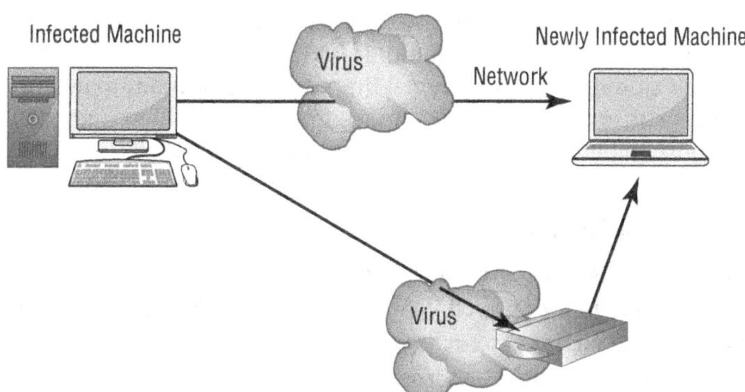

Many viruses are spread using email. The infected system attaches a file to any email that you send to another user. The recipient opens this file, thinking it's something you legitimately sent to them. When they open the file, the virus infects the target system. The virus might then attach itself to all of the emails that the newly infected system sends, which in turn infects the computers of the recipients of the emails. Figure 10.6 shows how a virus can spread from a single user to literally thousands of users in a very short time using email.

FIGURE 10.6 Email viruses can spread quickly.

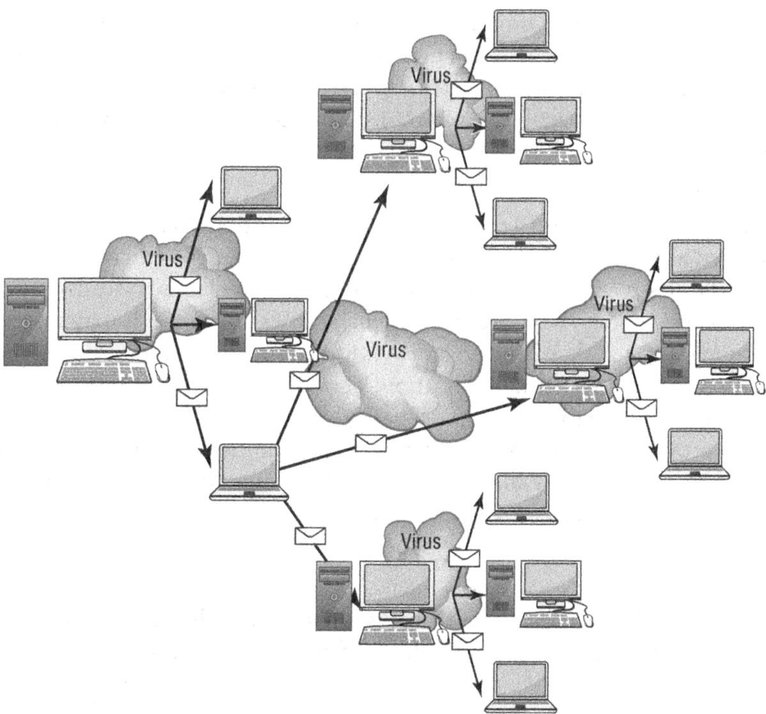

Antimalware programs are often able to detect malicious applications by looking for signatures. A *signature* is an algorithm or other element of malware that uniquely identifies it. Some viruses have the ability to alter their signature, so it is crucial that you keep your antimalware signature files current, whether you choose to download them manually or configure the antivirus engine to do so automatically.

Virus Transmission in a Network

Upon infection, some viruses destroy the target system immediately. The saving grace is that the infection can be detected and corrected. Some viruses won't destroy or otherwise tamper with a system; they use the victim system as a carrier. The victim system then infects servers, file shares, and other resources with the virus. The carrier then infects the target system again. Until the carrier is identified and cleaned, the virus continues to harass systems in this network and spread.

Viruses are detected and removed using antivirus software, which I covered in Chapter 5.

Worms

A *worm* is different from a virus in that it can reproduce itself, it's self-contained, and it doesn't need a host application to be transported. Many of the so-called viruses that have made the news were actually worms. However, it's possible for a worm to contain or deliver a virus to a target system. If a worm carries additional malware, that malware is called a *payload*.

Worms can be active or passive; active worms self-transport without human intervention, whereas passive worms rely on the user's innocence to transport themselves from one location to another, normally through email or social engineering. Active worms use email, vulnerabilities in your OS, TCP/IP, and Internet services to move their payload around a network infrastructure. Most antimalware programs can detect and remove worms.

Trojan Horses

A *Trojan horse* (often known as a Trojan) is a rogue application that enters the system or network disguised as another program. Some will pretend to offer services you want. For example, one insidious type of Trojan horse is a program that claims to scan your system for malware but instead causes system problems (which it tries to get you to pay to get rid of) or installs its own malware, such as a keylogger. A *keylogger* records all keystrokes and sends the information to a file or to a remote location. The hacker can get your usernames and passwords that way and use them to impersonate you.

Trojan horse programs don't replicate themselves, so they aren't viruses, technically speaking. The most common way that Trojan horse programs spread is via worms. Most antimalware programs can detect and remove Trojan horses.

Adware

Adware is a category of application that displays unrequested ads on your computer. The most common type of adware comes in the form of an add-on toolbar for your web browser that supposedly provides "advanced" or "helpful" search services but that also has the side effect of causing pop-up ads to appear whenever you use your web browser. Adware makers make money when people click the ads they display.

Strictly speaking, not all adware is illegal, and not all adware makers are involved in criminal activity. If you're seduced into downloading a particular web toolbar or application and then you aren't happy with what it does or there are too many ads to make it worth the value you're getting from it, you're free to remove it. Removal may not be easy, though; the uninstall option for the toolbar may or may not appear in Add Or Remove Programs in Windows, and you may need to connect to a website or go through some extra steps to complete the removal.

Some adware is an out-and-out annoyance, with no pretense of being anything else. Such programs are typically very difficult to remove, much like a virus infection. Your antimalware software may be of some help; you also may need to do a web search on the removal process to find Registry-editing instructions to help you stamp out the adware.

Always exercise caution when editing the Windows Registry. Improper settings could cause Windows to be inoperable and there is no "undo" feature.

Spyware

Spyware is software that (usually secretly) records your computer usage. Keyloggers are a form of spyware; so are programs that track the websites you visit and what ads you click and then send that information back to their owners. Spyware makers get revenue from collecting consumer marketing data, either specifically about you or about all users in general. Most spyware is illegal, works surreptitiously, and can be difficult to remove.

Spyware isn't self-replicating, and it relies on low-level social engineering to spread. The most common way to get infected with spyware is to install a free application from a website. Be very careful what sites you use to download executable files! Another way to get spyware is to run an ActiveX or Java component on a website you visit. A website may seem like a good deal because it's free, but there are many unscrupulous site owners, particularly in the adult entertainment industry, who exploit site visitors by infecting their computers with spyware or adware.

Some antimalware software detects and removes spyware. There are also applications designed specifically to remove spyware and adware from your system, such as Microsoft Defender (which was discussed in Chapter 5).

Ransomware

Ransomware is a particularly insidious type of malware that extorts the infected users for money. Even though it's been around since 1989, it's only gained significant popularity since about 2012. Generally contracted through a Trojan or exploits in software, the ransomware will pop up a message telling the user to pay up or else.

Some ransomware tries to look official. For example, one version attempted to look like an official notice from a police group, stating that the user had been in violation of several laws and needed to pay a fine to have the issue resolved. Others are far more direct—they will encrypt files on your hard drive and tell you that if you want them back, you'll pay the money. This type of threat is called *cryptoviral extortion*. The ransomware will give you a handy link to pay the fine, which redirects you to another site to enter your payment information.

Of course, this starts to introduce other problems. Clicking the link to visit the website means that other malware can be loaded onto your system, such as a rootkit, spyware, or keylogger. And, the hackers will give you the convenient option of entering your credit card information to pay them off. What could go wrong there? (If this does happen to you, one option is to get a prepaid credit card with a low limit and use that for the ransom payment. As soon as you have access to your files again, use antimalware software to remove the ransomware.)

Fortunately, most antimalware software will block ransomware as well. If you are infected and your files are locked or encrypted, your only recourse may be to wipe your system and restore from backup, provided of course that your backup files aren't infected as well.

Rootkits

Rootkits are software programs that have the ability to hide certain things from the operating system; they do so by obtaining (and retaining) administrative-level access. With a rootkit, there may be a number of processes running on a system that don't show up in Task Manager or network connections that don't appear in networking tools—the rootkit masks the presence of these items. It does this by manipulating the operating system to filter out information that would normally appear.

Unfortunately, many rootkits are written to get around antimalware programs that aren't kept up-to-date. The best defense you have is to monitor what your system is doing and catch the rootkit in the process of installation.

In Linux and UNIX systems, *root* is the name of the all-powerful administrator account. The term *rootkit* was coined because it's a tool that gives you root-level access to a system.

Backdoors

A *backdoor* is a method of circumventing the normal security system on a computer. Instead of needing a password, a hacker with a backdoor could log in by providing no credentials. Backdoors can be stand-alone programs or can be incorporated into other malware such as rootkits or worms.

Another source of backdoor issues is user error. Not changing a default password can allow for unauthorized access. In addition, debugging routines built into software, and not removed before release into production, can sometimes function as backdoors as well.

Spam

Spam is different than the software-based threats I've covered so far because it's not software that gets installed on your computer. Rather, *spam* is the deluge of unsolicited messages that you receive electronically. Most spam comes via email, but it can be generated in instant messaging, texts, online classifieds, smartphones, Internet forums, and message groups.

Most spam is advertisements, and there is little or no cost for the spammers to send these types of messages. All the spammer needs is a program to generate the spam (called a *spambot*) and email lists. There is a cost to Internet service providers (ISPs), businesses, and users, though, because ISPs and businesses need to install and maintain hardware or software solutions to deal with the volume. It's estimated that more than 9 trillion spam messages get sent each year. Clearly, legislation that has made spam illegal in many areas has not had much effect.

In addition, while a large percentage of spam is advertising, a lot of it is purely an attempt to defraud people who click links inside the email. It's becoming more common for users to realize that clicking a link in an email from someone you don't know is a no-no, but it still happens. In addition, spammers can often make the emails look like they come from a legitimate source, such as a real business, your ISP, or even a contact in your mailing list, making it more likely that someone will click a link and download a virus or other malware.

In addition to email spam, someone who posts the same message repeatedly in an online forum is considered a spammer. Their goal is usually to be obnoxious and hijack the thread or conversation for some reason.

The best way to deal with spam that gets into your inbox is to delete it. Most email clients will have a junk mail or spam filter, and you can flag the note as spam. This will redirect future emails from that sender straight into your junk email or spam folder.

Password Cracking

Most of us are used to typing in passwords, probably several times a day. It's kind of a fact of life that you need a username and password to get to most of your resources. Of course, there are people out there who would love to gain unauthorized access to your data as well, and one way they can do that is by attempting to crack your password.

Password cracking can take many forms. Perhaps the easiest is for the attacker to try the default password for a device or service. If the attacker knows your password for a different resource or website, they can try that one too, because a lot of us reuse our passwords across different sites. A third way is to guess passwords based on things they know about you, such as children's or pet's names, favorite teams or music, important dates, and things like that. Finally, there's the *brute-force* method. An automated computer program can start trying random strings of characters in an attempt to guess your password. Given enough time, password-cracking software will eventually guess your password—and it doesn't take as much time as you think. A regular desktop or laptop computer outfitted with password-cracking software can try about 9 billion password keys per second, meaning that a random eight-character password with numbers, mixed case, and symbols can be cracked in about 5 minutes. A computer designed specifically for password cracking can crank out about 90 billion password keys per second.

Password-cracking software is not illegal, and in fact there are many legal uses for it. If you have lost or need to reset a password, this type of software can be helpful. It's also useful for performing security audits. Trying to get into a system you don't own is illegal, though.

Fortunately, most websites and computer systems have limits to the number of login attempts that can be tried before the account is locked, usually around five attempts. Regardless, don't make it easy on someone to guess your password. You will learn more about specific steps to take for good password management in Chapter 11.

Understanding Access Control

The ultimate goal of a security system is to protect resources by keeping the bad people out and letting the good people in. It would be really easy to configure a system such that no one could access anything, and it would be equally simple to let everyone have open access. The first extreme defeats the purpose of having a network, and the second is just begging for trouble. The challenge then is to find a happy medium, where resources are available to those who should have them and nobody else.

In information security, there's a framework for access control known as *triple A*, meaning *authentication, authorization, and accounting (AAA)*. Occasionally auditing is added to the mix, making it *quad A*. And even further, nonrepudiation is also sometimes lumped in. Regardless, triple A is the umbrella term for describing systems of access control. In the following sections, I will describe the principles of authentication, authorization, and accounting, as well as nonrepudiation.

Authentication

To implement security, it's imperative to understand who is accessing resources on a computer or network. User *authentication* happens when the system being logged into validates that the user has proper credentials. Essentially, authentication asks the question, "Who are you?" Oftentimes, this is as simple as entering a username and password, but it could be more complex.

Authentication is part of Tech+ exam objective 6.1. Specifically, you should be able to explain the differences between single factor and multi-factor authentication as well as single sign-on.

Types of Authentication

The simplest form of authentication is *single-factor authentication*. A single-factor system requires only one piece of information beyond the username to allow access. Most often, this is a password. Single-factor authentication is quite common, but it's not the most secure method out there.

To increase security, your computer or network might require *multifactor authentication (MFA)*, which as the name implies requires multiple pieces of information for you to log in. Generally speaking, in addition to a username, multifactor authentication requires you to provide two or more pieces of information out of these four categories: something you know, something you have, something you are, or somewhere you are. An example of MFA is using a bank ATM. To get access, you typically need a bank card (something you have) along with a PIN or access code (something you know).

Something you know is usually a password. If you forget your password, a website might ask you to provide answers to security questions that you selected when you registered. These are questions such as the name of your elementary school, father's middle name, street you grew up on, first car, favorite food or musical artist, and so forth.

One-time passwords can be generated by sites to give you a limited time window to log in. These are far more secure than a standard password because they are valid for only a short amount of time, usually 30 minutes or less. The password will be sent to you via text or email or possibly a phone call.

Something you have can be one of a few different things, such as a smart card or a security token. A smart card is a plastic card, similar in dimensions to a credit card, which contains a microchip that a card reader can scan, such as on a security system. Smart cards often double as employee badges, enabling employees to access employee-only areas of a building or to use elevators that go to restricted areas, or as credit cards.

Smart cards can also be used to allow or prevent computer access. For example, a PC may have a card reader on it through which the employee has to swipe the card, or that reads the card's chip automatically when the card comes into its vicinity. Or, they're combined with a PIN or used as an add-on to a standard login system to give an additional layer of security verification. For someone to gain unauthorized access, they have to know a user's ID and password (or PIN) and also steal their smart card. That makes it much more difficult to be a thief!

A security token, like the one shown in Figure 10.7, displays an access code that changes about every 30 seconds. When received, it's synchronized with your user account, and the algorithm that controls the code change is known by the token as well as your authentication system. When you log in, you need your username and password, along with the code on the token.

FIGURE 10.7 RSA SecurID

Security tokens can be software-based as well. A token may be embedded in a security file unique to your computer, or your network may use a program that generates a security token much like the hardware token does. Figure 10.8 shows an example of PingID, which works on computers and mobile devices. This type of token saves you from having to carry around yet another gadget.

FIGURE 10.8 PingID

A system might also require you to log in from a specific location. For example, perhaps users are allowed to log in only if they are on the internal corporate network. Or, maybe you are allowed to connect from your home office. In that case, the security system would know a range of IP addresses to allow in based on the block of addresses allocated to your ISP.

Finally, the system could require something totally unique to you to enable authentication. These characteristics are usually assessed via *biometric devices*, which authenticate users by scanning for one or more physical traits. Some common types include fingerprint recognition, facial recognition, and retina scanning.

Law enforcement agencies have been using fingerprint recognition for more than 100 years, and no two prints have yet been found to be identical, even in genetically identical twins. That's because fingerprints develop in the womb, and they aren't preprogrammed at conception. More recently, computerized fingerprint scanners have taken the place of manual ink prints, and the technology for reading fingerprints has become so affordable that it's built into many computer systems, including consumer-level laptop PCs. Some fingerprint scanners use a rapid laser to detect the ridges in a person's fingers; others have an electrostatically sensitive pad that detects the current formed by the small quantities of water in a fingerprint.

Facial recognition software works in conjunction with a camera (like the webcams built into laptop computers) to scan the face of the person who is logging in. The facial scan is matched with existing previous scans of that same person stored on the computer. Some consumer-level laptops come with an option of logging into the OS via facial recognition as an alternative to typing a login password.

Retina scanning is similar to facial recognition, but it looks specifically at your eye and the pattern of blood vessels on your retina. Apparently, your retinal blood vessel pattern is as unique as your fingerprint.

Single Sign-On

One of the big problems that larger networks must deal with is the need for users to access multiple systems or applications. This may require a user to remember multiple accounts and passwords. The purpose of a *single sign-on (SSO)* is to give users access to all of the applications and systems they need with one initial login. This is becoming a reality in many large network environments.

Single sign-on is both a blessing and a curse. It's a blessing in that once the user is authenticated, they can access all the resources on the network with less inconvenience. It's a curse in that it removes potential security doors that otherwise exist between the user and various resources.

While single sign-on is not the opposite of multifactor authentication, they are often mistakenly thought of that way. One-, two-, and three-factor authentication merely refers to the number of items a user must supply to authenticate. After factor authentication is done, then single sign-on can still apply throughout remainder of the user's session.

Authorization

Once it's determined who the user is, the next step in access control is determining what the user can do. This is called *authorization*. Users are allowed to perform only specific tasks on specific objects based on what they are authorized to do. Most computers grant access based on a system of *permissions*, which you were introduced to in Chapter 4, "Operating Systems." Permissions are groups of privileges. For example, a user might be able to make changes to one file, whereas they are only allowed to open and read another.

One of the key foundations of an authorization system is the *least privilege model*. This states that users should be granted only the least amount of access required to perform their jobs, and no more. This principle applies to computers, files, databases, and all other available resources.

There are four access control methods about which you should be aware. They are role-based, rule-based, mandatory, and discretionary. I will cover each of them here.

Tech+ exam objective 6.1 includes authorization. You need to be familiar with what permissions are, administrator versus user accounts, and the least privilege model.

Mandatory Access Control

Of the four access control methods, *mandatory access control* is the most restrictive. It stipulates that all objects on the computer or network will have their security managed by a system administrator, including any files that a user may create on the system. This type of control is used in highly secure environments, such as many that are owned by governmental agencies.

While the upside is ultimate control over security, the downside is that it takes a lot of resources to manage properly.

In mandatory access control, each object (files, folders, resources) is assigned a security label. The label contains both the classification (top secret, confidential, restricted, and so forth) and category, which indicates which departments or groups can access the object.

Users also have a classification level and category. If a user attempts to access an object, they must have the appropriate classification level and category for permission to be granted. Classifications are hierarchical, so if a user has Top Secret clearance, they will be able to access less confidential levels as well.

Discretionary Access Control

In *discretionary access control*, users are allowed to set their own security settings for resources on their computer. This is commonly done in workgroup settings.

Instead of security labels, discretionary access control manages privileges based on an *access control list (ACL)*. The ACL lists the users or groups who have been granted access to the object and their level of access. For example, one user might have read-only access, whereas another user might have the ability to delete the file.

Users can set permissions only on resources that they own. If Joe owns a file, then Jenny can't set permissions on that file unless Joe has granted her the ability to do so.

Discretionary control is a lot more flexible than mandatory control, and it creates far less burden on the system administrators. It does place security in the hands of users, though, which might or might not be appropriate for a given set of users. There's certainly more risk to using this model.

Role-Based Access Control

Resource access in *role-based access control* is controlled through the use of administrator-defined roles. Usually these roles mimic departments or other logical definitions within organizations. For example, a school might have a Students role, a Faculty role, and a Staff role corresponding to various user account types. A business could have Marketing, Sales, Finance, and HR roles.

Most operating systems used role-based access control by default. For example, an administrator account is created when the OS is installed, and the administrator has the ability to access any file or service on the computer. There will likely be regular user accounts as well, who might have access to the files and folders they own, but don't have the ability to manage services on that computer or access another user's files.

Access is granted to an entire role at once, so all users who are in the Sales role have the same level of access. In true role-based systems, user accounts can be assigned to only one role at a time, and there is no way to grant permissions to individual user accounts. (Well, an administrator could start creating individual roles for certain users, but that could become cumbersome to manage very quickly.)

Rule-Based Access Control

The final access control method is *rule-based access control*. A rule-based system uses ACLs just like discretionary systems do, and an administrator defines the rules that allow or deny access to resources. When a user or group attempts to access a resource, the ACL is checked to determine whether the action is permitted.

Accounting

After users have been authenticated and authorized, it's time to think about tracking what the users did with their access. This is where *accounting* comes in. The principle of accounting seeks to keep a record of who accessed what and when, and the actions they performed.

Accounting is listed as a sub-objective in Tech+ exam objective 6.1. Be able to explain the concepts of accounting logs, location tracking, and web browser history.

The most common method of tracking user actions is through the use of logs. Nearly all operating systems have built-in logs that track various actions. For example, Windows-based systems contain Windows Logs, which are part of Event Viewer. To open Event Viewer, type **Event** in the Windows search bar and press Enter. Windows has logs that track Application events, Security events, and System events. Figure 10.9 shows the Security log. In an environment where multiple users log in, those logins will be shown here.

FIGURE 10.9 Security log in Event Viewer

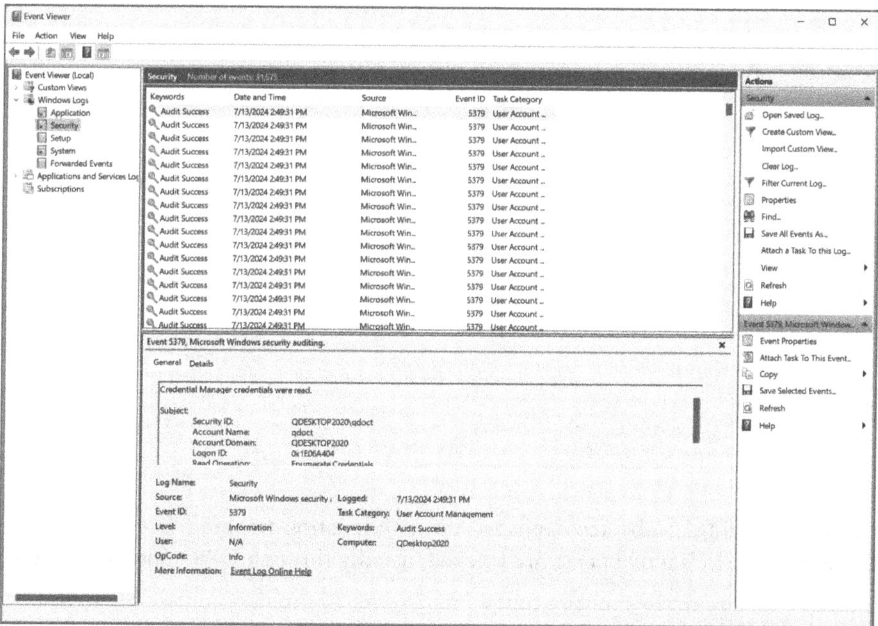

Another action that is frequently tracked is web browsing history. Web browsers retain a historical account of the sites that have been visited. To see viewing history in Microsoft Edge, click the Settings and More menu (three dots in a horizontal line, near the upper-right corner) and then History, as shown in Figure 10.10. (You can also press Ctrl+H at any time in the open browser.) Notice that there's an option to search clear the history, and you can clear it by clicking the garbage can as well. Note that this action clears it from the browser, but it won't clear it from any servers (such as a proxy server) that caches web requests. To view the history in Chrome, click the More menu (the three vertical dots) and then History or just open Chrome and press Ctrl+H.

FIGURE 10.10 Microsoft Edge site-viewing history

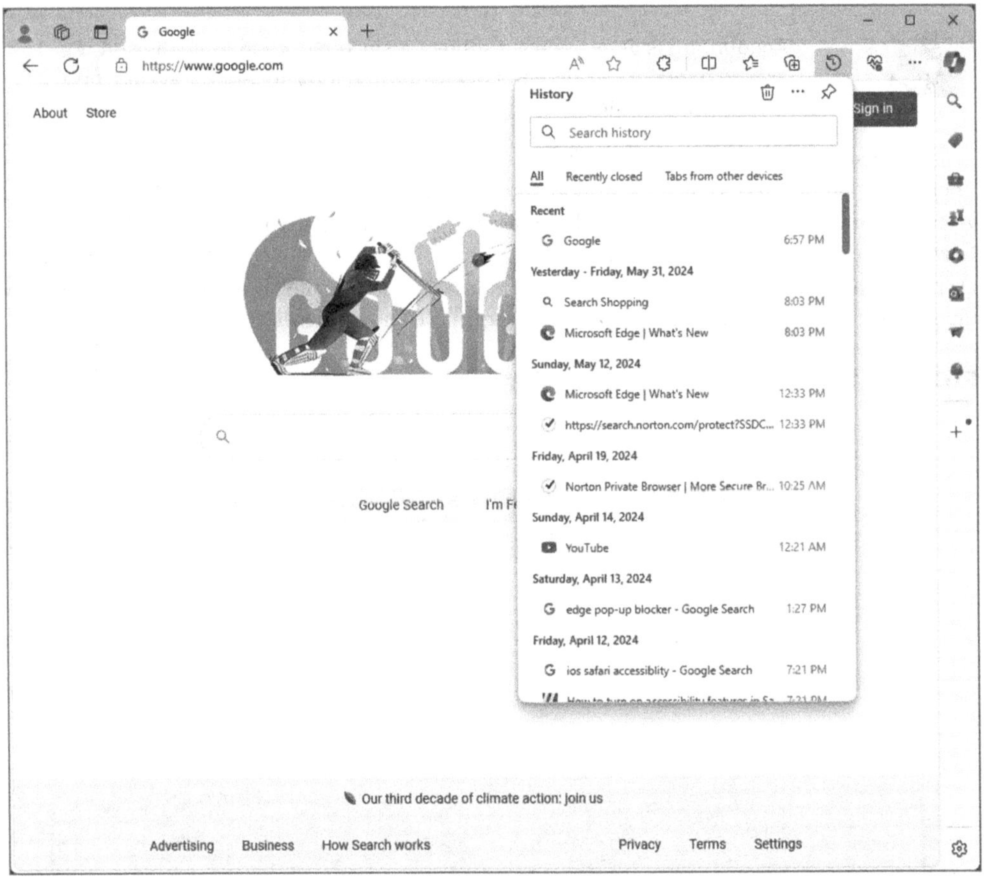

Finally, accounting can be accomplished through location tracking. Location tracking is when a user or device's movements are tracked, usually through GPS. Using GPS satellites, the device's latitude, longitude, and elevation can be determined to within a few meters. Mobile cellular devices can be tracked as well by using proximity to cell towers, but it's typically less accurate—within about 50 meters.

Nonrepudiation

Some people like to joke that "If there's no video, then it didn't happen." While it might be a fun joke among friends or colleagues, it can be a serious problem when it comes to information security. The goal of *nonrepudiation* is to make it so that people can't deny that an event took place. In other words, it provides proof that someone or something performed a specific action.

Nonrepudiation is listed in Tech+ objective 6.1 along with authentication, authorization, and accounting. Be able to explain what nonrepudiation is.

In the previous section, I talked about tracking behaviors through accounting, and tracking is indeed the first step. But what if someone got on your computer and visited a website that got you into trouble? The log would say that your computer visited the site. How would you prove that it was or wasn't really you who did it? Here are four methods of nonrepudiation:

Video Cameras are everywhere today, from security systems to the phone that everyone carries around. Video is generally considered a strong form of nonrepudiation. Technology now makes it possible to alter videos, but altered videos have traces of manipulation that experts can detect. If a video exists, it usually counts as proof.

Biometrics Police have used biometrics for ages to solve crimes—they look for fingerprints at crime scenes. Biometrics can be used as a factor for authentication, and they work just as well for nonrepudiation. If a system requires a fingerprint or a facial scan for access, odds are that the person who owns those traits accessed the system. Biometrics are a very strong form of nonrepudiation.

Signature For paper contracts, signatures have been considered binding for about as long as humans have been writing. In today's digital world, signatures can be captured using a stylus or touchscreen. Other systems consider an electronic document signed if the person types their name and date into a form, checks a box certifying that it's really them, and then submits the form.

The one problem with signatures is that they can be forged. Because of this, signatures aren't the strongest form of nonrepudiation. This can be overcome by the use of cryptography with digital signatures. Generally speaking, signatures as a form of nonrepudiation usually hold up in a court of law.

Receipt When someone makes a purchase transaction, they often get a receipt. This is considered proof that the transaction occurred. Receipts can be paper or digital.

Summary

This chapter introduced you to security threats that you can face every day. It started off with a discussion on hackers and their motives and the type of information they try to steal or the damage they try to cause. Hackers could be trying to steal data used to make business decisions or make money. They might want to monetize it themselves by selling it on the black market, or they might just want to damage the company's reputation or ability to conduct business.

Next, you learned about security threats and how they fit into the information security CIA triad. Confidentiality is ensuring that private data stays that way. Attacks against confidentiality include snooping, eavesdropping, wiretapping, social engineering, and dumpster diving. Integrity is ensuring that the data is true and correct and that users and computers are who they say they are. Integrity concerns include on-path attacks, replay attacks, impersonation, and unauthorized information alteration. Availability means that data is accessible when it should be, and potential attacks include denial of service, service outages, power outages, hardware failures, and hardware destruction. You then learned about privacy, laws that govern privacy, and what should be expected from various types of sites. Finally, there is a large group of threats that can cause multiple security issues, such as viruses, worms, Trojan horses, adware, spyware, ransomware, rootkits, backdoors, spam, and password cracking.

After that, you learned about access control using AAA—authentication, authorization, and accounting, with nonrepudiation added as well. Authentication ensures the identity of a user. While a single factor (such as a password) can be used to authenticate a user, a multifactor system provides greater security. Examples of factors include passwords, PINs, one-time passwords, software and hardware tokens, biometrics, a specific location, and security questions. A user can be validated among multiple systems at one time with single sign-on.

Authorization determines what the user can do. This is generally accomplished by the use of permissions, and administrators should always follow the least privilege model. Types of access control include mandatory, discretionary, role-based, and rule-based. Accounting tracks the actions of users through the use of logs or a web browser history. Finally, nonrepudiation ensures that people can't deny that an action took place. Factors for nonrepudiation include video, biometrics, signatures, and receipts.

Exam Essentials

Explain how data and information is an asset and is monetized. Companies use data to make money. Some use it to improve products or better reach customers. Others will sell data to different companies as their revenue stream. Critical data is data that can't be lost and should have the highest level of protection. Noncritical data can have less rigorous security standards.

Understand how data is used to drive business decisions. Data is captured and collected by companies to help make decisions. The data may be correlated with other datasets to develop insights, and data may be reported. Datasets are analyzed for patterns to help improve products or services, or better reach customers. Large, unstructured datasets are often referred to as big data.

Understand confidentiality concerns. Confidentiality concerns include snooping, eavesdropping, wiretapping, social engineering, and dumpster diving.

Understand integrity concerns. Potential integrity attacks include on-path and replay attacks, impersonation, and unauthorized information alteration.

Understand availability concerns. Threats to availability include denial of service, service outages, power outages, hardware failure, and hardware destruction.

Understand data privacy concerns. People have a right to privacy when it comes to their personal data, or personally identifiable information (PII). Companies that collect and use such data should take measures to secure it. However, not all companies do and there are hackers looking to find and exploit weak data security.

Understand regulations in place to protect PII. In the European Union, data privacy is protected through the General Data Protection Regulation (GDPR) law. The United States has the Privacy Act, and some states have stricter privacy laws as well.

Know what cookie consent is. Before a website can download a cookie onto your device, it must get your consent.

Understand privacy as it pertains to social media sites. Social media accounts can be set to public, in which everyone can see them, or some level of private where only friends or contacts can see the account.

Know several examples of authentication factors. Examples include passwords, PINs, one-time passwords, software tokens, hardware tokens, biometrics, a specific location, and security questions.

Understand what single sign-on does. Single sign-on allows a user to be authenticated among multiple systems with one set of user credentials.

Know what permissions are. Permissions are groups of privileges users have on a file or service. For example, one user may be able to edit a file whereas another user can only read it.

Understand what the least privilege model is. User accounts should only have the minimum amount of access (or privileges) to resources as possible.

Know what is used for accounting. To perform user tracking, logs, location tracking, and web browser histories are often used.

Understand what can be used for nonrepudiation. Video, biometrics, signatures, and receipts can all be used for nonrepudiation.

Chapter 10 Lab

You can find the answers in Appendix A.

Chapter 10 provided background on the large number of threats to your computer's security. Most threats are in the malware group, and new viruses and threats are released on a regular basis to join the cadre of those already in existence. It's a good idea to be aware of the threats that are out there and to keep up-to-date on new ones being introduced into the wild.

One great source to find this information is the CERT/CC Current Activity web page at `https://cisa.gov/news-events/cybersecurity-advisories`. There you'll find a detailed description of the most current viruses as well as links to pages on older threats. Another good option is the Broadcom security center at `https://broadcom.com/support/security-center` (click the Symantec Protection Bulletin link). Finally, you can also find updates on most antimalware companies' websites, such as `www.norton.com` (for Norton Security) and `www.mcafee.com`. Google searches can also make you aware of threats or provide news on recent attacks.

Here are a few specific questions for you to answer:

1. Pick a recent date. How many viruses and malware were "discovered" on that date? (Alternate question: How many were added to your antivirus program on a given date?)
2. Are there any serious security threats currently out there?
3. Which virus or worm caused the most damage in history? How many computers did it infect and how fast did it spread?
4. Can you find example names of some different types of viruses? Choose a few, such as a polymorphic virus, a boot virus, and a multipartite virus.
5. What is the most popular ransomware in history?
6. What is the name of the most common backdoor you can find?
7. What are examples of password-cracking software?

Review Questions

You can find the answers in Appendix B.

1. Which of the following are activities that a hacker might attempt?
   - **A.** Stealing usernames and passwords
   - **B.** Modifying website content
   - **C.** Disrupting network communications
   - **D.** Analyzing network traffic
   - **E.** All of the above
2. Your company has collected a lot of data on product performance that includes customer reviews, pictures, and schematics. Which term best describes the collection of data?
   - **A.** Data correlation
   - **B.** Data monetization
   - **C.** Big data
   - **D.** Critical data
3. Which of the following are threats to data availability? (Choose two.)
   - **A.** Service outage
   - **B.** Replay attack
   - **C.** Wiretapping
   - **D.** Destruction
4. What is the name of an application that appears to look like a helpful application but instead does harm to your computer?
   - **A.** Virus
   - **B.** Worm
   - **C.** Malware
   - **D.** Trojan horse
5. Someone was recently caught sifting through your company's trash looking for confidential information. What is this an example of?
   - **A.** Trash snooping
   - **B.** Dumpster diving
   - **C.** Phishing
   - **D.** Social engineering

6. You are implementing multifactor security on a computer. Which of the following is not a valid factor?
   A. Receipt
   B. Password
   C. Hardware token
   D. Specific location
7. You have been asked to lead a class on preventing social engineering. What two topics should you be sure to cover? (Choose two.)
   A. Viruses and worms
   B. Shoulder surfing
   C. Hardware theft
   D. Phishing
8. On a network, a user needs to access three different types of systems. However, they are required to enter their username and password only when they initially log in. Which term best explains this?
   A. Authentication
   B. Single sign-on
   C. Authorization
   D. Nonrepudiation
9. You receive an email from your bank telling you that your account has been compromised and that you need to validate your account details or else your account will be closed. You are supposed to click a link to validate your information. What is this an example of?
   A. A security breach at your bank that needs to be resolved
   B. Spam
   C. Ransomware
   D. Phishing
10. If you are concerned about confidentiality of client records, which of the following should you be on the lookout for? (Choose two.)
    A. Eavesdropping
    B. Denial of service
    C. Social engineering
    D. Replay attack
11. What is it called when a co-worker sitting next to you always seems to look your way when you try to enter your user ID and password to log onto the network?
    A. Phishing
    B. Social engineering
    C. Shoulder surfing
    D. Coincidence

12. Which of the following security terms best describes the process of determining what a user can do with a resource?
    - A. Authentication
    - B. Authorization
    - C. Accounting
    - D. Nonrepudiation
13. Which of the following operating systems are susceptible to viruses?
    - A. Windows
    - B. Windows and macOS
    - C. Windows, macOS, and Linux
    - D. Windows, macOS, Linux, and Android
14. A network administrator wants to enable accounting on her network. Which options should she use? (Choose two.)
    - A. Biometrics
    - B. Transaction logs
    - C. Software tokens
    - D. Web browser history
15. Which of the following can be used as an authentication factor and for nonrepudiation?
    - A. Password
    - B. One-time password
    - C. Biometrics
    - D. Security question
16. Your manager is concerned about potential wiretapping on the wireless network. What type of concern is this?
    - A. Availability
    - B. Authorization
    - C. Integrity
    - D. Confidentiality
17. To log into a network, you must use a password and answer a security question. What is this an example of?
    - A. Multifactor authentication
    - B. Single sign-on
    - C. Authorization
    - D. Nonrepudiation

18. Which of the following threats can directly impact data integrity on a network? (Choose two.)
    A. Snooping
    B. On-path
    C. Impersonation
    D. Denial of service
19. Your network's security model requires that the administrator configure permissions based on a user's job within the company. What does this describe?
    A. Rule-based access control
    B. Role-based access control
    C. Discretionary access control
    D. Mandatory access control
20. Which law protects consumer privacy in the European Union?
    A. Privacy Act
    B. CCPA
    C. PII
    D. GDPR

Security Best Practices

THE FOLLOWING COMPTIA TECH+ FC0-U71 EXAM OBJECTIVES ARE COVERED IN THIS CHAPTER:

✓ **6.0 Security**

✓ **6.2 Explain methods to secure devices and security best practices.**

- Security awareness
  - Social engineering
    - Phishing
  - Malicious or compromised content
- Securing devices (mobile/workstation)
  - Authentication
  - Anti-malware
  - Firewall
  - Patching/updating
  - Physical device security
    - Cable locks
    - USB locks
- Device use best practices
  - Licensing
    - Open source vs. proprietary
    - Subscription vs. one-time purchase vs. perpetual
    - Product keys and serial numbers
  - Software sources
    - Researching and validating legitimate sources

        - Original equipment manufacturer (OEM) websites vs. third-party websites
        - Application stores
    - Removal of software
        - Unwanted
        - Unnecessary
        - Malicious
    - Software piracy
- Safe browsing practices
    - Certificates
        - Valid
        - Invalid
- Privacy considerations
    - Social networking sites
    - Email
    - File sharing
    - Instant messaging
    - AI

✓ 6.3 Explain password best practices.

- Password length
- Password complexity
- Password history
- Password expiration
- Password reuse across sites
- Password managers
- Password privacy
- Password reset process
- Changing default usernames and passwords
- Enabling passwords

✓ **6.4 Identify common use cases for encryption.**

- Plain text vs. cipher text
- Data at rest
  - File level
  - Disk level
  - Mobile device
- Data in transit
  - Email
  - HTTPS
  - VPN
  - Mobile application

Chapter 10, "Security Concepts and Threats," introduced you to a wide range of possible attacks and threats to your computer. While it's true that you need to be vigilant in protecting your computer, the good news is that there are many steps you can take to help secure your system. Even if you follow all of the best steps to protect your computer, you can still find yourself the victim of an attack—there is no guarantee that you're safe. Your goal, though, is to make a would-be attacker's task as difficult as possible. The harder your computer is to infiltrate, the more likely it is that the attacker will look for easier victims. Following the proper steps dramatically decreases the odds of an attack being successful versus having an unprotected system.

This chapter builds upon Chapter 10 by showing you specific actions that you can take to protect your computer and your data. As part of these actions, you will learn how to harden your computer, manage users and passwords, and use data encryption. This chapter contains practical advice, as well as scenarios to help you understand preventive measures, what to look for in regard to suspicious activity, and what to do in case your system becomes compromised.

Understanding Security Best Practices

The best computer security plans are always multifaceted; there are parts of the plan to implement on the local computer as well as the network, and there are activities that you should avoid doing to be safe. Odds are you that wouldn't walk down a dark alley at night—this chapter will show you what the computerized version of that dark alley is so that you can avoid it.

First, I am going to talk about making a specific device more secure, which is referred to as *device hardening*. After that, I will discuss how to manage users, which includes behavioral concepts as well as password best practices. Then I will show you some examples of using data encryption.

Device Hardening

The term *device hardening* has to be one of the best terms in all of computing. It sounds strong and powerful and as if it will make your computer or device invincible. While the invincibility part is a bit of a stretch, device hardening helps protect your computer by reducing its vulnerabilities.

If you think about it, the very act of networking computers is what makes them vulnerable to attacks. An old adage in the IT industry is that "a server is totally secure until you install the network card." The pragmatic paradox is, of course, without that network card, the server can't really serve anyone. The adage holds true for all computers, and so does the paradox. Device hardening is one proactive step that you can take at the local machine to reduce the likelihood of a successful attack. The concepts behind device hardening can be applied to desktops, laptops, and mobile devices, although a few are clearly geared toward one type of device. Here I am going to break device-hardening techniques into the following six categories:

- Updating devices and enabling passwords
- Implementing physical security
- Using proper authentication
- Protecting against network threats
- Improving software security
- Browsing the Internet safely

Updating Devices and Enabling Passwords

The first step to ensuring that a device is as secure as possible is to keep the software on it up-to-date. Software applications, particularly operating systems, are incredibly complex. Even with great programmers and security mechanisms in place, operating systems have vulnerabilities. The question is how serious are these weaknesses, and have the hackers discovered them yet? Some vulnerabilities might not be critical. For example, say that a hacker found an exploit that made your computer reboot. While that's annoying, it's not as serious as data theft. Still, you'd want to fix it as soon as possible.

Tech+ exam objective 6.2, "Explain methods to secure devices and security best practices," has a long list of methods you need to know. Included in that list is patching and updating devices.

Whenever an operating system update or patch comes out, install it on your device. The same advice holds true for major software applications. There's no sense in leaving any doors open for a potential hacker.

Most OSs have a built-in update mechanism. As discussed in Chapter 5, "Software Applications," Windows comes with Windows Update, as shown in Figure 11.1. You can get to it several ways in Windows 11, such as by typing **Windows update** in the Windows search bar and pressing Enter, or by clicking Start Settings (the icon that looks like a gear) ➢ Windows Update.

Mobile operating systems need to be updated as well. Apple's iOS will tell you if an update is available within Settings ➢ General, as shown in Figure 11.2. Tapping Software Update will provide more details on the available update.

FIGURE 11.1 Windows Update

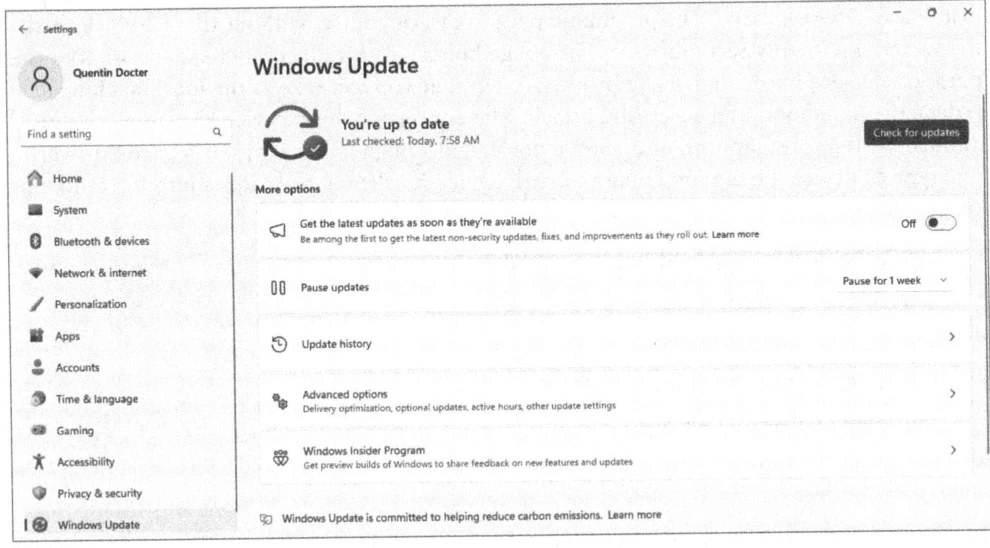

FIGURE 11.2 An iOS update is available.

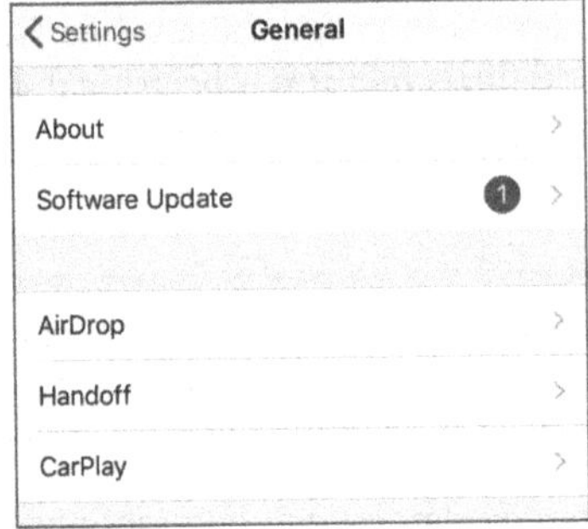

Android OS can be updated from Settings ➢ Software update, as shown in Figure 11.3. As a general rule, *patching* or updating automatically as soon as an update is available is a good practice.

The second immediate step to securing a device is to use system passwords and change the default password if there is one. This advice is particularly important for smaller, mobile devices that are easier to steal. Mobile devices let you set up a passcode on the lock screen, which is required to access the device. In Android OS, it's done through Settings ➢ Security And Privacy (Figure 11.4). An iOS lock screen password is configured through Settings ➢ Face ID & Passcode, also shown in Figure 11.4.

FIGURE 11.3 Android software update

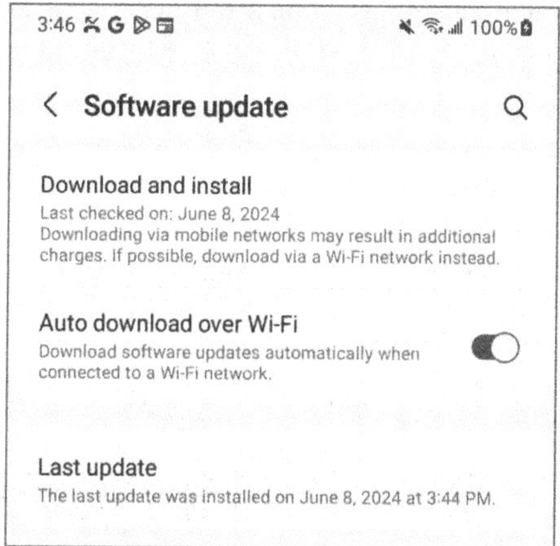

FIGURE 11.4 Android (a) and iOS (b) security settings

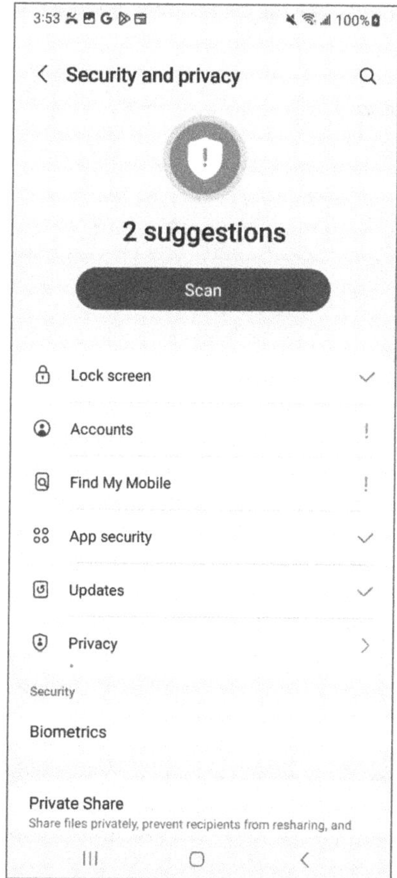

(a)

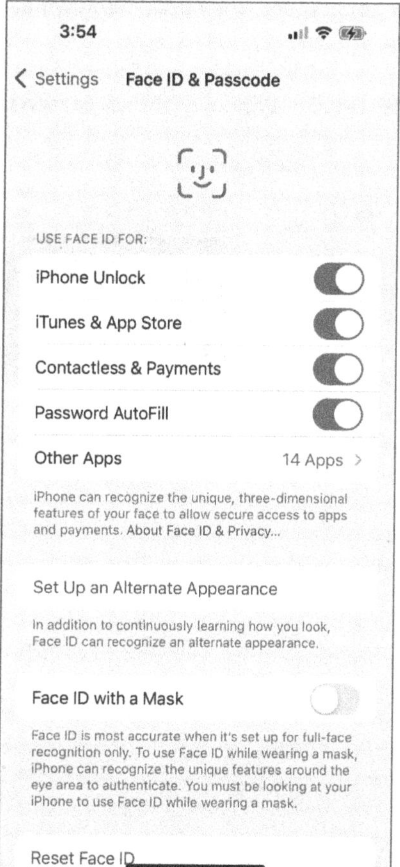

(b)

Mobile devices can be set to erase all of their data automatically (called a *wipe*) after 10 failed passcode attempts. This is an extra layer of security, but it can also pose a risk if the user is forgetful or has small children who might get to it.

For desktop and laptop computers, you can enable a system password through the BIOS. It will require the user to enter a password to boot the system. The BIOS can also be password protected to keep it from being altered.

Finally, when using a desktop or laptop in an open environment (such as an office), a good security step is to enable a screen-saver password and activate it every time you leave your desk. This will help reduce the risk of someone using your computer while you're away. In Exercise 11.1, you will practice setting up a secure screen saver.

EXERCISE 11.1

Securing a Windows 11 PC from Unauthorized Local Use

1. In Windows 11, right-click the desktop and choose Personalize.
2. Click Lock Screen. The Lock Screen window opens, like the one shown in Figure 11.5.

FIGURE 11.5 Windows 11 Lock Screen window

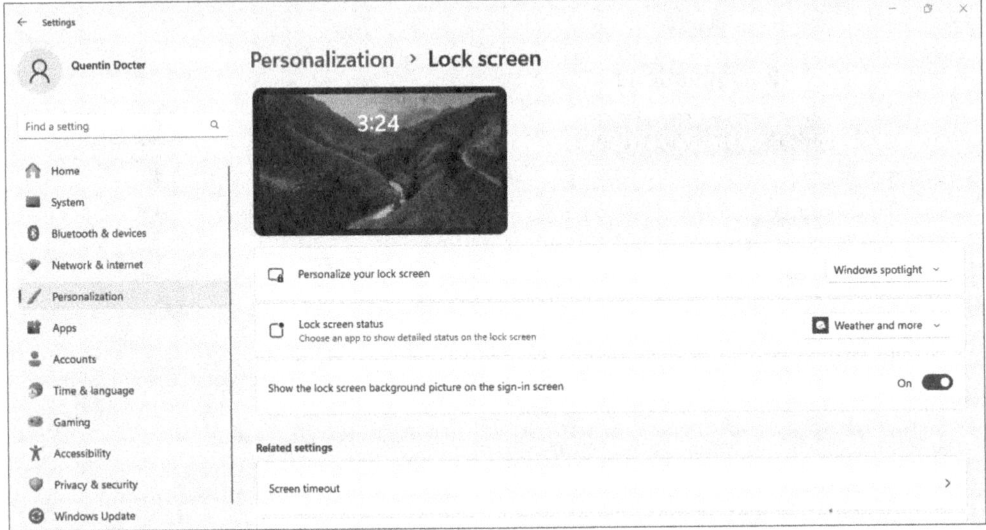

3. Click Screen Saver at the bottom of the window. It will open the Screen Saver Settings dialog box shown in Figure 11.6.

FIGURE 11.6 Screen Saver Settings dialog box

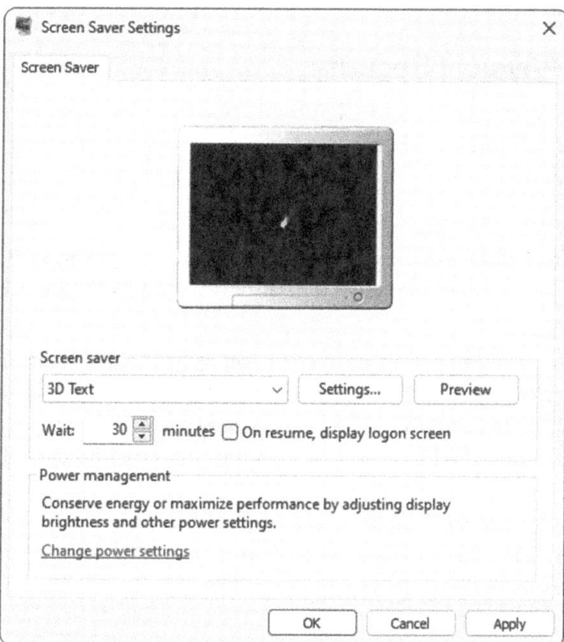

4. Choose a screen saver from the Screen Saver drop-down list, such as Bubbles.
5. In the Wait box, change the value to 1 minute.
6. Select the On Resume, Display Logon Screen check box. Click OK.
7. Wait 1 minute for the screen saver to start.
8. Move the mouse to awaken the computer. The logon screen appears.
9. Click your user account and retype your password to resume.

Another way to lock your Windows computer quickly when you leave is to use the Lock feature. Simply press Ctrl+Alt+Delete and click Lock. A somewhat catchy, if not slightly obnoxious security mantra is, "Control Alt Delete when you leave your seat!" (You can also press the Windows key + L, but there's no catchy phrase for that one.)

In addition to enabling passwords, always change them from the default to something secure. Keeping a default password in place is as bad as not having a password at all. I'll talk about creating secure passwords in the "Managing Passwords" section later in this chapter.

Implementing Physical Security

You learned about physical security in Chapter 3, "Computing Devices and the Internet of Things," as well as in Chapter 10. Because physical security is critical to device hardening, let's review it again here.

Physical device security, specifically cable locks and USB locks, are part of Tech+ exam objective 6.2. Understand how they work.

The first rule is to place important devices in secure or locked locations. Companies have server rooms locked down tight for a reason—if someone can get to and physically damage a machine, it doesn't matter how great your software security is. Of course, laptops and mobile devices are designed to travel, so locking them behind closed doors isn't always an option.

For laptops, use a laptop *cable lock* wherever possible. Figure 11.7 shows two standard Kensington locks (or K locks)—the one on the left is unlocked with a combination lock, and the one on the right, inserted into a laptop, uses a key.

FIGURE 11.7 Cable locks

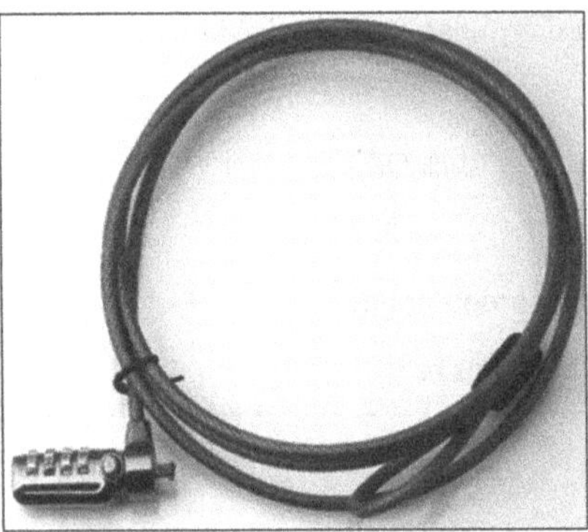

Another potential trouble spot for laptops is the USB ports. A potential attacker could insert a flash drive loaded with malware into the port, activate it, and cause all sorts of problems. Or perhaps someone could use a flash drive to copy sensitive data from a laptop or a network the laptop is connected to.

Another type of attack that's gained popularity is the "USB Drop" attack. The attacker will load malicious software onto a USB flash drive, and then drop it in a public place. The goal is to get an unsuspecting person to pick it up and put it into their USB port to see what's on it. When it gets inserted, AutoPlay will by default launch the executable file on the device, thereby infecting the device with malware.

The moral of the story is don't plug in any USB device that you don't trust. You will learn how to disable AutoPlay later in this chapter, in the "Disabling AutoPlay" section.

One way to physically protect USB ports is to use a device called a USB lock. A *USB lock* is a device that plugs into USB ports and blocks their access. Figure 11.8 shows several of them along with the key used to remove the locks from USB ports. USB ports can also be disabled though software means, such as in the BIOS or from Windows Device Manager. In Figure 11.9, you can see that by going into Device Manager and right-clicking on a USB port, you have the option of disabling the port. Of course, the downside to disabling the port is that it can't be used, but that's the trade-off for using this type of security.

FIGURE 11.8 USB locks

Using Proper Authentication

You learned about authentication in Chapter 10, so this again will be a quick review. Authentication, of course, helps keep computers and resources safe as it requires the user to validate their identity. The three types of authentication to remember are:

- **Single-Factor Authentication:** A username and one factor, such as a password, are required. Examples of a factor include something you know, something you are, something you have, or somewhere you are.

- **Multifactor Authentication:** It requires two or more items to validate the user, such as a password and a biometric scan, or a password and a temporary code. Using an ATM is an example, because it requires a bank card (something you have) and a PIN (something you know).
- **Single Sign-On (SSO).** This allows users to access multiple systems with only their initial login, as opposed to requiring the user to log in separately to each resource.

FIGURE 11.9 Disabling a USB port in Device Manager

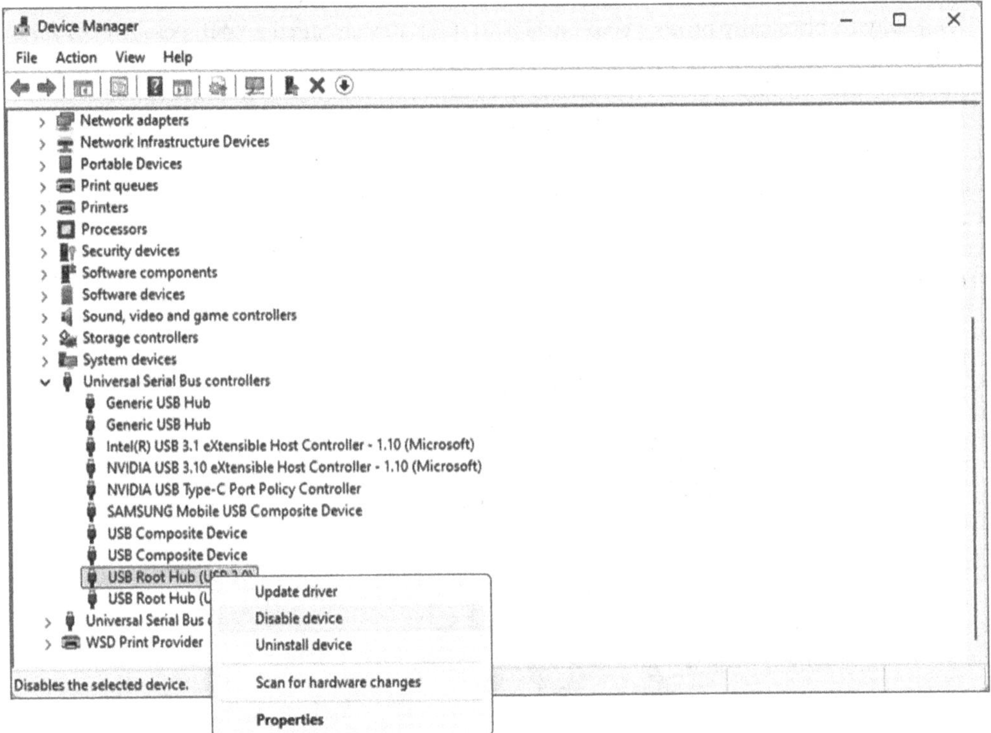

This might go without saying, but for any computer or network that has sensitive data, users should be required to authenticate before they are allowed to use them. If it's a public kiosk or something like that, authentication might not be as critical, but those systems should also have very limited access, such as Internet-only, or Internet and the ability to print.

Tech+ exam objective 6.2 includes securing devices through authentication. Be able to explain how authentication works and different types of authentication.

Protecting Against Network Threats

It's rare today to see someone using a computer that's not attached to some sort of network. Having access to network resources and the Internet is great, but it also opens up the computer to security risks. Malware infections are one of the most common security risks that you will encounter. These are four main classes of applications to help protect your system against malware and hackers:

- Antivirus software defends against viruses, worms, and Trojan horses.
- Antispyware software defends against adware and spyware.
- Antispam software reduces the amount of junk email you receive.
- Software firewalls block potentially dangerous network traffic.

There are also suites available that combine multiple security functions; for example, the Norton 360 suite includes antivirus, antimalware, and antispam features, along with identity protection tools, a software firewall, a backup tool, and a PC tune-up tool. McAfee has similar capabilities. In addition, there is some overlap between the types of threats each application guards against; for example, an antivirus program may also target some types of nonvirus malware.

Securing devices through the use of antimalware software and firewalls is part of Tech+ exam objective 6.2. The following sections cover different types of antimalware used to harden devices.

Antivirus Software

Antivirus software attempts to identify virus infections by scanning all of the files on your hard disk (or a subset of files that are most likely to contain viruses). Popular antivirus programs include Norton 360 (formerly Norton Antivirus) and McAfee Total Protection.

The website `www.av-comparatives.org` provides an independent, comprehensive comparison and review of current antivirus applications. Take the time to look through this site and draw your own conclusions about what may be the best antivirus application for you.

Viruses are often concealed by a simple deception. They embed themselves inside an application, redirecting the application's commands and code around themselves while running as a separate task. One way that antivirus programs detect a virus is by opening the file and scanning the code, looking for this type of redirection. Some programming languages, such as C++ and Java, generate code in a style that is sometimes wrongly accused by an antivirus program of being infected.

Another way that antivirus programs work is to scan the code of each executable file looking for virus signatures. A virus's *signature* is an identifying snippet of its code, sometimes called a *virus definition*. The antivirus program maintains a database of known virus definitions; when it finds a match between its database and some code it finds in a file that it scans, it signals a warning that there may be an infection. As new viruses and other threats are discovered, the company updates the virus definition file for its antivirus program and downloads it to users as an update. Having the most up-to-date definitions is critical for effective virus protection, so you must regularly update your antivirus software (or better yet, set it to update itself automatically).

A zero-day attack is one where an unknown software or firmware vulnerability is exploited—in other words, the attack occurs on "day zero." Of course, once the attack happens, it becomes a known vulnerability, and the software developers and antivirus companies start working on solutions.

In addition, many antivirus programs create an MD5 for each application. MD5 stands for Message Digest Version 5, a math calculation that results in a unique value used to reflect the data being checked. If the MD5 changes, this may be treated as a virus attack.

Antivirus applications are normally resident, meaning they're continuously running in the background and analyzing your system and any programs when they're opened or closed as well as any files that are opened or closed. Some antivirus programs check incoming and outgoing email too, as well as the web pages you visit. You can also tell your antivirus program to do a complete scan of all your files any time you like. (It will probably offer to do one right after you install the antivirus software.)

When your antivirus program finds something suspicious, a message appears, giving you the choice of deleting or quarantining the infected files. Deleting a file removes it from your system. Quarantining it places it in an off-limits area so that it can't be run but keeps it on your system. You might quarantine a file that you wanted to share with an IT professional who was tracking virus infections on your network, for example.

If your security software pops up an alert, it's best to act upon it immediately. The alert will tell you what the suspected problem is and recommend a course of action. Unless you have a specific reason not to, follow your security software's recommended actions!

Antispyware Software

Antispyware applications look for known spyware and adware programs and offer to disable them or remove them from your system. Like antivirus applications, antispyware programs look for definitions—that is, code snippets that identify a spyware or adware component.

Most antispyware applications can also remove lesser security and privacy threats, such as tracking cookies. Many antivirus applications include antispyware protection too, so you may not have to bother with a separate antispyware application.

Some antispyware applications run all the time in the background, like an antivirus application. Others run only when you specifically open them and initiate a scan.

Microsoft Defender is a free antispyware tool that comes with Windows. There are also many other free and commercial antispyware programs available, such as Spybot (`www.safer-networking.org`).

As with antivirus applications, antispyware applications are most effective when their definitions are up-to-date.

Antispam Software

Spam refers to unwanted junk email. People send spam to try to sell products because doing so is economical—it costs almost nothing to send millions of emails, so even if only a small percentage of people respond, it's still a money-making proposition. People also send spam to perpetrate fraud, either by trying to sell useless or nonexistent products or by trying to trick people into visiting phishing websites or sites where a virus or other malware will be downloaded.

Many email applications include filters and other tools to manage spam. Microsoft Outlook has its own junk-mail filter, for example. However, these built-in filters often fail to catch a lot of the spam because their algorithms for differentiating between spam and legitimate mail aren't sophisticated.

Some antivirus applications include an antispam component, and you can also buy add-on antispam programs or get them for free. For example, SpamBayes, available for free at `https://spambayes.sourceforge.io`, is an extremely sophisticated email differentiator that uses a ranking system that evaluates each message on multiple criteria to determine its spam probability. It's available for Windows, UNIX, Linux, and macOS.

Diagnosing and Fixing Malware Infections

Even if you have an antimalware application installed, it's not perfect. Occasionally a virus or other malware may get around it, especially a new threat (and especially if you haven't updated your definitions lately). When a system is infected with a virus, a worm, a Trojan horse, or other malicious software, you need to remove it immediately. Chapter 5 introduced you to the steps needed to remove malware, but here's a short reminder. The steps are as follows:

1. Identify malware symptoms.
2. Quarantine the infected system.
3. Remediate infected systems.
4. Schedule scans and updates.
5. Educate the end user to avoid a repeat performance.

Here are some of the symptoms that your computer may experience either immediately or on a particular day or time when the malware triggers itself:

- Your antivirus software may be disabled, and you can't reenable it. Or, if you didn't already have antivirus software and you're just now installing it, it may not install. This is a common side effect of virus infection because it makes it difficult for you to remove the virus.
- Your system may run sluggishly, taking much longer than normal to open windows or applications. Many malware infections bog down a system or cripple it.
- CPU and memory usage may be high even though you aren't doing anything that would cause them to act in this manner. This can happen if the malware is hijacking your system for its own computing purposes.
- A warning or message box may appear on-screen and refuse to go away. For example, there may be a message that your system is infected with a virus and demanding that you enter a credit card to "buy" software that will fix the problem.
- Your friends may let you know that they have been receiving strange emails from you that you didn't send.
- When you use your web browser, you may be bombarded with pop-up ads.

If you start experiencing these symptoms, your own antivirus program may not be much help because a virus may have gotten around it and disabled it. If it's running—great. Do a full virus scan immediately.

If you can't use your local antivirus program, your best bet is an online virus checker. Trend Micro offers a good free one at `www.trendmicro.com/en_us/forHome/products/housecall.html`, for example. Scan your system with that and then follow the advice the scanner recommends. If the system is infected to the point that it won't operate even to open a web browser, try booting into Safe Mode with Networking. Doing so may disable some of the virus's components temporarily. If you still can't rid of the virus, you may need to consult an IT professional at your local computer shop.

After you've removed the infection, you may need to repair or reinstall your antivirus software and download updates to it.

Software Firewalls

You learned about software firewalls in Chapter 5. If you will recall, firewalls can protect you in two ways. They protect your network resources from bad traffic generated by hackers, and they can simultaneously prevent computers on your network from accessing undesirable content on the Internet. Firewalls perform these tasks by monitoring and filtering network traffic.

There are two different types of firewalls: network-based and host-based. Windows comes with its own host-based firewall, appropriately named Windows Defender Firewall. If you want to obtain a different firewall, you can find them as stand-alone products or as part of a security suite such as Norton 360. If you are unsure of what security measures are in place on your system, the Security And Maintenance screen, shown in Figure 11.10, can show you what security measures are set on your system. To get to it, type **security and maintenance** in the Windows search box and press Enter.

FIGURE 11.10 Security And Maintenance screen

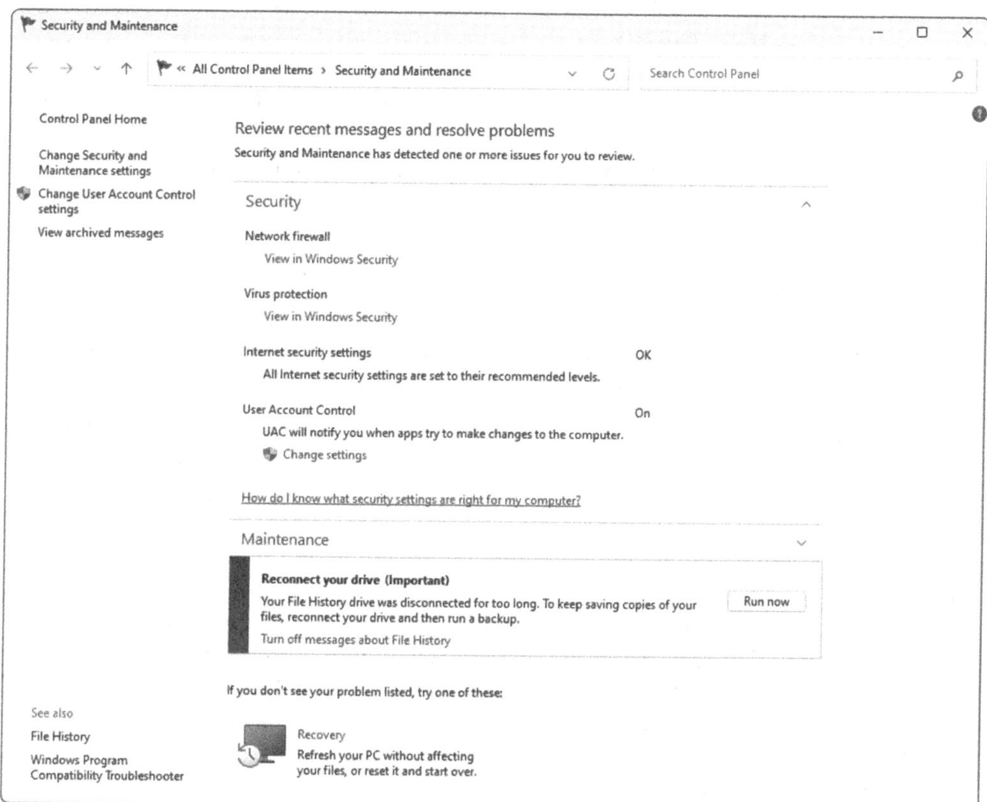

Improving Software Security

Software vulnerabilities present enticing targets to hackers. From a device security and hardening standpoint, ensuring that there are as few holes as possible is the best policy. Much like with operating systems, keeping the software on your devices up-to-date with the most current version is a great first step. But there are other best practices to follow as well. In this section, I will review some of these best practices—they will sound familiar if you've read Chapter 5. Because they were covered there, this will again be a quick review to refresh your memory. But then we'll look at disabling two additional features as well—services and AutoPlay—which can enhance security as well.

A big chunk of Tech+ exam objective 6.2 deals with software best practices related to securing devices. Be able to explain the following concepts:

- The use of licensing, including open source versus proprietary, subscriptions, one-time purchase, and perpetual licenses, and product keys and serial numbers
- Researching and validating legitimate sources, including original equipment manufacturer (OEM) websites and third-party websites as well as app stores
- Removal of unwanted, unnecessary, or malicious software and software piracy

Managing Software

As noted in the introductory paragraph, this section is a review from Chapter 5. For fuller coverage on these topics, please refer to that chapter. Don't ignore this section, though, because it is a great refresher and important for device security.

Ensuring proper licensing. Two types of software you may use are open source and proprietary. Open source software does not require a license. Proprietary software does. Using proprietary software without purchasing a license is illegal, but beyond that, you likely will not receive any software updates for the title. This can increase the risk that the software may be exploited.

There are three types of licenses with which you should be familiar. Subscription licenses renew periodically, typically every year, and charge the user upon renewal. The good news is, with subscriptions you are basically guaranteed to have the most current version. One-time purchase means the user pays once. Perpetual licenses are the same as one-time purchase licenses, in which you pay once and can use the software for perpetuity.

When you buy a license, you will get a product key to activate the software. Don't share the product key with anyone else. The software might or might not come with a serial number. The serial number can be handy for talking to technicians and is fine to share in forums like a message board if you're seeking troubleshooting help.

Using legitimate software sources. Software can be obtained from the OEM, which is the company that developed the software. This is always a safe option. There may be third-party websites as well that you can download software from. These might or might not be legitimate. Always research and validate that the website you are visiting is legitimate and won't download something unexpected to your device.

Finding Legitimate Software Sources Online

There's no shortage of websites from which you can download software. But considering the risk of spyware, ransomware, viruses, and other nasty malware, which sites can you trust?

For example, let's say you need a new printer driver. One way to look for it is to Google the printer name. I did this in Figure 11.11, and you can see that several results came up. The first one is from HP's support site. This is an example of an original equipment manufacturer (OEM) website. You can trust an OEM site. The others are third-party sites. Some might get creative and do their best to look as much like an HP site as possible with names such as `www.hpdrivers.net` and `https://support-hpdrivers.com`. These are not official HP sites but rather third-party sites. Can they be trusted? It's hard to say.

FIGURE 11.11 Printer driver search results

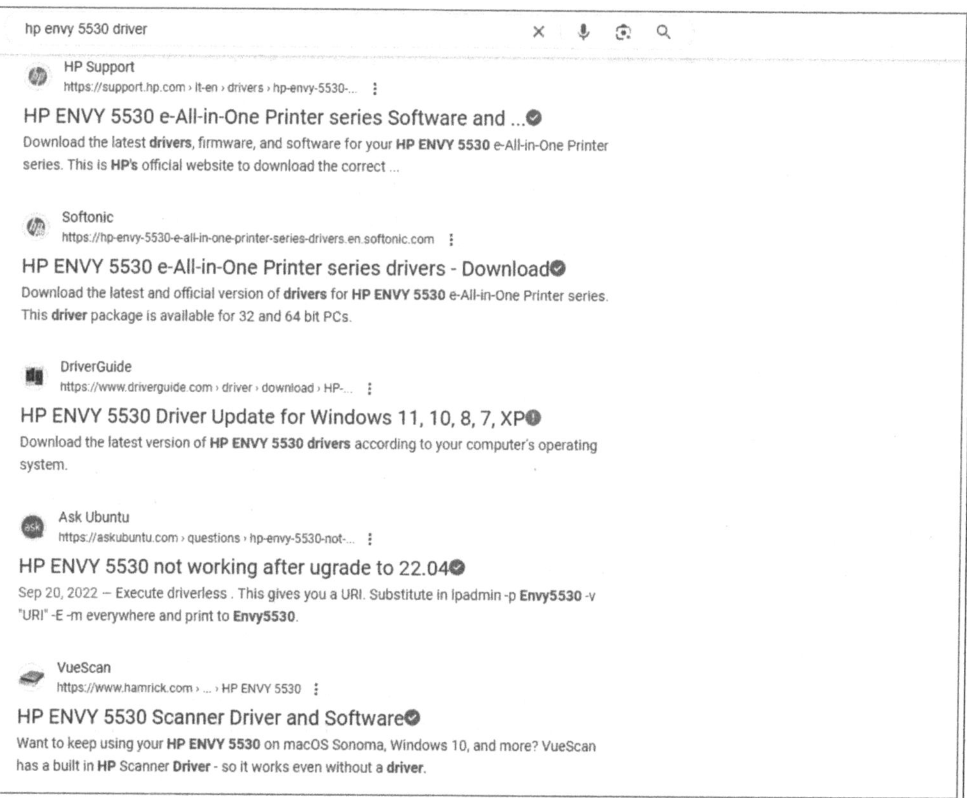

Before downloading anything from a website, including drivers and apps, research the site to see whether it's a legitimate source. Think of it this way—if some random person came up to you and offered you a pill that they said was medicine, would you take it? My guess is that you'd want to do some validation before ingesting it. If the person was your doctor and you were in the hospital, then the odds of the pill being legit are pretty good.

It's the same thing with software and drivers. Research the site to make sure that there are no known issues with it before ingesting a new download. Some antimalware programs can help. In my case, for example, my Norton subscription checks websites, and you can see that several of the results have a green check next to them. Those sites are probably fine. Norton is less sure about one of the sties in particular, and it has an orange circle with an exclamation point after it. If there are sites with known issues, Norton will place a box with a red X in it next to the link as a warning to stay away. The Web of Trust tool performs similar functionality and is installed as a browser extension.

Even without antimalware help, you can do things like Google the site name with the word *reviews* after it and see what pops up. Or, if you want to be more direct, search the site name with the word *problems* or *malware* or *virus*. If something pops up, check into it to see what happened or just avoid the site all together.

The moral of the story is that OEM websites are safe and preferred, while third-party ones might be just fine (or not). Do some research to help avoid getting hit with a nasty infection.

Removing unused software. If the software isn't on the computer, it can't pose a security risk. Remove apps that are unwanted or unnecessary. Of course, if you do end up with malicious software on your device, remove that immediately as well. For advice on where and how to remove software, refer to Chapter 5.

Avoiding software piracy. Piracy is the illegal copying and distribution of licensed software products. It's illegal, and you never can be sure if there are additional unwanted features attached to the copy. Just avoid pirated software.

Disabling Unused Services

As introduced in Chapter 4, "Operating Systems," various OS functions are implemented as services. For example, the process of managing a print job in Windows falls to the print spooler service, and logging into a domain controller is managed by a service called Netlogon. To run these services, your operating system logs itself on temporarily as a quasi-user with elevated privileges to perform the task and then logs itself back off.

An attacker could use an exploit of a service to attempt to gain unauthorized access to your machine. Most of the time, unused services are disabled by default, so the point is to not enable services unless you know you need them. Services are found in Windows in Computer Management. Exercise 11.2 shows you how to start and stop services in Windows 11.

EXERCISE 11.2

Starting and Stopping Services in Windows 11

1. Open Computer Management by typing **computer management** in the Windows search bar and pressing Enter.
2. On the left side of the Computer Management window, click Services under Services And Applications, as shown in Figure 11.12.

FIGURE 11.12 Windows Services

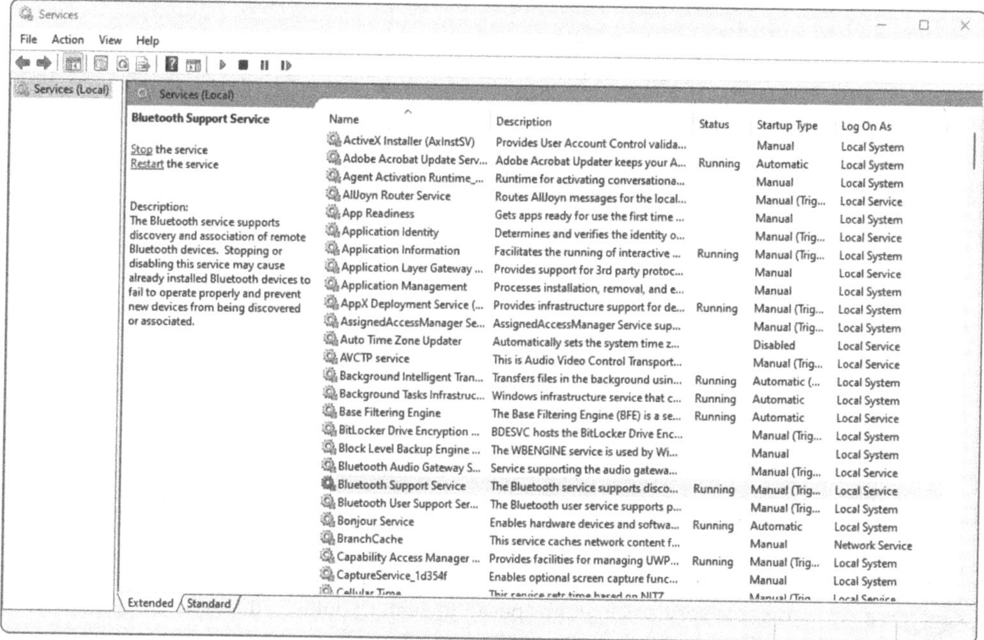

3. You will see the Bluetooth Support Service, as highlighted in Figure 11.12. Notice that it is running and starts up manually. The other broad choices for startup are Automatic and Disabled.
4. To stop the service, click the Stop button in the toolbar at the top, or right-click the service and choose Stop.
5. To start the service, either click the green Start arrow in the toolbar at the top or right-click the service and choose Start. The status will change.

EXERCISE 11.2 *(continued)*

6. To change the startup type for a service, right-click and choose Properties. Use the drop-down menu next to StartupType to make your selection, as shown in Figure 11.13, and then click OK.

FIGURE 11.13 Bluetooth Support Service properties

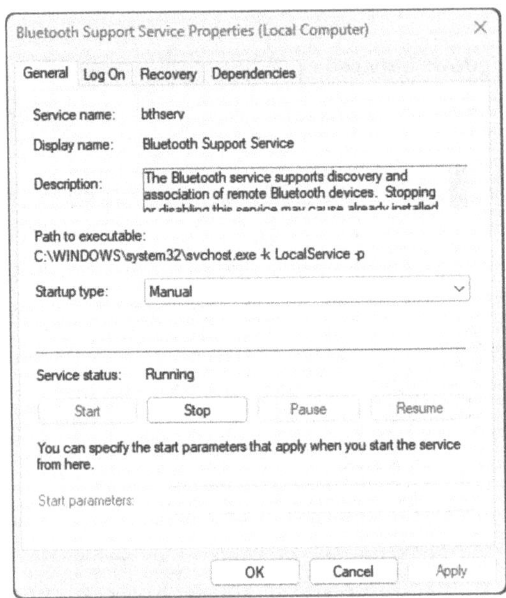

Although disabling unused services can help harden your system, don't disable services in your operating system unless you know what they do, and you know that you don't need them. Disabling necessary services can cause your system not to function properly.

Disabling AutoPlay

AutoPlay is branded as a convenient feature that lets you insert media into your system and have it run automatically. Unfortunately, this can also introduce a security risk.

It is never a good idea to put any media in a workstation if you do not know where it came from or what it is. The reason is that the media (Flash drive, DVD, CD) could contain malware. Compounding matters, that malware could be referenced in the `AUTORUN.INF` file on the media, causing it to be summoned simply by inserting the media in the machine and requiring no other action. AUTORUN.INF can be used to start an executable, access a website, or do any of a large number of different tasks. The best way to prevent your system from falling victim to such a ploy is to disable the AutoPlay feature on the workstation.

AutoPlay may also be called Autorun on your computer.

The AutoPlay settings can be accessed in a few ways. If you type **autoplay** in the Windows search bar and press Enter, it will open the AutoPlay Settings app shown in Figure 11.14. You can also open Control Panel and type **autoplay** in the Search Control Panel box in the upper-right corner to open the AutoPlay Control Panel app. It has more granularity than the Settings app, but both basically do the same thing.

FIGURE 11.14 AutoPlay options

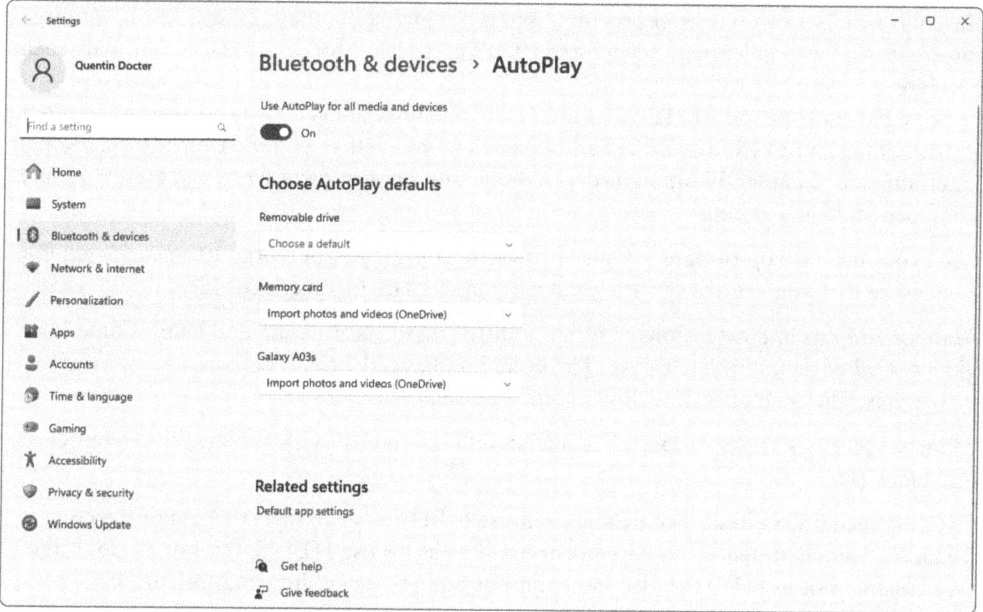

The easiest way to disable AutoPlay is to move the slider to the Off position at the top of the page. You can also control the settings for individual media types. For example, in Figure 11.14 you can see that you have options to configure different actions for different types of media. This is far better security than just running the media automatically.

Browsing the Internet Safely

When surfing the web was relatively new, most of the people who did it (or emailed regularly) were relatively computer-savvy early adopters. Over time, as the web and email became more mainstream, less-savvy people joined in the fun, which opened up many more opportunities for hackers to prey on them. A shadow industry of charlatans and other questionable business providers grew to take advantage.

Safe browsing practices is covered by Tech+ exam objective 6.2. Specifically for the exam, you need to understand valid and invalid security certificates.

At this point, it's probably safe to say that this whole "Internet" thing isn't just a passing fad. The Internet is cemented as an integral part of most of our daily routines, and now it seems that our goal is to have it on every electronic device imaginable. It's also safe to say that Internet users as a whole are savvier than ever before, either because they were a victim of a cybercrime themselves or because they know someone who was. Even though the collective user awareness of potential issues has increased, there are still plenty of targets out there. And as you learned in Chapter 10, it's pretty easy for attackers to automate their bad intent.

So, while most people are fairly aware of the potential dangers of browsing the Internet, it's still important to educate others and be vigilant yourself as you look for information and entertainment. Chapter 5 had an in-depth discussion on web browser safety. Here's a quick reminder of the key points:

Keep your browser up-to-date. Older browsers have greater potential for security exploits. Make sure that you are always using the most up-to-date browser possible.

Manage add-ons and extensions. While some of these features can add helpful functionality, not all of them are safe to use. The more you have, the more potential holes your system has. They can also slow down your browser.

Manage security settings properly. Understand how to deal with cookies, clear your cache, and block pop-ups.

Use only secure websites. Secure sites will use HTTPS instead of HTTP. As of the end of 2023, it's estimated that 90 to 95 percent of all websites use HTTPS, but not all do. If the website does not use HTTPS, absolutely do not put any secure information into it.

For a website to be able to use HTTPS, it needs to obtain a Secure Sockets Layer (SSL) certificate from a certificate authority (CA). A CA is kind of like a notary for websites, validating that they are legitimate sites, and SSL is the security protocol that enables data encryption over the Internet. If a website has a valid *SSL certificate*, you probably won't even think about it because your browser will automatically open the website when you try to visit. If the site does not have a valid certificate but is trying to use HTTPS, you will get a warning that pops up instead telling you that the certificate is invalid, and asking if you want to proceed. Certificates are valid for 13 months from the issue date, so it could be that the webmaster for a legitimate website forgot to renew it. Or it could be that the site is not legitimate. Sites using the unsecure HTTP do not use SSL certificates.

Microsoft Edge, by default, shows the full website URL so you can see if it uses HTTP or HTTPS. Chrome does not show the full URL by default. To change this, right-click a URL in the address bar, and then choose the Always Show Full URLs option from the menu.

Another security setting to be aware of is disabling Autofill. *Autofill* is a feature that automatically populates fields in a form on a web page for you. For example, say you visit a website that wants your name and address. Instead of needing to type it all in, once you start typing your first name in the First Name field, the rest of the fields will automatically fill in for you. Autofill can also save and enter in credit card payment information too. While this can be incredibly convenient, it can also pose a security risk.

If you are the only one using a home computer or it's just you and trusted members of your family, enabling Autofill is perfectly fine. One could argue that you shouldn't enable it on laptops because they are easier to steal. If it's a public workstation, though, definitely disable Autofill. If you are using a public workstation, and it asks you anything about saving your information for Autofill, politely decline.

The Autofill settings in Chrome are under Settings ➢ Autofill and passwords, as shown in Figure 11.15. There are separate sections for passwords (Google Password Manager), payments, and addresses.

FIGURE 11.15 Autofill in Chrome

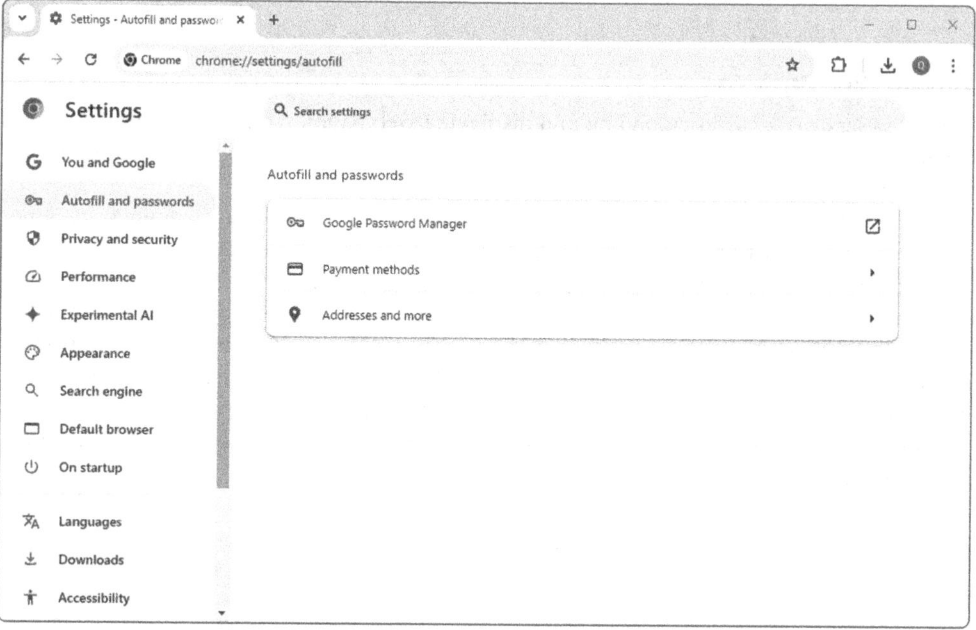

To enable or disable this feature in Microsoft Edge, go to Settings And More ➢ Settings and scroll to the bottom. There you will see the Microsoft Wallet option, as well as options to configure payments, passwords, and personal information such as addresses (Figure 11.16).

FIGURE 11.16 Edge settings

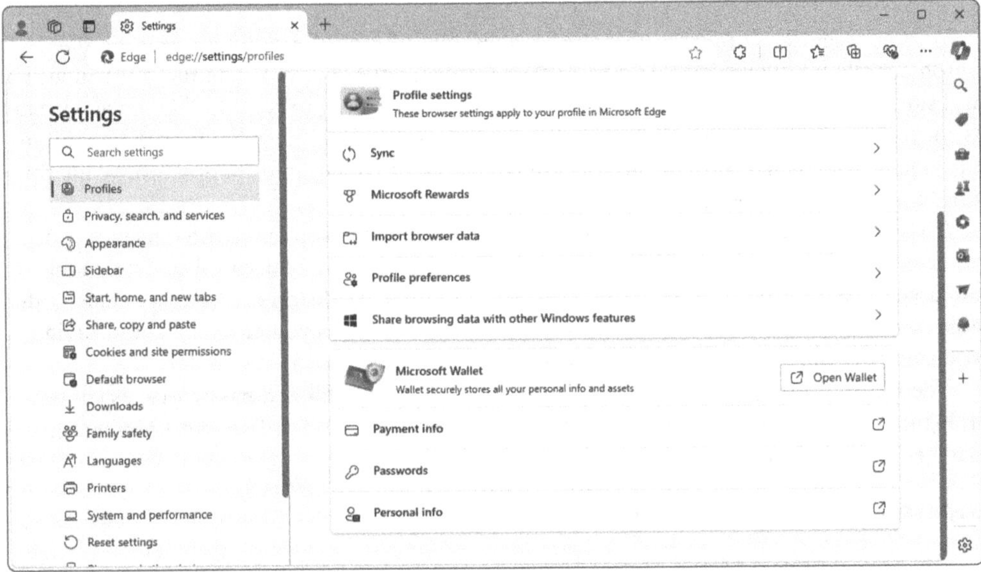

Tips for Safe Browsing

Web browsers work by downloading and displaying web pages, which are essentially programming scripts. The script is rendered as a formatted web page by your web browser on your local PC.

The trouble is, at the moment when that page is downloaded, there are numerous opportunities for a hacker to take advantage of the connection in various ways. For example, your requests for pages can be intercepted on their way to the server. This can compromise your privacy because someone can see what pages you're requesting. Moreover, it can compromise any login information that you may be sending to a financial or business site. Scripts can also contain malicious code that infects your system, making it perform unwanted activities such as sending your private information to a third party or displaying countless ads. Web pages can also have embedded Flash or Java applications that can do harm in some cases.

Before getting into specific things you should recognize, here are two basic safe web browsing tips:

Do not visit questionable sites. This one might seem self-evident, right? Part of the problem might be identifying a questionable site, much like you can't always identify a "bad person" simply based on their looks. Some sites are pretty obvious, though. Sites that claim to offer free software downloads for programs you know aren't normally free, sites that offer hate-themed material, and adult websites tend to be the most notorious for providing your computer with unwanted content.

Limit the use of personally identifiable information. *Personally identifiable information (PII)* is anything that can be used to identify an individual person on its own or in context with other information. This includes your name, address, other contact information, the names of your family members, and other details that you would consider private. You should also be judicious in providing your email address to websites to avoid getting spam.

Now on to specific tips for recognizing suspicious content.

Recognizing Suspicious Sites, Links, and Ads

It would be nice if sites that intended to download malware onto your computer would just let you know. Perhaps they could have a big flashing warning informing you that they intend to steal your identity and cause you hundreds of hours of misery. Obviously, that's not the case. Creators of sites who have bad intentions do everything they can to make sure their site resembles a legitimate one as much as possible. This can include copying web page layouts and company logos to convince people to visit the site and click the links.

Creating a site that masquerades as a legitimate secure site but actually steals your information is called *phishing* (or *spoofing*). Phishing employs many tactics, which are continually evolving. One common scheme to watch out for is getting an email that claims to be from your bank, ISP, or other institution, asking you to follow a link to its site to update your details. The email looks authentic, and when you follow the link, the site looks very much like the site of the bank or ISP—except the page probably isn't secure, and some links on the page may not be operational.

When people talk about phishing, it's generally in the context of suspicious email because that's how the term originated. Hackers sent out messages hoping to get someone to take the bait. The term has evolved a bit to encompass any electronic activity designed to defraud someone, which can and often does include the use of fake websites.

So, what does a suspicious site, link, or ad look like? Unfortunately, that's a bit like asking what a criminal looks like. There's no one specific answer. Here are some things you can look out for:

Secure Websites This was covered previously, but only visit sites that use HTTPS. The Firefox browser by default only allows access to sites using HTTPS, and other browsers can be configured to do this as well. Figure 11.18 later in this section shows you where to do that in Chrome.

Websites That Have Incorrect Spelling If someone is spoofing a website, they may try to get the spelling very close to the real site, hoping that people won't look closely and click. A made-up example is something like `www.micro.soft.com` or `www.micros0ft.com`. Neither of those are the Microsoft company, but the URLs could be chosen to attempt to impersonate Microsoft.

Incorrect Spelling or Bad Grammar Big companies do not send out mass emails to their clients unless they have been professionally edited and spell-checked.

Threats If you're being threatened that your account will close or your card won't work unless you enter your security information, it's probably not legitimate.

Deals That Are Too Good to Be True If it sounds too good to be true, it probably is. That's a good adage to follow in life, and it's especially true in cyberspace. The flashier or more attention-grabbing the banner ad, the more suspicious you should be of its legitimacy.

If you find yourself wondering whether a link or banner ad is legitimate, just don't click it!

Your web browser can likely help defend you against some phishing attacks because most browsers have some phishing protection built in.

In Microsoft-based browsers, the phishing filter is called the *SmartScreen filter*, and it can be enabled or disabled. In Windows 11, it's incorporated into Microsoft Defender. Normally you should leave it enabled because it provides information and doesn't prevent you from doing anything. Its assessment is fairly accurate as well. The only drawback (and it's minor) is that if you leave automatic checking turned on, the browser checks every page you visit, resulting in slightly slower browser performance. If you seldom visit secure sites and you want to check only the specific sites about which you have a question, you can turn off this feature. Exercise 11.3 shows you how to disable and enable the SmartScreen filter in Microsoft Edge.

EXERCISE 11.3

Configuring SmartScreen in Microsoft Edge

1. Open Microsoft Edge.

2. Click the Settings And More button (the three horizontal dots in the upper-right corner).
3. Click Settings.
4. Click the Settings hamburger menu in the upper-left corner, and choose Privacy, Search, And Services.
5. Scroll down to the Security section, shown in Figure 11.17.

FIGURE 11.17 SmartScreen filter

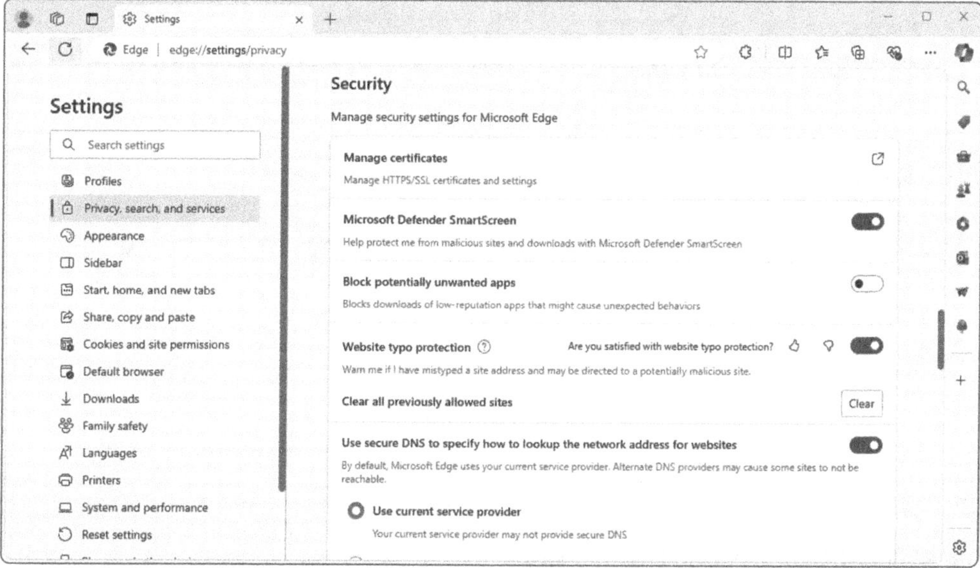

6. Slide the toggle off for Microsoft Defender SmartScreen.
7. Close Settings.

Google Chrome also has built-in phishing protection, enabled by default. It's configured by going to Settings ➢ Privacy And Security and then in the Privacy And Security section, clicking the Security link. It looks like the screen in Figure 11.18. Notice that on the Privacy And Security page you can also configure Chrome to always use secure HTTPS connections, which is a good option to enable as well.

FIGURE 11.18 Chrome Privacy And Security settings

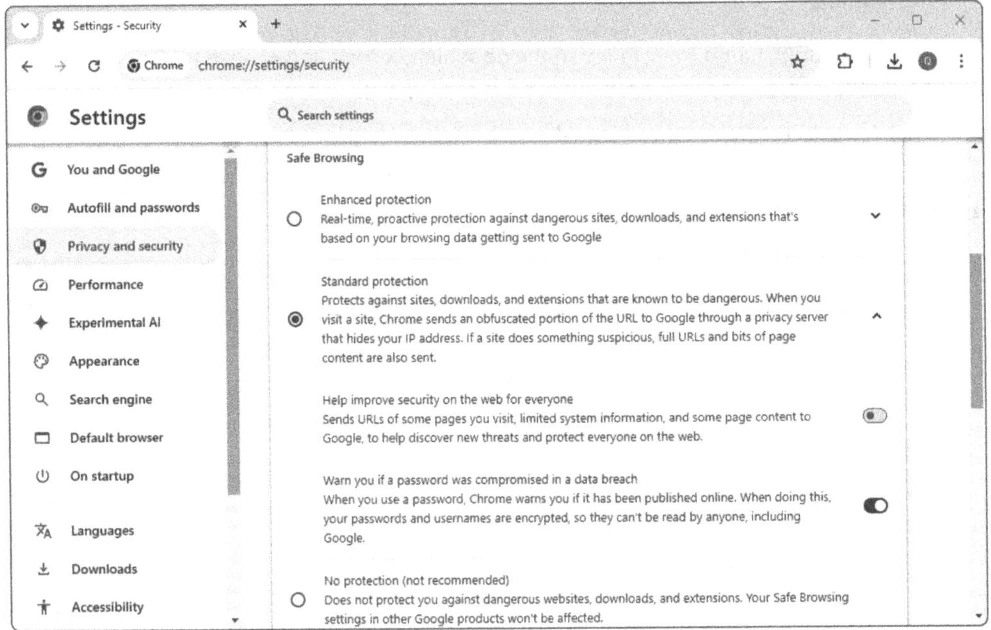

Real World Scenario

The Risks of Using Public Workstations

Every so often, you might find yourself in a situation where you want or need to use a public workstation. Perhaps you are stuck at the auto repair shop and they have convenient computers for their guests to use. Maybe you are staying at a hotel and they have computers available in their business center. No matter the reason, you should be aware of the risks of using public workstations.

Public systems can be fine to use, but they are also highly susceptible to attacks or acts of fraud because so many people use them. Some of the more severe risks include identity theft because a hacker or an unscrupulous owner could have installed a keylogger on the computer. Also, public computers often use unsecured Wi-Fi networks, which present a major issue because they transmit all communications without encryption. You don't want your credit card information announced to a crowd with a bullhorn. So, what can you do to protect yourself? Here are a few suggestions:

- If it's on an unsecured wireless network, don't use it except for basic web news surfing or entertainment. Don't enter in any personally identifiable information or usernames or passwords.
- Don't enter any confidential information, such as bank or credit card information.
- Make sure Autofill isn't being used and passwords are not being remembered.
- Don't save any files to the local computer.
- Delete your browsing history, cache, and cookies after you have finished.
- Always pay attention to your surroundings. Obviously, some locations are safer than others. Public places are great for shoulder surfing—don't be on the wrong side of that.

Managing Users and Passwords

Users represent the weakest link in the security chain, whether harm comes to them in the form of malware, social engineering, or simply avoidable mistakes. Aside from some of the obvious things, such as training users (or yourself) to be on the alert for social engineering, there are several tasks that you can perform to decrease the security risks related to user accounts. These include setting proper expectations with users on privacy and acceptable use policies and managing passwords.

Managing User Expectations and Behaviors

This is an area that needs a lot of attention because it can be one of the biggest problem areas for an organization. Users may have unrealistic expectations of what is permissible on a corporate or campus network. This can lead to inappropriate or potentially illegal behavior, which can in turn put the organization into legal jeopardy. It could be ignorance or malicious intent on the part of the user, but inappropriate behaviors should not be tolerated.

The key to managing user expectations and behaviors is to develop and deploy written policies and procedures identifying actions that are inappropriate and the consequences for performing those actions. This is referred to as a prohibited content policy or *acceptable use policy*.

Acceptable use policies can apply to any type of organization, such as a company, school, church, or community group. Throughout the rest of this section, I am simply going to say "company" for the sake of brevity, but understand that I am referring to all instances where this type of policy could apply.

What is in the policy depends on the company for which you work. Generally speaking, if something violates an existing federal or local law, it probably isn't appropriate for your computer either. Many companies also have strict policies against the possession of pornographic or hate-related materials on company property. Some go further than that, banning personal files such as downloaded music or movies on work computers. Regardless of what is in your policy, always ensure that you have buy-in from very senior management so that the policy will be considered valid. Here are some specific examples of content that might be prohibited:

- Adult content
- Content that advocates violence against an individual, group, or organization
- Unlicensed copyrighted material
- Content related to drugs, alcohol, tobacco, or gambling
- Content about hacking, cracking, or other illegal computer activity
- Violent or weapons-related content

A good policy will also contain the action steps to be taken if prohibited content or activities are spotted. For example, what should you do if you find porn on someone's work laptop?

The policy should explicitly outline the punishment for performing specific actions or possessing specific content. The appropriate penalty may be based on the type of content found. Something that is deemed mildly offensive might result in a verbal or written warning for the first offense and a more severe sentence for the second offense. If your company has a zero-tolerance policy, then employees may be terminated and possibly subject to legal action.

Finally, after the policy has been established, it's critical to ensure that all employees are aware of it and have proper training. In fact, it's highly recommended that you have all employees sign an agreement (remember nonrepudiation from Chapter 10?) saying that they have read and understand the policy and that the signed document be kept in their human resources file. Many companies also require that employees review the policy annually and re-sign the affidavit as well.

In Tech+ exam objective 6.2, there are a few different subobjectives covering users and security. Be sure to understand how security awareness plays a role in securing devices, specifically social engineering, phishing, and malicious or compromised content. Also be able to explain privacy considerations and expectations on social networking sites, email, file sharing, instant messaging, and with the use of AI.

Security Awareness

You learned about different security threats in Chapter 10, and one of the easiest ways to gain access to a device or network is through the user. Hackers can use social engineering tactics to extract information from the user to illegally gain access. This includes phishing emails and phone calls, as well as by delivering malicious or compromised content.

The key to prevention is education. Be sure that every user understands what to look for and the appropriate action to take. Companies should have training courses for users to take to understand risks. Of course, whenever in doubt, even the slightest bit of doubt, don't click that link!

Some companies will have their IT departments generate and send phishing emails as part of the security program. It will contain a link for users to click—fortunately it links to an internal site warning the user about clicking on links as opposed to something malicious. This can be a good way for IT to provide ongoing training as well as track who might need additional coaching about the risks of IT security.

Expectations of Privacy

Privacy considerations were initially covered in Chapter 10. In that chapter, you learned about different user privacy expectations for social networking sites, email, file sharing, instant messaging, and the use of artificial intelligence (AI). Instead of repeating that information, this section focuses on privacy expectations as it relates to a company's devices or networks.

Company use policies should also explicitly call out what the user can expect in terms of privacy while using the corporate network. The short answer is, they should expect none. Emails, instant messages, and files on a person's device generated from company-owned software and mobile apps are all company property and may be monitored, searched, or seized at any time. Just be sure that the company policy is clear about it.

Some companies may also choose to explicitly prohibit the use of work devices for anything other than work-related activities. This can include visiting social networking sites, personal email, instant messaging, file sharing, or the use of AI. Again, just be sure that the company policy is clear about what is and is not acceptable.

Handling Critical and Confidential Data

The final item that company policies should call out is the acceptable use and handling of critical and confidential information. This includes, but is not limited to, the following:

- Passwords
- Personally identifiable information
- Customer information
- Company confidential information

In general, each of these types of data should be treated carefully and not disclosed to anyone without explicitly stated access. Consequences for divulging confidential information can involve disciplinary action up to and including termination.

Managing Passwords

Imagine you just installed four computers on a wireless network, enabled the best Wi-Fi security (WPA3), and installed antimalware and a software firewall on all computers. Then you find out that one of the users has the word *password* for their login password. How secure is that?

Password management is a critical security feature that tends to get overlooked. It involves proper user training and is aided by restrictions a network administrator can set on users if their computers are part of a domain. Good password policy includes the following basic elements:

Enabling Passwords This might sound obvious, but it's not always done. If the device can be used to access any data that is personal, sensitive, critical, or confidential, be sure it requires a password.

Changing Default Usernames and Passwords The first thing a potential hacker will try to use is the default username or password for a device. Always change them.

Ensuring Password Privacy Users need to be educated on keeping their passwords private under all circumstances. Don't give it to the nice-sounding "IT person" asking for it over the phone to unlock their account, and don't write it on a sticky note attached to the monitor, for example.

Now that the basics are established, it's time to dive into further details of password management best practices.

Creating Effective Passwords

A *strong password* is one that is difficult for someone to guess. Strong passwords have these characteristics:

Long The longer, the better. At least eight characters should be the minimum.

Complex The password contains at least one capital letter and at least one number and/or symbol.

Unusual The password doesn't appear in a dictionary and isn't a proper noun.

Tech+ exam objective 6.3, "Explain password best practices," lists 10 best practices. They include enabling passwords, changing default usernames and passwords, and password privacy (covered already), and password length and password complexity.

Passwords that are easy to guess are considered *weak passwords*. Some of the worst passwords of all are things such as *qwerty*, *12345*, the user ID, and the word *password*. Only slightly better are the names of people, pets, and places. Even though a password should be difficult for others to guess, it's okay to make it easy for you to remember. To do this, try combining numbers and letters that make sense to you but won't make sense to other people. For example, suppose you have a cousin Sam who grew up in Wichita and you used to call him a lot, so you remember that his phone number was 555-1192. An effective password might be *Sam-Wich#1192*. Notice that this password is long (13 characters), varied (uppercase, lowercase, numeric, and symbol characters), and unusual, yet it's fairly easy for you to remember just by thinking about your cousin.

Here are some other techniques for creating passwords that are easy to remember but difficult to guess:

Substituting Zero for the Letter O in Words For example, *St0rageR00m*.

Substituting Numbers for Letters To make it easier to remember, use the numeral that represents the letter of the alphabet (for example, b=2) or use the numeral that represents the position in the word (for example, take the word *teacher* and substitute numerals for the second and fourth digits, like this: *t2a4her*.

Combining Two or More Unrelated but Memorable Words For example, *GroceryCandleFlowerpot*.

Substituting a Symbol for a Letter That It Resembles For example, $ looks like an *S*, as in *$ubstitution*, and ! looks like a capital *I*, as in *!temized*.

Creating Great Passwords

You will see lots of advice on how to make good passwords, such as using upper- and lowercase, numbers, and symbols. More complex passwords are in theory harder for hackers to crack. This advice is good, but even against brute-force cracking methods, you can protect yourself by simply using longer passwords. For example, a 7-character, numbers-only password can be cracked in about 4 seconds using today's technology. Lengthening it to 14 characters increases the time it may take to crack it to about 1 year. The following table gives you a rough idea how long it could take to brute-force-guess a password based on 2024 technology. It's not important to memorize the specifics of this table—the numbers are to give you a general idea and besides, technology is always improving to shorten these times. What is important is to understand that both password length and complexity are both critical to password security.

Number of characters	Numbers only	Lowercase letters	Upper and lowercase letters	Numbers, uppercase, and lowercase letters	Numbers, upper and lowercase letters, and symbols
4	Instantly	Instantly	3 seconds	6 seconds	9 seconds
5	Instantly	4 seconds	2 minutes	6 minutes	10 minutes
6	Instantly	2 minutes	2 hours	6 hours	12 hours
7	4 seconds	50 minutes	4 days	2 weeks	1 month
8	37 seconds	22 hours	8 months	3 years	7 years
9	6 minutes	3 weeks	33 years	161 years	479 years
10	1 hour	2 years	1k years	9k years	33k years
11	10 hours	44 years	89k years	618k years	2m years
12	4 days	1k years	4m years	38m years	164m years
13	1 month	29k years	241m years	2bn years	11bn years
14	1 year	766k years	12bn years	147bn years	805bn years
15	12 years	19m years	652bn years	9tn years	56tn years

Reusing Passwords and Password Managers

With the sheer number of passwords people need to remember today, it's quite common to reuse passwords across websites or systems. As tempting as it may be to reuse the same password, you're safer using a different password for every site you access. That way, if one site is hacked, it won't affect your security on another site.

As part of Tech+ exam objective 6.3, you should be able to explain password reuse across sites and password managers.

If you can't remember all the passwords in your head, one possible solution is to store them using a *password manager*. Password managers store passwords in a password-protected file on the device's hard drive. Yes, someone could steal that file and possibly even unencrypt it, but the chances of that happening are slim compared to the chances of a server being hacked where your password for a certain site is stored. Windows has a built-in password manager called Windows Credential Manager, and macOS uses Keychain Access. Some of the highest-rated third-party password managers are Bitwarden and 1Password.

Another possible solution is to reuse the same password for sites that don't store any financial information. For example, you might use the same password for logging into message boards and chat rooms at various sites, because if your password is discovered at those sites, the consequences are generally mild. Someone might log in and impersonate you, causing you some temporary embarrassment, but you haven't lost any money. On the other hand, you should use a different password for each of your important banking or other financial accounts because a thief could cause you significant financial problems on these sites.

Password Changes

Some companies' IT policies require that you change or reset your password at regular intervals, such as every 90 days. The rationale for having a *password expiration* policy is that the longer you keep a password, the more likely that someone has surreptitiously seen you type it, you've written it down somewhere, or some other security breach has occurred.

As part of Tech+ exam objective 6.3, you should be able to explain password expiration, password history, and the password reset process.

Even if a system doesn't require you to change your password on a certain timetable, you may want to take the initiative to change it yourself, especially on sites where you manage your financial affairs.

To help you remember your password in a frequently changing environment, you may want to develop a structured system of changes. For example, suppose your password is `video$Furrier`. When you change it, you might add the two-digit number of the month in which you changed it. For example, if you change it in February, you can make it `video$02Furrier`. Then, when you change it again in May, you can change it to `video$05Furrier`.

In addition to not reusing your password on different sites, you also shouldn't reuse a password after being required to change it. Recycling old passwords can make it easier for hackers to guess your password and gain unauthorized access.

Many companies have password policies in place that enforce strict requirements. For example, the policy might force users to have a minimum-length password with the complexity of uppercase, lowercase, a number, and a symbol. The policy can also make users reset their password every so often, such as 90 days, and prohibit users from reusing a number of their past passwords. Finally, policies will have a process defined for resetting a user's password in the event that they forget it or get locked out of the system. Examples include sending a one-time, temporary login code or having them answer security questions.

Using Data Encryption

Ever since writing was invented about 5,200 years ago, humans have been sending messages back and forth to each other. And for probably just as long, there's been someone who wanted to read the message for whom that message was not intended. Throughout history, all the interceding party needed to do was get a copy of the message and they could read it.

Five millennia later, and this concept hasn't changed. What has changed, of course, is the technology used to send and receive messages (data), as well as the ability to mask the data in an effort to make it unreadable by others.

In Chapter 10, I mentioned protocol analyzers, also known as sniffers. If someone were intercepting network packets that were sent in *plain text*, which is as it sounds—not encrypted at all, the data in those packets would be easily readable. Therefore, intercept enough packets, and the entire message would be crystal clear. The alternative for the sender and receiver is to encode or encrypt the text and turn it into what's known as *cipher text*. If read, the cipher text looks like gibberish.

To make cipher text work easily, the sender and receiver both need to understand how to encode and decode the message. As a child, perhaps you solved puzzles that used decoders, or maybe you even had an encoder/decoder toy that you used to write secret messages to friends. These are simple examples of cipher text.

In the world of computing, the process of encoding/encrypting and decoding/decrypting is thankfully far more complex than a free toy you might get in a cereal box or from a fast-food restaurant. There are dozens of encryption methods in the world, from symmetrical key models (where the same key encrypts and decrypts) to more secure asymmetrical models, where two keys are needed—one specifically to encrypt and a different one to decrypt. Knowing how all of these methods work is beyond the scope of the Tech+ exam, but I want to give you a quick example just to show you how it works.

A popular asymmetrical encryption technology is called *public key infrastructure (PKI)*. PKI uses two keys, a *public key* and a *private key*. To set up PKI, an individual or company would go to a CA to request a key. (CAs are the same entities that issue SSL certificates to secure websites.) The CA verifies the identity of the requester and then issues them a public key/private key matched pair.

Let's say that I requested a PKI, and I now have a private key and public key. You and I are doing business, and you want to send me an encrypted message. Electronically, I would send you my public key, which you would use to encrypt the message. You would then send the message to me, and I would decrypt it with my private key. My private key is the only one capable of decrypting the message, and I would never give it out to anyone.

You might wonder if someone were to intercept the message, couldn't they still try to hack it and read it? Of course they can try, but the keys are strong enough to make this code-breaking incredibly difficult. I'm not saying that it can't be done, but practically all hackers will give up on a small prize such as you and me because it takes too much effort.

Again, for the exam you don't need to know how specific encryption methods work. You do need to know the difference between plain text and cipher text, and you also need to know a few common uses of encryption. Next, I will give some examples of encryption of data at rest, as well as data in transit.

Encrypting Data at Rest

Laptops and mobile devices are enticing targets for thieves because of their portability. While encryption won't protect a device from getting stolen, it will prevent any thieves from accessing data stored on the computer—*data at rest*—if they manage to steal your device. Desktop computers can benefit from file encryption too. They can be stolen as well, or perhaps you share a computer with someone and have files that you absolutely don't want the other person to see. There are two levels at which you can encrypt data on a hard drive: at the file level and at the disk level.

File encryption in Windows is considered an attribute of the filesystem—NTFS is required to use encryption. When you encrypt folders, as long as you're logged in as the user who did the encrypting, the files are available normally, and the encryption is invisible to you. However, if you log in as some other user, the files are inaccessible. This includes users with Administrator privileges!

If your operating system does not natively support file and folder encryption, you can get third-party software that encrypts data. Examples include AxCrypt, CertainSafe, Folder Lock, VeraCrypt, and CryptoExpert. Third-party utilities often cost money, but they usually have more features than the OS-native versions.

Encryption is based on security certificates stored on the hard disk for each user. There's a risk involved, though, because if the security certificate becomes corrupted or deleted, you won't be able to access files that are legitimately yours. Remember, not even an administrator can unencrypt them. It's therefore important to back up your certificate before you start relying on encryption to protect your files locally. A lost or damaged certificate can be recovered but not easily. Exercise 11.4 has you practice encrypting files and shows you what happens when an unauthorized person tries to access an encrypted file. Exercise 11.5 provides practice in backing up a security certificate.

EXERCISE 11.4

Encrypting Local Folders in Windows 11

1. If you don't already have at least two user accounts on your PC, create one. If you have forgotten how, refer to Exercise 4.1.
2. Open the C: drive. Create a new folder named **`Private`**, and press Enter to accept the new name.
3. Right-click the `Private` folder and choose Properties.
4. On the Security tab, click Edit. The Permissions For Private dialog box opens, as shown in Figure 11.19.

EXERCISE 11.4 *(continued)*

FIGURE 11.19 Folder permissions

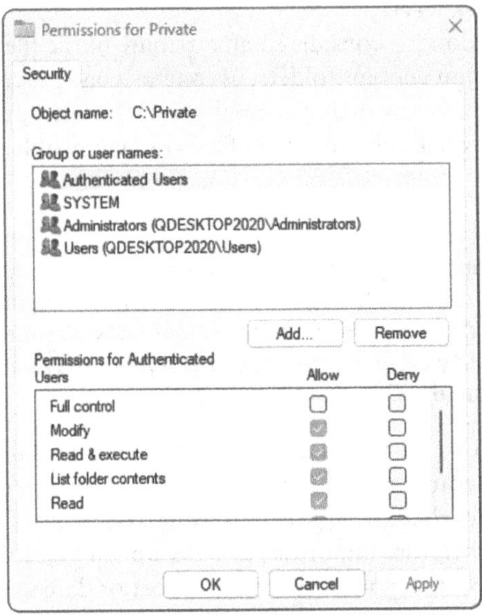

5. Click Add. The Select Users Or Groups dialog box opens.
6. In the Enter The Object Names To Select box, type the username for the other user on this PC that you want to use for the exercise.
7. Click Check Names. The username appears preceded by the computer name, as shown in Figure 11.20.

FIGURE 11.20 Select Users Or Groups dialog box

Select Users or Groups
Select this object type:
Users, Groups, or Built-in security principals
Object Types...
From this location:
QDESKTOP2020
Locations...
Enter the object names to select (examples):
QDESKTOP2020\TestUser
Check Names
Advanced...
OK
Cancel

8. Click OK. Now that user appears on the Group Or User Names list in the Private Properties dialog box.
9. With the user's name selected, notice the permissions in the lower pane. As Figure 11.21 shows, the Full Control and Modify check boxes aren't selected.

FIGURE 11.21 User permissions

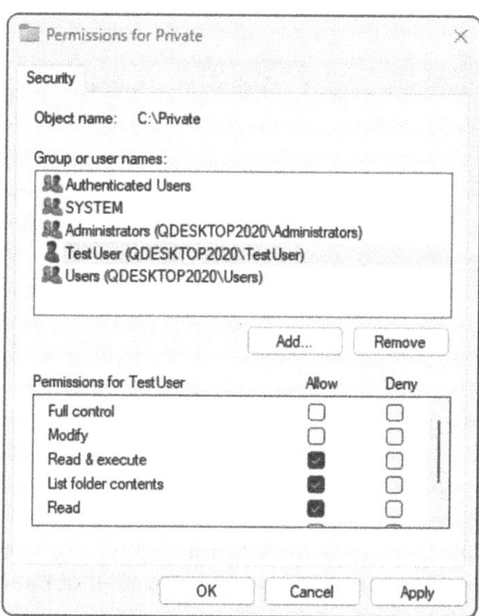

10. Click OK.
11. Click OK to close the Private Properties dialog box.
12. Copy a document file into the `Private` folder.
13. Log off your current user account and log in as the other user.
14. Attempt to open the document. Note what happens.
15. Attempt to save changes to the document. Note what happens.
16. Log off, and log in again using the original user account.
17. Find and right-click the `Private` folder and choose Properties.
18. On the General tab, click Advanced.

EXERCISE 11.4 *(continued)*

19. In the Advanced Attributes dialog box, select the Encrypt Contents To Secure Data check box, as shown in Figure 11.22.

FIGURE 11.22 Advanced Attributes dialog box

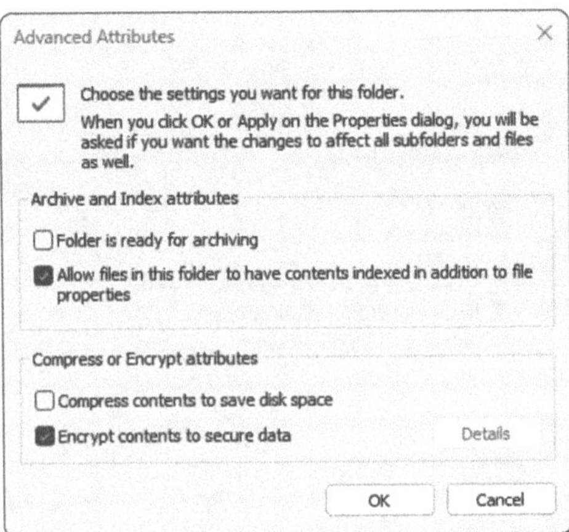

You must have a version of Windows that supports encryption to encrypt a folder's contents as detailed in step 19. If not, the check box will be grayed out.

20. Click OK.
21. Click OK to close the Private Properties dialog box.
22. Log off your current user account and log in as the other user.
23. Attempt to access the `Private` folder and note what happens. If you chose to encrypt the contents in step 19, it isn't accessible.
24. Log off, and log in again using the original username. Delete the `Private` folder.

EXERCISE 11.5

Backing Up a Windows Security Certificate

1. In Windows, click Start, type **certmgr**, and press Enter. The Certificate Manager utility opens, as shown in Figure 11.23. Depending on your UAC settings, you might get a security pop-up asking if you trust the Microsoft Management Console. Click Yes and then proceed.

FIGURE 11.23 Windows Certificate Manager

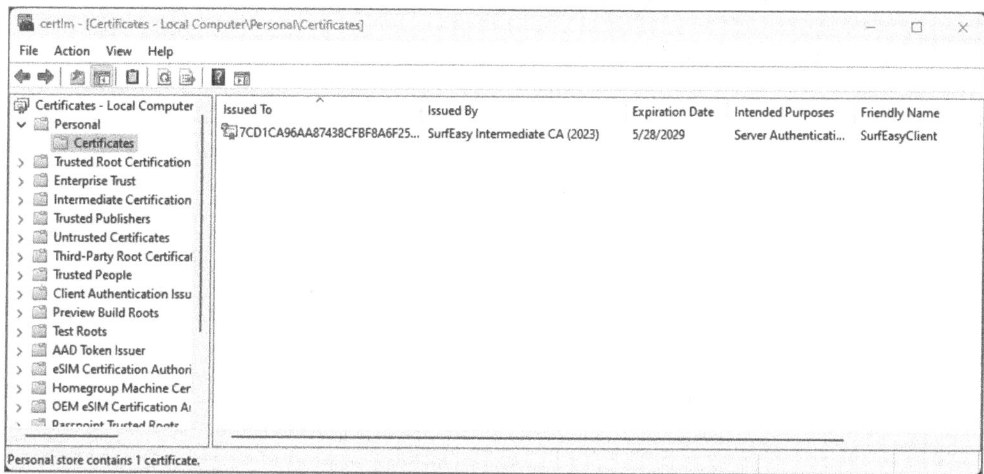

2. Click the `Personal` folder to expand it.
3. Click the `Certificates` folder.
4. Click a certificate in the right pane. If you have multiple ones, click the one that shows Encrypting File System in the Intended Purposes column.
5. Right-click the certificate, and then choose Action ➢ All Tasks ➢ Export. The Certificate Export Wizard runs.
6. Click Next.
7. Click Yes, export the private key, and then click Next.
8. Make sure Personal Information Exchange is selected and click Next.
9. In the Password box, type a password of your choice. Type it again in the Confirm Password box (Figure 11.24). Notice you can select the encryption type; the default is fine. Then click Next.

EXERCISE 11.5 *(continued)*

FIGURE 11.24 Certificate Export Wizard

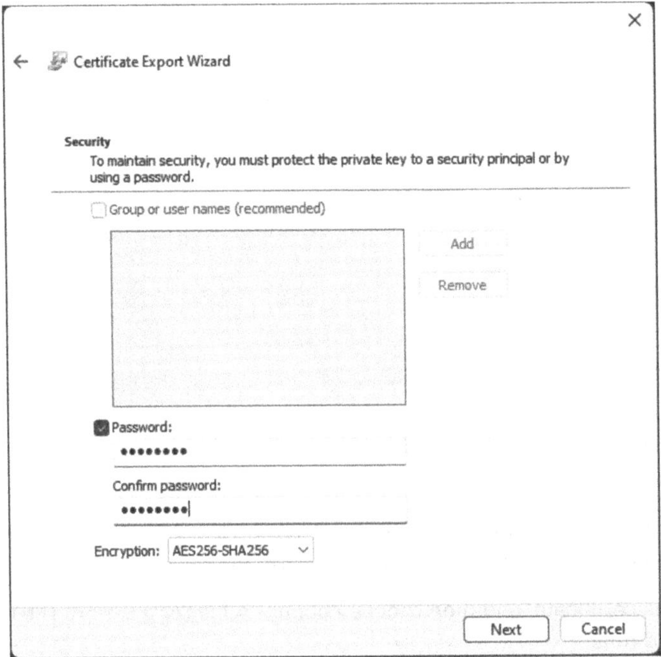

10. In the File Name box, type the name you want to use to save the backup file. For example, if your username is `jsmith`, you might use `jsmith-certbackup`.
11. The default storage location for the backup is the `C:\Windows\system32` folder. If you want to place it somewhere else, click Browse, change locations, and then click Save.
12. Click Next. The Completing The Certificate Export Wizard screen appears.
13. Click Finish.
14. In the confirmation dialog box, click OK.
15. Close the Certificate Manager window.

In macOS there are a few ways to encrypt files. To encrypt the full hard drive, use the FileVault utility, which is part of Security & Privacy, as shown in Figure 11.25.

FIGURE 11.25 The macOS FileVault

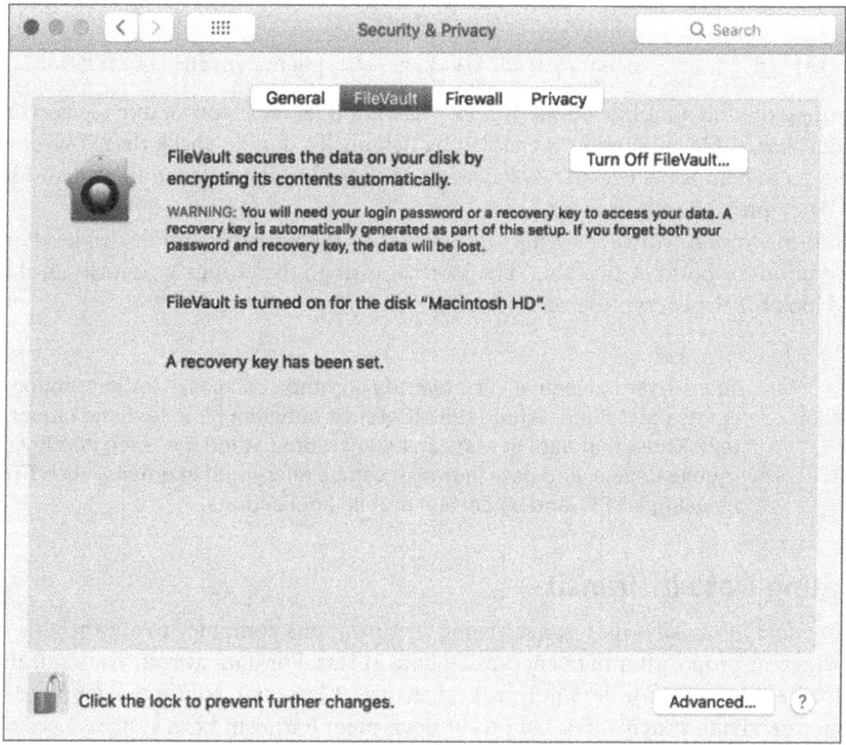

In macOS, local encryption can't be applied to individual folders and files; you must encrypt the entire disk. You can do this via the FileVault, which is part of Security & Privacy, as shown in Figure 11.25. Individual files or folders can be encrypted through the Disk Utility, or by Control-clicking the file or folder and selecting Encrypt from the menu.

The easiest way to encrypt files and folders on a Linux system is via the file manager in the graphical interface. Simply right-click the file and choose Encrypt. If the version of Linux you're using doesn't have the Encrypt option, another choice is the command-line interface using the `openssl` libraries. `openssl` allows encryption and decryption by selecting which cipher to use. For example, you can use Advanced Encryption Standard (AES) as the encryption algorithm. In Linux, you specify the cipher, followed by defining the key derivation routine, such as salt, when encrypting. Then you specify the original input file followed by the encrypted output file. An example looks like this:

```
openssl aes -salt -in originalfile.txt -out encryptedfile.txt
```

To decrypt, the only differences are that you use the -d option (which means decrypt), and you put the encrypted filename before the unencrypted output file. An example looks like this:

```
openssl aes -d -salt -in encryptedfile.txt -out unencryptedfile.txt
```

Encrypting files on a mobile device is pretty easy. In iOS, once you enable a password to secure your device, file encryption is enabled by default. To double-check that your device is encrypted, go to Settings ➢ Face ID & Passcode and scroll to the bottom. In a small font, it will say "Data protection is enabled."

Android encryption will vary by the version of the OS, but in general device-level or file-level encryption (or both) is available. The best bet is to go to Settings ➢ Security And Privacy, and look for the encryption option there.

Tech+ exam objective 6.4, "Identify common use cases for encryption," wants you to understand the difference between plain text and cipher text. Know that data at rest can be encrypted at the file level, disk level, or mobile device, and data in transit can be encrypted in emails, via HTTPS, by using a VPN, and by certain mobile applications.

Encrypting Data in Transit

Encrypting *data in transit*—that is, data being sent from one computer to another—is an entirely different proposition than encrypting data at rest. For data at rest, you're dealing with only one computer. For data in transit, there are at least two computers involved—the sending and receiving systems. For data to be encrypted in transit, both systems need to support the same encryption technology. Here are a few examples of where data is encrypted in transit:

Email All major corporate email providers and the big public ones (Gmail, `Outlook.com`, Yahoo! Mail, and so on) support the encryption of emails in transit. Gmail does state that it uses different levels of encryption, depending on what the receiving email server can handle. If Gmail detects that the receiving email server doesn't support encryption (which would be rare), then it can't send it encrypted because the receiving server wouldn't be able to translate the message. This isn't a knock on Gmail because all providers are bound by the same limitations; it's just that Gmail is more forthcoming in their documentation than other providers.

Internet Browsing You've learned before that secure Internet sites use a secure version of the HTTP protocol named HTTPS. If a website starts with `https://`, you can rest assured that the data it transmits to and from your client will be encrypted.

Virtual Private Network A *virtual private network (VPN)* is a secured, encrypted connection between two specific computers that occurs through a public network such as the Internet. It works by creating a virtual, private tunnel by encapsulating the traveling data into secure packets. An illustration of this is shown in Figure 11.26.

FIGURE 11.26 A VPN

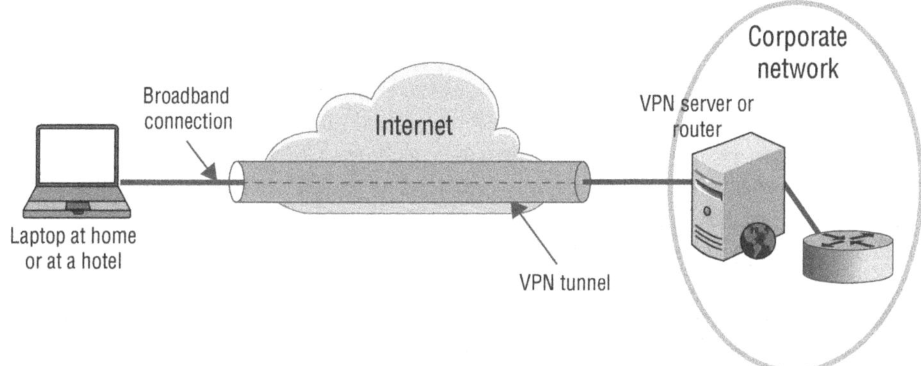

The private network provides security over an otherwise unsecure environment. VPNs can be used to connect LANs together across the Internet or other public networks, or they can be used to connect individual users to a corporate network. This is a great option for users who work from home or travel for work. With a VPN, the remote end appears to be connected to the network as if it were connected locally. From the server side, a VPN requires dedicated hardware or a software package running on a server or router. Clients use specialized VPN client software to connect, most often over a broadband Internet link. Windows 11 comes with its own VPN client software accessible through Start ➢ Settings ➢ Network & Internet ➢ VPN (or by typing **VPN** in the Windows search box), as do some other operating systems, and many third-party options are also available.

Mobile Applications Almost all mobile applications will encrypt data in transit, but it's not guaranteed. The same standards used for PC transmissions apply. In other words, if you are using email, visiting a secure website, or are logged into a network using a VPN, then the data is encrypted in transit. If not, then it's up to the individual application. Check its documentation for more information.

Summary

In this chapter, you learned about security best practices. The first section was on securing your devices, including computers and mobile devices. The section focused on device hardening, which starts with keeping the software up-to-date and enabling passwords. Then, make sure authentication is enabled for any device that can access private, sensitive, or confidential data. Next, protect against network threats by using antivirus and antimalware software and software firewalls. When installing software, ensure that it's licensed and that you are getting it from a reputable site, and always practice safe Internet browsing. Finally, disable unused or unwanted services and AutoPlay. You should also lock your system, both physically to the desk in the case of laptops (and some desktops) and by using a software lock when you are away from your computer. Control Alt Delete when you leave your seat!

The next section was on user and management. Ensure that your company has written policies and procedures that outline acceptable use of company devices and that they spell out expectations of privacy when using these devices. Train users on security awareness to help aid the cause. Policies should also provide specifics on how to handle confidential information. Passwords need to be carefully managed as well. They should be sufficiently complex, changed regularly, and not reused.

The last section was on encryption. Encryption scrambles the data using cipher text to make it unreadable to a potential hacker. Data at rest can be protected via encryption at the file or disk level, and mobile devices can be encrypted as well. Plain-text data in transit is a major risk, so you should encrypt data in transit too. Email, secure websites, VPNs, and most mobile applications provide encryption in transit.

Exam Essentials

Understand the actions you can take to accomplish device hardening. Device hardening makes it more difficult for attackers to exploit. Some actions you can take include using antimalware software and software firewalls; enabling passwords and changing them from the default; browsing the Internet safely; patching software; researching valid software sources before downloading anything; and removing or disabling unused software and services, and disabling AutoPlay.

Know how to lock your system. If you have a laptop or other mobile device, it should be secured to the desk with a security cable. If you leave your workstation, use Control Alt Delete when you leave your seat!

Know what encryption of data at rest does. Encryption scrambles your files so no other local users can read them, not even someone with Administrator access. Only the user who encrypted the files can decrypt them.

Know how to encrypt data in transit. Most commercial email systems will encrypt data in transit. Using secure websites with HTTPS will also encrypt data, as will VPNs.

Know how to protect your computer against malware. The best way is to avoid malware in the first place, but this isn't always possible. To protect yourself, use antimalware software, such as antivirus, antispam, and antispyware applications.

Understand what expectations for privacy should be. When using social networking, instant messaging, or file-sharing sites, the expectations of privacy should pretty much not exist.

Know good practices for password management. Always change default passwords. Passwords should be sufficiently complex to avoid being guessed or hacked, kept confidential, changed regularly, and not reused on other sites or in the future after they have been changed.

Know how to configure your browser for safe Internet browsing. Update it to the latest version, including any necessary add-ons and extensions. Disable Autofill, enable security, and manage cookies properly.

Understand how to browse the Internet safely. Avoid unscrupulous sites. If you are going to enter confidential information such as passwords or financial information, make sure that the site is secure. Avoid suspicious links and ads.

Know how to tell whether a website is secure. Secure websites will start with `https://` instead of `http://`.

Chapter 11 Lab

Chapter 11 covered a wide range of security measures that you can implement on your computer, on your network, and when you browse the Internet. This lab provides you with a checklist of things that you can do to improve your security. It's recommended that you go through each of the tasks and understand how to perform them on your system.

Tasks you should be able to do are as follows:

1. Educate others on the risk of social engineering.
2. Install and configure antimalware software.
3. Enable and configure a software firewall.
4. Update or patch software.
5. Install a cable or USB lock.
6. Find license numbers for installed software.
7. Research legitimate sources for downloading software.
8. Remove unwanted, unnecessary, or malicious software.
9. Disable unused services.
10. Disable AutoPlay.
11. Be able to tell if a website is secure or not.
12. Create complex passwords that are easy for you to remember.
13. Explain password complexity and reuse to a coworker.
14. Draft (or find online) an acceptable use policy for your company.
15. Set up a screensaver password and engage it.

16. Update your web browser to the latest version.
17. Configure Autofill.
18. Configure browser security.
19. Manage and delete browser history and cookies.
20. Enable file encryption.

There are no specific answers for the Chapter 11 lab.

Review Questions

You can find the answers in Appendix B.

1. Due to a recent string of thefts in your office, you need to harden your local system. What two actions are most appropriate for your situation? (Choose two.)
   A. Install a hardware lock.
   B. Disable unused services.
   C. Install antimalware.
   D. Enable encryption.
2. What option can you configure on your workstation to increase security when you leave your desk?
   A. File encryption
   B. Multifactor authentication
   C. Single sign-on (SSO)
   D. Screensaver password
3. You are visiting a website that starts with `https://`. Which of the following statements about the website are true? (Choose two.)
   A. It has a CA certificate from an SSL.
   B. It has an SSL certificate from a CA.
   C. HTTPS websites are not required to have a security certificate.
   D. Traffic to and from this website is in cipher text.
   E. Traffic to and from this website is in plain text.
4. Claire, a coworker, is browsing the Internet and wants to know if it's safe to enter her credit card information into a website. What do you tell her to look for?
   A. `HTTPS://`
   B. `HTTP://`
   C. `SSL://`
   D. `TLS://`
5. You enabled file encryption on your local computer. While you were on vacation, one of your coworkers managed to get onto your computer and share your important files with other users. How did they do this?
   A. They logged on and disabled encryption.
   B. They used the Disk Recovery tool to access the encrypted files.
   C. All users logging into the system have access to encrypted files.
   D. They logged on with your username and password.
   E. They used an administrator account.

6. Which of the following types of data should be considered confidential and handled appropriately? (Choose two.)
   A. Financial information
   B. Social networking site
   C. Customer information
   D. Contact information
7. Which type of software will help protect your computer from malicious network traffic?
   A. Software firewall
   B. Password complexity tool
   C. Antispyware
   D. Antivirus
8. You are using Google Chrome and you want to ensure that when you type in your first name to a web page, all of your other information fills in the fields for you. What should you do?
   A. Enable cookies.
   B. Enable cache.
   C. Enable Incognito.
   D. Enable Autofill.
9. Which of the following methods of securing a laptop works by giving users access only to certain files?
   A. Authentication
   B. Antimalware
   C. Firewall
   D. Patching
10. Which of the following actions is not considered a web-browsing best practice?
    A. Limiting the use of PII
    B. Disabling Autofill
    C. Closing untrusted source warnings
    D. Updating add-ons and extensions
11. The managers at your company have decided to implement stricter security policies on the company's local network. Which of the following should they do? (Choose two.)
    A. Enforce password policies.
    B. Develop written policies and procedures.
    C. Disable host firewalls.
    D. Enable HTTPS on the corporate web server.

12. Your coworker Rachel has recently discovered that when she starts typing her name into a field in a web browser, her whole name appears as well as her address in the appropriate boxes. What is this due to?
    - A. Adware infection
    - B. Single sign-on
    - C. Suspicious hyperlinks
    - D. Autofill
13. You have been asked to give training on network security. For your section on password management, which options should you recommend to users? (Choose two.)
    - A. Do not use complex passwords because they are easy to forget.
    - B. Change default passwords on systems.
    - C. Use the same password on multiple systems so that they are easy to remember.
    - D. Do not reuse the same password after you are required to change it.
14. You are in a library that has free computers to use for Internet browsing. Which of the following should you possibly be concerned about?
    - A. Shoulder surfing
    - B. Keyloggers
    - C. Unsecured wireless network
    - D. A and B
    - E. A, B, and C
15. You have remotely logged into your corporate network. Which of the following is used to ensure encryption of data in transit between your laptop and corporate servers?
    - A. HTTPS
    - B. Email encryption
    - C. VPN
    - D. Host firewall
16. Which of the following are considered characteristics of a strong password? (Choose two.)
    - A. Long
    - B. Uses patterns
    - C. Uses symbols, numbers, and letters
    - D. Contains PII
17. You just read an article about an Internet worm recently causing problems. What type of software should you install to protect yourself from this worm?
    - A. Software firewall
    - B. Authentication protocol
    - C. Antivirus
    - D. Security certificate

18. You receive an email in your Inbox from your friend Sara. The title of the email is "This is so cool!" and inside the email is a link to a website. What should you do?
    A. Delete the email.
    B. Click the link to see why she thinks it's cool.
    C. Run virus scan, then click the link.
    D. Call Sara to see if she sent you the email.
19. You recently received a new workstation and need to secure it properly before browsing the Internet. Which actions should you take? (Choose two.)
    A. Enable Autofill.
    B. Enable acceptance of cookies.
    C. Upgrade your browser to the newest version.
    D. Install an antivirus.
20. Which of the following statements is true regarding web browser add-ons and extensions?
    A. They should be updated to the newest versions.
    B. They are dangerous and should be deleted.
    C. They will be detected and removed by antivirus software.
    D. They only function in Microsoft Edge or Internet Explorer.

Data Continuity and Computer Support

THE FOLLOWING COMPTIA TECH+ FC0-U71 EXAM OBJECTIVES ARE COVERED IN THIS CHAPTER:

✓ **1.0 IT Concepts and Terminology**

✓ **1.4 Explain the troubleshooting methodology.**

- Identify the problem.
- Establish a theory of probable cause (question the obvious).
  - Research knowledge base/Internet, if applicable.
- Test the theory to determine the cause.
- Establish a plan of action to resolve the problem and implement the solution.
- Verify full system functionality and, if applicable, implement preventive measures.
- Document findings/lessons learned, actions and outcomes.

✓ **5.0 Data and Database Fundamentals**

✓ **5.4 Explain basic data backup concepts.**

- Data
  - File backups
  - System backups
  - Restoring data
- Location
  - Stored locally
    - Flash drive
    - External hard drive
    - Secure digital (SD) card
  - Cloud storage

Computer systems, whether they are powerful servers or portable handheld devices, have become an omnipresent part of society today. People use them for business, recreation, and entertainment, for keeping in touch with friends and family, and for multiple other reasons. At the beginning of the 2000s, it was just starting to become more common for households and businesses to have PCs. Now, if you include mobile devices (which you should), practically every household and business has several. Computers are so common that we tend to take them for granted—until they don't work like they're supposed to.

This chapter covers two key topics related to dealing with computer problems—data continuity and troubleshooting and support. Data continuity means trying to prevent problems from happening to data in the first place and planning for when the inevitable hardware failure or software loss happens. This includes the major topics of fault tolerance and disaster recovery.

When that inevitable problem does happen, you need to be familiar with the best methods to isolate and fix the problem to get the computer up and running as quickly as possible. For example, if the problem is with the hard drive, then what do you do? In this chapter, you will learn a methodology to troubleshoot effectively any computer problem you come across.

Understanding Data Continuity

Although this section is titled "Understanding Data Continuity," the concepts here easily apply to any organization or person who is interested in protecting their digital assets. Data continuity focuses on keeping systems up and running consistently, as often as the users need to access them. And, if and when something does happen to a computer or network, what plans are in place to recover from that problem as quickly as possible?

Data continuity will be broken down into two major concepts: fault tolerance and disaster recovery. Fault tolerance covers topics such as replication, redundancy, backups, and contingency plans. Disaster recovery deals with restoring data and access based on predefined priorities.

Fault Tolerance

Fault tolerance is defined as the ability to lose a component or data and still have a functional system. Built into this definition is the word *tolerance*, which in this case refers to how much risk you are willing to accept. For example, if you don't care about the data on a laptop, and you can stand to be without the system for a few days if it dies, then you don't really need to worry about developing a fault-tolerant solution. On the other hand, if the data is the key to running your business and you can't survive without it, then a fault-tolerant plan is required.

Fault-tolerant systems help protect against single points of failure. There are different variants of fault-tolerant plans that can be implemented, from full-time, always-on solutions to offline backups that might take a day or two to restore. I'll explore some of those concepts after discussing contingency planning.

Contingency Plans

Data continuity concepts should all be part of a company's *contingency plan*, which is simply a plan for action in the event of a problem. Having a plan in place will help drive the appropriate actions when a problem happens. Without a plan, chaos can ensue.

Contingency plans will vary by company, but in general, here are some steps to take to create one:

Step 1: Perform a business impact analysis. The first thing to understand is what impact, if any, failures of components or loss of data would have on the business. If there is no impact, then there's really no need for a contingency plan, but at least you're making an informed decision. This should be done for all critical systems, including computers and infrastructure.

Step 2: Identify preventive systems. What systems does the company have in place to prevent issues from happening? Start with environmental things such as smoke detectors and sprinkler systems as well as security systems to control access. Then move on to more specific computer-related items such as power backups and security policies.

Step 3: Develop a recovery plan. In the event of a problem, what is the plan? Specifically understand who is responsible for specific actions and what the chain of authority is. Recovery plans need to account for all types of problems, such as data loss from hackers, equipment failure, and natural disasters.

Step 4: Test the recovery plan. Just because the plan is created doesn't mean it will work properly! Test it in live simulations including the people involved. The testing phase can help identify potential issues and inspire revisions to the plan.

Step 5: Set up a maintenance and review schedule. Plans need to adapt over time based on changing circumstances. Maybe a company added five more servers and 50 more clients; the plans need to change. Review as often as needed and make appropriate changes. Also test the preventive equipment identified in step 2.

Step 6: Implement training. Training is critical to ensure that the first responders know what to do and the people that follow after them understand their roles as well. Delivering periodic training should be incorporated into the maintenance and review schedule.

No plan is entirely foolproof, but having a plan will help things run smoothly if and when an event happens.

Replication and Redundancy

Replication is what it sounds like—it's a full working copy of whatever data, computer, or network that's being considered. If you're talking about replicating data, it could mean that the same data is written to two hard drives, databases, or servers at the same time. On a larger scale, some organizations have entire networks replicated (called *hot sites*) in case of failure. If not having any fault tolerance plan is at one end of the risk aversion spectrum, replication is at the other. It leaves no room for any failures to impact data or systems. The downside to replication is that it's the most expensive of the fault-tolerant options.

One step down from replication is redundancy. With *redundancy*, there are devices or data in place to help keep things running normally for a short period of time, until the original problem can be fixed. Redundancy can be implemented on data, networks, and power sources.

Data Redundancy

If having one hard drive is good, then having two hard drives is better, right? Perhaps you need additional storage space, so you add another drive. There's nothing wrong with doing that, but what happens if one (or both) of your hard drives fails? Having that extra drive didn't help. In fact, it added another potential point of failure for your computer, so it actually increased your risk of hardware failure and data loss.

There are ways that you can add additional hard drives to a computer and get benefits beyond increased storage capacity. Having an additional hard drive can make your disk reads/writes a little faster, and you can also create fault tolerance by having extra protection against disk failures. You do this by implementing *RAID*.

RAID stands for *redundant array of independent* (or inexpensive) *disks*, which is multiple physical hard disks working together as a team for increased performance, increased reliability, or both. There are more than 10 different implementations of RAID. The three most popular (and important) versions are as follows:

RAID 0 Also known as *disk striping*, RAID 0 is where at least two drives are combined to create one logical volume. Equal amounts of space are used on each drive, and data is written across the volume like a stripe. *RAID 0* is not RAID in every sense because it doesn't provide the fault tolerance implied by the *redundant* component of the name. Data is written across multiple drives, so you essentially have two drives reading or writing the same dataset at once. This makes for faster data access. However, if any one of the drives fails, all content is lost. To protect data, an additional form of redundancy or fault tolerance should be used in concert with RAID 0.

RAID 1 Also known as *disk mirroring*, *RAID 1* is a method of producing fault tolerance by writing the same data simultaneously to two separate drives. If one drive fails, the other contains an exact copy of the data and will become the primary drive. However, disk mirroring doesn't help access speed, and the cost is double that of a single drive.

RAID 5 Combines the benefits of RAID 0 and RAID 1, creating a redundant striped volume set. Unlike RAID 1, however, *RAID 5* does not employ mirroring for redundancy. Each stripe places data on all drives except one, and parity is computed from the data that is placed on the remaining disk. The parity is interleaved across all of the drives in the array so that neighboring stripes have parity on different disks. If one drive fails, the parity information for the stripes that lost data can be used with the remaining data from the working drives to derive what was on the failed drive and rebuild the set once the drive is replaced. It's easier to understand when you can see it. Take a look at Figure 12.1; RAID 1 is on the left, and RAID 5 is on the right.

FIGURE 12.1 RAID 1 and RAID 5

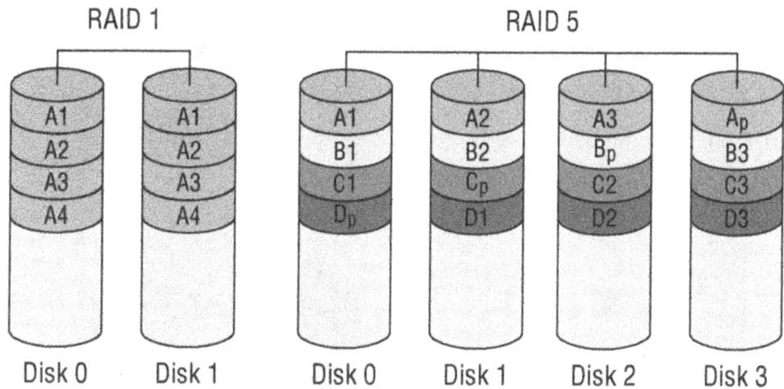

A minimum of three drives is required for RAID 5. If one drive fails, the system will continue to operate, but slowly. The loss of an additional drive, however, results in a catastrophic loss of all data in the array. RAID 5 does not eliminate the need to do data backups.

Network Redundancy

For businesses reliant on their network connections, a network device failure could be problematic. Networks can be configured with redundant connections to avoid having a single point of failure. The redundant connection could potentially be alive and working full-time, or it could be an offline backup that springs into action if a failure is detected in the main link.

Power Redundancy

There's no two ways about it—computers need power to run. Even laptops and mobile devices can use battery life for only so long before they need to be recharged. Power redundancy helps out in the case of an unexpected power outage.

The best device for power protection is called an *uninterruptible power supply (UPS)*, which you first learned about in Chapter 2, "Peripherals and Connectors." These devices can be as small as a brick or as large as an entire server rack. Some just have a few indicator lights, while others have LCD displays that show status and menus and come with their own management software. The back of the UPS will have several power plugs. It might divide the plugs such that a few of them provide surge protection only, whereas others provide surge protection as well as backup power. Figure 12.2 shows you the front and back of a small UPS.

FIGURE 12.2 Front and back of a UPS

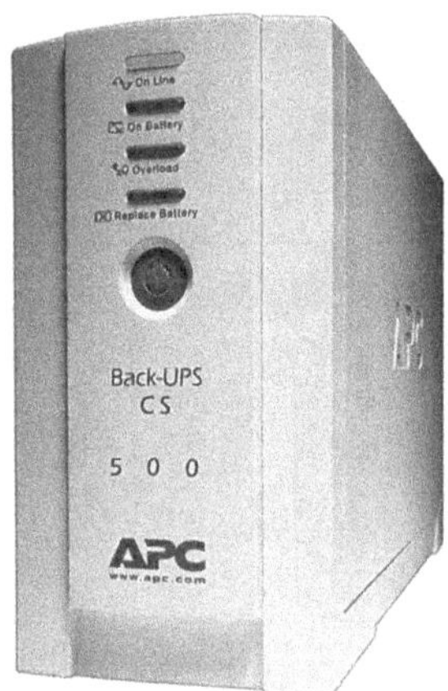

Inside the UPS are one or more batteries and fuses. Much like a surge suppressor, a UPS is designed to protect everything that's plugged into it from power surges. UPSs are also designed to protect against power sags and even power outages. Energy is stored in the batteries, and if the power fails, the batteries can power the computer for a period of time so that the administrator can then safely power it down. Many UPSs and operating systems will also work together to power down automatically (and safely) a system that gets switched to UPS power. These types of devices may be overkill for Uncle Bob's machine at home, but they're critically important fixtures in server rooms.

The UPS should be checked periodically to make sure that its battery is operational. Most UPSs have a test button that you can press to simulate a power outage. You will find that batteries wear out over time, and you should replace the battery in the UPS every couple of years to keep the UPS dependable.

UPSs all have a limit as to how many devices they can handle at once. These power limitations should be strictly observed. Overloading a UPS can cause a short, which could potentially result in fire.

Data Backups

Simply put, your data is probably the most important thing you have. Hardware can be replaced, but if you lose your data, you could be in serious trouble. From a personal standpoint, you could lose important pictures or other information that you can never replace. For businesses, large-scale data losses often lead to catastrophic results.

The way to prevent total data loss is to ensure that you are backing up your data. A *backup* is a restorable copy of any set of data that is needed on the system. Sometimes, you will hear people call it an archive, but technically an *archive* is any collection of data that is removed from the system because it's no longer needed on a regular basis.

If you work for a company, that organization's *backup policy* dictates what information should be backed up and how it should be backed up. If you are concerned only with your own system, you should still create a plan for backups, including what type you will make and how often you'll make them. Along with making the backup, you also need to consider who can get to the backup. If data is valuable enough to spend the resources required to back it up, it is clearly important enough to protect carefully.

When considering a backup solution, the following questions are pertinent:

- How often do you plan to back up? For business-critical data that changes often, every day is appropriate. For casual home users and their personal files, once a week or even once a month may be enough.
- What do you want to back up? You can perform a *file backup*, which backs up one or more files on a computer, or you can perform a *system backup*, which backs up an entire computer system.
- How large are the files? Backing up a large amount of data takes more time and takes up more disk space. You may choose to back up large files like videos and music less often than other files for this reason.
- What backup software is available? Many different applications will do local and online backups and system images. Some have more features and higher price tags than others.
- Should each backup recopy all files, or should there be smaller backups done that copy only files that have changed?

Tech+ exam objective 5.4, "Explain basic data backup concepts," lists file backups and system backups as subobjectives. Be sure to understand the difference between the two.

Understanding the Importance of Backups

Computer users often take their data for granted, forgetting the large quantity of important and irreplaceable documents, images, and music files they collect over the years. A hard disk failure or virus can wipe out years of stored memories, not to mention files of significant value to a business.

There are many ways to ensure that a system failure doesn't result in data loss. For example, you can use a multidisk RAID system to protect against data loss caused by a physical hard disk failure by mirroring a drive (RAID 1) or striping data across multiple drives (RAID 5). RAID isn't enough, though, because multiple hard disk failures will still doom you. Even if you use RAID, you should perform backups of your data.

Real World Scenario

The Importance of Data

Several years ago when I did technical support, I received a call from a user with hard drive problems. After some quick troubleshooting, I determined that his hard drive had failed and it would need to be replaced. After telling him the news, he asked, "So how do I get my data back?" I asked if he had backed up his data, and he had not.

He was a doctoral student in his final year, and his dissertation was stored on that hard drive. (Key word: was.) He had no backups. I could hear the desperation and agony in his voice as he frantically sought options to get his data back. He had spent years of his life hard at work on something that was now gone—simply gone. Had he taken a few moments to back up the data, there would have been no problems. At the time, data recovery cost several thousand dollars per megabyte.

Now, data recovery companies that will take damaged hard drives and attempt to recover data from them are not as expensive as they used to be, but their services are not cheap. Some of the least expensive online services cost $200–$300, and others can cost several thousand dollars. Back up your data, and you won't have to feel the sting of paying that cost.

While the general theme of this section is "Back up your data," it might not be necessary based on the situation. If what's on the hard drive is unimportant and it's not a big deal to lose it, then don't bother backing up. This could be the case for a public workstation. Otherwise, it's a critical step that most people forget to do.

Understanding How Backups Work

Backup programs generally work by looking at an attribute of the file known as an *archive bit*. When a file is created or modified, the archive bit is set to 1, indicating that the file has not been backed up in its current state. When a backup is made, that archive bit may be cleared—that is, set back to 0—to indicate that the file has been backed up. Some backup types do not clear the archive bit.

There are a couple of quick and easy ways to see whether the archive bit for a file is or is not set. The first is in Windows File Explorer. Navigate to a file, such as a Word document, right-click it, and choose Properties. At the bottom of the General tab, you will see an Advanced button. Click the Advanced button to display a window like the one shown in Figure 12.3.

FIGURE 12.3 Advanced file attributes

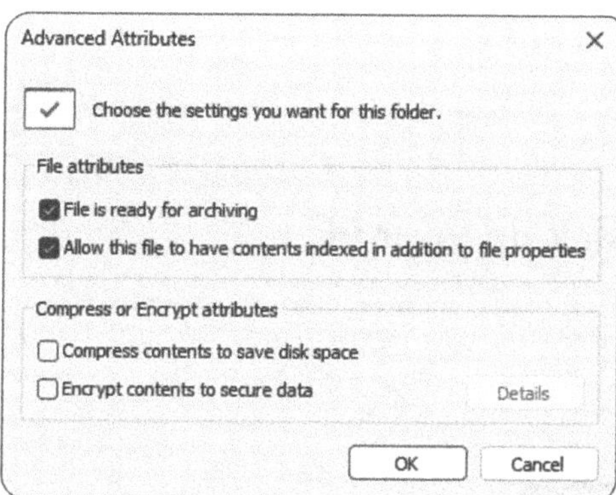

If the File Is Ready For Archiving option is selected, it means the archive bit is set. If you deselect the option, then the archive bit is set back to 0.

The second way to tell whether the archive bit for a file is set is from a Command Prompt. In a directory, type **attrib** and press Enter. You will see a directory listing. If off to the left of the filename you see the letter A, that means that the archive bit is set. The `attrib` command can be used to clear and set this bit. For help with this, type **attrib /?** at the Command Prompt.

Understanding Backup Options

When performing a data backup, you will have several decisions to make on various options. The first is which backup program you want to use. Windows comes with a backup utility, named Windows Backup, which will meet the needs of most users. To get to it, type **Windows backup** in the Windows search bar and press Enter. There are also network-based backup programs that can back up multiple systems across a network. Finally, online and cloud-based backup utilities are popular as well.

Other options that you will need to think about are the type of backup you want to perform, the location in which you will store the backup files, and the frequency and scheduling of backups.

Backup Types

Some backup programs are rather simplistic in the types of backups they offer—you choose the files to back up, and they get backed up. Others give you far more options as to how you want to back things up. Windows Backup, for example, doesn't give you too many options (see Figure 12.4). In Figure 12.4, the Folders option is expanded and it provides sliders to choose whether or not to back up the `Desktop`, `Documents`, and `Pictures` folders. The files are automatically backed up to OneDrive on the Microsoft cloud. Other programs let you choose how often to back up, how long to keep backups, which folders to back up, and the backup location. The intent for most backup programs is to back up user files and not the standard files that the operating system requires to run.

FIGURE 12.4 Windows Backup

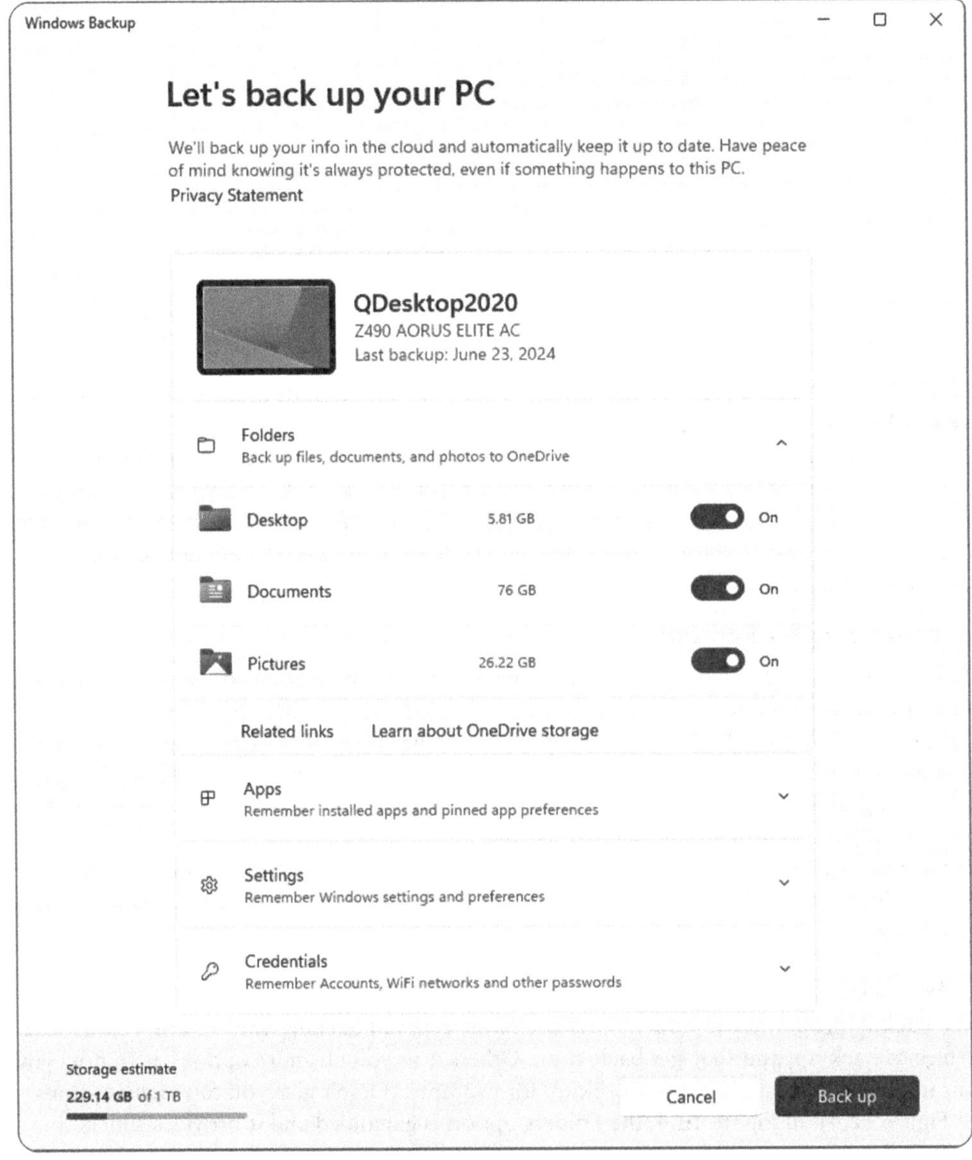

Windows 11 also contains a legacy backup program called Backup and Restore (Windows 7). It's accessed through Control Panel. We will look at using it later in this chapter in Exercise 12.1.

Other programs give you far greater options on the type of backup you want to do. In general, there are five different types of backups that you can perform:

Normal or Full Backs up selected files and clears the archive bit. It takes the longest to back up, but it is the fastest to restore. This option will be called Normal or Full, depending on the software used.

Copy Backs up selected files but does not clear the archive bit.

Incremental Backs up selected files only if they were created or modified since the previous backup and clears the archive bit. This tends to be the fastest in terms of backup speed but is slower to restore.

Differential Backs up selected files only if they were created or modified since the previous backup, but it does not clear the archive bit. It is in between Normal and Incremental on backup and restore speeds.

Daily Backs up files that were created or modified today. It doesn't look at the archive bit but only the date when the file was modified.

The most thorough backup is Normal because it will back up everything you've selected. When you choose to back up files using Windows Backup, this is the type of backup performed. But since this backs up everything, it can take the longest amount of time. At one company where I used to consult, it took more than 16 hours to make a full backup of one of their file servers! This is obviously something they couldn't do every night, nor did they need to since not all files changed every day. Their solution was to start a full (Normal) backup on Saturday evening and to make incremental backups every night during the week.

For security purposes, you must have administrative rights to be able to back up files belonging to people other than yourself.

There's one additional type of backup to discuss, and that's called a *system image*. Some backup utilities can make a system image, which is an exact copy of an entire hard disk. This includes user files as well as operating system files. You use a system image to create a snapshot in time of your system, and then you restore that copy if something ever happens to the original. There are two drawbacks. First, it's a whole-drive image, so it takes a long time to make. Second, when you restore, it doesn't let you choose what to restore—it restores everything. For these two reasons, it's not commonly used as a backup type.

Backing up critical data and important user files should be the top priority. In addition, if the company has a database, that should be backed up as well. To back up a database, use the database's native utility or a third-party utility designed for database backup. Operating system files don't usually need to be backed up for users. If a user's system fails, a clean version of the OS can be reinstalled and then the user's data on top of that.

Backup Locations

When you back up files, you need to choose where to back them up. The one option you will *not* have is to back up files to the same hard drive on which they are located. Doing so wouldn't make a lot of sense, considering that you would still be at a loss if the hard drive failed. Your choices boil down to the following:

- Locally attached storage, such as an internal hard drive, external hard drive, flash drive, secure digital (SD) card, or an optical drive
- Network-attached storage (NAS), such as a hard drive on a server or an actual NAS device
- Internet or cloud-based

Local backups will always be the fastest. To back up your computer locally, you can use a second internal hard drive, an external hard drive, flash drive, SD card, or an optical drive. If you are using external media such as a flash drive, hard drive, or optical drive, be sure to secure the drive or disc after the backup has been made. It could be very easy for someone to casually walk away with the flash drive that contains all of your personal data.

Be able to explain the differences between local backups, such as those on flash drives, external hard drives, and SD cards, and cloud storage. They are part of Tech+ exam objective 5.4.

Network backup solutions can be handy for corporate networks. These types of backups are generally configured by an administrator, and the user doesn't need to do anything. Security is also controlled centrally. As the end user, you probably don't know if it's being backed up on a server or an NAS device or somewhere else, but it really doesn't matter as long as you can get your files back when you need them. For a lot of companies, backing up everyone's local workstation is far too cumbersome, and they rely on the individual users to make backups of their own systems.

Internet and cloud-based backups are very popular options for home users and corporations alike. You pay for a certain amount of storage space, and your cloud provider takes care of the backups and security. Before using one of these services, be sure you understand how often they perform backups and what security measures they have in place.

Finally, if you do make backups to physical media (and not the cloud), consider where to store the backup drives or discs. If you store them on-site, they are convenient to get to if you need them. The downside is that if something happens to the building (such as a fire or natural disaster), then the backup could be ruined as well. Consider storing at least some of the backups off-site with a reputable vendor. That way, you're protected in case of damage to your facility.

For many organizations, regulations determine how often backups need to be done, where backups can be stored, and how long they must be retained. These organizations may be subject to audits to ensure they are complying with the regulations.

Frequency and Scheduling

This is one of the areas most users, and even most companies, fail to manage properly. At the same time, it's one of the most important. Backups serve several key purposes, such as protecting against hard drive failure, protecting against accidental deletion, protecting against malicious deletion or attacks, and making an archive of important files for later use. Any time you make major changes to your system, including installing new software, you should perform a backup of important files before making those changes.

All Windows versions since Windows 2000 allow you to schedule backups, which is a great feature that not all versions of Windows have had.

Now that you know you can schedule backups to make your life easier, and of course you want to make backups because it's the right thing to do, the question becomes: how often do you need to back up your files?

The answer depends on what the computer does and what you do on the computer. How often does your data change? Every day? Every week or every month? How important are your files? Can you afford to lose them? How much time or money will it cost to replace lost files? Can they be replaced? By answering these questions, you can get an idea of how often you want to run scheduled backups. As a rule of thumb, the more important the data is and the more often it changes, the more often you want to back up. If you don't care about losing the data, then there's no need for backups—but most of us do care about losing our stuff. Exercise 12.1 walks you through setting up a backup in Windows 11.

EXERCISE 12.1

Setting Up a Backup in Windows 11

1. Open Control Panel.
2. Click Backup And Restore (Windows 7). If you are viewing by categories, it will be listed under System And Security.
3. If you have not previously used Backup And Restore, it will look similar to Figure 12.5. Click Set Up Backup.

EXERCISE 12.1 *(continued)*

FIGURE 12.5 Backup And Restore

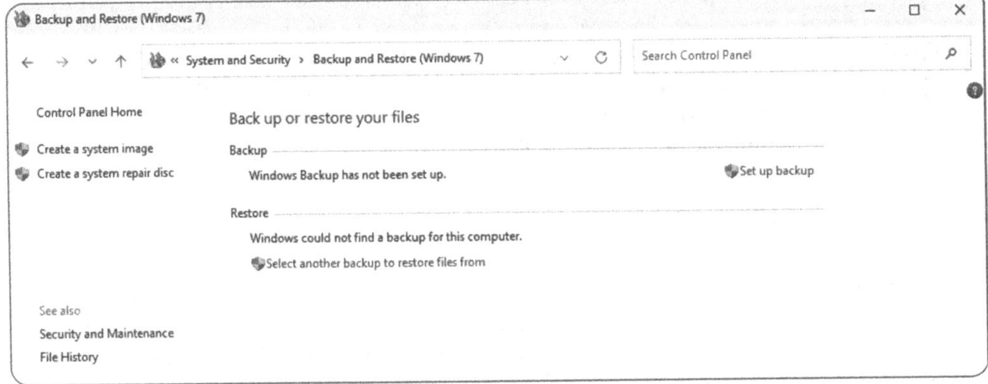

4. On the next screen (Figure 12.6), you will be asked to select a location to back up the files. In Figure 12.6 there are two choices, and a Save On A Network button. Notice that because I have a removable device selected, there is a warning message saying I can't create a system image. (Windows doesn't allow system images to be saved to removable media.) Select a location and click Next.

FIGURE 12.6 Select a backup location

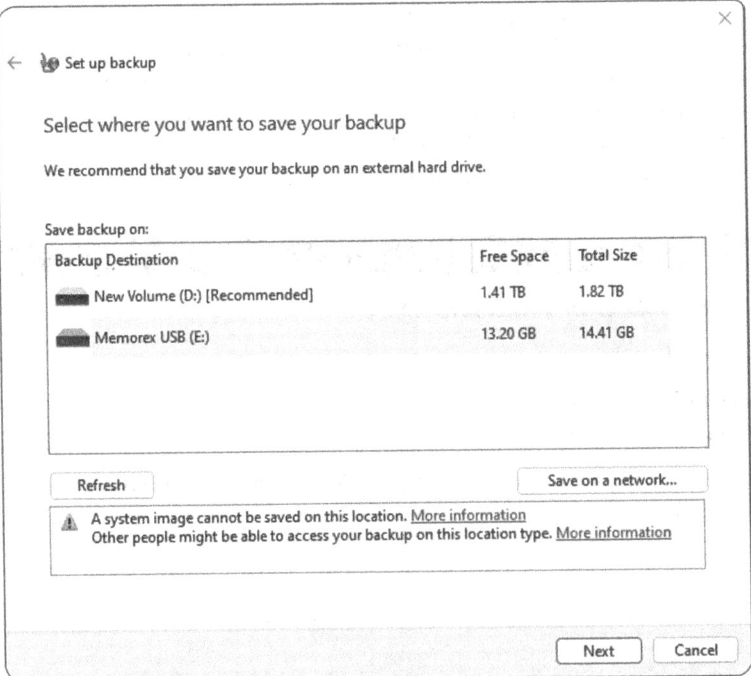

5. Let Windows choose which files to back up, or choose them yourself. For this exercise, select Let Me Choose and click Next.
6. You will be presented with choices of what to back up, including all of the current user's libraries, or specific folders on local hard drives. Here you can also choose to create a system image (that is, of the system partition and C: to do a full system restore). Choose a small folder to back up, such as the `Downloads` folder, and then click Next.
7. Finally, you can review your backup settings. An important option on this page is you can schedule backups as well. (In the Windows Backup tool you learned about earlier, scheduling is not an option.) Click Change Schedule.
8. Choose how often and when to back up the files (Figure 12.7). For example, you can choose daily, weekly, or monthly. Then you can choose the day and time. Click OK.

FIGURE 12.7 Schedule options

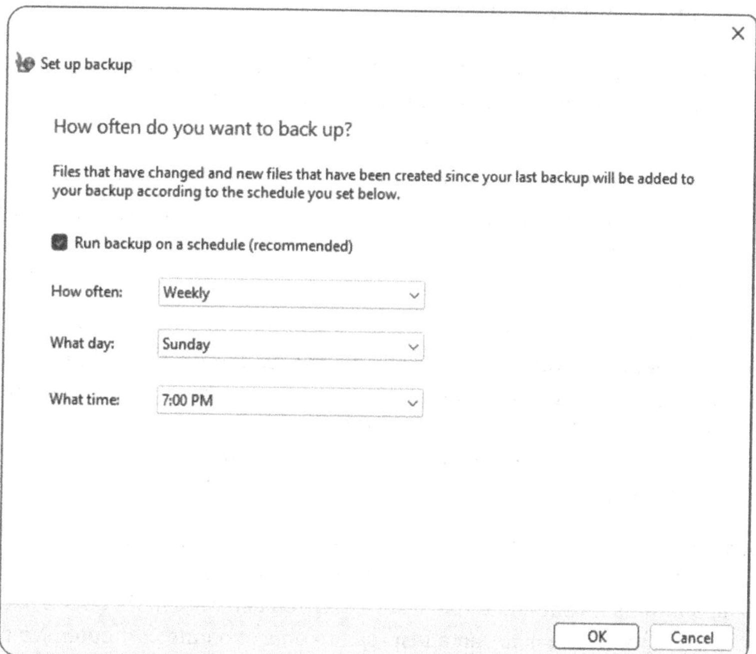

9. Click Save Settings And Run Backup.
10. The Backup And Restore setup window will close and take you back to the Backup And Restore control panel, where you can see the progress of the backup you are creating. Save this backup because you will use it in Exercise 12.2.

Different backup programs will have slightly different steps, but overall the process is the same: Choose what you want to back up, decide where to back it up to, and set up a schedule. Backup programs will include options to restore folders and files from a backup as well.

Verifying and Testing Backups

Creating a backup should give you a feeling of security. Now if something happens to your system, at least your data is protected. Before feeling too comfortable, though, you need to complete one more step—verifying your backups. This is a step that many people completely forget, but it's critical. To understand why, it's probably best to share a real-world example.

Real World Scenario

Learning Lessons About Backups

People don't back up data enough, plain and simple. Scheduling regular backups is a good protective measure, but just because you are backing up your data doesn't mean you're completely saved if something goes wrong.

Several years ago, one of my former students related a story to me about a server crash at his company. A server had mysteriously died over the weekend, and the technicians were greeted with the problem first thing Monday morning. Not to worry, they thought, because they made regular backups.

After several attempts to restore the backup tape, a second, more serious problem was readily apparent. The backup didn't work. They couldn't read the data from the tape, and it was the only backup tape they had. (Tape backup drives were the most popular option for quite a while, until Internet-based cloud backups exploded in popularity.) It wasn't going to be a very good Monday. Ultimately, they ended up losing extensive data from the server because their backup didn't work.

How do you prevent tragedies like this from happening? Test your backups. After you make a backup, ensure that you can read from it. If you've just backed up a small amount of data, restore it to an alternate location and make sure that you can read it. If you are backing up entire computers, a good idea is to run a test restore on a separate computer. No matter what your method, test your backup, especially when it's the first one you've made after setting up backups or you have made backup configuration changes. It isn't necessary to test each backup fully after that, but it is a good idea to spot-check backups on occasion.

Here are two more ideas that will help if you back up locally:

- If you use removable media, rotate the backup media. Alternate media every other backup period, or use a separate flash drive or disc for each day of the week. This lessens the risk of having bad media bring you down.
- Store your backups off-site. If your backup is sitting on top of the server, and you have a fire that destroys the building, then your backup won't do you any good. There are data archiving firms that will, for a small fee, come and pick up your backup tapes and store them in their secure location.

Be vigilant about backing up your data, and in the event of a failure, you'll be back up and running in short order.

Disaster Recovery

If an event such as data loss or equipment failure does happen, restoring access will be the most important task to complete. The *disaster recovery* plan should be a key component to the contingency plan, which will identify the priorities to take in the event a disaster strikes.

First, if a disaster does strike, ensure that it's under control before beginning to recover from it. For example, while it might sound silly to say it, make sure that the fire is out before you begin restoring access to systems. That might be kind of obvious, but for some situations, such as hackers attacking a network, it can be a little trickier to understand when everything is under control.

When recovering from a disaster, follow the priorities as outlined in the contingency plan. Usually, you work from the biggest stuff to the smallest. For example, restoring access to servers would take priority over fixing someone's email client. And, of course, hardware needs to be in good working order before data restoration can begin. Once the disaster is under control and hardware is in working order, you can restore missing data. Exercise 12.2 shows you how to do that in Windows 11.

EXERCISE 12.2

Restoring Files in Windows 11

1. Locate your backup media and insert it, if applicable.
2. Open Control Panel.
3. Click Backup And Restore (Windows 7). It will look something like Figure 12.8. (Note that here is also where you can turn off scheduling, create a system image, or create a system repair disc.)

EXERCISE 12.2 *(continued)*

FIGURE 12.8 Restoring files

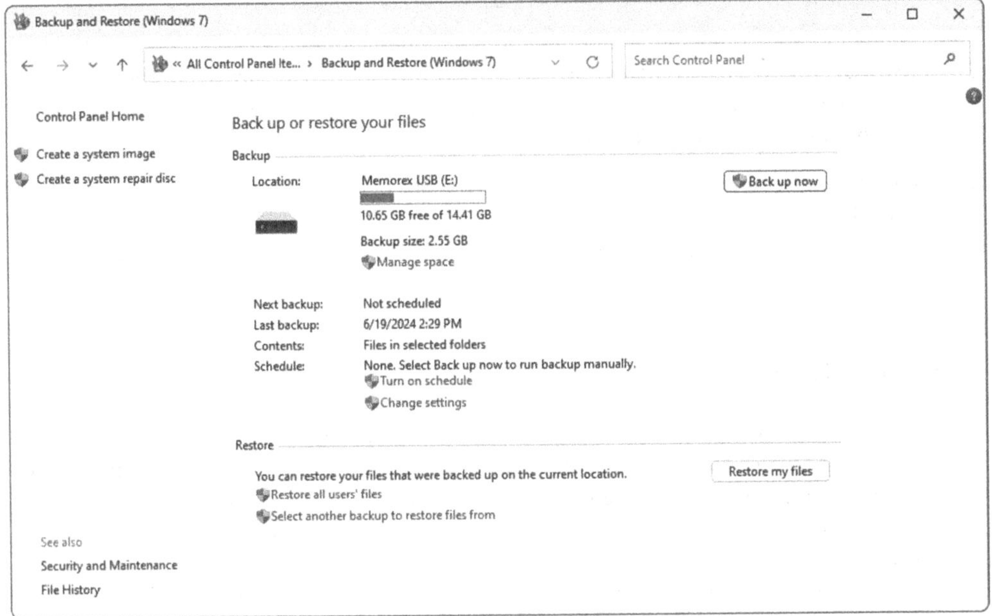

4. Click Restore My Files.
5. Specify which files you want to restore. Click Browse For Folders.
6. In the next window that appears (Figure 12.9), click Backup Of C: (or the name of your backup file), and then click Add Folder.

FIGURE 12.9 Adding the backup file

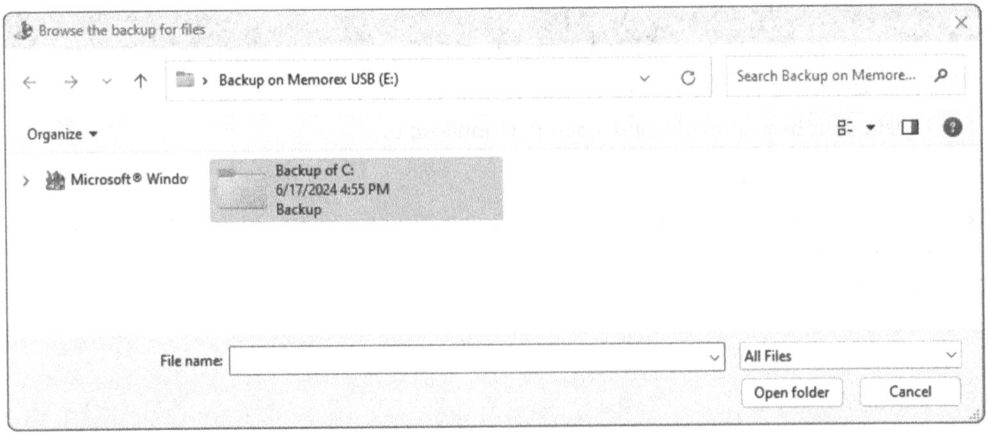

7. Click Next.
8. Choose where to restore the files to—the original location or browse for an alternate location.
9. Click Restore.
10. Watch the magic happen.
11. When you receive the message that your files have been restored, click Finish.
12. Close Backup And Restore.

Exploring Computer Support Concepts

Computer support isn't typically thought of as one of the sexy jobs in IT, but it's definitely one of the most critical and visible jobs. Users don't care how elegant your network design is, how bulletproof your security model is, or how user-friendly your website is if their computer won't boot up. And when it won't boot up, their best friend is the computer support person.

Sometimes you will fix computers in person, while at other times you'll deal with challenging situations over the phone. In either case, you need to be prepared to diagnose the problem quickly and implement a solution. The user will be counting on you—and you get to be the hero! Okay, so maybe the user won't treat you like a hero and there probably won't be a parade in your honor, but you will definitely know that they appreciate your help.

Computer support is synonymous with troubleshooting. To troubleshoot well, you need to understand the theory and process of troubleshooting. This includes the basic concepts and resources that apply in most situations. In addition, there are common scenarios that you will encounter—knowing how to solve the common issues will help you think about how to solve the difficult ones as well.

Understanding the Troubleshooting Methodology

When troubleshooting, you should assess every problem systematically and try to isolate the root cause. Yes, there is a lot of art to troubleshooting, and experience plays a part too. But regardless of how "artful" or experienced you are, haphazard troubleshooting is doomed to fail. Conversely, even technicians with limited experience can be effective troubleshooters if they stick to the principles. The major key is to start with the issue and attempt to isolate it. Whittle away at it until you can get down to the point where you can pinpoint the problem—this often means eliminating, or verifying, the obvious.

Although everyone approaches troubleshooting from a different perspective, a few things should remain constant. First, always back up your data before making any changes to a system. Hardware components can be replaced, but data often can't be. For that reason, always be vigilant about making data backups.

Second, establish priorities—one user being unable to print to the printer of their choice isn't as important as a floor full of accountants unable to run payroll. Prioritize every job and escalate it (or de-escalate it) as needed.

Third, but perhaps most important, document everything—not just that there was a problem but also the solution you found, the actions you tried, and the outcomes of each.

The troubleshooting methodology can be broken down into the following steps to pursue:

1. Identify the problem.
2. Establish a theory of probable cause (question the obvious).
3. Test the theory to determine the cause.
4. Establish a plan of action to fix the problem and implement the solution.
5. Verify full system functionality and, if applicable, implement preventive measures.
6. Document findings/lessons learned, actions, and outcomes.

In the next few sections, I will take you through each step of the troubleshooting process.

Identifying the Problem

While this may seem obvious, it can't be overlooked: If you can't define the problem, you can't begin to solve it. Sometimes problems are relatively straightforward, but other times they're just a symptom of a bigger issue. For example, if a user isn't able to connect to the Internet from their computer, it could indeed be an issue with their system. But if other users are having similar problems, then the first user's difficulties might just be one example of the real problem.

Ask yourself, "Is there a problem?" Perhaps "the problem" is as simple as a customer expecting too much from the computer.

Problems in computer systems generally occur in one (or more) of four areas, each of which is in turn made up of many pieces:

- A *collection of hardware pieces* integrated into a working system. As you know, the hardware can be quite complex, what with motherboards, hard drives, video cards, and so on. Software can be equally perplexing.
- An *operating system*, which in turn is dependent on the hardware.
- An *application* or software program that is supposed to do something. Programs such as Microsoft Word and Microsoft Excel are bundled with a great many features.
- A *computer user*, ready to take the computer system to its limits (and beyond). Sometimes it's easy to forget that the user is a complex and important part of the puzzle.

Tech+ exam objective 1.4, "Explain the troubleshooting methodology," wants you to understand six key steps for troubleshooting computer problems. The first is "Identify the problem." In this section, you will learn several techniques for how to do so.

Talking to the Customer

Many times, you can define the problem by asking questions of the user. One of the keys to working with your users or customers is to ensure, much like a medical professional, that you have a good bedside manner. Most people are not as technically fluent as you, and when something goes wrong, they become confused or even fearful that they'll take the blame. Assure them that you're just trying to fix the problem but that they can probably help because they know what went on before you got there. It's important to instill trust with your customer. Believe what they are saying, but also believe that they might not tell you everything right away. It's not that they're necessarily lying; they just might not know what's important to tell.

Real World Scenario

Is the Power On?

It's a classic IT story that almost sounds like a joke, but it happens. A customer calls technical support because their computer won't turn on. After 20 minutes of troubleshooting, the technician is becoming frustrated . . . maybe it's a bad power supply? The technician asks the user to read some numbers off the back of their computer, and the user says, "Hold on, I need to get a flashlight. It's dark in here with the power out."

Help clarify things by having the customer show you what the problem is. The best method I've seen for doing this is to say, "Show me what 'not working' looks like." That way, you see the conditions and methods under which the problem occurs. The problem may be a simple matter of an improper method. The user may be performing an operation incorrectly or performing the operation in the wrong order. During this step, you have the opportunity to observe how the problem occurs, so pay attention.

Here are a few questions to ask the user to aid in determining what the problem is:

Can you show me the problem? This question is one of the best. It allows the user to show you exactly where and when they experience the problem.

How often does this happen? This question establishes whether this problem is a one-time occurrence that can be solved with a reboot or whether a specific sequence of events causes the problem to happen. The latter usually indicates a more serious problem that may require software installation or hardware replacement.

Has any new hardware or software been installed recently? New hardware or software can mean compatibility problems with existing devices or applications. For example, a newly installed device may want to use the same resource settings as an existing device. This can cause both devices to become disabled. When you install a new application, that application is likely to install several support files. If those support files are also used by an existing application, then there could be a conflict.

Has the computer recently been moved? Or did it fall? Moving a computer can cause things to become loose and then fail to work. Perhaps all of the peripherals of the computer didn't complete—or weren't included on—the move, meaning there's less functionality than the user expects. Laptops and mobile devices are more prone to unexpected "falls." Asking if they have been dropped seems more accusatory, so asking if the user knows if the device fell (it makes it sound like it's the device's fault for jumping out of their hand and tumbling down the stairs) is more innocuous.

Has someone who normally doesn't use the computer recently used it? That person could have mistakenly (or intentionally) done something to make the computer begin exhibiting the irregular behavior.

Have any other changes been made to the computer recently? If the answer is yes, ask if the user can remember approximately when the change was made. Then ask them approximately when the problem started. If the two dates seem related, there's a good chance the problem is related to the change. If it's a new hardware component, check to see that it was installed correctly.

Be careful of how you ask questions so you don't appear accusatory. You can't assume that the user did something to mess up the computer. Then again, you also can't assume that they don't know anything about why it's not working.

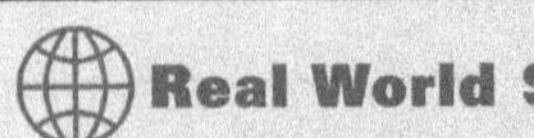

The Social Side of Troubleshooting

When you're looking for clues as to the nature of a problem, no one can give you more information than the person who was there when it happened. They can tell you what led up to the problem, what software was running, and the exact nature of the problem ("It happened when I tried to print"), and they can help you re-create the problem, if possible.

Use questioning techniques that are neutral in nature. Instead of saying, "What were you doing when it broke?," be more compassionate and say, "What was going on when the computer decided not to work?" Frame the question in a way that makes it sound like the computer did something wrong and not the person. It might sound silly, but these things can make your job a lot easier!

While it's sometimes frustrating dealing with end users and computer problems, such as the user who calls you up and gives you the "My computer's not working" line (okay, and what *exactly* is that supposed to mean?), even more frustrating is when no one was around to see what happened. In cases like this, do your best to find out where the problem is by establishing what works and what doesn't work.

Gathering Information

Let's say that you get to a computer and the power light is on and you can hear the fan spinning, but there is no video, and the system seems to be unresponsive. At least you know that the system has power and you can start investigating where things start to break down. (It sounds like there is a reboot in your future!)

The whole key to this step is to identify, as specifically as possible, what the problem is. The more specific you can be in identifying what is not working, the easier it will be for you to understand why it's not working and to fix it. If you have users available who were there when the thing stopped working, you can try to gather information from them. If not, you're on your own to gather clues.

So now instead of having users available to pose questions to, you need to use your own investigative services to determine what's wrong. The questions you would have otherwise asked the user are still a good starting point. Does anything appear amiss or seem to have been changed recently? What is working and what is not? Was there a storm recently? Can I reboot? If I reboot, does the problem seem to go away?

If a computer seems to have multiple problems that appear to be unrelated, identify what they are one at a time and fix them one at a time. For example, if the sound is not working and you can't get on the Internet, deal with those separately. If they seem related, such as not being able to get on the Internet and you can't access a network file server, then one solution might solve both problems.

The key is to find out everything you can that might be related to the problem. Document exactly what works and what doesn't and, if you can, why. If the power is out in the house, as in the story related earlier, then there's no sense in trying the power plug in another outlet.

Determining Whether the Problem Is Hardware- or Software-Related

This step is important because it determines the part of the computer on which you should focus your troubleshooting skills. Each part requires different skills and different tools.

To determine whether a problem is hardware or software-related, you can do a few things to narrow down the issue. For instance, does the problem manifest itself when the user uses a particular piece of hardware (a DVD-ROM or USB hard drive, for example)? If it does, the problem is more than likely hardware-related, which can also mean a problem with the device driver.

This step relies on personal experience more than any of the other steps. You'll without a doubt run into strange software problems. Each one has a particular solution. Some may even require reinstallation of an application or the operating system. If that doesn't work, you may need to resort to restoring the entire system (operating system, applications, and data) from a data backup done when the computer was working properly.

Determining Which Component Is Failing (for Hardware Problems)

Hardware problems are usually pretty easy to figure out. Let's say that the sound card doesn't work, you've tried new speakers that you know do work, and you've reinstalled the driver. All of the settings look right, but it just won't respond. The sound card is probably the piece of hardware that needs to be replaced.

With many newer computers, several components such as sound, video, and networking cards are integrated into the motherboard. If you troubleshoot the computer and find a hardware component to be bad, there's a good chance that the bad component is integrated into the motherboard and the whole motherboard must be replaced—an expensive proposition to be sure.

Laptops and lots of desktops have components (network card, sound card, video adapter) integrated into the motherboard. If an integrated component fails, you may be able to use an expansion device (such as a USB network adapter) to give the system full functionality without a costly repair.

Establishing a Theory of Probable Cause (Question the Obvious)

Way back when, probably in your middle school or junior high school years, you learned about the scientific method. In a nutshell, scientists develop a hypothesis, test it, and then figure out if their hypothesis is still valid. Troubleshooting involves much the same process.

Once you have determined what the problem is, you need to develop a theory as to why it is happening. No video? It could be something to do with the monitor or the video card. Can't get to your favorite website? Is it that site? Is it your network card, the cable, your IP address, DNS server settings, or something else? Once you have defined the problem, establishing a theory about the cause of the problem—what is wrong—helps you develop possible solutions to the problem.

The second step in the troubleshooting methodology, per exam objective 1.4, is "Establish a theory of probable cause (question the obvious)." Included in that is researching knowledge bases or the Internet, if applicable. Understand these steps prior to taking the exam.

Question the Obvious

Occam's razor says that the simplest explanation is often the correct one. It definitely applies to troubleshooting computers, which is quite prescient coming from someone in the 14th century! All jokes aside, if something seems obvious, check it out first before working on more elaborate theories.

Research Knowledge Sources, If Needed

Sometimes you will run into an issue and know exactly what the solution is. More often than not, you won't be quite so lucky. The good news is that there's a wealth of knowledge available online. Many manufacturers have knowledge bases with detailed information about known issues, and if not, there is likely a message board somewhere with users or technicians discussing problems similar to yours. The key is finding it.

I've joked before that Google knows everything, but if you have a specific error message or code, a Google search will probably give you a solution or point you in the right direction. If not, you can try various keywords to explain the symptoms to see what you can find. You might not find answers associated with the specific device or model number on which you're working, but maybe something similar or related will give you a good idea of what could be causing the problem. It could take some creative searching but have patience and take the time to look around if needed. It's better than just shooting in the dark.

Besides the manufacturer's documentation and website (which should generally be your first resources), there may be technical community groups that can help. If a similar question to yours has been posted, there could be an answer. If you don't see your problem, post the question on the board. Always remember to be as clear as possible about the problem, and be polite and friendly. No one is going to answer a question if they think you are a troll. If none of that works out, you can always call the manufacturer's technical support line to seek help.

Finally, if you're lucky enough to have experienced, knowledgeable, and friendly coworkers, be open to asking for help if you get stuck on a problem.

Before starting to eliminate possibilities, check the vendor's website for any information that might help you. For example, if you are getting an error message saying, "PC Load Letter," and you don't know what it means, typing it into the vendor's website might take you directly to specific steps to fix the problem.

Eliminating Possibilities

Theories can state either what can be true or what can't be true. However you choose to approach your theory generation, it's usually helpful to take a mental inventory to see what is possible and what's not. Start eliminating possibilities and eventually the only thing that can be wrong is what's left. This type of approach works well when it's an ambiguous problem; start broad and narrow your scope. For example, if the hard drive won't read, there is likely one of three culprits: the drive itself, the cable it's on, or the connector on the motherboard. Try plugging the drive into the other connector or using a different cable. Narrow down the options.

A common troubleshooting technique is to strip the system down to the bare bones. In a hardware situation, this could mean removing all interface cards except those absolutely required for the system to operate. In a software situation, this usually means booting up in Safe Mode so that most of the drivers do not load.

Once you have isolated the problem, slowly rebuild the system to see whether the problem comes back (or goes away). This helps you identify what is really causing the problem and determine whether there are other factors affecting the situation. For example, I have seen memory problems that are fixed by switching the slot in which the memory chips are installed.

Divide and Conquer

I said it earlier in this chapter, but it bears repeating: If there are multiple problems, tackle each one individually. To paraphrase an ancient axiom, "He who chases two rabbits catches neither." Focus on one problem and separate it from other issues, and it reduces the complexity of the task at hand.

Testing the Theory to Determine the Cause

You've eliminated possibilities and developed a theory as to what is the problem. Your theory may be pretty specific, such as "the power cable is fried," or it may be a bit more general, like "the hard drive isn't working" or "there's a connectivity problem." No matter your theory, now is the time to start testing solutions to see whether your theory is correct. If the theory is confirmed, then you can move to fixing the problem. If not, it's time to establish a new theory. Again, if you're not sure where to begin to find a solution, the manufacturer's website is a good place to start!

The third step in the troubleshooting methodology, per exam objective 1.4, is "Test the theory to determine the cause." Know how to do this.

Check the Simple Stuff First

This step is the one that even experienced technicians overlook. Often, computer problems are the result of something simple. Technicians overlook these problems because they're so simple that the technicians assume they *couldn't* be the problem. Here are some examples of simple problems:

Is it plugged in? And is it plugged in at both ends? Cables must be plugged in at *both ends* to function correctly. Cables can easily be tripped over and inadvertently pulled from their sockets. Rule number one is always to check the cables first.

Real World Scenario

"Is It Plugged In?" and Other Insulting Questions

Think about how you feel if someone asks you this question. Your likely response is, "Of course it is!" After all, you're not an idiot, right? You'll often get the same reaction to similar questions about the device being turned on. The reality is, making sure it's plugged in and turned on are the first things you should always do when investigating a problem.

When asking these types of questions, it's not what you say but how you say it. For example, instead of asking if it's plugged in, you could say something like, "Can you do me a favor and check to see what color the end of the monitor plug is? Is that the same color of the port where it's plugged into on the computer?" That generally gets the user to at least look at it without making them feel dumb. For power, something like, "What color are the lights on the front of the router? Are any of them blinking?" can work well.

Ask neutral and nonthreatening questions. Make it sound like the computer is at fault, not the user. These types of things will help you build rapport and be able to get more information so that you can solve problems faster.

Is it turned on? This one seems the most obvious, but we've all fallen victim to it at one point or another. Computers and their peripherals must be turned on to function. Most have power switches with LEDs that glow when the power is turned on.

Is there physical damage? Sometimes physical damage is obvious, such as if someone hit a computer with a hammer. Other times it will be subtler. For example, you might see a brown patch on a motherboard where it got burned or get a faint whiff of burnt plastic because of a power issue.

Is the system ready? Computers must be ready before they can be used. *Ready* means the system is ready to accept commands from the user. An indication that a computer is ready is when the operating system screens come up, and the computer presents you with a menu or a Command Prompt. If that computer uses a graphical interface, the computer is ready when the mouse pointer appears. Printers are ready when the Online or Ready light on the front panel is lit.

Do the chips and cables need to be reseated? You can solve some of the strangest problems (random hang-ups or errors) by opening the case and pressing down on each socketed chip, memory module, and expansion card (known as *reseating*). This remedies the chip-creep problem, which happens when computers heat up and cool down repeatedly as a result of being turned on and off, causing some components to begin to move out of their sockets. In addition, you should reseat any cables to make sure they're making good contact. Of course, make sure that the power is off before you attempt this!

Always be sure you're grounded with an antistatic wristband before operating inside the case! If you're not, you could create an electrostatic discharge (ESD) that could damage components. A great example of ESD is when you reach out to touch a doorknob or other metal surface and feel a small shock. The shock might just annoy you, but it can ruin computer components.

Check to See Whether It's User Error

User error is common but preventable. If a user can't perform some common computer task, such as printing or saving a file, the problem is likely because of user error. As soon as you hear of a problem like this, you should begin asking questions to determine whether the solution is as simple as teaching the user the correct procedure. A good question to ask is, "Were you *ever* able to perform that task?" If the answer is no, it could mean they are doing the procedure wrong. If they answer yes, you must ask additional questions to get at the root of the problem.

If you suspect user error, tread carefully in regard to your line of questioning to avoid making the user feel defensive. User errors provide an opportunity to teach the users the right way to do things. Again, what you say matters. Offer a "different" or "another" way of doing things instead of the "right" way.

Real World Scenario

Problems Faxing

Several years ago when I was doing computer support over the phone, I had a user call with a problem with their fax modem. (I told you it was a long time ago!) He said he tried faxing several times, but nothing would ever go through.

I started with the basics, like determining whether the computer was on (it was) and the phone line was connected (it was). We even checked the modem to be sure it picked up the line properly and dialed numbers. The hardware seemed fine. My thoughts turned to an issue in the fax software. I had him open the application, verify that he typed in the right phone number, and confirm several other options. Just like with the hardware, everything seemed fine. I was getting really confused as to why it wasn't working.

Finally, I started asking the right questions. When I asked what he was trying to fax, he said it was a piece of paper he needed to send to his insurance company. Okay, that's a good start . . . a piece of paper? I followed up by asking him to walk me through the steps of how he was trying to fax it. He responded by telling me that he opened the fax program and typed in the number. He then held the piece of paper up to the monitor and clicked the Send button on the fax program. And—he thought it was difficult to click the Send button when he couldn't see it because the paper was in the way. But it didn't work.

Clearly, the process he was following wasn't going to work, so it was an opportunity for user education. And while it's always good to start with the basics, such as checking the connections, the moral of the story is always to understand what the user is actually doing when they try to accomplish a task.

Restart the Computer

It's amazing how often a simple computer restart can solve a problem. Restarting the computer clears the memory and starts the computer with a clean slate. If restarting doesn't work, try powering down the system completely and then powering it up again (*rebooting*). More often than not, that will solve the problem.

If you (or the user) experience a problem on a computer for the first time, reboot the computer and see whether the problem goes away. If it does, then you've finished fixing it. If the problem is a persistent one, though, it indicates a larger issue that needs further investigation. There could be failing hardware or an application that needs to be reinstalled.

Establishing a Plan of Action and Implementing the Solution

At this point, one of three things has happened. The first is that you've fixed the entire problem, and you can congratulate yourself for being brilliant. The second is that you've fixed it in one spot but it's still happening on other computers or programs, and you need to further implement a solution. The third is it still isn't working.

The fourth step in the troubleshooting methodology, per exam objective 1.4, is "Establish a plan of action to resolve the problem and implement the solution."

For example, say you tried the hard drive with a new (verified) cable and it still doesn't work. Now what? Or, your sound card won't play and you've just deleted and reinstalled the driver. Next steps? Move on and try the next logical thing in line.

When trying solutions to fix a problem, make only one change to the computer at a time. If the change doesn't fix the problem, revert the system to the way it was and then make your next change. Making more than one change at a time is not recommended for two reasons:

- You are never sure which change actually worked.
- By making multiple changes at once, you might accidentally cause additional problems.

When evaluating your results and looking for that golden "next step," don't forget other resources that you might have available. Use the Internet to look at the manufacturer's website. Read the manual. Talk to your friend who knows everything about obscure hardware (or arcane versions of Windows). When fixing problems, two heads can be better than one.

Once you have found the right fix for the problem it's time to implement the solution. Of course, if the problem is isolated to one computer and your last troubleshooting step fixed it, that's great. But some problems you deal with may affect an entire group of computers.

For example, perhaps some configuration information was entered incorrectly into the router, giving everyone the wrong configuration. The router is now fixed, but all of the clients need to renew their IP configuration information.

If instead you feel completely over your head, it might be time to escalate the situation to a more senior technician or manager. This depends on the severity of the problem and the amount of time you've spent on it. If you still have ideas and the problem isn't urgent, keep at it. But if you've hit a dead end and you have people screaming at you to get it running *now*, call in some reinforcements if you can.

Take notes as you are working through problems, especially ones that appear complex. This will help you remember what you've done and will also help you when you document the solution at the end of the process.

Verifying Functionality

After fixing the system or all of the systems affected by the problem, go back and verify full functionality. For example, if the users couldn't get to any network resources, check to make sure they can get to the Internet as well as internal resources.

The fifth step in the troubleshooting methodology, per exam objective 1.4, is "Verify full system functionality and, if applicable, implement preventive measures."

Some solutions may accidentally cause another problem on the system. For example, if you update software or drivers, you may inadvertently cause another application to have problems. There's obviously no way you can or should test all applications on a computer after applying a fix, but know that these types of problems can occur. Just make sure that what you've fixed works, and that there aren't any obvious signs of something else not working all of a sudden.

Another important thing to do at this time is to implement preventive measures, if possible. If it was a user error, ensure that the user understands ways to accomplish the task that don't cause the error. If a cable melted because it was too close to someone's space heater under their desk, resolve the issue. If the computer overheated because there was an inch of dust clogging the fan . . . you get the idea.

Documenting the Work

Lots of people can fix problems. But can you remember what you did when you fixed a problem a month ago? Maybe. Can one of your coworkers remember something you did to fix the same problem on that machine a month ago? Unlikely. Always document your work so that you or someone else can learn from the experience. Good documentation of past troubleshooting can save hours of stress in the future. Unfortunately, it's often the most neglected step.

The sixth and final step in the troubleshooting methodology, per exam objective 1.4, is "Document findings/lessons learned, actions, and outcomes."

Documentation can take a few different forms, but the two most common are personal and system-based.

Probably the best thing that you can do is always to carry a personal notebook and take notes. The type of notebook doesn't matter, such as electronic or paper—use whatever works best for you. The notebook can be a lifesaver, especially when you're new to a job. Write down the problem, what you tried, and the solution. The next time you run across the same or a similar problem, you'll have a better idea of what to try. Eventually, you'll find yourself less and less reliant on it, but it's incredibly handy to have!

System-based documentation is useful to both you and your coworkers. Many facilities have server logs of one type or another, conveniently located close to the machine. If someone makes a fix or a change, it gets noted in the log. If there's a problem, it's noted in the log. It's critical to have a log for a few reasons. One, if you weren't there the first time it was fixed, you might not have an idea of what to try, and it could take you a long time using trial and error. Two, if you begin to see a repeated pattern of problems, you can make a permanent intervention before the system completely dies.

There are several different forms of system-based documentation. Again, the type of log doesn't matter as long as you use it! Often, it's a notebook or a binder next to the system or on a nearby shelf. If you have a rack, you can mount something on the side to hold a binder or notebook. For client computers, one way is to tape an index card to the top or side of the power supply (don't cover any vents!), so if a tech has to go inside the case, they can see whether anyone else has been in there to fix something too. In larger environments, there is often an electronic knowledge base or incident repository available for use; it is just as important to contribute to these systems as it is to use them to help diagnose problems.

Troubleshooting Examples

There isn't one single book that you can read to learn everything you need to know to troubleshoot every situation. There are just too many pieces of hardware, software applications, operating systems, and security configurations in the market for there to be one comprehensive guide. A lot of what you will know comes from experience. Remember, though, even if you're relatively inexperienced, you can still do a good job of troubleshooting by following a disciplined and methodological approach. It isn't always the fastest way, but it's the best, and you will get faster as you gain experience.

Knowing that there isn't one book that can cover all troubleshooting scenarios, I am still going to provide some examples of issues you might run into and possible solutions. This will give you a good foundation for working on problems. Here, I've created four groups of common types of problems:

- Computer won't boot up
- Operating system errors

- Application failures
- Hardware failures

Computer Won't Boot

Telling someone that a computer won't boot is a pretty general statement. It can mean anything from a hardware failure to an operating system problem. In these scenarios, the key is that the OS won't load. And because the operating system provides the platform from which you launch all of the activities you do with a computer, nothing productive can happen until you fix it. Depending on the OS and version, the steps involved for troubleshooting will vary. The following sections present some general guidance and introduce some troubleshooting tools that may be useful.

Nothing on the Monitor

If you turn on the computer and nothing happens—no fan spinning, no nothing—you probably have some type of power problem. Check that the computer is plugged in. A bad power supply unit (PSU), motherboard, or CPU can also cause the computer to appear dead. Those failures, however, are less likely if the computer has been working in the past than if you're assembling a new one from scratch.

If you hear fans spinning but nothing shows up on the screen, there's probably an issue with the monitor, display adapter, memory, or motherboard. It can be difficult to figure out which of these may be faulty without an error message to guide you. If you have a spare display adapter or memory module, you can try swapping it out, but it may be easier to take the computer to a repair shop at this point.

If you're determined to troubleshoot on your own, a device called a *POST card* may be useful. POST stands for "power-on self-test," and it's a diagnostic routine built into the BIOS. Some desktop computers will beep once after a successful POST, where all critical components are checked. If you hear no beeps, or a series of beeps, you might have a hardware problem. A POST card is a circuit board you insert into an open slot in the motherboard or into a USB port, which can help you diagnose the issue. The card displays a two-digit numeric code on its LED to tell you where the system is in the booting process. A book that accompanies the POST card tells what each number represents. When the boot process stalls, read the code on the POST card and look it up to figure out where the boot process has broken down, which may tell you which component has failed.

Black-Screen or Blue-Screen Error Message

A plain-text error message (gray text on a black screen) is usually a message from the BIOS prior to the OS load. A failed or soon-to-be-failed hard disk most often triggers such a message. The exact wording of the BIOS-thrown error messages varies depending on the BIOS company and version; you may see a message like "Disk Drive Failure" or "No Boot Disk Found."

Although hard disk errors are the most common errors that appear before the OS load, they aren't the only possible errors at this point. You may see a message that the keyboard has a key stuck, for example, or that there is an error involving RAM.

If the error message appears as gray or white text on a bright blue background, that's a *STOP error*. It's called a STOP because the first word on the screen is usually `STOP`, and the PC freezes up when it appears, requiring you to power the PC off and back on again to continue. Some techie types call this error a *Blue Screen of Death (BSOD)*. This type of error often means that a piece of hardware (usually something like a network adapter, sound card, or modem) is defective or incompatible with your Windows version, but there are also other reasons for STOP errors, specific to the error code that displays.

To diagnose a STOP error, look up the error code on a website that provides a directory of such errors. Here are a few good sources to get you started:

```
www.lifewire.com/blue-screen-error-codes-4065576
www.aumha.org/a/stop.php
```

Based on what you discover, you may need to remove or replace a hardware component or reinstall or repair the OS.

Windows Won't Load

Windows requires certain files to be present, usable, and in the expected location to start up. These files are mostly stored in the `C:\Windows\System32` or `C:\Windows\SysWOW64` folder, and they include `WinLoad.exe`, `Ntoskrnl.exe`, `Hal.dll`, and `WinLogon.exe`, among others. If any of these files are unavailable, Windows won't load, and an error message will tell you what's missing. You may need to reinstall or repair Windows in order to fix the problem. This is normally done through the Windows Recovery Environment (WinRE), available in Windows Vista or newer. (See the section "Using the Recovery Environment" later in this chapter for details.) Remember, this is used when Windows won't load.

Assuming Windows has all the critical files it needs to load, it reads information from the Registry as it boots up. The Registry informs it of the settings to use, what device drivers to load, and what programs should start up automatically in the background. If any of the files called for during this process are unavailable, an error message appears or the boot process simply hangs, usually after the Windows logo has briefly appeared on-screen.

You may be able to boot the PC using Safe Mode, which bypasses all noncritical startup options; if the problem is with one of the noncritical files, that problem will be temporarily disabled enough to start the system. After starting up Windows (in Safe Mode if necessary), if the problem was caused by a recently installed item of hardware or software, you may be able to use System Restore to return the system configuration to its earlier state, undoing whatever action caused the problem to occur.

Using Safe Mode

When Windows won't start normally, you can often boot into Safe Mode for access to your Windows Desktop. *Safe Mode* is a low-functionality mode that bypasses all optional components, both hardware and software, loading only the minimum required to display the desktop. You shouldn't use the computer for normal tasks in Safe Mode because of its limited functionality; stay in Safe Mode only long enough to implement whatever fixes are needed to allow Windows to boot normally again.

Safe Mode can be accessed in one of two ways. If Windows is running, you can get to it through Windows Settings ➢ System ➢ Recovery ➢ Advanced Startup. At the login screen, Advanced Startup is activated by holding the Shift key down and clicking Power ➢ Restart. You will get to access Advanced Startup in Exercise 12.3.

EXERCISE 12.3

Booting into Safe Mode in Windows 11

This exercise assumes Windows is running. If you are the login screen, hold down the Shift key and click Power ➢ Restart to open Advanced Startup and skip to step 5.

1. Open Windows Settings by clicking Start ➢ Settings or by pressing Windows + I.
2. In the left pane, click System.
3. Click Recovery. You will see a screen similar to the one in Figure 12.10.

FIGURE 12.10 Recovery options

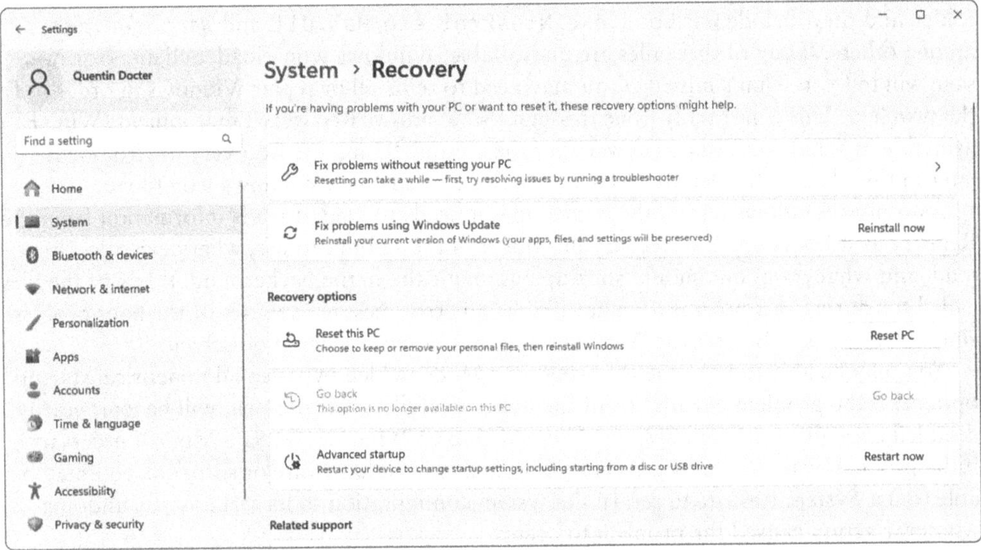

4. In the Advanced Startup area, click Restart Now.

The next screen you are presented with will be titled Choose An Option.

5. On the Choose An Option screen, click Troubleshoot.
6. Click Advanced Options.
7. Click Startup Settings.
8. Click Restart.

   The computer will restart.

9. The Startup Settings screen will present nine options. There are three Safe Mode options: Safe Mode (option 4), Safe Mode With Networking (option 5), and Safe Mode With Command Prompt (option 6). For this exercise, choose Safe Mode (option 4).
10. Windows will boot into Safe Mode. Notice how it looks more basic than a normal Windows boot.
11. When you are done, reboot to return to Windows in normal mode.

In Safe Mode, the display adapter uses a generic driver, so the screen resolution is very low and uses only a limited color set. Nonessential hardware doesn't work, such as sound cards and modems, and unless you chose Safe Mode With Networking at the Startup Settings menu, the network doesn't work either (and that includes the Internet).

If the computer starts fine in Safe Mode but doesn't start normally, you can assume that the startup problem lies in one of the nonessential hardware drivers or software applications that Safe Mode blocks from starting. From here it's just a matter of elimination.

Here are some things to try once you're in Safe Mode:

- Disconnect all nonessential external hardware devices, such as modems, external hard disks, webcams, and so on. Try to boot normally. If you can, then plug the devices back in one at a time, rebooting after each one, until you find the one with the problem.
- If you've recently installed new internal hardware, remove it and see whether the problem goes away.
- If you've recently installed a new application, remove it (see Chapter 5, "Software Applications") and reboot to see whether the problem goes away.
- Use System Restore, as described in the next section, to return your computer to an earlier configuration point before the problem started.
- Run the System Configuration utility (MSCONFIG), as described later in this chapter, to prevent all noncritical applications from loading at startup. Then reenable them one by one, rebooting each time, until you find the problem.

Using System Restore

The *System Restore* feature in Windows makes a backup copy of the important system configuration files once a day (by default), called a *restore point*. You can also make additional copies at any time, such as immediately before you install new and untried hardware or software. Then, if the system doesn't work anymore after you install the new item, you can revert the system files to the earlier versions, removing all traces of anything the new item may have brought with it.

System Restore backs up Windows configuration files only, *not* personal data files!

If Windows won't start normally or if it runs poorly all of a sudden after previously running fairly well, it's often easier to revert to a System Restore point than to spend a lot of time trying to pinpoint what happened. Start System Restore from System Properties. Exercise 12.4 provides an opportunity to manage restore points in Windows 11.

EXERCISE 12.4

Using System Restore in Windows 11

1. Open the System Properties by typing **restore point** in the Windows search box and clicking Create A Restore Point.
2. The System Protection tab, shown in Figure 12.11, will appear.

FIGURE 12.11 System Protection tab in System Properties

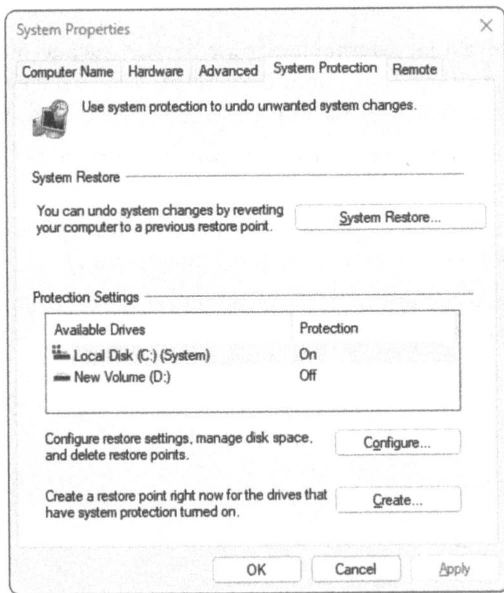

3. Click the Create button. A System Protection dialog box opens.
4. Type **Test 1** in the text box.
5. Click Create to create the restore point and wait for the restore point to be created. It should take a minute or two.
6. Click Close to close the message box that tells you the restore point was created.
7. Close all open windows and dialog boxes.
8. Right-click the desktop and choose Personalize.
9. Select a different desktop background and then close the Personalization window.
10. Open System Properties again and click the System Protection tab.
11. Click System Restore. The System Restore application opens.
12. Click Next to continue.
13. In the list of restore points, click Test 1, as shown in Figure 12.12.

FIGURE 12.12 Choosing a restore point

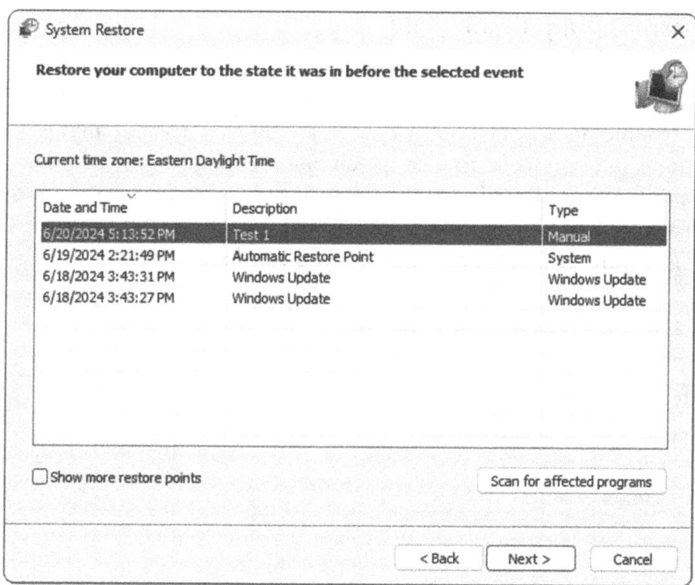

14. Click Next and then click Finish. A warning appears that says once started, System Restore can't be interrupted. Click Yes.

EXERCISE 12.4 *(continued)*

15. Wait for your system to restart. After it restarts, click Close to dismiss the dialog box that tells you the System Restore operation completed successfully. Note what the desktop background looks like.
16. Open the System Properties dialog's System Protection tab again.
17. Click System Restore.
18. Click Next to continue.
19. In the list of restore points, click Restore Operation. Notice that its type is Manual; you're going to undo the system restore you just did.
20. Click Next and then click Finish. A warning appears that says once started, System Restore can't be interrupted. Click Yes.
21. Wait for your system to restart. After it restarts, click Close to dismiss the confirmation dialog box. Notice what the desktop background looks like.

Using the System Configuration Utility

The *System Configuration utility*, also known by its executable filename of MSCONFIG, allows Windows users to manage the startup process. This can be a great benefit when you're trying to troubleshoot a startup problem that you're fairly sure involves one of your startup applications, but you have no idea which one.

This utility isn't found in the Windows menu system, so you have to run it using its name. In the Windows search bar, type **msconfig**, and press Enter to open the System Configuration window shown in Figure 12.13. It's available in Safe Mode too.

FIGURE 12.13 System Configuration utility

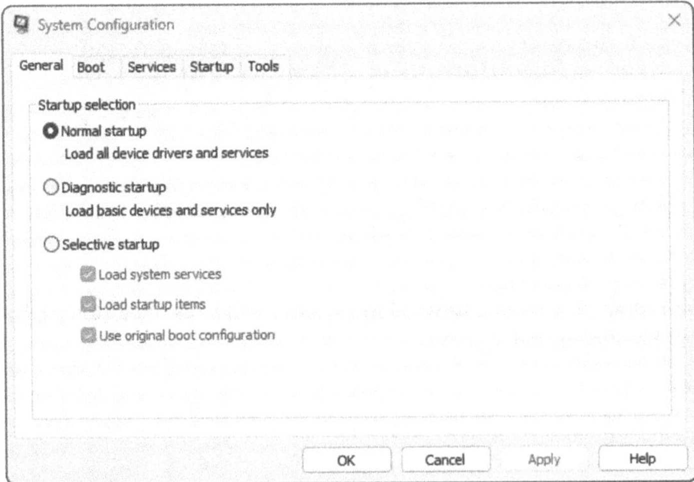

There are three options for startup. Normal startup means everything that the Registry specifies should be loaded is loaded. The alternatives are Diagnostic Startup (which turns off everything nonessential and is useful in determining, in general, whether something loading at startup is causing the problem) and Selective Startup (which starts up using only the specific items you haven't excluded).

The Startup tab was a main feature of this utility, but the functionality was moved to Task Manager starting in Windows 10. If you click Startup, it will give you a link to open the Startup section of Task Manager to see a list of all of the programs that load at startup. The length of the list may surprise you. Exercise 12.5 walks you through how to use System Configuration.

EXERCISE 12.5

Using the System Configuration Utility in Windows 11

1. In the Windows search box, type **msconfig** and press Enter. The System Configuration window opens.
2. Click the Startup tab.
3. Click the link to open Task Manager. It will take you to the Startup apps section, as shown in Figure 12.14.

FIGURE 12.14 Task Manager Startup apps

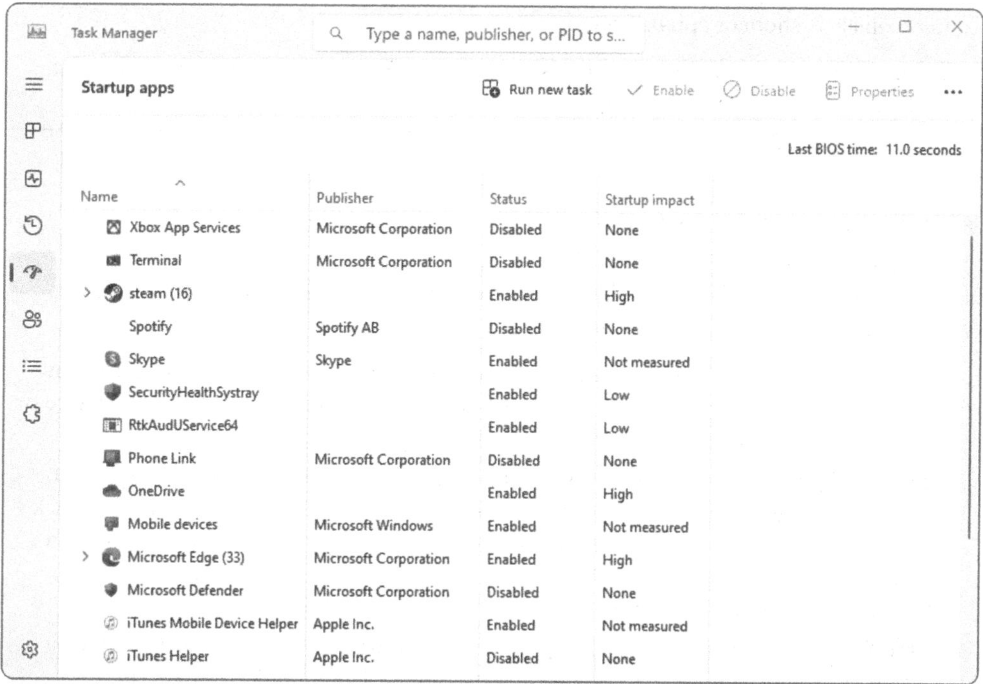

4. To prevent any of the apps from loading at startup, right-click the app and choose Disable.

You might want to go through the list of items on your Startup tab to see what's loading when you boot. There may be applications starting about which you are unaware and might not want on your computer. In addition, the more items you load on startup, the slower your operating system will boot. Some items are critical, but if they're not, you can speed up the boot process by disabling them from starting up automatically.

The System Configuration utility not only provides easy access to your startup options but also offers links to many of the most commonly used troubleshooting utilities in Windows, all on the Tools tab. Therefore, you may want to create a shortcut for it on your desktop. Exercise 12.6 shows you how to do this.

EXERCISE 12.6

Creating a Desktop Shortcut for MSCONFIG

1. Right-click the desktop and choose New ➢ Shortcut. The Create Shortcut dialog box opens.
2. In the Type The Location Of The Item text box, type **msconfig**. Click Next.
3. In the Type A Name For This Shortcut text box, type **System Configuration Utility**, replacing the default name that's there.
4. Click Finish. A shortcut appears on the desktop.
5. Double-click the shortcut to confirm that it opens the System Configuration utility. Then close the utility window.

Using the Recovery Environment

If Windows is being stubborn and won't boot, you might want to look to the *Windows Recovery Environment (WinRE)*, which gives you access to some troubleshooting and recovery commands. WinRE can be accessed five different ways:

- Through Windows Settings ➢ System ➢ Recovery ➢ Advanced Startup ➢ Restart Now (the same way you accessed Safe Mode). After the system restarts, click Use A Device or click Troubleshoot and then Reset This PC.
- From the login screen, hold down the Shift key and click Power ➢ Restart. (Again, the same way you got to Safe Mode.) After the system restarts, click Use A Device or click Troubleshoot and then Reset This PC. Note that this method also works from within Windows by pressing Ctrl+Alt+Del to open the Lock screen, and then holding down Shift and clicking Power ➢ Restart.
- In the Windows search bar, type **cmd**, and then click Run As Administrator in the list that appears under the Command Prompt app. At the Command Prompt, type `shutdown /r /o` and press Enter.

- Boot from a recovery or installation USB flash drive. (You may need to change the boot sequence in BIOS Setup so that it boots from the USB drive rather than the hard disk.)
- Hard reboot. *If* the computer won't boot, hold down the power button until it turns off. Then press the power button again to turn it on. This is called a *hard reboot* or *hard reset*. You might need to repeat this a few times, but if Windows is inoperable, you should get a screen that is titled Recovery. There, choose the option See Advanced Repair Options and it will take you into the Choose An Option screen.

Follow the prompts until you get to Advanced Options and then click Startup Repair. Follow the advice that Startup Repair gives to repair your Windows installation.

macOS Won't Load

Macs go through the same basic process for startup as PCs. If there's a disk error, such as the ones on the black screen that a PC's BIOS may display, you'll see a flashing question-mark icon.

The flashing question-mark icon means that the startup process can't find a hard disk or can't find a system folder on the hard disk. The hard disk may be disconnected, its driver may be bad, or its cable may be loose, or if it's an old enough system to have an optical media drive, there may be a disc in that drive that the OS is trying to boot from instead of the hard disk.

For macOS to load, the hard drive must have a `System` folder that contains such items as accessories, fonts, and system utilities, plus the System file and Finder. Without these, the computer won't boot. The question-mark icon appears if this folder is missing or corrupted or doesn't contain the needed files.

Any other OS problem in macOS results in a red circle with a diagonal line through it, called a *prohibition icon*. (Earlier versions of macOS used a "sad Mac" icon in these cases.) Along with this icon, you'll see an error code that you can look up online. Try a Google search or the Apple support website.

Operating System Error Messages

Each OS has its own error messages that it displays in various circumstances. In most cases, you can look up these error messages online at the OS maker's website or third-party sites to determine what they mean.

For example, to troubleshoot issues with macOS, see the article "Troubleshooting Mac Startup Issues" on Apple's support knowledge base: `https://it-training.apple.com/tutorials/support/sup080`.

Other OS manufacturers will have their own support sites as well, listing common error messages and fixes. Here are a few Windows error messages that you may encounter and what they mean:

Windows Has Recovered From A Serious Error This message means something major has crashed, and Windows has restarted itself as a result. If you see this error once, it's probably a fluke; if you see it frequently, you may need to repair Windows or take a critical look at what programs are loading at startup that may be causing the error.

The System Is Low On Virtual Memory. Windows Is Increasing The Size Of Your Virtual Memory Paging File. This message describes what is happening when your system has run out of memory. Do you have too many applications running for the amount of memory installed? As a result, Windows increases the paging file size so that it won't happen again (presumably). If the PC is running slowly, try rebooting.

Data Error Reading/Writing Drive This message means Windows is having trouble reading from or writing to whatever drive letter it lists in the error message. Run `CHKDSK` (it's called Error Checking when you right-click on the drive and then choose Properties, and go to the Tools tab and click Check) and click Scan Drive to start scanning the drive.

The Event Viewer utility in Windows can sometimes provide information about an error event that has occurred, helping you to narrow down what may have caused it. You can access the Event Viewer (Figure 12.15) from Control Panel in the Windows Tools section.

FIGURE 12.15 Event Viewer

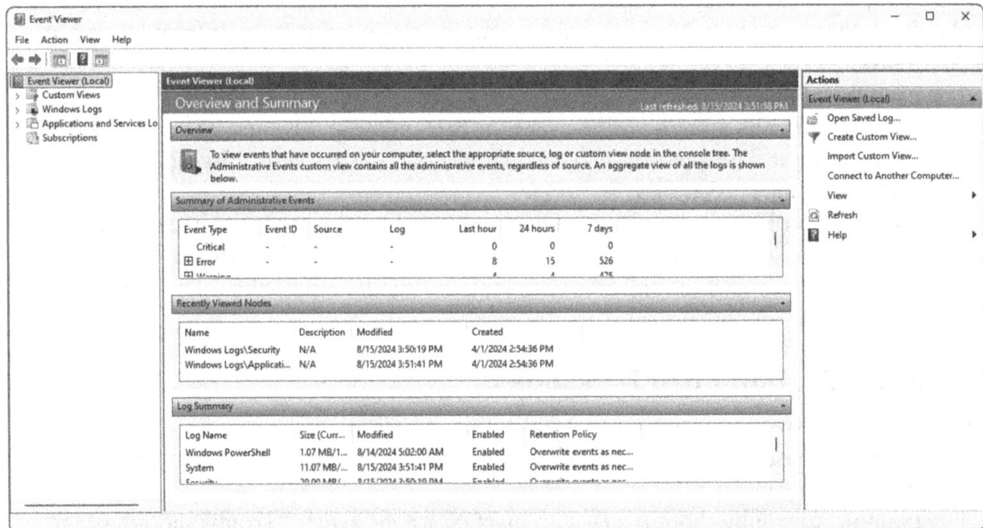

OS Slowdown or Lockup

Sometimes you may be working along in your OS when, all of a sudden, everything slows to a crawl. Simple things like opening an application and closing a window take much longer than usual. There are two basic reasons why slowdowns happen. One is that the physical memory is mostly used up, so the system is relying more on its paging file than usual. Because the paging file is on the hard disk and the hard disk is slower than real RAM, operations involving heavy use of the paging file take longer. The other reason is that the CPU is being heavily used, so each operation that needs the CPU's attention has to wait its turn.

That begs the question: What causes the RAM and/or the CPU to be used heavily? They can be legitimately used by applications if you run a lot of applications at once, especially those that require a lot of processing power. Big graphics-editing programs like Adobe Photoshop qualify, for example. The RAM and CPU can also be improperly hijacked by a malfunctioning program or by a virus or other malware application.

When you first start up the OS, it's normal for application-related activities to take longer than normal because the OS continues to finish loading behind the scenes for up to several minutes after the OS interface becomes usable. If you try to start up several applications immediately after starting the PC and they don't start up quickly enough to suit you, be patient. Within a few minutes, your computer should be running normally.

To check the memory and CPU usage in Windows, use the Task Manager. Right-click the Taskbar and choose Task Manager. Then, in the Processes section, sort by the Memory column and look for a process that is using an inordinate amount of memory. Terminate it if necessary to get back normal control of your computer. You can also look in the Performance section to see the CPU, Disk, and Network usage statistics.

If the OS locks up completely, usually including the mouse pointer, the most common cause is overheating. If the CPU or another chip on the motherboard overheats, the system locks up. The OS can lock up like that for reasons other than overheating, such as a corrupted system file (repair the OS to fix that), but that's less likely. By halting rather than continuing to operate in an overheated state, the motherboard preserves the valuable CPU chip, which may be damaged if it continued to run. The monitor may go blank, or it may keep displaying the last information it was sent, so the image on the screen appears frozen in time.

If your OS has locked up, shut off the PC if it didn't shut itself down. Open the case, and let the PC sit for 10 to 15 minutes so everything cools off. Then, with the case open, turn on the computer again and see whether any fans aren't spinning. The problem may be as simple as a faulty fan. There should be a fan inside the power supply, a fan on (or very near) the CPU, and possibly other fans that circulate air through the case. No faulty fans? Let the PC boot up the OS again, and let it sit. Don't run any applications. If it boots up just fine but then locks up after a few minutes without you doing anything to it, something is definitely overheating.

Application Failures

Applications are more likely to cause problems than OSs because there are so many different applications, all made by different manufacturers, and all are expected to play nicely with each other, with your hardware, and with different versions of the OS.

Application Fails to Install or Fails to Run

Usually, when an application fails to install or fails to run, it's because it's somehow incompatible with your system. It could be that your OS version isn't supported or the application doesn't like a piece of hardware you've installed (most likely the sound or display adapter). The hardware may be inadequate (check the minimum requirements for the application) or simply incompatible.

Check the application's specs to make sure that your system meets the minimum requirements in every way. If your system meets the requirements but the application still won't install, check out the Support section of the application manufacturer's website. There may be a patch you can download that will fix the problem, or there may be suggestions regarding workarounds. For example, in some cases, installing an updated driver for your display adapter or sound card can make an application work that previously didn't.

If the program meets all of the hardware requirements but not the OS requirements, you can try running the Setup program in *compatibility mode* (in Windows). Compatibility mode tricks the application into thinking you have a different version of the OS than you actually have, bypassing any version requirements that may be built into the software. It doesn't always work because different applications implement version requirements in various ways, and some of those ways have nothing to do with the version-specific bits and pieces that compatibility mode offers the application.

Another possible source of trouble when installing applications is overzealous security. The OS itself may prevent you from installing an application, for example. If you're logged in as a standard user, you may need to log out and then log in again as an administrator. If the application being installed requires Internet access to complete the installation, you may need to tell your firewall that it's okay to let that application through. Finally, the application may make a system change that your antivirus program or security suite detects as a threat (falsely), causing the security program to prevent the change from being made. Exercise 12.7 shows you how to run an application in compatibility mode in Windows 11.

EXERCISE 12.7

Running an Application in Compatibility Mode

Note that for this to work, you will need a shortcut for an app on your desktop. Create a shortcut for an app that is not preinstalled in Windows. Do this by right-clicking the desktop and choosing New ➢ Shortcut and specifying the location of an executable file.

1. Right-click a shortcut on the desktop and choose Properties.
2. Select the Compatibility tab.
3. Select the Run This Program In Compatibility Mode For check box.
4. Open the drop-down list below the check box, and examine the available OSs. Select an older version of Windows, such as Windows 98/Windows Me or Windows 7.

5. In the Settings area, select the Reduced Color Mode check box and choose 8-bit (256) color, as shown in Figure 12.16.

FIGURE 12.16 Configuring an application for compatibility mode

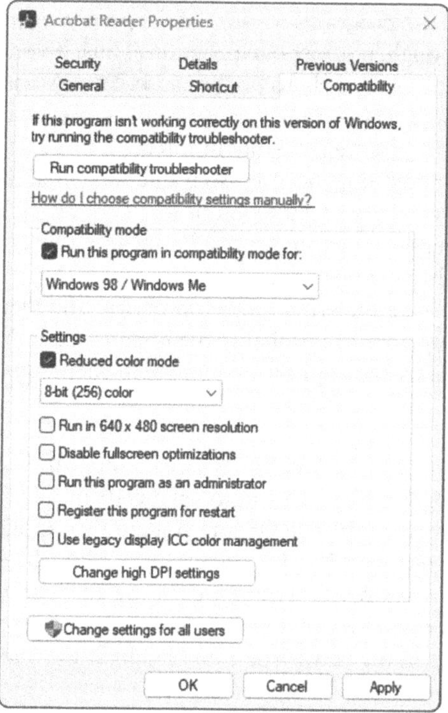

6. Click OK.
7. Double-click the program shortcut to run it. It may run, or it may not. It doesn't matter; you're just testing.
8. Close the application (if it ran).
9. Right-click the shortcut again and choose Properties again.
10. Click the Compatibility tab and deselect the Run This Program In Compatibility Mode For check box.
11. Deselect the Reduced Color Mode check box.
12. Click OK to close the Properties box.

A Previously Working Application Won't Work Anymore

If an application stops working that previously worked, something has changed on your system—obviously. But what was it? If any of the files belonging to the application have been deleted, you may need to reinstall the application. Or, you can try to repair it in Programs And Features in Windows Control Panel.

A virus infection can cause programs to run slowly, poorly, or not at all. Many viruses affect the entire system, though, not just one program. Thus, if you're having troubles with only one application, a virus isn't likely to be the cause. There's one exception to that: Viruses sometimes target antivirus software specifically, so if everything is working other than your antivirus software, you're probably infected.

Some programs have limited-time licenses, so it's possible that an application that previously worked may stop working because of a license expiration. In such cases, though, a helpful dialog box will usually appear to let you know how to pay the software maker, so there's not much doubt what's happening.

If you've recently installed an OS or application update and then suddenly an old familiar application won't work anymore, it's probably the update's fault. You can try removing the update (if possible) or contact the application manufacturer's support department for help.

Application Crashes

Crash is the term used to describe a situation when an application stops working. It may stop working due to a programming error in its own code or due to a conflict or compatibility issue with a device driver, with the OS, or with another application.

When an application stops working, it may terminate all by itself, or you may have to terminate it manually. To do so in Windows, right-click the Taskbar and choose Task Manager. Then, in the Task Manager window, on the Processes page, click the application. The task may have Not Responding in the Status column. Highlight the app, right-click, and click End Task.

In macOS, to force-quit an application, choose Force Quit from the Apple menu (or press Command+Option+Esc) and then select the unresponsive application in the Force Quit window and click Force Quit.

If an application crashes only once, it may be a fluke. However, if the same application keeps crashing repeatedly, it's time to do a little detective work to try to figure out what may be the problem. If an error message appears, make a note of it. Try closing all other applications, including any background applications you don't need, and running the application again to see if that helps. If it does, the problem stems from a conflict with some other program. You may need to uninstall and reinstall the crashing application or check the manufacturer's website for troubleshooting tips.

Device Failures

Any hardware component can fail, and the longer you keep your computer, the more likely it is that you'll experience at least one hardware failure. Usually, you'll know a device has failed simply because functionality you were expecting to work doesn't work.

Hardware/Driver Compatibility

Many times, device failure isn't a hardware issue but the result of a driver problem. As you learned in Chapter 5, a *driver* is a file (or set of files) that contains information needed for the OS to communicate with a hardware device. One way to think of a driver is as a language translator between the OS, which speaks one language, and the hardware, which speaks an entirely different one.

The skill of the interpreter makes all the difference in any communication, and a driver that can accurately translate between the OS and the hardware is essential for satisfactory hardware functionality. Therefore, it's important to pick the best driver available. If an unsatisfactory driver is installed (perhaps one that's not designed specifically for the OS or device being used or one that has been corrupted), the device may behave strangely or not work at all.

The best driver is one that is specifically for that device (most important), specifically for that OS (moderately important), and the most recent version available (least important).

When you install a hardware device, you have a choice of drivers, and your challenge is to figure out which of them fits the criteria the best. Your choices may include the following:

- The OS may supply a driver for the device and install it automatically.
- The device may come with a setup USB flash drive that contains an appropriate driver.
- A driver may be available on the device manufacturer's website that is even more current than the one that came with the device.

If the device has never worked, the driver is a good place to start. If it was working but just stopped, it's more than likely not a driver issue, unless the driver was somehow uninstalled.

Malfunctioning Input Devices

An input device, such as a keyboard or mouse, may malfunction for a variety of reasons. For example, the wrong driver may be installed for it (see the previous section), or it may be incompatible with your OS. For example, some mice and trackballs are specifically designed for Macintosh computers, and they won't work if you plug them into a Windows-based PC.

After you've eliminated incompatibility and bad drivers as the cause of an input device malfunction, next look at the device itself. Is there anything physically wrong with it? If it's an optical mouse, does the light turn on? (It could be a dead battery.) If it's a keyboard, will all the keys press? Is the cord or connector damaged? Has something spilled on the device? Has it been dropped or hit?

If there's nothing physically wrong with the device, try reseating it first, and then if it still doesn't work, plugging it into a different computer if possible. If it works there, then the problem is the relationship between the device and the original computer and not the device itself. Investigate things such as driver issues, incompatibility, and the connector on the PC into which the device connects. If it doesn't work on the other computer, the device is probably defective.

An input device that gradually stops working well over time or that malfunctions only in a specific way (such as a certain key not working on a keyboard or a mouse that moves in only one direction) may be dirty. Try cleaning the device.

Troubleshooting Network Connectivity

Hardware is often, but not always, to blame when a user can't log onto the local network or can't connect to the Internet. Here are some general troubleshooting tips:

1. If you can't browse network resources:
   a. Confirm that the computer's network adapter is installed and working. In Windows, look in Device Manager to make sure that it's there and doesn't report any errors.
   b. Confirm that a cable or wireless connection is established between the network adapter and the router, switch, or wireless access point. If it's a wired connection, trace the cable from the PC to the router or switch. If wireless, check to make sure that the OS recognizes the wireless connection.
   c. Make sure that the right networking protocols are in place (TCP/IP being the most common). Exercise 12.8 shows you how to do this in Windows and how to use TCP/IP to troubleshoot an Internet connection problem.
2. If your network login keeps getting rejected on a corporate network:
   a. Check that Caps Lock isn't on and that you're typing your username and password accurately.
   b. Check with your network administrator to make sure that there are no known problems with the network that may be preventing everyone from logging on (not just you).
   c. Check with the network administrator to ensure that the account has not been locked out, for example, due to a number of incorrect login attempts.
3. If the problem is lack of Internet connectivity:
   a. You may need to reset or power-cycle your connectivity device, such as the cable or DSL modem.
   b. Your Internet service provider (ISP) may be temporarily unavailable. Sometimes, there are brief outages with even the most reliable services. Wait it out for a few hours before contacting your ISP.
   c. The Internet itself may be experiencing temporary delays or outages. This is likely the case if you can get to some but not all websites or you can get email but not web access, or vice versa.

EXERCISE 12.8

Checking TCP/IP Connectivity

This exercise has you check IP connectivity. You will work "closest to furthest," testing connectivity and functionality of the local network adapter first, and then moving out toward the Internet.

1. In Windows, open a Command Prompt window. To do so, type **cmd** in the Windows search box and press Enter. You can also do this exercise on Linux or Mac systems by opening a Command Prompt.
2. At the Command Prompt, type **`ping 127.0.0.1`** and press Enter (as shown in Figure 12.17). 127.0.0.1 is the *loopback address*—that is, the IP address that refers to the machine that is issuing the command. If you get a reply from this command, you know your network adapter is working. This eliminates all problems within the PC from the troubleshooting process. You can also type **`ping localhost`** to get the same results.

FIGURE 12.17 Pinging the loopback address

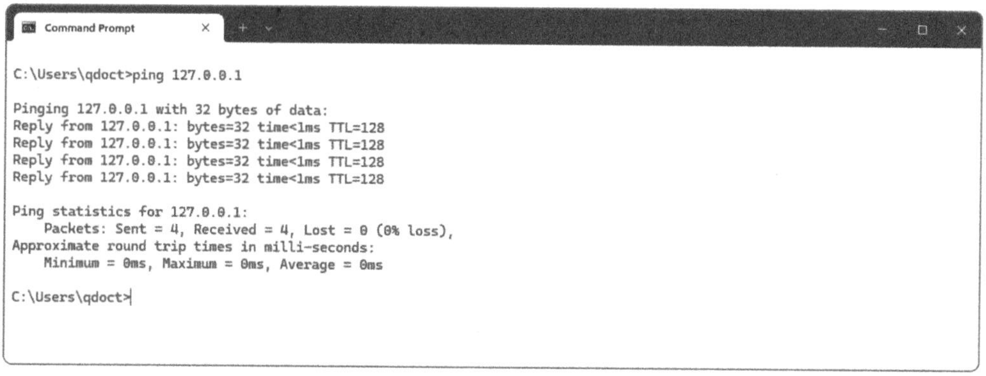

```
Command Prompt

C:\Users\qdoct>ping 127.0.0.1

Pinging 127.0.0.1 with 32 bytes of data:
Reply from 127.0.0.1: bytes=32 time<1ms TTL=128
Reply from 127.0.0.1: bytes=32 time<1ms TTL=128
Reply from 127.0.0.1: bytes=32 time<1ms TTL=128
Reply from 127.0.0.1: bytes=32 time<1ms TTL=128

Ping statistics for 127.0.0.1:
    Packets: Sent = 4, Received = 4, Lost = 0 (0% loss),
Approximate round trip times in milli-seconds:
    Minimum = 0ms, Maximum = 0ms, Average = 0ms

C:\Users\qdoct>
```

3. At the Command Prompt, type **`ipconfig`** and press Enter. The IP addresses for all the network adapters in your system appear. Some of them may show Media Disconnected, meaning that the adapter isn't in use. (macOS users should use **`ifconfig`** and Linux users **`ip`** instead.)
4. Find the network adapter you use to connect to the network and look at the IPv4 address for it. For example, in Figure 12.18, the Wireless Lan adapter Wi-Fi IP address is 192.168.1.81. IP addresses that begin with 192.168 are common on small home networks.

EXERCISE 12.8 *(continued)*

FIGURE 12.18 `ipconfig` results

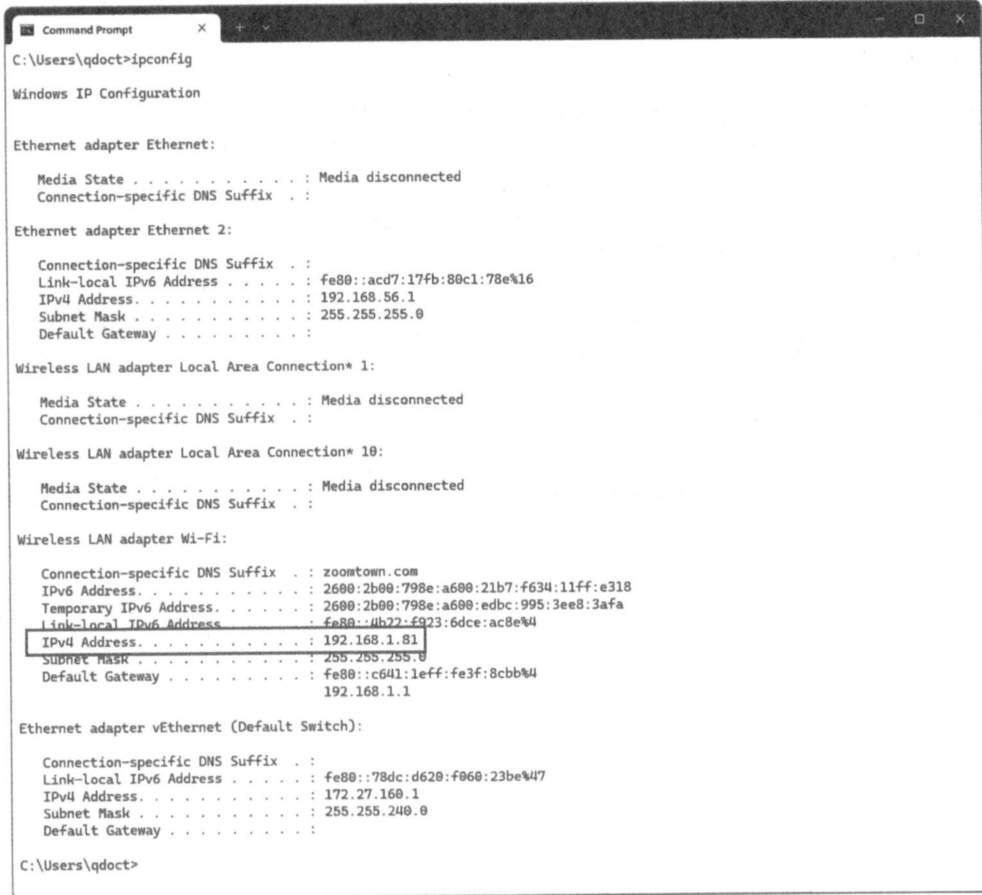

Command Prompt
C:\Users\qdoct>ipconfig
Windows IP Configuration
Ethernet adapter Ethernet:
Media State . . . . : Media disconnected
Connection-specific DNS Suffix . :
Ethernet adapter Ethernet 2:
Connection-specific DNS Suffix . :
Link-local IPv6 Address . . . . . : fe80::acd7:17fb:80c1:78e%16
IPv4 Address. . . . . : 192.168.56.1
Subnet Mask . . . . : 255.255.255.0
Default Gateway . . . . :
Wireless LAN adapter Local Area Connection* 1:
Media State . . . . : Media disconnected
Connection-specific DNS Suffix . :
Wireless LAN adapter Local Area Connection* 10:
Media State . . . . : Media disconnected
Connection-specific DNS Suffix . :
Wireless LAN adapter Wi-Fi:
Connection-specific DNS Suffix . : zoomtown.com
IPv6 Address. . . . . : 2600:2b00:798e:a600:21b7:f634:11ff:e318
Temporary IPv6 Address. . . . . . : 2600:2b00:798e:a600:edbc:995:3ee8:3afa
IPv4 Address. . . . . : 192.168.1.81
Default Gateway . . . . : fe80::c641:1eff:fe3f:8cbb%4
192.168.1.1
Ethernet adapter vEthernet (Default Switch):
Connection-specific DNS Suffix . :
Link-local IPv6 Address . . . . . : fe80::78dc:d620:f060:23be%47
IPv4 Address. . . . . : 172.27.160.1
Subnet Mask . . . . : 255.255.240.0
Default Gateway . . . . :
C:\Users\qdoct>

5. For that same network adapter, make a note of the default gateway. That's the address of the router that provides the exit point from the local network and connects you to the larger network (for example, the Internet). In the previous figure, it's 192.168.1.1.

6. Ping the default gateway to make sure it's reachable. To do this, type **`ping`**, a space, and then the address of the default gateway that you noted in step 5—for example, **`ping 192.168.1.1`**. If the default gateway is reachable, you should get back multiple Reply lines. If not, you'll get back multiple Timed Out lines.

7. Ping a website to see whether you have web connectivity. To do so, type **`ping`**, a space, and then either an IP address or a URL of a website. For example, type **`ping www.google.com`** and press Enter, as shown in Figure 12.19. If you don't get a reply from the first site you try, try some other addresses. Some websites block `ping` inquiries as a matter of company policy.

FIGURE 12.19 Successful `ping` results

```
C:\Users\qdoct>ping www.google.com

Pinging www.google.com [2607:f8b0:4002:c1b::67] with 32 bytes of data:
Reply from 2607:f8b0:4002:c1b::67: time=54ms
Reply from 2607:f8b0:4002:c1b::67: time=25ms
Reply from 2607:f8b0:4002:c1b::67: time=22ms
Reply from 2607:f8b0:4002:c1b::67: time=23ms

Ping statistics for 2607:f8b0:4002:c1b::67:
    Packets: Sent = 4, Received = 4, Lost = 0 (0% loss),
Approximate round trip times in milli-seconds:
    Minimum = 22ms, Maximum = 54ms, Average = 31ms

C:\Users\qdoct>
```

8. If you can't get through to a particular website, you can use another command, `tracert` (short for "trace route"), to see the hops the message takes from router to router across the Internet. This can help you see where the transmission is breaking down. Type **`tracert google.com`**, and press Enter. Information comes back about each of the routers the message passes through on the way, up to a maximum of 30 hops. Your results will look different than the one shown in Figure 12.20 because your computer will take a different path to Google's servers than mine did.

   In Figure 12.20, hops 15 through 20 timed out. This is because the owner of those routers has configured the router to not respond to `tracert` requests. The trace still completed though (hop 21), so you know the connection is good.

FIGURE 12.20 Successful `tracert` results

```
C:\Users\qdoct>tracert google.com

Tracing route to google.com [2607:f8b0:4002:c05::65]
over a maximum of 30 hops:

  1     1 ms     1 ms     1 ms  2600:2b00:798e:a600:c641:1eff:fe3f:8cbb
  2     5 ms     1 ms     3 ms  2607:f500:0:1::a02:279
  3     6 ms     5 ms     2 ms  2607:f500:0:1::8e
  4     3 ms     2 ms     5 ms  2607:f500:0:1::8d
  5    16 ms    17 ms    15 ms  et330.ash1.core.fuse.net [2607:f500:0:1::d844:e95]
  6    17 ms    18 ms    18 ms  2001:4860:1:1::41e
  7    17 ms    18 ms    15 ms  2607:f8b0:82de::1
  8    16 ms    16 ms    15 ms  2001:4860:0:1::53bc
  9    17 ms    18 ms    15 ms  2001:4860:0:eaf::2
 10    23 ms    27 ms    50 ms  2001:4860::c:4002:3325
 11    26 ms    25 ms    25 ms  2001:4860::c:4002:a29a
 12    26 ms    26 ms    23 ms  2001:4860::c:4002:cd33
 13    26 ms    24 ms    25 ms  2001:4860::c:4002:8e71
 14    25 ms    24 ms    25 ms  2001:4860::cc:4002:d6
 15     *        *        *     Request timed out.
 16     *        *        *     Request timed out.
 17     *        *        *     Request timed out.
 18     *        *        *     Request timed out.
 19     *        *        *     Request timed out.
 20     *        *        *     Request timed out.
 21    24 ms    26 ms    24 ms  yw-in-f101.1e100.net [2607:f8b0:4002:c05::65]

Trace complete.

C:\Users\qdoct>
```

9. Close the Command Prompt window by typing **`exit`** and pressing Enter.

Summary

In this chapter, you learned about data continuity and computer support concepts. First, you learned about data continuity, which means keeping data and systems as reliable as possible but also preparing for inevitable failures.

The first data continuity topic was fault tolerance. Make sure that your organization has a contingency plan to deal with potential issues. Then, implement replication, redundancy, or backups to protect systems and critical data. Redundant systems can be used for data, network, and power. Backups are critically important yet often overlooked. Of course, the problem is that users don't always realize how important backups are until it's too late and they have lost data. Backups often work by utilizing the archive bit on a file. When you set up a backup, you need to choose the type of backup, the location (such as local storage, a network server, or the Internet/cloud), and the frequency and schedule. Finally, always verify your backups by testing them, so you don't get a bad surprise when trying to restore them.

When disasters do strike, be prepared with a disaster recovery plan (part of contingency planning) that identifies priorities for restoring access and data.

Next, you learned about the troubleshooting methodology. Troubleshooting can be a combination of art and science, but if you follow some basic concepts, you can be an effective troubleshooter even without much experience.

In the troubleshooting methodology, the first step is to identify the problem. This includes talking to the customer, gathering information, and isolating the issue. After that, establish a theory of probable cause (question the obvious). Research knowledge bases or the Internet if needed. Sometimes the theory is easy to identify. Other times, you need to eliminate possibilities to narrow down the problem. Once you have established a theory about what caused the problem, test the theory to determine the cause. Start with the simple stuff first, such as loose cables or connections, loss of power, or physical damage. It could also be user error or simply require a reboot.

Establish a plan of action to resolve the problem—you might need to fix one computer or one hundred computers with this issue—and implement the solution. If you've implemented the solution, verify full system functionality, implement preventive measures if needed, and finally, document the findings/lessons learned, actions, and outcomes of your work.

Finally, you reviewed some common troubleshooting examples. Groupings of problems you read about included the computer not starting, operating system errors and slowdowns, application failures, and device failures.

Exam Essentials

When given a scenario, know the right steps to take to identify and solve a problem. The steps include identifying the problem, establishing a theory of probable cause, testing the theory to determine cause, establishing a plan of action and implementing the solution, verifying functionality, and, if applicable, implementing preventive measures, and finally documenting the findings/lessons learned, actions, and outcomes.

When given a scenario, know some of the basic external issues to check. Always check the easy stuff first, such as loose cables or connections, if the system has power, and if there is physical damage.

Know the external resources you can use to help troubleshoot a problem. The manufacturer's documentation and website should always be at the top of your list. In addition, you might find help from online technical community groups, Internet searches (ask Google!), or technical support.

Understand the difference between a file backup and a system backup. File backups back up user data as a set or as individual files. A system backup will often back up user data, but backs up core operating system files as well.

Know the common locations to store backup files. Common locations are local storage (flash drives, external hard drives, or SD cards), network locations, or off-site or in the cloud.

After backing up, know the next step to take. Don't consider a backup complete until it has been tested and verified that it will work if it's needed.

Understand the importance of data backups and how it relates to scheduling and frequency. The more important data is, the more important backups are. The more frequently the data changes, the more frequently it should be backed up. Scheduling backups is a good idea to keep people from forgetting to do them.

Chapter 12 Lab

You can find the answers in Appendix A.

Chapter 12 covered troubleshooting concepts and computer backups. It's challenging to write a lab about troubleshooting—breaking your computer (or a friend's computer) just for the sake of fixing it can be risky. Instead, this lab will focus on establishing and enacting a good backup plan.

Step 1: Determine the scope of your backup plan. Are you backing up just one computer? Or do you have a small group of computers to back up? The answers here will determine many of the answers for future steps.

Step 2: Understand the importance of the data. Does anyone care if the data is lost? Or, on the other end of the spectrum, would a business fail or your life be ruined if you were to lose the data?

Step 3: Understand how much data there is to back up and how often the files change. Perhaps there are terabytes of data on the system or systems you need to back up, but only a few hundred megabytes of data change frequently. Or maybe if it's your local computer, there are only a few hundred megabytes with which you are concerned.

Step 4: Where do you want to store the backup files? In general, your choices are on local media (such as external hard drive or optical disc), on a network server, or in the cloud. The answer will likely depend on how important the data is, how often it changes, and how much there is.

Step 5: Decide on backup software. If it's just your computer, perhaps the OS backup program is fine. Or you can purchase an external hard drive backup system and use its software. Third-party backup solutions are needed for bigger jobs, or you might find a viable cloud solution online.

Step 6: Configure the backup and run it. Simple enough, right? Run the backup based on the solution you chose in step 5. Also note that if the backup is difficult to configure or run, you might want to reevaluate your choice of backup software.

Step 7: Test and verify the backup. Don't forget this step! Restore some files from your backup just to make sure that it's working properly.

Step 8: Schedule recurring backups. How often depends on your needs. If the data is critical and changes daily, then daily backups may be in order. Once a week tends to be a common schedule, as does once per month for less critical data.

Step 9: Document the backup process and schedule. If you're just backing up your own computer, this step probably isn't needed. If it's multiple systems, though, and if multiple people are involved, documentation is critical. Write down the software, the settings, and the overall plan so others know what is happening and when. If other administrators are involved, you will also need to share critical security information such as backup passwords so that they can perform backup and restoration tasks as needed.

Review Questions

You can find the answers in Appendix B.

1. When troubleshooting a computer problem, which of the following are steps you can take to identify the problem? (Choose two.)
   - **A.** Use external resources such as the Internet.
   - **B.** Talk to end users.
   - **C.** Isolate the issue.
   - **D.** Attribute it to user error.
2. You are troubleshooting a MacBook Pro. When it turns on, you receive a screen with a flashing question mark. What is the likely cause?
   - **A.** Device driver failure
   - **B.** Video card failure
   - **C.** Memory failure
   - **D.** Hard drive failure
3. When providing computer support and testing solutions, what should you always do first?
   - **A.** Assume user error.
   - **B.** Test the simple stuff.
   - **C.** Check Internet resources for solutions.
   - **D.** Establish a plan of action.
4. Your computer has been running backups for a year. Today, you make a change from backing it up to an external hard drive to backing it up to the cloud. What should you do next?
   - **A.** Secure the cloud backup location.
   - **B.** Schedule regular cloud backups.
   - **C.** Destroy the old hard drive.
   - **D.** Verify that the cloud backup works.
5. You are troubleshooting a computer problem. After testing the theory to determine the cause, what should you do next?
   - **A.** Establish a plan of action to resolve the problem and implement the solution.
   - **B.** Verify functionality.
   - **C.** Document the work.
   - **D.** Identify the problem.

6. After installing several new software applications, your friend notices that their computer boots very slowly. Which tool can they use to disable programs from running at startup on Windows?
   - A. Recovery Console
   - B. System Configuration
   - C. System Restore
   - D. Safe Mode
7. Raul has just installed an older application on his Windows 8 computer and it will not run. He asks you for advice. What should you tell him to try to make it run?
   - A. Delete and reinstall.
   - B. Run it as an administrator.
   - C. Use Safe Mode.
   - D. Use compatibility mode.
8. You are troubleshooting a Windows PC that will not load the operating system. You insert the Windows USB flash drive and reboot. Which utility can you use to repair Windows?
   - A. Recovery Environment
   - B. MSCONFIG
   - C. System Restore
   - D. Safe Mode
9. What is the last step in the process of troubleshooting a computer?
   - A. Verify Internet functionality.
   - B. Document the findings.
   - C. Clean up the mess.
   - D. Retest the solution.
10. You have been asked to design a backup solution for your manager's workstation. Which option will be the fastest?
    - A. Cloud storage.
    - B. Network storage.
    - C. Local storage.
    - D. They are all the same speed.
11. What type of computer backup will back up all selected files and then clear the archive bit?
    - A. Normal
    - B. Differential
    - C. Incremental
    - D. Copy

12. You have just installed a new printer on your computer, and while it seems to be recognized by the operating system, it will not print. What is the first source to check for information on the problem?

    A. The OS manufacturer's website

    B. The printer manufacturer's website

    C. Google search

    D. Internet technical community groups

13. You need to run an emergency backup of your computer, and you need it to finish as fast as possible. You just backed up about three weeks ago. Which backup option should you use?

    A. Normal

    B. Differential

    C. Incremental

    D. Copy

14. While troubleshooting a Windows computer that may have a bad memory module, the computer freezes and displays a blue screen with white text and a STOP error. What generated that error message?

    A. The memory module

    B. Windows

    C. BIOS

    D. MSCONFIG

15. Ron's computer behaves normally for a time, and then his screen completely freezes up. The mouse and keyboard do not respond. What is the most likely cause of his problem?

    A. Faulty video driver

    B. Faulty mouse or keyboard driver

    C. Failing hard drive

    D. Overheating

16. You are troubleshooting a PC and see a gray text-based message about the boot disk on a black screen. What is the most likely source of this error message?

    A. Windows

    B. CHKDSK

    C. BIOS

    D. POST card

17. You are helping a neighbor buy a computer, and based on a recent experience, they insist that their system needs to remain working even if a hard drive fails. What should you suggest they buy?

    A. SATA

    B. PATA

    C. RAID 0

    D. RAID 1

18. You are asked to troubleshoot a computer, and your friend recommends you take a POST card with you. What can the POST card help you diagnose?
    - A. Application problems
    - B. Overheating problems
    - C. Startup problems resulting in a BIOS error message
    - D. Startup problems where nothing is displayed on the screen
19. What type of backup will make a copy of all files on the computer, including user files and operating system files, to use in the event of a complete failure?
    - A. System image
    - B. Full backup
    - C. Incremental backup
    - D. Complete backup
20. You're asked to troubleshoot a PC that's not working properly. You push the power button but don't see anything on the screen or hear any fans spinning. What is the most likely reason?
    - A. Defective monitor
    - B. Defective power supply
    - C. Broken fan
    - D. Defective network adapter driver

Appendix A Answers to Written Labs

Chapter 1 Lab Answers

For this lab, there are not necessarily any right answers. The goal was to get you to compare specifications and get more familiar with the language used to describe PCs. As I mentioned, all three of these desktop PCs were the same price on a major electronics retailer's website. It's almost shocking how much specifications can differ from computer to computer, even at the same price point. It's always best to shop around; sometimes you will find a computer on sale that has far better gear than others in its price range. Here are my thoughts on answers to this lab:

Based on the system specifications, which one would you recommend and why? System J is probably the best fit, although you probably can't go wrong with any of them. The large hard drive in System J will give it the edge if the user needs a lot of storage space for photos and videos, and it also has the largest screen. If it's a toss-up, it might come down to product reviews, which brand you like better, or even which case you think looks better.

What specifications made you not choose the others? System L has the smallest screen size and only one USB port, which can limit expandability. System S has a very small hard drive for someone with a lot of photos and the least amount of RAM.

If you were looking for a computer for someone who played a lot of online action games, would you change your recommendation? Why? System J, as configured, is probably the best for a gamer. More RAM is a plus, as is dedicated video memory and a larger screen. Really, though, if they want a gaming laptop they need to increase their budget!

If this laptop were for a relative who traveled a lot, would you change your recommendation and why? For a frequent traveler, System L is probably the best choice. It's the lightest—one pound can make a huge difference—and also has the longest battery life. This can be a big deal if power outlets are in short supply.

Chapter 2 Lab Answers

This lab could have several different answers. Here I'll provide some principles that I would use to think about the situation.

First, consider Elise's goals. She wants more storage, so that takes you toward external hard drives. She wants it to be easily accessible for multiple people. That steers you toward NAS, which basically means multiple hard drives. She also would like some sort of fault tolerance, which, fortunately, many NAS devices can provide.

Second, let's think about technology. Elise has a Mac, so you are probably safe going with Thunderbolt. If she gets a new Mac or James upgrades to a new Mac, you know that those computers will have Thunderbolt support. That's good because then they won't have wasted money on peripheral devices that they can no longer use.

Third, look at potential expansion. If Elise gets the right NAS device, additional users will be able to use it without a problem.

So, you should go looking for a NAS device that supports Thunderbolt. In addition, you should probably start with a NAS with SSDs because they are so much faster than HDDs. They are more expensive, so you might want to consider HDD options as well. Just be sure to let Elise know that they will be a lot slower on data transfers, which she will be doing a lot of. If NAS is out of her range, she can consider simply purchasing additional external hard drives.

One last option to consider (and to be fair, I didn't cover it in this chapter) is cloud-based storage. I'll cover some cloud concepts in Chapter 9, "Cloud Computing and Artificial Intelligence." The upside to cloud is that it's easily accessible from anywhere with an Internet connection and relatively cheap. The downside is that file transfers, especially uploads, can be slow. Price it out for Elise and give her some options! If this was your business, what solution would you choose?

Chapter 3 Lab Answers

1. From left to right, the three buttons are Back, Home, and Recents (or Recent Apps). They take you one screen back, open the home screen, or pull up the recent apps you've used.
2. Use the Google search bar on the home screen.
3. The apps appear as icons on the home screen.
4. Open Settings in System Apps and scroll down to Accessibility.
5. Use the Airplane mode icon in the right sidebar.
6. There are two ways. One is the icon in the right sidebar just below airplane mode. The other is to open Settings (the gear in the lower-right corner) and go to Display.
7. Ideally, installing the app was easy! It should create an icon for you on the home screen, and you can tap the app to open it. To delete it, double-tap and choose Remove. This will not uninstall the app but just remove the shortcut from the home page.

Chapter 4 Lab Answers

Using Lubuntu will probably feel quite a bit like using Windows. The interfaces have quite a few similarities in terms of navigation. Here are some hints on where you can find the utilities you need to complete the exercises you did in this chapter.

Exercise 4.1: Creating a User Account You can do this by clicking the launcher (it looks like a button with a bird on it, about where you would expect the Start button to be in

Windows) and then going to Preferences ➤ LZQt Settings ➤ Users And Groups. Click the Add button to create a new user.

Exercise 4.4: Managing Storage Space Open the launcher and go to Preferences ➤ Disk Utility. Or click the Computer icon, find the hard drive, right-click, and choose Properties. This one won't work exactly like the one in Windows since it's on a virtual hard drive.

Exercise 4.5: File Attributes Open the launcher, and go to Accessories ➤ File Manager. Once that opens, you can right-click files to look at their attributes. There will be limited options available in the GUI and many operations such as making a file read-only are done through a command prompt.

Exercise 4.6: Manipulating Files Open the launcher, and go to Accessories ➤ File Manager. Once that opens, you can right-click files to perform your tasks or choose File Manager using the icon to the right of the launcher.

Exercise 4.7: Creating a Shortcut Shortcuts can be created by dragging an icon from the launcher menu or File Manager to the desktop.

Extra question: Changing the Desktop The wallpaper and other aesthetics can be changed by going to the launcher and then Preferences ➤ LZQt Settings ➤ Desktop.

Chapter 5 Lab Answers

Answers will vary depending on the user.

For the LibreOffice lab, the versions should work similarly to their Microsoft counterparts. If you open basic text or worksheet files, you should be fine as well. Opening more intricately formatted documents or worksheets with fancy graphics could pose some issues.

The security portion of the lab will have different answers as well. The key is to raise awareness of key security concepts so that readers are familiar with the best ways to protect their computers versus malicious software.

Chapter 6 Lab Answers

These answers to the Chapter 6 lab pertain to `www.youtube.com` as of April 2024. It's entirely possible the website has changed between then and when you're doing this exercise!

1. The website is written in HTML. You can see the first line of the page starts with the tag `<!DOCTYPE html>`.
2. The developers used some braces to indicate code blocks. They also indented lines of code in a several places as well. There is some pseudocode too. HTML uses `<!-- tag -->` to indicate comments. If you didn't see any, search for `<!--`.

3. There are several `if` statements in the code, but as of this writing there were no `while` statements.
4. As of this writing, the page did have several functions. To find them, search for `function(`.
5. JavaScript was used (search for `javascript`).
6. This will depend on the string you chose. But if you see something that is represented as text on the source code, you should be able to locate the corresponding source code on the web page.
7. Search for `color`. There should be several instances where colors were set. Bonus points—look up what those colors are!

Chapter 7 Lab Answers

1. The sales coordinator for Northwind Traders is Laura Giussani. (You can find her in the Employee List form or the Employees table.)
2. Woodgrove Bank has placed three orders, one for $479.95, one for $481.75, and one for $1012.65. (Look on the Order Details form and filter by customer. Bonus points if you created a query!)
3. Northwind sold 9 units of coffee. It's on the product list, or you can use the Sales Reports Dialog form under Reports to generate this report.
4. Northwind's top-three sellers were coffee, clam chowder, and brownie mix.
5. Order 48 was done by Robert Zare with Proseware, Inc.

Chapter 8 Lab Answers

There are no right answers to Part 1 of the lab; the intent is to give you experience properly setting up a wireless router.

For Part 2, answers may vary. Note that if you were to get onto another unsecured network, you would be able to open up the Network And Sharing Center in Control Panel and see other devices on the network. This means that if you were on your neighbor's network, you could probably see the other computers on their network. As a big warning, I do not recommend doing this, because in many places it is illegal to snoop on someone else's network. Just know that if you do not secure your network, unsavory people could get on your network and see your computers and very possibly your files as well. Secure your network!

Chapter 9 Lab Answers

1. There are a few ways to turn on the virtual machine.
   a. In the Virtual Machines pane, right-click the virtual machine and choose Start.
   b. Highlight the New Virtual Machine and in the Action menu, click Start.
2. By default, there is 4,096 MB of memory allocated to the virtual machine. (Right-click the virtual machine, then choose Settings.)
3. Right-click the virtual machine and choose Connect. (Or highlight it and choose Action ➢ Connect.)
4. Connecting to the virtual machine will fail. You will likely get an error message such as a boot failure, shown in the graphic.

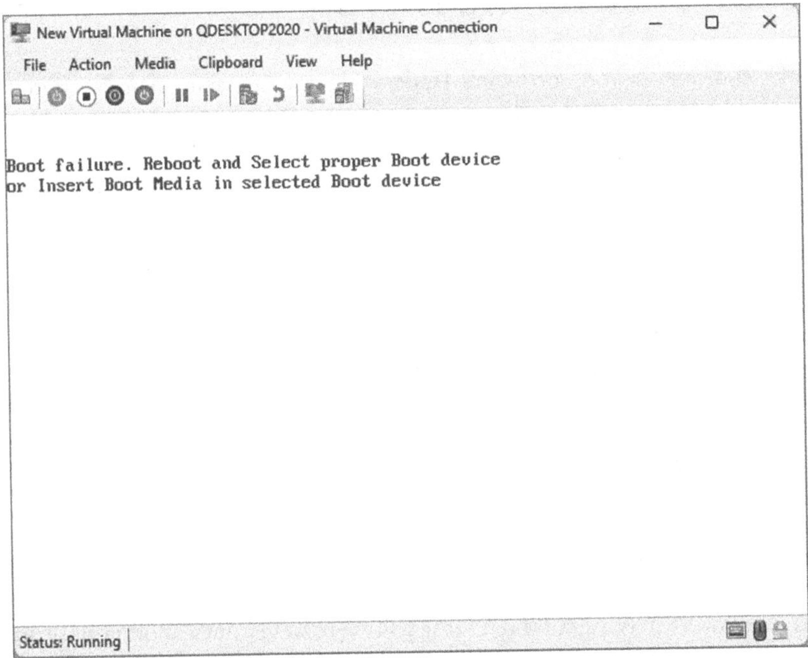

The boot failure happened because there is no guest operating system installed in the virtual machine.

Chapter 10 Lab Answers

As with many labs, answers can vary. The goal of this lab is to familiarize you with the different types of threats out there and the damage they can do. Education is the best way to help prevent attacks or at least mitigate the damage they can do. Ideally, this lab exposed you (safely!) to some common threats so that you have a better idea of what to watch out for.

1. The number will vary based on the date you pick. Take a look at `www.broadcom.com/support/security-center/protection-bulletin` and odds are there will be multiple entries for any date.
2. It depends on the day you pick, but most security sites will give you a security indicator from low risk to high risk.
3. A Google search will turn up several sites with "worst virus" rankings. According to `www.hp.com/us-en/shop/tech-takes/top-ten-worst-computer-viruses-in-history`, MyDoom was the worst of the bunch, causing $38 billion in damage. Other sites claim it affected 2 million PCs in about 2 hours. And, even though it hit in 2004, it's still around today. That's pretty impressive and scary.
4. An example of a polymorphic virus is the Virus.Win32 series, including Virus.Win32.Virut and Virus.Win32.Virut.ce. Phoenix, Evil, and Proud are the names of some other polymorphs. Michelangelo, Stone, and Disk Killer are some of the more infamous boot viruses. Multipartite viruses include Invader, Flip, and Tequila.
5. CryptoLocker is probably the most infamous, but WannaCry and LockBit are two other big examples.
6. Back Orifice is relatively well known and is really the first widely-used backdoor. ShadowPad is more recent, as are the worms Sobig and MyDoom, which contained backdoor components.
7. There are many commercial password crackers, including John the Ripper, Ophcrack, Brutus, and RainbowCrack.

Chapter 11 Lab Answers

The Chapter 11 lab provided you with a checklist of things that you can do to improve your security. It's recommended that you go through each of the tasks and understand how to perform them on your system. There are no specific answers for this lab.

Chapter 12 Lab Answers

There are no right or wrong answers to the Chapter 12 lab. The answers will vary based on the computer or computers you need to back up. Here's a table that will help you collect your answers:

Chapter 12 Lab: Information gathered

Step	Information/Notes
Scope of backup plan	
Importance of data	
How much data	
How often data changes	
Where to store	
Backup software to use	
Configuring the backup	
Test and verify	
Backup schedule	
Documentation and notes for others	

Answers to Review Questions

Chapter 1: Core Hardware Components

1. A, B, E. RAM is memory, which is a temporary data storage area. SSD is a type of hard drive, and BD-ROM discs store data as well. PCI is an expansion slot type, and PSU is a power supply unit.

2. B. A network interface card (NIC) lets your computer participate on a network, either wired or wireless. Modems require telephone lines. PSU is a power supply unit, and PCIe is an expansion slot type.

3. C. PCIe is the fastest expansion slot standard on the market today. PCI is much older and slower. Of the PCIe slots, PCIe x16 is the fastest. There is no PCIe x64 (not yet anyway).

4. D. Blu-ray discs (BD-ROM) store 25 GB per side per layer. That's far more than DVDs or CDs.

5. B. RAM provides the fastest access to data. It is volatile (not persistent), meaning that when it loses power, all data in RAM is lost. SSDs and HDDs are persistent but slower than RAM. A database would need to be stored on a hard drive.

   The chipset on the motherboard controls communications between the processor (CPU) and memory (RAM). The motherboard itself just provides connectivity.

6. A. Joe needs to make sure his power supply has a free connector, as well as enough power to supply the drive. Hard drives do not use expansion slots. The CPU and RAM are indifferent to how many hard drives a computer has installed.

7. B. For gamers, the graphics processing unit (GPU) on the video card is a critical component. If there is a dedicated video card, the CPU will not be involved in processing video output. The power supply unit (PSU) won't be relevant unless it can't support the upgraded video card. NVMe is an SSD storage technology.

8. C. A solid-state drive (SSD) will provide faster bootup times than a conventional hard disk drive (HDD). Neither RAM nor CPUs provide storage space.

9. D. Virtual memory is hard drive space used as extra memory if your system runs low on physical memory. It's slower than physical memory, though.

10. C. From largest to smallest is petabyte (PB), terabyte (TB), gigabyte (GB), megabyte (MB), kilobyte (KB), byte, and bit. In this example, the largest option in the correct answer is terabyte (TB).

11. A. The BIOS stores configuration information such as time and date, but it is powered by the CMOS battery when the system is off. If the CMOS battery fails, the system will no longer retain its BIOS configuration.

12. B. Monika will definitely need SODIMMs, which are made for laptops. DIMMs are for desktop computers. SODIMMS come in DDR4 and DDR5, so without more information you don't know which one she needs.

13. D. The power supply is connected to the motherboard with a 24-pin block connector.

14. A, D. The three types of internal storage connectors are PATA (or IDE), SATA, and M.2. (Hard drives may also come in a PCIe package.) HHD and SSD are types of hard drives, and NVMe is an SSD data transfer technology.

15. D. Small devices, such as smartphones and tablets, are most likely using ARM processors. They could be 32-bit or 64-bit. A GPU is for video processing, and Intel does not currently produce ARM chips.

16. C. If you want to upgrade a BIOS, the best way to do so is to flash it.

17. B. The processor, or CPU, produces the most heat of any internal component. Care must be taken to ensure that the heat is properly dissipated or the processor will fail.

18. A, B. Solid-state drives (SSDs) and hard drives (HDDs) are nonvolatile storage choices for user data. RAM is a volatile storage medium. ROM is nonvolatile storage—it does not hold user data, but holds preset routines such as the BIOS.

19. A, B, C. Solid-state drives (SSDs) are faster, generate less heat, and quieter than conventional HDDs. They are not cheaper per megabyte than HDDs, though.

20. A, B. Network interface cards (NICs) and modems are devices that allow your computer to communicate with other computers and therefore are communications devices.

Chapter 2: Peripherals and Connectors

1. C. Thunderbolt was developed by Apple in partnership with Intel. eSATA and USB are industry standards but not developed by Apple. There is no Mac Video port.

2. C, D. Keyboards can be plugged into either USB or PS/2 ports. Parallel ports were used for printers, and serial ports were used for modems and older mice.

3. B. Twisted-pair network cables are terminated with RJ45 connectors. RJ11 is at the end of telephone lines. HDMI is a video connector. There is no TPI connector.

4. A. HDMI is the best video connection standard available today. DVI and VGA video are older standards. HEMI is not a video connector.

5. D. Thunderbolt is the only connector that currently provides support for two 4k displays. USB provides support for one. DVI is a video standard but does not support 4k. RJ45 is a networking connector.

6. D. Laser printers use toner, which is an ink-like plastic powder. The toner is held to the paper via weak electrical charges and then melted onto the paper via the printer's fuser.

7. B. A touchpad is a pointing device similar to a mouse. It's located on most laptop keyboards just below the keys.

8. A, D. Near-field communication (NFC) and Bluetooth are wireless networking technologies. DVI is a video connection, and RJ45 is a wired Ethernet connector.

9. B. With plug-and-play, you plug the device in, the operating system installs the driver, and the device should work properly. There should be no need for additional steps.

10. A. The device you are looking for is network attached storage (NAS). External hard drives will give you extra storage, but they do not have built-in fault tolerance.

11. C. SuperSpeed is a trade name for USB 3.x, so your friend is talking about USB devices. SSDs are solid-state hard drives (SSDs), and OLEDs are displays. eSATA is an outdated external standard used mostly for hard drives.

12. B. Color inkjet printers use cyan, magenta, yellow, and black ink. Those cartridges are called CMYK.

13. D. A webcam allows you to record or transmit video, which is needed for a video teleconference.

14. A. An uninterruptible power supply (UPS) can provide power in the event of a power failure. A PSU is a power supply unit. USB is a connector type, and RF is radio frequency, a wireless network type.

15. C. VGA is the oldest video standard currently used today. It is analog only. DVI can produce analog or digital output, and HDMI and Thunderbolt are both digital.

16. A. From fastest to slowest are terabits per second (Tbps), gigabits per second (Gbps), megabits per second (Mbps), kilobits per second (Kbps), and bits per second (bps).

17. B. A crimper is used to attach RJ45 connectors to twisted-pair cabling, and a cable tester can test to see if it works. Splicing is connecting two cables to each other. A multimeter is an electrical testing tool but not used to create cables.

18. C. DVI connectors are digital in nature, but they are backward-compatible with analog VGA devices.

19. B. Printer properties is where sharing is enabled. Printing preferences are tailored to each printer and can set things like the quality of output and color versus black and white. The print queue is where print jobs are located. There is no IP printing configuration utility in Windows.

20. D. Although the answer of "stop typing" might be tempting, it's probably not the best answer if Robert wants to get work done. Disabling the touchpad will keep this problem from happening.

Chapter 3: Computing Devices and the Internet of Things

1. A. To scroll down, you need to "pull" the page up, so swipe up. Swiping down will move the page down. Pinching fingers together will zoom out, and a reverse pinch will zoom in.

2. B, D. Gaming consoles are used to play video games, watch Blu-ray or DVD movies, and sometimes connect to the Internet. A laptop or a workstation is better suited to edit Word documents or create spreadsheets.

3. D. To zoom in on a map, you use reverse pinch. Pinching zooms out. Tap or double-tap will open items.

4. C. A server is used to provide services to others on a network. In this case, it sounds like a file server is what's needed.

5. D. The gyroscope detects rotational movement within a mobile device.

6. A. Thermostats are used to control temperature.

7. B. Not all apps support rotation, and Settings is one of them. The app needs to be specifically programmed to support rotation.

8. C. To have two Bluetooth devices communicate with each other, they need to be paired.

9. C. With biometrics enabled, she can use either the passcode or her fingerprint to access a locked device. Devices often have facial recognition but not an iris scan.

10. D. A display is needed to project the AR image onto. VR requires headsets, but not AR. Earbuds and/or headphones may help enhance the AR experience but are not required.

11. B. The Wi-Fi settings are in the Settings app in Android as well as in iOS.

12. A. Smartphones are likely to be the smallest devices, and therefore will have the least amount of storage space.

13. D. The proper steps in order are to verify wireless capabilities, turn on Wi-Fi, locate SSID, enter the wireless password, and verify the Internet connection.

14. B, C. For syncing and backing up iPhones (and iPads), you can use iCloud to back up to the Internet or use iTunes to back up to a local computer.

15. A. A pacemaker is a medical device that helps patients maintain a regular heartbeat.

16. C. Airplane mode turns off the cellular connection on an iPhone. On an Android, it turns off Bluetooth as well. (In older versions of iOS and Android, Airplane mode turned off all wireless connections.)

17. B. Video is a key component of security, and IP cameras allow you to capture video as part of a security system.

18. D. The Google Play Store has apps for Android devices. iTunes is for iOS devices only. Google Drive is the name of Google's cloud-based storage.

19. C. An Xbox Series X is a gaming console, along with PlayStation and the Switch.

20. A. For games and other apps for an iPad, she should use the iTunes store. It's accessed by tapping the App Store icon on the home page.

Chapter 4: Operating Systems

1. B. An operating system provides an environment for the software to function, but it does not coordinate between software applications.

2. D. Linux is the only open source desktop OS discussed in this book. Some versions of Android are open source, but Android is a mobile OS.

3. A. A piece of software written for an OS will work only on that type of OS.

4. C. Chromebooks often have very small hard drives, and they are not used for file storage. By default, all files are stored on Google's cloud.

5. A. When you delete a shortcut, nothing happens to the file to which the shortcut pointed. The shortcut is just an easy way to access the file.

6. D. With the FAT and NTFS file systems, you cannot rename a file, or change any of the metadata, while the file is open or in use.

7. A. iPhones come with the iOS operating system.

8. B. Firmware is an example of an embedded OS. They are small and require very few resources to run.

9. C. A website should be hosted from a web server. Any server should be using a server operating system.

10. D. Access control is managed by the operating system, not the file system.

11. C. Linux is a kernel, which is the core of an OS. Linux packages are put together as distributions and marketed as such.

12. A. Processes are stopped (killed) in the Task Manager program.

13. D. When you copy a file, the original file remains intact, and a new version of that file is created elsewhere on the hard drive. The new version is associated with the new folder.

14. A. Compression makes files smaller to save space, but it also slows down file access. Encryption secures files. Compression and encryption are file attributes, but attribution is not the correct option. Journaling is what an operating system does to note that a file has changed.

15. A. A Linux-based OS is called a distribution, which is a combination of the kernel, shell, and utilities needed for a fully functional OS.

16. C, D. Windows Task Manager allows you to stop processes and services. Drivers are managed through Device Manager.

17. D. Before the hard drive can be used for file storage, it needs at least one partition. Once it's partitioned, you can format the drive, which will install a file system.

18. A. In Windows, drivers can be upgraded and managed from Device Manager.

19. B. Any data or information inside a file is part of the file itself, not the metadata for the file. Metadata is information about the file, such as its name, size, creator, and security.

20. A. Permissions define who or what can access a resource. Read-only is an attribute that can make the file immune to changes, but it can still be accessed. Archive is a backup attribute. Compression makes the file smaller but does not prevent access.

Chapter 5: Software Applications

1. D. The browser windows the user is getting are known as pop-up windows. Configure a pop-up blocker, which should resolve the problem. If not, it's possible the computer has malware.

2. A. If a software product is giving you a limited number of uses, you must activate that software with the manufacturer. This typically requires you to have a software license and a product key.

3. C. Web browsers cache information about websites. It's possible that the browser's cache is being read instead of the new data on the site. Clear the cache.

4. B. The product key will be required to install or use any licensed software product. The manufacturer will include this on the installation media or email it to you.

5. A. Remote support software will help the technicians connect to client computers to fix problems easier. Instant messaging and document sharing will probably be helpful as well, but remote support software is the best choice for fixing problems.

6. B. The best bet is to always download software from the original equipment manufacturer (OEM) website and not a third-party site. Disabling the pop-up blocker and then downloading from a random site is probably the worst advice possible. If it's PC-based, the software will not be in the Apple Store.

7. A. A user's profile contains the color scheme, security settings, and favorites (or bookmarks), so the profile should be set up for synchronization in this case. Bookmarks (or favorites) are links to websites. Accessibility is for ease-of-use enhancements. The browser does need to be compatible for applications, but this isn't a requirement in this situation.

8. A. Word processing, spreadsheets, and presentation software are three examples of productivity software.

9. C. Subscriptions require the user to pay yearly. Perpetual would incur a one-time charge. There are no proprietary or recurring licenses.

10. A. Drivers are designed to let the OS talk to hardware. Each piece of hardware must have a driver to work with the operating system.

11. B. The users need an online workspace, which will allow them to share files and work with them online.

12. B, C. The two most important things to consider are if the software was written to work with that operating system and if the computer has enough or the correct hardware to run the application.

13. C. If you're ever missing a driver, go to the manufacturer's website to download it and then install it.

14. A. Accessibility options are those that add ease-of-use features to a web browser, such as for those who have limited eyesight.

15. D. There is no browser kernel. The kernel is the core of the operating system (from Chapter 4).

16. A. For security software, such as antivirus protection, you should update the definition file at least once per week. Better yet, set the software to update automatically.

17. B. Open source software is generally free, and users can modify the application if they so choose.

18. A, B. Software product keys are typically included on the package in which the installation media was shipped, if there was any. If the software was downloaded, then the manufacturer usually sends the software key via email.

19. D. Private browsing doesn't guarantee anonymity, but it doesn't use any of your cache or cookies, making it less likely that the site you visit can determine your identity.

20. B. When you click a button on a web page, it may activate a script for a pop-up window. If pop-ups are blocked, then the button may not work properly.

Chapter 6: Software Development

1. C. Hexadecimal is also known as base-16. It uses the numbers 1 to 9 and letters A to F.

2. A, D. Functions and methods are used to break code into small, reusable segments.

3. A, C. Java and Python are considered object-oriented languages, as are C++, C#, PHP, Perl, and Ruby.

4. D. Arrays and vectors are containers for data. An array can have only one data type and is fixed in length. Vectors are more flexible, containing multiple data types, and are dynamic in length.

5. B. ASCII and Unicode are used for numerical representations of letters and symbols. ASCII covers English letters and some symbols. For non-English, use the superset of ASCII called Unicode.

6. C, D. The three classes of interpreted languages are scripting, scripted, and markup languages.

7. A. Compiled language programs are compiled once and then executed as many times as needed. Scripted, scripting, and markup languages are interpreted languages, which are not compiled with a compiler.

8. D. Assembly is the lowest-level programming language, and it is used when developers want to access computer hardware directly.

9. C. The logic says that anyone younger than 20 is a teen, while anyone younger than 65 is an adult. Since this person is 20 exactly, they are in the Adult category.

10. B. A string is a group of characters—technically, zero or more characters, but not having a fixed length.

11. A. Looping logic is characterized by the `while` statement.

12. B, C. Objects are made up of properties, attributes, and methods. Arrays and variables could be part of an object but do not have to be.

13. D. It's a float data type, which is a number with a decimal place. It could be binary, but binary is a notational system, not a data type.

14. D. Arrays are of a fixed length, so you can't just add another variable if it's at its maximum length. Vectors can have their length dynamically adjusted and might work better in this situation.

15. A. Query languages are used to obtain data from databases.

16. D. The threat level should be red. Anything from 9 to 11 is in the red range.

17. B. Extensible Markup Language (XML) is an example of a markup language. The other primary markup language is Hypertext Markup Language (HTML).

18. C. A flowchart is designed to depict visually the sequence of events and logic within a program.

19. D. Assembly is the lowest-level programming language. Interpreted and compiled are high-level languages, and query languages are used to get data from a database.

20. A. A flowchart is a visual depiction of a program. It includes the logic components, inputs, and all other properties of the program.

Chapter 7: Database Fundamentals

1. A. For a small number of rows, with only two people accessing the data, a spreadsheet is fine in this situation.

2. C. Data persistence means that the data is permanently available. Hard drives store data in a persistent way, so the answer is SSD.

3. D. A relational database has structured data, which is predictable and organized, with tables containing columns and rows of text or numerical data.

4. B. After a database is created, data needs to be imported or inputted.

5. D. Permissions are considered part of data definition.

6. C. With different types of data, including images, the best choice for a database is a nonrelational database such as a document database or a key-value database.

7. A. A primary key is one or more fields whose data is used to uniquely identify a record.

8. D. Constraints can be placed on fields such that they will accept only certain types of data. For example, if a field is set to accept only integers, users will not be allowed to enter text data.

9. A. Pictures by themselves would be nonstructured data, but since metadata is included, these pictures are classified as semi-structured data.

10. A. Using a JDBC connection to a database is an example of direct access.

11. B. Oscar will not be able to view the database because if there is a permission conflict, a specific deny overrides a specific grant.

12. C. The `CREATE TABLE` command is used to create new tables in a database.

13. D. You can use `ALTER` to add, delete, and modify columns.

14. C. Sometimes you need to delete tables or databases, and in database terms this is known as dropping. The `DROP` command is used for dropping a database or a table in a database.

15. C. A primary key is one or more fields whose data is used to identify a record uniquely. They are required, and there can be only one primary key per table.

16. B. The `INSERT` command is used to insert records into an existing table.

17. D. The `SELECT` command is used to create queries to search for data.

18. A. The `DELETE` command is used to remove records (rows) from a table.

19. D. In a key-value database, data is represented as a collection of key-value pairs. Keys are an arbitrary string of characters, such as a filename or a URL, and must be unique. Values are stored as blobs, meaning that they don't conform to a schema.

20. D. The `UPDATE` command is used to update existing data in the database.

Chapter 8: Networking Concepts and Technologies

1. A, D. For network communications on a TCP/IP network, an IP address and a subnet mask are required. If you want to communicate outside of your network, a default gateway is also required. DHCP servers automatically assign clients IP configuration information.

2. B. DSL and broadband in general, can get up to around 50 Mbps without exploring fiber options. This is faster than a T1 (1.544 Mbps), ISDN (basic rate is 128 Kbps), or cellular (up to 20 Mbps).

3. C. A small network with no dedicated administrator and no mention of a server is a peer-to-peer network. It is likely that this network also qualifies as a LAN, but LAN/WAN are not networking models but are topologies or types of networks.

4. D. Wireless routers will have a reset button on their bottom or back. Press and hold the button for about 30 seconds, and the router will reset to factory specifications. If you never changed the password, then using admin would work, but I am hoping you changed the password!

5. B. For such a connection, a wireless option is needed, so fiber-optic is off the table. Satellite is the best. Cellular and RF have more limited ranges and would not work in the middle of the ocean.

6. C. The network password for clients to use is `Tx$pr4y2`.

7. C. A firewall helps protect networks by blocking potentially dangerous network traffic. A DNS server resolves hostnames to IP addresses. A DHCP server assigns TCP/IP configuration information. DSL is a type of Internet service.

8. A. Ports are like channels within TCP/IP that designate which top-level protocol is being used. An IP address is the network address of the host. MAC addresses are hardware addresses built into network cards. Ports are based on protocol, not the networking model.

9. C. WPA3 would be the best choice. However, of the options listed, WPA2 is the most secure wireless security protocol.

10. A. Cellular networks give you the best mobility, with a range of up to several miles. Even then, unless you go out of the range of a tower completely, you will be handed over to the next cell tower.

11. B. The 802.11ax standard is the fastest one available on the market today. Of the options listed, 802.11ac is the fastest, followed by 802.11n, 802.11g, and then 802.11a.

12. A. Generally speaking, the higher the frequency, the shorter the range. The correct choice is 6 GHz. 1180 kHz is not a Wi-Fi band option, but within the U.S. AM terrestrial radio range.

13. D. Cellular has the longest delay, because the signal needs to travel the farthest distance.

14. B. Routers connect networks to each other. A switch is a central connectivity point for computers on a network. Firewalls are security devices that can block network traffic. Access points are wireless central connectivity devices.

15. D. File Transfer Protocol (FTP) is designed specifically for file transfers. HTTPS is the protocol for secure websites. POP3 and SMTP are email protocols.

16. B, D. The three email protocols are POP3, SMTP, and IMAP. Of those, POP3 and IMAP are used to download email. SMTP is used to send email.

17. A. The `ifconfig` command is used in macOS to show your IP address and other TCP/IP configuration information.

18. A. The Service Set Identifier (SSID) is the wireless network name.

19. B, C. You should always change the SSID and the administrator password on a wireless router.

20. B. The guest network password for clients to use is `tpg$2015`.

Chapter 9: Cloud Computing and Artificial Intelligence

1. D. In this instance, macOS is running as a guest OS inside a hypervisor. It's a virtual machine running the guest OS.

2. A. The hypervisor is software that enables virtualization, or the ability to install a guest operating system within an existing operating system.

3. B. A Type 1 hypervisor sits directly on the hardware, whereas a Type 2 hypervisor sits on a host OS. The guest OS is the OS that resides within the hypervisor.

4. B. Client-side virtualization is enabled by a Type 2 hypervisor. A Type 1 hypervisor is also called a bare-metal hypervisor, sits on the hardware, and is typically used for server-side virtualization.

5. D. The guest OS is virtual, so it uses virtual hardware. Therefore, it will use the vNIC. The vNIC will be linked to one or more physical network cards for communication on the physical network.

6. C. If cloud infrastructure is both on-premises (like the servers are) and online, it's a hybrid cloud.

7. D. If the cloud service includes apps, it is Software as a Service (SaaS). Platform as a Service (PaaS) includes hardware and software development platforms. Infrastructure as a Service (IaaS) includes just the hardware. Some define GaaS as Gaming as a Service, but that's not something you need to know for the Tech+ exam.

8. C. The highest level of the three standard cloud services is Software as a Service (SaaS), which includes infrastructure, access to development platforms, and software.

9. A. Platform as a Service (PaaS) provides both hardware and software development platform tools. Infrastructure as a Service (IaaS) would not provide developers with the needed tools, and Software as a Service (SaaS) provides more than is necessary. GaaS is Gaming as a Service but is not listed in the Tech+ exam objectives.

10. D. Rapid elasticity is when clients can get more resources instantly (or at least very quickly) without supplier intervention. Measured service is how providers track client resource usage. High availability means the services are always or almost always available, and resource pooling is when the provider groups resources together to divide them up among clients.

11. B. High availability is the term that refers to uninterrupted and responsive cloud services. Measured service is how providers track client resource usage. Broad network access means that users can access services regardless of where they are or what type of device they are using. Virtualization is the technology that enables cloud computing.

12. B. Amazon Web Services (AWS) runs a public cloud. An on-premises or private cloud is one run by a company on its own site, not intended for use by other companies. A hybrid cloud is a mix of public Internet cloud-based and private.

13. A, B, C. Virtual routers and network infrastructure are provided with Infrastructure as a Service (IaaS), which is the lowest level of common cloud service available. Platform as a Service (PaaS) is one level higher and can provide IaaS services as well. Software as a Service (SaaS) is the highest common level and can provide the functionality of IaaS and PaaS in addition to applications.

14. D. The customer service "person" is most likely an AI chatbot. It can answer specific questions, help retrieve information about your account, and transfer you to a human customer service representative if needed. It's going to be able to answer specific questions about your bank account, though, and not general questions about other topics such as how to bake cookies.

15. A. Alexa and Siri are examples of AI assistants. An AI assistant can help answer general questions (by searching the Internet), set timers, play music, and perform general tasks.

16. B. Natural language processing (NLP) is the study of understanding written or spoken human languages.

17. C. ChatGPT is an example of generative AI. Amazon Alexa is an AI assistant. A customer service pop-up window on a website is most likely an AI chatbot. Autocorrect is an example of AI predictions and suggestions.

18. C. Generative AI can be specialized to generate computer programming code.

19. D. This is a predictive AI, which aims to predict future actions or suggest items you might be interested in, based on past behavior (such as searching for an item).

20. C. Artwork can be created by custom generative AIs.

Chapter 10: Security Concepts and Threats

1. E. Hackers may have different motivations, but their activities can include stealing usernames and passwords, modifying website content, disrupting network communications, and analyzing network traffic.

2. C. A large, unstructured dataset of different data types is called big data. Analytics might find correlations within the data that can in turn be monetized. Some of the data may be critical, but other data (such as online customer reviews) may be easily replaceable.

3. A, D. Examples of availability threats include denial of service, power outage, hardware failure, destruction, and service outage.

4. D. A Trojan horse might look like helpful software but will actually do harm to your computer. An example could be a program that looks like a security scanner but actually installs malware. (Ironic, isn't it?)

5. B. Going through the trash to find confidential information is considered dumpster diving, and it's illegal in most areas. Social engineering means trying to get information out of another person. Phishing is social engineering via email.

6. A. Receipts are used for nonrepudiation, not for authentication. Examples of factors include passwords, PINs, one-time passwords, software tokens, hardware tokens, biometrics, a specific location, and security questions.

7. B, D. Social engineering occurs when attackers ask people for information to help them gain access to sensitive information. Examples of this are shoulder surfing and phishing.

8. B. Single sign-on gives users access to all the applications and systems they need with one initial login.

9. D. Phishing is a form of social engineering where an attacker sends an email asking for personal information to use in an attack. This might also be considered spam, but phishing is more specific here.

10. A, C. Confidentiality concerns include snooping, eavesdropping, wiretapping, social engineering, and dumpster diving. Denial of service is an availability concern, and replay attacks threaten integrity.

11. C. Shoulder surfing is trying to see private information on someone else's computer. This can include information on the computer screen, but also can be something like trying to see a password.

12. B. Authentication identifies who a user is, authorization determines what the user can do, and accounting tracks what the user did. Nonrepudiation provides proof that someone or something performed a specific action.

13. D. All current end-user operating systems are susceptible to viruses and malware.

14. B, D. Accounting on a network tracks what users do. The administrator can use logs or web browser history to do this.

15. C. Biometrics are a security factor, but it can also be used for nonrepudiation. This is because biometrics are incredibly difficult to be duplicated or stolen from someone, practically guaranteeing an identity.

16. D. Wiretapping is a confidentiality concern. Other examples of confidentiality concerns are snooping, eavesdropping, social engineering, and dumpster diving.

17. A. When users are required to use more than one authentication factor for logging in, that is called multifactor authentication. Examples of factors include passwords, PINs, one-time passwords, software tokens, hardware tokens, biometrics, a specific location, and security questions.

18. B, C. Four examples of integrity concerns are on-path, replay attack, impersonation, and unauthorized information alteration. Snooping is a confidentiality concern, and denial of service is an availability concern.

19. B. In role-based access control, users are assigned a role, which determines all of their permissions on the system.

20. D. The General Data Protection Regulation (GDPR) law protects data privacy in the European Union. The Privacy Act is a U.S. law, and the California Consumer Protection Act (CCPA) is in California. Personally identifiable information (PII) is the data these laws seek to protect.

Chapter 11: Security Best Practices

1. A, D. All four answers are device-hardening options. If you are worried about local theft, installing a hardware lock is a must. In addition, if your device does get stolen, encryption will prevent thieves from accessing your files unless they know your username and password.

2. D. A screensaver password will require someone to enter your password to gain access to the computer. File encryption won't help if the attacker has access to the computer as you. Multifactor authentication and SSO are both used when a user initially logs in.

3. B, D. Websites using HTTPS need to get a security certificate, called an SSL certificate, from a certificate authority (CA). If a website uses HTTPS, then traffic to and from the site is encrypted (is in cipher text).

4. A. Secure websites start with `HTTPS://`.

5. D. The only plausible answer is that someone else had your username and password and logged onto the computer as you. Even administrator accounts can't access other users' encrypted files.

6. A, C. Financial information and customer lists are confidential and should be protected. Some contact information may also be confidential, but in many cases external people need to know how to reach people in a company.

7. A. A software firewall protects your computer against malicious network traffic. Antispyware and antivirus software packages are good, but they protect against malicious programs.

8. D. Autofill is the name of the service that remembers your personal information. When you begin to type your information into an online form, Autofill will populate more of it (whatever it has stored) for you.

9. A. Authentication is where a user provides a username and password (or other security factor) to log into a system. This allows access to certain files through the use of permissions. Antimalware protects against viruses and other malicious software. A firewall can block malicious network traffic. Patching refers to updating software.

10. C. You should recognize untrusted source warnings and act on them appropriately. Good practices include limiting the use of personally identifiable information (PII), disabling Autofill, and updating browser add-ons and extensions.

11. A, B. Written policies and procedures should be established for enabling stricter security policies. Password policies that enforce length, complexity, expiration, and limited reuse are good to implement.

12. D. Rachel is experiencing Autofill, which is a feature in a browser that automatically populates your information in the right fields when you start entering any of the information. It can be convenient, but it can also be a potential security risk.

13. B, D. You should use complex passwords that are still easy for you to remember. Changing default passwords is a good idea, as is not reusing a password on multiple systems or after it has been changed.

14. E. Shoulder surfing, keyloggers, and unsecured wireless networks are all potential security risks associated with public workstations.

15. C. A virtual private network (VPN) is a secured, encrypted connection between two computers. When logging into a corporate network, VPNs are often used to secure communications.

16. A, C. Strong passwords are long, complex, and use a variety of symbols, numbers, and letters. Passwords should not contain any personally identifiable information (PII), and patterns in passwords make them easier to guess.

17. C. Antivirus software programs protect against worms and Trojan horses. Software firewalls can prevent malicious network traffic but do not recognize viruses or worms. Authentication protocols are used to validate login credentials, and security certificates validate the legitimacy of secure websites.

18. D. It's possible that your friend sent you a very cool link. It's also possible that her email has been hijacked and you've just been sent a virus or other malware. Don't click it until you talk to her first and verify that it's legitimate.

19. C, D. Two things that you can do are to upgrade your browser to the newest version (as well as any add-ons and extensions) and ensure that you have a good antivirus package. Enabling Autofill and accepting all cookies can increase your security risk.

20. A. Web browser add-ons and extensions can add functionality to your web browser. To make sure that you maintain the best security possible, ensure that they are updated to their most current versions.

Chapter 12: Data Continuity and Computer Support

1. B, C. To identify the problem, you can talk to users, gather information, and isolate the issue. Using external resources such as the Internet is part of the process to establish a theory of probable cause.

2. D. If the hard drive is not detected or if a specific folder needed to load macOS is not detected, the Mac will display a flashing question mark.

3. B. Always test the simple stuff first. Assuming user error is not a good way to endear yourself to your clients.

4. D. Whenever setting up a new backup system or making a change to an existing backup solution, verify that the backup works. Once you have done that, then you can perform other tasks.

5. A. The solution might have worked, and it might not have. Based on whether it appeared to or not, you should establish a further plan of action. If it worked, you can move on to verifying full functionality. If not, you may need to go back to trying additional solutions.

6. B. The System Configuration utility, or MSCONFIG, allows users to see which applications are loading at the startup of Windows. If too many programs load on startup, it will slow down the boot process.

7. D. Older applications might not work with current operating systems unless you use compatibility mode.

8. A. The Windows Recovery Environment is a feature of Windows Vista and newer setup programs that lets you repair an installation of Windows when booting to the installation flash drive. All of the other options require the OS to load before using them.

9. B. The last step in the troubleshooting process, and one that is often overlooked, is to document the findings/lessons learned, actions, and outcomes. (Cleaning up is important to do if you made a mess, but it's not specifically a step in the troubleshooting methodology.)

10. C. Local backup solutions will always be faster than network storage or cloud-based solutions. This is because the transfer rate to a local hard disk or USB flash drive is faster than network connections.

11. A. A normal (or full) backup will back up all selected files and then clear the archive bit. An incremental backup will clear the archive bit as well, but it will not back up files that have not been changed since the last backup.

12. B. Always check the manufacturer's website first. Since it's hardware, check that manufacturer and not the OS manufacturer.

13. C. Incremental backups will back up only the files that have changed since the last backup. They are the quickest backups to make.

14. B. STOP errors, also known as the Blue Screen of Death (BSOD), are generated by Windows. The faulty memory module may have caused the error, but Windows generated the message.

15. D. The most likely cause of intermittent hard locks like this is an overheating system. Power the system down, give it a chance to cool off, and then inspect for damage or excessive dust in the fans. With the case open, power it back on and ensure that all cooling fans are running.

16. C. A black-screen error usually comes from the BIOS, such as a message indicating that the hard disk is not bootable.

17. D. Your neighbor needs RAID 1, also known as disk mirroring. It writes data to both hard drives simultaneously. If one hard drive fails, the other will still be operational.

18. D. A POST card is a circuit board you insert into an open slot on the motherboard. It displays a two-digit code to tell you where the system is in the booting process. This is useful when nothing is displayed on-screen.

19. A. A system image makes a copy of the entire hard drive, which can be used in the case of a complete system failure. It takes a long time to make and you can't restore individual files from one like you can with a normal backup program.

20. B. The most likely cause is the power supply, since there are no fans spinning. Of course, don't forget first to check that it's plugged in!

Index

B

C

D

E

F

G

H

I

J

K

L

M

N

O

P

Q

R

S

T

U

V

W

X-Y-Z

Online Test Bank

To help you study for your CompTIA Tech+ certification exam, register to gain one year of FREE access after activation to the online interactive test bank—included with your purchase of this book! All of the chapter review questions and the practice tests in this book are included in the online test bank so you can practice in a timed and graded setting.

Register and Access the Online Test Bank

To register your book and get access to the online test bank, follow these steps:

1. Go to `www.wiley.com/go/sybextestprep`. You'll see the **"How to Register Your Book for Online Access"** instructions.
2. Click "here to register" and then select your book from the list.
3. Complete the required registration information, including answering the security verification to prove book ownership. You will be emailed a pin code.
4. Follow the directions in the email or go to `www.wiley.com/go/sybextestprep`.
5. Find your book on that page and click the "Register or Login" link with it. Then enter the pin code you received and click the "Activate PIN" button.
6. On the Create an Account or Login page, enter your username and password, and click Login or, if you don't have an account already, create a new account.
7. At this point, you should be in the test bank site with your new test bank listed at the top of the page. If you do not see it there, please refresh the page or log out and log back in.